Oracle Press™

Oracle Discoverer Handbook

Michael Armstrong-Smith
Darlene Armstrong-Smith

Osborne/**McGraw-Hill**

Berkeley New York St. Louis San Francisco
Auckland Bogotá Hamburg London Madrid
Mexico City Milan Montreal New Delhi Panama City
Paris São Paulo Singapore Sydney Tokyo Toronto

Osborne/**McGraw-Hill**
2600 Tenth Street
Berkeley, California 94710
U.S.A.

For information on translations or book distributors outside the U.S.A., or to arrange bulk purchase discounts for sales promotions, premiums, or fund-raisers, please contact Osborne/**McGraw-Hill** at the above address.

Oracle Discoverer Handbook

1234567890 VFM VFM 019876543210

ISBN 0-07-212635-3

Publisher
Brandon A. Nordin

Vice President and Associate Publisher
Scott Rogers

Acquisitions Editor
Jeremy Judson

Acquisitions Coordinator
Ross Doll

Technical Editor
Karlene Jensen

Copy Editor
Dennis Weaver

Indexer
Valerie Perry

Computer Designers
Jani Beckwith and Gary Corrigan

Illustrator
Michael Mueller

Series Design
Jani Beckwith

Cover Design
William Voss

This book was composed with Corel VENTURA™ Publisher.

**This book is dedicated to our children—
Mark, Sarah, Stephanie, Byron, Grant, and Sean—
and our grandson Ronnie.**

About the Authors

Michael Armstrong-Smith is the Worldwide Information Delivery Manager for Logitech, Inc., and secretary of the data warehousing SIG of the OAUG. A fellow of the Institute of Analysts and Programmers, and a member of Oracle's customer advisory board on information delivery, he has over 18 years systems development experience. Michael is a leader in the field of information delivery, with specialist knowledge of data warehouses, electronic data interchange and, of course, Oracle Discoverer.

Situated in Fremont, CA, Logitech designs, manufactures, and markets human interface devices and supporting software that link people to the Internet and enable them to work, play, learn, and communicate more effectively in the digital world.

Darlene Armstrong-Smith is an instructional designer as well as a standup trainer. She has experience designing and implementing system conversion training, and also as a vocational education teacher. Darlene has served as a training consultant to a major financial institution, and has written training manuals and policies and procedures for various organizations.

Contents

PART II

Editing the Query

PART III
Advanced Discoverer Techniques

PART IV
Appendixes

Acknowledgments

We would be remiss if we did not mention the names of some key people who have helped immensely in the writing of this book. Karlene Jensen from Oracle Corporation acted as our technical editor and encouraged us to dig into all features of Discoverer. She pointed us in the right direction more than a few times, and gave us loads of valuable information that made the work go easier. Much of the information she gave us you will not find in any other location.

We would also like to acknowledge our editorial team at Osborne/McGraw-Hill. Jeremy Judson believed in us and was always the voice of encouragement and understanding. Patty Mon, who served as our project editor, was endlessly patient and helpful. Monika Faltiss and Ross Doll were our acquisitions coordinators, and at home, we affectionately referred to them as our bulldogs. They were always after us to stay on track. Finally, we want to thank our copy editor, Dennis Weaver, for taking our words and making them better, and for taking Michael's "British English" and converting it into "American English."

Our final thanks go to our children—Stephanie, Byron, Grant, and Sean—for the many nights they had leftovers and cold sandwiches for dinner, and to our cat Eliza Doolittle for keeping us company as we burned the midnight oil.

Introduction

Our first step in writing this book was to determine who our audience was. We knew when we began writing that there was (as yet) no book on Discoverer on the market. We also knew that end users at all levels were in need of a tutorial on this powerful and very complex piece of software. We made the decision to reach out to all users—from the novice to the true power user.

We feel that there is something in this book for every Discoverer user. The novice will be taken from the very first step of each task through to its successful completion. The power user will find information that they may have otherwise needed to look for in myriad places. We have organized the steps for every task into useful and easy-to-follow workflows, and have tried to be as detailed as possible.

The second decision we needed to make was what versions of Discoverer we should address here. The choices we made were Discoverer 3.1.36 and 3.1.41, and Discoverer 3*i* (3.3.48). We have not tackled either of the Discoverer Viewer editions in this book. So as not to confuse the user, we did not cover the Discoverer Admin Edition. There is, however, a section in Chapter 14 on what the Discoverer administrator can do for you.

When we took on the challenge of writing this tutorial, our desire was to bring all of Discoverer's powerful features into one source. You will find many hitherto undocumented Discoverer features in this book.

How This Book Is Organized

This book is divided into three sections and four appendixes.

- **Part I** "Getting Started" contains five chapters that cover the basic history and philosophy of Discoverer. Part I also contains an extensive description of the types of databases with which Discoverer can interface. Following these introductory chapters, we deal with the login sequence and all steps of the Discoverer Workbook Wizard.
- **Part II** "Editing the Output" contains four chapters and is focused on turning a basic Discoverer query into much more. We begin with formatting issues, such as font, colors, headings, and numbers. We then move on to graphing in Discoverer and turning a query into a well-formatted and ready-to-deliver report. The final chapter of Part II covers using Discoverer to analyze data. This is a powerful tutorial on the elements of analysis as well as how to use Discoverer's various tools to analyze your data.
- **Part III** "Advanced Discoverer Techniques" contains five chapters. The first three chapters take all of the Discoverer tools and give detailed instructions on how to use them effectively, including refining items, drilling, and building effective conditions, along with refining parameters, calculations, sorting, and percentages. The final two chapters of Part III deal with query management, user preferences, the toolbar, and the Discoverer administrator.
- **Part IV** There are four appendixes in this book. Appendix A contains a detailed list of all of Discoverer's functions, including syntax, descriptions, and examples. It also contains a detailed list of format masks. Appendix B contains a description of various databases and views. Appendix C is a comparison of 3.1 and 3*i*. Appendix D gives a description of the tutorial database we used throughout this book.

PART I

Getting Started with Discoverer

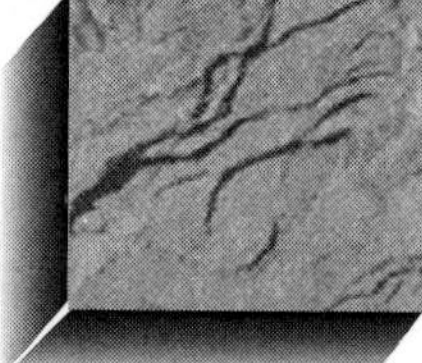

CHAPTER 1

An Overview of Discoverer

his chapter will introduce you to Discoverer, the award-winning reporting and analysis tool from Oracle. We will discuss the whole scenario of information delivery and see how Discoverer is perfectly suited to be your company's tool of choice. The recent introduction of a Web version of the product is very exciting, and places Oracle firmly at the helm of the information revolution.

We continue the overview by discussing the benefits of using the standard Windows GUI, and how adoption of point-and-click technology is essential in the modern world. We follow with a discussion of some of the more general aspects of query writing by telling you the differences between ad hoc and predefined queries. The final section in this overview tells you how to use various sources of help to find out more about Oracle Discoverer.

Information Delivery and Your Business

Oracle creates the worlds finest and best-known (and most used) database systems. The word "Oracle" has become synonymous with relational databases and all that is good with database technology. However, when one speaks of Oracle, the words "easy-to-use query, analysis and reporting tools" do not as readily spring to mind. Other companies have been left with the task of developing these tools to use with Oracle databases. That is, until now.

As one of the leading providers of both traditional and, more recently, Internet business intelligence, Oracle Corporation has gone to great lengths to try to understand the links and interactions between databases (and database technologies) and delivering information. Anyone interested in delivering information within his or her business should look to Oracle. The terms "information delivery," "business intelligence," and "decision support" are all included under the same umbrella. In fact, these terms are often used interchangeably. While the definitions remain vague, an organization's need is clear. Companies are investing billions of dollars, pounds, francs, marcs, yen, and so forth into information technology. The goal for all of these companies is to gather data and make use of it, enabling faster and better-informed business decisions.

Companies can no longer be satisfied in knowing how many sales were made today. They want to know how many sales were made last week, last month, last year. They want to know if their company's bottom line is improving and be able to forecast trends with better accuracy. As a company executive once said to one of the authors, "Tell me something about my company that I don't already know."

This technique, otherwise know as *data mining,* is not generally associated with Discoverer, but this tool in the hands of an expert data analyst will surprise even the most seasoned users of other products.

You may gather from the previous statements that the authors are converts to Discoverer. Never before in an 18-year career in the information industry have we seen a product surface with such ease of use and power. If you don't already have it and you have an Oracle database, this tool is a must have. Another pleasant surprise is that Discoverer will link to just about any open database connectivity (ODBC)-compliant database. So, if you have not yet made the switch to using Oracle databases, you can still benefit from the power and ease of use built into the Discoverer product.

Organizations today are generating unprecedented amounts of data to support their day-to-day functions—but collecting and collating data is no longer enough. An organization must have a means of turning that data into that most precious of business commodities, information. Anyone with decision-making power needs the ability to view and manipulate company data. Oracle Discoverer does just that. It can unleash your data, turning it into a true asset for your business.

Discoverer's Role in Information Delivery

As stated earlier, Oracle has firmly positioned Discoverer right at the heart of their information delivery strategy. But Discoverer is more than just a component of a suite of tools (albeit an extremely powerful suite). It has the ability to stand on its own two feet, to make a place for itself within your company, and to be your analysis tool of choice. This book, therefore, will concentrate on Discoverer itself. So just where does this tool come from, and how can it fit in with your company's information delivery strategy?

Oracle Introduces Discoverer

With the introduction of the Windows version of Discoverer in the late 1990s, Oracle gave anyone working in information delivery an award-winning, easy-to-use ad hoc query and analysis tool. It was developed as a means to view data stored in Oracle databases, and analyze and create reports based upon that data. Discoverer is a tool that places power in the hands of the user—power that until Discoverer came along was the domain of developers.

Subsequent improvements have moved it out into a league of its own. Its simple to use graphical user interface (GUI) makes navigation easy. It is highly intuitive, and its Workbook Wizard guides you through all the steps you need in order to create a query. The seasoned computer user will adapt to its point-and-click features quickly and easily. The novice will be guided by wizards to create what may be their first database queries and reports.

If your background is PC-based, you will be familiar with tools such as Microsoft Excel. Discoverer has a similar look and feel and is extremely easy on the eyes. There are no cumbersome screens or navigation paths, there are shortcuts to most of the functionality, and (just like many Windows products) there are usually two or even three ways to do the same thing. Many of these shortcuts are undocumented and only surface when you say to yourself something like, "I wonder if Discoverer can do this?"—and then click your mouse. More often than not the authors have been pleasantly surprised to find that Discoverer can.

Discoverer Comes to the Internet

With the Windows version so popular and easy to use, the launch of a fully working Web version (as opposed to a Web viewer) has been eagerly awaited and anticipated. The release of Oracle's Internet version, Discoverer 3*i*, came out in the spring of 2000, and the authors were lucky enough (and owe a debt of gratitude to Oracle Corporation for being allowed) to have received a prerelease version for testing and evaluation.

While not currently having all of the features of its Windows counterpart, this product is sure to be a hit with the e-commerce fraternity who have been longing to use Discoverer on the Web. Oracle is promoting 3*i* as being an integral part of their suite of Internet business intelligence tools. These tools—Oracle Discoverer, Oracle Reports, and Oracle Express—are together designated the key components of Oracle's Business Intelligence System (BIS) suite of products. Together, they will provide superior ease of use and exceptional performance, enabling companies to make better, quicker, and more-informed decisions.

As stated above, 3*i* does not yet have all of the features of 3.1, but don't let this fool you into thinking that it is an inferior product. In fact, prompted by feedback from users of 3.1, Oracle has enhanced the Internet version. They have assured the authors that they are working hard to add all of the missing functionality, and more, to their Web version, and they are planning an update for later in 2000.

NOTE

Throughout this book, whenever there is a difference between Discoverer 3.1 and Discoverer 3i*, both functionalities will be explained. When no difference is discussed, you can be confident that both products work the same way.*

Windows and Internet Compatibility

Oracle is aware that many companies already have a significant investment in the Windows version of Discoverer. During the construction of 3*i*, they took great strides to avoid you having the embarrassment of building a query in one environment and then finding that it would not work in the other. Even though there are currently limitations on the functionality of 3*i*, such as the inability to create queries that use subqueries, Oracle has made sure that any query written in 3.1 will run on the Web version, no matter how complex or formatted.

In the case of the example highlighted where 3*i* will not let you create subqueries, if you actually build a query in 3.1 that uses subqueries and you bring it into 3*i*, it will still work. Even though you cannot edit the subquery, Discoverer 3i will recognize its existence and use it correctly. Therefore, do not be overly alarmed by the omission from 3*i* of some of the features that you have come to love in the Windows version. A full list of the differences between 3.1 and 3*i* will appear in Appendix C. Whichever version you use, this book is for you.

How to Use This Book

This book focuses on the current releases of both the Windows and Web versions of Discoverer. Primarily aimed at end users, it is valuable to the beginner as well as the superusers. The book will not concentrate on technical issues such as setup and installation, and therefore is not intended to be a technical reference manual. However, reference will be made to administrative functions when they will improve the user's awareness of what features are available within the product. This will enable end users to know what their administrators can do for them.

Discoverer administrators will find much useful information for optimizing the product for maximum performance. By seeing and understanding how end users will use the tool, they will also learn how to provide a better service. Working together as a team, your Discoverer administrator, superusers, and end users will be able to use this product to its maximum effectiveness.

You may have already purchased Discoverer and are wondering what it can do for your company. You have probably heard about its easy-to-use interface, its ability to link to just about any database you can name, or maybe you're just caught up in the information delivery revolution that is shaping our modern world. Whatever your reason for purchasing this book, and whatever your level of expertise with Discoverer, the authors feel that there is something here for everyone.

Example Database

Throughout this book we have used an Oracle Personal Lite database and created sales records for a fictitious company called Global Widgets. This database has been used to demonstrate the creation of useful and meaningful queries. We have also added a mix of examples showing both Discoverer 3.1 and Discoverer 3*i* functionality. When there is a functional difference between the two systems, we will show both together. When the difference is cosmetic only, we will give the description but not necessarily add a figure or illustration.

In the example database, our fictional company, Global Widgets, uses a fiscal year that begins on the Saturday following the last Friday in September. Thus Q1 (quarter one) runs from October to December, Q2 from January to March, and so on. We have done this to demonstrate Discoverer's ability to deal with fiscal years, because we are aware that not all companies base their fiscal year on the calendar year. Global Widgets used to deal exclusively with orders received and processed using traditional channels, but during 1999 they started using e-commerce. We have done this so that we can show you examples of queries where we analyze sales performance of the two channels.

You will also be shown how to analyze data from various sales districts and regions as a means of demonstrating Discoverer's drilling and filtering capabilities. The fiscal date hierarchy also allows us to demonstrate drilling, but this time from year to quarter to month to day.

Appendix D provides an entity relationship diagram (ERD) of the example database and a list of tables and indexes.

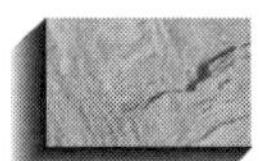

NOTE
In order to access Oracle Lite, we have used ODBC. There are some features of Discoverer that are not supported by ODBC, and there are some features of ODBC that are not supported by Discoverer.

A New Direction in Reporting

In the past, it was the job of the developer to take the requirements of the business unit and turn them into queries and reports. Often, this was accomplished with the use of a middle layer of people: the analyst and the database administrator (DBA).

The business unit representative explained to the analyst what information was needed in the report. The analyst, in conjunction with the DBA, looked at the information available in the database and determined the best way to extract it and how it should be presented. This information was conveyed to the developer, who wrote the programming code for the report.

The developer passed the programming code on to the DBA, who implemented the new programming into the system.

The final step gave the report to the business unit, who would usually say it was all wrong—and the process would begin again.

This example may seem a bit extreme, but the truth is that this type of organization can sometimes resemble the children's game "telephone." Of course, there are many companies with excellent communications in the links between the users, analysts, developers, and DBAs. However, even under the best of circumstances this can be a time-consuming and labor-intensive way for queries and reports to be created.

No one knows better what information is needed and how it should be organized than the person who will be using it. With Discoverer, the end user is now able to do the following:

- Create queries
- Analyze data in seconds rather than days or weeks
- Create their own custom reports

The Discoverer GUI

Oracle has developed a graphical user interface (GUI) in Oracle Discoverer that is a natural to use for those well acquainted with standard spreadsheets, databases, Web browsers, and Microsoft Windows. The authors commend Oracle for embracing the traditional Windows environment and creating a user interface that will be comfortable and familiar to most end users. Many of the readers will remember, and may still be using, mainframe, UNIX, VMS, and DOS-based legacy systems. You have probably been hoping for a better interface. With Oracle Discoverer, you now have one.

Figures 1-1 and 1-2 show the GUI startup screens for Discoverer 3.1 and 3*i*.

The Benefits of a GUI

Back in the 1950s and 60s, the standard interface available in computing was poor. The user was usually faced with a black screen with green letters on a mainframe terminal. They were forced to memorize commands and screens, and there were no such things as icons, dialog boxes, and windows. During the mid-60s, research was taking place to allow the direct manipulation of graphical objects. By 1975, when David Canfield Smith coined the term "icon" in a Stanford Ph.D. thesis, the

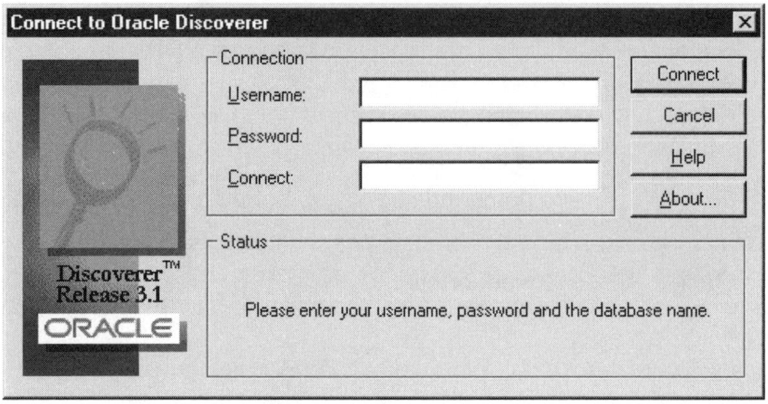

FIGURE 1-1. *The Discoverer 3.1 startup screen*

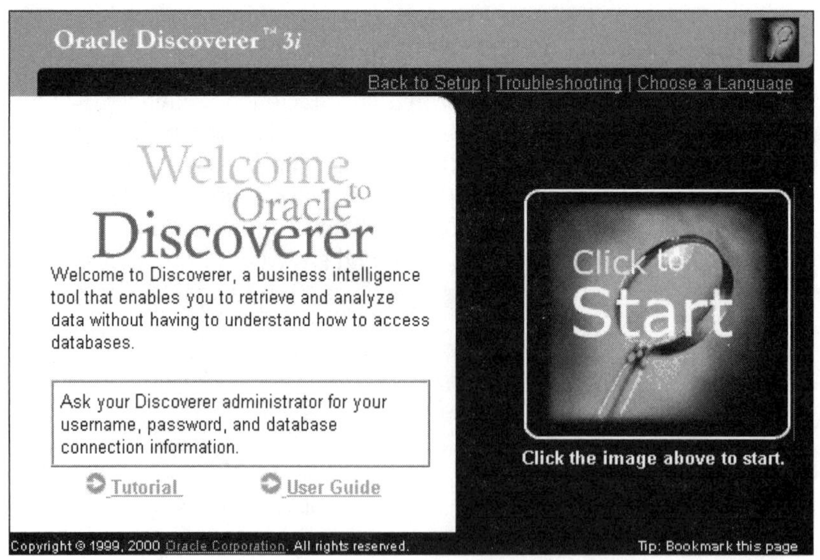

FIGURE 1-2. *The Discoverer 3*i *startup screen*

computing world was gearing up for a revolution. This revolution culminated in the first real GUI interface on the Apple Macintosh in 1984. The following are some of the benefits of a GUI:

- You can have your database on a non-PC platform, and enjoy the features of the PC on your desk.
- Use your mouse to point and click, drag and drop, use shortcuts, and context-sensitive (bubble) help. Export files to other applications.
- Print to local or network printers.
- Attach reports to your email system.
- WYSIWG – What you see is what you get.

The Power of a Mouse in Reporting

During the 1960s and early 70s, research was being conducted into a new type of computer device at Stanford Research Institute by Doug Engelbart. His team developed the mouse to navigate and manipulate systems.

The ability to use a mouse is one of the strongest features of Discoverer. Using a mouse with the Query Wizard and seeing a query building before your eyes is a revelation. Previously, this was considered a "nice to have." Now it is a "must have." Once you have used Discoverer, you will never want to go back. Old legacy tools let you build your query, but you couldn't go back and even change the order of the columns in your query. You were forced to begin again, not able to make the most minor of edits. It was in the realms of fantasy to have multiple outputs from the same query. Today, with Discoverer's point-and-click capability, your query is as easy to change as it is to manage a spreadsheet or surf the Web.

Ad Hoc Queries vs. Predefined Queries

Predefined reports and queries are at the heart of most information systems. Companies invest millions in development. Most database systems come with a myriad of predefined reports. You either use the same reports everyone else uses, or spend a great deal of money and time having them modified to meet your company's needs.

Ad hoc queries are a relatively new concept, one that can be difficult to come to terms with. Given they have had some education in how it is done, users can build queries. With a good foundation in the principles of query writing, the end user can produce queries and reports almost instantly. However, a person without an understanding of these principles may spend hours on a query and end up with data that is completely useless. You will begin learning to create queries and reports that will give you the information you need in Chapter 4. You will also learn how to avoid writing "the query from the Twilight Zone." Later, in Chapter 8, you will be shown how to turn a Discoverer query into a report.

Nonpredictability vs. Predictability

Prewritten reports and queries are predictable—predictable in their output, formatting, and internal processing. Every time you run them, they will give you the same data, same formatting, same font, same sort order, and same day different numbers. Predictability is fine to a point, but sometimes a company needs to think outside of the box to compete in today's market. You may need to know something today that you did not need to know yesterday. To wait two or three weeks for a programmer to define a new report might be too late, and the opportunity will be lost.

Ad hoc reports, by their very nature, are unpredictable. The same data can be output and formatted in an endless variety of ways. When you start the Query Wizard and begin to select the bits of information you think you need, you don't know what the return will be. When the query has been run, the real fun begins.

Easy to Change vs. Fixed Queries

In an ad hoc query, the data can be rearranged, unneeded information removed or masked, cross tabs can be created, and drill-downs formed to dig deeper and deeper. Oracle Discoverer performs these tasks with one click of the mouse.

A fixed query is impossible for a user to change. Most users can see a better way to do it, but don't have the power to make the change. It would be great if the Management Information Systems (MIS) department could have programmers poised in the aisles waiting for a user to raise their hand. They could then rush to the user's side, find out what was needed, and make the programming change before lunch. This is of course impossible, so ad hoc queries are the answer.

The Benefits of Both Types of Queries

It may sound as though there is no place in the modern organization for a fixed query or report. This is not the reality. In many cases, the report is so complex and the amount of knowledge required about the database structure is so vast, there is no choice but to have a fixed report that has been created by a skilled programmer. Another benefit to the fixed report is that some reports will never change. A Total Quantity Shipped report will be the same quarter after quarter, year after year.

Some benefits of the ad hoc query and report are as follows:

- Instantaneously accessing data
- Creating cross tabs (pivot tables)
- Drilling (slicing and dicing)
- Sorting
- Adding calculations and percentages

Some of these terms you may be familiar with, some not. We will cover these various concepts and more as we teach you to use this powerful tool.

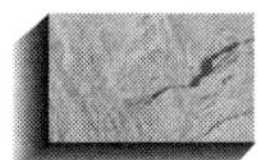

NOTE
There needs to be a balance between the fixed report and the ad hoc report. It is impractical for an organization to rely solely on one type or the other. Some companies may see the use of Oracle Discoverer as a means of downsizing their information delivery departments with a "users can do it all" mentality. This would be folly, and the authors are not suggesting it. Discoverer should be seen as a complement to the fixed report and a means of seeing "what you don't already know."

Oracle Applications Standard Reports vs. Discoverer Reports

Now that you are familiar with the generic terms of fixed and ad hoc queries and reports, let's be specific. Oracle Applications is probably being used by most of the readers of this book. You might be using Discoverer already, or are considering whether or not to add it to your list of tools. This section may help you in your decision, and should help you to position Discoverer in your suite of reporting tools.

If you have implemented all of the modules of Oracle Applications, you may be aware that Oracle provides more than 700 prewritten standard reports. Getting to know these reports is a mammoth undertaking and not to be underestimated. These reports are an excellent resource to your organization, and it is to your benefit to take full advantage of them. It is a sad waste of time and effort to use Discoverer to create reports that already exist in Oracle Apps. In other words, *don't reinvent the wheel.*

A consulting company with expertise in Oracle Apps can help you sift through the standard reports and find the ones that are best suited to your needs. Some companies have a great enough demand for reporting that a full-time reports analyst should be employed. This analyst is responsible for taking the users' requirements and finding the reports that fill them. They can then make recommendations to either use a standard report "as is," rework an existing report, or say that no standard report fulfills the requirements.

This is where Discoverer comes into the picture. Discoverer should not be seen as the replacement for Oracle standard reports. It is an enhancement to give you greater power to access your data—and wow, what power!!

Getting Help About Discoverer

Oracle has provided comprehensive resources for getting help about Discoverer.

The very first place to look for help is within the product itself by selecting from the menu bar. For those familiar with standard Windows applications, this will be second nature.

To access the Help menu, click on the Menu bar and select Help. You will be presented with the drop-down menu, shown here:

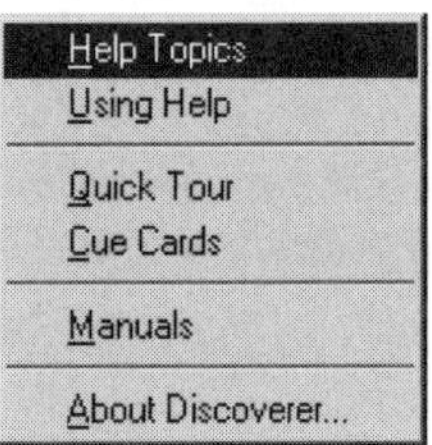

From the Help menu you can select the following:

- **Help Topics** An Oracle-provided index of help topics (see Figure 1-3).
- **Using Help** Instructions from Microsoft on how to use the Windows help features.
- **Quick Tour** A brief overview of the main features of the Discoverer End-User Edition.
- **Cue Cards** A set of crib sheets to step you through some common topics.
- **Manual** This feature takes you to the online end-user manual provided by Oracle.

The following figure shows the Discoverer 3.1 Help window.

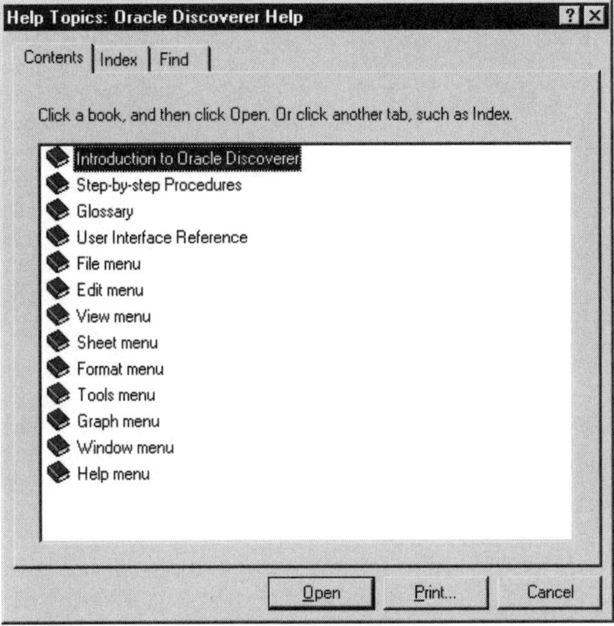

FIGURE 1-3. *The Help window*

Other sources of help can be found on the Web. Listed below are some of the most useful help sites.

Source of Help	Web Site	Contents and Features
Oracle's Web site	www.oracle.com/tools/discoverer/index.html	Here you will find white papers, FAQs, Quick Tours, demos, etc.
Oracle's Metalink site	www.oracle.com/support/elec_sup/ml_login.html	This site is available to companies who have purchased support from Oracle. You will be required to register. In order to register, you will need to know your company's customer support identifier (CSI) number. The site contains technical libraries, forums, and even a means of creating technical assistance requests (TARs) online.

Source of Help	Web Site	Contents and Features
ODTUG Web site	www.odtug.com/	This is a members-only site for the Oracle Development Tools User Group. You can join by completing the online registration form. The site contains case studies, feature articles, links to related material in the ODTUG *Technical Journal* and a technical journal online.
OAUG Web Site	www.oaug.org/	This site belongs to the Oracle Applications User Group. It contains information on upcoming conferences and meetings. There are even special interest groups (SIGs) that have been set up. The Data Warehouse SIG, soon to be renamed the Information Delivery SIG, is the group for Discoverer.
IOUG Web Site	http://www.ioug.org/	This site belongs to the International Oracle Users Group. It contains information on discussion forums and has a technical repository.

Summary

The current releases of Discoverer, 3.1 for Windows and 3*i* for the Web are slick, easy to use, and intuitive. From the introduction of the Windows version in the 1990s, through to the 2000 Web release, Discoverer has played an ever-increasing role in information delivery. With the release of Discoverer 3*i*, the product has brought a full release of the User Edition to the Internet. Today, Oracle has defined this tool as being an integral part of their BIS suite.

You have learned that this book is primarily aimed at the end user with helpful advice for the Discoverer administrator. Throughout the book you will be shown examples of queries and reports taken from a fictitious company database. We are sure that the examples accurately reflect "real-world" situations that will be useful in teaching you good query design using Discoverer.

In the section entitled "A New Direction in Reporting," we have described how things used to be in many companies and how Discoverer can overcome many obstacles in reporting. The Discoverer GUI and the use of a mouse make Discoverer intuitive and user friendly. You have also learned how ad hoc queries differ from predefined queries and the benefits of both.

Finally, we have given you a table showing the variety of help resources available to the end user and Discoverer administrator alike.

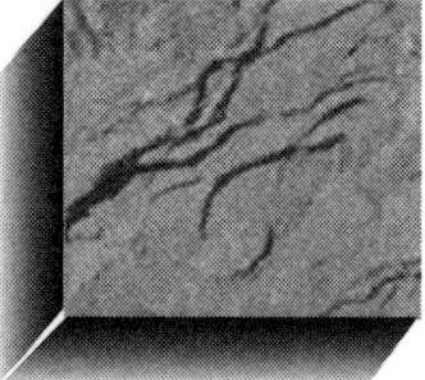

CHAPTER 2

Users and Databases

verybody is familiar with the terms "hardware" and "software". When something goes wrong with a system, it is to these that people usually look when seeking out the reason why. Because of this, not all companies invest as much as they should into the other, and probably more important, resources: the users. That said, there is a lot that users can do to help themselves when they are required to start working with Discoverer.

This chapter will deal with the responsibilities of the end user and then go on to discuss the concept of superusers. Throughout this chapter we will make reference to other staff members, such as DBAs and Discoverer administrators, but will leave the discussions about these people until the next chapter.

The Responsibility of the End User

If you don't understand your responsibilities as a Discoverer end user, you are lost. Queries cannot be defined if you are not aware of the data available to you, if you don't know which folders contain the data, and what the end result is that you are after. Therefore, before you begin to explore the power of Discoverer, you will need to understand the following:

- Your business
- Your reporting requirements
- Your database

Your Business

The most important question you can ask yourself is "What is my business?" Are you the CEO of your own small company? Perhaps you are an analyst in the accounting department of a large manufacturing firm. Whatever your business, the first step in viewing company data is to understand what it is you need to know about your business, and then try to get a feeling for what it is that you don't already know.

If you don't know about your company—what it does and how you fit into the scheme of things—how can you begin to create reports that can have a meaningful impact upon your business? You need to at least understand your company's objectives and then get someone to explain how your role fits in to the overall plan. Once you have ascertained exactly how important you are to your company, you can begin to make some headway into the area of query creation for your department. But where do you start?

The best way to begin is by looking at any predefined queries and reports that already exist. These may arrive on your desk in the form of a weekly or monthly report. Perhaps a clever programmer developed this report based on some long forgotten request. That request might have come from your department, perhaps even from your predecessor. It is also possible it came from another department and that someone in your unit felt it would be useful.

If that report was designed and created more than a year ago, chances are that no one remembers why it was built in the first place. You may be lucky and find that someone actually documented the report and what it does. More likely, you will have nothing other than the query itself, a query that probably means very little to you today.

Each time the report is found in your In box, you read it with some frustration because it does not really answer the questions you have. Sure, it answers questions A, B, and C, but what you really need to know is D and what you want to know is E. Because you know your business, you know the answers that are missing from your existing reports. More importantly, you know the questions to pose in order to get the answers you need.

Your Reporting Requirements

Now that you know how to look for what is missing, it is time to brainstorm. Write down everything you want to know about your business. Be as detailed as you can, but bear in mind that you will not likely get everything you want. It is something like a Christmas wish list. Don't just write down what you need to know, but also what you would like to know. The following story illustrates how understanding what you want to know leads to more questions.

A successful commercial real estate firm realized the need to automate and centralize information, and had a database built. The database contained the names of building owners, building information, building tenants and all of their lease information, maintenance companies, and other information. Not understanding the kinds of questions to ask, the database was used timidly at first. The DBA was asked questions like, "Can you tell me which tenants leases expire in the next six months?" Then she was asked "Which tenants have an increase in their rent in the next three months?" Soon, the users asked more and more questions and the DBA responded by creating more queries and more reports.

The people in this company had come to realize the power of the information in the database and were asking the right questions. It is your responsibility to do the same. Once you have ascertained what is missing, you need to formulate a plan to aid you in getting what you need.

Determining End-User Requirements

Your best resource for defining end-user requirements is your current pool of end users, your business unit managers, and your database administrators. These people can be a great source of help and inspiration when all seems lost. Remember to find out if anyone else is using Discoverer, and see whether they know how to get the data that you need for your report. Your Discoverer administrator is also a great source of help, and should be used as well.

Employ an Incremental Approach

Don't try to answer every question by using one query, and don't try to answer all your questions in one session. Take your time, and remember that whatever fit the bill perfectly last year may not do so now. Requirements change, business direction changes, and people change. Try to remember this when you are analyzing requirements.

Remaining flexible is a great asset to have and using a "develop, demonstrate, and revise" approach will work wonders. Develop a report that will handle the current needs, demonstrate that it works and satisfies requirements, then be prepared to revise it when the time arises. Discoverer is a powerful tool and will allow you to change your query at any time. When your manager realizes that you have that power under control, he or she will naturally see other ways to harness your Discoverer talents.

Documenting Your Requirements

Perhaps one of the hardest and most unenvied of all tasks is documentation. We all try to avoid doing this as if it were some terminal disease from which there is no hope of recovery. Yet, when the chips are down, the first thing we all go looking for is the selfsame documentation, and how pleased we are when we find that we did in fact write down why management wanted our query to only pull in data from four of the five sales regions.

So, what should you document? Well, you at least need to identify who it was who told you that something had to be done this way rather than that. You need to give examples of report layouts and specify any special requirements (which will later become conditions) that need to be applied in order to make the query do what you want.

This may all seem to be overkill, and in some cases this may be so. But we can tell you that not documenting is usually far worse than over documenting. Remembering that requirements change is itself a reason to write down why you have done something. Having documented what it is your query is supposed to do, you need to be aware of the data that is available to you and where you can go to find help about that data.

Your Database

Perhaps the most daunting responsibility anyone tasked with creating queries can have is to understand the database they are working with. You cannot know what questions to ask of the database if you don't know what data is available to you. It is in this step that you must become a partner with your Discoverer administrator. The Discoverer administrator can familiarize you with the database structure you are using and the data that is available to you.

NOTE
It is important to remember that just because there is data in the database, it might not be available to you. Security issues and "need to know" are important parts of access. If there is some part of the database that you have not been granted access to and want, you will need to make a case for why you should be granted access.

It is also important for you to know what type of database system you are using. Is it a live production system, a copy of production, or a data warehouse? Each system has different characteristics and parameters that you need to familiarize yourself with if you are to become an expert in Discoverer.

OLTP Systems

These are the "live" databases, otherwise known as online transaction processing (OLTP) systems. This is where the work is being done. Invoices are being entered, orders taken, payments recorded, inventory counted, and other tasks are being performed. It is in "production" that the data is the freshest because it is all happening now. So the question might be asked, "Why don't we just do all of our querying and reporting from the production database and forget about those other systems?" The answer is simple.

An OLTP has been designed and built for entering and storing transactions quickly. It is not built for querying or reporting. You may ask, "What is the difference?" There are several reasons why the transaction systems and reporting systems are different:

- The database structures are different.
- Reporting from an OLTP is slow.
- The data is volatile.
- OLTP table names are not easy to understand.
- OLTP systems are frequently purged of their data.

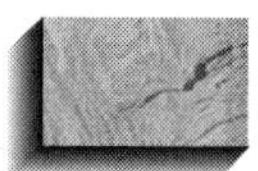

NOTE
The comment about table names being not easy to understand is a moot point if your Discoverer administrator renames the folders. If your system does not have user-friendly table names, you should speak with your Discoverer administrator and ask him or her if it is possible to change them.

The Database Structures Are Different If you are familiar with database design, you will have heard of *normalization*. This technique uses many tables and never repeats an item of data. It uses small indexed tables to hold everything. On your transaction tables, an OLTP stores ID numbers or codes as cross-references (foreign keys or lookups) to other tables. For example, in the OLTP, the city San Francisco is only listed in the City lookup table with a code of 430. Every customer in San Francisco is listed in the Customer table with the code 430.

Reporting from an OLTP is Slowwwww Because an OLTP is optimized for entering transactions, it is not optimized for reporting. The database that can do both quickly and efficiently has not yet been invented. However, Oracle is making great strides in this direction. One day this will no doubt be possible. Until then, the reality is that when you use your OLTP for reporting, it can be deadly slow.

You might find yourself beginning to run your query, go get a cup of coffee, visit a friend, call to make a vet appointment for Muffy to get her teeth cleaned, and then come back to find that your query has timed out. To make matters worse, you will have impacted your online colleagues who will already have been complaining that the database is running slow. You may even find that the DBA terminated your query because it was drawing too many system resources. How wonderful it would be if the company built a database just for you!

The Data Is Volatile In an OLTP system, the data is changing constantly. If you run a report at 9:00 A.M. and your coworker runs the same report at 11:00 A.M., and you both bring the report to the 3:00 P.M. staff meeting, the reports will be different. In the two hours between the reports, new orders will have been placed, invoices paid, shipments made, and so on.

To further compound the problem, your supervisor will see the difference in your reports and may decide to check the figures for herself at 3:30 P.M. Guess what—her answers will be completely different, so maybe she decides you are both incompetent and the two of you get the sack! Of course, this is an extreme example, but it does illustrate one problem with using an OTLP for reporting.

OLTP Table Names Are Not Easy to Understand When you are selecting the criteria for your query, you need to know where the data comes from. In an

OLTP system, the table names are not obvious. You might think that the City table would be called "City". You will probably be wrong. It might have a simple, but still difficult to decipher, name like "location_names_all", or it might be called "table_19975". Just imagine the nightmare in trying to report using these names. This may sound far-fetched, but the truth of the matter is that system designers frequently don't take the needs of end users into account when designing databases.

If you have Oracle Applications and want to build a report showing all shipments and returns, did you know that the tables you need are so_headers_all, so_lines_all, so_line_details, so_picking_lines, mtl_so_rma_receipts, mtl_so_rma_interface, and ra_addresses_all? Not only do you need to know the names of all these tables, you need to know how to link them together. The typical end user would have no idea how this is done because the system was built for storing transactions—not reporting.

If your company has decided not to invest in another alternative, you have no choice but to report from the OLTP system. Perhaps your company is small and only has one person in MIS, or simply cannot afford one of the alternative systems. Whatever the reason, you should work with your Discoverer administrator, who is able to at least change the names of the tables to something more meaningful. He or she may even be able to build some views of the database for you, bringing together common tables for your reporting needs. A view, by the way, is a means of hiding the logic that goes into joining tables together. Not only do they look like tables, but you can query from them as if they are tables.

If you are using Oracle Applications, your company may have purchased products called Noetix Views from Aris Software or BIS from Oracle. These companies have analyzed common end-user requirements and have put together a complete set of views for all of the modules. Both BIS views and Noetix views will be explained in greater detail in Appendix B.

OLTP Systems Are Frequently Purged of Their Data Most OLTP systems do not store large amounts of history. Since these systems are designed for immediate response, their data is often purged within a few months of capture. Therefore, you cannot get any significant historical information from an OLTP system.

Snapshot Databases

These are copies of your data. They can be one of the following two types:

- A complete copy of your OLTP system
- A partial copy of the database saved to a local server

Complete Copy of the OLTP System The preceding section outlined the drawbacks of reporting from an OLTP system. Many companies minimize these drawbacks by making a complete copy of their OLTP database for use in reporting. The benefits of a complete copy are as follows:

- The data is constant. If you run your report at 9:00 A.M. and your colleague runs the same report at 11:00 A.M., you will both have the same information for your 3:00 P.M. meeting—and hopefully keep your jobs.
- There is no impact on the OLTP system. You will not have unhappy coworkers complaining about your query mucking up the system.

Some companies take a full copy of their OLTP system every night following the close of the working day, placing that copy on a different machine from the OLTP system.

The disadvantages to the complete copy are as follows:

- You could still have the problems over database structure and table names (see the note below).
- It is still inherently an OLTP system, thus meaning it is not designed for reporting.
- The data is not up-to-date—in some cases, 24 hours or more old. This may not be seen as a disadvantage, depending on what you will use the data for. If you want to analyze shipments made yesterday, the snapshot is to your advantage. If you want to analyze today's shipments, you must wait until the next refresh cycle.
- Because it is a copy of the OLTP system, you cannot do historical reporting.

NOTE
One of the reasons for having a database administrator is to present the data to you in a meaningful way. This includes simplifying the view of the database, although this should be transparent to the end user.

Complete snapshot copies are becoming increasingly popular. They overcome some of the disadvantages of reporting from an OLTP system, as long as you are aware of your company's refresh cycle.

A Partial Copy of the Database Saved to a Local Server If your company uses a centralized database, it could be located many thousand of miles or kilometers from your office. In order to improve performance, you can make local copies of some of the tables you need for your reports. Snapshots can be used to copy all or part of a table. If your database is in Paris and your office is in Denver and you are only interested in reporting on North American data, your DBA can arrange to copy only the data you need.

The simplest forms of partial copy take the tables in their entirety, rather than the more complex forms, which use queries to extract just the portions you need. The advantages of this approach are as follows:

- The data is constant.
- There is no impact on the OLTP system.
- The performance in relation to speed is increased.
- The DBA can define some indexes specifically designed for your reporting needs.

The disadvantages are as follows:

- You still have the problems over database structure and table names.
- It is still inherently an OLTP system, thus meaning it is not designed for reporting.
- The data is not up-to-date—in some cases, 24 hours or more old.
- If you have only copied parts of the database and you now need to report on something outside of the copied data, you cannot.
- Because it is a copy of the OLTP system, you cannot do historical reporting.

Data Mart or Data Warehouse

Data marts and data warehouses are commonly discussed together, and some industry experts will tell you that the two cannot exist side-by-side. We will not involve ourselves in that debate. We will simply tell you what they are.

Data Warehouses According to Bill Inmon, commonly regarded as the father of data warehousing, a data warehouse is a "subject-oriented, integrated, non-volatile, time-variant collection of data used in support of management decisions." What the heck does that mean?

Quite simply this means that a data warehouse is a business-relevant (subject-oriented) collection of data from various sources. The data can come from the OLTP system, spreadsheets, word processor documents, even from your customers. In essence, the data warehouse will contain all of the items needed to satisfy the reporting requirements for your business area.

Because the data can come from various sources, it has to be manipulated into a common format (integrated). For example, your customers may all provide you with information about their sales of your products, but they probably will send you that data using their own in-house codes and ID numbers. It is necessary to convert these numbers into your codes. This is accomplished by the integration process.

Once the data has been collected into the data warehouse, it will not change and cannot be deleted (non-volatile), implying that you will have historical data. As a data warehouse is a read-only database, users cannot change it. The only way the data can change is during the refresh cycle when new data is added.

Because the data is collected periodically you will be able to report trends over time according to the refresh cycle. What this means is that if you collect your data every day, you can analyze your daily sales. If you only refresh your data weekly, you can analyze weekly sales, and so forth (time-variant). You need to specify what your requirements are so the data warehouse is built accordingly. If you are working from an existing data warehouse, you might not have the necessary clout to change the refresh cycle, but you certainly need to know what it is.

The advantages of a data warehouse are as follows:

- It is optimized for reporting.
- It contains historical data.
- It does not impact the OLTP system.
- It has meaningful table names.
- It is not subject to change.
- You can perform data mining ("tell me something I don't already know").
- It contains data from multiple sources, not just your OLTP system.

The disadvantages of a data warehouse are as follows:

- It can be extremely expensive to build and maintain. You may need to have buy-in from senior management to get approval for a data warehouse.
- You need large amounts of storage space, potentially one terabyte or more.
- Because there is a huge amount of data, it is possible to write queries that seem to run forever and never come back with an answer (the query from the Twilight Zone).
- The data is not up-to-date—in some cases, 24 hours or more old.

- They are not easily changed. If you spot an error in the data warehouse, you will have to correct it in the source system. If that system cannot be changed, the data warehouse cannot be changed and you will have to live with incorrect data. For example, company "ABC Widgets" could be stored in the database as "A.B.C. Widgets", "AB and C Widgets", or "AB&C". Unless you know about these possible irregularities, you will get incomplete results. You may have a difficult time persuading your company to change their procedures to satisfy the data warehouse.
- Because the data is coming from different sources, you may not be able to get the same answer from your OLTP system as you do from the data warehouse. It will be difficult, if not impossible, to identify if any OLTP transactions are missing from the data warehouse.

Data Mart A data mart is a table or set of tables that has been created for a specific reporting requirement. They provide a subject-oriented view of the data in your system and contain significantly smaller amounts of data than in your OLTP or data warehouse systems. Where they exist, they will be the prime focus of the online analytical processing (OLAP) by the end users. The table structure(s) will be simple, the table names will correspond to folders within business areas, and the data items should have user friendly, meaningful names.

NOTE
The names of the data items should not be an issue if your DBA has created user friendly, meaningful names. In the vast majority of cases, this will be true; however, sometimes you may need to speak with the DBA and request that the names be changed.

Data marts are like snapshots in that they are refreshed periodically. In fact, most data marts are actually refreshed from a data warehouse if you have one, making your data marts a subset of your data warehouse. When you don't have a data warehouse, they are refreshed from the OLTP system. Unlike snapshots—but like data warehouses—they have been optimized for reporting purposes. In fact, their sole purpose in life is reporting.

Typically, one data mart contains all of the data you need to satisfy the reporting requirements for a single business area. Using the Oracle example highlighted in the previous section, where you had to pull from at least seven tables to obtain a complete shipping report, all of this data is now found in a single shipping table. It also has been given the delightful name Shipping.

The advantages of a data mart are as follows:

- It is a single source of data for a business area.
- It has no impact on the OLTP system.
- It is optimized for reporting.
- It is fast, because it has special indexes created to enable you to extract the data quickly.
- When sourced directly from an OLTP system, they can be quick to build and less expensive than a data warehouse. They could even be used as a prototype for a future data warehouse.

As with all things, there are disadvantages, namely:

- It usually contains data to satisfy predefined reports. If you suddenly decide you need more data in a report, you can't have it easily. You will need to submit a request to your administrator to have the data mart structure, and possibly the data warehouse, changed. This can be a difficult and time-consuming process.
- Data marts are not typically built to cross-link one business area to another. This is not a Discoverer limitation, but a business rule implementation. For example, your company may have sales regions across the world and have built a data mart for each region. If your company has decided to prevent users in one region querying the sales data from another, your Discoverer administrator will not be prevented from cross-linking the data marts.
- If they are pulling from an OLTP system, they are not historical.
- Because the data is usually a subset of another system, you may not be able to get the same answer from your OLTP system as you do from the data mart. In fact, if your data mart is sourced from a data warehouse, you are two steps away from the source.

For a more detailed explanation of data warehouses and data marts, we recommend you read, *Oracle8 Data Warehousing: A Practical Guide to Successful Data Warehouse Analysis, Build, and Roll-Out,* by Michael J. Corey, Michael Abbey, Ian Abramson, and Ben Taub (Oracle Press, 1998). If you are interested in reading more by Bill Inmon, you should read his book, *Building the Data Warehouse* (John Wiley and Sons Inc., 1996).

The Superuser Concept

The concept of superusers has been around for some time, and so the principals being proposed here will not come as a surprise to many of you. However, there will be some of you to whom this is a new idea.

The Definition of a Superuser

A superuser is defined as being a subject matter expert with:

- An expert knowledge of the functionality of Discoverer
- A sense of business acumen—basically a pretty good idea of what their part of the business does, knows their formulas, definitions, and so forth
- A sense of their business unit's strategic goals and objectives
- A temperament suited to helping others
- A very good understanding of the database(s) used by their business unit

Most companies have one or two Discoverer users who stand out from the rest because they possess the above qualities. Pooling these staff as an additional resource can have great benefits for a company, as we will show.

The Benefits of Having Superusers

There are a number of reasons for having superusers in your organization. The following list is not exhaustive but is given as a means to show how beneficial it might be to designate superusers within your company:

- They are a first line of support for Discoverer-related issues to other end users.
- They would have additional know-how to go about solving problems with queries and reports.
- They will be able to give at least some introductory Discoverer training to other end users.
- They would be responsible for producing your company's standard queries.
- They could be given some Discoverer admin rights so that they can undertake some tasks normally performed by the Discoverer administrator.

The Benefits of Being a Superuser

It may seem at first that becoming a superuser would simply mean more work. There are, however, a number of benefits:

- You would receive additional Discoverer training, thus becoming an expert in this growing field (not a bad addition to your résumé, but don't tell that to your boss when you ask for additional training).
- You will have a direct line to the Discoverer administrator for help and guidance in solving problems.
- You will have greater database access rights than a normal end user.
- You should be included in strategic planning for your business unit when Discoverer issues are discussed.
- You will have the ability to help other end users by being their first line of support for Discoverer-related issues.

Choosing your Superusers

You may not be in a position to become a superuser, but you might be the person who will choose your company's or department's superusers. When first choosing a superuser, there are a number of questions you should ask yourself about the person under consideration:

- Is the person a subject matter expert in the business area they will be serving?
- Does the person have an expert knowledge of Discoverer or the ability to become an expert?
- Does the person have the respect of their fellow users?
- Does the person have the ability to act as a first line of support to other end users?

You may find that there is some resistance amongst some managers, who could see the idea of a superuser as a means for the IT department to reduce its level of support. After all, IT members are supposed to be the experts in everything to do with computers, aren't they? Well, this used to be true in the days of mainframe computers, when the IT staff were locked away behind glass walls. But ask most modern users about computers and they nearly all have one at home. They know how to use the Internet, they know how to use spreadsheets and word-processors, and no longer need to have their hands held by the IT department.

Companies are looking to employ computer-literate staff, the same staff who will soon become experts in Discoverer. Whether or not your company chooses to embrace this pool of knowledge at this time is an internal matter. What we can say is that Discoverer is a powerful tool, it has been designated by Oracle as being a key component of its BIS suite, and the ability to master this product will be a much sought after commodity. The IT department, not being fully aware of business issues, will not be in a position to fill this role.

Summary

In this chapter, we have discussed in detail the roles and responsibilities of the end user in connection with Discoverer. It is important for you to understand your business, your reporting needs, and how your data is stored. Once you understand these things, you are ready to determine exactly what your reporting requirements are.

You have also learned how things change in business and how your reporting needs will change with those things. An incremental approach will lead to a need for documentation as you build queries and reports.

How your data is stored and the differences between OLTP systems, snapshots, data warehouses, and data marts were discussed in detail. You have learned the benefits and drawbacks of each type of system and how you will need to interact with them.

Finally, we discussed the superuser concept and how to implement it in your company. You learned the benefits of having superusers, being a superuser, and the attributes of a good superuser. We also discussed why the IT department is not a good replacement for superusers.

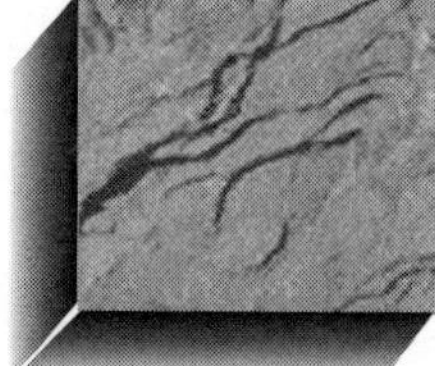

CHAPTER 3

Getting Started in Discoverer

n this chapter, you will learn about the importance of some key members of your Discoverer team: the Discoverer administrator, the DBA and the superuser. Developing good relationships with these key personnel can be very beneficial in your successful use of Discoverer.

We will introduce you to some important terms that will be useful to your success in using Discoverer. You will also learn how Discoverer manages SQL queries and their interaction with your source database. You will come to understand the process that must be followed prior to gaining access to the system, and gain some insight into what happens behind the scenes.

We will introduce you to Discoverer's "memory," referred to by Oracle as its "Sticky Feature." Just before we show you how to launch Discoverer, we give you a list of cool things it can do. Then, at last, you will be launching and logging on to Discoverer.

Key Personnel

In all companies, no matter what you call them, there are a number of key personnel with whom you should become familiar. If the size of your organization gets in the way of knowing these people personally, you should at least have a basic understanding of their job function. The key personnel with whom you need to form a relationship are as follows:

- Your Discoverer administrator
- Your database administrator
- Your superuser

In some smaller organizations, you may not have both a Discoverer administrator and a DBA, and the roles may be combined. For the purposes of clarity, we will describe the basic functions of each role separately.

Discoverer Administrator

The Discoverer administrator is probably the most important member of the support staff with whom you need to maintain contact. The Discoverer administrator is responsible for the following:

- Maintaining the end-user layer (EUL)
- Maintaining user access to the EUL
- Defining Discoverer strategy and monitoring Discoverer performance

- Setting the default item names and table characteristics (essential for 3*i*)
- Being a source of help

The Discoverer administrator works with the individual business units to identify the data required for each business area (sometimes called business functions). Oracle has provided a separate tool, called the Discoverer Admin Edition, in which the Discoverer administrator works to create the seamless interface with which you will be working. This tool provides a highly secure, centralized link to the EUL.

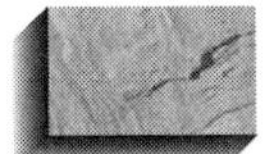

NOTE
The EUL is the interface between you and the database. What you see when you log onto Discoverer is the EUL. It maintains all of the links between you and the underlying database. Whenever you create a Discoverer query, it is converted into a Structured Query Language (SQL) statement by the EUL. When you submit your query, Discoverer converts it into efficient SQL code and sends it to the database, keeping you from needing to know (1) the underlying database and (2) SQL. In other words, thank goodness for the EUL!!

For more information about the roles and responsibilities of the Discoverer administrator, including what it can do for you, please refer to Chapter 14.

DBA

Besides being the person we all love to hate, the DBA is a crucial piece of the Discoverer jigsaw puzzle. Without these warm and charming people, the databases would cease to function. Their main responsibilities are as follows:

- Maintaining the databases
- Maintaining user access to the databases
- Defining database strategy and monitoring database performance
- Being yet another source of help

DBAs are a much-maligned group of people and are misunderstood by many. They have an unenviable role in the organization and bear the brunt of everyone's frustrations whenever the system goes down. The fact of the matter is that systems go down by their very complex nature, and it is the DBA that gets the system going again.

We are so used to having our systems up and running for 100 percent of the time that even a break in service of 15 minutes seems like a lifetime. The DBA has to find where in this complex system the breakdown is and repair it. Most of the time you don't even know that a problem existed, because they monitor the system constantly and correct many problems before they even affect the uptime. So, next time your system goes down and you feel like venting at your DBA, get them a pack of cookies from the vending machine instead and go answer some emails.

Superusers

Within your company, you may be lucky to find that you have designated superusers. It is your responsibility to locate and pick the brains of the superuser for your business unit. These people are users just like yourself, but have been given added responsibilities and training. Their responsibilities may include the following:

- Being your primary source of help for all Discoverer-related issues
- Being a subject matter expert in Discoverer
- Knowing your business unit's goals and objectives
- Being the link between the user community and the Discoverer administrator

For more information about the roles and responsibilities of superusers, please refer back to Chapter 2.

Having learned about the key personnel within your organization, you are now ready to turn to Discoverer itself, but first you will need to have everything set up.

Gaining Access to Discoverer

Before you can even begin to think about logging on to Discoverer, the following steps will need to have been completed:

1. If your company is installing Discoverer directly on to your PC, a request will have to be submitted for this to be done. Perhaps your company has decided not to install Discoverer this way, and to use a terminal server instead (see the following note explaining terminal servers). In this case, a request will have to be made for that software to be installed. If your access to Discoverer is to be via the Web, someone should ensure that you have your company's standard browser correctly installed and configured. Whichever method your company uses to provide access to Discoverer, we would hope that you will be provided with an icon on your desktop that can be double-clicked to launch the login sequence.

   This step may sound elementary, but it is amazing how many times these basic requirements are overlooked.

2. You or your manager will need to request that access to Discoverer be made available to you. In the request, you will need to specify which database you need and which business areas you should be granted access to. The request should also contain your telephone number, your position, and whether you need to have full Discoverer access or just the ability to run prewritten queries.

   If you are new to the company, your manager should complete this on your behalf. Perhaps he or she can name another person within your department who has the same access you need and ask the Discoverer administrator to duplicate it. The more information you can give to your Discoverer administrator, the easier will be the setup.

3. Your Discoverer administrator will take your request and coordinate it with the DBA. The DBA will create a database account for you, assigning a username and password as determined by your company's standards.

4. After your DBA has created the database account, your Discoverer administrator will complete his or her tasks. The administrator will grant you access to the required business areas and possibly arrange for you to attend a training course. This course could either be an official Oracle-given course at one of their many training centers or it could be given internally if your company has a training department. You might even be in training right now using this book as your text!

5. Finally, once all of the above has been completed, you should receive notification from your Discoverer administrator that your account has been set up and has been activated. In this notification, you will be informed of your username, password, and any database connect string that you may need. If you are going to be connecting to Discoverer via the Web, you will also be given the appropriate URL.

NOTE

If your main database is not located at your work site, your company may well have decided to use one or more terminal servers. These powerful PCs (usually Windows NT servers) are used as a link between you and the database and have a full working copy of Discoverer 3.1 on them. They are usually installed in your data center with a direct connection to the database. You connect to a terminal server from your PC using your network, and then you can use it just as if it were your own PC. The benefits of this approach are reduced network traffic and improved performance. Anyone who has tried running Discoverer from their own PC connected to a database more than 1,000 miles away will know what we mean.

Having had the correct setups completed, you are now ready to use Discoverer.

Key Definitions

Before we get into the Discoverer login sequence, we need to explain two key definitions that you need to know.

Workbooks and Worksheets

Discoverer uses workbooks. Anyone familiar with spreadsheets should understand the concept of workbooks. A workbook is a group of worksheets. Each worksheet in the *workbook is related in some way to the others.* For example, you may have a workbook that pulls in the date for the sales in your eastern region. One worksheet might have sales broken down by salesperson, another might have sales sorted showing highest sales to lowest by customer, and yet another shows the regional sales compared to last year. The worksheets are related, but each one puts a different spin on the data and answers a different business question.

NOTE
Multiple worksheets should be used cautiously at first, and perhaps you should not use them at all in your first few workbooks. The idea behind Discoverer is its ease of use. Getting bogged down in worksheets is not always to your advantage.

Each worksheet in a workbook is related to its own query.

Queries

We have already used the term "query" a number of times in this book. However, some of you might not know what a query is. A query is simply asking the database a question. When you tell Discoverer to run a worksheet, it generates a SQL query and sends the code to the database. Hopefully, the answer you expect comes back. An example of a query is "how many blue widgets did we sell in the southwest region last week?" If the query was created correctly, the answer will come back to you in a matter of seconds.

Sticky Features

Discoverer has a memory. From time to time, Discoverer will make a note in the system registry of "last used" options. The next time you are given a choice for one of these options, Discoverer will remember what you last did and default to that setting. Oracle calls this Discoverer's Sticky Feature. We will tell you whenever this is available with a *Sticky Feature* note.

Main Features of Discoverer

We have told you how great Discoverer is and how easy it is to use. According to *PC Week*, "Oracle's Discoverer breaks new ground with its high-performance mix of dynamic and pre-computed queries, while its useable interface ensures its power can be put to immediate use."

We have not told you some of the terrific things Discoverer does. It might be in your mind that all you can do is view data and create queries. This is far from the truth. If you are used to working with spreadsheets or even DOS-based systems, you may not be aware of some of the features that Discoverer has available. Below is a list, though not exhaustive, of some of those features:

Folders based on tables and views	Items based on columns
Descriptions of folders and items	Lists of values
Joins based on primary- and foreign-key definitions	Default date hierarchies (year-quarter-month)
Drills to related items	Complex objects (pivots, filters, calculations)
Complex joins (folders joined to other folders)	Derived items (items based on other items)
Graphing	Percentages
Exceptions	Exporting to other applications
Sorting (simple, group sorting, sort within sort)	Totaling (grand totals and subtotals)
Formatting (fonts, colors, justification, italics, bold, numeric)	Adding bitmaps to reports
Applying titles	Adding page breaks and pagination
Queries based upon other queries (subqueries)	Printing and print preview
Scheduling	Sharing queries with other users
Shortcuts	Right mouse support (context menus)

The above list is by no means all of the features of Discoverer, but is meant to give you a flavor of what to expect in the coming chapters. Okay, now the bit you have been waiting for. In the next section, you will learn to log on and get started in Discoverer.

Discoverer Login Sequence

From this point forward in the book, we will be describing step-by-step instructions for using Discoverer. We suggest you perform these steps for yourself as a way of reinforcing the skills you are learning. Imagine you are in a classroom and the book is your instructor.

As we were going through the login sequences for Discoverer 3.1 and Discoverer 3*i*, we noticed that there are enough differences between the sequences to warrant documenting each separately. We therefore will give you a small section on each login process. This is the only time in the book when we do this. In all other instances, we describe one of the processes and tell you how that differs, if at all, from the other.

We will begin with the Windows version, Discoverer 3.1.

Launching Discoverer 3.1

You launch Discoverer 3.1 using the same process you use for all of your Windows applications. You can either use the Start menu, or you can double-click on an icon on your desktop. If you are using the Start menu, the normal sequence is Start | Programs | Oracle Discoverer 3.1 | User Edition, as shown in Figure 3-1.

If your company uses a terminal server for the connection to Discoverer, you should first connect to the terminal server, then launch Discoverer from the Start menu of that machine. Whichever approach your company has adopted, follow the procedures that are the standard in your company. If you are not sure how to log on, you should either contact your superuser or call your Discoverer administrator.

Having successfully launched Discoverer 3.1, you will be presented with the following login screen:

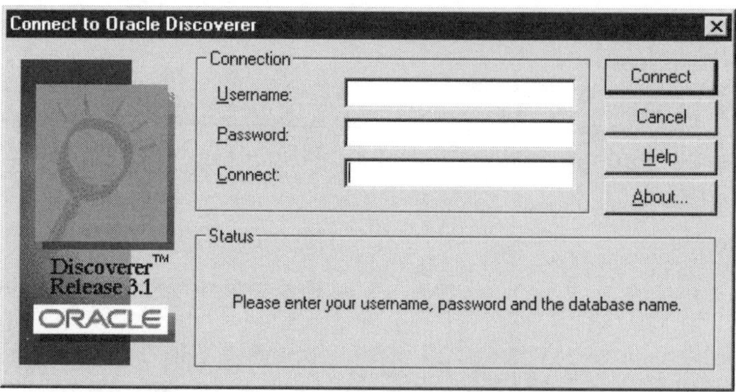

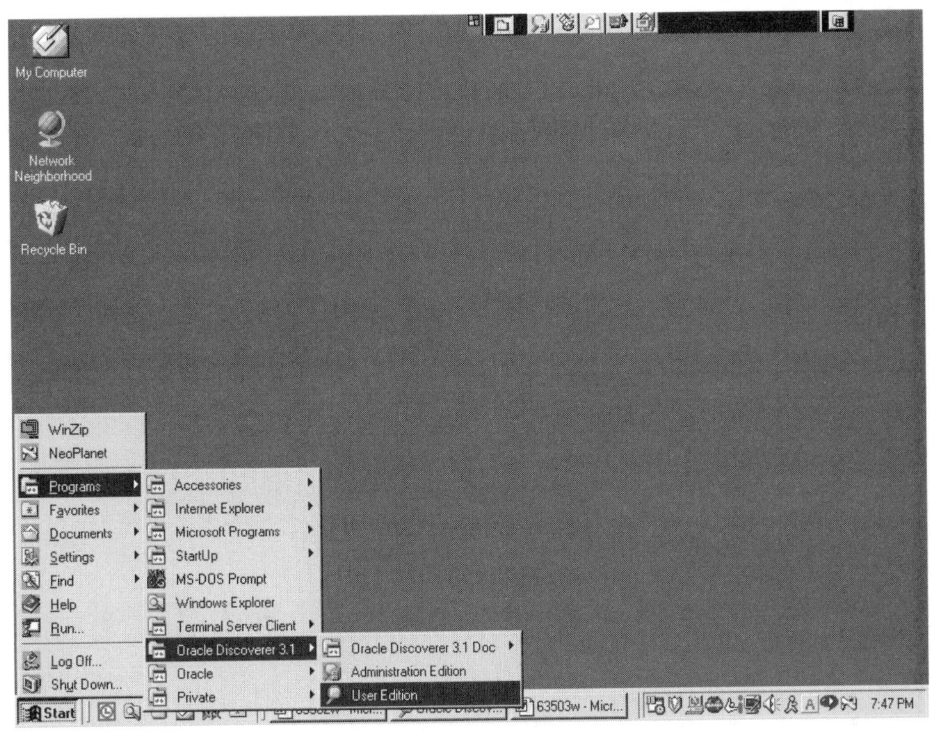

FIGURE 3-1. *Discoverer 3.1 Start menu*

Enter your username and password in the appropriate fields in the startup screen. You will also need to know and enter the name of the database you want to access. This takes us back to the earlier part of this chapter on your Discoverer administrator and the DBA. Since each company will address these issues uniquely, we can only give you generic instructions.

When you have entered your username, password, and database, click Connect. You will be allowed three attempts to get this right before Discoverer terminates your connection. However, don't worry because Discoverer does not lock you out, it only closes and makes you start again.

Launching Discoverer 3*i*

Logging onto Discoverer 3*i* is done via your Web browser. Your Discoverer administrator will give you a Uniform Resource Locater (URL) for the application as it is stored on your company's Web server. This may sound complicated, but it really isn't. Just remember to ask for the instructions for launching, and then follow those instructions.

TIP
Don't forget to add the URL to your bookmarks or Web favorites.

When you first launch the URL to start Discoverer 3*i*, you will see the welcome screen shown in Figure 3-2.

To start Discoverer 3*i*, click the large Start button (Discoverer even tells you to click it). You may need to wait while it initializes (Discoverer will give you a message that this is what it's doing).

Having successfully launched Discoverer 3*i* you will be presented with the following connect screen:

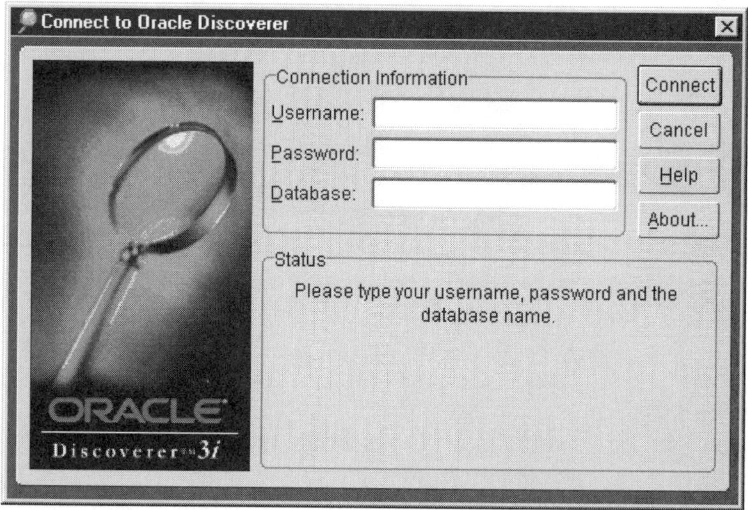

When you have entered your username, password, and database, click Connect.

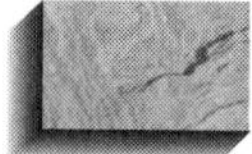

STICKY FEATURE
Unlike 3.1, 3i is not sticky when it comes to logging you on. If you close your browser, it will not remember who you are or where you were last connected. You will have to type these again. The authors hope this will be fixed in a future release.

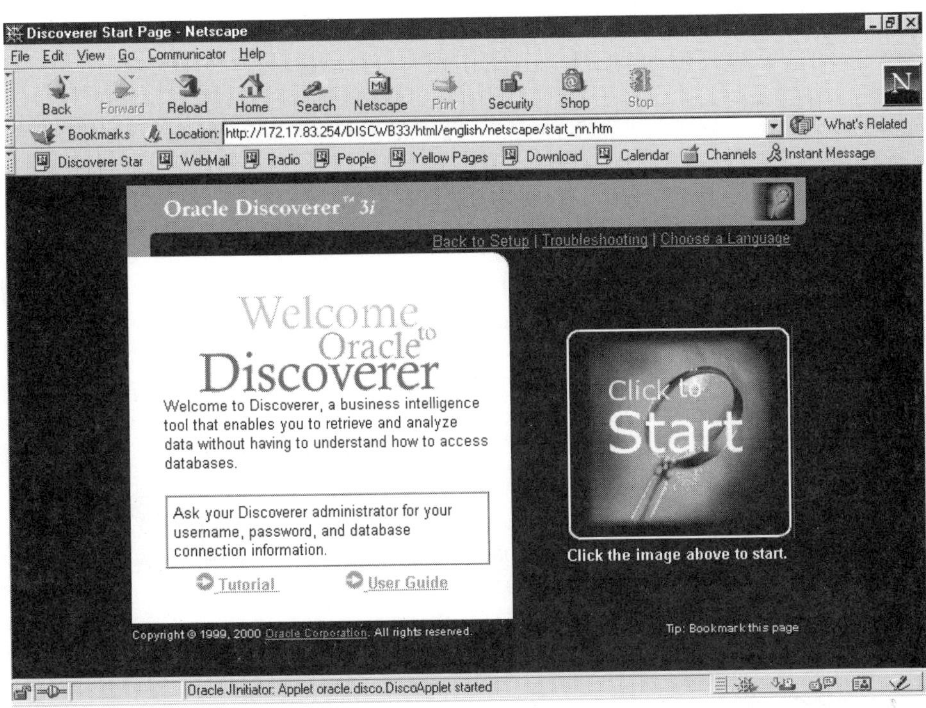

FIGURE 3-2. *Discoverer 3*i *Welcome screen*

Starting a Workbook

Assuming you have successfully logged on to either 3.1 or 3*i*, you are now in the first screen of the Discoverer Workbook Wizard.

In Discoverer 3.1, this wizard has the following six workflow steps:

1. Choose whether to open an existing workbook or create a new one. If you elect to create a new workbook, you will also be prompted to choose the display type. If you open an existing workbook, the workbook opens and the wizard will close.
2. Select items for your worksheet.
3. Define the screen layout.
4. Define any conditions.

5. Define any sort criteria.
6. Define any calculations.

This wizard—already one of the best, and very intuitive in the 3.1 version—has been improved in 3*i* by the addition of the following three extra steps:

1. Define any percentages.
2. Define any totals.
3. Define any parameters.

By following the instructions step by step, you can quickly be creating queries.

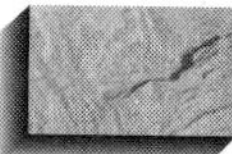

NOTE
It may seem simple enough to use the Workbook Wizard, and you might be asking yourself, "Why do I need this book?" The answer is that using the wizard is easy, but creating an effective query is not. Chapters 10, 11, and 12 will focus on advanced query techniques to help you to create better and more complex queries.

Summary

You have learned the importance of your Discoverer team: the Discoverer administrator, the DBA, and the superuser. Forging a good relationship with each of these important contacts will be of benefit as you become an expert in Discoverer.

We have introduced you to some important terms and features of Discoverer. You have also learned about SQL queries and how Discoverer manages them. We have explained about Discoverer's Sticky Feature. In addition, we have given you a step-by-step procedure for gaining access to the system. Finally, we showed you how to launch both versions of the system in preparation to begin using the Workbook Wizard.

In the next chapter, the fun begins! You will be taken through the first four steps of the Workbook Wizard to create what might be your first Discoverer query. In Chapter 5, the remaining steps of the Workbook Wizard will be covered, showing how more complex criteria can be added to your queries using the wizard.

The Workbook Wizard: The Essential Steps

n Chapter 3, you were shown how to launch Discoverer and log on to your database. In this chapter you will learn about the Workbook Wizard and how to go about creating your first query. We call the first four steps the essential steps, in that these are the base steps that you need to use in order to produce a working query.

We will teach you a simple workflow that you should follow to build your queries. If you follow this workflow, you will find that this is the quickest way to get a new query up and running. We will also teach you how to use constraints in order to avoid creating "The Query from the Twilight Zone," the dreaded query that seems to run forever.

Finally, we show you how to make Discoverer run your query and then teach you how to save it using a meaningful name. We know you will enjoy coming to grips with this brilliant tool, so let's begin.

The Workbook Wizard

As discussed in Chapter 3, the Discoverer 3.1 Workbook Wizard has six steps and 3*i* has nine. However, the quickest way to build a new query is to only use the first four steps. These steps form a simple workflow and will be covered in this chapter.

A Simple Workflow

In this chapter, we will take you through these steps by applying the following workflow:

1. Choose a display type.
2. Select the items.
3. Arrange the layout of the data.
4. Define conditions to avoid the Query from the Twilight Zone.

If you follow the above workflow, omitting the latter steps of the Workbook Wizard, you can quickly generate a new query.

Workbook Wizard Options

When you first open the Workbook Wizard seen in Figure 4-1, you are prompted whether to create a new workbook or open an existing workbook. As you can see,

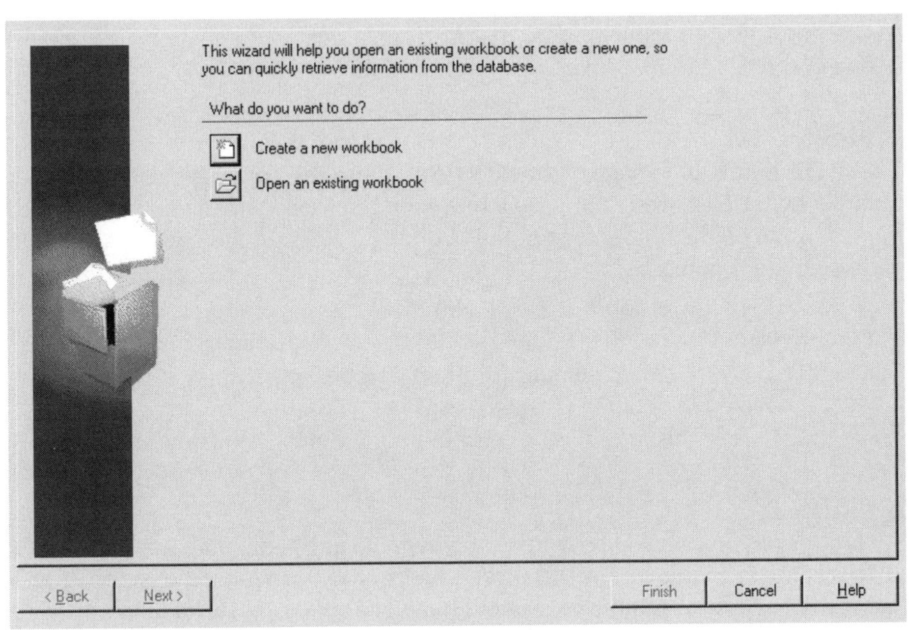

FIGURE 4-1. *The Workbook Wizard, screen one*

Discoverer displays a graphic on the left-hand side. As you move through the steps of the Workbook Wizard, the graphic changes to represent the step that you are currently working in.

At the bottom of each Workbook Wizard screen are six buttons (only five of them appear on screen one of 3.1, the sixth shows up from screen two onward). The order of the buttons is different in 3.1 and 3*i*, but the functionality is the same.

The illustration that follows shows the buttons on the 3.1 Workbook Wizard.

< Back | Next > | Options... | Finish | Cancel | Help

The next illustration shows the buttons on the 3*i* Workbook Wizard.

Cancel | Help | Options... | « Back | Next » | Finish

< Back

Back

Use this button to move back to the previous screen. When you are on screen one of the Workbook Wizard this button is inactive (gray).

Next >

Next

Use this button to move to the next screen. On screen one, this button is inactive until you tell Discoverer to create a new workbook or open an existing workbook. When you are on the final screen of the Workbook Wizard, this button is inactive (because there is no next!).

Options...

Options

Use this button to set up defaults for query formats and display settings. These will be covered in detail in Chapter 14. When you are on screen one of the Workbook Wizard, this button is not visible in 3.1, but is visible and inactive in 3*i*.

Finish

Finish

Use this button to tell Discoverer that you have finished creating the query. This is not available on the first screen unless you have moved to screen two, then come back. It is possible to create a query that does not select anything from the database. This is not a bug, and there may be good reasons to do just this. For example, you could create a query that returns the current fiscal month, using functions only. This query could be saved as a template for future queries that may need to use the fiscal month.

NOTE

You can click on Finish at any time; however, choosing Finish too soon can result in The Query From the Twilight Zone (this will be covered later in this chapter).

Cancel

Cancel

Use this button to tell Discoverer that you don't want to continue with the current query.

Help

Help

In 3.1, this button opens a standard Windows help file on using the Workbook Wizard. In 3*i*, it opens a second browser and displays the Discoverer 3*i* online help (in HTML format).

NOTE
If you are familiar with other Windows applications, you might be in the habit of using keyboard hot keys or shortcut keys instead of your mouse. Both versions of Discoverer make these keys available throughout, although there are some minor differences between the versions. If you have not used hot keys or shortcut keys before, they are a combination of either the ALT *or* CTRL *keys with another key. For example; on screen one of the Workbook Wizard,* ALT-*N selects Next. You can tell which key to press by looking for the letter that has the underscore.*

Workbook Wizard Step 1: Create a New Workbook or Open an Existing Workbook

Upon successfully getting past the startup screen, you will go to the first screen of the Workbook Wizard. This window has two buttons for "Create a new workbook" or "Open an existing workbook." We will begin by creating a new one.

Create a New Workbook

From the Workbook Wizard screen, select "Create new workbook." This brings up the second part of the initial screen of the Workbook Wizard. Discoverer asks you "How do you want to display the results" and has four buttons for Table, Page-Detail Table, Crosstab, and Page-Detail Crosstab, as shown in Figure 4-2. Notice how Discoverer has changed the graphic on the left-hand side of the screen.

When you have chosen to create a new workbook, the Workbook Wizard prompts you to choose the display type for your query. Discoverer 3.1 asks, "How do you want to display the results?", and 3*i* asks "How do you want to display the information?" There are four choices:

- Table
- Crosstab
- Page-Detail Table
- Page-Detail Crosstab

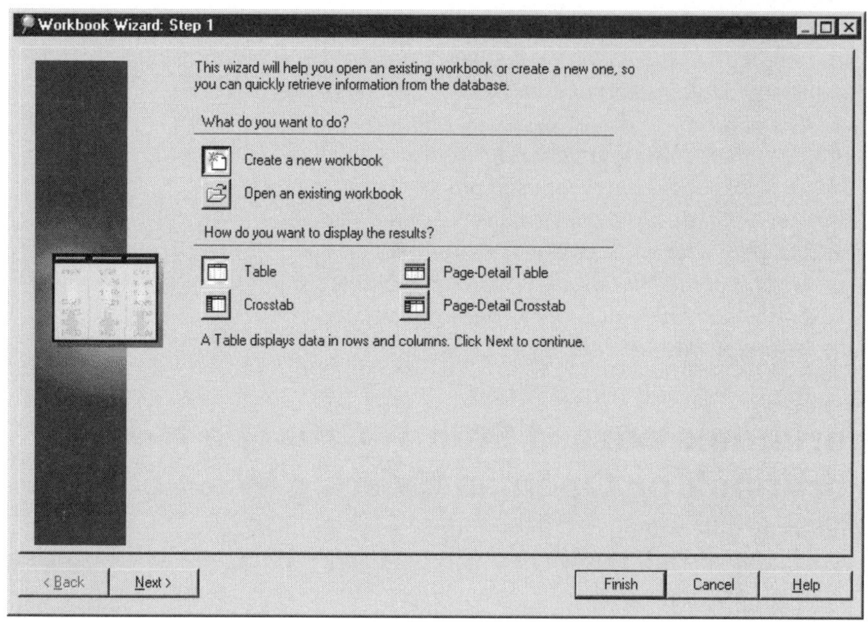

FIGURE 4-2. *Workbook Wizard: Step 1, with display type buttons*

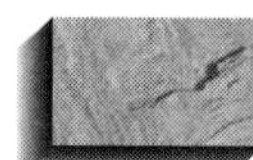

STICKY FEATURE

Discoverer 3.1 remembers the type of display you used last and offers it as the default for your next worksheet.

Table

For anyone experienced with spreadsheets, the table is a familiar sight. In the table, data is organized in rows (across) and columns (down). Discoverer numbers the rows on the left and the column heading names come from the source. Tables are essentially data organized in a list. In 3.1, you can rename the column headings to make them more meaningful. This will be covered later in the chapter.

Oracle Discoverer - [Workbook1]

File Edit View Sheet Format Tools Graph Window Help

Double-click here to edit this title.

	Line Name	Widget Model	Size	Cost AVG	Sell AVG
1	MEGA-WIDGET	AB-2500	SMALL	5.99	12.75
2	MEGA-WIDGET	CD-100	MEDIUM	6.21	15.25
3	MEGA-WIDGET	CD-200	MEDIUM	6.21	15.25
4	MEGA-WIDGET	CD-500	LARGE	10.62	22.18
5	MEGA-WIDGET	CD-550	LARGE	10.62	22.18
6	MEGA-WIDGET	CD-625	LARGE	10.62	22.18
7	SUPER-WIDGET	AB-3000	SMALL	9.88	21.25
8	SUPER-WIDGET	AVR-500	MEDIUM	11.48	26.95
9	SUPER-WIDGET	AVR-550	MEDIUM	11.48	26.95
10	SUPER-WIDGET	AVR-800	LARGE	15.94	34.65
11	SUPER-WIDGET	AVR-900	LARGE	15.94	34.65
12	WONDER-WIDGET	AB-2000	SMALL	7.22	13.50
13	WONDER-WIDGET	QB-1000	LARGE	12.42	23.45
14	WONDER-WIDGET	QB-2000	LARGE	12.42	23.45
15	WONDER-WIDGET	QB-3000	LARGE	12.42	23.45
16	WONDER-WIDGET	QB-5000	MEDIUM	8.33	17.66
17	WONDER-WIDGET	QB-5500	MEDIUM	8.33	17.66
18	WONDER-WIDGET	QB-6000	MEDIUM	8.33	17.66

Sheet 1

NUM

FIGURE 4-3. *A standard Discoverer table*

3*i* NOTE

*You cannot rename the column headings in 3*i*. Until Oracle corrects this (we anticipate this will be in Discoverer 4*i*) you will have to discuss column names with your Discoverer administrator. He or she has the ability to rename data items on your behalf.*

Crosstab

Crosstab (Pivot Table)

The Crosstab option, short for cross-tabulation, will be less familiar to some end users than the standard table. In a crosstab, the interrelationship of two or more sets of data is viewed. This multidimensional view of data is one of the most exciting features of Discoverer. Crosstabs can look at data from various sources and allow the user to view the interrelationships of the data "on the fly." For those familiar with the Excel pivot table, the functionality is similar. However, the Discoverer crosstab is far easier to use and the data much easier to access.

NOTE
You might hear of the output of a crosstab being referred to as multidimensional. That is because a crosstab is made up of at least three dimensions of data; one item on the top axis (columns), one item for the side axis (rows), and one for the data point (the data you actually see in the table). In Discoverer, you can have multiple items in the top and side axes, giving you greater power in your analysis of the data. We will look more closely at multidimensional data in Chapter 9, when we discuss analysis.

In Figure 4-4, the data from the Products folder is shown as a table.

In the standard table, you see the data as a list of related items. This is fine for most types of output, but where more analysis is needed, or where the list is pages long, the crosstab can be a better choice. In Figure 4-5, the same data is shown as a crosstab.

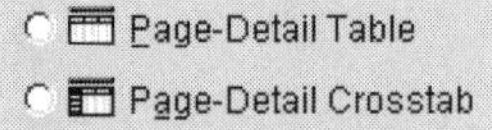

Page-Detail Tables and Page-Detail Crosstabs

A page detail is used when there is a large amount of data to display. In this type of worksheet, an element or elements of the data are moved to the page axis.

NOTE
Page detail refers to the overall concept of opening up the page axis, and is the final result that you see in your query. The page axis is the space at the top of the worksheet labeled Page Items. It is into this area that you place data items from the table or crosstab.

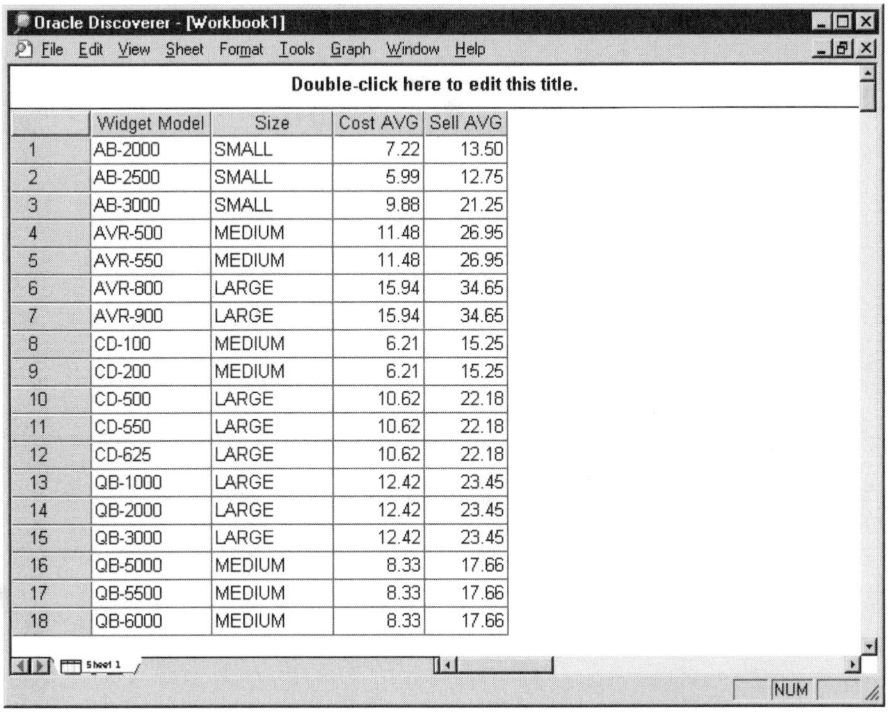

Oracle Discoverer - [Workbook1]

File Edit View Sheet Format Tools Graph Window Help

Double-click here to edit this title.

	Widget Model	Size	Cost AVG	Sell AVG
1	AB-2000	SMALL	7.22	13.50
2	AB-2500	SMALL	5.99	12.75
3	AB-3000	SMALL	9.88	21.25
4	AVR-500	MEDIUM	11.48	26.95
5	AVR-550	MEDIUM	11.48	26.95
6	AVR-800	LARGE	15.94	34.65
7	AVR-900	LARGE	15.94	34.65
8	CD-100	MEDIUM	6.21	15.25
9	CD-200	MEDIUM	6.21	15.25
10	CD-500	LARGE	10.62	22.18
11	CD-550	LARGE	10.62	22.18
12	CD-625	LARGE	10.62	22.18
13	QB-1000	LARGE	12.42	23.45
14	QB-2000	LARGE	12.42	23.45
15	QB-3000	LARGE	12.42	23.45
16	QB-5000	MEDIUM	8.33	17.66
17	QB-5500	MEDIUM	8.33	17.66
18	QB-6000	MEDIUM	8.33	17.66

Sheet 1

NUM

FIGURE 4-4. *Products folder as a standard table*

There are two reasons for using page detail:

- When you have a large amount of data to display and you want to use drop-down lists. This will, in essence, give you multiple sheets, one behind the other.
- When you have a unique constraint (applied as a condition). For example, take a look back at Figure 4-4. If we had opted to place a condition on the product size so that only medium sizes were selected, we would be wasting a column by leaving the size item in the main body of the table. We should move the product size to the page axis.

Oracle Discoverer - [Workbook1]

File Edit View Sheet Format Tools Graph Window Help

Double-click here to edit this title.

Size	Widget Model	Cost AVG	Sell AVG
LARGE		12.63	25.77
	AVR-800	15.94	34.65
	AVR-900	15.94	34.65
	CD-500	10.62	22.18
	CD-550	10.62	22.18
	CD-625	10.62	22.18
	QB-1000	12.42	23.45
	QB-2000	12.42	23.45
	QB-3000	12.42	23.45
MEDIUM		8.62	19.63
	AVR-500	11.48	26.95
	AVR-550	11.48	26.95
	CD-100	6.21	15.25
	CD-200	6.21	15.25
	QB-5000	8.33	17.66
	QB-5500	8.33	17.66
	QB-6000	8.33	17.66
SMALL		7.70	15.83
	AB-2000	7.22	13.50
	AB-2500	5.99	12.75

Sheet 1 Sheet 2 NUM

FIGURE 4-5. *Products folder as a crosstab*

Figure 4-4 shows all sizes of widgets and widget model numbers. In a real business database there might be thousands of part numbers or even millions. By moving one or more items from the body of the table to the page axis, you can choose to see only one part of the table at a time. In Figure 4-6, you can see that we have moved the product size to the page axis.

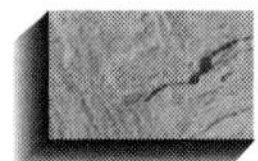

TIP

After you have selected your data and run the query, look to see if you have a single item being selected in a column. If you have, turn on the page-detail feature and move the item to the top of the page. To turn on page-items, from the menu bar, select View | Page Items.

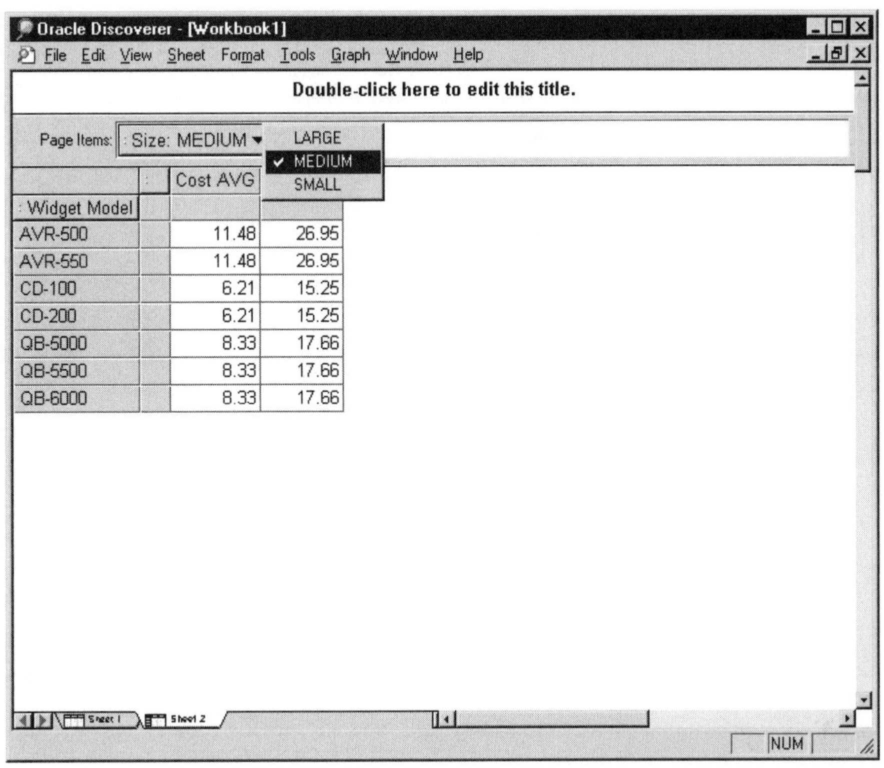

FIGURE 4-6. *Crosstab with Medium page detail selected*

In Figures 4-6 and 4-7, the Size element has been moved to the page detail. Size becomes a drop-down list and you can view each size individually.

Open an Existing Workbook

Whenever you open an existing workbook, Discoverer does one of three things, depending upon your preferred options. The three alternatives are as follows:

- Ask for confirmation (the default).
- Run the query automatically.
- Don't run the query and leave the sheet empty.

The mechanism for setting these options is explained in Chapter 14.

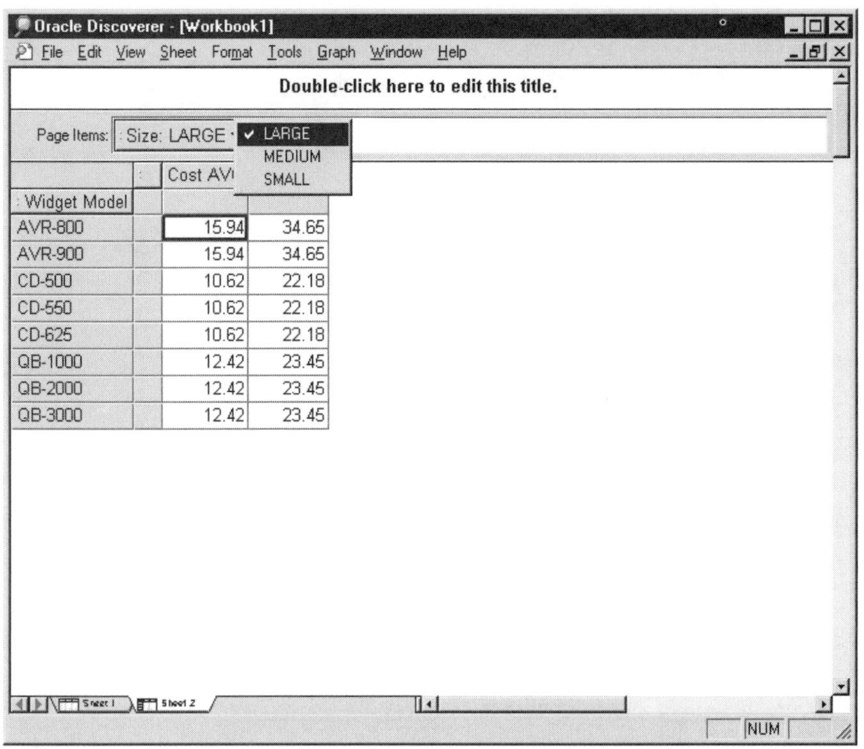

FIGURE 4-7. *Crosstab with Large page detail selected*

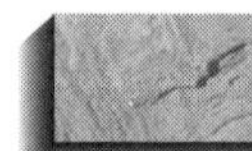

3*i* NOTE

*If you don't allow Discoverer 3*i *to run the query, a nice new feature warns you that the data for the sheet has not yet been queried. It even tells you which command you need to use in order to run the query later.*

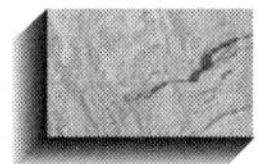

STICKY FEATURE

If your preference is to be prompted, and you have multiple worksheets, then one of Discoverer's Sticky Features remembers which worksheet you had open last. Discoverer calls this the active worksheet. This is the one that is prompted. As you navigate into each of the other worksheets, Discoverer will prompt you again. However, if your preference is for the worksheets to run automatically, and you have multiple worksheets, Discoverer runs the last one you had open. As you navigate to the other worksheets, Discoverer runs them automatically.

Workbook Wizard Step 2: Selecting the Data

The next step in creating a query is to select the data you want. After selecting the display type, click Next.

This brings up the second screen of the Workbook Wizard, shown in Figure 4-8. This window has the following three boxes:

- A folders, items, and business area selection box with the heading Available.
- A box with the heading Selected where you place your choices.
- A **Find** button, in 3.1 only, with the icon of a flashlight. Clicking this button opens the **Find** dialog box.

You can select from a business area to which you have access. Each business area contains folders, and within the folders are the items you will select to create your query.

Choosing a Business Area

The first thing you must do is choose the business area you want to work with from the Available drop-down list. If the one you want is not shown, press the down arrow and select the business area from the list, as shown here.

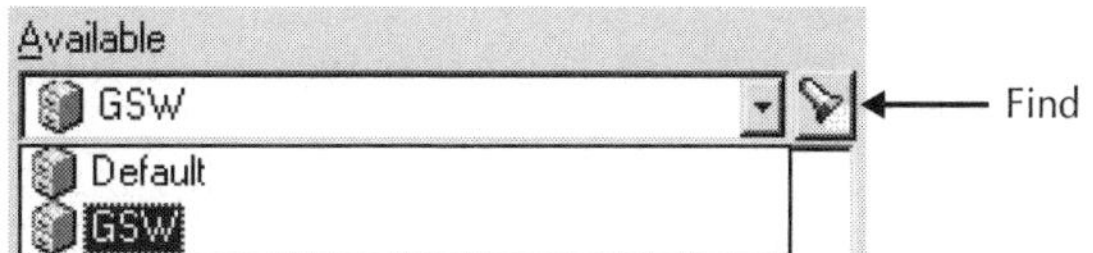

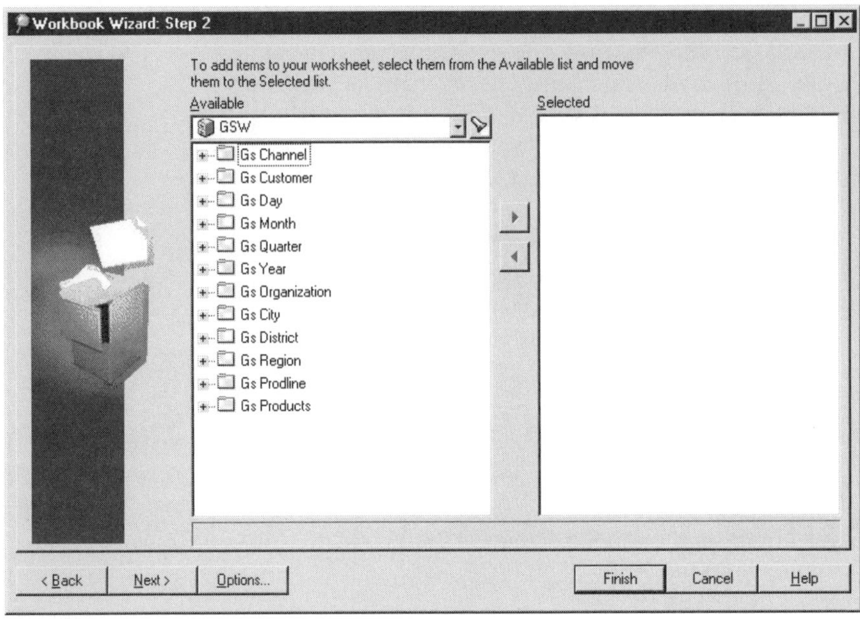

FIGURE 4-8. *Workbook Wizard: Step 2*

STICKY FEATURE

*Discoverer 3.1 remembers the name of the business area you were last working with. When you come back to create another workbook, Discoverer inserts as the default that business area. In the current release, 3*i *does not do this. It is hoped that this feature will be incorporated into a future release of 3*i.

Choosing a Folder

Having selected the business area you want, Discoverer displays a list of all the folders that are available to you from that business area, as shown in Figure 4-9. Open a folder you want to use by clicking on the plus sign to the left of the folder. Each folder contains a list of items. These items form the basis of your query.

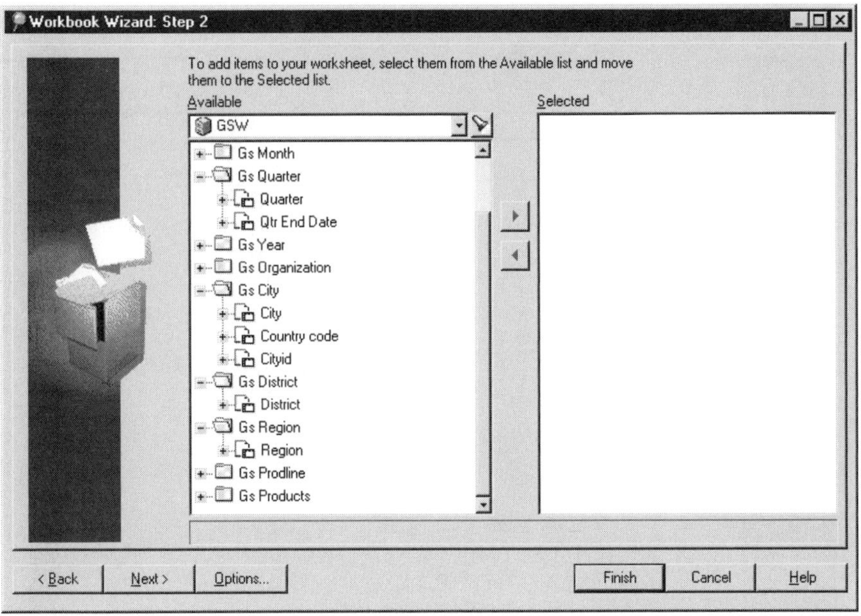

FIGURE 4-9. *Folders open, showing the items*

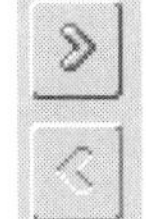

Choosing an Item

Having chosen a folder to work with, you are ready to select the item(s) from that folder. There are two ways to do this:

- **Point and click** Point to the item you want, click on it to highlight it, then click on the selection arrow as shown here.
- **Drag and drop** Click on the item you want and drag it over into the Selected box.

TIP

If you have decided to include more than one item from the same folder, you can select multiple items by holding down the control (CTRL) key and clicking on each of the items you want to select. As you click them they will be highlighted. When you have them all selected, click on the selection arrow, or click on one of the highlighted items and drag it (and the others) into the Selected box, as shown in Figure 4-10.

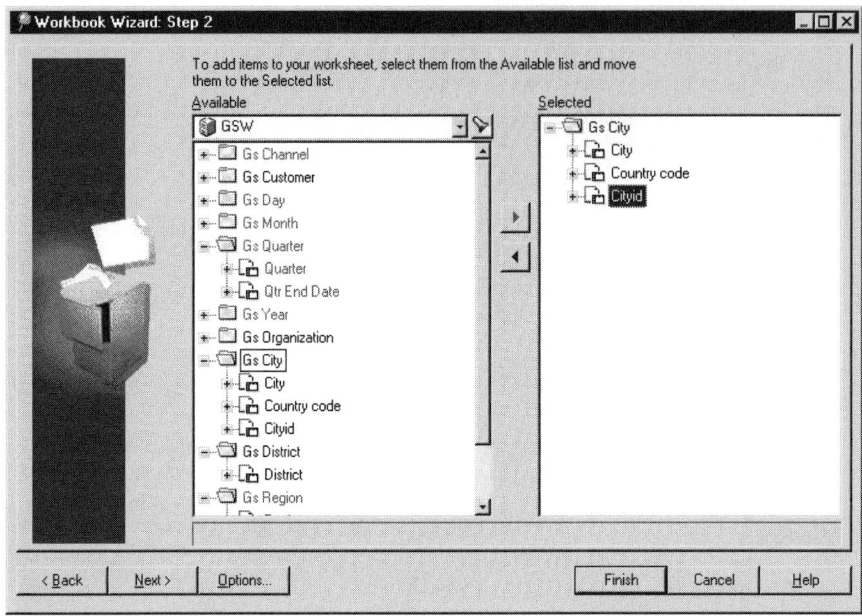

FIGURE 4-10. *Items selected for the query*

When an item is selected, the top selection arrow becomes active. When there is one or more items in the Selected box and you highlight one of them, the bottom selection arrow is activated. Use the bottom selection arrow to remove unwanted items from the Selected box.

Finding an Item in 3.1

When using Discoverer 3.1, if you are not sure whether or not an item exists within the business area that you have selected, use the Find dialog box. This dialog box allows you to search for items in the business area, producing a list of all items that match the search criteria.

To use the Find dialog box to locate an item, follow this workflow:

1. Click the Find button. Discoverer opens the Find dialog box shown here:

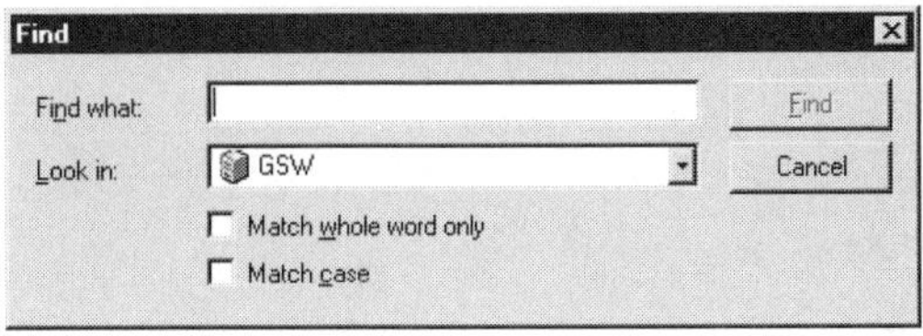

NOTE
The Find button is located to the right of the Discoverer 3.1 business area drop-down list. This button has the icon of a flashlight on it.

2. Type the name or partial name of the item that you want to search for.
3. Check Match Whole Word if you want Discoverer to find an exact match.
4. Check Match Case if you want Discoverer to match the case.
5. Click Find. Discoverer searches the business area and displays a list of all items matching the criteria you entered. In the following illustration, we asked Discoverer to search for items containing the word "cost". As you can see, Discoverer located an item called "Cost Price" in the sales folder, and a second item called "Unit Cost" in the products folder.

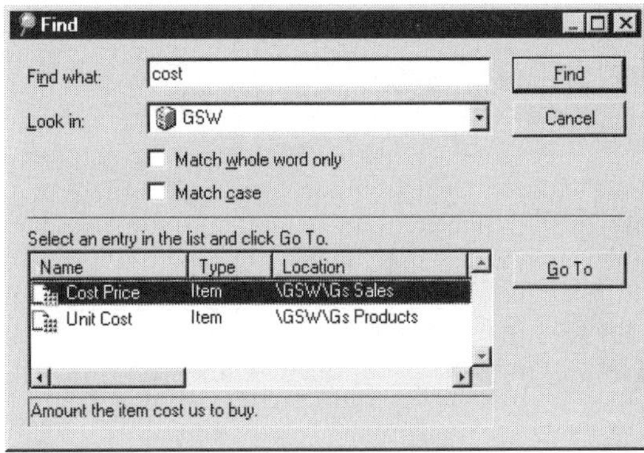

6. From the list of items, highlight the one that you want to use.

7. Click Go To. Discoverer closes the Find dialog box and returns you to the Workbook Wizard Step 2. The folder containing the item is automatically opened, the item that you found will be highlighted, and available for selection.

8. If Discoverer could not find an item matching the search criteria, the following dialog box is displayed. As you can see, Discoverer informs you that the search has failed and prompts you to try again. To abandon the search at this point, click Cancel.

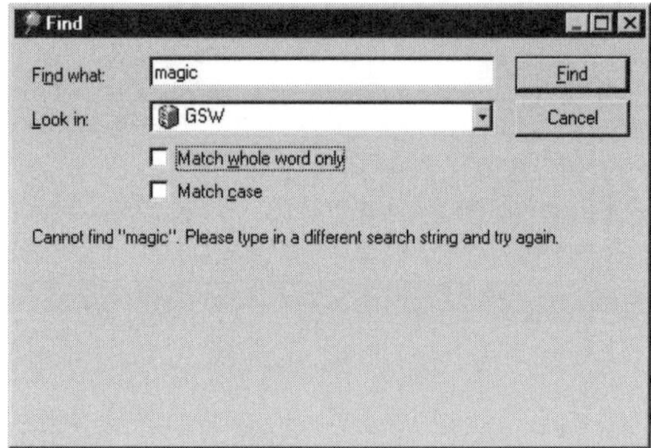

In our opinion, this ability of Discoverer to locate items in business areas is excellent. We recommend that you use the above workflow frequently, especially when you are not sure whether or not the item exists.

3*i* NOTE
*Discoverer 3*i *does not have a Find button, and so the section above only applies to Discoverer 3.1. We like this feature very much and hope that Oracle introduces the ability to find items this way in an upcoming release of 3*i.

Item Types

Discoverer uses icons to represent different types of data and the options you have to choose from when making your selections. These types of data and options are as follows:

- Strings and dates
- Numbers
- Predefined conditions

Strings and Dates The icon to the left is the one you will see most often. It represents either strings (names, cities, customers, etc.) or dates. If the item has a plus sign to the left of it, you have some options for placing constraints on the data. This is called a list of values (LOV).

For example, if the Customer folder contains an item called postcode and this item has a plus sign, clicking on the plus sign gives you a list of customer postcodes. If you are only interested in seeing the data for selected postcodes, you can choose only those postcodes you want to see, thus applying a constraint.

NOTE

If you cannot see a plus sign next to a data item, and you believe that a list of values would help you create your queries more efficiently, you should speak with your Discoverer administrator. He or she has the ability to create these lists for you.

Numbers The data represented by this icon (it is supposed to look like a numeric keypad) is numeric, like selling and cost prices. When you click on the plus sign next to an item with this icon, you have at least six subitems to choose from. If you don't choose, the choice is made for you and defaults to whatever the Discoverer administrator has set up. Most often this will be SUM (the default will be in boldface, as shown in Figure 4-11).

The following is the list of available choices and their definitions. You will not always see all of these options, as the type of data and how your Discoverer administrator has set it up determines what is available. It is also possible to have an LOV with numeric items. When such a list exists it will appear before the other available functions.

- **SUM** Returns a sum of all the values.
- **COUNT** Returns the number of values in the query where the expression is not null.
- **MAX** Finds the maximum value of the expression.
- **MIN** Finds the minimum value of the expression.
- **AVG** Computes the mathematical average.
- **Detail** This does not apply any aggregation. For example, if you have a line-detail table that is showing shipments for the same line over several days, select Detail if you want to see one row per shipment. If you select SUM, you will see a single row with all of the shipment details totaled (including the line number!).

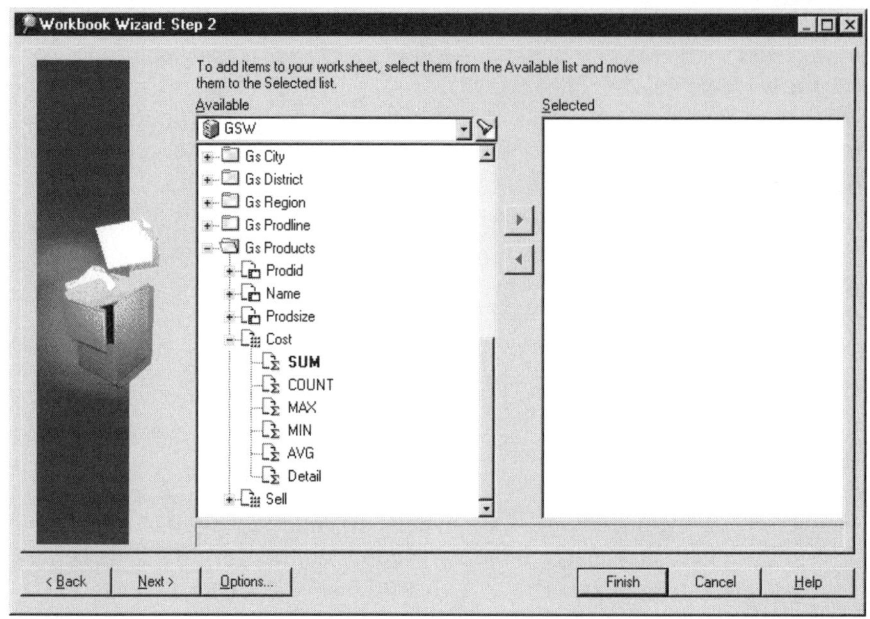

FIGURE 4-11. *Numeric item with default in bold*

NOTE
If you forget what each of the items does, simply click on the item and the Workbook Wizard status bar gives the description.

Predefined Conditions For those familiar with Microsoft Excel and Access, you will recognize this as the Filter by Item icon. In Discoverer, it serves a similar function. Your Discoverer administrator can set predefined conditions and add them to the business area.

For example, assume you don't give credit to some of your customers. You need a report showing which of your customers have a credit limit and what the amounts are. It makes sense to ask your Discoverer administrator to create a predefined condition on the item Credit Limit, which would filter out all customers with a credit limit greater than zero. The condition appears in the folder like any of the other items and can be identified by the Predefined Condition icon (the filter). You can select the condition for your query, but if you don't want to use it, you don't have to.

By selecting a predefined condition, you won't need to create one of your own when setting up your queries. Predefined conditions can be applied or deactivated at any time, as shown in Figure 4-12. You will be shown in Chapter 11 how to use predefined conditions and apply other conditions to your queries.

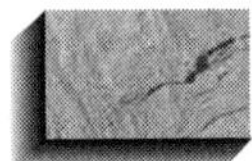

NOTE

Pre-defined conditions are created by the Discoverer administrator. They cannot be modified except by the Discoverer administrator. However, the end user can combine two or more conditions defined by the administrator to create a complex condition. If the condition you want is not covered by any predefined condition or combination of conditions, you will need to create one of your own.

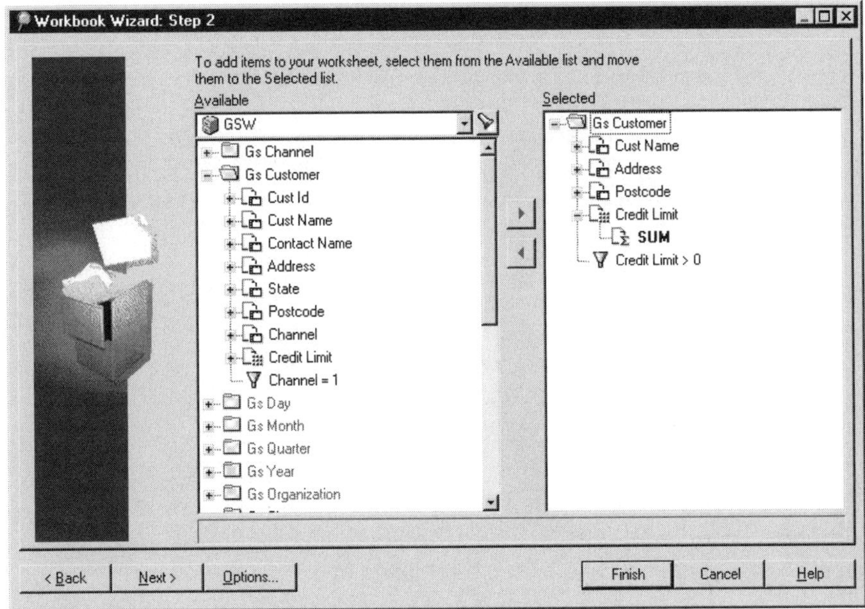

FIGURE 4-12. *Query using a predefined condition*

Selecting Items for Your Query

The order in which the chosen items are displayed in the Selected box is governed by the following:

- The folder in which the item resides.
- The ordering of the items in that folder. If your Discoverer administrator listed the folders alphabetically, then the order of the folders in the Selected box will be alphabetical—no matter in what order you made your selections.

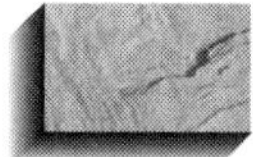

NOTE
This note is for administrators who may be reading this section. If you arrange the ordering of the folders in the order in which your users will most likely need them, this will speed up the selection process. Similarly, you might order the items within a folder by placing the most commonly used items near the top of the list. Both of these tips will help your users make their selections quicker.

A very useful feature of the product is when an item has been selected, only the folders that have links to the chosen item remain active. This helps you to know where the links are, and what data is available to use in the query. When folders are not available to you for selection, they will be grayed out. However, you can still see the items inside the folder by clicking on the plus key.

NOTE
Your Discoverer administrator can set the ordering of the folders and items in the most logical order for you to select. If you believe that the ordering is not correct you can ask him or her to change it.

Discoverer knows about the links between the folders, and you should make a point to read your company's documentation in order to know which folders link together. You will have to select from the folders in a logical sequence.

NOETIX

If you are using Noetix Views, we recommend that you have the Noetix Views Help file open when you are making your selections. The help provided by Noetix is probably one of the best online help manuals around. Not only does the help file describe the folders and the items in them, but it also tells you which folders can be joined to from the current folder. For more details on using Noetix Views, refer to Appendix B.

Workbook Wizard Step 3: Arranging the Order of the Output

The next step in creating a query is to arrange the order of the output. After selecting the data you want to view, click Next.

This brings up the third screen of the Wookbook Wizard, in which you arrange the order you want the data displayed. No matter which order you selected the items, Discoverer will always display them in the order of their listing within the business area. The Wizard Step 3 screen, shown in Figure 4-13, is the place where Discoverer first gives you a chance to change that order and make two other choices.

You can choose to:

- Show Page Items
- Hide Duplicate Rows

Show Page Items

Show Page Items

Check this box if you want to turn the table or crosstab into a page-detail table or crosstab (we will show more examples of page-detail tables and crosstabs in Chapter 9).

Hide Duplicate Rows

Hide Duplicate Rows

Depending upon the data you have selected, you may find that your query has two or more identical rows. If you only want to see one of these you should check this box.

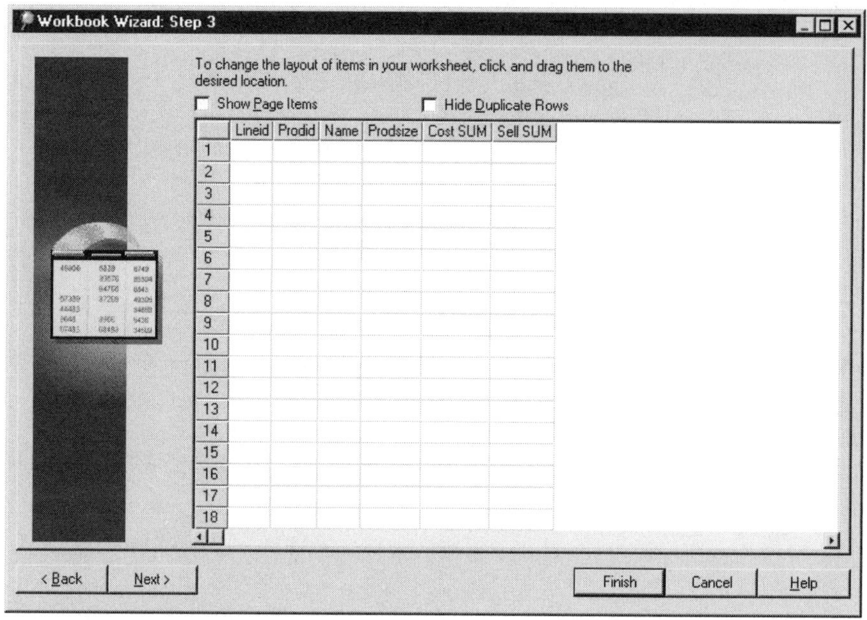

FIGURE 4-13. *Workbook Wizard: Step 3*

The following example shows Global Widgets selling products to 23 customers in 16 countries. We want a report that shows which countries have customers. The City table has been created to contain a record for every city that contains customers. Selecting only the country code from the City table, without checking this box, will produce a list with 23 country codes, some of which are duplicates.

In Figure 4-14, US is listed six times and both BR and GB are listed twice. For the sake of the example above, we only want to see each country listed once.

With the Hide Duplicate Rows box checked, the list now contains only the 16 countries in which we have customers. Looking at the list in Figure 4-15, you will see that US, BR, and GB are only listed once. This satisfies the requirement to see what countries have customers.

NOTE

You won't always want to hide duplicate rows; in fact, your report might be inaccurate if you do. You can use duplicate rows for a more complex view of the data.

	Country code
1	PH
2	US
3	GB
4	PT
5	BR
6	GB
7	FR
8	IT
9	ES
10	US
11	US
12	CA
13	MX
14	BR
15	JP
16	HK
17	KR
18	CH
19	US
20	US
21	US
22	PE
23	PL

FIGURE 4-14. *Country code from city with duplicates*

Arranging the Order of the Columns

To change the order of the columns, simply click on the column you want to move and drag it to the desired location. If you have selected a large number of items for the query, you may not be able to see them all onscreen. You should start by locating the item you want to display in column 1 and move it first, following with each of the other items in turn.

TIP
If you cannot see column 1 onscreen and you need to move the current column to that position, you should click on the column you want to move, hold down the mouse button and drag the item off the active screen (which will reset). Now move the item to the desired position and then release the mouse button. This only works in 3.1. In 3i, you have to move the item over as far as you can, then scroll over and move it again.

	Country code
1	BR
2	CA
3	CH
4	ES
5	FR
6	GB
7	HK
8	IT
9	JP
10	KR
11	MX
12	PE
13	PH
14	PL
15	PT
16	US

FIGURE 4-15. *Country code from city with no duplicates*

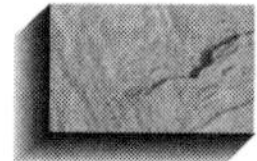

3*i* NOTE
*Although in Oracle Discoverer 3.1 you can change the order of the columns directly in the workbook, you cannot do this in 3*i*. It is important to do all of this while still in the Workbook Wizard. If you get into the workbook and decide the columns need to be reordered, you will need to edit the sheet to make the changes. This is a feature the authors hope can be incorporated into a future Web release.*

Workbook Wizard Step 4: Setting User-Defined Conditions

The next step in creating a query is to set the conditions. After arranging the table layout, click Next.

This brings up the fourth screen of the Workbook Wizard, shown in Figure 4-16. This window contains three boxes.

- **View Conditions for** A drop-down box where you can choose to view conditions for all items, the active items, or a specific item only.

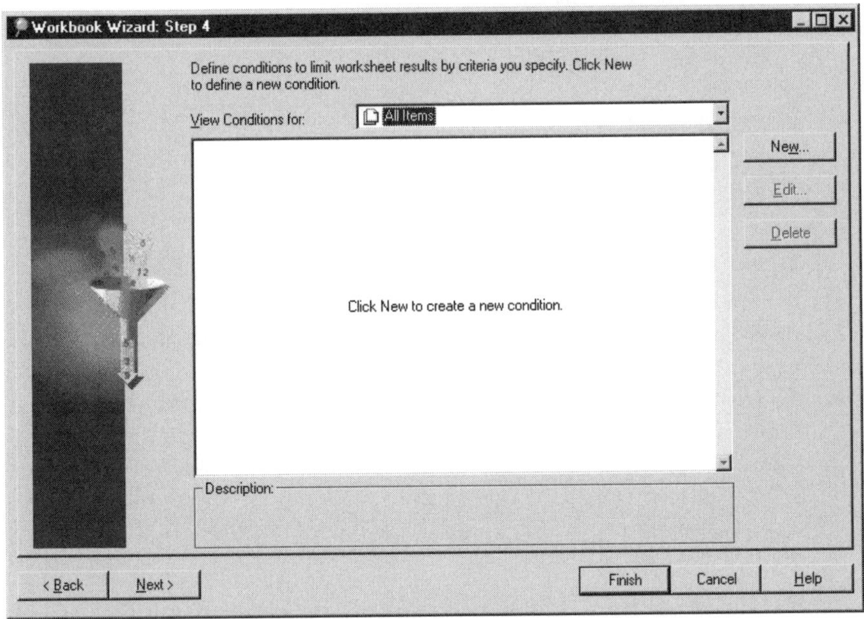

FIGURE 4-16. *Workbook Wizard: Step 4*

- **Conditions** A list box showing all of the conditions based upon the selection made in the drop-down box above.
- **Description** A box showing the description of the condition highlighted in the conditions box.

The screen also contains three new buttons:

- **New** This button is used to create a new condition.
- **Edit/Show** This button toggles between Edit, for conditions that you can edit, and Show, for predefined conditions that you cannot edit but can view in the Show Conditions window.
- **Delete** Be careful using this one. It does just what it says and without prompting!

View Conditions for: Drop-down Box

You will need to select one of the items from the "View Conditions for" drop-down box. The choices are described below.

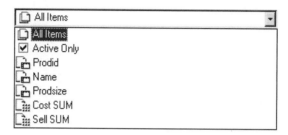

- **All Items** This is the default and will show all conditions used within the entire workbook. If you have more than one worksheet in the workbook, viewing conditions for all items will list those conditions from the other worksheets as well as the one you are working on. This could be confusing, and you might delete a condition by accident because you believed you did not need it.

  If you try to select a condition that applies to an item that is not used in your worksheet, you will get the following error message in 3.1

And the following error message in 3*i*.

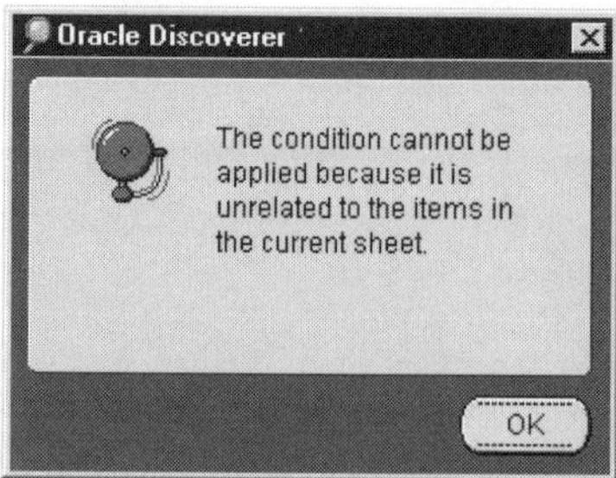

- **Active Only** This option allows you to view only those conditions which are being used in the current worksheet.

  If you have multiple worksheets in the workbook and they use completely different sets of items, perhaps even from different business areas, you may want to select this option. It will, in some situations, help reduce confusion to use the Active Only option; however, *use this option with care*. You might already have the exact condition created, but will not know it if you select Active Only.

- **Specific Items** Discoverer maintains a list of all the items in your query, whether or not they have conditions. Clicking on the down arrow not only lists the options referred to above, but also includes all the items in the query. You may choose to view the conditions for just one of these items.

  If you have multiple conditions on the same item and your query is producing unexpected results, you will probably find that you have a wrongly defined condition. Selecting to view the conditions for just the item concerned will allow you to ascertain where the error lies.

NOTE
After you have finished debugging your conditions, don't forget to switch the view back to All Items or Active Only. If you save the query and exit, when you come back into the worksheet Discoverer will reset the view to All Items.

Conditions

The large box in the middle of the window shown in Figure 4-17 contains the conditions (predefined and user defined) being used in this workbook. When you have more than one condition, Discoverer will highlight by default the first condition in the box.

STICKY FEATURE
There is a Sticky Feature that will remember the last condition you selected and that will be the one highlighted when you come back to the conditions step of the Workbook Wizard.

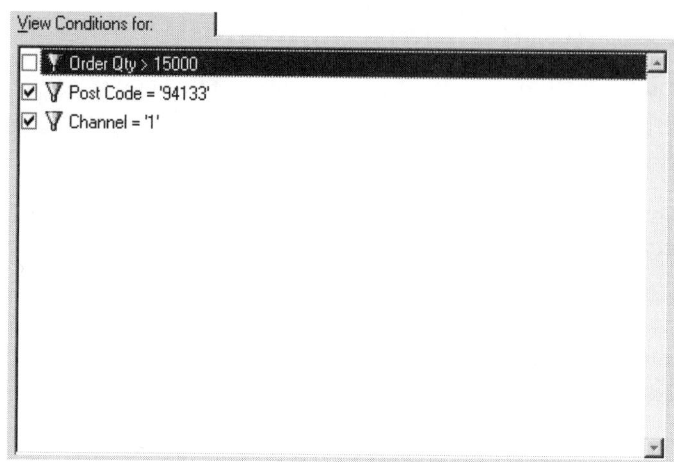

FIGURE 4-17. *Workbook Wizard Step 4 Conditions box*

Description

The gray box below the list of conditions contains a description of the selected condition in the box above.

In this box, Discoverer will display a description of the highlighted condition. You may use this "at a glance" feature to get help on the condition. Many conditions are short and sweet, and you can view the entire condition without even looking in the Description box. However, some conditions are complex and the Description box can display the user- or administrator-defined description of the condition. If no description has been provided, Discoverer will display the condition itself.

What Are Conditions?

Conditions are constraints, criteria, or filters that you apply to your query. All of these terms can be used interchangeably. For those who have used other products such as Microsoft Access, you are used to the terms *criteria* and *filters* in query writing.

Discoverer 3.1 defines a condition as "a set of criteria that filters data in a sheet. You use a condition when you want to limit the amount of data or refine the level of detail in the sheet."

Discoverer 3*i* defines a condition as "a statement for finding specific data. Turning on a condition filters out the data that does not meet the condition, and displays only the data that you want to see."

As you can see, Oracle has given slightly different definitions for conditions in a query. We believe that the 3*i* definition is more accurate and easier to understand for those familiar with other query tools.

The following three examples illustrate the concept of conditions in queries:

- You know that fiscal quarter 2 is always the best for sales and you want to analyze sales data from that quarter in order to produce a presentation for the shareholders. You can set a condition that will only return the numbers for quarter 2 and filter out everything else. The condition quarter=Q2 will satisfy this example.
- Your company has one salesperson per district and rewards them by giving a vacation to all who have generated sales in excess of ten million. By setting a condition that reports district sales revenue in excess of ten million, you can tell at a glance who gets the all-expense paid trip to the Bahamas for two. The condition Revenue>10000000 will meet the requirement for this query.
- You have decided to create a report analyzing the margin between sales and costs. In order to do this correctly, you need to exclude zero-cost items from the query. Setting a condition Cost<>0 will give you the numbers you need.

You are not restricted to the number of conditions you may create. However, there is a trade-off between applying conditions and query performance. Ideally, you should attempt to apply your conditions to items that are indexed. If you do this, you will improve the performance of the query. Applying conditions to nonindexed items could have a negative impact on performance. The more nonindexed conditions you apply, the longer your query could take to run. Check with your Discoverer administrator or system documentation to see which database items are indexed.

NOETIX

If you have Noetix Views you should look inside the Noetix Views Help file. Open the folder containing the item you want to apply the condition to and look to see if the item name begins with A$. Noetix uses this prefix to indicate which items are indexed. It is strongly recommended to always apply conditions to these items, if at all possible.

The New, Edit, and Show Buttons

These buttons open three windows that appear to be identical, but function in slightly different ways. The only evidence you have of which window you are in is the title bar.

- **New** Use this button to open the New Condition window, shown in Figure 4-18, to create a condition to use in your query.
- **Edit** Use this button to open the Edit Condition window. This button is only visible when you have selected a condition that you can edit. An example of an editable condition is one you or another user has defined or a constraint you applied in step 2 of the Workbook Wizard.
- **Show** Use this button to open the Show Conditions window. This button is only visible when you have selected a condition that cannot be edited. Predefined conditions cannot be edited, but you can view how the condition was created.

These windows will be shown in greater detail in Chapter 7, as well as how to create useful and meaningful conditions.

The Query from the Twilight Zone and How to Avoid It

The term "The Query from the Twilight Zone" was first introduced to one of the authors by an Oracle trainer during a course on data warehousing. It describes perfectly the type of query that users should avoid writing.

So what is it? Well to put it simply, it is a query that never—or seems like never—returns any information. Once submitted, the query just appears to run forever; apparently having been submitted to that "big database in the sky" from whence nothing ever returns. Somewhere out there in the bowels of dataland are millions of queries still searching for their elusive data, and hopefully the users are not still sitting at their desks waiting for the results!

Having all the data from your company available to you, coupled with the newly unleashed power of Discoverer, makes for a tempting dabble into querying everything. Look at the following example:

Let's say you work for a company that produces widgets and you currently have 10,000 finished products. Your bill of materials defines what components make up those widgets and the current monthly cost of each of those components. So let's say each of your widgets has 50 components and that you are a fairly large company with 20 manufacturing plants worldwide. You therefore have to maintain monthly costs for 10 million (10,000 × 50 × 20) different components.

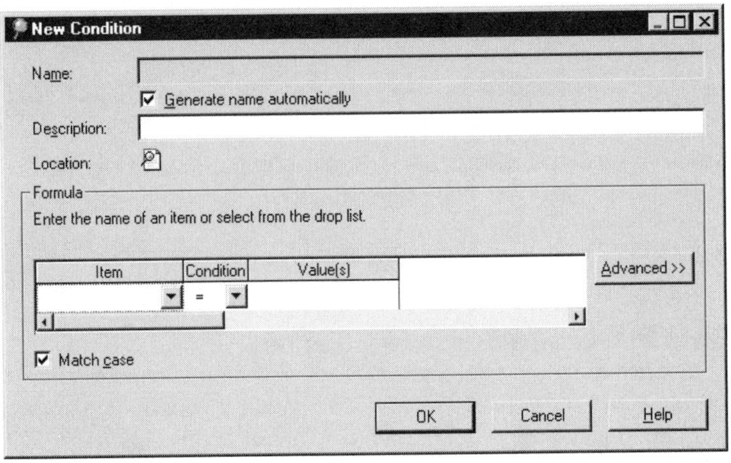

FIGURE 4-18. *New Condition window*

If you were trying to build a query to analyze your current costs, you would not want to let your first attempt run against all of those records. To further compound the issue, imagine trying to compare the current month's costs against those during the past year. This query would compare the current 10 million with the 110 million from the previous 11 months. This example may seem somewhat extreme, but it isn't. There are thousands of companies like this, many of which are actually bigger and more complex.

The query above that analyzes 10 million records may, depending upon what kind of hardware your company has, actually produce a result inside four or five hours. Realistically, though, your Discoverer administrator will probably have set a limit for the maximum length of time he or she will allow you to run your query, and your query will have timed out. We therefore have to explore ways of reducing the length of time required to build your query.

There are many ways to reduce the length of time when building a query. Five of these are as follows:

- Using data marts and summary tables
- Applying constraints to avoid creating long-running queries
- Applying a sort order after the query results have been ascertained
- Creating totals and subtotals on a subset of the data
- Applying calculations after the query has run

The first two will be covered in this chapter and the last three will be covered in Chapter 5.

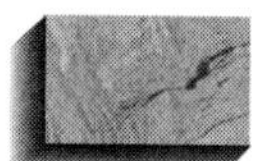

NOTE
You may want to look at the previous list as a workflow. By applying the steps listed above, you should be able to effectively manage large data selections without creating "The Query from the Twilight Zone."

Using Data Marts and Summary Tables

Data marts and summary tables can greatly reduce the time taken to produce reports that require large amounts of data. Therefore, whenever you have to create a query that needs to report a large amount of data, you should consult with your Discoverer administrator and inquire whether or not there are any data marts in existence. As described earlier, a data mart is basically a table that has been specially created for reporting and has indexes specially built for reporting. Summary tables can be created by your Discoverer administrator. Where these exist, Discoverer will analyze your query and, if all the items you want can be found within a summary table, redirect your query to use that table.

While you yourself cannot point your query to a summary table, discussing your requirements with your Discoverer administrator may well reveal that such a table exists. Where these do exist, you may want to consider amending your requirements so that you only include those items that are contained within the summary table.

If there are no data marts or summary tables in existence, you may want to discuss your requirements with your superuser or Discoverer administrator. These people may be able to help you start the process for having one of these objects created for you. Do not feel that you need to give up on any queries that you want to create. There is always something you can do, and you should make use of the resources available.

Applying Constraints to Avoid Creating Long-Running Queries

The first thing every good query writer learns is how to apply constraints. Discoverer calls these conditions. You need to work with your Discoverer administrator and possibly your DBA to find out as much as you can about the nature of the data you will be working with.

You need to know which tables contain large numbers of items and what the values are within your main indexes so that you can define suitable conditions. Very large tables need to be constrained on their index items. If you attempt to create your conditions on nonindexed items, then this will hardly make any impression on the time taken to run your query because the system will still have to search all of the items in order to decide whether each of those items meets your condition.

In the example query we are using, where we have 10 million current cost records, you would need to find out what code your system uses to define the current month's costs (Oracle calls the current cost the *frozen cost,* and usually it has the code value 1). This will at least reduce the number of items being searched to those 10 million records.

Applying Temporary Constraints to Quickly View Preliminary Output

If you get to work closely with your Discoverer administrator and spend some time learning about the data in your system, you will soon become aware that querying from some tables will take a very long time. This experience, coupled with some common sense, will tell you to look for ways to minimize the time it takes to at least get some preliminary output. You don't want to wait several hours to see the column ordering, nor wait that long only to discover you left something out or included something you didn't need.

NOTE
Setting temporary constraints in order to get preliminary output is an essential tool in your armory and will result in a rapid building process.

Returning to our example query: We have already ascertained what the code value is for the current month, but this would still result in a query of 10 million records. While the end result may be that we do in fact want to produce a report of that magnitude, during the construction of the query we do not want to be running against that volume of data. We would therefore look to reduce the number of items being queried. This is done by, 1) limiting the query to search only one manufacturing facility (reducing the query down to 500,000 items), and 2) limiting it further by restricting the query to, say, only 10 finished products (reducing it down to a manageable 500 items). This query will run very quickly, and you can now concentrate on defining your sort criteria, totals, subtotals, and the final data formatting characteristics.

Viewing the Results

Although there are more steps to the Workbook Wizard, we feel the best way to proceed is to leave the wizard now and run the query. Don't worry—the remaining steps of the wizard will still be available to you after running the query. There is a good reason for this. We feel that people new to creating queries should keep them simple to begin with, and build them up by steps. If you continue through the remainder of the wizard, you could find that after all of your work you have created a query that will return no data, or so much data that you are timed out of the system before it can finish running. Build the foundation of the query and see the basic data, then go on from there.

To view the results of the query, click Finish. Discoverer closes the Workbook Wizard, runs the query, and displays the results. Figure 4-19 shows the results from a typical query.

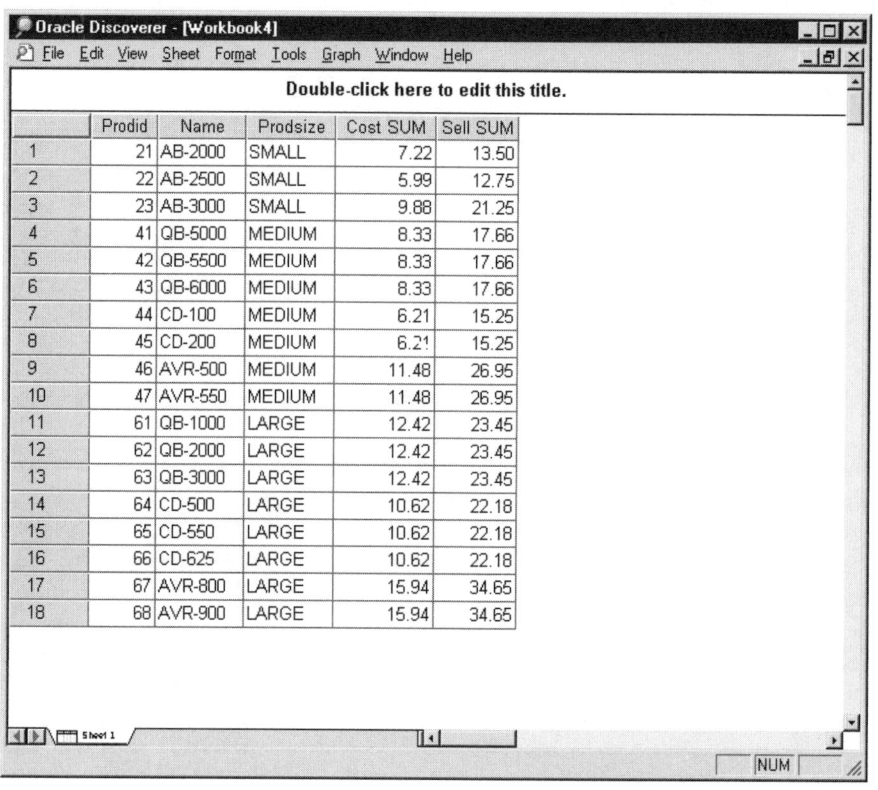

	Prodid	Name	Prodsize	Cost SUM	Sell SUM
1	21	AB-2000	SMALL	7.22	13.50
2	22	AB-2500	SMALL	5.99	12.75
3	23	AB-3000	SMALL	9.88	21.25
4	41	QB-5000	MEDIUM	8.33	17.66
5	42	QB-5500	MEDIUM	8.33	17.66
6	43	QB-6000	MEDIUM	8.33	17.66
7	44	CD-100	MEDIUM	6.21	15.25
8	45	CD-200	MEDIUM	6.21	15.25
9	46	AVR-500	MEDIUM	11.48	26.95
10	47	AVR-550	MEDIUM	11.48	26.95
11	61	QB-1000	LARGE	12.42	23.45
12	62	QB-2000	LARGE	12.42	23.45
13	63	QB-3000	LARGE	12.42	23.45
14	64	CD-500	LARGE	10.62	22.18
15	65	CD-550	LARGE	10.62	22.18
16	66	CD-625	LARGE	10.62	22.18
17	67	AVR-800	LARGE	15.94	34.65
18	68	AVR-900	LARGE	15.94	34.65

FIGURE 4-19. *A basic query*

Interrogating the Results of a Query in 3.1

When viewing the results of a query that has been run in Discoverer 3.1, you may want to check if a certain piece of data has been retrieved. The long, laborious way of doing this is to use the mouse to page through the results until you find the item that you want. In Discoverer 3.1 only, the quickest way to check whether an item has been retrieved is to use the Find Results dialog box.

To check if an item has been returned amongst the results of a query, use the following workflow:

1. With the results of the query visible on screen, from the menu bar select Edit | Find. Discoverer opens the Find Results dialog box shown here:

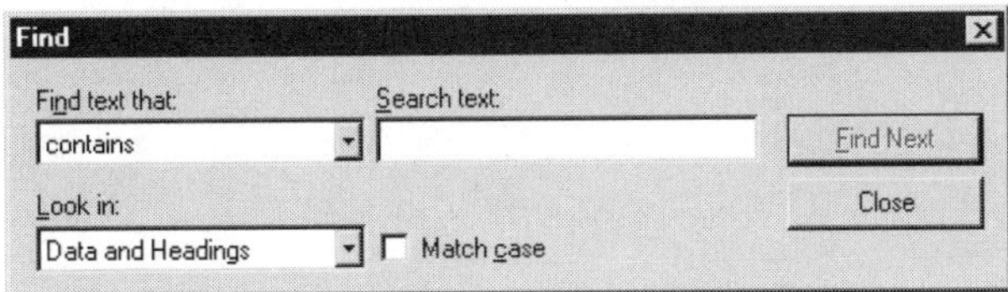

2. In the box entitled Find Text That, use the drop-down list to select the type of search that you want to do. The options are Exactly Matches, Contains, Begins With, Ends With, and Is NULL. The default is Contains.
3. In the box entitled Look In, use the drop-down list to indicate whether you want Discoverer to search in the Data and Headings or Data Only.
4. In the Search Text box, type the item that you want Discoverer to search for.
5. Check the Match Case box if you want Discoverer to search for results that match exactly the case of the item that you entered in step 4.

NOTE
If you are certain that the item can only be in the case that you have specified, checking Match Case will increase the efficiency of the find and perform the search faster.

6. Click Find Next. Discoverer will now search for the item that you entered.
7. If the item is found, Discoverer displays, in the background, the first row containing that item. In the following illustration, you can see that Discoverer has located the value 1277 in our results.

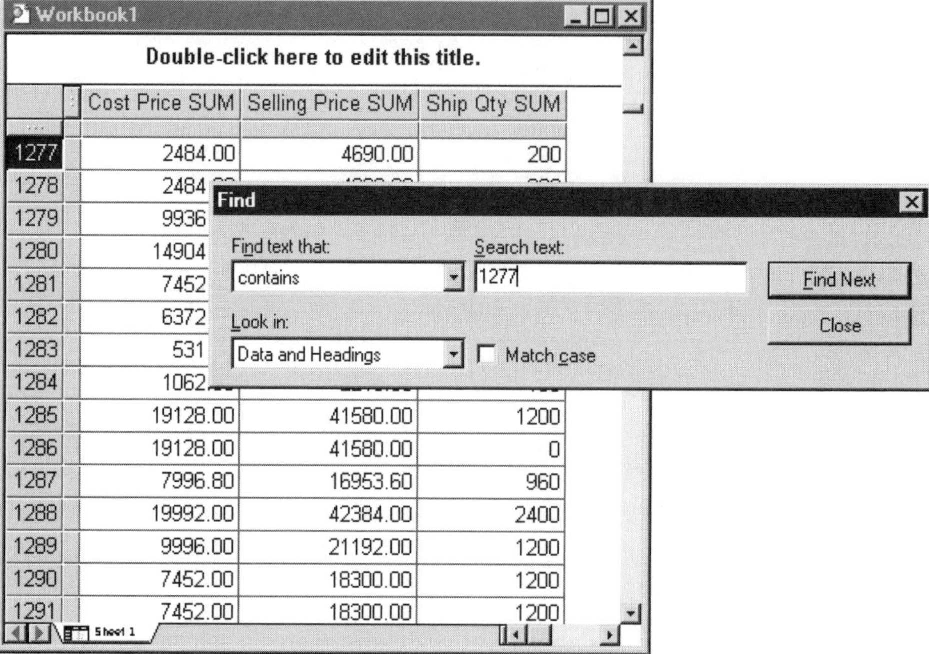

8. Repeat steps 6 and 7 as many times as required, viewing all rows that contain a match of the search criteria.
9. If the item you are looking for is not located within the results, or there are no more items matching the search criteria, Discoverer displays the following error message.

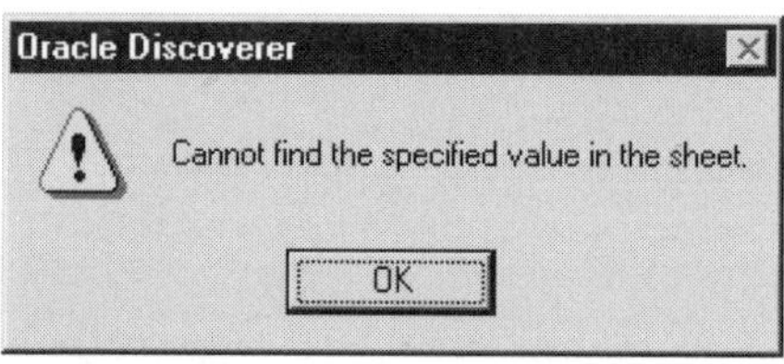

We recommend that you invest some time learning the previous workflow. Making effective use of this search capability of Discoverer 3.1 will save you a great deal of time when checking the results of queries.

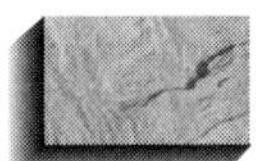

3*i* NOTE

*Unfortunately, Discoverer 3*i *does not have the above functionality. We hope that Oracle will introduce this functionality into a future release. In 3*i*, the only way to check whether or not an item has been retrieved is to page through the results. When there are hundreds of pages, this will take some time.*

Saving the Query

Computers never crash, do they? One of the quirky things about computers is that they sometimes appear to have minds of their own. They know when you're busy, they know when you've got an important document or query on screen that you haven't yet saved, and they know that you're taking a risk by not saving your work! Of course, if you save your work regularly, guess what? The system never crashes—but hold off on saving and you know what will happen. Yes, the evil elf inside the system decides to teach you a lesson, crashes your computer, and you lose everything. The authors don't know which chip on the motherboard has been programmed to do this, but if we did we wouldn't need to write this section.

The truth of the matter is that computer systems do crash, network connections fail at the most awkward of times, and laptops run out of battery power. What we are trying to instill into you is the discipline to save your work regularly.

Therefore, before doing anything else, save the query. Don't take a coffee break, don't admire the output of your first query, and don't tempt fate! There is nothing more frustrating than creating the best query anyone has ever built and then losing it before you get a chance to save it. And how is it that the second attempt never produces the same result? We don't know, but with the foundation of your query built and saved, you can refine it by formatting it, applying sort orders, calculations, totals, and so on, or you can use it as the basis for creating more complex queries.

NOTE

Discoverer saves your query, the items, the layout, and the formatting characteristics, along with any calculations or conditions you may have applied. It does not save the output of your query. This will be dealt with in Chapter 8.

There are five ways to make Discoverer save a new query:

- Press CTRL-S
- Click the Save icon on the toolbar
- Click File | Save
- Click File | Save As
- Click File | Close

When you take the last option, Discoverer asks if you would like to Save Changes to Workbook1?, as shown next, and gives you the following three options:

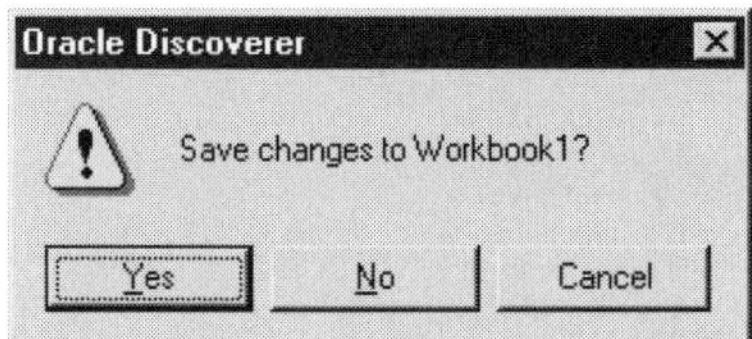

- **Yes** Displays the Save Workbook dialog box—see Figure 4-20
- **No** Closes the workbook without saving
- **Cancel** Exits the Close dialog box, and keeps the workbook open without saving it

Whichever way you decide to save your query, Discoverer 3.1 displays the Save Workbook dialog box shown in Figure 4-20.

FIGURE 4-20. *Save Workbook dialog box*

3*i* NOTE

*Because you are working on the Web, Discoverer 3*i *cannot give you the option of saving to My Computer. Therefore, you will not be prompted to choose where to save the workbook. Discoverer 3*i *takes you straight to the Database dialog box.*

Discoverer prompts you with Where Do You Want To Save This Workbook? and gives you the following two options:

- **My Computer** This allows you to save your workbook on your computer, a floppy drive, or to a network account on your server. When you first create a new query, we recommend that you take this option.
- **Database** This allows you to save your workbook to your database server. You should only save fully completed and working queries to the database.

My Computer

Choosing this option will allow you to save your worksheet to either your hard disk, a floppy disk, or your network account, and by default will give it the extension DIS. If you are going to save your workbooks on either your hard disk or a network account, we recommend that you create a special area where you can safely save them. This way, you can store all your queries in the same place, categorize them, and organize them into folders.

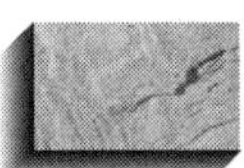

NOTE

If you are on a terminal server, remember that the hard disk you see is not on your PC, but on the terminal server itself. Your company will probably have defined a folder or folders on the server for your use. Make sure that you always save your files into your assigned area. If you want to see your work after logging off the terminal server, copy it back to your PC hard disk or network account before you exit.

Having opted to save your workbook, click Save.

Discoverer now opens up the Save As dialog box shown in Figure 4-21.

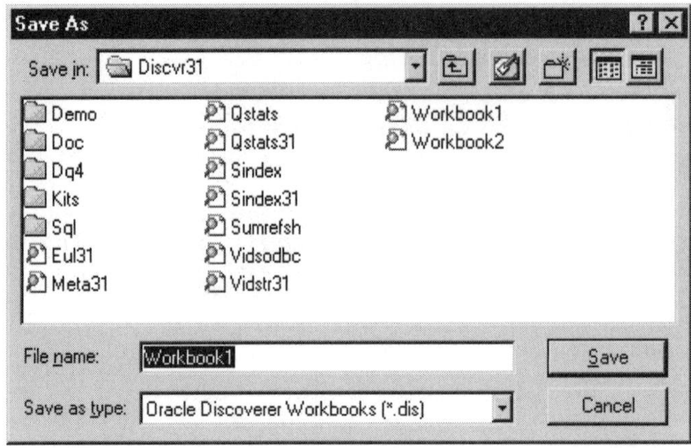

FIGURE 4-21. *The Save As dialog box*

This box has four main areas:

- Save in
- Available Workbooks
- File name
- Save as type

Save In This area displays the current folder into which your worksheet will be saved. If you do not want to save your worksheet in this folder, you should switch to another folder or create a new folder by pressing the New Folder icon.

Available Workbooks This area lists all of the workbooks that you currently have saved in the folder highlighted.

File Name This area enables you to type in a meaningful name for your workbook. By default, Discoverer will name your query Worksheet1.DIS.

NOTE
We don't recommend saving workbooks using the default name; instead, you should give your query a meaningful name (see the following section).

Save as Type This area allows you to change the file format you can save your query in. By default, Discoverer will give your workbook the extension .DIS and save it as an Oracle Discoverer workbook. If you do not want to save your query using this extension, you can click on the down arrow and select All Files (*.*) You can now save your query using any extension of your choosing. However, the file type is still an Oracle Discoverer workbook and can only be used as such.

NOTE
We don't recommend saving workbooks using any extension other than the default. If you do decide to save your workbooks using different extensions, you will make it more difficult for yourself to later locate and maintain your workbooks.

Having given your query a name and chosen where to save it, click Save. Your query is now safe, and if your system decides to crash, it will make no difference.

Database

Choosing this option will save your workbook to your Discoverer account on the database server. You should take great care not to waste space on your server and only save fully working "production" worksheets to the database.

Having opted to save your workbook to the database, click Save.

Discoverer now opens up the Save Workbook to Database dialog box shown in Figure 4-22.

This box has five areas:

- Available workbooks
- Name
- Save
- Cancel
- Help

Available Workbooks This area lists all of the workbooks that you currently have saved under your account in the database.

Name (New Name in 3*i*) This area enables you to type in a meaningful name for your workbook.

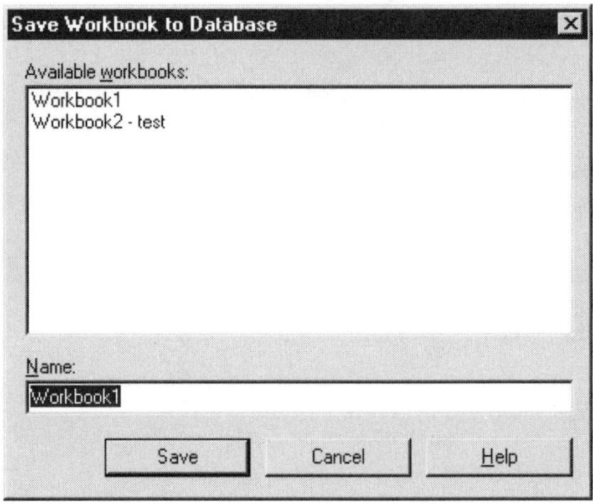

FIGURE 4-22. *Save Workbook to Database dialog box*

Save Clicking Save saves the workbook. If you choose to save using the same name as an existing workbook, Discoverer warns you that a workbook already exists by that name and asks if you would like to overwrite it, as shown in Figure 4-23.

You have the following three options:

- **Yes** This will overwrite the file.
- **No** This exits the Warning dialog box, and allows you to type in a new name for the workbook.
- **Cancel** This also exits the Warning dialog box, and allows you to type in a new name for the workbook.

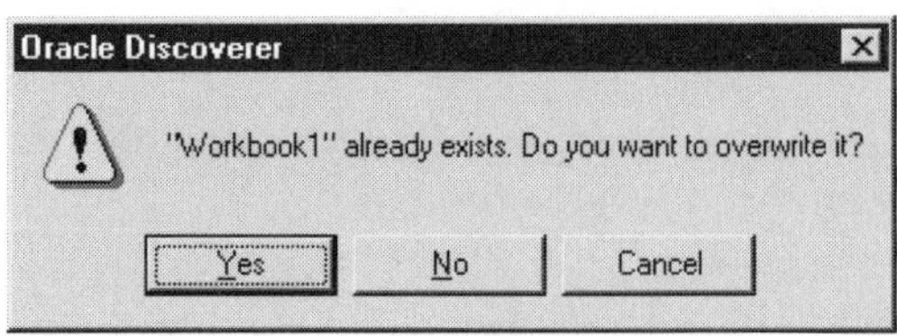

FIGURE 4-23. *Save Warning dialog box*

Cancel Clicking on this cancels the Save and returns you to your results.

Help Clicking on this calls up the Discoverer Help screen.

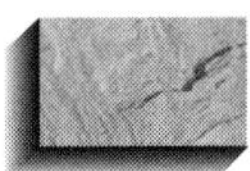

NOTE

In Discoverer 3.1, if you do not see the option to save to the database, this is because your Discoverer administrator has disabled this option. You may need to speak with him or her if you think you should be able to do this.

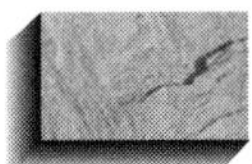

3*i* NOTE

If your Discoverer administrator has disabled the option to save to the database, you are up the river without a paddle! Obviously, if you cannot save to My Computer and you are barred from saving to the Database, you have nowhere to save your query. Run, do not walk, to your Discoverer administrator and have him or her enable saving to the Database. But seriously, there may be good reason why some users are barred from saving queries over the Web. Perhaps they are novices to Discoverer, or perhaps your company restricts creation of queries to staff working in-house. If this applies to your company, you will only be able to run queries, not create them.

If you are working in Discoverer 3*i* and have created a new query, but your Discoverer administrator has barred you from saving to the database, the above note has explained that you will not be able to save the query at all. Any attempt to leave the query will receive a warning that you have insufficient privileges.

Giving the Query a Meaningful Name

As with all files that you save to your computer, especially to a networked computer, you should get into the good habit of giving your Discoverer workbooks and worksheets meaningful names. There can be nothing more frustrating than having a database full of workbooks with meaningless names when you are looking for the one that will give your manager your end-of-year results.

Avoid naming your queries names like Bob's first query, Bob's test query, or My query. This will only end up frustrating you and your colleagues. Describe what the query is referencing, such as Q2 sales by region 2000 or Gross Margin by Product

Feb 2000. These names tell you exactly what the query is about and will not leave you guessing. It will also keep you from saving queries that you don't use (because the name does not tell you what it is for, but you are afraid to delete it) and will prevent you and your colleagues from reinventing the wheel. The authors have seen the same queries duplicated many times simply because they were not given meaningful names and were therefore not reused but re-created.

The age of the eight-character DOS naming convention is long gone. Let it die and give your files meaningful names!

Summary

In this chapter, you have learned a simple workflow for creating new queries. We explained that in Discoverer 3.1 there are six steps to the Workbook Wizard, while in Discoverer 3*i* there are nine steps.

By following the first four steps of the Workbook Wizard, you learned to create a working query and to avoid "The Query from the Twilight Zone." Feels good, doesn't it? You also learned to view the results and save your work. As a novice in Discoverer, this is a good approach, and should be used until you have become more experienced in creating queries. In fact, even seasoned Discoverer users adopt this approach, and rarely use the remaining steps of the wizard before viewing the initial output.

However, it would be remiss of us to not explain the remaining steps of the Workbook Wizard. These will be covered in the next chapter.

CHAPTER 5

The Workbook Wizard: The Optional Steps

In Chapter 4, you were shown the essential steps in using the Workbook Wizard to create a working query. In this chapter, you will learn the remaining steps of the Workbook Wizard: sorting, calculations, percentages, totals, and parameters. These steps are optional and can be added after you have a functional query.

Because the steps of the Workbook Wizard covered in this chapter are optional, it is necessary that you learn how to reopen the Workbook Wizard to add them to your query. In the second part of this chapter, you will learn how to open the Edit Sheet dialog box in order to edit an existing query. This form contains all of the steps of the Workbook Wizard in a multitabbed configuration, thus making Discoverer's functionality easy to access.

The Optional Steps of the Workbook Wizard

The following two steps are in both the 3.1 and 3*i* Workbook Wizards:

- Creating a sort order
- Creating user-defined calculations

This completes the 3.1 Workbook Wizard; however, in 3*i*, there are three additional steps. The Percentages, Totals, and Parameters dialogs are launched via the menu bar or toolbar in 3.1:

- Creating user-defined percentages
- Creating user-defined totals
- Creating user-defined parameters

NOTE

Throughout the final steps of the Workbook Wizard, you may decide to run your query at any time by clicking the Finish button. You can even skip a step if you wish, simply by clicking Next. As long as you stay in the Workbook Wizard, you can return to a previous step by clicking Back.

Workbook Wizard Step 5—Creating a Sort Order (Tables Only)

Let us assume that you have not run and saved your query. For a table query, the next step after creating user-defined conditions is creating a sort order. For crosstab queries, this step is omitted and the Workbook Wizard continues with the setting of calculations. While it is possible to add sort criteria to crosstab queries, the Workbook Wizard does not allow you to do this. If you are using a crosstab, you need to complete your query, display the results onscreen, and then apply or refine your sort.

The following section therefore only applies to table queries. To see how sort orders are applied to crosstabs, refer to the section on crosstab sorting later in this chapter. From here until the end of this section on sorting, we will assume that you are working with a table query. After applying conditions, click Next.

This brings up the fifth screen of the Workbook Wizard. As shown in Figure 5-1, this window consists of the following features:

- **Sorting box** This box will be empty until you add a sort order. As you apply sorts to your items, Discoverer will display them in here in the order in which you defined the sort.
- **Add** Click this to add an item to sort.
- **Delete** Click this to delete a sort.
- **Move Up** Click this to promote a sort.
- **Move Down** Click this to demote a sort.

Sorting—What Is It?

Sorting arranges text in alphabetical order and numbers in numerical order in either Lo to Hi (ascending, a–z, 1–10) or Hi to Lo (descending, z–a, 10–1) order. This creates an orderly means of viewing data, such as employees alphabetically or customer sales from highest to lowest. Anyone familiar with Excel has used sorting before and will probably be looking for a Sort button. Discoverer has these also, but not in the Workbook Wizard. In here, you need to take a more complicated approach. This is one of the reasons we suggest not defining your sort orders in the Workbook Wizard.

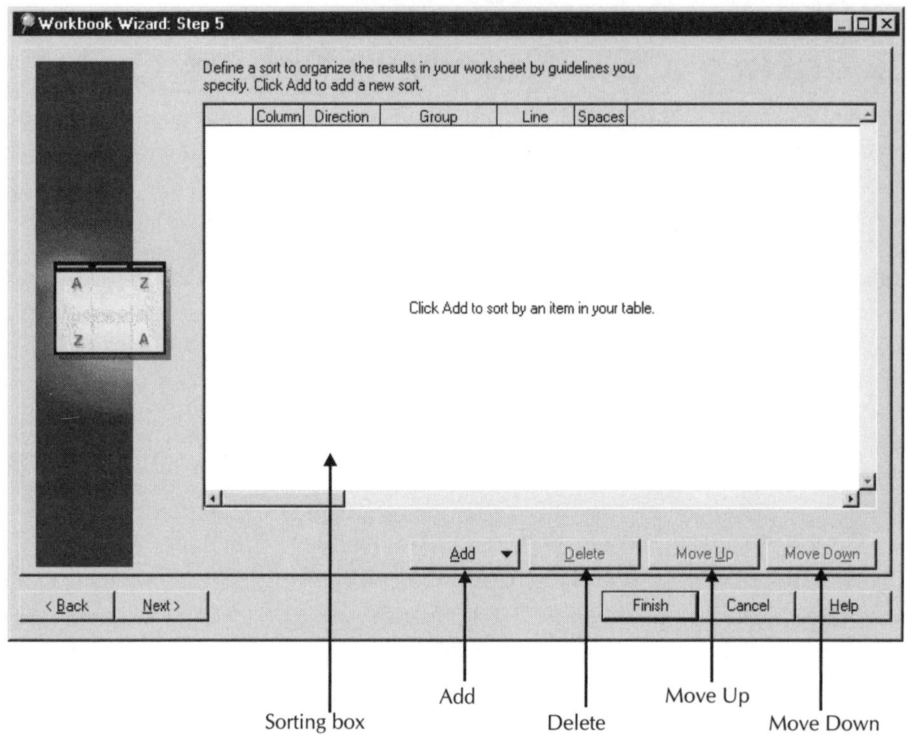

FIGURE 5-1. *Workbook Wizard step 5*

NOTE
*In Discoverer 3*i*, Lo to Hi and Hi to Lo are spelled out in full (Low to High and High to Low). Throughout this chapter, whenever we use the terms Hi and Lo, we are referring to Discoverer 3.1. When the terms High and Low are spelled out, we are referring to Discoverer 3*i*.*

Figure 5-2 shows an example of a numeric sort in Lo to Hi order.

Discoverer also allows for group sorting. For those not familiar with group sorting, a group sort is a more specialized form of Lo to Hi or Hi to Lo sort. When you select this type of sort, Discoverer leaves blank all repeating items, thus making your reports much easier to read and more aesthetically pleasing.

Figure 5-3 shows the same data used in Figure 5-2, sorted as a group sort.

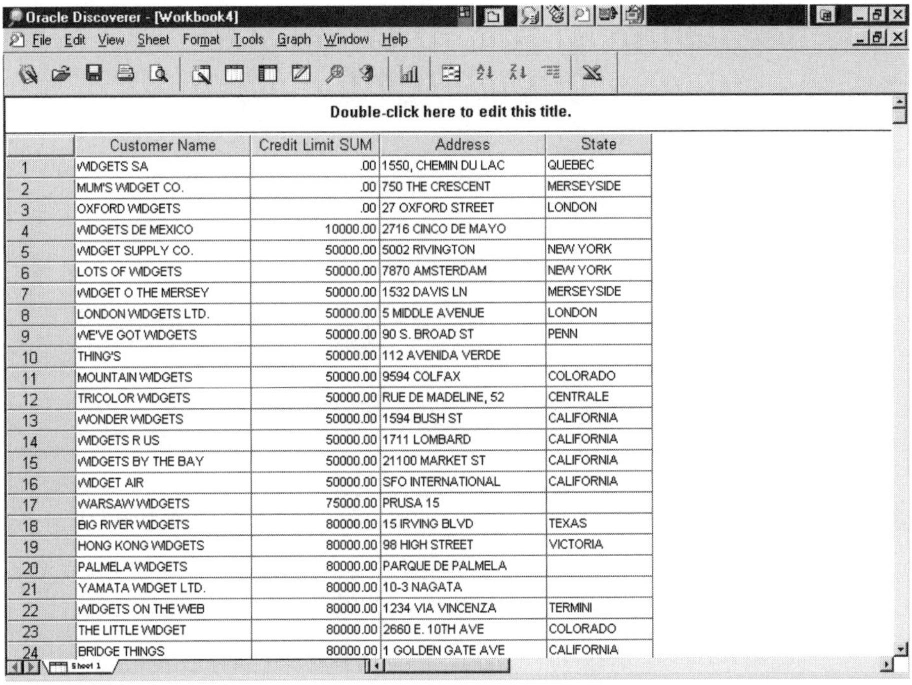

Oracle Discoverer - [Workbook4]

File Edit View Sheet Format Tools Graph Window Help

Double-click here to edit this title.

	Customer Name	Credit Limit SUM	Address	State
1	WIDGETS SA	.00	1550, CHEMIN DU LAC	QUEBEC
2	MUM'S WIDGET CO.	.00	750 THE CRESCENT	MERSEYSIDE
3	OXFORD WIDGETS	.00	27 OXFORD STREET	LONDON
4	WIDGETS DE MEXICO	10000.00	2716 CINCO DE MAYO	
5	WIDGET SUPPLY CO.	50000.00	5002 RIVINGTON	NEW YORK
6	LOTS OF WIDGETS	50000.00	7870 AMSTERDAM	NEW YORK
7	WIDGET O THE MERSEY	50000.00	1532 DAVIS LN	MERSEYSIDE
8	LONDON WIDGETS LTD.	50000.00	5 MIDDLE AVENUE	LONDON
9	WE'VE GOT WIDGETS	50000.00	90 S. BROAD ST	PENN
10	THING'S	50000.00	112 AVENIDA VERDE	
11	MOUNTAIN WIDGETS	50000.00	9594 COLFAX	COLORADO
12	TRICOLOR WIDGETS	50000.00	RUE DE MADELINE, 52	CENTRALE
13	WONDER WIDGETS	50000.00	1594 BUSH ST	CALIFORNIA
14	WIDGETS R US	50000.00	1711 LOMBARD	CALIFORNIA
15	WIDGETS BY THE BAY	50000.00	21100 MARKET ST	CALIFORNIA
16	WIDGET AIR	50000.00	SFO INTERNATIONAL	CALIFORNIA
17	WARSAW WIDGETS	75000.00	PRUSA 15	
18	BIG RIVER WIDGETS	80000.00	15 IRVING BLVD	TEXAS
19	HONG KONG WIDGETS	80000.00	98 HIGH STREET	VICTORIA
20	PALMELA WIDGETS	80000.00	PARQUE DE PALMELA	
21	YAMATA WIDGET LTD.	80000.00	10-3 NAGATA	
22	WIDGETS ON THE WEB	80000.00	1234 VIA VINCENZA	TERMINI
23	THE LITTLE WIDGET	80000.00	2660 E. 10TH AVE	COLORADO
24	BRIDGE THINGS	80000.00	1 GOLDEN GATE AVE	CALIFORNIA

Sheet 1

FIGURE 5-2. *Simple Lo to Hi sort (Credit Limit sorted, unsorted Customer Name)*

Creating Your First Sort

When creating a new sort you should use the following workflow:

1. Click Add.
2. Select the item you want to sort on.
3. Define the sort parameters.
4. Click OK to finish.

When you first enter step 5 of the wizard, the main box in the center of the screen will be empty (see Figure 5-1). You need to think about what item or items you want to apply a sort on. Unfortunately, unlike conditions, there are no administrator-created sorts, so it is all up to you.

Because you can create multiple sorts in your query, you should try to create them in a logical sequence, defining the primary sort first. There is no limit on the number of sorts you can define, other than the number of items in your query, but

Oracle Discoverer - [Workbook1]

File Edit View Sheet Format Tools Graph Window Help

Double-click here to edit this title.

	Customer Name	Credit Limit SUM	Address	State
1	WIDGETS SA	.00	1550, CHEMIN DU LAC	QUEBEC
2	OXFORD WIDGETS		27 OXFORD STREET	LONDON
3	MUM'S WIDGET CO.		750 THE CRESCENT	MERSEYSIDE
4	WIDGETS DE MEXICO	10000.00	2716 CINCO DE MAYO	
5	WIDGET SUPPLY CO.	50000.00	5002 RIVINGTON	NEW YORK
6	WIDGET O THE MERSEY		1532 DAVIS LN	MERSEYSIDE
7	WIDGET AIR		SFO INTERNATIONAL	CALIFORNIA
8	WE'VE GOT WIDGETS		90 S. BROAD ST	PENN
9	TRICOLOR WIDGETS		RUE DE MADELINE, 52	CENTRALE
10	THING'S		112 AVENIDA VERDE	
11	WIDGETS BY THE BAY		21100 MARKET ST	CALIFORNIA
12	MOUNTAIN WIDGETS		9594 COLFAX	COLORADO
13	LOTS OF WIDGETS		7870 AMSTERDAM	NEW YORK
14	LONDON WIDGETS LTD.		5 MIDDLE AVENUE	LONDON
15	WIDGETS R US		1711 LOMBARD	CALIFORNIA
16	WONDER WIDGETS		1594 BUSH ST	CALIFORNIA
17	WARSAW WIDGETS	75000.00	PRUSA 15	
18	PALMELA WIDGETS	80000.00	PARQUE DE PALMELA	
19	WIDGETS ON THE WEB		1234 VIA VINCENZA	TERMINI
20	THE LITTLE WIDGET		2660 E. 10TH AVE	COLORADO
21	HONG KONG WIDGETS		98 HIGH STREET	VICTORIA
22	BRIDGE THINGS		1 GOLDEN GATE AVE	CALIFORNIA
23	BIG RIVER WIDGETS		15 IRVING BLVD	TEXAS
24	YAMATA WIDGET LTD.		10-3 NAGATA	
25	WIDGETS MARKET	100000.00	1665 MARKET ST	CALIFORNIA
26	WIDGETS Y GADGETS		CALLE MARTINEZ, 208	

Sheet 1

FIGURE 5-3. *Simple Lo to Hi group sort (credit limit as a group sort/customers unsorted)*

we recommend you restrict your choices to a maximum of two or three within the Workbook Wizard. Creating complex sort sequences greater than this is very difficult to visualize and we strongly advise you to create these later.

When you have decided what column(s) needs to be sorted, click the Add button. This displays a drop-down list (as shown in the following illustration) of all the items in your query. Pick the item you have decided on for the primary sort from the list.

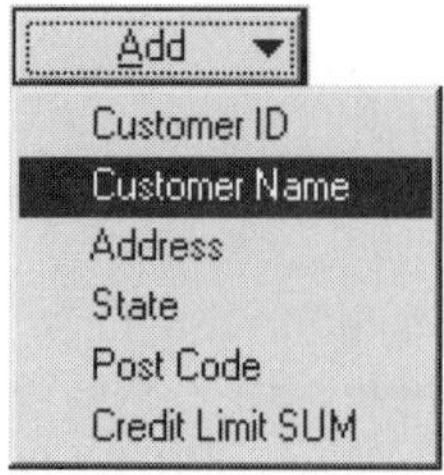

This will place your first sort in the box and give you the following additional choices:

- **Column** Displays the name of the item you chose for your sort.
- **Direction** The sort order (defaults Lo to Hi) for the item.
- **Group** Click this for a drop-down list of group sort options.
- **Line** Click this if you want to change the width of the line between group-sorted items.
- **Spaces** Click this if you want to add extra line spacing between group-sorted items.

The 3.1 sort criteria are shown in the following illustration:

	Column	Direction	Group	Line	Spaces
1	Customer Name	Lo to Hi	None	---	---

At this point, you will notice that the Delete button is activated. If you have made a mistake and selected the wrong item for your sort, click Delete and it will be removed.

Assuming you have chosen the correct item, Discoverer defaults the sort into ascending order; it is not a group sort (as indicated by the word None under the Group heading), and for 3.1 only, there is no setting for either line width or line spacing (as indicated by the characters **...** in the box). In 3*i*, the Hidden check box will be blank.

The 3*i* sort criteria are shown in the following illustration:

	Column	Direction	Group	Hidden
1	Customer Name	Low to High	None	☐

- **Column** Displays the name of the item you chose for your sort.
- **Direction** The sort order (defaults Low to High) for the item.
- **Group** Click this to choose between None and Group Sort.
- **Hidden** Check this box if you do not want the item to be displayed. By default, it is unchecked.

Refining Your First Sort

Having created your first sort, you may find that it needs refining. Perhaps you want to have the data sorted Hi to Lo, or use a group sort:

- In 3.1, to toggle between Lo to Hi and Hi to Lo, click the up or down arrow beneath the heading Direction. You will see the direction indicator change accordingly.
- In 3*i*, to switch between Low to High and High to Low, click on the down arrow alongside the current setting and select from the drop-down list.
- To apply a group sort, click the down arrow beneath the heading Group.

Building a Group Sort

We will now explain in detail how you can add and refine your own group sort. Having clicked on the down arrow beneath the heading Group, Discoverer produces a drop-down list of the available options. In 3.1 the list has the following options:

- **None** Select this option if you do not want to use a group sort.
- **Group Sort** Select this option to convert your existing sort into a group sort. This automatically opens up the Line and Spaces options, both of which are explained below.
- **Page Break** Select this option if you want Discoverer to insert a page break into the final output every time the group sort encounters a new value. In the final display onscreen, Discoverer indicates that there is a page break by inserting a broken line between the sorted items. Whenever you print a report containing a page break, Discoverer will begin each sorted item on a new page.
- **Hidden** Select this option if you do not wish to display any of the data values for that item onscreen. You should apply this type of sort with great care, because it may not be obvious to someone looking at your report that the query is applying a sort on a hidden item.

Having elected to use a group sort, in Discoverer 3.1 you have two more options that you can set. You can opt to insert line spacing between the group-sorted items and you can change the width of the line separators. By default, Discoverer 3.1 sets both to 1.

3i FEATURE

*Discoverer 3*i *only displays the options None and Group Sort. The current Web version does not support page break sorts, line width, or line spacing. The Hidden option has been moved and is no longer a subset of the Group Sort option. It has become a valid option for both types of sort.*

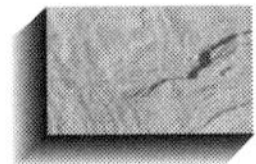

NOTE
The Hidden option can be very powerful, and the following are good examples of its usage. First, suppose HR wants to produce a report, by department, of the employees based on their salaries, but does not want to print out the actual salary amounts. Applying a sort on the salary figures and then hiding those items from the report will print out the employees in order of salary. Second, suppose you want a report showing your best performing departments in terms of sales, without printing the actual sales figures. You would simply create a sort on the sales figures and hide them.

Line Width

In Discoverer 3.1, if you want to change the width of the line separators, click the down arrow alongside the number 1 under the heading Line. This displays the following drop-down list:

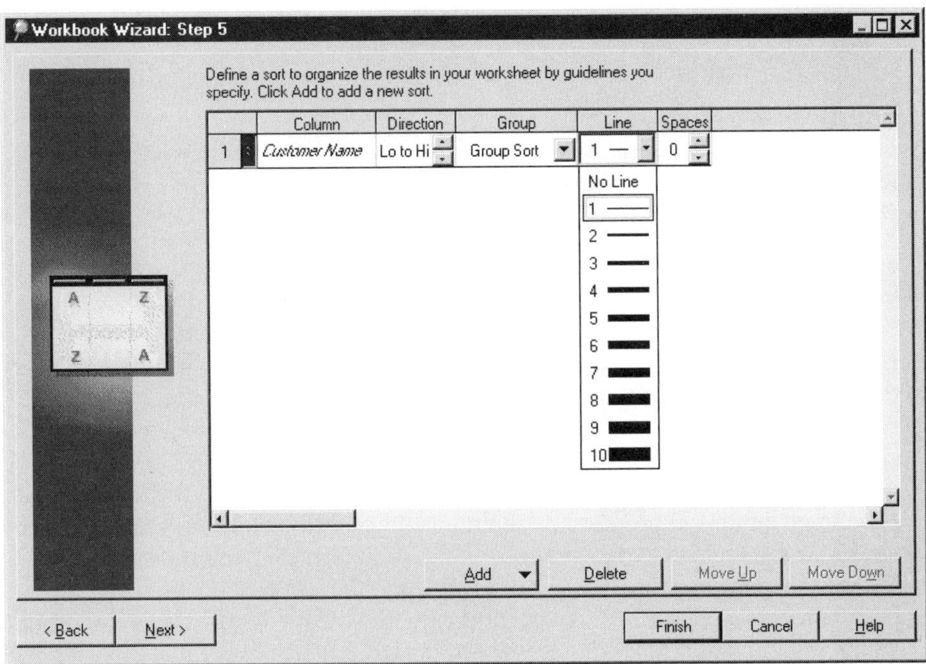

As you can see, you can choose to use no lines or you can choose a line width of between 1 and 10.

Line Spacing

In Discoverer 3.1, if you want to change the spacing between group-sorted items, click on the down arrow alongside the number 1 under the heading Space.

Use the up and down arrows to set the number of spaces you want to appear between each change of group-sorted items.

Adding Another Sort

Having created one sort you may decide to add a second, third, and so on. This will cause items to sort within other items.

For example, in our original sort shown above, we have a group sort by credit limit. However, the customers are not sorted. It would be a better report to have the customers also sorted alphabetically. We therefore need to add a second sort to our query. To do this, click Add. This will once again display the drop-down list of available items.

NOTE

Any item that has already been selected for sorting will not appear in the drop-down list again. You can only apply one sort to an item. When there are no more items available for sorting, the Add button is deactivated.

Figure 5-4 shows a Discoverer 3.1 example of a multiple-sort sequence. We have taken the previously group-sorted list (see Figure 5-3) and applied a second sort on the Customer column.

Rearranging the Sort Order

Whenever you have two or more sorts in use, you should look carefully at the relationship between the items and determine if the sort sequence is correct. Earlier, we suggested that you should try to create your sorts in the order that you want to see them in the final report. However, with even the best design or analysis, sometimes you may have created them in the wrong order.

If you decide you have a sort in the wrong place, you can use the Move Up and Move Down buttons to promote or demote items. These buttons only become active when you have created two or more sorts. You can also use your mouse to click and drag the items to change their position within the sort sequence.

For example, suppose we had created a query with the items' ship date, product number, and quantity shipped. We want to have our final display in date order with the products in alphabetical order by date. However, by mistake we created the sort on the products before we created the sort on the dates. The result will appear as in Figure 5-5. By promoting the ship date above the product, our display will be correct as shown in Figure 5-6.

Oracle Discoverer - [Workbook1]

File Edit View Sheet Format Tools Graph Window Help

Double-click here to edit this title.

	Customer Name	Credit Limit SUM	Address	State
1	MUM'S WIDGET CO.	.00	750 THE CRESCENT	MERSEYSIDE
2	OXFORD WIDGETS		27 OXFORD STREET	LONDON
3	WIDGETS SA		1550, CHEMIN DU LAC	QUEBEC
4	WIDGETS DE MEXICO	10000.00	2716 CINCO DE MAYO	
5	LONDON WIDGETS LTD.	50000.00	5 MIDDLE AVENUE	LONDON
6	LOTS OF WIDGETS		7870 AMSTERDAM	NEW YORK
7	MOUNTAIN WIDGETS		9594 COLFAX	COLORADO
8	THING'S		112 AVENIDA VERDE	
9	TRICOLOR WIDGETS		RUE DE MADELINE, 52	CENTRALE
10	WE'VE GOT WIDGETS		90 S. BROAD ST	PENN
11	WIDGET AIR		SFO INTERNATIONAL	CALIFORNIA
12	WIDGET O THE MERSEY		1532 DAVIS LN	MERSEYSIDE
13	WIDGET SUPPLY CO.		5002 RIVINGTON	NEW YORK
14	WIDGETS BY THE BAY		21100 MARKET ST	CALIFORNIA
15	WIDGETS R US		1711 LOMBARD	CALIFORNIA
16	WONDER WIDGETS		1594 BUSH ST	CALIFORNIA
17	WARSAW WIDGETS	75000.00	PRUSA 15	
18	BIG RIVER WIDGETS	80000.00	15 IRVING BLVD	TEXAS
19	BRIDGE THINGS		1 GOLDEN GATE AVE	CALIFORNIA
20	HONG KONG WIDGETS		98 HIGH STREET	VICTORIA
21	PALMELA WIDGETS		PARQUE DE PALMELA	
22	THE LITTLE WIDGET		2660 E. 10TH AVE	COLORADO
23	WIDGETS ON THE WEB		1234 VIA VINCENZA	TERMINI
24	YAMATA WIDGET LTD.		10-3 NAGATA	
25	ABC WIDGET CO	100000.00	123, YOCKSAM-DONG	KANGNAM-GU
26	ACE MANUFACTURING		VASCO DE GAMA, 78	

Sheet 1

FIGURE 5-4. *Credit Limit/Customer query group sorted by credit limit and customer ascending*

Why Not Sort in the Wizard?

When you are working with queries that need to pull a large amount of data, we recommend that you do not attempt to create your sort sequences inside the Workbook Wizard. We recommend against this because sorting adds to the length of time it takes to run a query, and if you have defined complicated sorts you will add an unnecessary overhead to your query. This overhead could actually cause your query to exceed the maximum query time set by your Discoverer administrator, and your query could time out.

When you have a working copy of your query, you can concentrate on the sort criteria. You should look at the data that your query has brought in and try to define the best way to display that data. Presenting your data using appropriate and meaningful sort criteria should be done only after you have some data onscreen as a result of a reduced set of constraints.

In Chapter 8, you will learn how different types of sorts affect your report and how to create a useful sort order.

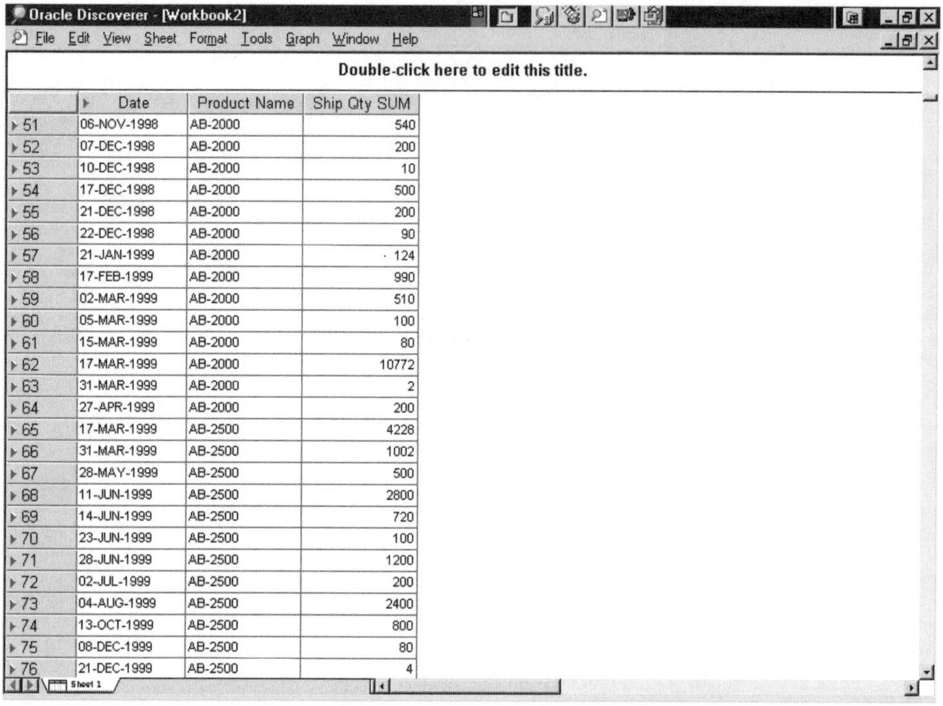

Oracle Discoverer - [Workbook2]

File Edit View Sheet Format Tools Graph Window Help

Double-click here to edit this title.

	Date	Product Name	Ship Qty SUM
51	06-NOV-1998	AB-2000	540
52	07-DEC-1998	AB-2000	200
53	10-DEC-1998	AB-2000	10
54	17-DEC-1998	AB-2000	500
55	21-DEC-1998	AB-2000	200
56	22-DEC-1998	AB-2000	90
57	21-JAN-1999	AB-2000	124
58	17-FEB-1999	AB-2000	990
59	02-MAR-1999	AB-2000	510
60	05-MAR-1999	AB-2000	100
61	15-MAR-1999	AB-2000	80
62	17-MAR-1999	AB-2000	10772
63	31-MAR-1999	AB-2000	2
64	27-APR-1999	AB-2000	200
65	17-MAR-1999	AB-2500	4228
66	31-MAR-1999	AB-2500	1002
67	28-MAY-1999	AB-2500	500
68	11-JUN-1999	AB-2500	2800
69	14-JUN-1999	AB-2500	720
70	23-JUN-1999	AB-2500	100
71	28-JUN-1999	AB-2500	1200
72	02-JUL-1999	AB-2500	200
73	04-AUG-1999	AB-2500	2400
74	13-OCT-1999	AB-2500	800
75	08-DEC-1999	AB-2500	80
76	21-DEC-1999	AB-2500	4

Sheet 1

FIGURE 5-5. *Ship date, product, and ship quantity, sorted by product and date*

After applying crosstab conditions or adding sort orders to a table, click Next. This brings up the sixth screen of the Workbook Wizard.

Workbook Wizard Step 6—Creating User-Defined Calculations

As shown in Figure 5-7, Workbook Wizard step 6 contains three boxes and three buttons:

- **View Calculations For box** A drop-down box where you can choose to view calculations for all items or a specific item only. In Discoverer 3*i*, you also get an option to view active-only calculations.

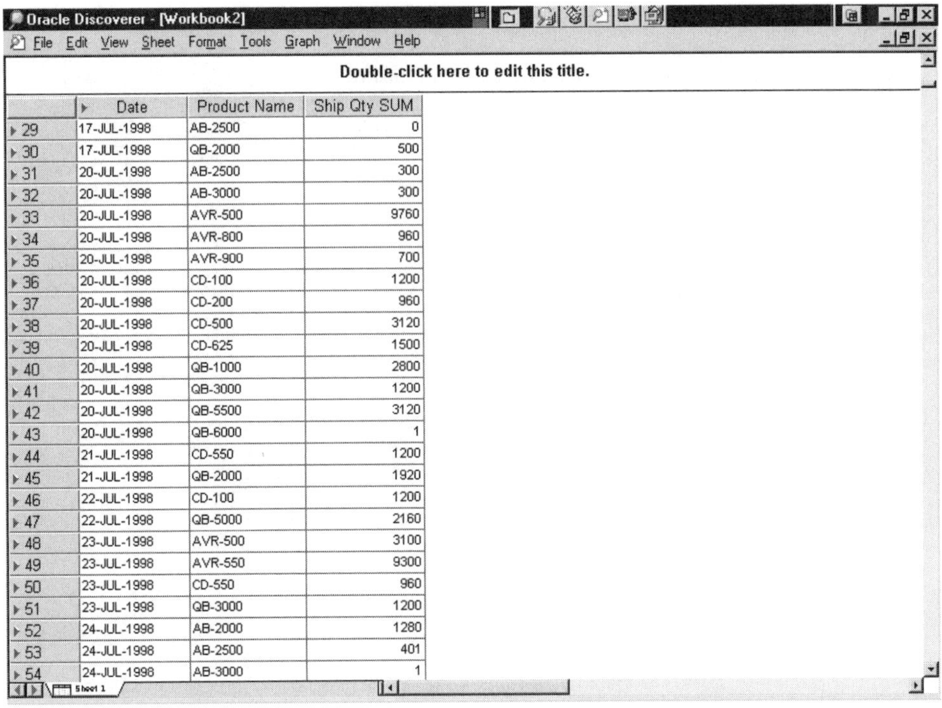

Oracle Discoverer - [Workbook2]

File Edit View Sheet Format Tools Graph Window Help

Double-click here to edit this title.

	Date	Product Name	Ship Qty SUM
29	17-JUL-1998	AB-2500	0
30	17-JUL-1998	QB-2000	500
31	20-JUL-1998	AB-2500	300
32	20-JUL-1998	AB-3000	300
33	20-JUL-1998	AVR-500	9760
34	20-JUL-1998	AVR-800	960
35	20-JUL-1998	AVR-900	700
36	20-JUL-1998	CD-100	1200
37	20-JUL-1998	CD-200	960
38	20-JUL-1998	CD-500	3120
39	20-JUL-1998	CD-625	1500
40	20-JUL-1998	QB-1000	2800
41	20-JUL-1998	QB-3000	1200
42	20-JUL-1998	QB-5500	3120
43	20-JUL-1998	QB-6000	1
44	21-JUL-1998	CD-550	1200
45	21-JUL-1998	QB-2000	1920
46	22-JUL-1998	CD-100	1200
47	22-JUL-1998	QB-5000	2160
48	23-JUL-1998	AVR-500	3100
49	23-JUL-1998	AVR-550	9300
50	23-JUL-1998	CD-550	960
51	23-JUL-1998	QB-3000	1200
52	24-JUL-1998	AB-2000	1280
53	24-JUL-1998	AB-2500	401
54	24-JUL-1998	AB-3000	1

Sheet 1

FIGURE 5-6. *Ship date, product, and ship quantity, sorted by date and product*

- **Available Calculations box** This box will be empty until you add a calculation. As you add calculations to your query, Discoverer will display them here in the order in which you create them.
- **Description box** A box showing the description of the calculation highlighted in the Calculations box.
- **New button** Click this to add a new calculation.
- **Edit button** When active, click this to edit an existing calculation.
- **Delete button** Click this to delete a calculation. As with conditions, be careful using this one because it does just what it says and without prompting!

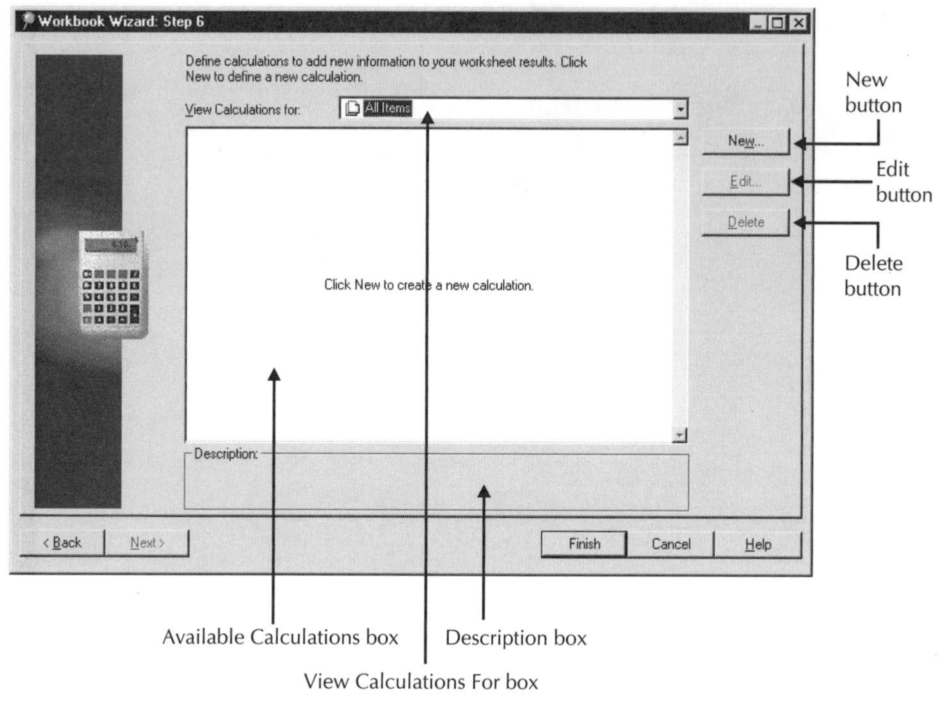

FIGURE 5-7. *Workbook Wizard step 6*

Calculations—What Are They?

The word "calculate" means to compute mathematically, to ascertain by computation, to reckon, to estimate, or to plan. Calculations have been with us almost from the dawn of time, and throughout the ages man has been trying to devise new and quicker ways to perform them. The computer you are working on right now has the capability to perform millions of calculations per second (MIPS). In a business environment, you will most likely want to use calculations to aid you in estimating, trending, and forecasting.

Calculations give you more power in ad hoc reporting. When there is no underlying item in the database that contains the data you want, Discoverer allows you to create new items. The formulas used to create these items can be very simple, or they can be complex mathematical or statistical expressions.

When using calculations, you can use existing items from the database, the operators multiply (*), divide (/), add (+), and subtract (-), literals such as 1, 100, and 65.5, and functions. You can also use calculations that have been created for you by your Discoverer administrator.

It is possible to see profits, costs, and margins calculated and grouped in a matter of minutes. Using mathematical formulas, calculations enable you to produce more complex queries. They usually apply some sort of algorithm or equation to the query results. A simple example of a calculation in a query is subtracting a product's cost price from its selling price to see the profit. A more complex calculation would be to see the profit margin, which is the sum of the profit (itself a calculation) divided by the sum of the selling price.

Figure 5-8 shows a simple calculation being used in a query. You can see the selling price minus the cost price is being shown as the profit Calculation0.

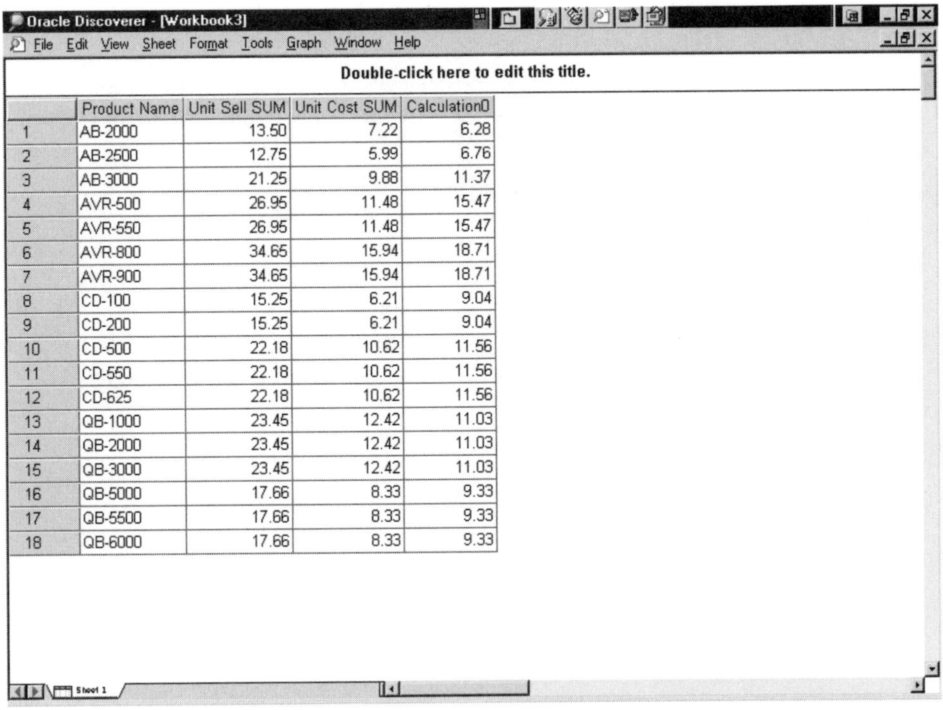

Oracle Discoverer - [Workbook3]

File Edit View Sheet Format Tools Graph Window Help

Double-click here to edit this title.

	Product Name	Unit Sell SUM	Unit Cost SUM	Calculation0
1	AB-2000	13.50	7.22	6.28
2	AB-2500	12.75	5.99	6.76
3	AB-3000	21.25	9.88	11.37
4	AVR-500	26.95	11.48	15.47
5	AVR-550	26.95	11.48	15.47
6	AVR-800	34.65	15.94	18.71
7	AVR-900	34.65	15.94	18.71
8	CD-100	15.25	6.21	9.04
9	CD-200	15.25	6.21	9.04
10	CD-500	22.18	10.62	11.56
11	CD-550	22.18	10.62	11.56
12	CD-625	22.18	10.62	11.56
13	QB-1000	23.45	12.42	11.03
14	QB-2000	23.45	12.42	11.03
15	QB-3000	23.45	12.42	11.03
16	QB-5000	17.66	8.33	9.33
17	QB-5500	17.66	8.33	9.33
18	QB-6000	17.66	8.33	9.33

Sheet 1

FIGURE 5-8. *Workbook Wizard, step 6—selling price minus the cost price*

Creating Your First Calculation

When creating a new calculation, you should use the following workflow:

1. Click New.
2. Give a meaningful name for your calculation. This name will appear as the column heading. By default, Discoverer inserts the word calculation followed by an integer.
3. Click Show to see a list of available expressions.
4. Build your calculation using a combination of expressions and operators.
5. Click on OK to finish.

When you first enter step 6 of the wizard, the main box in the center of the screen will be empty (see Figure 5-7). You need to think about what item or items you want to use in your calculations. Like conditions, there are administrator-created calculations for you to choose from. You can select these predefined calculations in exactly the same way as you select the items in your query. In Chapter 4, you were shown the different icons for the types of items you could select. Simple predefined calculations appear as a numeric item and aggregate calculations appear as a calculator.

In the example below, the Discoverer administrator has created simple calculations for standard margin, markup, and profit. There is also an administrator-defined aggregate calculation called "profit margin." The first three appear as normal items, and you can use the usual mathematical functions of SUM, AVG, and so forth on these. The item called profit margin, however, is an aggregate based on dividing the SUM of one item into another. This type of aggregated calculation stands alone in that it cannot have any other function applied to it, hence the absence of any (+) character.

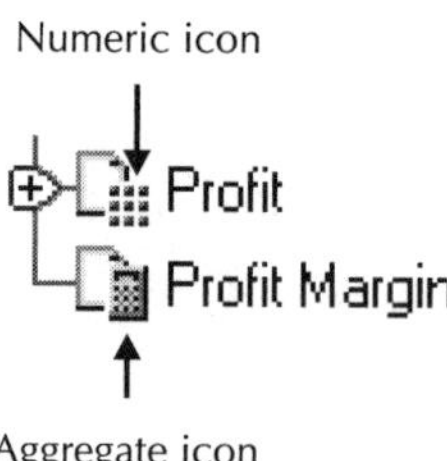

Because you can create multiple calculations in your query, you should try to create them in a logical sequence, defining simple calculations first. There is no limit on the number of calculations you can define. Creating complex calculations requires a great deal of preplanning, perhaps working out your calculations on paper before you begin to define them in the Workbook Wizard. One of the most common mistakes made by end users is defining or attempting to define extremely complex calculations in the Workbook Wizard.

When you have decided what columns you need for a calculation, click the New button.

Figure 5-9 shows the Edit Calculation dialog box used in Discoverer 3.1. Figure 5-10 shows the New Calculation dialog box used in Discoverer 3*i*. These dialog boxes consist of the following sections:

- **Name** The name given here will appear as the column heading.
- **Calculation box** Type or paste the components for your calculation here.
- **Show box** This is a drop-down list of the items, functions, parameters and other calculations available to use in this calculation.

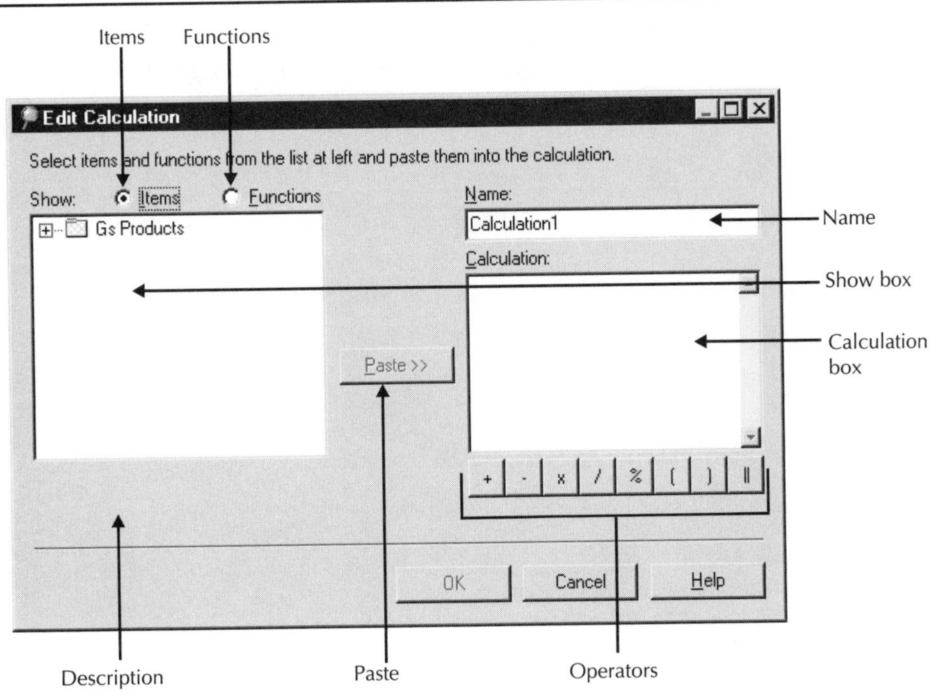

FIGURE 5-9. *3.1 Edit Calculations dialog box*

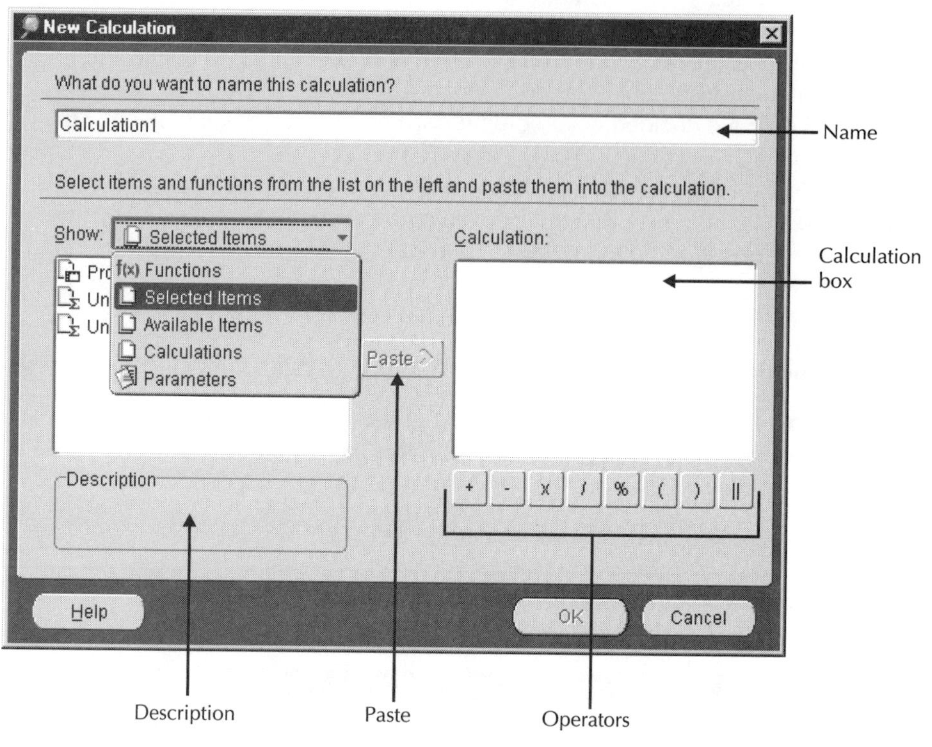

FIGURE 5-10. *3*i *New Calculation dialog box*

- **Paste** Click this button to add an item, function, parameter or other calculation to the Calculation box.
- **Operators** A set of buttons for standard mathematical operators. Clicking on these pastes the operator into the calculation.
- **Description** Displays a description of an item, calculation or function.
- **Name** The name given here will appear as the column heading.
- **Calculation box** Type or paste the components for your calculation here.
- **Show box** This is a drop-down list of the items or functions available to use in this calculation.
- **Items** Click this radio button to display a list of the items available to create your calculation.

- **Functions** Click this radio button to display a list of functions available to create your calculation.
- **Paste** Click this button to add an item or function to the Calculation box.
- **Operators** A set of buttons for standard mathematical operators. Clicking on these pastes the operator into the calculation.
- **Description** Displays a description of an item, calculation, or function in this part of the screen.

When you have created a calculation, click OK. This causes Discoverer to test the mathematical properties of your calculation. If you have defined an incorrect calculation, Discoverer will warn you and you will have to correct your formula before continuing.

Assuming you have created a valid calculation, Discoverer inserts it into the box for calculations and ticks the check box automatically. Also at this point, you will notice that the Edit and Delete buttons that were shown inactive in Figure 5-7 are now activated, and Discoverer has inserted the formula into the Description box. If you have made an error in your formula, use the Edit button to reopen the Calculation dialog box and change it. If you decide you no longer need this calculation, click Delete and it will be removed.

Discoverer adds the calculations into the box in the order you create them. You can use your calculations or administrator predefined calculations to create more complex algorithms.

NOTE

Be very careful creating calculations that employ division. You need to ensure that the divisor column does not contain any zero values; otherwise, you will encounter the dreaded divide-by-zero error, which will cause your query to fail. You will either have to apply a condition on the column that is being used as the divisor (Column<>0), or create your calculation using a DECODE function to tell Discoverer what to do when it encounters this situation. A DECODE calculation can be thought of as an IF...THEN clause. This will be explained fully in Chapter 12. If you are debugging a query that contains division, the first step is to check for the required nonzero condition and implement one of the two solutions outlined here. This is probably the single most common reason why calculations fail.

Why Not Calculate in the Wizard?

Applying calculations is one of the most challenging and complicated aspects of query design. It is recommended that you do not attempt to create calculations using the Workbook Wizard until you have become proficient in the use of Discoverer. The authors have spoken with numerous expert Discoverer users, and none of them said they attempt to add calculations in the wizard. They wait until they have a working query with the data needed and then begin to create their calculations.

As with all querying tools, the more complicated the query, the higher the risk becomes that you will make an error—usually with no data being returned. This becomes even riskier when adding calculations, especially calculations using division. One expression in the wrong place and you could wait several minutes for a query to run, only to come back with a message that no data was found. The best way around this type of frustration is to build yourself a basic working query and then add your calculations.

NOTE
If your Discoverer administrator has predefined calculations for your use, you will probably be safe adding these by using the Workbook Wizard.

If you are working in 3.1, you have now completed all the steps of the Workbook Wizard and you should click Finish. In 3*i*, there are three more steps, and you should click Next to move to step 7.

Discoverer 3*i* Workbook Wizard Steps 7–9

The next section of the Workbook Wizard is only applicable to Discoverer 3*i*. If you are only using 3.1 and have no interest in 3*i*, you may want to skip this section. However, most companies are moving towards Web-based analysis and we would recommend that you continue reading.

Having completed step 6 (calculations), Discoverer 3*i* added the following three additional steps to the Workbook Wizard:

- Creating user-defined percentages
- Creating user-defined totals
- Creating user-defined parameters

All of these options are available in 3.1, but not as part of the Workbook Wizard. We will show you later in the chapter how to use these in 3.1.

Workbook Wizard Step 7—Defining Percentages

Figure 5-11 shows step 7 of the 3*i* Workbook Wizard. This dialog box contains the following three boxes and three buttons.

- **View Percentages For box** A drop-down box where you can choose to view percentages for all items, a specific item only, or active-only percentages.
- **Available Percentages box** This box will be empty until you add a percentage. As you add percentages to your query, Discoverer will display them here in the order in which you create them.

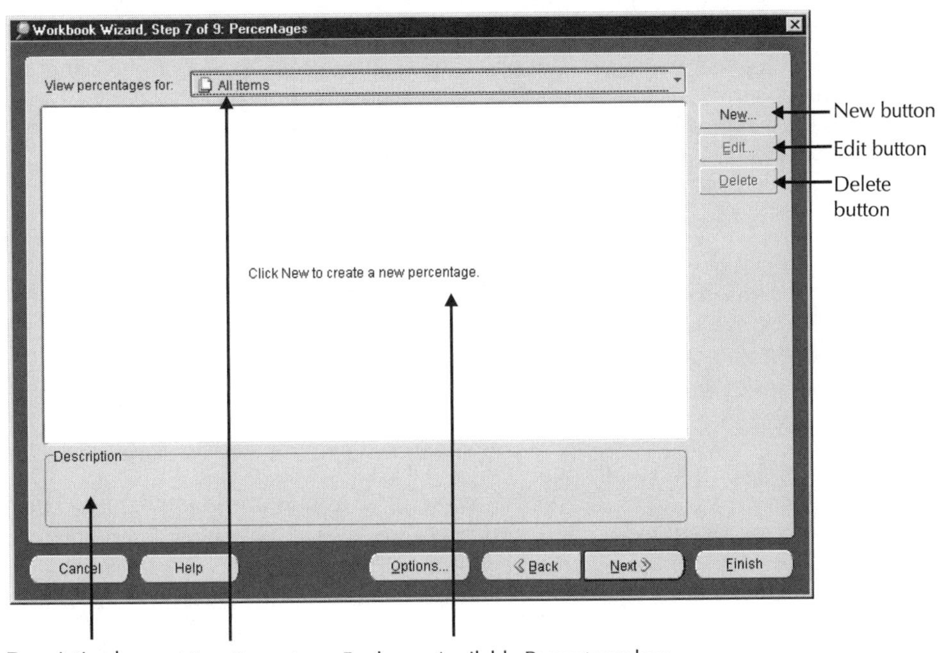

FIGURE 5-11. *Workbook Wizard step 7*

- **Description box** A box showing the description of the percentage highlighted in the Percentages box.
- **New button** Click this to add a new percentage.
- **Edit button** When active, click this to edit an existing percentage.
- **Delete button** Click this to delete a percentage. As with conditions, be careful using this one because it does just what it says and without prompting!

Percentages—What Are They?

The word "percent" comes from the Latin words "per" (meaning by) and "centum" (meaning hundred). A percentage is quite simply the rate of an item per hundred, or in accounting terms, a commission, duty, or interest based on one hundred. Most countries in the world use a currency based on one hundred parts: one hundred cents in a dollar, one hundred centimes in a franc, one hundred pennies in a pound. These allow for very simple percentage calculations, but it wasn't always this way. As recently as 1970, England had 240 pennies in one pound, but to make it worse they had 12 pennies in a shilling and 20 shillings in a pound (incidentally, the guinea that is still used in race horse trades is 21 shillings).

Calculating percentages of numbers with the answer being part of one hundred is a typical data analysis task. Discoverer allows you to choose both the data to use for the percentage calculation itself and for the value used to represent the percentage (grand total, subtotal, etc.). Don't worry about the terms used at this stage, as these will all be fully covered.

NOTE
As percentages are just a specialized form of calculation, many of the comments that were given in the preceding section on calculations are valid for percentages as well.

Percentages are mathematical formulas that enable you to analyze your data more effectively. They apply standard mathematical algorithms to the item you have chosen. A simple example of a percentage in a query is "Show me the percentage of my sales by channel for the month of January, 2000." A more complex percentage would be to see the same query extended for the whole of fiscal quarter Q2, with the percentages being applied over the whole quarter's profit margin—which is the sum of the profit (itself a percentage) divided by the sum of the selling price.

Figure 5-12 shows a simple percentage being applied in a query. You can see that the selling price has been totaled by channel and that the percentage of sales is shown by channel and by total. Because the month is only used to define a condition, it has been moved to the Page Items box.

NOTE
Because of rounding in percentages, don't expect your percentage totals to always add to up 100 percent. This is a common phenomenon, and anyone familiar with spreadsheet programs such as Excel has encountered this situation.

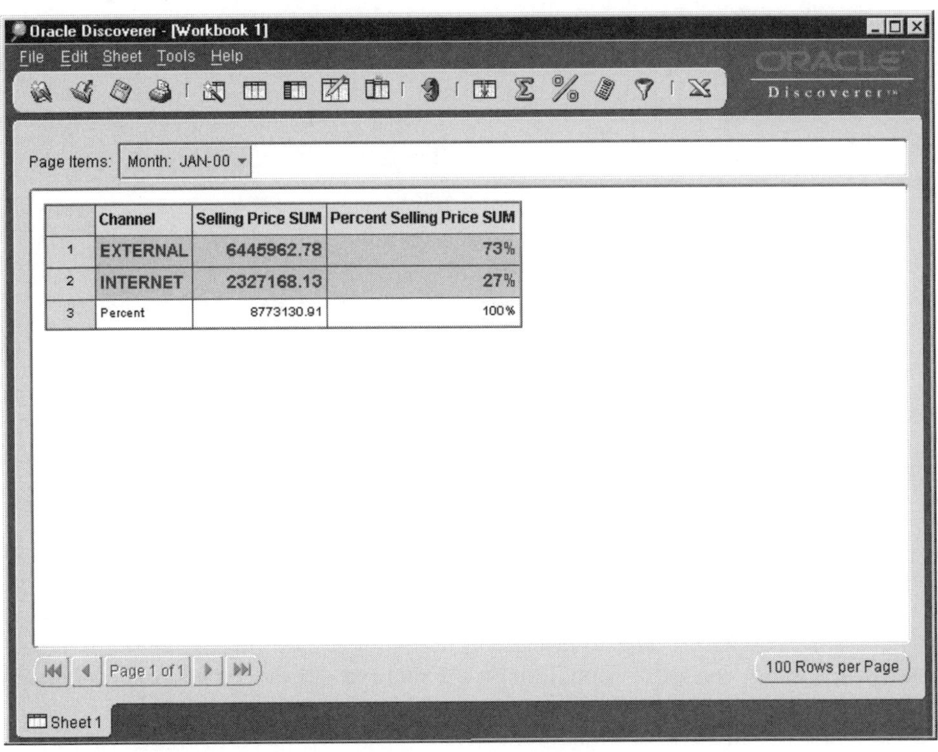

FIGURE 5-12. *Selling price as percentage by channel for January 2000*

Creating Your First Percentage

When creating a new percentage you should use the following workflow:

1. Click New.
2. Give a name for your percentage. This name will appear as the column heading. If you leave this blank, the percentage column will have no label.
3. Click the Data Point drop-down box to see the list of available data points, and select the data item you want to apply the percentage on from the list. If you have only one item that can be used, Discoverer inserts that item by default and disables the drop-down.
4. Choose whether you want your percentage to be based on a grand total of all values or on a subtotal.
5. Choose whether to calculate percentages using only items displayed on the current page or whether to calculate using the page items as well. The latter is a 3*i*-only feature and cannot be used in 3.1. If you create a percentage in 3*i* that uses page items, you can still open and run the query in 3.1; however, the percentage will not display.
6. Choose whether to include totals in your percentages. If you do so, you may also give a label for the percentage. This is not mandatory, and you may leave it either with the default or nothing at all.
7. Click OK to finish.

When you first enter step 7 of the wizard, the main box in the center of the screen will be empty (see Figure 5-11). You need to think about what item or items you want to use in your percentages. Unlike calculations, there are no administrator-created percentages for you to choose from. However, you can have calculations that give the answer as a percentage, but these cannot be edited as percentages.

Because percentages usually stand alone as data items, it doesn't really matter in what order you create them. Although you probably wouldn't have more than one or two in your query, there is no limit on the number of percentages you can define. Creating valid and meaningful percentages can be somewhat taxing at first, but don't worry because most of the fun of working with Discoverer is based upon examining and trying things out for yourself.

When you have decided what data item you need for a percentage, click the New button. This opens the New Percentages dialog box, which contains the following sections:

- **Name** The name given here will appear as the column heading. Discoverer will create a name for you if you don't specify one. Figure 5-13 shows Discoverer inserting default names. We recommend you review Discoverer's names and change them to something more meaningful.
- **Data Point box** This is a drop-down list of the data points that you can use to base percentages on.
- **Grand Total of All Values** Click this radio button if you want your percentages to be based on the grand total of all values.
- **Subtotal at Each Change In** Click this radio button if you want your percentages to be based on a subtotal. Having clicked on this button, select the item on which you want to create the subtotal from the drop-down list.
- **Calculate Only for Current Page Item** Click this radio button if you want percentages to be based only on the items displayed onscreen. This is a 3*i*-only option.

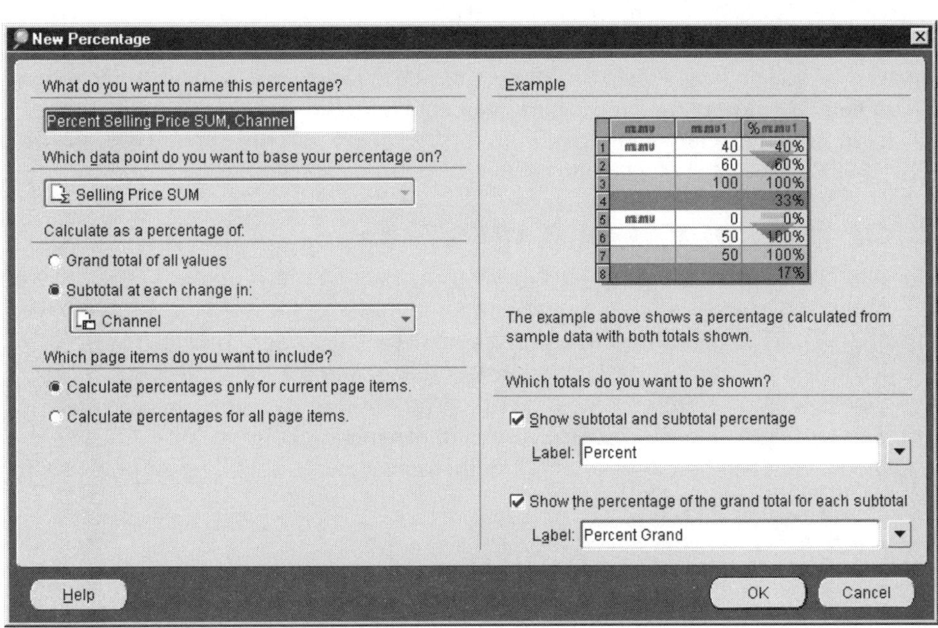

FIGURE 5-13. *3i New Percentages dialog box*

- **Calculate for All Page Items** Click this radio button if you want percentages to be based on the page items. This is a 3*i*-only option.
- **Show Subtotal and Subtotal Percentage** Check this box if you want to show the subtotal and subtotal percentages onscreen. You can also then use the drop-down list to select items for labeling the subtotal.
- **Show the Percentage of Grand Total for Each Subtotal** Check this box if you want to show the grand total percentages onscreen. You can also then use the drop-down list to select items for labeling the grand total.

When you have created a percentage, click OK. This causes Discoverer to calculate the percentage. Unlike calculations, where Discoverer has to test the mathematical properties of the calculation, percentages always work. There is no such thing as having defined an incorrect percentage, although the results you see onscreen may not be that obvious at first—as we shall show you in a moment.

Assuming you have created a valid percentage, Discoverer inserts it into the box for percentages and ticks the check box automatically. Percentages are added into the box in the order you create them.

Also at this point, you will notice that the Edit and Delete buttons are activated and Discoverer has inserted the formula into the Description box. If you have made an error in your formula, use the Edit button to reopen the Percentage dialog box and edit it. If you decide you no longer need this percentage, click Delete and it will be removed.

When you have completed adding percentages to your query, you can either click Finish, which causes Discoverer to run the query, or you can move to step 8 of the Workbook Wizard by clicking Next.

Examples of Percentages

Because there are many options available to you within the Workbook Wizard, we will show you examples of each type. For the purpose of these examples, we have specified a query that pulls in the selling price SUM, the sales channel, the fiscal year (with a condition to constrain to just FY1999), and the fiscal quarter. The fiscal year has been moved to the Page Item box. We will start by using a very simple percentage calculation and progress through all of the options so that you can see at a glance what each option does. In all of these examples, the only data point open to us is the selling price SUM.

Example 1: A Simple Percentage

In this example, we will apply the following options:

- Calculate as a percentage of the grand total
- Calculate percentages for current page items only
- Do not show any totals

This is by far the easiest type of percentage to create and apply within your query, and probably the easiest for anyone viewing your output to understand. By setting the options as shown below, and then clicking OK, Discoverer will create the percentage calculation shown on the right. Discoverer has sorted the query by channel and quarter. You can see at a glance that Global Widgets' best quarter was Q1, 1999, with 46 percent of sales for the year. You may also spot that there were no sales from the Internet in that quarter; this is because they didn't start their e-business until the beginning of Q2.

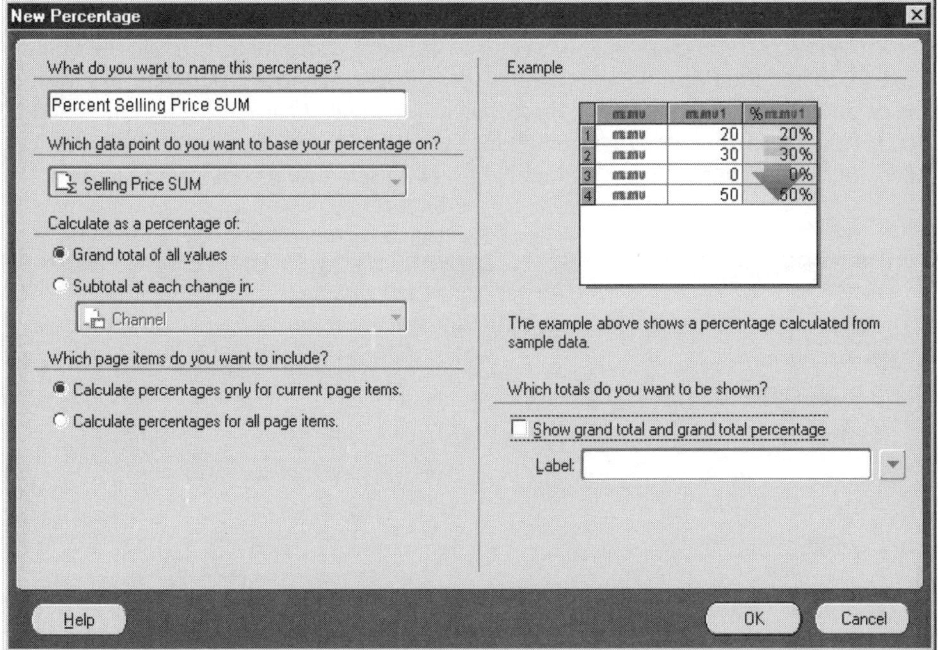

	Channel	Quarter	Selling Price SUM	Percent Selling Price SUM
1	EXTERNAL	1999-Q1	4653005.02	46%
2		1999-Q2	2208282.19	22%
3		1999-Q3	1754457.39	17%
4		1999-Q4	468566.29	5%
5	INTERNET	1999-Q2	404521.85	4%
6		1999-Q3	470116.40	5%
7		1999-Q4	191039.43	2%

Example 2: Showing the Grand Total

In the next example, we have edited the previous percentage and redefined it as follows:

- Calculate as a percentage of the grand total
- Calculate percentages for current page items only
- Show grand total and grand total percentage, and use the label "Percent"

By setting these options, Discoverer will refine the percentage calculation to be as shown below. As you can see, Discoverer is showing grand totals for both the Selling Price SUM and the Percentage columns. You can also see that Discoverer has inserted the default name "Percent Selling Price SUM". As advised earlier, we recommend that you review these default names and change them to something more meaningful. We have not done so here in order to highlight how Discoverer inserts default names.

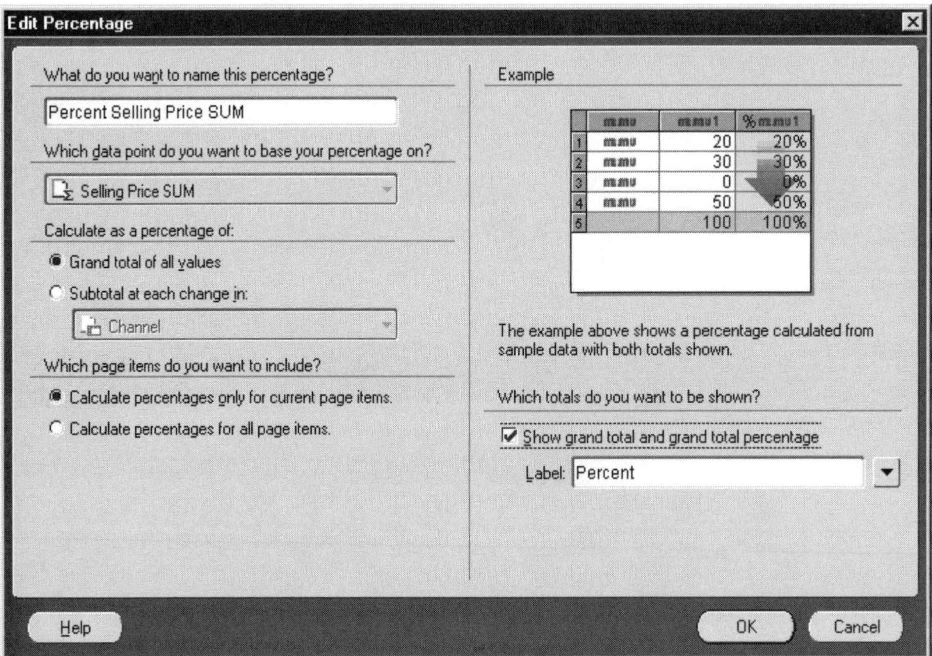

	Channel	Quarter	Selling Price SUM	Percent Selling Price SUM
1	EXTERNAL	1999-Q1	4653005.02	46%
2		1999-Q2	2208282.19	22%
3		1999-Q3	1754457.39	17%
4		1999-Q4	468566.29	5%
5	INTERNET	1999-Q2	404521.85	4%
6		1999-Q3	470116.40	5%
7		1999-Q4	191039.43	2%
8	Percent		10149988.57	100%

Example 3: Showing Subtotals

In the next example, we have further edited the percentage and redefined it as follows:

- Calculate as a percentage of the subtotal based on the channel
- Calculate percentages for current page items only
- Show subtotals and subtotal percentages, using the label "Percent"

By setting these options, Discoverer will refine the percentage calculation to be as shown below. Discoverer is showing subtotals by channel for both the Selling Price SUM and the Percentage columns. We can see at a glance that the best quarter for Global Widgets via their external channel was Q1, which accounted for 51 percent of that channel's annual sales. Their best quarter from the Internet came in Q3, with 44 percent of annual sales.

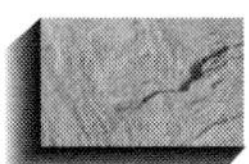

NOTE

In order to correctly apply a percentage using subtotals, you need to define sorts on the items you want to subtotal. Using the example above, we have created a group sort on the channel and applied a normal ascending order sort on the fiscal month.

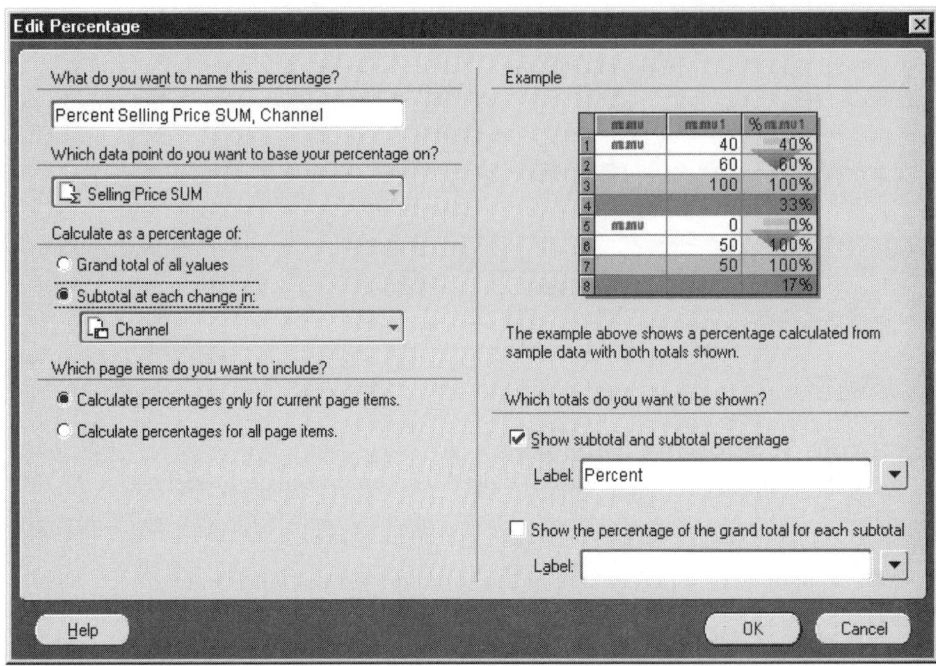

	Channel	Quarter	Selling Price SUM	Percent Selling Price SUM, Channel
1	EXTERNAL	1999-Q1	4653005.02	51%
2		1999-Q2	2208282.19	24%
3		1999-Q3	1754457.39	19%
4		1999-Q4	468566.29	5%
5	Percent		9084310.89	100%
6	INTERNET	1999-Q2	404521.85	38%
7		1999-Q3	470116.40	44%
8		1999-Q4	191039.43	18%
9	Percent		1065677.68	100%

Example 4: Showing Subtotals and a Grand Total

In the next example, we have further edited the percentage and redefined it as follows:

- Calculate as a percentage of the subtotal based on the channel
- Calculate percentages for current page items only
- Show subtotals and subtotal percentages, using the label "Percent"

- Show grand totals and grand total percentages, using the label "Percent Grand"

By setting these options, Discoverer will refine the percentage calculation to be as shown below. Discoverer is now showing not only the subtotals by channel for both the Selling Price SUM and the Percentage columns, but also the percentage of each as compared to the grand total. We can now see that the external channel accounted for 90 percent of all sales for FY 1999, with the Internet accounting for just 10 percent.

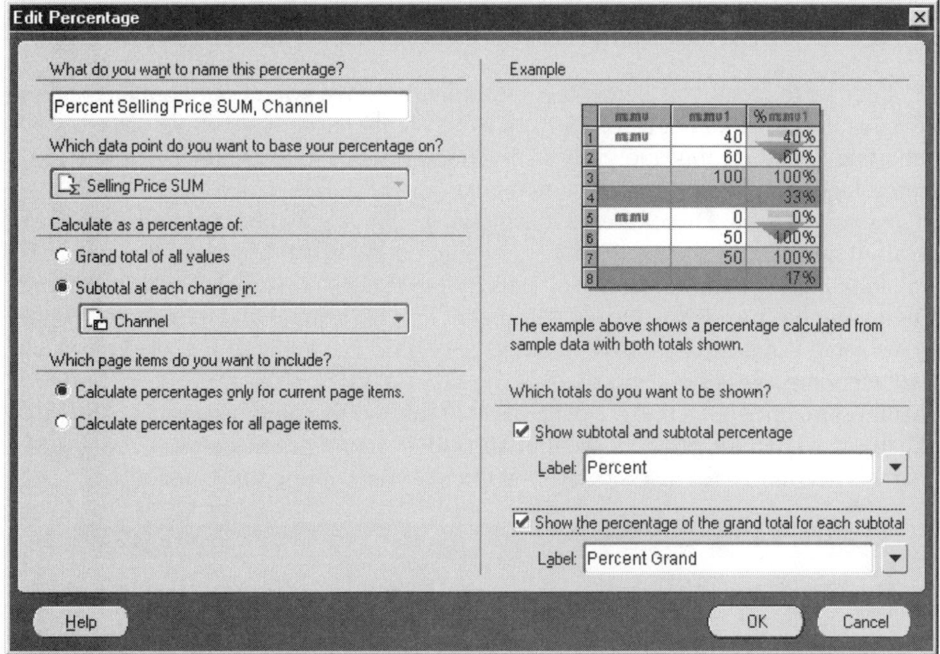

	Channel	Quarter	Selling Price SUM	Percent Selling Price SUM, Channel
1	EXTERNAL	1999-Q1	4653005.02	51%
2		1999-Q2	2208282.19	24%
3		1999-Q3	1754457.39	19%
4		1999-Q4	468566.29	5%
5	Percent		9084310.89	100%
6				Percent Grand: 90%
7	INTERNET	1999-Q2	404521.85	38%
8		1999-Q3	470116.40	44%
9		1999-Q4	191039.43	18%
10	Percent		1065677.68	100%
11				Percent Grand: 10%

Example 5: Showing Subtotals and a Grand Total Using Page Items

In the next example, we have further edited the percentage and redefined it as follows:

- Calculate as a percentage of the subtotal based on the channel
- Calculate percentages for all page items
- Show subtotals and subtotal percentages, using the label "Percent"
- Show grand totals and grand total percentages, using the label "Percent Grand"

In order to create this percentage example, we have edited our condition on the fiscal year, bringing in data for 1998 as well. We therefore have a two-year reporting period for this query. By setting these options, Discoverer will refine the percentage calculation to be as shown next.

As you can see, Discoverer is still showing subtotals by channel and a grand total. At first glance, the results may appear to be incorrect; however, they are not. If you look closely at the percentage totals for the external channel, you will see that Discoverer has inserted values of 45 percent for the subtotal and 42 percent for the grand total. What this means is that in FY 1999, Global Widgets had external sales that accounted for 45 percent of all of the external sales in the two-year period, and that this amount equated to 42 percent of *all* sales in the same period. Looking at the Internet channel, you can see that *all* of their Internet sales came in 1999, and that this accounted for just 5 percent of the total sales in the same period.

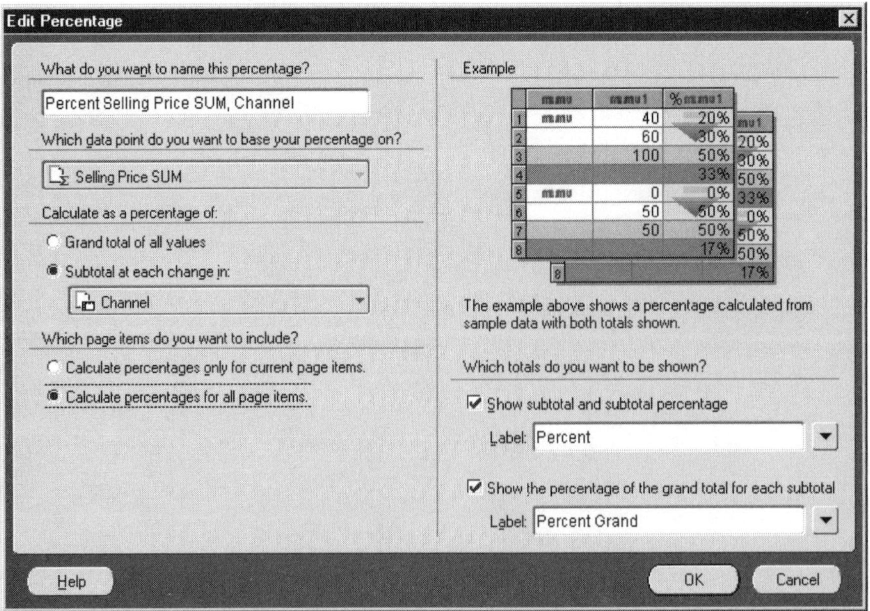

	Channel	▸ Quarter	Selling Price SUM	Percent Selling Price SUM, Channel
1	EXTERNAL	1999-Q1	4653005.02	23%
2		1999-Q2	2208282.19	11%
3		1999-Q3	1754457.39	9%
4		1999-Q4	468566.29	2%
5	Percent		9084310.89	45%
6				Percent Grand: 42%
7	INTERNET	1999-Q2	404521.85	38%
8		1999-Q3	470116.40	44%
9		1999-Q4	191039.43	18%
10	Percent		1065677.68	100%
11				Percent Grand: 5%

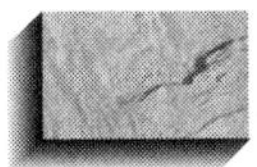

NOTE
*Oracle added the capability to create percentages based on page items when they introduced their Web version of Discoverer. The above example can therefore only be created in 3*i.

Why Not Perform Percentages in the Wizard?

As the above examples have shown, applying percentages and understanding what the various Discoverer options mean can be quite daunting, even to a seasoned query writer. Percentages can also take some time to compute, and it may not be the best use of your time to worry about percentages until after you have a working version of your query. For this reason, we again recommend that you do not attempt to create percentages using the Workbook Wizard until you have become proficient in the use of Discoverer.

You have now completed step 7 of the 3*i* Workbook Wizard. Click Next to move to step 8.

Workbook Wizard Step 8—Defining Totals

Figure 5-14 shows the Workbook Wizard step 8. Like most other steps in the Workbook Wizard, this dialog box contains the following three boxes and three buttons:

- **View Totals For box** A drop-down box where you can choose to view percentages for all items, a specific item only, or active-only totals.
- **Available Totals box** This box will be empty until you add a total. As you add totals to your query, Discoverer will display them here in the order in which you create them.

- **Description box** A box showing the description of the total highlighted in the Totals box.
- **New button** Click this to add a new total.
- **Edit button** When active, click this to edit an existing total.
- **Delete button** Click this to delete a total. As with conditions, again be careful because it does just what it says and without prompting!

Totals—What Are They?

Discoverer 3.1 defines a total as "The result of a calculation that summarizes data in a sheet. Examples of totals are minimum, maximum, average, and sum." The definition within 3*i* states "When working with numeric information, you often need to see various summations of the data. Totals can sum rows and columns of

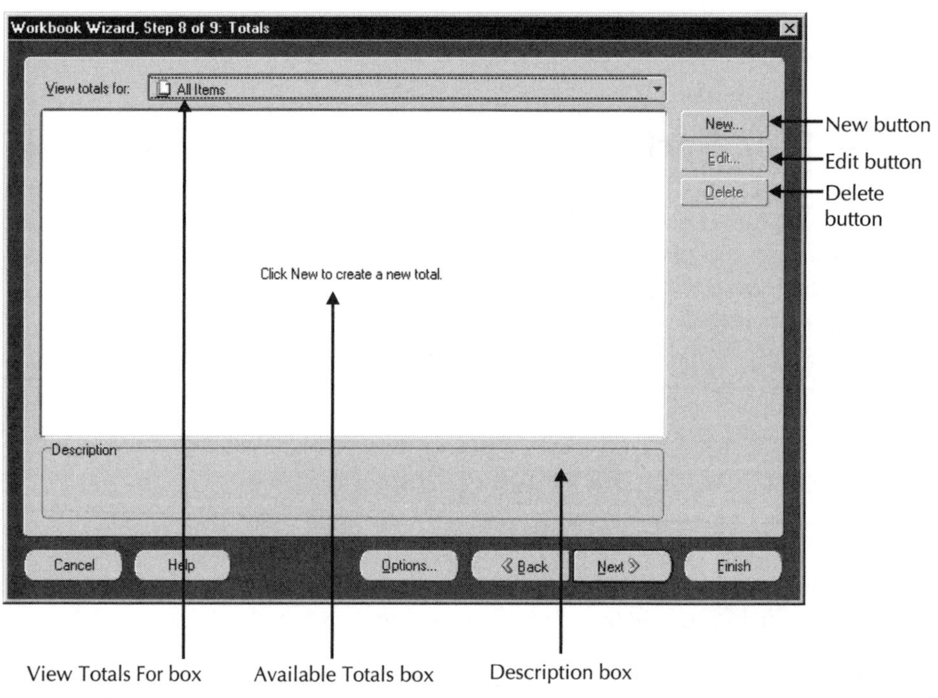

FIGURE 5-14. *Workbook Wizard step 8*

numbers, find averages and standard deviation, compute subtotals and grand totals and so on. When you add a total to a worksheet, Discoverer automatically adds a column or row to the worksheet for the totals data."

If you read both definitions closely, there is a clue in the 3*i* definition that Oracle has enhanced the totaling capabilities of Discoverer in their Web version. This is absolutely true, and 3*i* has more options for totaling than are available in the Windows version.

Calculating totals of numbers is again a typical data analysis task. Discoverer allows you to choose both the data to use for the total itself and for the value used to represent the total (grand total, subtotal, etc.). Don't worry about the terms used at this stage, as these will all be fully covered.

NOTE
If in step 7 you created a percentage based on either a grand total or a subtotal, you would not want to create it again here. If you have decided not to create totals based on percentages, you should create them in step 8 of the Workbook Wizard.

Like percentages, totals are mathematical formulas that enable you to analyze your data more effectively. They apply standard mathematical algorithms to the item you have chosen. A simple example of a total in a query is "Show me the grand total of product ordered for the month of January, 2000." A more complex total would be to see the same query extended to include subtotals for each change of product.

Figure 5-15 shows a simple total being applied in a query. You can see the total amount of product sold. Again, because the month is only used to define a condition, it has been moved to the page item.

Creating Your First Total

When creating a new total, you should use the following workflow:

1. Click New.
2. Give a name for your total. This name will appear as the column or row heading.
3. Click on the Data Point drop-down box to see the list of available data points, and select the data item you want to apply the total on from the list. If you have only one item that can be used, Discoverer inserts that item by default and disables the drop-down.

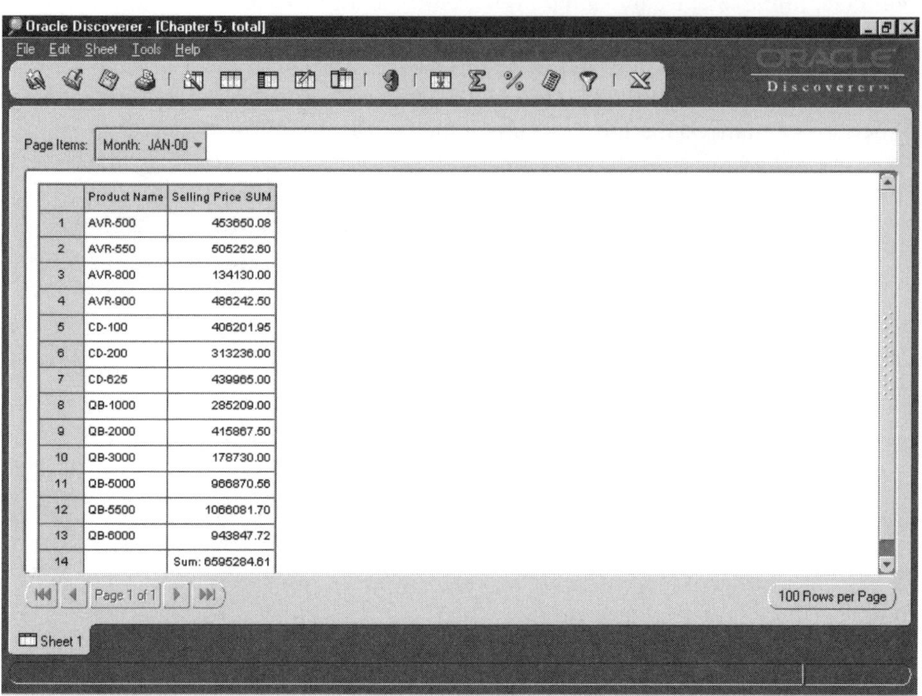

FIGURE 5-15. *Workbook Wizard step 8—grand total of product for January 2000*

4. Choose the type of total you want to apply. See below for a list of the valid types.
5. Choose whether you want your total to be based on a grand total of all values or on a subtotal.
6. Choose whether to display totals for a single row or not.
7. Choose whether to calculate totals using only items displayed on the current page or whether to calculate using the page items as well. This is a 3*i*-only feature and cannot be used in 3.1.
8. Click OK to finish.

When you first enter step 8 of the wizard, the main box in the center of the screen will be empty (see Figure 5-14). You need to think about what item or items you want to use in your totals. Unlike calculations, there are no administrator-created totals for you to choose from. However, you can have totals that are based on percentages, but these cannot be edited as totals.

Because totals usually stand alone as data items, it doesn't really matter in which order you create them. Although you probably wouldn't have more than one or two in your query, there is no limit on the number of totals you can define.

When you have decided what data item you need for a total, click the New button. This opens the New Total dialog box.

- **Name** The name given here will appear as the column heading. Discoverer will create a name for you if you tick the check box.
- **Data Point box** This is a drop-down list of the data points that you can use to base totals on.
- **Total Type box** This is a drop-down list of all of the functions that are available to you.
- **Grand Total at Right** This option only appears if the query is using a crosstab layout.
- **Grand Total at Bottom** Click this radio button if you want to see a grand total at the bottom based on the grand total of all values.
- **Subtotal at Each Change In** Click this radio button if you want your totals to be based on a subtotal. Having clicked this button, select the item on which you want to create the subtotal from the drop-down list.
- **Calculate Only for Current Page Item** Click this radio button if you want totals to be based only on the items displayed onscreen. This is a 3*i*-only option.
- **Calculate for All Page Items** Click this radio button if you want totals to be based on the page items. This is a 3*i*-only option.
- **Show Subtotal and Subtotal Total** Check this box if you want to show the subtotal and subtotal totals on screen. You can also then use the drop-down list to select items for labeling the subtotal.
- **Show Total of Grand Total for Each Subtotal** Check this box if you want to show the grand total totals onscreen. You can also then use the drop-down list to select items for labeling the grand total.

NOTE
*The 3*i* dialog box looks and operates almost exactly the same as the one for 3.1, except that it has two additional areas that can be filled in.*

When you have created a total, click OK. This causes Discoverer to calculate the total. Unlike calculations, where Discoverer has to test the mathematical properties of the calculation, totals always work. There is no such thing as having defined an incorrect total, although the results you see onscreen may not be that obvious at first, as we shall show you in a moment.

Assuming you have created a valid total, Discoverer inserts it into the box for totals and ticks the check box automatically. Totals are added into the box in the order you create them.

Also at this point, you will notice that the Edit and Delete buttons are activated and Discoverer has inserted the formula into the Description box. If you have made an error in your formula, use the Edit button to reopen the Total dialog box and edit it. If you decide you no longer need this total, click Delete and it will be removed.

When you have completed adding totals to your query, you can either click Finish, which causes Discoverer to run the query, or you can move to step 9 of the Workbook Wizard by clicking Next.

Workbook Wizard Step 9—Defining Parameters

Figure 5-16 shows the Workbook Wizard step 9. This step in the Workbook Wizard has a dialog box containing the following two boxes and five buttons:

- **Available Parameters box** This box will be empty until you add a parameter. As you add parameters to your query, Discoverer will display them here in the order in which you create them.
- **Description box** A box showing the description of the parameter highlighted in the Available Parameters box.
- **New button** Click this to add a new parameter.
- **Edit button** When active, click this to edit an existing parameter.
- **Delete button** Click this to delete a parameter. As with conditions, again, be careful because it does just what it says and without prompting!
- **Move Up button** If you have multiple parameters, click this to promote the highlighted parameter. The order controls the sequence in which the parameters are prompted when the query is run.
- **Move Down button** If you have multiple parameters, click this to demote the highlighted parameter.

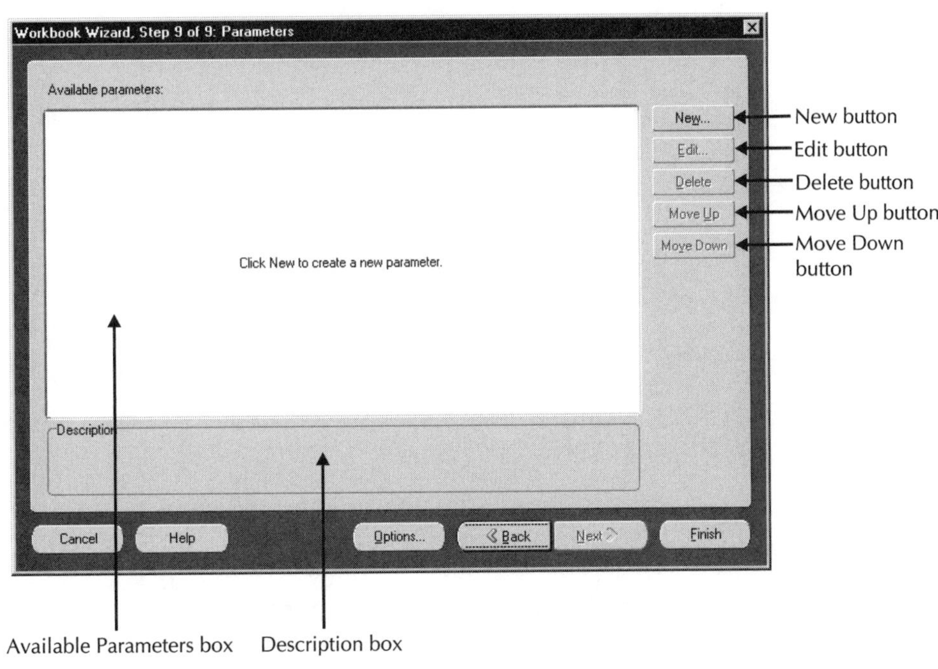

FIGURE 5-16. *Workbook Wizard step 9*

Parameters—What Are They?

Parameters offer choices each time the query runs. They are placeholders that give you an opportunity to add specific values to a condition. Whenever you create a parameter where no condition currently exists, Discoverer will create a condition and will link the parameter to the condition. Parameters are unlike regular conditions in that they allow you to use different criteria each time the query is run. For example, say you have created a query that shows total sales for the past seven years with a condition Year>=1993. Every time you run this query, you see all of the sales from 1993 until today. If you want to run the query for just the last five years, you would need to edit the condition and save the query. If you add a parameter to the condition, Year>=[Year Entered], you will be prompted before the query runs to add the value for the earliest year you want to see. This avoids the need to edit and resave the query.

Figure 5-17 shows the prompt you will see before the query runs.

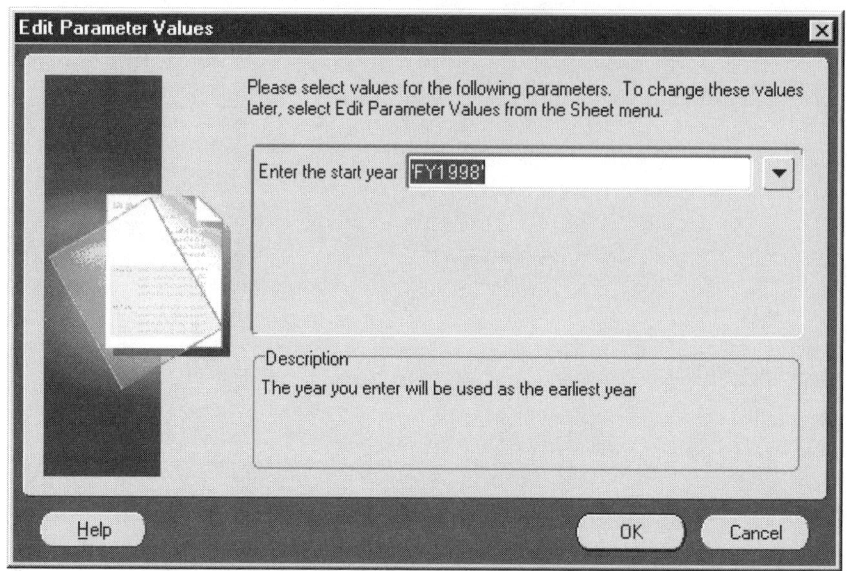

FIGURE 5-17. *Workbook Wizard step 9—Edit Parameter Values dialog box*

As you can see, Discoverer displays a dialog box allowing you to enter the exact filter you want to apply to your query based upon a certain condition. This capability allows the same query to be used by many people with different reporting needs.

Differences Between Conditions and Parameters

One of the things that new Discoverer users find difficult to understand is the difference between a condition and a parameter, and when to apply them. Both are filters, and both are used to constrain your query.

Conditions are fixed filters so you see exactly the same results every time you run the query. The only way to change the output is to edit the query and change the condition. However, some users don't have the ability to edit queries because a constraint has been applied to their profiles by the Discoverer administrator. This constraint is primarily used for new Discoverer end users who haven't yet taken training and learned how to edit correctly. Another reason all end users don't have editing rights is system integrity. You would not want to have a query you spent many hours creating edited by a novice end user, and find that it no longer works.

Parameters are variable filters, so you don't see exactly the same results every time you run the query. They are the solution to the above problem. A well-written parameterized query can satisfy dozens of different user requests without the need to edit the query or jeopardize its integrity. This is an excellent reason for having superusers. It allows queries to be built by them on behalf of your department, end users can then be granted access rights to run the query. They would simply fill in the parameter(s) that fits their needs without having to rebuild or create a new query. In other words, no need to "reinvent the wheel."

Another difference between conditions and parameters is that parameters help you to open a workbook quickly to see only the data you need. Your day-to-day mission-critical queries need to be parameterized, allowing them to be used by many people time and time again. Conditions, being designed more for analysis, are aimed at helping you find very specific data. For example, suppose you are puzzled because the sales from Europe for a particular product are lower than expected. You could not have anticipated this, and therefore you will not have a prewritten query. You will need to create an ad hoc query using conditions to isolate by both Europe and the product in question. This query will probably be used only once and will never need to be parameterized. Parameters and conditions can be mixed for creating more sophisticated filtering procedures.

The rule of thumb on parameters and conditions is that parameters should always be utilized in queries that are used more than once and by multiple users, whereas conditions should be created in queries that are more for analysis.

Creating Your First Parameter

When creating a new parameter, you should use the following workflow:

1. Click New.
2. Give a name for your parameter. This is only an internal name used by the system; however, you should still give it a short, meaningful name. If you leave this blank, Discoverer will insert a name for you.
3. Click on the Item drop-down box to see the list of available items, and select the data item you want to apply the parameter on from the list. If you have only one item that can be used, Discoverer inserts that item by default.
4. Enter the text you want to prompt the user with. For example, **Enter the year**. Leaving this blank causes Discoverer to generate a prompt for you.
5. Enter a description of the parameter that is easy to understand. Discoverer will display this to the user as context-sensitive help. Unlike the previous steps, if you leave this blank, Discoverer will not create a description for you. The user will therefore get no context-sensitive help.

6. Enter a default value for the parameter or choose from the drop-down list of values. Discoverer does not require a default to be entered.
7. Choose whether to allow users to select multiple values. For example, if you check this box and the prompt was for a product, the user would be given a list of all products and allowed to check the ones they want. We think this is a really clever feature, as you will see later. Leaving this box unchecked allows users to only enter single values when prompted.
8. Choose whether to create a condition based on this parameter. Parameters only get used in a worksheet when they are associated with a condition. Leaving this box unchecked will create a parameter but not link it to a condition. Having ticked the box to create a condition, you can now choose an operator from the drop-down list. By default, Discoverer inserts the operator =.
9. Click OK to finish.

When you first enter step 9 of the wizard, the main box in the center of the screen will be empty (see Figure 5-16). You need to think about what item or items you want to use in your parameters. Unlike calculations, there are no administrator-created parameters for you to choose from.

It does not make any difference to Discoverer what order you create your parameters. In fact, it makes no difference in what order they are run. However, you will probably want to present them to the user in a logical sequence. This sequence could simply be alphabetical, or you may want to offer the parameters in their sort order. Whatever method you choose, you should always do it the same way—thus creating query standardization.

If your company already has reporting standards, you should follow them. For example; if your company always prompts for a date before a customer, so should you. Similarly, if your company has standards for naming prompts, you should use these—thus making your queries look professional. The last thing you want to do is create a wonderful query that does not adhere to your company standards.

When you have decided that you need a parameter, click the New button. This opens the New Parameter dialog box that consists of the following sections:

- **Name** The name given here will be used internally by Discoverer when referencing the parameter.
- **Item box** This is a drop-down list of the items that you can use to base parameters on.
- **Prompt box** Enter a meaningful prompt for the end user.

- **Description box** Enter a meaningful description for the parameter. Discoverer displays this as help to the end user.
- **Default Value box** Enter a default value for the parameter. If a list of values exists, you may select an item from the drop-down list.
- **Let Users Select Multiple Values box** Check this box if you want your users to be able to select multiple values for the parameter.
- **Create Condition box** Check this box if you want Discoverer to automatically create a condition using this parameter.
- **Use Operator box** This is a drop-down list of all of the operators that are available to you.

Figure 5-18 shows the New Parameter dialog box.

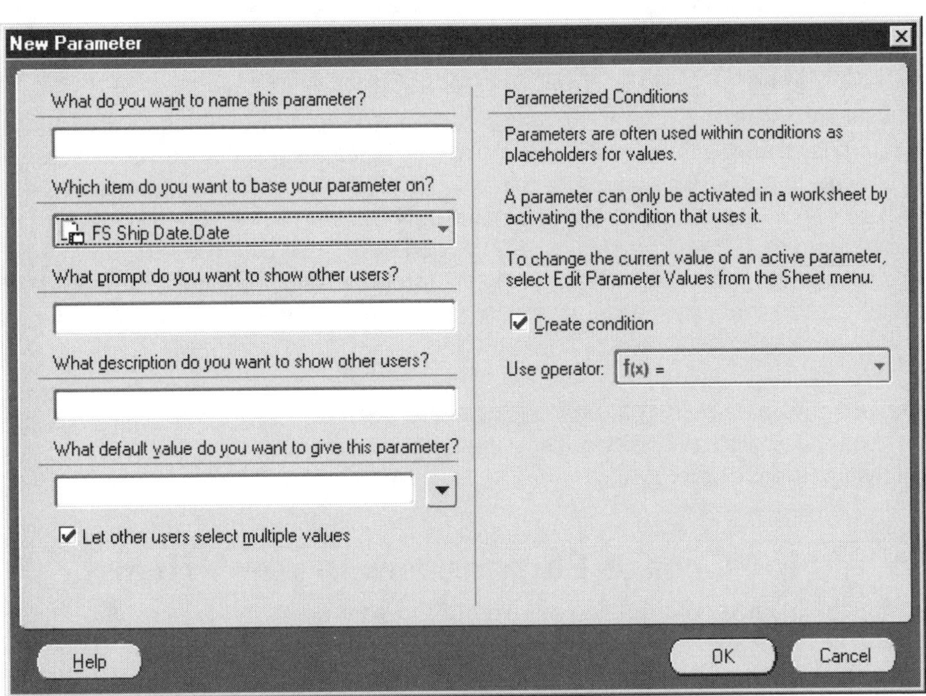

FIGURE 5-18. *3i New Parameter dialog box*

When you have created a parameter, click OK. Unlike calculations, where Discoverer has to test the mathematical properties of the calculation, parameters always work. There is no such thing as having defined an incorrect parameter, although the results you see onscreen may not be that obvious at first, as we shall show you in a moment.

Assuming you have created a valid parameter, Discoverer inserts it into the box for parameters. If you checked the box to create a condition, Discoverer will insert a check mark alongside the parameter. Parameters are added into the box in the order you create them.

Also at this point, you will notice that the Edit and Delete buttons are activated and Discoverer has inserted the description you created into the Description box. If you have made an error, use the Edit button to reopen the Parameter dialog box and edit it. At this stage, you will no longer be allowed to change the operator being used for the condition. If you need to change this, you will have to edit the condition itself. If you did not create a condition, editing the parameter will not allow you to do this either. The only way to do this now is to create a new condition by going back to step 4 of the Workbook Wizard. If you decide you no longer need this parameter, click Delete and it will be removed.

Rearranging the Parameter Order

Whenever you have two or more active parameters, you should look carefully at the list and determine if the parameter sequence is logical. If you decide you have a parameter in the wrong place, you can use the Move Up and Move Down buttons to promote or demote items. These buttons only become active when you have created two or more parameters linked to conditions. You can also use your mouse to click and drag the items to change their position within the sequence. The sequence determines the order in which parameters are offered to the end user.

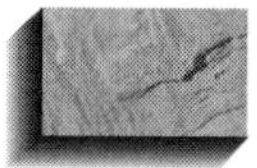

NOTE
An active parameter is a parameter that has been associated with a condition. Only these parameters will be used as prompts.

Why Not Create Parameters in the Wizard?

Although parameters do not add an overhead to your query in the same way that calculations, sorting, totaling, and percentages do, when working with new queries we still recommend that you do not create them inside the Workbook Wizard. We do strongly recommend that you create conditions, and these should suffice for getting the query up and running.

When you have a working copy of your query, you can concentrate on the conditions and look to see which ones can be parameterized. You are also in a better position to ascertain whether you need any new conditions and have the choice whether to do this as a parameter or not. Finally, taking the time in the Workbook Wizard to create parameters, when your query may not even work, can be very frustrating and time-consuming.

When you have completed adding parameters to your query, you have finished with the Workbook Wizard. You can either click Finish, which causes Discoverer to run the query, or you can click Back to go back to validate previous steps.

Editing the Sheet After the Query Has Run

Because we recommend that you only use the Workbook Wizard for the first four steps of a query, we need to show you how to reopen the Workbook Wizard after you have a working query.

From the menu, select Sheet…Edit Sheet or click the Edit Sheet icon on the toolbar. This opens a multitabbed form with one step of the Workbook Wizard per tab.

Figure 5-19 shows the Edit Sheet form used in Discoverer 3.1, and Figure 5-20 shows the Edit Worksheet form used in Discoverer 3*i*.

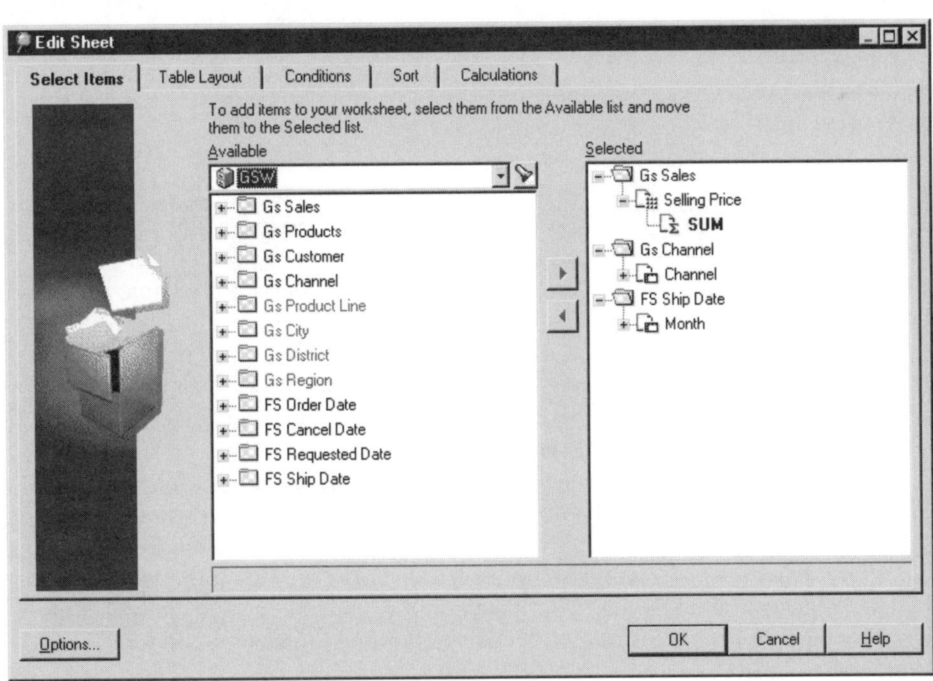

FIGURE 5-19. *3.1 Edit Sheet window*

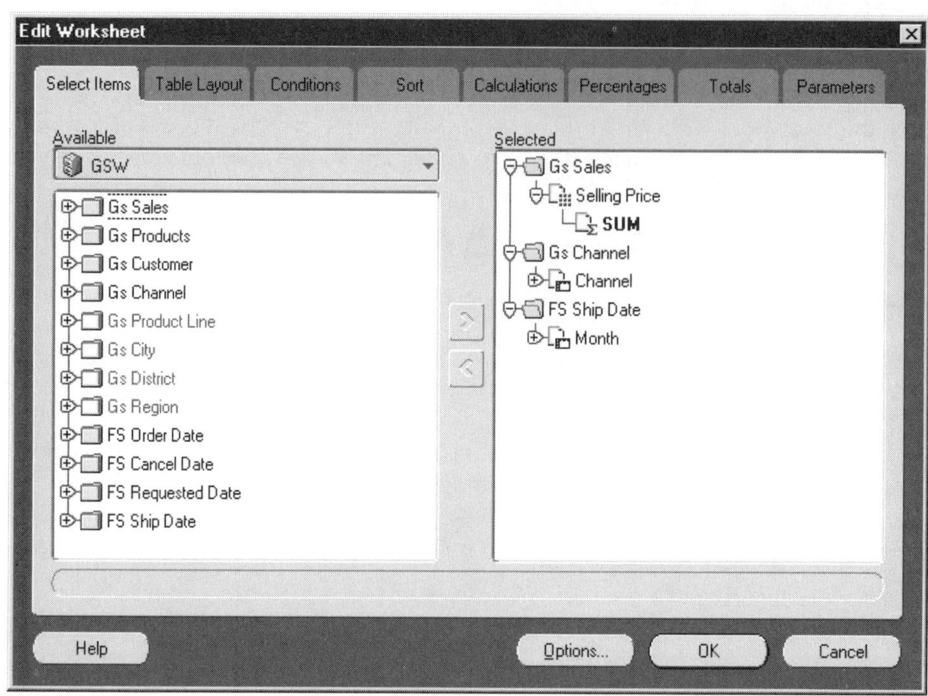

FIGURE 5-20. *3*i *Edit Worksheet window*

Use the tabs to select the step you want to apply to the query. This method allows you to add criteria to your query step by step. You can now build your query, being sure that it is showing exactly what you want before you move on and add another criteria.

The forms function in the exact manner of the Workbook Wizard sheet, but you do not have the Back and Next buttons. You can click randomly from dialog to dialog, adding the criteria you want to your query. When you are done adding criteria, click the OK button and your query will run with the changes you have made.

In addition to the Edit Sheet dialog box, each of the forms from the Workbook Wizard can be accessed directly from the menu bar. In both versions of Discoverer, the Tools menu option gives you a drop-down list of available forms. In addition, 3.1 offers an analysis bar, while 3*i* has an analysis area on the toolbar containing buttons to access the tools. For more detail on the analysis bar and analysis area, see Chapter 9. For more instruction on using all of the tools offered in the Workbook Wizard, see Chapters 10, 11, and 12.

Summary

In this chapter, you have learned the optional steps of the Workbook Wizard as well as how to reopen the Workbook Wizard with the Edit Sheet form. We have given the definitions of sorts, calculations, percentages, totals, and parameters, and how they can be used in a query. You have also been shown the steps used to add these functions to a query.

In each section we have explained why it is recommended to complete the first four essential steps and run your query prior to adding sorts, calculations, percentages, totals, and parameters.

These topics and those in Chapter 4 have given definitions of the Workbook Wizard steps and an overview of each function. This will get you started creating simple queries. More in-depth examples will be given and skills taught in Chapters 11 and 12.

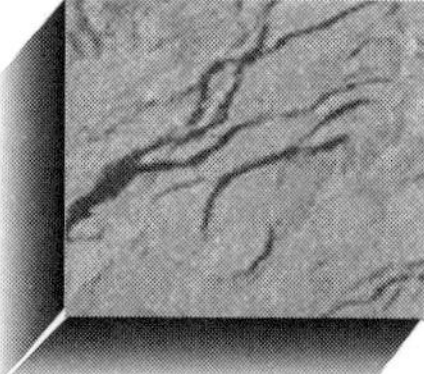

PART II

Editing the Query

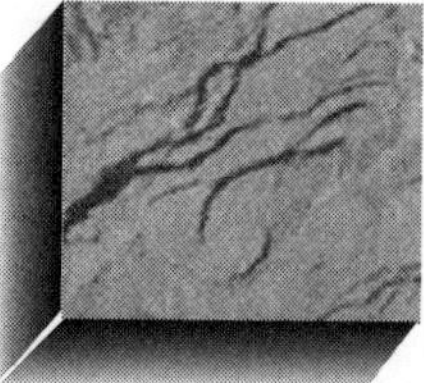

CHAPTER 6

Formatting the Output

As we have already explained, Discoverer can be used to produce both ad hoc queries, which answer a specific one-off question, and queries that will be used by multiple users. Both can remain as queries, but as soon as you decide that the output needs to be viewed by somebody else, it becomes a report. This is especially true if you are planning on giving the results to senior management.

When you have a fully working query of this type, it needs to be formatted. Put in its simplest form, formatting is the shape, size, typeface, and general appearance of a document. Formatting is an important step in turning your query into an easy to read, attractive, and well-organized report. This is true whether or not you intend the output to be viewed onscreen, printed, or exported. The latter two will be dealt with in Chapter 8.

In this chapter, you will learn how to rename and reposition column headings in order to fit your needs. You will be shown how to rearrange the order and position of the output.

Another way to use formatting to improve a query is to change fonts and font sizes, font and background colors, and text justification. This chapter will show you in detail how to perform these functions. You will also be taught how to format numbers as currency, with commas, and with the correct number of decimal places.

You will be taught to add titles to your query, and how to format them with font, sizes, and colors, as well as how to add bitmaps to the title. Finally, you will be shown how to add graphics to the background of a query to add interest and flair.

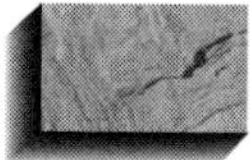

3*i* NOTE

*Discoverer 3*i *currently has no formatting capabilities, and most of what we will cover in this chapter applies only to 3.1. However, any report formatted in 3.1 will retain its formatting in 3*i*, even though you will not be able to change it. You will have to go back to your 3.1 query and change it there.*

*If you have created a query in 3*i *that needs formatting, and you have 3.1 available to you, you should save the query to the database, reopen it in 3.1, and make your formatting changes there. We know this sounds complicated, but currently it is your only option. Oracle plans to include formatting in the next release of the Web product.*

Giving Your Headings Meaningful Names

As was discussed in a previous chapter, your Discoverer administrator can give items in business areas meaningful names. However, one business area could be used by a variety of departments, and what is meaningful to one department might not be to you.

Throughout the book, whenever you have had an opportunity to create new items, such as calculations, percentages, parameters, and totals, we have recommended giving these meaningful names as well. Even though in many cases Discoverer will insert a name for you, this is not a good habit to get into. What is meaningful and obvious to Discoverer, and even to you at the time, may not be so obvious to you later. Therefore, as soon as you have a working query, the first thing you should do is look at the column names and decide if they are meaningful. If they are not, you need to change them.

How to Rename Columns

To change the name of a column, use the following workflow.

1. Place your cursor on the column heading.
2. Right-click. This displays the following pop-up list of options.

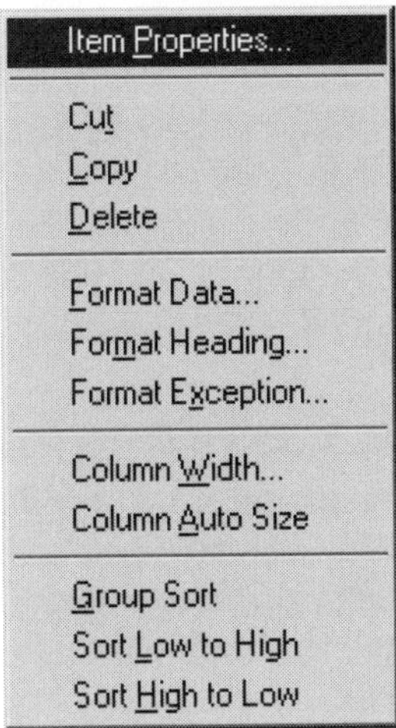

3. Select Item Properties. This displays the following Item Properties dialog box.

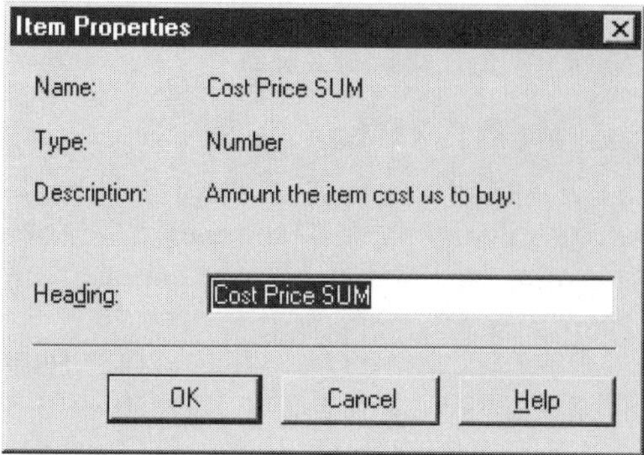

4. Change the heading name in the Item Properties dialog box.
5. Click OK or press ENTER to finish.

Discoverer adds the word SUM, AVG etc, to each numeric heading. While this may be okay for an ad hoc query, you should change this on your report by removing it from each heading. You must change each heading individually.

As you change column names, Discoverer resizes the width of the column to match the name, even if that means you won't be able to see all of your data. If Discoverer has resized the column to be too small, see the section on resizing later in this chapter to correct it.

Rearranging the Order of the Output

After you have renamed your columns, the next step is to make sure that the columns are really in the order you want them. When you were in the Workbook Wizard, you arranged the order of the columns. After running the query, you may find that the order just does not look right, and you can see how rearranging them will make your report easier to read.

How to Rearrange Columns

There are two ways to rearrange columns. You can rearrange them in the worksheet or in the Edit Sheet dialog box. We will give you both methods, but always suggest you use the simplest. For rearranging single columns, we recommended using the worksheet. When rearranging multiple columns, you can use either method. If you are certain of the order you desire, do it in the worksheet. If you are not sure how you want the columns arranged, use the Edit Sheet dialog box. This option allows you to "try out" an arrangement; however, you can click Cancel if you want the order returned to its original configuration.

Moving a Single Column

To move a single column, use the following workflow:

1. Click and hold on the column heading you want to move.
2. Drag the column heading to the desired location, then release the mouse button.

Figure 6-1 shows a column being moved to the left. Notice how the mouse pointer has changed to a double-headed arrow.

Moving Multiple Columns

To move multiple columns, or to "try out" a configuration, use the following workflow:

1. From the menu bar, select Sheet | Edit Sheet, or from the toolbar click the Edit Sheet icon—either of these methods displays the Edit Sheet dialog box (Figures 5-20 and 5-21 in the previous chapter). In 3*i*, a new button has been added to take you to the Layout tab directly.
2. Click the Table Layout tab. Drag and drop the columns into their desired location, as seen in the illustration below.

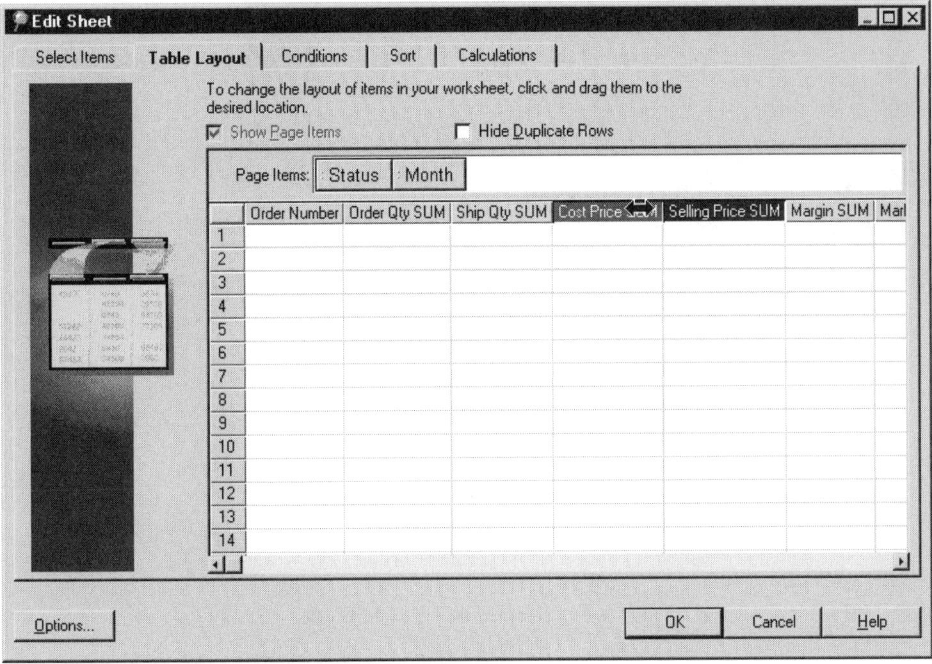

3. Click OK or press ENTER to finish.

Oracle Discoverer - [Profit Test]

File Edit View Sheet Format Tools Graph Window Help

Double-click here to edit this title.

Page Items: Status: SHIPPED ▾ Month: FEB-00 ▾

	Order Number	Order Qty	Ship Qty	Cost Price	Selling Price	Marg	Mark Up
1	2692	1200	1200	7,452.00	18,300.00	59.27	145.57
2	2691	2400	2400	19,992.00	42,384.00	52.83	112.00
3	2689	504	504	4,198.32	8,900.64	52.83	112.00
4	2688	1200	1200	19,128.00	41,580.00	53.99	117.37
5	2687	48	48	765.12	1,663.20	53.99	117.37
6	2682	2400	2400	29,808.00	56,280.00	47.03	88.80
7	2681	4800	4800	59,616.00	112,560.00	47.03	88.80
8	2680	96	96	1,192.32	2,251.20	47.03	88.80
9	2679	4800	4800	59,616.00	112,560.00	47.03	88.80
10	2678	1200	1200	14,904.00	28,140.00	47.03	88.80
11	2675	1200	1200	19,128.00	41,580.00	53.99	117.37
12	2674	1200	1200	19,128.00	41,580.00	53.99	117.37
13	2672	1200	1200	12,744.00	26,616.00	52.11	108.85
14	2671	6000	6000	63,720.00	133,080.00	52.11	108.85
15	2670	2400	2400	23,712.00	51,000.00	53.50	115.08
16	2669	96	96	575.04	1,224.00	53.01	112.85
17	2668	72	72	519.84	972.00	46.51	86.98
18	2667	1200	1200	13,776.00	32,340.00	57.40	134.75
19	2666	2400	2400	27,552.00	64,680.00	57.40	134.75
20	2664	50	50	310.50	762.50	59.27	145.57
21	2663	50	50	416.50	883.00	52.83	112.00

Sheet 1

FIGURE 6-1. *Rearranging columns directly in the worksheet*

NOTE
If you have started to reorder the columns and wish to abort the changes you have made, do not click OK or press ENTER. *Clicking Cancel causes Discoverer to abandon all column moves and reinstate the ordering as it was before you started.*

We don't recommend using this method for moving a single column because it involves unnecessary keystrokes.

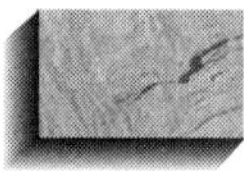

3*i* NOTE
*The only way to change the ordering of the columns in Discoverer 3*i *is to use the Table Layout tab from the Edit Sheet dialog box.*

Formatting Data

After you have changed your column names, you should look at the data items in each column and decide whether they need formatting. Discoverer recognizes three different types of data—text, dates, and numbers—and each can be formatted in a variety of ways.

Formatting Bar

Discoverer provides a toolbar called the formatting bar. This bar contains buttons that perform many of the standard formatting functions. We will explain what each button does later in the appropriate section of this chapter.

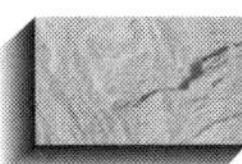

NOTE

If you cannot see the formatting bar, click View | Formatting Bar to make it appear.

3*i* NOTE

*There is no formatting bar in 3*i. *However, your Discoverer administrator can create many default formats for you. You should speak with him or her to find out what the defaults are.*

Format Data Dialog Box

Discoverer provides a Format Data dialog box that has four tabs: one each for formatting fonts, setting the alignment, and changing the background color, and a fourth tab that changes depending on the type of data in the column. For example, a column for text will have a tab named Text, while a column for numbers will have a tab named Number, and so on.

Many of the functions that are available within the Format Data dialog box are also available on the formatting bar. There are two ways to access the Format Data dialog box:

- From a pop up list
- From the menu bar

From a Pop-Up List

To access the Format Data dialog box from a pop-up list, use the following workflow:

1. Right-click anywhere in the column you want to format. This displays the following pop-up list of options.

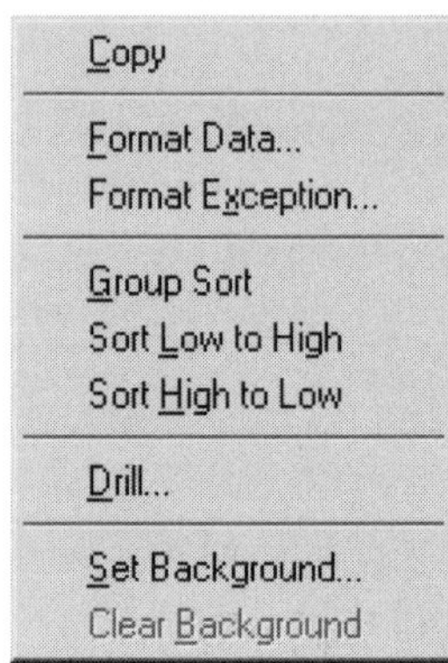

2. Select Format Data. This displays the dialog box.

NOTE
To apply the same format to multiple columns, hold down the CTRL *key and select the columns you require. If you select columns of different types, only the Font, Alignment, and Background Color tabs will be available. Selecting multiple columns of the same data type with the same formatting characteristics causes all tabs to be active.*

3*i* NOTE
*Right mouse button support is not available in Discoverer 3*i.

From the Menu Bar

To access the Format Data dialog box from the menu bar, use the following workflow:

1. Click anywhere in the column you want to format.
2. From the menu bar, select Format | Data, as shown in the following illustration.

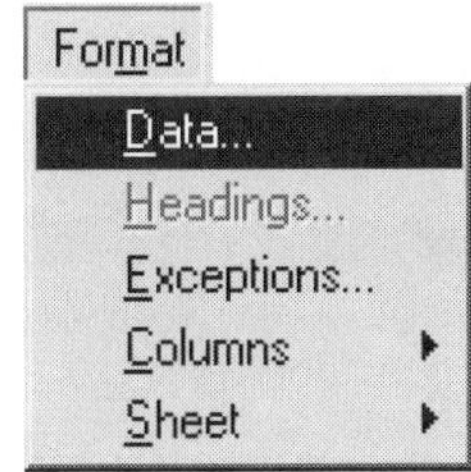

3. Discoverer opens the following Format Data dialog box.

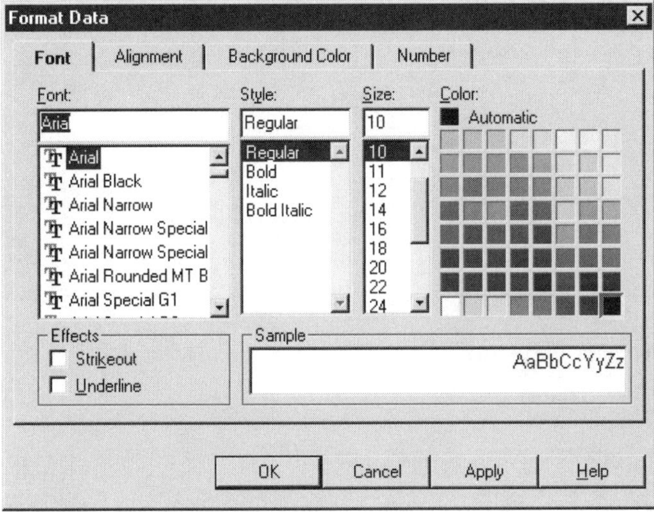

As you can see in the illustration above, there are four tabs to this dialog box. These are:

- **Font** Select this tab to change the font, style, size, color, and effect.
- **Alignment** Select this tab to change the horizontal and vertical alignment.
- **Background Color** Select this tab to change the background color of your data.
- **Date, Text, or Number** Select this tab to set specific formatting requirements for the data type of the column. The heading will change based on the data type.

Font Tab

Clicking on the Font tab displays the Font dialog box, as shown here:

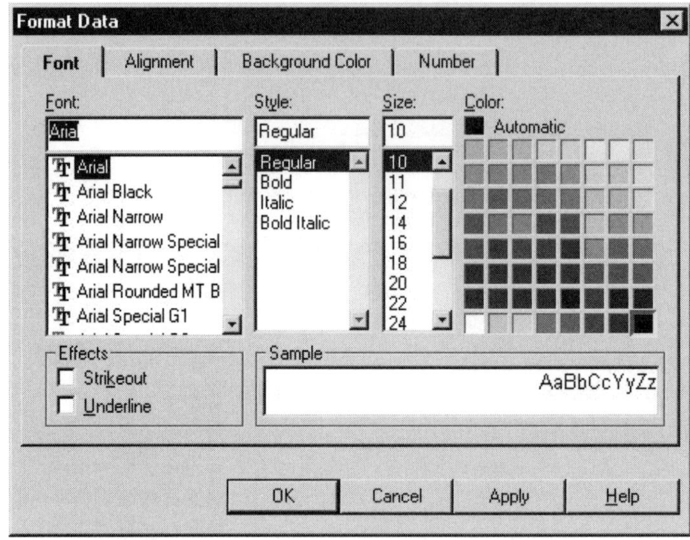

- **Font** Select the font you require from the list provided.
- **Style** Select Regular, Bold, Italic, or Bold Italic.
- **Size** Select the font size you require.
- **Color** Select the foreground color for the data.
- **Effects** Select Strikeout or Underline.
- **Sample** This shows you how your selections will look. As you move from tab to tab, this will show whatever effect you have applied so far.

If you have no more formatting to do, click OK. This will apply your changes to the data and close the dialog box. If you have more formatting to do, click on one of the other tab headings and proceed.

Apart from the strikeout effect, all of the above font characteristics can also be applied directly from the formatting bar.

The formatting bar has several buttons that provide shortcuts to the most popular formatting functions, as shown here:

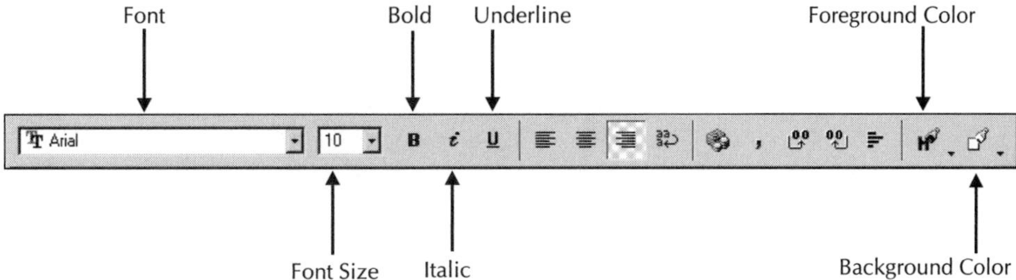

- **Font** Select the font you require from the list provided.
- **Font Size** Select the font size you require.
- **Bold** Click this button to display your data in bold.
- **Italic** Click this button to display your data in italics.
- **Underline** Click this button to display your data underlined.
- **Foreground Color** Click this button to change the foreground color.
- **Background Color** Click this button to change the background color.

3*i* NOTE

*There are no Discoverer administrator settings that can be applied to help you set fonts. However, you can create your own general default fonts that Discoverer will apply to all queries created in 3*i*. See the section on applying user default formats later in this chapter.*

Alignment Tab

Clicking on the Alignment tab displays the following Alignment dialog box:

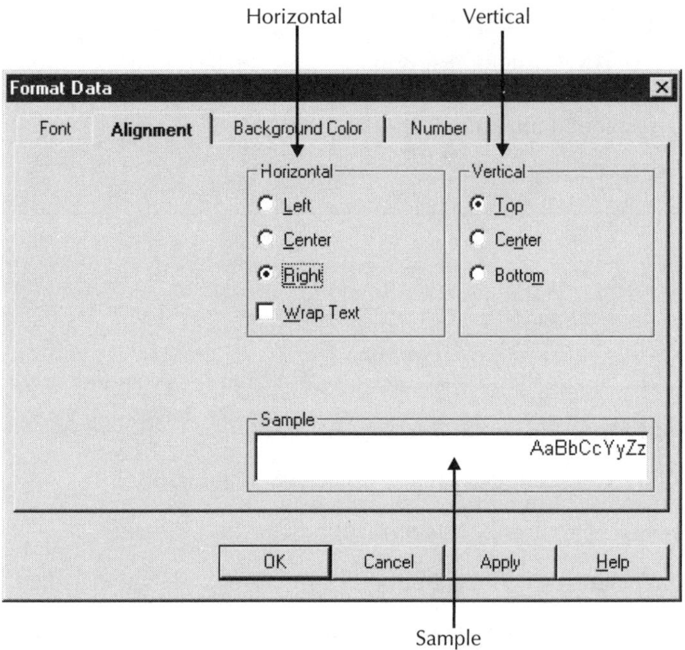

- **Horizontal** Select Left, Center, or Right alignment, and also choose whether to allow your data to wrap within the column.
- **Vertical** Select whether to display the data in the Top, Center, or Bottom of the cell.
- **Sample** This shows you how your selections will look.

Only the following horizontal alignment characteristics can be applied directly from the formatting bar:

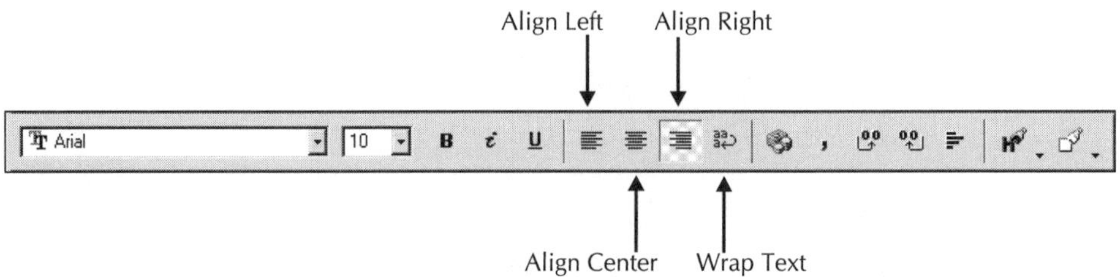

- **Align Left** Click this button to align the data to the left.
- **Align Center** Click this button to align the data to the center.
- **Align Right** Click this button to align the data to the right.
- **Wrap Text** Click this button to wrap the text in the column. You cannot wrap text in the headings and text will only wrap when there is a space in the data.

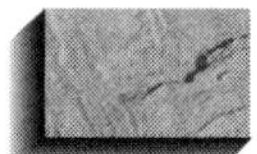

3*i* NOTE

*Your Discoverer administrator can set default horizontal alignment characteristics and can set a default for word wrapping. You can also create your own general default vertical alignments that Discoverer will apply to all queries created in 3*i*. See the section on applying user default formats later in this chapter.*

Background Color Tab

Clicking on the Background tab displays the following Background Color dialog box.

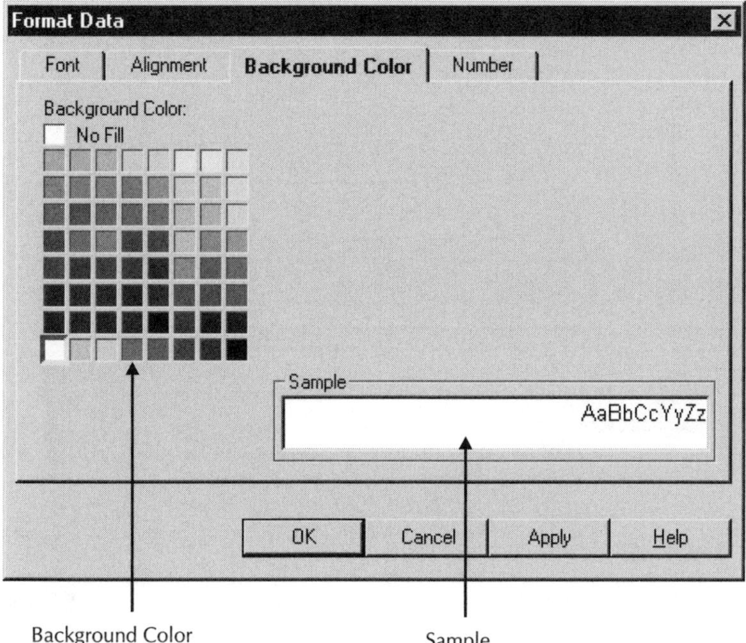

- **Background Color** Select the color you wish for the background. Check No Fill to display no background color.
- **Sample** This shows you how your selections will look.

3*i* NOTE

*There are no Discoverer administrator settings that can be applied to help you set background colors. However, you can create your own general default colors that Discoverer will apply to all queries created in 3*i*. See the section on applying user default formats later in this chapter.*

Date Tab

We often use dates in reports, and there are a multitude of ways to format them. Clicking the Date tab displays the following Format Date dialog box.

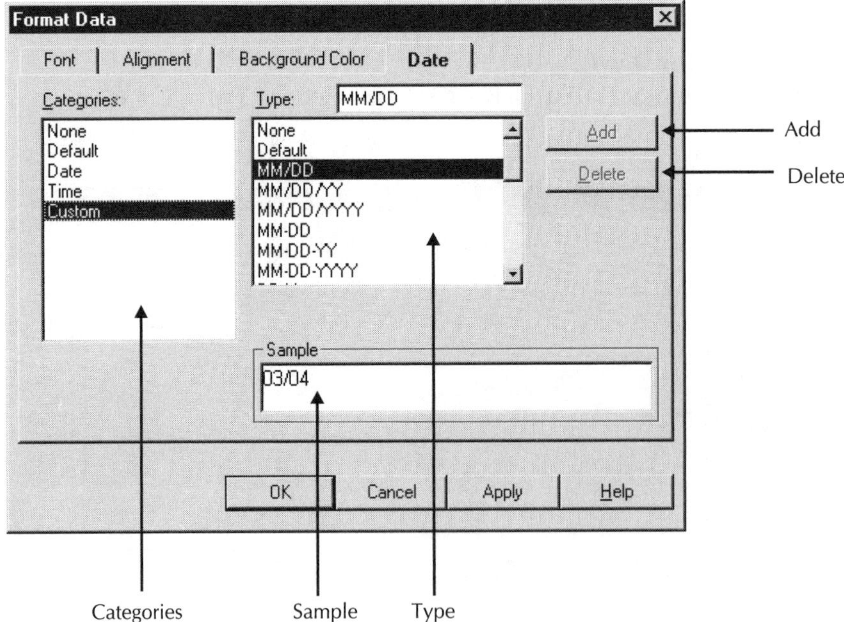

The Date tab above gives you five categories to choose from.

- **Categories** Select from None, Default, Date, Time, and Custom.
- **Type** This selection list appears if you have selected a category other than None and Default. It is a list of all types available. If you are working with the category Custom, an edit box will open allowing you to create custom types.

- **Add** This button is displayed when you select the category Custom. If you have created a custom type, click this button to add it to the list.
- **Delete** This button will remove a custom type.
- **Sample** This shows you how your selection or custom type will look.

None This displays the date in the format exactly as it is stored in the database. If you are unsure what the format is for your database, click Custom. The top item on the custom list is the date format used on your database.

Default This is the default selection and displays dates using the format mask set up by your Discoverer administrator. The most common format mask in use within Oracle is DD-MON-YYYY, which would display March 4, 1996 date as 03-MAR-1996. If you are unsure what the format is that has been set by your Discoverer administrator, click Custom. The second item on the custom list is the date format specified by your Discoverer administrator.

Date/Time/Custom The Date selection gives you a list of the most common date formats available. Discoverer displays the list using the actual format as it would appear in your query.

The Time selection gives you a list of the most common time formats available. Discoverer displays the list using the actual format as it would appear in your query.

The Custom selection gives you an opportunity to create a customized date and/or time. Discoverer gives you a list of the most common types, this time using standard masks. For example, instead of showing a format of 03-Mar-1996, the mask would display as DD-Mon-YYYY.

When you view the custom list, the top two items on the list are given the name None and Default, indicating that these are the default date formats for your database as set by your Discoverer administrator, respectively.

The following table displays the relationship between the formatted dates and times and their format masks.

Date	Time	Custom Mask
03/04		MM/DD
03/04/96		MM/DD/YY
03/04/1996		MM/DD/YYYY
03-04		MM-DD
03-04-96		MM-DD-YY
03-04-1996		MM-DD-YYYY

Date	Time	Custom Mask
04-Mar		DD-Mon
04-Mar-96		DD-Mon-YY
04-Mar-1996		DD-Mon-YYYY
04 March 1996		DD fmMonth YYYY
March 4, 1996		fmMonth DD, YYYY
Monday, March 04,1996		fmDay, fmMonth DD, YYYY
04-Mar-96 12:15 PM	04-Mar-96 12:15 PM	DD-Mon-YY HH:MI AM
04-Mar-96 12:15:30	04-Mar-96 12:15:30	DD-Mon-YY HH24:MI:SS
	12:15	HH:MM
	12:15 PM	HH:MM AM
	12:15:30	HH:MM:SS
	12:15:30 PM	HH:MM:SS AM
	12:15	HH24:MM
	12:15:30	HH24:MM:SS

In the list above, you see various format masks. By combining uppercase and lowercase characters, you can create additional masks.

For example, in the list above there is a mask for DD-Mon-YYYY that would display October 14, 1958 as 14-Oct-1958. If you wished to display this date as 14-OCT-1958, you would simply create a new type using the mask DD-MON-YYYY.

For a full list of all date and time format masks, please see Appendix A.

NOTE
If you are not sure about the relationship between dates, times, and their format masks, select a date or time from the date or time list. You can see its mask by clicking Custom. This can be very helpful when creating complex calculations that use date functions.

NOTE
There are no date formatting features available from the formatting bar.

Adding a New Date or Time Mask To add a new date or time format to the list available, you must follow this workflow:

1. Open or create a query containing a date.
2. Place your cursor in any column containing a date.
3. Right-click. This displays a pop-up list of options.
4. Select Format Data. This opens the Format Data dialog box.
5. Select the Date tab.
6. Select the Custom category.
7. In the box titled Type, enter the mask for the format you require. As you type, Discoverer will convert that mask into a date or time and display this in the Sample box. See Appendix A for a list of available masks.
8. When you have entered the new type, click Add. The new type will be added to the bottom of the list.
9. If you want the new format to be applied to the column, click OK or Apply. If you only want to create the new format but do not wish to use it, click Cancel.

3*i* NOTE
*As the current release of 3*i* has no means of formatting dates, your Discoverer administrator can create default date formats for you. You should speak with him or her to find out what the defaults are, or to ask him or her to create them if there are none.*

Number Tab

By default, Discoverer formats numbers with no decimal places, no comma separator, and with negative numbers displayed using a minus sign in front of the number—for example, -1234.

The Number tab is quite a busy little box and changes depending upon the category you choose. It has three areas that are common to all of the number categories: a list of categories, a check box for showing graphic bars, and a Sample window.

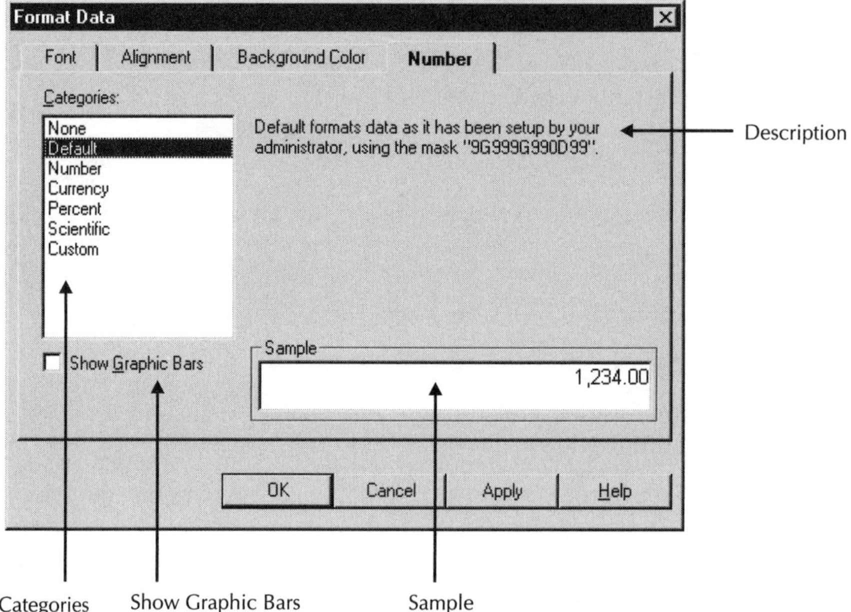

- **Categories** Always present. Select from None, Default, Number, Currency, Percent, Scientific, and Custom.
- **Show Graphic Bars** Always present. Check this to add a graphic bar indicating the size of your numbers in relation to each other.
- **Sample** Always present. This shows you how your selection or custom type will look.
- **Description** Only displayed for None and Default. This area displays a brief description of the current setting.

The categories Number, Percent, and Scientific, in addition to the areas we've just detailed, contain the three additional areas:

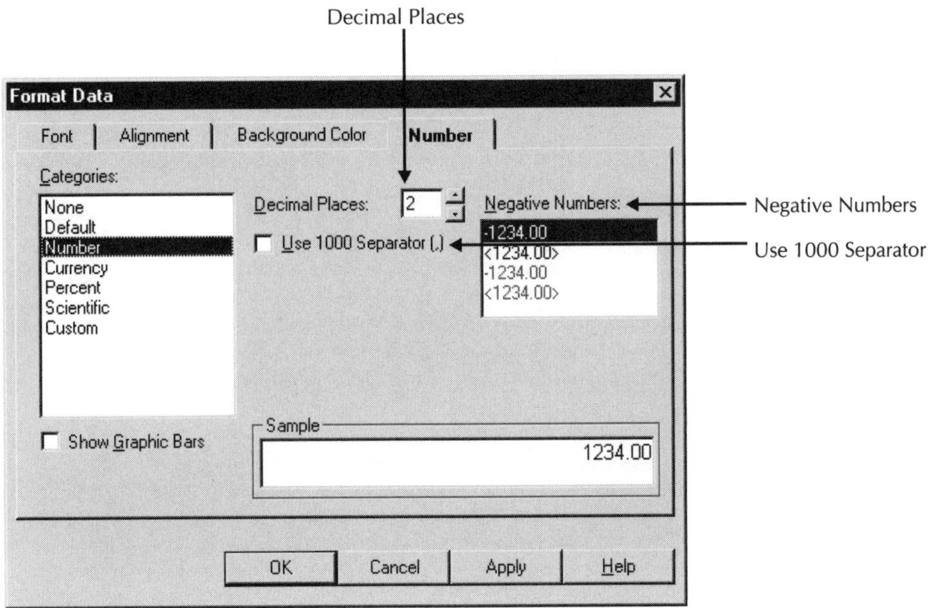

- **Decimal Places** Increase or decrease the number of decimal places to display.
- **Use 1000 Separator** Check this to display a comma separator in large numbers. Not available for percentages or scientific.
- **Negative Numbers** Choose from the list how you want Discoverer to display negative numbers. Not available for scientific numbers.

As shown next, the Currency category also has a check box for determining whether or not to use the dollar sign. Check this box to add a dollar sign before the number.

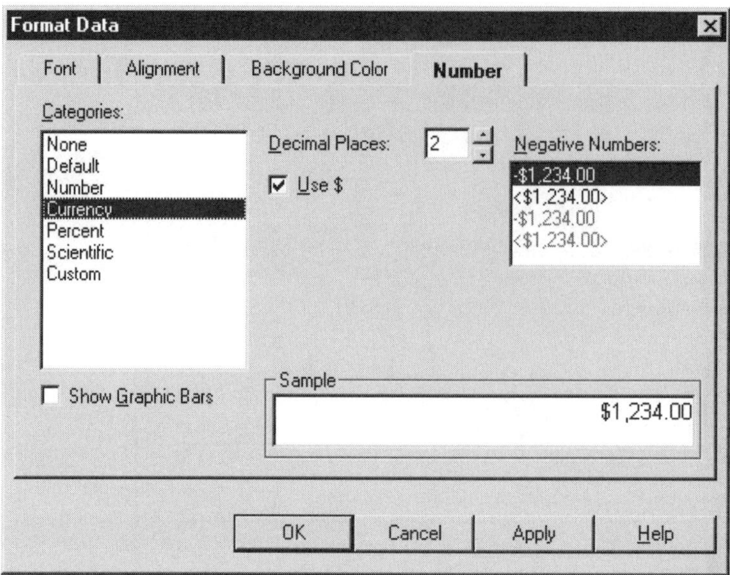

The final number category is for adding custom number formats, as shown here:

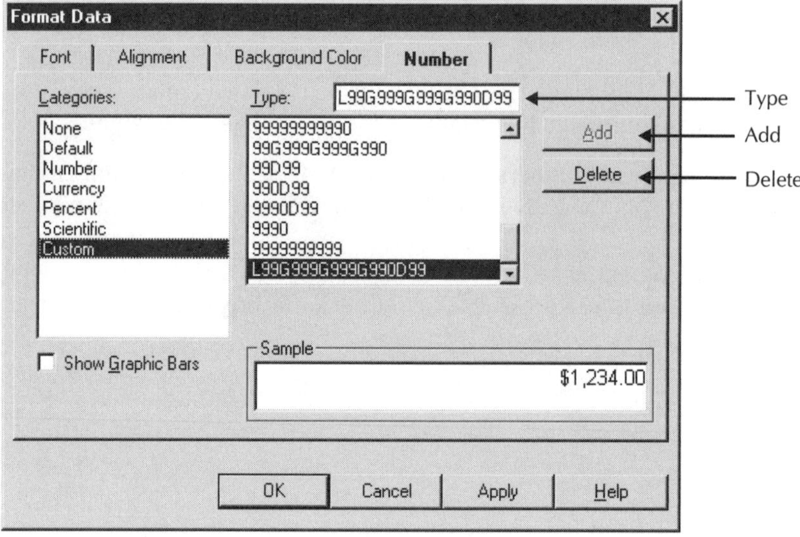

- **Type** This selection list appears if you have selected the category of Custom. It is a list of all types available. An edit box will allow you to create custom types.

- **Add** This button is displayed when you select the category Custom. If you have created a custom type, click this button to add it to the list.
- **Delete** This button will remove a custom type.

The following table displays the standard number formats and how they will appear onscreen.

Format Mask	Will display 1234 as
999999990	1234
999999990D99	1234.00
999990D99	1234.00
999G990	1,234
999G990PR	1,234
999G9990D99	1,234.00
9990V99	123400
9.99EEEE	1.23E+03
HH:MI:SS	20:34 (20 minutes 34 seconds)
0HH:MI:SS	00:20:34
9EEEE	1E+03
9D99EEEE	1.23E+03
99G999G990D99	1,234.00
99999999990	1234
99G999G999G990	1,234

For a full list of all number format masks, please see Appendix A.

The following illustration shows the numeric buttons of the formatting bar:

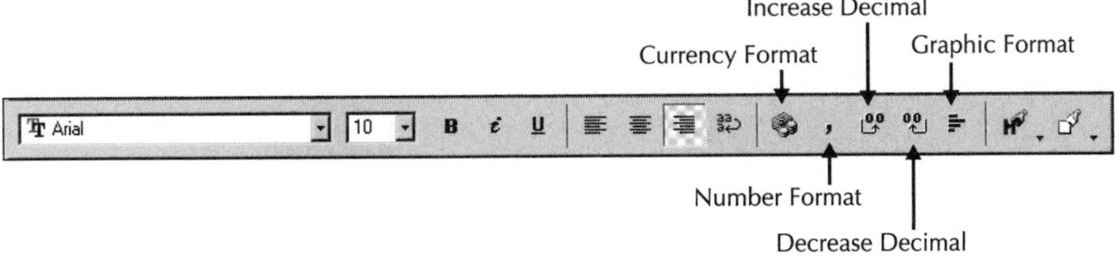

- **Currency Format** Click this to apply standard currency formatting that places a dollar sign, two decimal places, and comma separators.
- **Number Format** Click this to apply standard number formatting that is two decimal places and no comma separators.
- **Increase Decimal** Click this to add one decimal place to your number.
- **Decrease Decimal** Click this to remove one decimal place from your number.
- **Graphic Format** Click this to display a graphic bar.

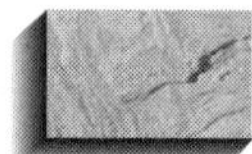

3*i* NOTE
Since the current release of 3i *has no formatting bar, your Discoverer administrator can create default number formats for you. You should speak with him or her to find out what the defaults are, or to ask him or her to create them if there are none.*

Adding a New Number Mask To add a new number format to the list available you must follow this workflow:

1. Open or create a query containing a number.
2. Place your cursor in any column containing a number.
3. Right-click. This displays a pop-up list of options.
4. Select Format Data. This opens the Format Data dialog box.
5. Select the Number tab.
6. Select the Custom category.
7. In the box titled Type, enter the mask for the format you require. See Appendix A for a list of available masks.
8. When you have entered the new type, click Add. The new type will be added to the bottom of the list and an example displayed in the Sample box.
9. If you want the new format to be applied to the column, click OK or Apply. If you only want to create the new format but do not wish to use it, click Cancel.

Text Tab

Clicking on the Text tab opens the Text dialog box, as shown here:

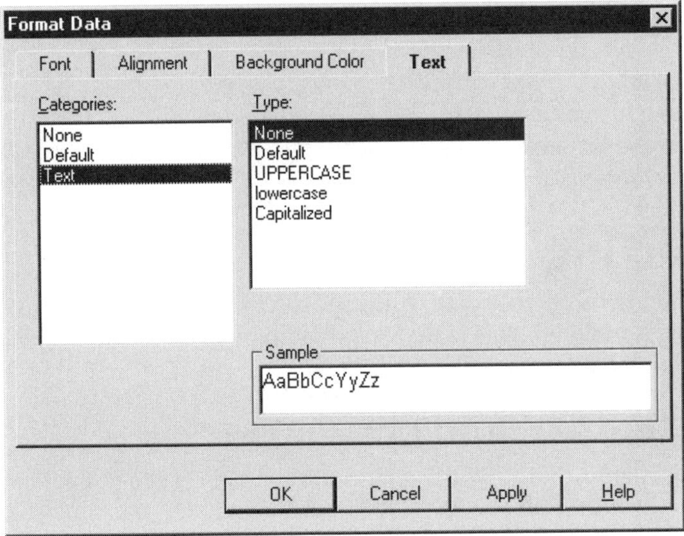

- **Categories** Select from None, Default, or Text.
- **Type** When you select the category Text, you can choose from None, Default, Uppercase, Lowercase, or Capitalized.
- **Sample** This shows you how your selection or custom type will look.

None of these features are available from the formatting bar.

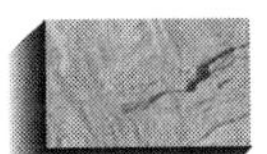

NOTE
Throughout the above section, whenever we have referred to a category of None, this means that the data will be displayed in the format as defined on the database. Whenever we refer to the Default category, the data will be displayed as formatted by the Discoverer administrator.

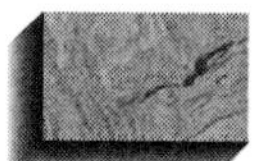

3*i* NOTE
The Discoverer administrator is capable of setting some default text formatting characteristics. He or she is able to format the text as being General (displays the text exactly as it appears on the database), Initcap (initial letter of each word capitalized), Lowercase, or Uppercase. The most normal default is General. He or she is also able to set a default setting for Word Wrap. This usually defaults to No.

Formatting Columns

After you have formatted your data, you should look at the columns and decide if any formatting is required. This includes formatting column headings, deleting columns and resizing columns.

Formatting Column Headings

Like formatting data, Discoverer provides a Format Heading dialog box. There are two ways to access the Format Heading dialog box:

- From a pop up list
- From the menu bar

From a Pop-Up List

To access the Format Heading dialog box from a pop-up list, use the following workflow:

1. Click the heading you want to format.
2. Right-click on the heading. This displays the following pop-up list of options:

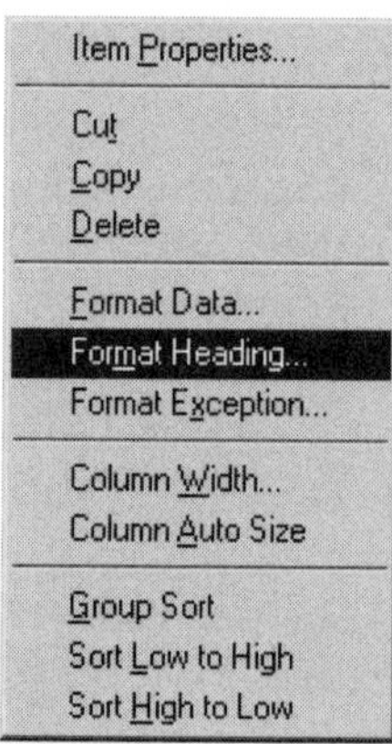

3. Select Format Heading. This displays the following dialog box.

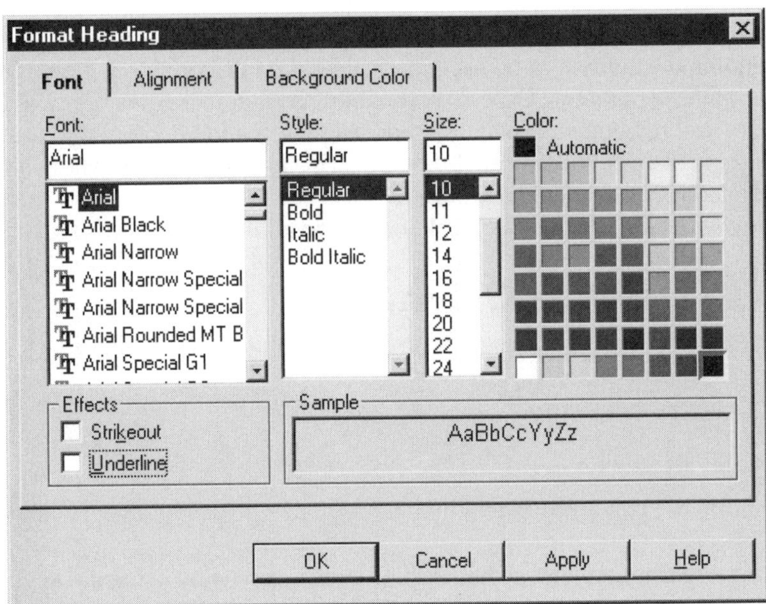

The above box has the same functionality as the Format Data dialog box that was explained in the section titled "Formatting Data." The only difference is that the Format Heading dialog box only has the first three tabs, for font, alignment, and background color.

NOTE
To apply the same format to multiple headings, hold down the CTRL *key and select the columns you require.*

From the Menu Bar

To access the Format Heading dialog box from the menu bar, use the following workflow:

1. Click on the heading you want to format.
2. From the menu bar, select Format | Headings. This displays the dialog box.

While you were rearranging and formatting the column headings, you may have spotted a column that is unnecessary. You may have included something that has no bearing on the final wanted result. For example, Global Widgets always ships what is ordered. Including Order Qty and Ship Qty in the same query would be redundant, and you could remove one of them.

Another reason for removing a column is when the sole purpose for including it was to enable the column to be used in a calculation or condition. Now is the time to get rid of these columns. Do not worry about your calculations or conditions, as Discoverer will remember which columns were used and will continue using them after you have deleted them from the output. This holds true even when the item being deleted was the only item being selected from a folder. We think this is a really clever feature. This will be explained in detail in Chapter 11.

How to Delete a Column

There are three ways to delete a column from the output of your query:

- From the keyboard
- From a pop up list
- From the Edit Sheet dialog box

Always use the simplest method, which in this case is by using the keyboard.

NOTE
Be careful when deleting columns using the first two ways because Discoverer will not prompt you or warn you if you are about to delete a column that is needed within the query.

From the Keyboard

To delete a column using the keyboard, use the following workflow:

1. Click on the column heading for the column you want to delete.
2. Press the DELETE key.

From a Pop-Up List

To delete a column from a pop-up list, use the following workflow:

1. Right-click on the heading of the column you want to delete. This displays a pop-up list of options.
2. Select Delete.

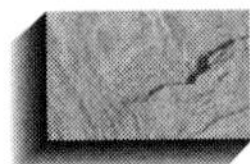

NOTE
For both of the workflows on the previous page, you can delete multiple columns by holding down the CTRL *key as you make your selections.*

From the Edit Sheet Dialog Box

If you are not sure which columns you want to delete and simply want to see how the worksheet will look without some of the columns, you should use this method.

To delete columns from the Edit Sheet dialog box, use the following workflow:

1. From the menu bar, select Sheet | Edit Sheet, or from the Toolbar click on the Edit Sheet icon. Either of these displays the Edit Sheet dialog box (Figures 5-19 and 5-20 in the previous chapter).
2. Click the Table Layout tab.
3. Highlight the column you want to delete.
4. Press the DELETE key on your keyboard.
5. Click OK or press ENTER to finish.

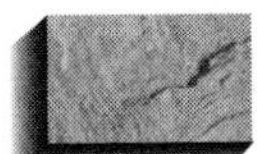

NOTE
If you have deleted the wrong column, do not click OK or press ENTER*. Clicking on Cancel causes Discoverer to abandon the delete and reinstate the column.*

Resizing Columns

There are four ways to resize columns in Discoverer (unfortunately, none of which apply to 3*i*). Some of these are very precise, while others are free format and simply resize to whatever manual width setting you apply to the column.

The four ways you can resize a column are as follows:

- Drag the column edge to the required width.
- Double-click on a column edge (precise).
- Manually resize a single column using the Format menu.
- Auto-size using the Format menu (precise).

NOTE
To view the current width of a column, place the cursor on the right-hand edge of the column, then click and hold the left mouse button. This causes Discoverer to embolden all of the column's right-hand edge and to display the current width at the bottom of the screen (see Figure 6-2).

Single-click the right-hand edge of the column header

Oracle Discoverer - [Profit Test]

File Edit View Sheet Format Tools Graph Window Help

Double-click here to edit this title.

Page Items: Status: SHIPPED Month: FEB-00

	Order Number	Order Qty SUM	Ship Qty SUM	Cost Price SUM	Selling Price SUM	Margin SUM	Mark Up SUM
1	2692	1200	1200	7,452.00	18,300.00	59.27	145.57
2	2691	2400	2400	19,992.00	42,384.00	52.83	112.00
3	2689	504	504	4,198.32	8,900.64	52.83	112.00
4	2688	1200	1200	19,128.00	41,580.00	53.99	117.37
5	2687	48	48	765.12	1,663.20	53.99	117.37
6	2682	2400	2400	29,808.00	56,280.00	47.03	88.80
7	2681	4800	4800	59,616.00	112,560.00	47.03	88.80
8	2680	96	96	1,192.32	2,251.20	47.03	88.80
9	2679	4800	4800	59,616.00	112,560.00	47.03	88.80
10	2678	1200	1200	14,904.00	28,140.00	47.03	88.80
11	2675	1200	1200	19,128.00	41,580.00	53.99	117.37
12	2674	1200	1200	19,128.00	41,580.00	53.99	117.37
13	2672	1200	1200	12,744.00	26,616.00	52.11	108.85
14	2671	6000	6000	63,720.00	133,080.00	52.11	108.85
15	2670	2400	2400	23,712.00	51,000.00	53.50	115.08
16	2669	96	96	575.04	1,224.00	53.01	112.85
17	2668	72	72	519.84	972.00	46.51	86.98
18	2667	1200	1200	13,776.00	32,340.00	57.40	134.75
19	2666	2400	2400	27,552.00	64,680.00	57.40	134.75

Sheet 1

Width: 22.00 NUM

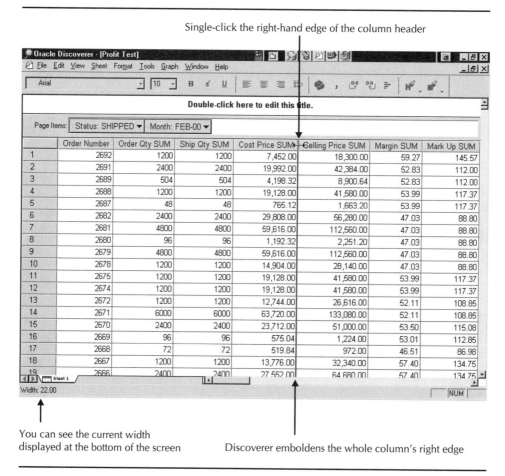

You can see the current width displayed at the bottom of the screen

Discoverer emboldens the whole column's right edge

FIGURE 6-2. *Viewing the width of a column*

Resizing by Dragging the Column Edge to a Required Width

Resizing a column using this method is quick but imprecise, and comes down to user preference. This method is sufficient for working on the screen, but not usually accurate enough for printing or creating a report. Discoverer will resize a column to any width you choose, even if that means being unable to see all of the data. There are valid occasions when you may want to do this. For example, a company using long product names may decide that the first 20 characters in the name are sufficient for the purpose of displaying on reports.

To resize a column by dragging its edge, follow this workflow:

1. Place the mouse pointer on the right-hand edge of the column header you want to resize. This causes the pointer to change to the resize pointer.
2. Hold down the left mouse button and drag the pointer to the left or right. As you do this, the column width will increase or decrease.
3. When the column is the width you require, release the mouse button.

Resizing by Double-Clicking on a Column's Edge

Resizing a column using this method is very precise and causes Discoverer to auto-size the width of the column. Auto-sizing means that Discoverer automatically works out the width of the column based upon the width of the header and the width of the longest data item in the column. It will resize the column to make it one character bigger than either the width of the header or the width of the longest data item.

To auto-size a column by double-clicking on its edge, follow this workflow:

1. Place the mouse pointer on the right-hand edge of the column you want to resize. This causes the pointer to change to the resize cursor.
2. Double-click the left mouse button. This causes the column width to auto-size.

Manually Resizing a Single Column Using the Format Menu

This method of resizing a column is again imprecise and somewhat hit-and-miss. You will probably repeat the resizing several times before you get the column to the width that appears correct. If you want to resize a number of columns, you will have to repeat the method for each column.

To manually resize a single column using the Format menu, follow this workflow:

1. Click anywhere in the column you want to resize. This causes Discoverer to highlight the column.
2. From the menu, select Format | Columns | Width. This displays the following Column Width dialog box.

3. Enter a number for the width of the column. The number you enter is the number of characters that will display, based on an 8-point font. You can enter decimal places if you wish.
4. Click OK.

Auto-Sizing Using the Format Menu

This method of resizing columns is very precise and should be used when creating a report or printing, or when you want to resize multiple columns. There is nothing hit-and-miss about this method because the columns are auto-sized.

To auto-size a column or columns using the Format menu, follow this workflow:

1. Highlight the column or columns to be auto-sized. You do this by clicking in a column, holding down the CTRL key, and then clicking on any other desired columns. To select all columns, click on the blank item immediately to the left of the first data item. The following illustration shows where to click:

Oracle Discoverer - [Profit Test]

File Edit View Sheet Format Tools Graph Window Help

Double-click here to edit this title.

Page Items:

Click here to highlight all columns

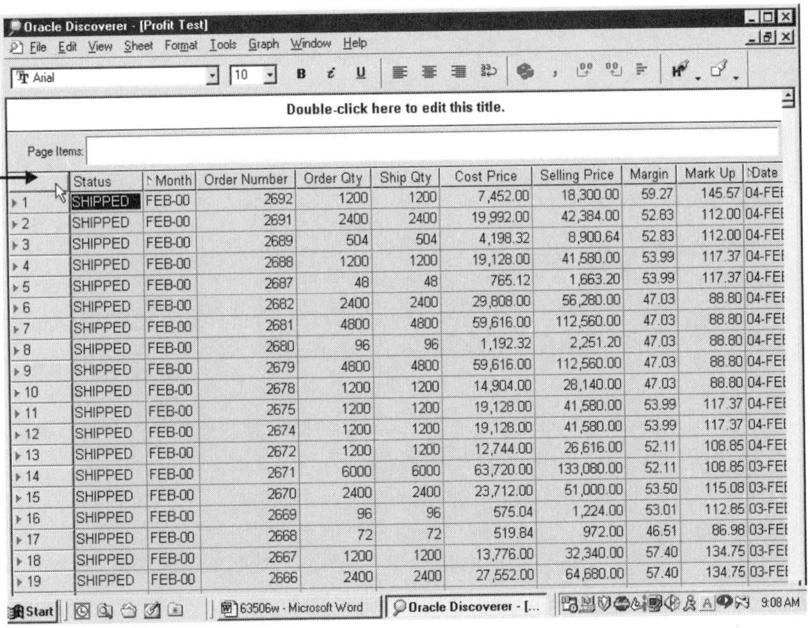

	Status	Month	Order Number	Order Qty	Ship Qty	Cost Price	Selling Price	Margin	Mark Up	Date
1	SHIPPED	FEB-00	2692	1200	1200	7,452.00	18,300.00	59.27	145.57	04-FEI
2	SHIPPED	FEB-00	2691	2400	2400	19,992.00	42,384.00	52.83	112.00	04-FEI
3	SHIPPED	FEB-00	2689	504	504	4,198.32	8,900.64	52.83	112.00	04-FEI
4	SHIPPED	FEB-00	2688	1200	1200	19,128.00	41,580.00	53.99	117.37	04-FEI
5	SHIPPED	FEB-00	2687	48	48	765.12	1,663.20	53.99	117.37	04-FEI
6	SHIPPED	FEB-00	2682	2400	2400	29,808.00	56,280.00	47.03	88.80	04-FEI
7	SHIPPED	FEB-00	2681	4800	4800	59,616.00	112,560.00	47.03	88.80	04-FEI
8	SHIPPED	FEB-00	2680	96	96	1,192.32	2,251.20	47.03	88.80	04-FEI
9	SHIPPED	FEB-00	2679	4800	4800	59,616.00	112,560.00	47.03	88.80	04-FEI
10	SHIPPED	FEB-00	2678	1200	1200	14,904.00	28,140.00	47.03	88.80	04-FEI
11	SHIPPED	FEB-00	2675	1200	1200	19,128.00	41,580.00	53.99	117.37	04-FEI
12	SHIPPED	FEB-00	2674	1200	1200	19,128.00	41,580.00	53.99	117.37	04-FEI
13	SHIPPED	FEB-00	2672	1200	1200	12,744.00	26,616.00	52.11	108.85	04-FEI
14	SHIPPED	FEB-00	2671	6000	6000	63,720.00	133,080.00	52.11	108.85	03-FEI
15	SHIPPED	FEB-00	2670	2400	2400	23,712.00	51,000.00	53.50	115.08	03-FEI
16	SHIPPED	FEB-00	2669	96	96	575.04	1,224.00	53.01	112.85	03-FEI
17	SHIPPED	FEB-00	2668	72	72	519.84	972.00	46.51	86.98	03-FEI
18	SHIPPED	FEB-00	2667	1200	1200	13,776.00	32,340.00	57.40	134.75	03-FEI
19	SHIPPED	FEB-00	2666	2400	2400	27,552.00	64,680.00	57.40	134.75	03-FEI

Start 63506w - Microsoft Word Oracle Discoverer - [... 9:08 AM

2. When you have selected a column or columns, from the menu select Format | Columns | Auto Size. This causes Discoverer to automatically resize all of the highlighted columns.

Formatting Totals

If you have added totals to your query, you can format them. Discoverer uses the Format Data dialog box to let you format totals. However, when formatting totals, only the Font and Background Color tabs are available. Discoverer also allows you to use some of the formatting bar buttons when working with totals.

Formatting Totals Using the Format Data Dialog Box

The Format Data dialog box is accessible in two ways:

- From the menu bar
- From the Total pop up list

From the Menu Bar

To access the Format Data dialog box from the menu bar, use the following workflow:

1. From the menu bar, select Tools | Totals, this displays the Edit Totals dialog box.
2. Highlight the total you want to format.
3. Click the Edit button. This opens the Editing dialog box.
4. Click the Format button. This opens the Format Data dialog box.

From the Total Pop-Up List

To access the Format Data dialog box from the Total pop-up list, use the following workflow:

1. Right-click on the row containing the total.
2. From the pop-up menu, select Edit Total. This opens the Editing dialog box.
3. Click the Format button. This opens the Format Data dialog box.

If you have only one total in your worksheet, clicking on any cell in the row containing the total displays the Edit box for that total. When you apply the format to a single total, Discoverer applies the format to the complete row. If you have multiple totals in your worksheet, clicking the cell containing a total displays the Edit box for that total. Clicking on any other cell in the Totals row displays the Edit Totals dialog box, from where you will have to select the total you want to format.

NOTE

There is no way to format all totals at once. When you have multiple totals in your worksheet, you can only apply a format to those cells that are totals.

Formatting Totals from the Formatting Bar

After you have created a total or totals in your worksheet, rather than calling up a dialog box, Discoverer allows you to format totals directly from the formatting bar.

To format from the formatting bar, you should do the following:

1. Click on the row containing the total. Discoverer then activates some of the formatting buttons on the formatting bar.
2. Click on any of the buttons: Font, Font Size, Bold, Italic, Underline, Wrap Text, Foreground, and/or Background Colors. This applies that format setting to the total.

If you have only one total in your worksheet, clicking on any cell in the row containing the total activates the formatting bar. When you click on one of the formatting buttons, Discoverer applies that format to the whole row. If you have multiple totals in your worksheet, the formatting bar is only activated when you click on one of the cells containing a total. In this situation, Discoverer applies the format only to that total. Clicking on any cell that does not contain a total disables the formatting bar.

Formatting Exceptions

One of the analysis features of Discoverer is the ability to format data exceptions. We will explain how to create and format these in Chapter 9 when we discuss using Discoverer to analyze data.

Adding a Title to Your Query

Discoverer handles titles by offering the Edit Title dialog box. The box has two tabs, one for formatting the text and one for adding bitmaps to the title. The Bitmaps tab also serves the purpose of allowing you to preview the title. You can also insert text codes into the title, such as workbook name or any conditions present in the query.

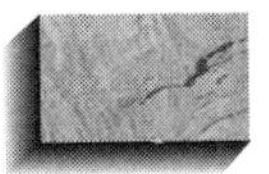

NOTE
You can give an individual name to each worksheet in a workbook.

Editing the Title

To Edit the title of a query, use one of the following three methods:

- Double click the title bar. The title bar is directly above the column headings and page details.

- Right-click on the title bar, and from the drop-down menu select Edit Title.

NOTE
If you cannot see the title bar, you can activate it from the Tools | Options menu. Click the Crosstab or Table tab and check the box Title. This displays a title.

- From the menu bar, select Sheet | Edit Title.

If you haven't created a default title, Discoverer will display "Double-click here to edit this title" as the title. This doubles for the instructions, so don't be confused when the Edit Title dialog box opens and still seems to be giving instructions to double-click.

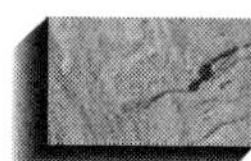

NOTE
You can create your own default title from the Crosstab or Table tab on the Options menu. This default is created in exactly the same way as you create a normal title, so all that you read in this section equally applies to creating a default title. The following illustration shows the Table Options tab.

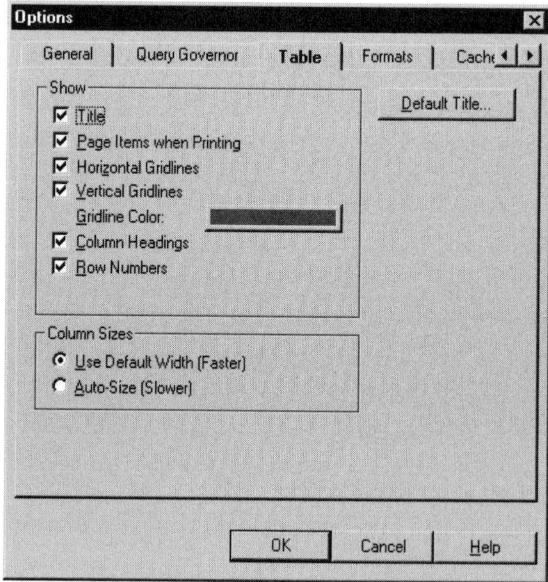

Whichever method you chose to edit the title, Discoverer now displays the Edit Title dialog box. This box has two tabs, a Text tab and a Bitmap tab.

The Text Tab

Using the Text tab, you can change the font, font size, font properties and alignment, as well as foreground and background color. You are also given a drop-down list of special text codes that you can add to the title, as shown here:

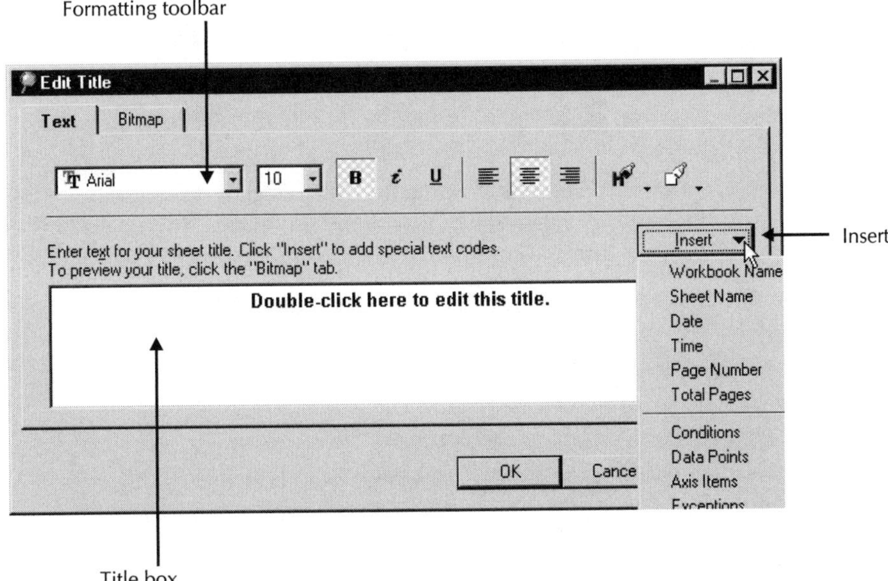

- **Formatting toolbar** These buttons work in the same way as on the main Discoverer formatting bar.
- **Insert** Select from a list of special text codes. See the following table.
- **Title Box** As you select options for your title, Discoverer inserts the options here. You can also type text into the box.

The following table explains the special text codes available:

Text Code Name	Description
Workbook Name	The name of your workbook.
Sheet Name	The name of the current sheet.

Text Code Name	**Description**
Date	The date the query is run.
Time	The time the query is run.
Page Number	The current page number.
Total Pages	A count of all pages in the worksheet.
Conditions	The name of each condition in the worksheet is displayed, separated by a comma.
Data Points	The column name for each data point (mathematical expression) in the worksheet is displayed, separated by a comma.
Axis Items	The column name for all items in the worksheet is displayed, separated by a comma.
Page Items	The column name for every page item in the worksheet is displayed, separated by a comma. You can edit the list and remove any that you don't want to display.
Exceptions	The description for every exception in the worksheet is displayed, separated by a comma.

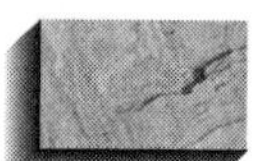

NOTE
The above text codes display on the Text tab with an ampersand (&) as the first character. This character is programming code and will not display as part of the title. You can force Discoverer to show an individual column name by typing its name into the Title box preceded by an ampersand. To preview the title, click the Bitmap tab.

To create a new title, select the text "Double-click here to edit this title" and type in your new workbook title. You might want to make the worksheet name the title, in which case select Worksheet from the Insert drop-down list.

With the text of the new title selected, use the formatting tools at the top of the dialog box to format the text. If you want more than one line for the title, press ENTER to go to the next line. There are no tabs, or multiple areas for the title like in the header and footer, so creating a complex and well-formatted title is not easy. The authors recommend that you use the Header and Footer options of Page Setup to create a better title and stick to a simple one- or two-line title with a graphic here.

NOTE
Headers and footers will be covered in detail in Chapter 8,"Turning a Discoverer Query into a Report."

The Bitmap Tab

Using the Bitmap tab, you can insert bitmaps into the background of your title. For example, perhaps you want to insert your company's logo.

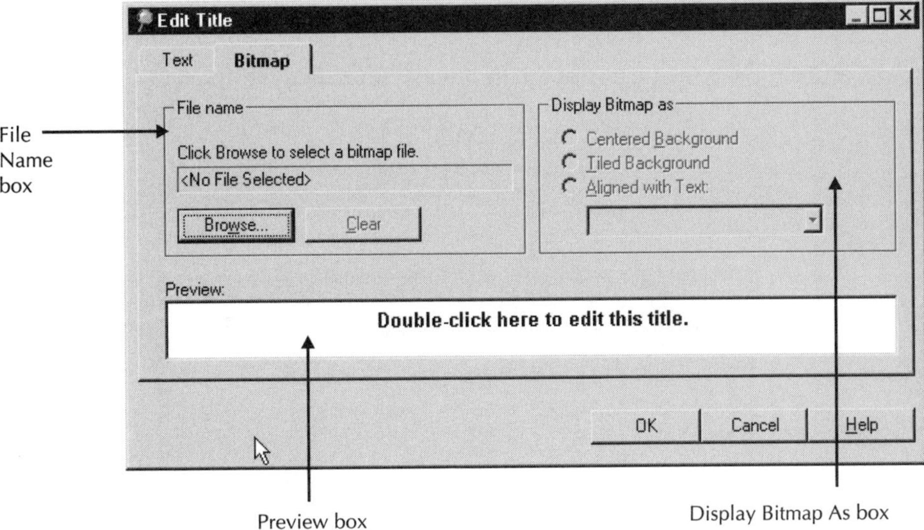

The Bitmap tab consists of the following three sections:

- **File Name box** Use the Browse button to locate a bitmap, and the Clear button to delete it. When a bitmap is selected, Discoverer displays the path and name of the file.
- **Display Bitmap As box** Check the radio buttons to center the bitmap in the background, to tile the bitmap in the background, or to display the bitmap aligned with the text. You can align a bitmap above, below, to the left, or to the right of the text.
- **Preview box** Discoverer displays how the bitmap will look when combined with the options selected from the Text tab.

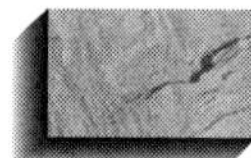

NOTE
You can create a bitmap of your company's logo by scanning it from a piece of stationery. Let us give you a word of warning about scanned images. These images are rarely as good as original artwork and certainly not good enough for printing onto reports that will be sent externally. It is likely that your company has standard artwork, and you should speak with your Discoverer administrator to find out where the images are stored.

To add a bitmap to a title, use the following workflow:

1. Click the Bitmap tab on the Edit Title dialog box.
2. Click the Browse button. This causes Discoverer to display the following Open dialog box:

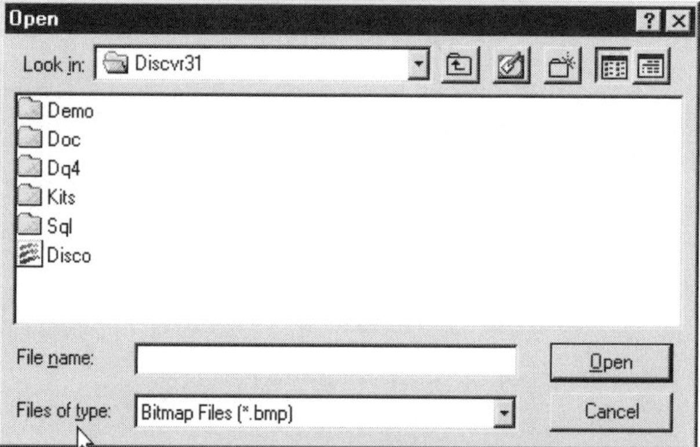

3. Find the bitmap you want to insert.
4. Click Open. Discoverer displays the full path and name of the bitmap, and also shows you how the bitmap will look.
5. Select an option for displaying the bitmap. You can choose from Centered Background, Tiled Background, or Aligned With Text. If you choose Aligned With Text, you will need to select how it will be aligned. You can choose from Left of Text, Right of Text, Above Text, or Below Text.
6. When you are satisfied that you have the correct bitmap, and that it is displayed correctly, click OK. This will display the title in your query.

7. The following example shows a title with a bitmap aligned to the left.

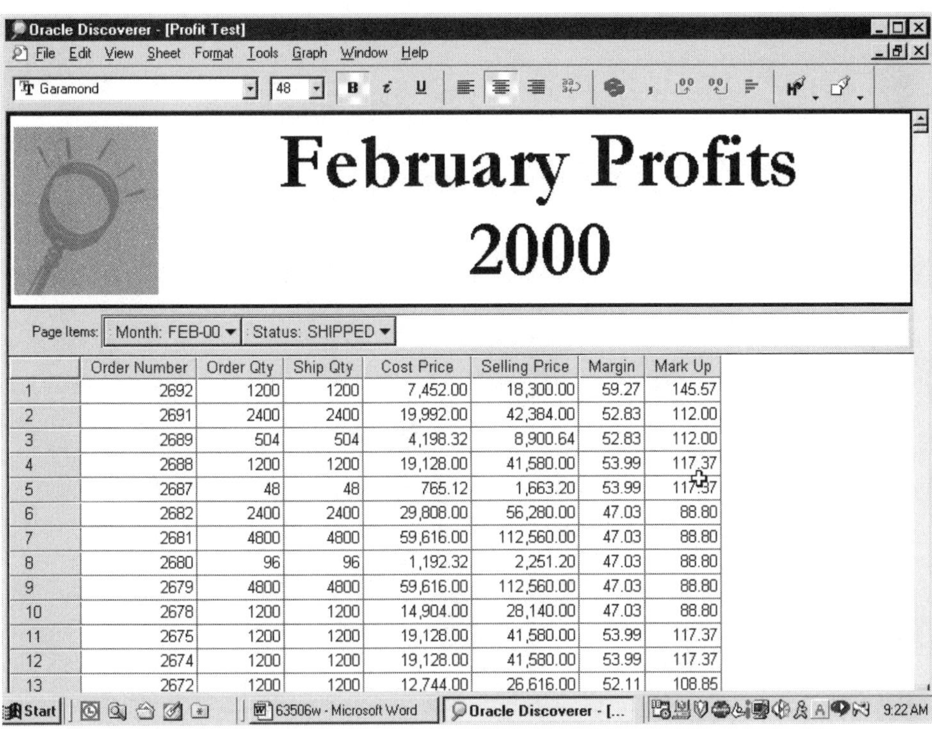

	Order Number	Order Qty	Ship Qty	Cost Price	Selling Price	Margin	Mark Up
1	2692	1200	1200	7,452.00	18,300.00	59.27	145.57
2	2691	2400	2400	19,992.00	42,384.00	52.83	112.00
3	2689	504	504	4,198.32	8,900.64	52.83	112.00
4	2688	1200	1200	19,128.00	41,580.00	53.99	117.37
5	2687	48	48	765.12	1,663.20	53.99	117.37
6	2682	2400	2400	29,808.00	56,280.00	47.03	88.80
7	2681	4800	4800	59,616.00	112,560.00	47.03	88.80
8	2680	96	96	1,192.32	2,251.20	47.03	88.80
9	2679	4800	4800	59,616.00	112,560.00	47.03	88.80
10	2678	1200	1200	14,904.00	28,140.00	47.03	88.80
11	2675	1200	1200	19,128.00	41,580.00	53.99	117.37
12	2674	1200	1200	19,128.00	41,580.00	53.99	117.37
13	2672	1200	1200	12,744.00	26,616.00	52.11	108.85

NOTE
If you do not want to use the selected bitmap, you can remove it and start again by clicking Clear.

STICKY FEATURE
Discoverer remembers the way you last displayed a bitmap and offers this as the default the next time you insert a bitmap.

Formatting the Title

There are two ways to format the title. The first has already been described above in the section for the Text tab. The second way to format the title is to use the Format Title dialog box. This box can be accessed in two ways, as follows:

- Right click the title. From the drop-down menu, select Format Title.
- From the menu bar, select Format | Sheet | Title.

NOTE

Before you can select a method to access the Format Title dialog box, you must have a title showing.

The following illustration shows the Format Title dialog box:

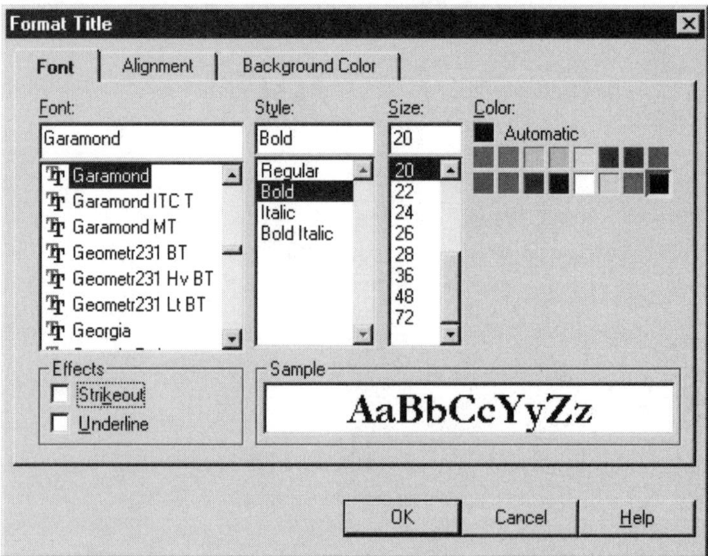

The above box has the same functionality as the Format Data dialog box that was explained in the section titled "Formatting Data." The only difference is that the Format Title dialog box only has the first three tabs for font, alignment, and background color.

Suppressing a Title from Displaying

To suppress a title from displaying, use the following workflow:

1. From the menu bar, select Tools | Options.
2. Select the Crosstab or Table tab.
3. Uncheck the Title check box.

NOTE
Suppressing a title from displaying does not delete the title. It still exists and can be reactivated by rechecking the Title check box.

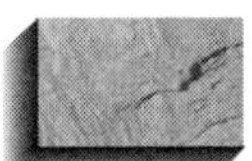

NOTE
*There is no way to edit a title within Discoverer 3*i. *This is scheduled for the next major release. However, if you create a query in 3.1 that has a title, Discoverer 3*i *will correctly display the title.*

Adding a Background Bitmap

This final section on formatting shows you how to add a bitmap as a background to your whole worksheet. Again, as we explained in the section dealing with bitmaps in titles, you should try and use existing artwork rather than scanning in your own image.

Try to use bitmaps that have light colors and do not distract the eye away from the report itself. We therefore recommend using caution when using bitmaps as a background.

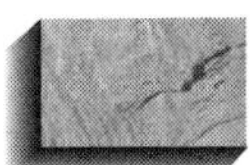

3*i* NOTE
When using any form of bitmap, you should ensure that you are not infringing on any copyright or proprietary rights. If you are not sure whether you can use a bitmap or not, you should consult your company's legal department for advice. The best advice we can give you is, if in doubt, don't use it. You don't want to invoke a lawsuit on your company just because you infringed on a copyrighted image.

Setting a Background

There are two ways to set a background:

- From a pop up list
- From the menu bar

From a Pop-Up List

To set a background from a pop-up list, use the following workflow:

1. Right-click anywhere on the worksheet that you want to add a background to. This displays a pop-up list of options.
2. Select Set Background. This causes Discoverer to display the Open dialog box.
3. Find the bitmap you want to insert.
4. Click Open. Discoverer displays the bitmap tiled in the background.

From the Menu Bar

To set a background from the menu bar, use the following workflow:

1. From the menu bar, select Format | Sheet | Set Background. This displays the Open dialog box.
2. Find the bitmap you want to insert.
3. Click Open. Discoverer displays the bitmap tiled in the background.

Clearing a Background

If you already have an existing background and now wish to remove it, you must use the Clear Background command. There are two ways to clear a background:

- From a pop up list
- From the menu bar

From a Pop-Up List

To clear a background from a pop-up list, use the following workflow:

1. Right-click anywhere on the worksheet that you want to clear a background from. This displays a pop-up list of options.
2. Select Clear Background.

From the Menu Bar

To clear a background from the menu bar, use the following workflow:

1. From the menu bar, select Format | Sheet | Clear Background.

Summary

In this chapter, you have learned the need to give meaningful names to query column headings and any item that might become a heading. You have been shown how to rearrange the order of the columns and rename the headings.

You have been shown how formatting can improve a query by changing fonts and font sizes, font and background colors, and text justification.

This chapter has shown you how to format numbers as currency, with commas and with the correct number of decimal places.

Finally, you have been taught to format totals and add titles to your query. You have also learned how to add graphics to a query by placing bitmaps into the title as well as adding graphics to the background.

By adding formatting to a query, you will add interest, and make them easier to read and more pleasing to view. Formatting the query gives you an excellent beginning in turning a query into a report. In Chapter 8, you will learn more about reporting in Discoverer.

CHAPTER 7

Using Graphs to Present Data

n important feature of good reporting is the use of graphs. Graphs are a powerful, visual representation of the data from your database. Discoverer uses a Graph Wizard to take you through the steps of creating a graph. For those familiar with creating graphs in other applications, don't expect the same ease of use and flexibility. Also unfortunate is the fact that graphing is completely unavailable in the current release of 3*i*.

You can use both tables and crosstabs to create a graph, but you cannot select certain parts of the data to use in the graph. Discoverer uses all of the data points to create the graph and decides for you what it is you want. You are left with only the power to format it.

If you want to use only some of the data points of a table or crosstab, Discoverer will allow you to move those unwanted data points to the page items. However, you should be wary of doing this as unexpected results could arise.

If you want to use only some data points of a table or crosstab, it is necessary to turn on the page-item feature and move the data points you don't want included in the graph to the page axis. Later, when you have finished graphing, you will need to return the columns to the body of the worksheet. To do this, you will have to use the Edit Sheet dialog box.

If you only want data that meet certain conditions, you will have to create those conditions. This will be a big change for those used to creating graphs in Excel, where you can select only the data you want to use in the graph from your table. The upside is that once the graph has been created, it is easy to tweak until you get it right. If you make a change to the worksheet, the changes are made to the graph instantly with no intervention from the user. The graph will also be automatically updated each time the query is run.

There are enough different types of graph styles to choose from, including 3D models, that you should be able to find a format that meets your needs. There are also bountiful formatting options, including a nifty little paint can to pour your color selection in place.

In this chapter, you will learn to create, modify and format graphs. You will be shown how to begin with the Graph Wizard and then use the graph toolbar as well as the Modify Graph dialog box to make changes to the graph. You will learn about the various types of graphs available and how to create titles and add legends. You will also be shown how to create a snapshot of a graph to use in other applications, such as Word documents.

The Discoverer Graph Window

Discoverer displays graphs in the Graph window. The first time you open the window, you will be taken through the Graph Wizard to assist you in creating the graph. After you have created a graph in Discoverer, it becomes a permanent part of the worksheet that it is based on.

Figure 7-1 shows a simple query and Figure 7-2 shows the graph based upon the query.

	Sales	Quarter
1	$1,996,801	1998-Q3
2	$9,243,165	1998-Q4
3	$4,653,005	1999-Q1
4	$2,612,804	1999-Q2
5	$2,224,574	1999-Q3
6	$659,606	1999-Q4
7	$231,788	2000-Q1
8	$23,367,614	2000-Q2

FIGURE 7-1. *A Discoverer worksheet*

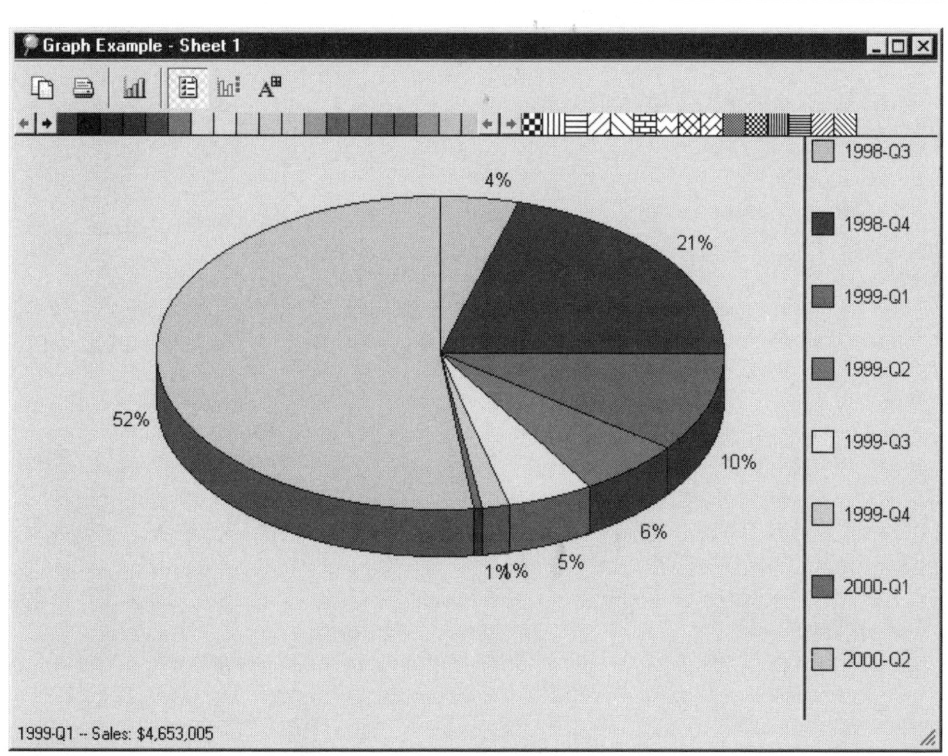

FIGURE 7-2. *The graph based on the worksheet*

The Features of the Discoverer 3.1 Graph Window

Unlike Excel, Discoverer does not embed the graph into the worksheet. Instead, the graph is created in its own sheet that can be opened for viewing as the associated worksheet is changed or updated. This is a nice feature, and we especially like the way the graph automatically refreshes itself with the changing data.

Figure 7-3 shows the features of the Discoverer Graph window.

Toolbar

The Discoverer Graph window has a toolbar used to work with the graph details, as shown here:

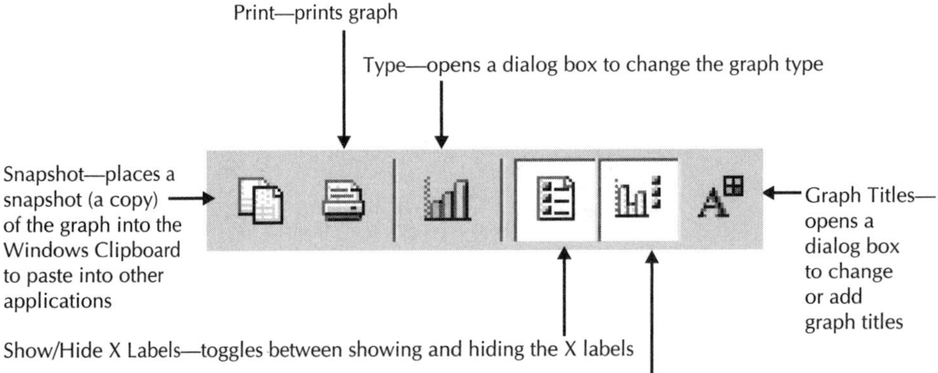

Y Axis

Discoverer creates a scale appropriate to the data of the original worksheet. This is shown in the Y axis (along the left side of the graph). For example, if the worksheet is based on sales for the first quarter of Q-1 by region, and the highest sales were $534,109, Discoverer would create a scale in increments from $0 to $535,000. You can format the scale yourself as well as add decimal points.

Scroll Bar

Some types of graphs, such as bar charts, contain a large number of bars. You might need to use the scroll bar to see all of the data items of the graph.

Status Bar

As you point to various data items on the graph, Discoverer will display the associated data in the status bar.

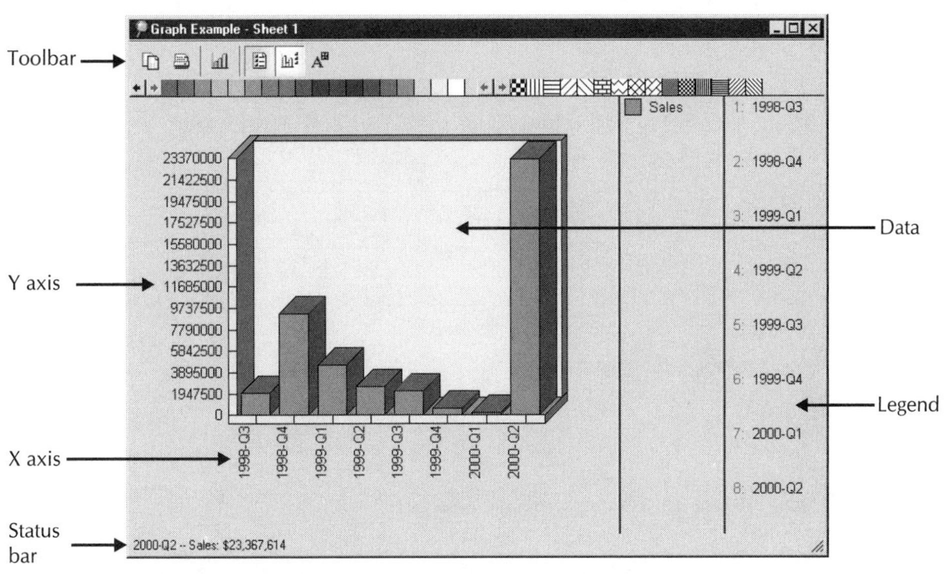

FIGURE 7-3. *The Graph Window*

Legend

The legend shows the color and the label used to display the corresponding worksheet data.

Horizontal and Vertical Gridlines

The gridlines are vertical and horizontal lines that can be turned on or off. You can select to use either vertical, horizontal, or both. This can be helpful in reading the graph details.

Data

The data is simply the bars of the bar chart, or the slices of the pie chart. It is a graphical representation of the data in your worksheet.

X Axis

The X axis shows the labels used to identify the data. When your data has long names, they will be replaced by numbers. If you have short names, they will be shown below the associated data and will eliminate the need to show the legend.

The Available Graph Styles

There are 14 different graph styles available, and each graph type has one or more formats available. In this section, we will show you the same query as each type of graph.

The query used to show the graphs is a comparison of sales for Global Widget's four regions in Q-2 of 1999 and 2000.

Global Widget's Q-2 by Region for 1999 and 2000

	Region	Profit SUM	Quarter
1	EUROPE	$413,006	1999-Q2
2		$4,014,862	2000-Q2
3	FAR EAST	$108,713	1999-Q2
4		$1,366,098	2000-Q2
5	NORTH AMERICA	$671,937	1999-Q2
6		$5,959,886	2000-Q2
7	SOUTH AMERICA	$126,259	1999-Q2
8		$865,758	2000-Q2

Sheet 1

Area

The area graph shows trends in values across categories.

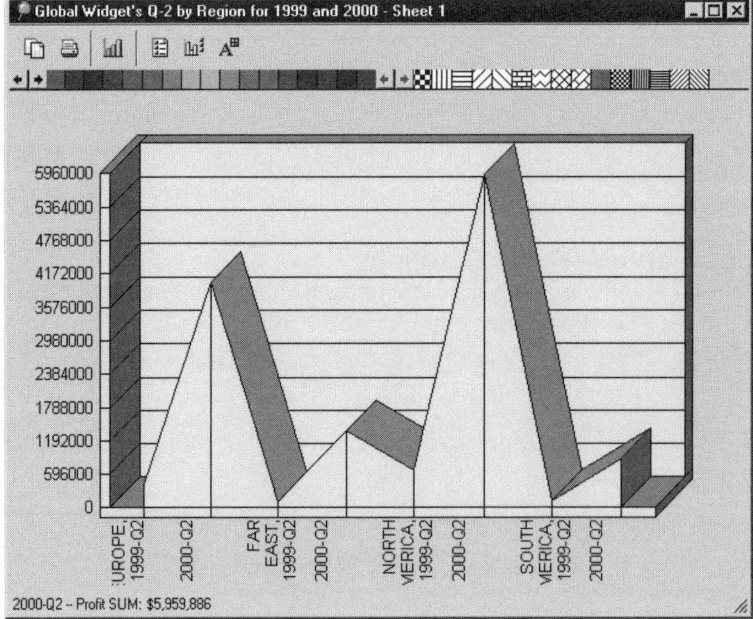

Bar

The bar graph shows values in comparison to beginning and ending values. This is useful in graphing financial data and stock prices. The Y axis shows the values and the X axis shows the categories.

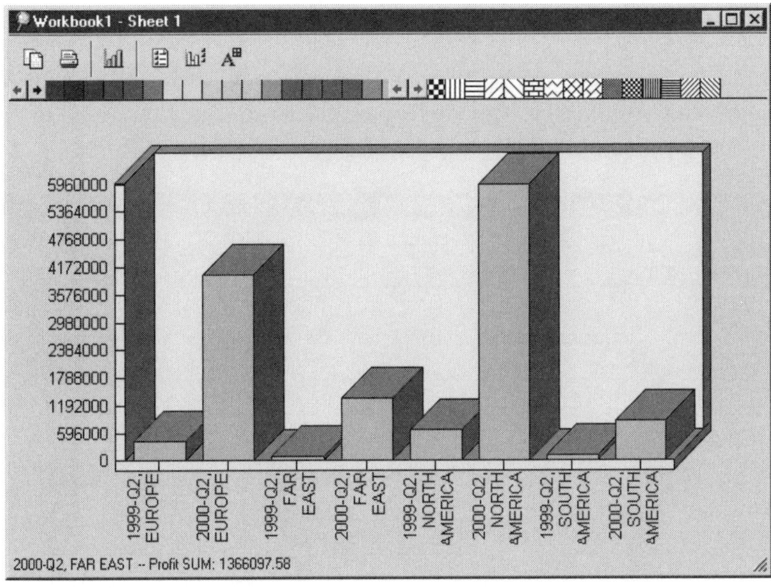

Cube

The cube graph shows trends in values across categories, separated by category. The top of the cube represents the value. The Y axis shows the values and the X axis shows the categories.

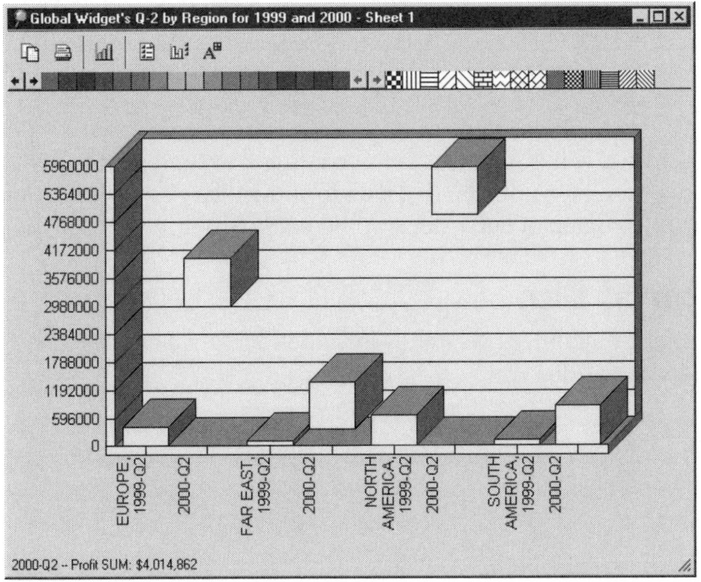

Fit to Curve

The fit-to-curve graph shows trends in values across categories. The points represent values separated by category. The line is used to demonstrate the trend in the value changes.

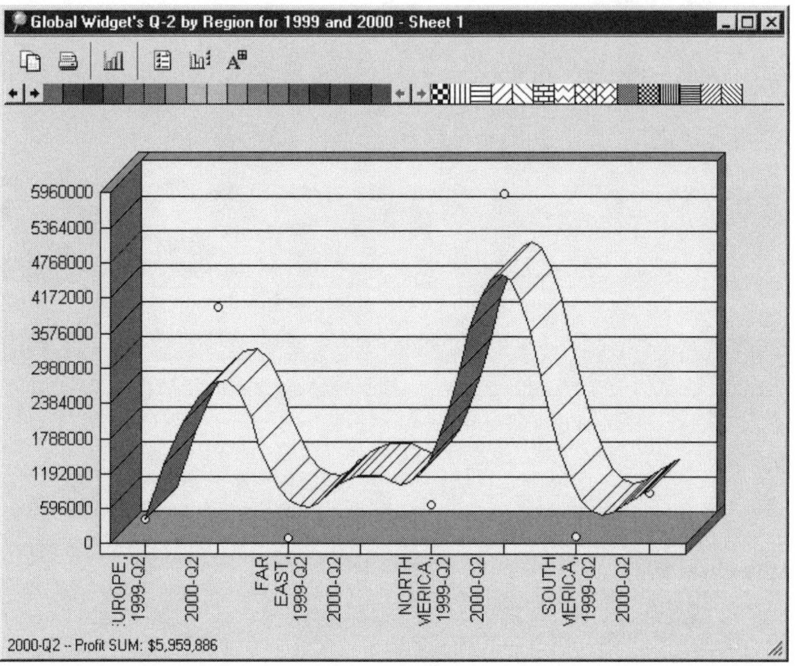

Hi-Low-Close

The hi-low-close graph is identical to the bar graph in our example. This type of graph is more useful for stock market data to show the relationship of the high, low, and closing price of a particular stock or the market itself.

Horizontal Bar

The horizontal bar graph shows trends in values across categories. It is a regular bar graph turned on its side.

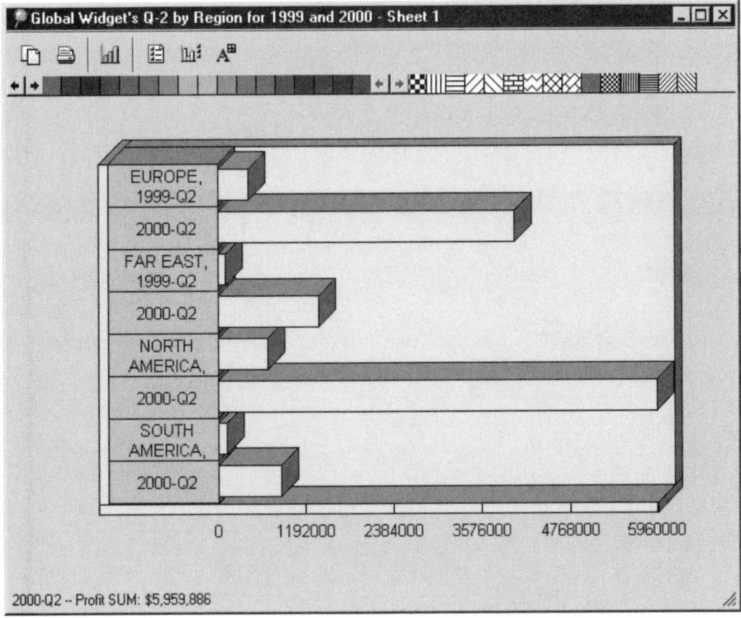

Line

The line graph shows trends in values across categories. The values are shown as dots separated by categories and a line is drawn to emphasize the trend.

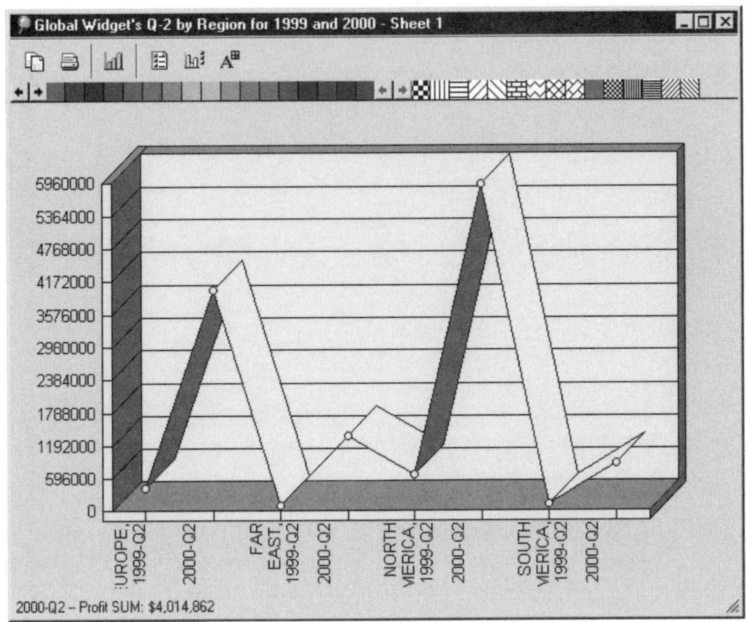

Parteo

The parteo graph shows trends in categories across categories. A line is drawn above to show the trend associated with each change.

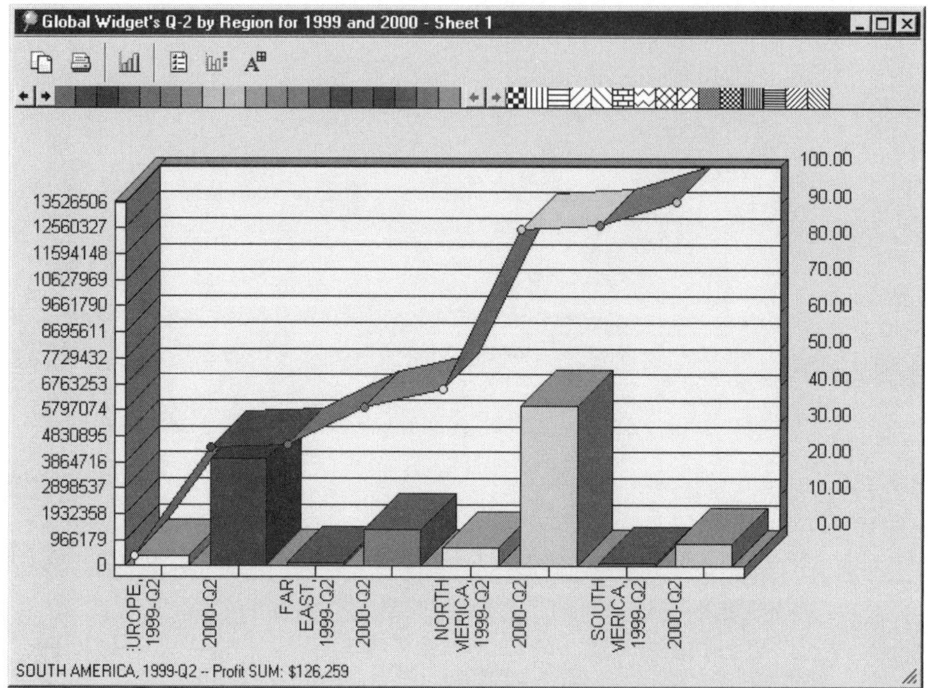

Pie

The pie graph shows values across categories. Each value is shown as a portion of the whole pie.

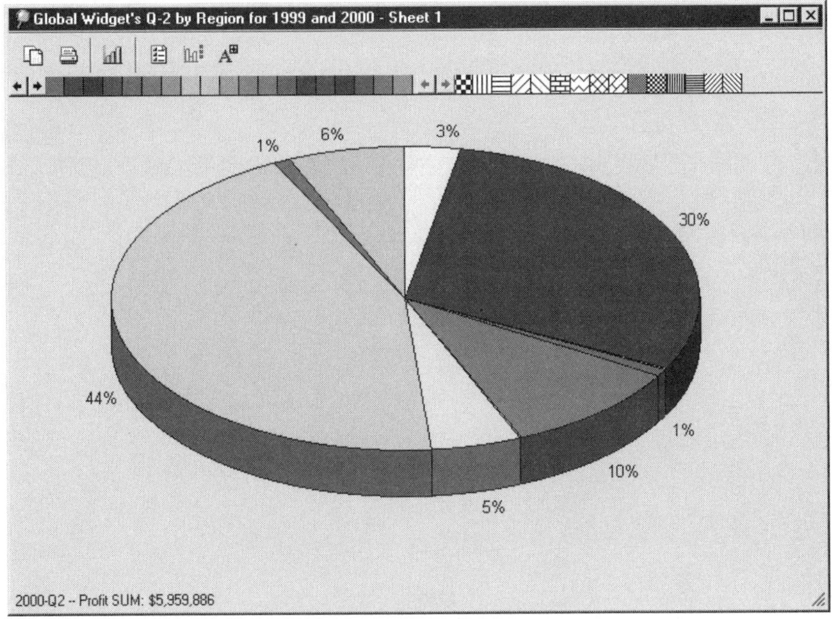

Point

The point graph shows trends in values across categories. The points show data separated by values and categories.

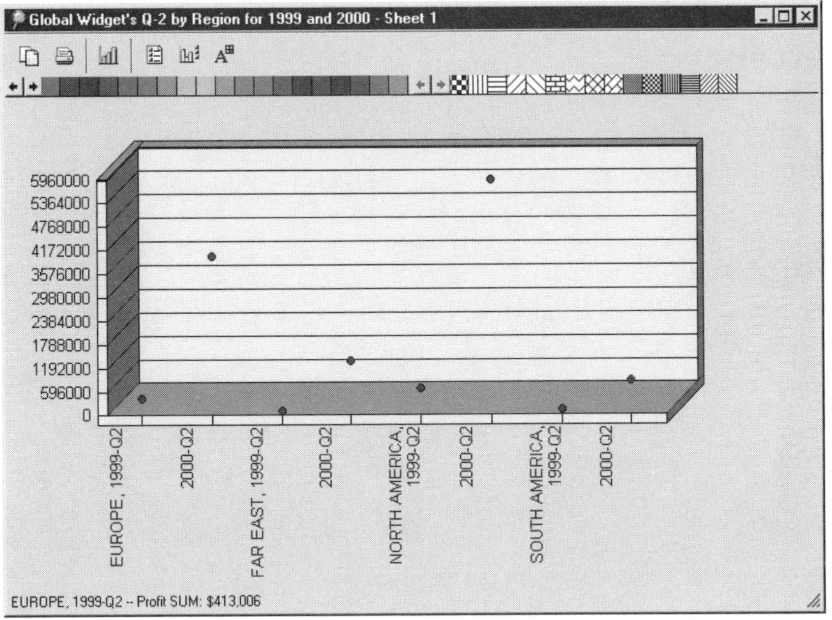

Polar

The polar type of graph plots data as angle-length points.

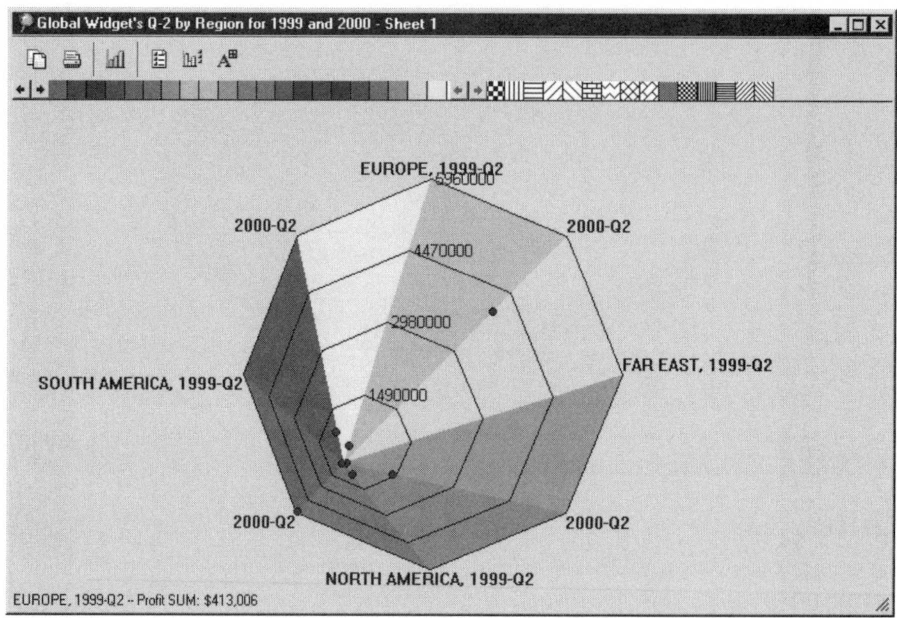

Scatter

The scatter graph shows changes in values in comparison to other values. Each axis must represent a number. Using our example query, the results are the same as the point graph.

Doughnut

The doughnut graph shows values across categories. Each value is shown as a portion of the whole.

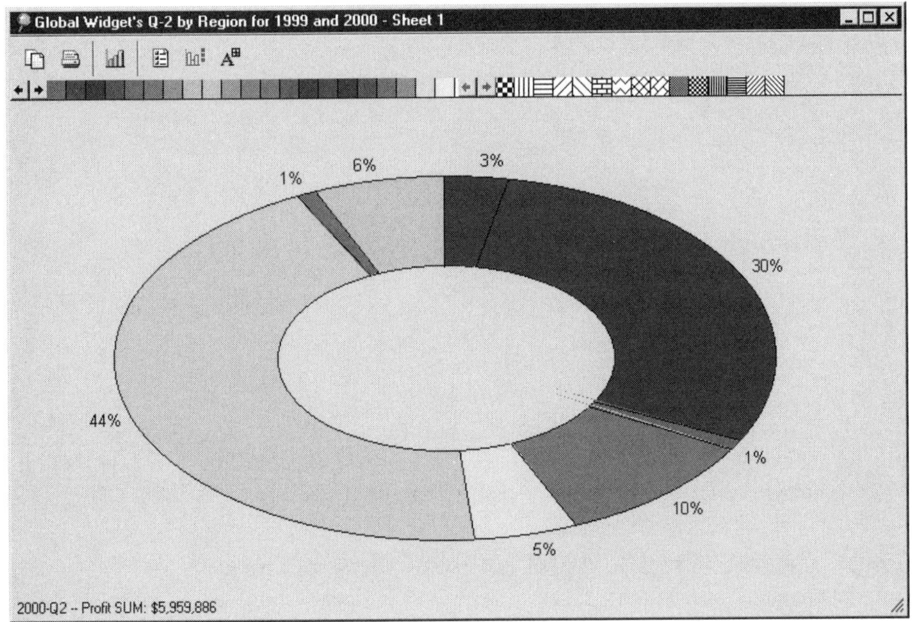

Surface

This graph shows values across categories; however, with the example query, there was no data shown on the graph.

Creating a Graph

To create a graph, you can use the Graph button on the main Discoverer toolbar or use the menu bar.

To begin using the Discoverer graphing tool, click on Graph | New Graph from the menu bar or click on the Graph button on the toolbar.

The Graph Wizard

Following one of the two methods previously described will open the Graph Wizard. There are four steps to the Graph Wizard that take you step-by-step through the process of building your graph. The four steps are as follows:

- Selecting the graph type
- Formatting the graph type
- Titles and legends
- Adding special graph options

Don't worry if you are not sure how your graph will turn out. If you are not satisfied with the results, it is easy to edit the graph until you are. You can also click on the Back button at any time to return to the previous step(s).

Graph Wizard Step 1: Selecting the Graph Type

The first step in creating your graph is to select the graph type. The features of the Graph Wizard step 1 are as follows:

- **Graph types** Select the type of graph you want to use to best represent your data.
- **Graph example** Shows an example of the graph type.
- **Description box** Description of the graph type. If the description is too long for all of it to be seen, click on the Description box and the box will expand to show the complete description.

Figure 7-4 shows the first step of the Discoverer 3.1 Graph Wizard.

To select the graph type, use the following workflow:

1. Click on the graph type you want to use.
2. Click OK.

Graph Wizard Step 2: Selecting the Graph Format

After selecting the graph type, Discoverer will advance you to step 2 of the Graph Wizard—selecting the graph format. Discoverer gives you, in most cases, several

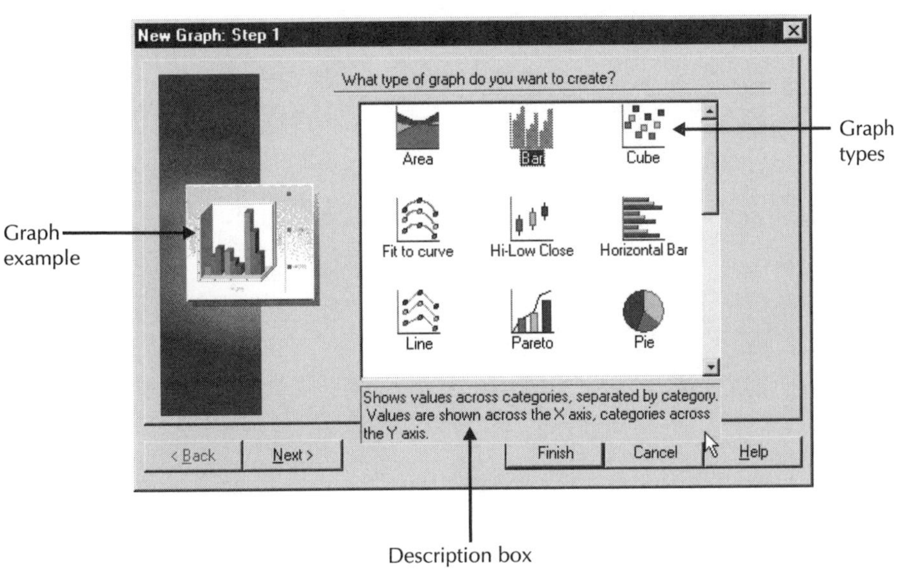

FIGURE 7-4. *Step 1 of the Graph Wizard*

format choices for the graph type you have selected. The features of the Graph Wizard step 2 are as follows:

- **Graph format style** Select the type of graph you want to use to best represent your data.
- **Graph format style example** Shows an example of the graph with the format selected.
- **Description box** Description of the graph format style. If the description is too long for all of it to be seen, click on the Description box and the box will expand to show the complete description.

Figure 7-5 shows the second step of the Discoverer 3.1 Graph Wizard. To select the graph type, use the following workflow:

1. Click on the graph format style you want to use.
2. Click OK.

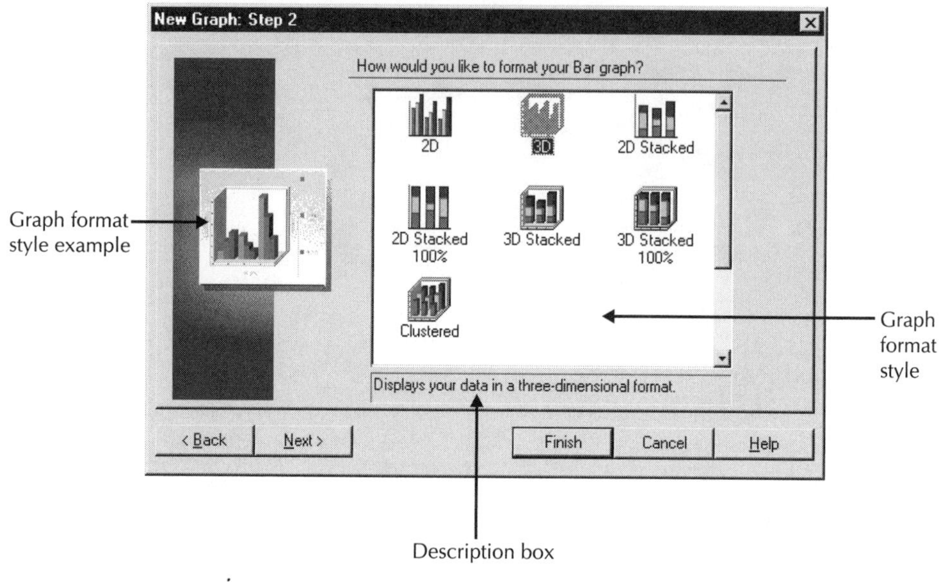

FIGURE 7-5. *Step 2 of the Graph Wizard*

Graph Wizard Step 3: Titles and Legends

The next step is to add titles to your graph. You can have titles on the top, bottom, and both sides. You can also format the font type, style, size, and color, as well as using underline or strikeout effects. Step 2 also gives you an opportunity to show the graph legend and to format it, and format the fonts for the X and Y axes. The features of the Graph Wizard step 3 are as follows:

- **Titles** Add titles for top, left, bottom, and right of the graph.
- **Legend** Select to show and format the font of the legend.
- **Axis** Format the font of the X and Y axes.

Figure 7-6 shows the third step of the Discoverer 3.1 Graph Wizard.

To add titles, a legend, and format the font of the X and Y axes of your graph, use the following workflow:

1. Decide where you want to add titles to your graph.
2. Click in the field for the title you want to add and format.

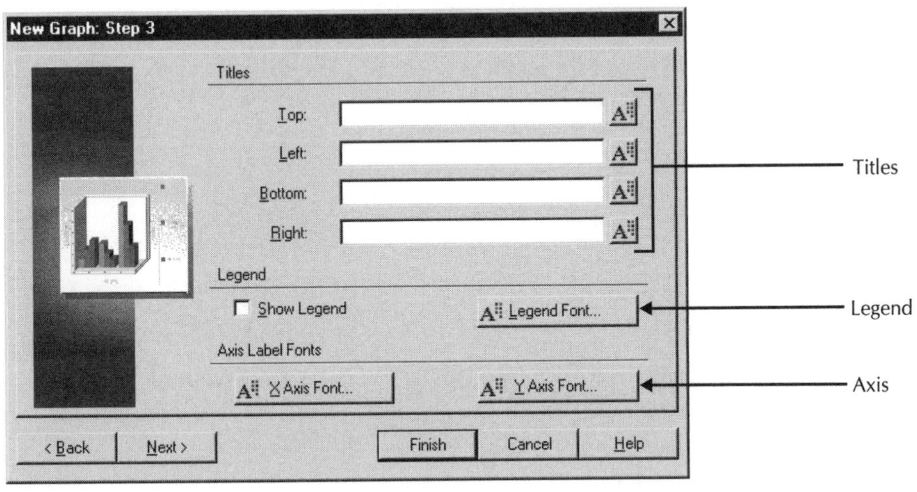

FIGURE 7-6. *Step 3 of the Graph Wizard*

3. Type in the title.
4. Click the Font button to the right of the title.

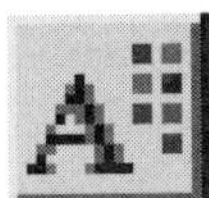

5. Select the font type, style, size, color, and effect.
6. Click OK.
7. Decide whether or not you want to show the graph legend.
8. Format the legend using the same method described above.
9. Format the X and Y axes.
10. Click OK.

Graph Wizard Step 4: Adding Special Graph Options

Step 4 of the Graph Wizard allows you to change some options of the graph. This is where you can either accept the default scale Discoverer chooses or create your own. You can also add decimal places to the scale. The features of the Graph Wizard step 3 are as follows:

- **Y axis scale** Use the scale created by Discoverer, or type in the scale of your choice.
- **Decimals** Use this to determine how many decimal places will be displayed.
- **Show gridlines** Click to show horizontal or vertical gridlines.
- **Graph series by** Select to use the data in the columns or rows of the workbook to be the X axis for the graph.

Figure 7-7 shows the fourth step of the Discoverer 3.1 Graph Wizard. To format the options of your graph, use the following workflow:

1. Decide if you want to create your own scale or use the default set by Discoverer.
2. If you choose to change the scale, click in the Maximum field and type the highest number you want to use for the scale.
3. Click in the Minimum field and type the lowest number you want to use for the scale.
4. To add decimal places to the scale, click in the Decimal field and type the number of decimal places you want to use for the scale.
5. Decide if you want to add gridlines to your graph and click in the check box for the gridlines you want to use—vertical, horizontal, or both.
6. Decide whether you want to use the data from the worksheet's rows or columns for the X axis and select the corresponding radio button. If you are not sure which series you want to use, a hint is displayed below the radio buttons.
7. Click Finish.

You have completed creating your graph and Discoverer will close the Graph Wizard and open the Graph window (see Figure 7-3).

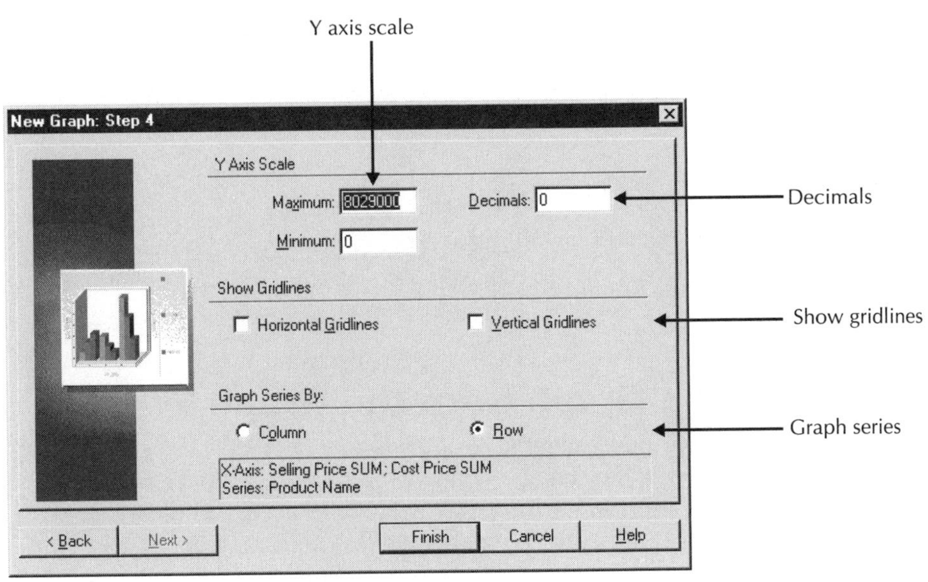

FIGURE 7-7. *Step 4 of the Graph Wizard*

Modifying a Graph

After the graph has been created, it is easily modified. The Modify Graph dialog box is viewed one of two ways. If you open it from the worksheet, it is displayed in exactly the same format as the Graph Wizard. If, however, you open it from the graph itself, it opens as a four-tab form with the same steps as the Graph Wizard. Each of the tabbed dialog boxes is used in exactly the same way as the four steps of the wizard.

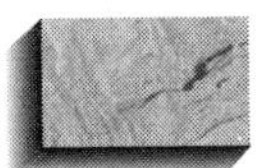

NOTE
Remember that you do not need to do anything for the data to be updated with changes to the query. Discoverer does this for you automatically.

To Modify the Graph from the Worksheet

When the graph is closed, you can use either the Graph button on the toolbar or use the menu bar. If you use the menu bar, you will notice that only two options are available to you: Show and Edit Graph. The rest of the items are available only when the graph is open and the Graph window is maximized. After you modify the graph, the Graph window will open.

To open the Modify Graph dialog box from the worksheet, use the following workflow:

1. Click on Graph | Edit Graph.
2. Follow the instructions given in the previous section—"The Graph Wizard."
3. After making the desired modifications, click OK.

To Modify the Graph from the Graph Window

It is easier to modify the graph with the Graph window open because you have the toolbar available. Many of the changes you will want to make can be made from the toolbar. With the Graph window open, you can also access all of the options on the Graph drop-down list on the menu bar. Unless the Graph window is maximized, it seems as though the menu bar is not available to you, but it is. Click on the menu bar of the worksheet and it will become active, leaving the Graph window open in the front, in an inactive state.

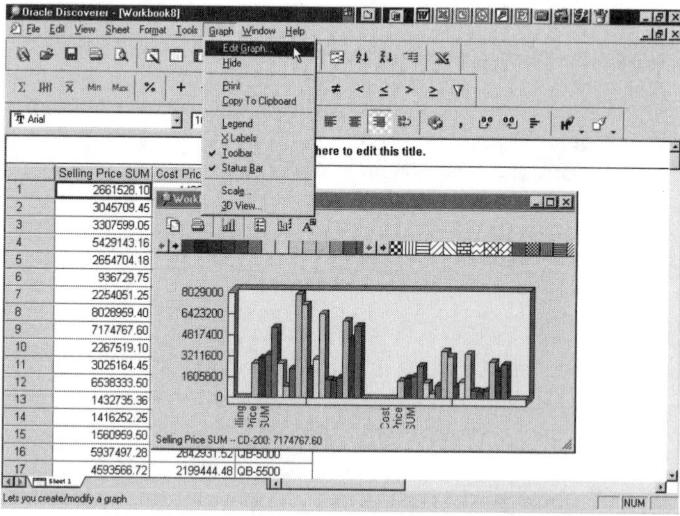

You can also access all of the same options by left-clicking in the Graph window. This opens a pop-up list of options for working with the graph.

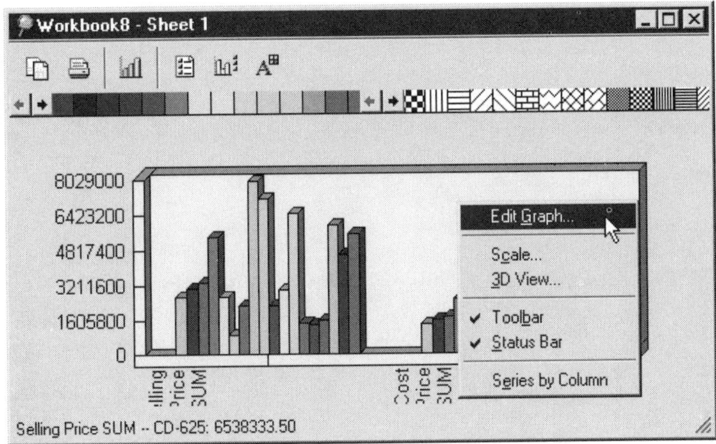

To open the Modify Graph dialog box from the Graph window, use the following workflow:

1. From the menu bar click on Graph | Edit Graph or right-click on the Graph window and select Edit Graph.
2. Select the tab you want to use.
3. Follow the instructions given in the previous section—"The Graph Wizard."
4. After making the desired modifications, click OK.

Resizing the Graph

You will, in most cases, need to resize the graph or some of its components. Most of the graph elements can be resized.

Figure 7-8 shows the resizable elements of a graph.

To resize a graph element, use the following workflow:

1. Click on the resizable element until the mouse pointer changes to a double-headed arrow.
2. Drag until the desired size is obtained.

Modifying the Scale

Although you set the scale in the Modify Graph dialog box, there is a separate dialog box that allows for the setting of more options. Along with minimum and

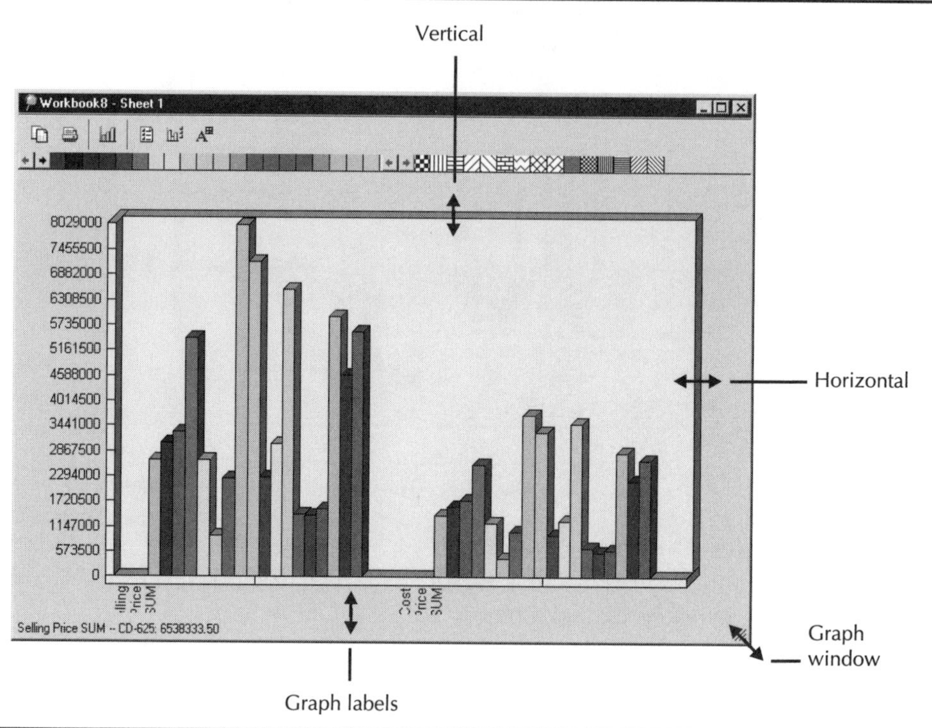

FIGURE 7-8. *The resizable elements of a graph*

maximum, you can also set the scale unit. For example, if you are analyzing sales based on units sold, and you want a graph that shows sales in thousands of units, you should set the scale unit to one thousand. This is equally effective for showing dollar values in the millions. Simply set the scale unit to one million and you will reduce the size of the numbers on the Y axis, while still showing the relationship of the data. The number of the scale is shown in the upper-left corner of the Graph window as a fraction, such as 1/1000 for setting the scale unit to one thousand.

Discoverer sets the increments between the numbers on the Y axis based upon the lowest and highest number being analyzed. The increments are divided equally and will change automatically when the query updates. By choosing Fixed instead and selecting a number, you can create smaller or larger increments. Be careful when choosing, however; if you choose too large a number, the gaps between increments may be so small you might not be able to see them all. If you make the increment too small, it may be difficult to effectively analyze the data.

One other thing you can do in the Scale and Numbers dialog box is to change the scale from linear to logarithmic. We recommend leaving the setting at linear unless you are analyzing scientific or complex mathematical formulas.

To open the Scale and Numbers dialog box from the Graph window, use the following workflow:

1. From the menu bar, click on Graph | Scale or right-click on the Graph window and select Scale.

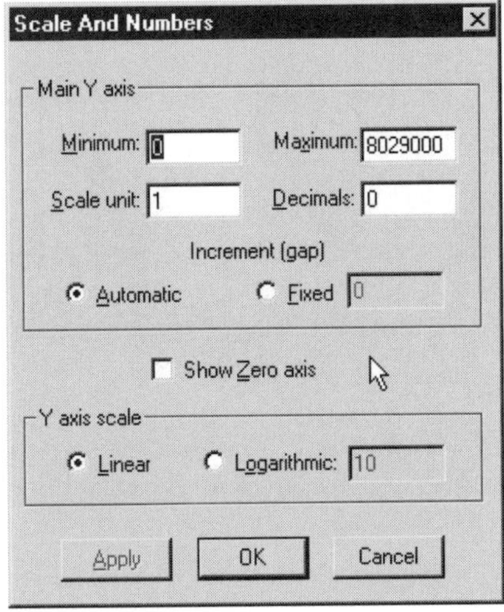

2. Make the modifications desired.
3. Click OK.

Changing Colors

After the graph is created, use the color and pattern section of the toolbar to change colors. Discoverer uses a drag-and-drop system for changing colors and patterns.

To change a color or pattern on the graph, use the following workflow:

1. Click on the color or pattern you want to use.
2. Hold down the mouse button until the mouse pointer changes to a paint can.

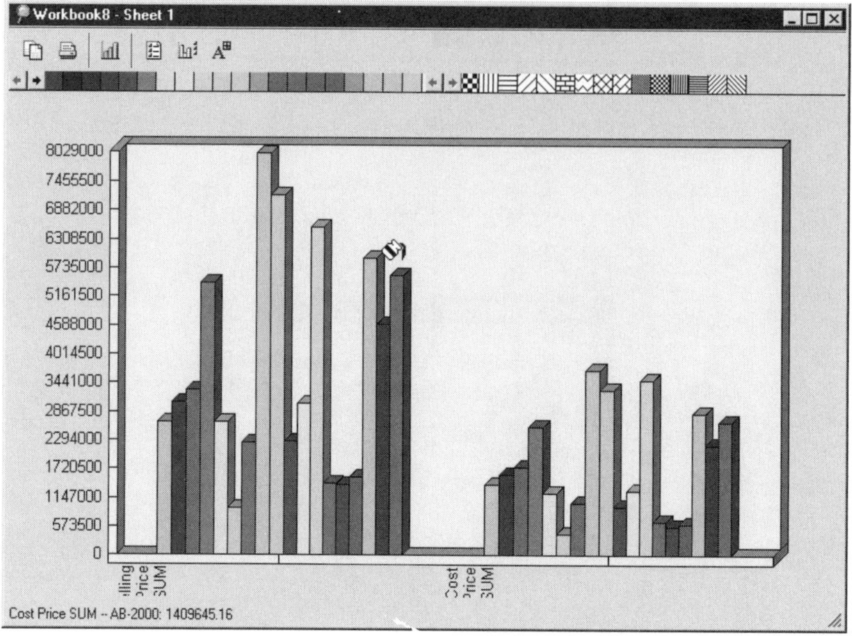

3. Drag the paint can (mouse pointer) to the data on the graph you want to change.
4. Release the mouse button.

Using Pull-Outs

When using a pie or doughnut type of graph, you can "pull out" one or more sections of the graph. Do this to emphasize certain data, such as the highest and lowest sales regions or Q-1 for the past 3 years.

To pull out an element on a pie or doughnut graph, use the following workflow:

1. Click on the data section of the pie you want to pull out.
2. Drag it away from the center of the graph.
3. Continue the steps above until you have pulled out all of the data you want to emphasize. This is shown in the following illustration:

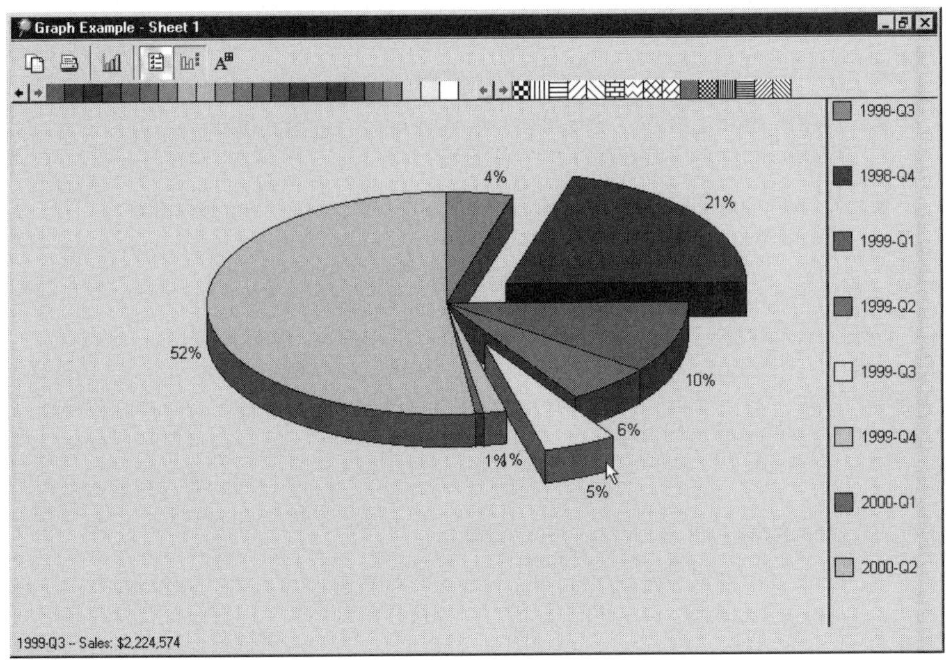

Modifying 3D Effects

When you select the type and format for the graph in the wizard, you have limited control over the formatting. Some of the graph types have one or more 3D formatting options. Using 3D formatting can add interest and character to a graph, and most graph types default to a 3D format. If you choose to use a 3D format, you can modify it after you have finished creating the graph with the 3D View Properties dialog box. The options available include changing the angle of the graph, applying a full 3D view, and making the graph deeper or more shallow.

To open the 3D View Properties dialog box, click on Graph | 3D View or right-click on the graph and click on 3D View. The box contains the following features:

- **3D check box** Applies standard 3D effects.
- **Full 3D view check box** Adds full 3D effects.
- **Shadow check box** Adds or removes shadows in the graph.

- **X Angle box** Changes the X axis angle.
- **Y Angle box** Changes the Y axis angle.
- **Depth sliding scale** Slide this scale to increase and decrease the depth of the 3D effects.
- **X and Y axes diagram** Drag the dots to change the angle of the X and Y axes.

Figure 7-9 shows the 3D View Properties dialog box.

Oracle makes an excellent recommendation when working with the 3D View Properties dialog box. Write down all of the settings before you begin to modify the 3D effect so you can return them to the default if you wish. Then you are free to experiment with different rotations and angles.

To change the 3D effects of a graph, use the following workflow:

1. Check the Full 3D View check box.
2. Click and drag the dots on the X and Y axes diagram, the numbers in the X and Y Angle boxes will change as you do this.

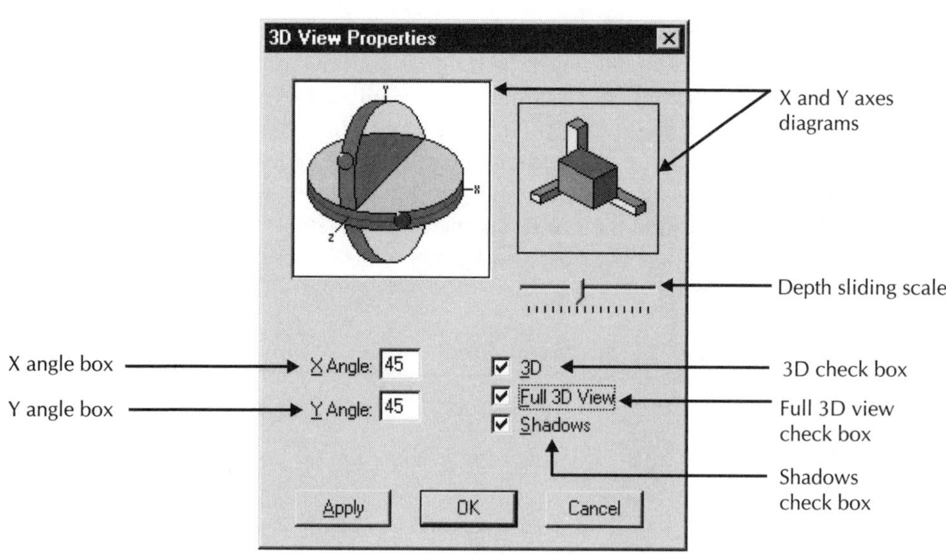

FIGURE 7-9. *The 3D View Properties dialog box*

3. Move the depth sliding scale to increase or decrease the depth of the graph.
4. Click on Apply to view the changes to the graph.
5. When done with the modifications, click OK.

Summary

In this chapter, you have learned how to use the Graph Wizard to create graphs based on your queries. You have learned to add interest and detail by adding titles, changing fonts, and adding legends and labels. You have been shown how to modify your graphs in a variety of ways, including using pull-outs, adding 3D effects, and changing the scale of the Y axis.

Graphs are an excellent way to represent your data visually. By using the Discoverer graph tool, you will add a new dimension to your queries.

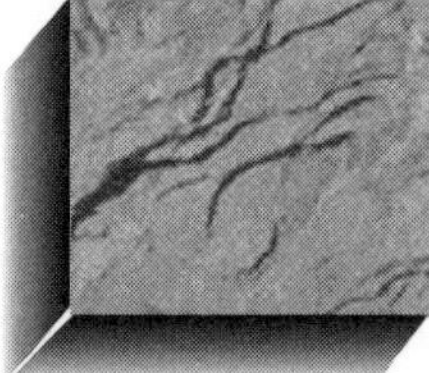

CHAPTER 8

Turning a Discoverer Query into a Report

It may seem premature at this point to show you how to create a report. However, we feel that once you have a working query, you should know how to turn it into a report. In the coming chapters, you will learn more advanced Discoverer techniques on building bigger and better queries. As you do, the lessons you learn here will enable you to create reports based upon those queries.

A Discoverer report is simply a well-formatted query. There is no wizard to guide you, or button to click, that will magically turn your query into a stunning printable report. You have a bit of work to do, but we think it is fun to format reports!

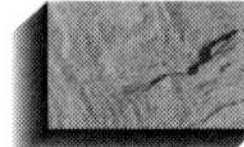

3*i* NOTE

*Since you have little control over formatting in 3*i*, we don't feel you can create a good report using it. If you create a report in 3.1, you can print it from 3*i*; however, it will display the original headers and footer.*

Report aesthetics are all-important. If you present your report in a logical order, using meaningful business-friendly column names and fonts that are pleasing to the eye, you are well on the way towards having your report accepted by those who will read it. Sloppy reports with bad formatting, misspelled column names, and illogical ordering invite criticism such as "If he or she can't even give me a report with a good layout, maybe I should get someone to double-check the figures." A well-written report induces confidence in the author.

Many companies have a standard for reporting. If your company is one of those that do have a standard, it is important to learn it and use it in your reports. It is possible, however, that there is no established standard. If this is the case, you may be the one that introduces such a standard to your company.

Avoid using frilly or unusual fonts. Times New Roman and Arial are normal default fonts for a reason. They are easy to read and pleasing to the eye. Also, adding too much detail to headers and footers, or using too many different colors, can distract from the data. The old adage "keep it simple, stupid" is a good one to adopt in reporting.

We have already covered the steps for creating and formatting titles, column headings, widths, and colors, and changing fonts in the data, so we will not repeat them here. These formatting steps have been added to the workflow to give you an idea of where to do them if they were not done as the query was created. Many queries are around for a long time just waiting to become a report, and so have a good deal of the formatting already done. We call these "wish queries" because they are queries that wish they were reports, or, in more likelihood, there is someone who is saying, "I wish I had a report that did this or answered that" when there is already a query that does. It simply needs to be turned into a printable report.

In this chapter, you will learn a workflow that will prepare your queries to be turned into reports. You will learn how to format the report for printing, format the sheet, headers, footers, and margins, and format the table options to determine if the printable report will have gridlines or not, and how to insert page breaks. We will show you how to use the Page Setup feature to give you greater flexibility in how your pages will print. We will also teach you to use the Print Preview feature of Discoverer as a tool for fine-tuning the report.

Discoverer has the ability to export reports into other applications. You will be shown the steps to follow for exporting your reports as spreadsheets, HTML, and text files.

A Workflow for Building Reports

Although you have already been taught the basic concepts included in the reports workflow, we offer them here to help you save time and unneeded effort in report building. The workflow ensures that you perform your formatting in the right order, so you don't need to do the same thing twice. For example, if you format the width of your columns and then rename them, the column might not be wide enough to accommodate the new name and you will need to format the width again. This is a waste of time. Thus, by following the workflow, you can avoid duplication of effort.

Included in the workflow are reminders on when to save your query. It may seem elementary, but we feel that there are good times to save based upon changes you have made to your report. It might also be a good idea for you to save your query by some other name as a backup in case you get carried away and want to begin again from the base query.

Report Workflow

Use the following workflow to begin turning a query into a report:

1. Create a working query that avoids the "Twilight Zone."
2. Rearrange the columns in the query and move to the Page Items those columns that have the same data repeated in every row.
3. Decide whether any columns could be better displayed on their own sheet and move these also to the Page Items (using Page Items will be discussed in more detail when we explain analysis in Chapter 9).
4. Rename any item that does not have a meaningful name.
5. Adjust column widths.
6. Save the query.

7. Refine temporary conditions and create new ones to select only the data from the database that you want to use in the final report—if you make a mistake, you can always reload from the saved copy. Conditions should be refined, honed, and so forth as many times as needed. This step is also included in the analysis workflow that will be covered in detail in the next chapter.
8. Create any calculations that you need. This step adds or replaces data items that cannot be pulled in directly from the database. You may want to concatenate some items, create new items based on values in other columns or even replace difficult-to-understand codes with more meaningful values. This step is also included in the analysis workflow that will be covered in detail in the next chapter.
9. Save the query again.
10. Upon completion of your calculations, you should review the final arrangement of the columns. Even though you may have done an initial column order during step 2, now that you have added calculations you should make sure that these new items are also in the right place. In particular, you should place all items that will be sorted in the first columns, with the primary sort item in column 1 and so on.
11. Delete unwanted columns—yes, you can delete columns that have been used in calculations and in conditions, and the calculation or condition will still work. This step will be covered in Chapter 11 when we cover advanced queries.
12. Apply any sorting that you need. By this stage, your query should contain all of the database and calculated items that will be used to produce the final result, with all items in their correct order. You should now apply all of the sort criteria that will be used to make an understandable and presentable report.
13. Save the unfinished report.
14. Create subtotals and totals that you need. Having created a sort order, you should decide whether or not you need to include any subtotals and totals. These are an essential element if your report will be used for analysis. This step is also included in the analysis workflow that will be covered in detail in the next chapter.
15. Save the report.
16. Create and format a report title.

17. Format headings.
18. Format data.

If you have followed the above workflow, you are ready to do the following:

1. Format the report for printing.
2. Format the sheet, headers, footers, and margins.
3. Format the table options to determine if the printable report will have gridlines or not.

Formatting the Report for Printing

It may seem premature to begin with print setup, but we have a good reason to start here. There is not a place in the Page Setup dialog box to format the paper size, so it must be done in the Print Setup dialog box. Since you will be using Print Preview as a tool for fine-tuning the report before printing, it is essential that the paper size be set before moving on. We have also discovered that in the Print Setup dialog box, there are some performance issues in 3.1 that need to be covered to save you some frustration.

Print Setup in 3*i*

Because there is very little you can do as far as formatting is concerned in 3*i*, you are limited to printing the query as it is. There is not even a print preview so you can view how it will print. You can print reports developed in 3*i*, but they might not print exactly as they do in 3.1, because 3*i* is WYSIWYG and your report will print just as you see it on the screen. It will not display headers and footers that are created in 3.1, but instead adds the sheet number in the upper-right corner and the page number at the bottom in the center of the page.

When you press the Print button, the printer's Windows dialog box opens and allows you to set up printer properties such as page size and orientation. Use the page size that is most appropriate for the report, but you might need to guess since there is no Print Preview option.

There is a Print Wizard dialog box, but it is nothing to write home about. It is a one-screen dialog box that allows you to answer the following two questions:

- What do you want to print?

Here, you can select to print the sheet you are currently viewing or you can select to print all of the sheets in the workbook.

- What type of printing do you want to perform?

If you choose Supervised, you will be asked to resolve any issues that arise during the printing process.

If you choose Unsupervised, Discoverer will automatically run all queries before worksheets are printed and will ignore all alert messages.

You can also select to skip sheets with long-running queries. We are not sure what Oracle considers a long-running query, but if you are concerned about this, select the box and later print the sheets that don't print with the others on their own.

The Print Wizard is shown in the following illustration.

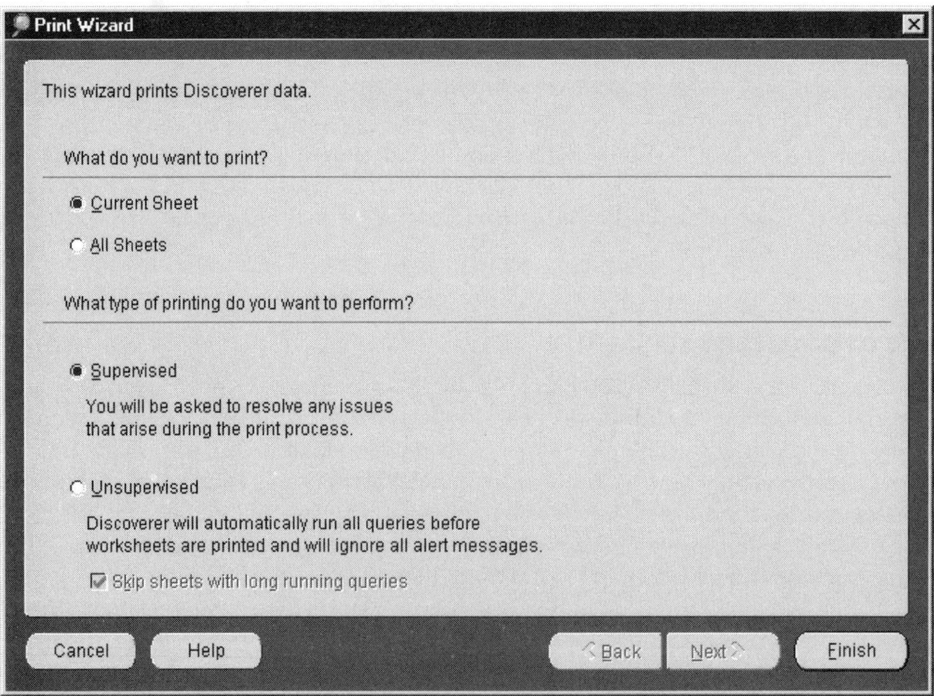

To print using the Print Wizard, use the following workflow:

1. Click File | Print on the menu bar.
2. Make your selections.
3. When you are done making your selections, click Finish.

4. The Windows Print dialog box will open.

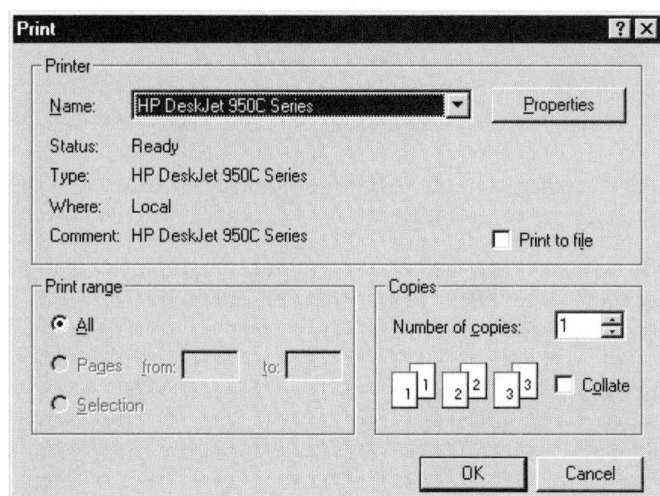

5. Click Properties.
6. Select the correct paper size and any other properties that you might want from your printer.
7. Click OK.
8. Make any appropriate selections from the Print dialog box.
9. Click OK.

To print using the Print button, use the following workflow:

1. Click the Print button.
2. The Windows Print dialog box will open.
3. Click Properties.
4. Select the correct paper size and any other properties that you might want from your printer.
5. Click OK.
6. Make any appropriate selections from the Print dialog box.
7. Click OK.

Print Setup in 3.1

You have a good deal more flexibility in creating and printing your reports in 3.1; however, it has no Print Wizard. When you click the Print button, be prepared for your report to print, because you will not be prompted in any way.

To prepare your report for printing, use the following workflow:

1. Select File | Print, and the Windows Print dialog box will open. Here, you have a standard print setup.
2. Select the printer that will be used to print the report. It is important to use the correct printer because they all print differently.
3. Set the print range.
4. Select the number of copies.
5. Click the Properties button. This opens the Printer Setup window. Depending upon the printer you have, you will have different setup options. There are usually several tabs. The ones that we are concerned with here are the orientation and paper size.
6. Set the paper size that you feel will best display your report.
7. Set the orientation that will best suit the layout of your report.
8. Click OK, and the Properties dialog box closes, taking you back to the Print dialog box.

   This is where it becomes a little tricky. You have set up your paper size and orientation, but are not ready to print your report. If you are like us, we expected, when we clicked on OK, that our property selections had been saved. This is not the case. If you click on Cancel at this point, the paper size and orientation, as well as any other changes you made, will return to what they were before you started. You must click on OK from the Print dialog box as well as the Properties box to save your print setup, thus causing your print job to run.

   Your report is not ready to print, so you might want to do what we did, and turn off the printer if possible. If your computer is slow enough, you might be able to hit the Cancel button in time. Or, if your printer is slow, you can open the Print Queue window and cancel it there. Of course, another possibility is to simply let it print and see what your preliminary output is.
9. Click OK.

Page Setup

When creating a report in Discoverer, you have many of the same page setup options as some familiar word processors and spreadsheets. You can set page margins, add headers and footers, change the orientation from portrait to landscaped, as well as set up print features.

3*i* NOTE
*Page setup features are not available in Discoverer 3*i.

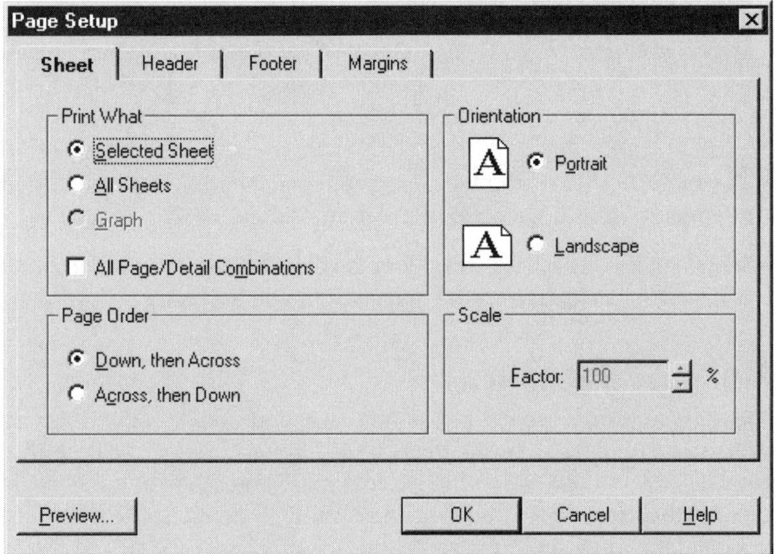

Discoverer provides a Page Setup dialog box that has four tabs; one each for setting up the Sheet, setting up the Header, setting up the Footer, and a fourth tab for setting up Margins.

None of the functions of the Page Setup dialog box are available on the formatting bar.

To open the Page Setup dialog box, click on File | Page Setup.

Sheet

The Sheet tab is divided into four sections:

- **Print What** In this area, you can select whether to print only the Selected Sheet (the sheet you are working on), All Sheets in the workbook, and any Graphs you have included in the workbook.

There is also a selection box you can check to show All Page Detail/Combinations. If your worksheet includes page detail, selecting this will print all combinations available. For example, say the page detail is Year with 1998, 1999, and 2000 in the drop-down list, but only 1999 is showing in the worksheet. If you check this box, all three years will print.

- **Page Order** This area allows you to determine the order the pages will print when the data on the worksheet is too large to print on one page. For example; if the worksheet is twelve columns wide, but only eight columns will fit on a page, using the default, "Down, then Across", will print all pages with the first eight columns first and then the pages with the remaining four columns.

The second option is "Across, then Down". We prefer this option, because it prints each page with the first eight columns followed immediately by a page with the remaining four columns, thus keeping all of the items together.

- **Orientation** Here, you will select whether to print in Portrait or Landscape orientation (select the same orientation used in the Print setup).
- **Scale** In this area, you can select to scale the report so it will fit better on to a page. This feature is only available if you are using a PostScript printer.

Header and Footers

Headers and footers are a great way to add to a report detail that will repeat on each page, such as page numbers, or the date the report was printed, or even the name of the report's author. In Discoverer, the Header and Footer tabs of the Page Setup dialog box function in exactly the same way. We will demonstrate the steps for creating a header and footer at the same time.

The first time you use these screens, the Available Headers or Available Footers list will show "none." As you create headers and footers, you can add them to the list of available headers and footers. Thus you can use the same ones each time to create continuity and consistency in your report writing.

There is also an Insert button. Use this button to insert codes for items such as date, time, file name, and location. It is a good idea to place these codes in the same locations each time you use them. Those who read your reports will appreciate the continuity and find your reports easier to navigate than if you use a variety of formats. You can also add a line between your header and the body of the report. The Line button allows you to select from predefined line widths. Play with these options, look at other reports that you find attractive and easy to read, and then adapt them to your own reports. Headers and footers are an excellent way to add distinction to your reporting.

The Header and Footer tabs contain:

- **Available Headers** or **Footers** A drop-down list of available headers or footers
- **Add & Remove** Two buttons used to add and remove headers or footers
- **Line Width** A drop-down box to set the line width that separates the header or footer from the body of the report
- **Insert** A drop-down button used to insert predefined codes
- **Font** Opens the Fonts dialog box to allow formatting of the header or footer
- **Left Section**, **Center Section**, **Right Section** Sections where you create the header or footer
- **Preview** A button to see a print preview of the report

The illustration below shows the Header tab of the Page Setup dialog box. Remember that the Header and Footer tabs are identical in appearance and functionality.

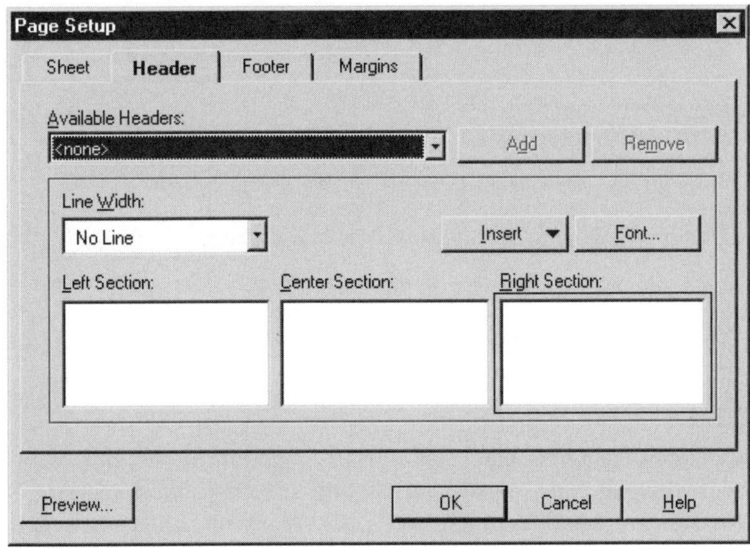

To create a header or footer, use the following workflow:

1. Click the Header or Footer tab.
2. Select an available header or footer or create your own.

3. To create your own header or footer, click in the Left, Center, or Right section.
4. Type in the text you want, or use the Insert drop-down button as seen in the illustration below to select from predefined codes.

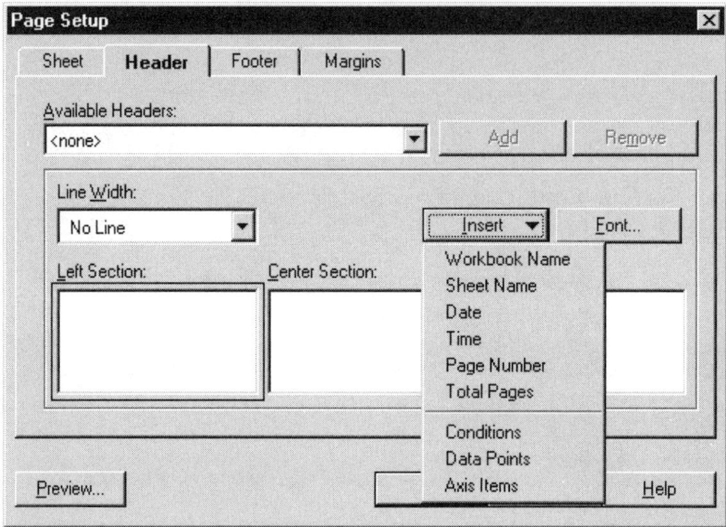

5. Format the font type, size, and color.
6. Select a line width, if desired.
7. Click on Preview to see the report as it will print.
8. Make any adjustments to the header or footer.
9. When you are satisfied with the header or footer, click OK.

Margins

Adjusting margins is a good way to give you added control over how your report will print. The default margins are 1 inch for the top and bottom margins and .75 inch for the side margins. This might work for you if you have a small report, but for larger reports, some fudging may be in order. There are times the data is just a wee bit too much for a good page layout, and by adjusting the margins you can get it all on one page—or at least get the data to break better.

Use some caution when adjusting margins. It is possible to make them so small that data will actually print over the header or footer. Most printers also have a printable area, and you could lose some data from the printout where the printer could not print.

Another formatting option you have in the Margins tab is whether or not to center the report on the page. You can select horizontally or vertically or both. You will probably always want to center the report horizontally. This will give a nice look to the report; however, vertical centering should be used sparingly. Sometimes the report is small and vertical centering will bring the report too far down the page.

The Margins tab has the following sections:

- **Margins** Four up/down boxes used to adjust the margins
- **From Edge** Two up/down boxes used to adjust how far from the edge of the page the header or footer will print
- **Center on Page** Two check boxes used to center the report on the page horizontally or vertically
- **Preview** A button to see a print preview of the report

To set the margins, use the following workflow:

1. From the Page Setup dialog box, click the Margins tab.
2. Use the up/down buttons in the Margins section to set the margins, or type in the margin you want in inches.
3. Use the up/down buttons in the From Edge section to determine how far from the edge of the paper you want the margins to print. Be careful to not set these larger or the same as the margins, and do not set them outside your printer's printable area.
4. Center the report on the page horizontally, vertically, or both.
5. Click on Preview to see the report as it will print.
6. Make any adjustments to the margins.
7. When you are satisfied with the margins, click OK.

Before moving on to the next section, you might want to revisit column widths at this time. It is possible that by slightly widening or narrowing the column widths, your report will fit better on the page. By going back and forth between column widths and margin sizes, you can fine-tune the report layout. You might even want to take another look at font sizes to see if your report will fit better on the page. Use Print Preview often as you prepare your report to print.

Table and Crosstab Gridlines

Remembering that Discoverer is WYSIWYG—you will need to format the table itself if you don't want to see gridlines printed in your report. This is done through the Options dialog box. The Options dialog box defaults to the Table or Crosstab tab, depending upon the type of query you are working with.

We are disappointed that the gridlines cannot be turned off for printing only, as you can in Excel. Most of us like to work on a table with the gridlines showing, but turned off for a final report. It is a nuisance to have to change back and forth. We hope this functionality will be incorporated into a future release of Discoverer.

If you chose to leave the gridlines on for your report, you might want to change the gridline color. Be careful with this type of formatting and be sure that it is not just pretty, but actually helps display the data in a meaningful way.

Table Gridlines

The following illustration shows the table tab of the Options dialog box:

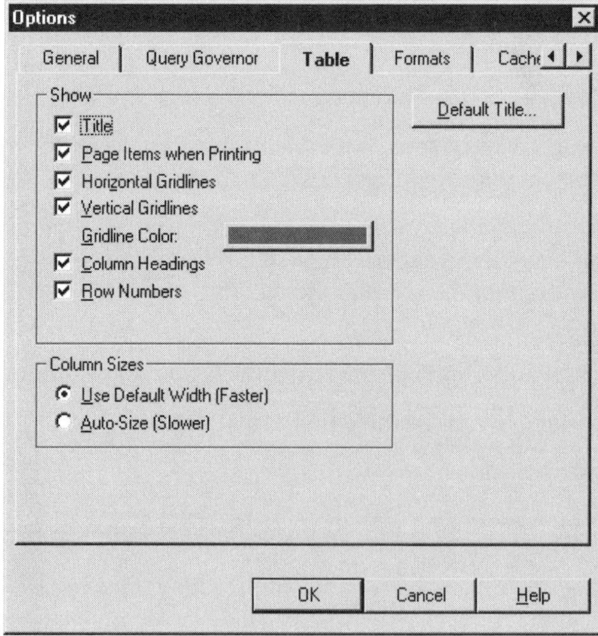

To change the gridline properties of a table, use the following workflow:

1. From the menu bar, select Tools | Options.
2. Deselect the Horizontal and Vertical gridlines as desired.

3. If leaving the gridlines on, but changing the gridline color, click the box to the right of Gridline Color.
4. Select a new color from the color selection box.
5. Click OK.

Crosstab Gridlines

Crosstabs have two more choices associated with the crosstab. You can also choose whether or not to show the axis item labels and whether to show axis gridlines in 3D. Additionally, you can choose the style of your crosstab here. You can choose to show crosstab labels inline (labels stacked on top of each other) or in an outline format (staggered labels and data items). The latter of the two requires more space, so if the size of the report is a concern, you might try inline. Work with it until you have it in a format that is easy to read and aesthetically pleasing. The illustrations below show an inline and an outline crosstab.

			Percent Order Qty SUM			
		Status	CANCELLED	HOLD	OPEN	SHIPPED
Channel	Product					
EXTERNAL	QB-1000		13.419%	0.003%	4.080%	82.497%
	QB-2000		12.746%		3.222%	84.031%
	QB-3000		2.904%		33.328%	63.768%
	QB-5000		3.742%	0.296%	24.835%	71.127%
	QB-5500		0.877%		5.980%	93.143%
	QB-6000		7.294%	0.213%	8.885%	83.608%
INTERNET	QB-1000		28.733%		31.712%	39.556%
	QB-2000			0.321%	41.572%	58.107%
	QB-3000		48.898%		13.045%	38.057%
	QB-5000		1.873%	0.002%	69.847%	28.279%
	QB-5500		5.179%	0.216%	30.586%	64.019%
	QB-6000		0.155%	0.002%	66.805%	33.038%
Sum						

		Percent Order Qty SUM			
	Status	CANCELLED	HOLD	OPEN	SHIPPED
C Product					
EXTERNAL		5.180%	0.137%	14.761%	79.922%
QB-1000		13.419%	0.003%	4.080%	82.497%
QB-2000		12.746%		3.222%	84.031%
QB-3000		2.904%		33.328%	63.768%
QB-5000		3.742%	0.296%	24.835%	71.127%
QB-5500		0.877%		5.980%	93.143%
QB-6000		7.294%	0.213%	8.885%	83.608%
INTERNET		7.060%	0.102%	49.770%	43.068%
QB-1000		28.733%		31.712%	39.556%
QB-2000			0.321%	41.572%	58.107%
QB-3000		48.898%		13.045%	38.057%
QB-5000		1.873%	0.002%	69.847%	28.279%
QB-5500		5.179%	0.216%	30.586%	64.019%
QB-6000		0.155%	0.002%	66.805%	33.038%

The following illustration shows the Crosstab tab of the Options dialog box.

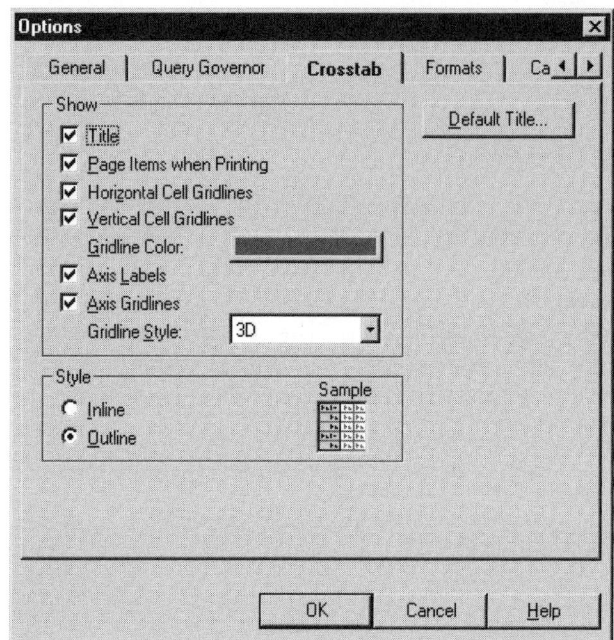

To change the gridline properties of a crosstab, use the following workflow:

1. From the menu bar, select Tools | Options.
2. Deselect the Horizontal and Vertical gridlines as desired.
3. If leaving the gridlines on, but changing the gridline color, click the box to the right of Gridline Color.
4. Select a new color from the color selection box.
5. Check the Axis Labels box if you want the names of the axis items to appear in your report.
6. Check Axis Gridlines if you want gridlines to appear around the axis items.
7. Select the crosstab Style.
8. Click OK.

Inserting Page Breaks in Tables (Sorry, No Page Breaks in Crosstabs)

Page breaks are useful when you want to add logical breaks between data items. For example, your reports show the sales for all of your regions. You want a page break between each of the regions. By group sorting by region in your report, you can also add a page break between them. When you add a page break to items that cover more than one page, the column headings repeat as well as the item name at the top of each column.

To create a page break, follow the workflow below:

1. Click Tools | Sort.
2. Click the item you want to group sort and create a page break on.
3. From the Group drop-down list, select Page Break.
4. Click OK.

Exporting Your Report to Another Application

Once you have a great report formatted and ready for printing, you might also want to send the file to someone who does not have Discoverer. Discoverer files can be exported in many different formats, the most common being Excel, HTML, Comma Separator Delimited (CSV), and Tab Delimited (Text).

Excel is an excellent spreadsheet program, and many companies use it. However, with some experimentation, we have discovered that exporting to Excel can be extremely time-consuming. It is recommended that instead of exporting into an Excel format, you use CSV that Excel imports easily. This method will save you time and frustration.

HTML is also a popular format and creates files that anyone with a browser can view. The downside, of course, is that the data can only be viewed in HTML and not worked with. Discoverer Viewer result sets are displayed as HTML and allow users to open predefined queries and perform some limited analysis, such as drilling down a hierarchy. HTML data can, however, be copied and pasted into a spreadsheet or word processor. The data will have to be reformatted, but it can be worked with.

To export a Discoverer report to another application, use the following workflow:

1. Click on File | Export. This opens the Export dialog box shown here:

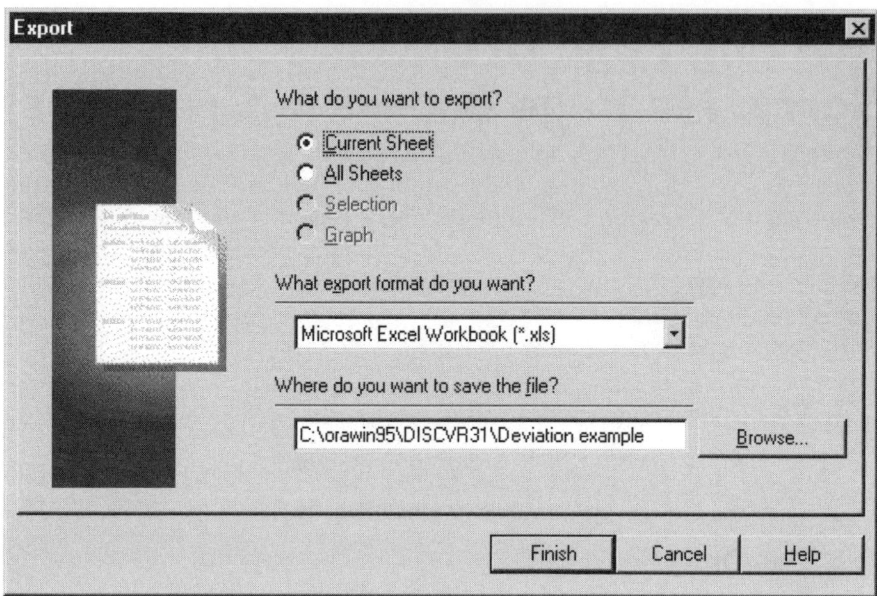

2. Select the part of the workbook you want to export. If you want to export a graph, the graph needs to be the active window and will export as a wmf file.
3. From the drop-down list, select the format you want to export the file in.
4. Give the location you want to save the file to.
5. Click Finish. The file is now ready to be used in another application.

Summary

In this chapter, you have learned a workflow to use in preparing your queries to be turned into reports. You have been shown how to format the report for printing, and how to format the sheet, headers, footers, and margins. We have also shown you how to format the table options to determine if the printable report will have gridlines or not, and how to insert page breaks.

We have shown you how to use the Page Setup feature to give you greater flexibility in how your pages will print, as well as how to use the Print Preview feature of Discoverer as a tool for fine-tuning the report. You have also learned how to export reports into other application such as spreadsheets, HTML, and as text files.

CHAPTER 9

Using Discoverer to Analyze Data

"Now, what I want is, facts... facts alone are wanted in life"
—Charles Dickens, *Hard Times*

here is an almost endless variety of possible combinations of facts in table and crosstab design, and it would be impossible for us to describe them all to you in this book. In fact, as we have explored the various permutations that Discoverer allows, we have come to the conclusion that we could almost write an entire book on just table layouts and their relationship with analysis.

Therefore, in this chapter, we will teach you how we go about analyzing data in Discoverer using basic and clear-cut methods. As you become more skilled in the use of the product, you should begin experimenting and see how it will work for you.

In this chapter, you will learn the meaning of analysis and the four basic types of analysis: statistical, classification, deviation, and trend. You will learn how to perform these types of analysis, using Discoverer 3.1 and 3*i*. We will introduce an analysis workflow that we hope will help you go about analyzing your data more effectively.

We will show you more ways to access the tools that were introduced to you in Chapters 4 and 5. You will be introduced to the analysis toolbar and shown how to cut your analysis time by using its terrific features. In this chapter, we will talk about analysis and statistics and describe some of the fundamentals involved.

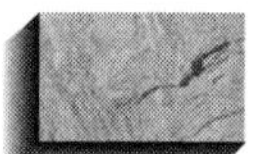

3*i* NOTE
*Unfortunately, Discoverer 3*i *does not have an analysis bar and, therefore, the section on the analysis toolbar of this chapter will not be applicable if you only have the Web version.*

What Is Analysis?

Analysis provides the capability to discover new and meaningful information by using existing data. Analysis techniques massage the data in some way, by either constraining the initial selection by restricting the data to just a subset of what is available, or by reducing the final output to make it more meaningful. Facts are taken, then dissected, compared, rearranged, put back together, and finally reported.

Having decided upon the data items you need for your query, and having ordered those items into columns and rows and formatted them, you have completed the first part of your task. However, before you can turn your query into a report, you need to decide whether any analysis of the data is required.

Think about what it is that your analysis is trying to do. Throughout this chapter on analysis, you must stay focused and remember to always keep in mind what question it is that you are trying to answer. If you do this, you will be visualizing at least a part of the final display, and already be anticipating what to do if the figures do not in fact produce the result you wanted.

Types of Analysis

The world of analysis is full of different methodologies and approaches. There are also many types of analysis techniques available to you, and we want to give you an understanding of four of them that we believe are most useful. They are as follows:

- Statistical analysis
- Classification analysis
- Deviation analysis
- Trend analysis

We will also enclose some ideas and examples from our own database to show you the results that can be obtained from these different analysis techniques. Full details on how to build these examples can be found at the end of this chapter.

Statistical Analysis

The statistical approach uses rules or conditions and is based on data relationships. Usually what you will end up with are statistics, but how are statistics derived? Online analytical processing (OLAP) is an example of this statistically oriented approach, and is one of the forms of analysis that Discoverer is particularly good at. An example of a statistical application may determine that all sales orders beginning with a 5 are regular sales orders, while orders beginning with a 7 are returns. By analyzing only the returns and determining that 18 percent of the sales orders begin with a 7, you can accurately state that 82 percent of sales orders are regular orders—without ever querying those orders that begin with 5.

There is a popular saying in England that "one could drive a bus through someone else's statistics." While this may sound somewhat exaggerated, in fact there is more than a grain of truth to this statement. Many statistics are produced to satisfy corporate or personal objectives. Perhaps someone is looking for data to prove that a particular product has sold exceptionally well, accidentally overlooking the fact that the product also had an exceptional number of returns. The end result of that analysis may have produced a set of statistics that do not tell the complete story.

For example, suppose you were asked to write a query that analyzed all of the sales for the past year, showing how each region had fared when compared to the other regions. It should be evident that your query needs to be constrained to just one year and so, adding a condition on this item will be the first technique you apply. Having constrained or filtered your query to only include the year in question, you would run the query and take a look at the output to decide what other analysis tools need to be applied. These rules are the building blocks for further analysis.

Let us therefore build the above query using our database. As the specification states, we need to include the year, the region, and the sales amount (the selling price). If we build this as a crosstab, we can place the region on the side axis and the year in the page axis. Finally, adding a percentage on the selling price makes the query look like what is shown in Figure 9-1.

As you can see in the example, the percentage of sales for Europe was 32.55 percent, which means that the sales for all other regions must be 77.45 percent. There is no need to add them up because by deduction this statistic must be true.

We know this example is very simple, but it is given just to show you how you can take one figure that you do know to derive another statistic that you do not.

Classification Analysis

The classification approach groups data according to some similarity in the data or based upon some derived commonality. Knowledge of your company—and more to the point, the database itself—can be an important string to your bow in this scenario. This background knowledge of how your data is being used can be a tremendous asset to helping you understand whether the classifications that you have determined are valid.

You can see that what we are implying is that you should use sorting and paging to manipulate your data. Moving the data around onscreen like this is another of the

Page Items: Year: FY1999

Region	Selling Price SUM	Percent Selling Price SUM
EUROPE	3303568.77	32.55%
FAR EAST	1197140.00	11.79%
NORTH AMERICA	4932897.65	48.60%
SOUTH AMERICA	716382.15	7.06%

FIGURE 9-1. *Statistical example—sales for 1999 based on region*

things that Discoverer does very well. Unless you change the selections or conditions, you can manipulate the data onscreen without any impact to the system. This is because once Discoverer has completed the base query, it stores all of the resulting data in memory, allowing you the pleasure of manipulating it to your heart's content—although probably not your manager's!

Let us show you what we mean. Figure 9-2 shows the cost price, selling price, and total amount of profit made in each quarter of 1999, by each product, with the query grouping the products by their respective product line.

By moving some of the items around, we can display exactly the same data using a completely different classification. In Figure 9-3, the same query has been manipulated to show the profit only for all products in all product lines.

See the section entitled "How to Build the Example Queries" at the end of this chapter for full instructions on how to construct and manipulate this query.

Deviation Analysis

In its simplest form, deviation analysis uses percentages and exceptions to the rule to identify areas for improvement. A series of numbers such as sales figures, electrical consumption, and attendance records are excellent types of data for this kind of analysis. To perform this analysis, you would work out a percentage of each item when compared to the total. Then you would apply an exception to identify those items that are deviating too high or too low.

Page Items: Product Line: MEGA-WIDGET

Product	Quarter	Cost Price	Selling Price	Profit
AB-2500	1999-Q1	36812.88	69505.80	32692.92
	1999-Q2	78419.88	148063.30	69643.42
	1999-Q3	63615.24	120110.90	56495.66
	1999-Q4	47196.00	89110.00	41914.00
CD-100	1999-Q1	262707.14	571066.65	308359.51
	1999-Q2	38096.60	82813.50	44716.90
	1999-Q3	241395.36	524739.60	283344.24
	1999-Q4	51406.50	111746.25	60339.75
CD-200	1999-Q1	274646.20	597019.50	322373.30
	1999-Q2	84195.08	183021.30	98826.22
	1999-Q3	120697.68	262369.80	141672.12
	1999-Q4	3219.88	6999.30	3779.42
CD-500	1999-Q1	68432.28	160648.95	92216.67
	1999-Q2	41557.60	97559.00	56001.40

FIGURE 9-2. *Classification example—profit by quarter of 1999, by product*

Page Items: Data Point: Profit

Product Line	Product	Quarter: 1999-Q1	1999-Q2	1999-Q3	1999-Q4
MEGA-WIDGET	AB-2500	32692.92	69643.42	56495.66	41914.00
	CD-100	308359.51	44716.90	283344.24	60339.75
	CD-200	322373.30	98826.22	141672.12	3779.42
	CD-500	92216.67	56001.40	41614.30	17017.00
	CD-550	94073.07	32053.84	23205.00	154.70
	CD-625	364051.60	233258.04	93251.72	41674.08
SUPER-WIDGET	AB-3000	55381.63	139275.81	62087.87	8272.50
	AVR-500	271605.63	88607.01	55214.94	21925.50
	AVR-550	53740.80	14741.40	44802.66	2276.52
	AVR-800	6712.68	19171.36	49010.00	67.60
	AVR-900	58384.95	20124.90	53268.45	12734.40
WONDER-WIDGET	AB-2000	23317.42	139110.36	43149.36	4412.00
	QB-1000	37515.93	25209.66	21365.70	933.00
	QB-2000	50913.28	39414.40	14238.00	45.20

FIGURE 9-3. *Classification example—profit by quarter for all product lines*

In Figure 9-4, we have analyzed the sales for all of Global Widgets products that begin with "QB", by status and channel. We wanted to know whether there was any difference between the channels. In particular, we wanted to analyze the percentage of orders shipped and cancelled, and see if there was anything for us to report. For us, a percentage shipped of 60 percent or more is considered acceptable, while cancellations greater than 20 percent are considered unacceptable. We know from experience that products that begin with "QB" are the highest sellers.

In Figure 9-4, we have taken the percentage of the order quantity for each status, by product and channel. The results surprised us, and only went to underline the benefit of doing this type of analysis. As you can see, all of our "QB" products in the External channel—that is, our normal non-Internet channel—have a percentage shipped of 63 percent or higher. Looking at the Internet channel, we were amazed to see that only one product, QB-5500, made the cut.

If you look at the report in more detail, you can see that we have a high percentage of open, nonshipped orders in the Internet channel. Looking further, you can see that we also have very high percentages of cancellations for two of our products (coincidentally from the Internet). These figures will make for an

		Percent Order Qty SUM			
	Status	CANCELLED	HOLD	OPEN	SHIPPED
Channel	Product				
EXTERNAL	QB-1000	13.419%	0.003%	4.080%	82.497%
	QB-2000	12.746%	0.000%	3.222%	84.031%
	QB-3000	2.904%	0.000%	33.328%	63.768%
	QB-5000	3.742%	0.296%	24.835%	71.127%
	QB-5500	0.877%	0.000%	5.980%	93.143%
	QB-6000	7.294%	0.213%	8.885%	83.608%
INTERNET	QB-1000	28.733%	0.000%	31.712%	39.556%
	QB-2000	0.000%	0.321%	41.572%	58.107%
	QB-3000	48.898%	0.000%	13.045%	38.057%
	QB-5000	1.873%	0.002%	69.847%	28.279%
	QB-5500	5.179%	0.216%	30.586%	64.019%
	QB-6000	0.155%	0.002%	66.805%	33.038%
Sum					

FIGURE 9-4. *Deviation example*

interesting discussion the next time we have a board meeting with the VP of Internet Sales!

See the section entitled "How to Build the Example Queries," at the end of this chapter, for full instructions on how to construct and manipulate this query.

Trend Analysis

Trend analysis, as the name suggests, looks for trends and makes assumptions or forecasts based on those trends. Many people today, either through lack of understanding or lack of available time, focus their reporting mainly on status and identifying problems. An example of a status report could be a list of orders shipped yesterday or the number of employees who came into work on time, while a problem report could be the list of orders that did not ship or the employees that did not get in on time. These reports are based on facts and figures within the database, and are obtained by constraining the data to look at a particular flag or status.

An organization that concentrates on status or problem reports will typically be in "fire-fighting" mode, reacting after the event to something that has already happened. By its very nature, this reactive form of reporting does not offer much in the way of trending or performance reporting—the latter being required if the organization is to establish guidelines to determine whether performance expectations are being met.

Let's look at one of the examples above and see if we can use trending to give us a better type of report. We will take the example of the late employees. While it is important to know how many were late, wouldn't it also be useful to know who was habitually late or whether a particular day—perhaps the Monday following a holiday—was more likely to have a higher rate of latecomers or absenteeism? By knowing these figures, you could easily extrapolate—that is, you can infer or estimate other values by projecting outwards from a known value or values.

If your company is in the business of selling products, one of the hardest things to do is to try and forecast how many of these products will be required each quarter. Traditionally, the company will turn to its sales force and ask each salesperson to submit a forecast, based on discussions with each person's customers. By looking back over time and comparing how products have actually sold, and comparing those with the forecast's received from the sales force, perhaps a better forecast could be made this time.

Now we'll try and build the example within Discoverer. Using a crosstab, we created a query to find total sales by district for each of our past quarters. We then added a percentage and obtained the results shown in Figure 9-5. As you can see, the trend shows that, on average, the NA North district has about 34 percent of sales in any one quarter, whereas the FE district has 15 percent, and the SA district around 9 percent.

Using the above information, we will take whatever sales have been forecast for these districts and extrapolate total quantities required for our factory. Therefore, if the NA North district sales force forecasts 210,000 during the next quarter, we can estimate that we need to have 617,640 products available altogether. Now, if the SA district forecasts 55,500, based on their average of 7 percent, this would produce a total requirement of 611,110 units. Finally, if the FE forecasts 92,500, this equates to 616,665 units. You can see that these three forecasts validate each other and we could issue an order for our factories to build 620,000 units.

		Percent Ship Qty SUM							
	Quarter	1998-Q3	1998-Q4	1999-Q1	1999-Q2	1999-Q3	1999-Q4	2000-Q1	2000-Q2
District									
EU-EAST			3%	2%	3%	1%	0%	0%	2%
EU-NORTH		20%	18%	21%	9%	20%	12%	5%	18%
EU-SOUTH		3%	13%	10%	20%	9%	13%	17%	13%
FE-ALL		27%	14%	14%	8%	10%	26%	9%	11%
NA-NORTH		30%	28%	34%	41%	35%	29%	44%	31%
NA-SOUTH		6%	16%	12%	10%	19%	15%	8%	17%
SA-ALL		14%	7%	7%	9%	5%	5%	17%	8%
Sum									

FIGURE 9-5. *Trend example—quarterly sales by district*

Let's now assume that our EU East district comes in with a forecast of 27,000 units. Based on their average of 1 percent, this would require a total of 2,700,000 units, an amount that is way out when compared to the other three districts. In this situation, we would probably ask our EU East sales department to recheck their forecast and come back with a reason why the sales should be that high. We would not just accept the forecast because, if we did, we would almost certainly end up with excess inventory at the end of the quarter.

Fundamentals of Analysis

Knowledge discovery is what most enterprises strive for, wish for, yet mostly dream about. In our opinion, not enough resources are being dedicated to finding out what information is available. Vast amounts of money are being spent on transactional systems, with superfast servers and dedicated data lines, yet reporting databases are frequently relegated to secondary, and sometimes outdated, machines.

The amount of data being collected and stored in databases today far exceeds the capability of humans to reduce and analyze that data with any accuracy. What we need is some sort of methodology to overcome the difficulties involved in accurately transforming the raw data into knowledge. Therefore, getting the most from your stored data depends on the following:

- Your understanding of discovery techniques.
- Your understanding of how to apply those techniques.
- Your ability to use all of the features of Oracle Discoverer.

Many OLTP business databases are growing at an unparalleled rate. Yet, it is the very fact that we have this large amount of data available to us that makes it possible to analyze with any accuracy in the first place. The irony of this situation is that the more data we have, the longer our queries take to run—yet the more accurate becomes our analysis.

Therefore, in order to effectively analyze data from large databases, you need to understand the following fundamentals:

- Good analysis is based on large amounts of data (a data warehouse for example).
- Accuracy is essential (filtering out unwanted data).
- Some form of methodology or workflow is required.
- A query tool is required (Discoverer, of course).

- Analysis sometimes produces interesting or unexpected results.
- The results should be presented in a manner that is understandable to humans.

This book has tried to address all of the above fundamentals. We have used workflows wherever we can, and the previous chapter explained how to turn your query into a report that is capable of being understood by human beings.

Uncontrolled queries can very quickly exceed the capacity of the system. Therefore, before you begin to analyze anything, some questions need to be asked:

- Do you want to include detail or summary data?
- Do you want to work from the top down or from the bottom up?
- Do you want to focus on one piece of your organization or the complete entity?
- Do you want to export the information to a spreadsheet tool to do more complex analysis?

Before you take any more steps in the analysis of your data, answer these questions. It will save you time and keep you from "spinning your wheels." After you have answered these questions, you are ready to proceed to the analysis workflow.

An Analysis Workflow

While this book is not designed to teach analysis, it would be deficient of us not to include some basic tips on how to go about analyzing data. We understand that many of you are already experienced analysts who do not need another lesson in analysis. However, there will also be many readers who are employed as analysts for the first time, and may be wondering how Discoverer can help them achieve their objectives.

Throughout an early career in the field of analysis, one of us was employed to analyze data for a large company that specialized in the leasing and management of vehicles to corporate clients. Being asked to analyze any form of data for the first time is a daunting task, but when the results of the analysis will be sent to customers who will then take actions based upon that report, the task can become frightening. So, just where does one start and how does one analyze something?

During those early days with the company referred to above, the author spent many hours with senior analysts defining and refining the best way to use the tools available. While the tools may have improved, the fundamental steps to analyze data have not. We would like to share with you those same steps, and we believe that, by following this workflow, you will quickly be able to achieve at least a rudimentary understanding of how to analyze data.

In the previous chapter, we gave you a reporting workflow. Within that workflow were several analysis steps. These steps have been extracted to form the following analysis workflow. This workflow is applicable to both Discoverer 3.1 and Discoverer 3*i*, although only the first five steps can be used in Discoverer 3*i* because the current version does not allow you to create exceptions.

1. Revisit any existing conditions and create new conditions to select only the data from the database that you want to use in the final report.
2. Create calculations.
3. Create percentages.
4. Create subtotals and totals.
5. Apply sorting.
6. Create exceptions (Discoverer 3.1 only, although 3*i* will display them).
7. Use the information and produce a report.

Not all of the above steps will be used in all cases. However, we recommend that as you analyze your data you follow the above workflow; omitting unneeded steps will benefit you.

Core Examples Used in This Chapter

After many hours of experimentation, the authors have come to the conclusion that analyzing data in a crosstab is slicker and more user friendly when compared to a standard table.

Using Discoverer 3.1 against our database, we created two identical queries, a table and a crosstab. These queries will form the basis for most of the analysis examples in the rest of this chapter. The first illustration below is a table, while the second is a crosstab. Both queries produced the same basic result by selecting the quantity shipped and selling price for all products sold in financial year 1999. We have moved the product to the page axis and opted to view the results for just the product AB-2500.

Page Items: Product Name: AB-2500

	Quarter	Ship Qty SUM	Selling Price SUM
1	1999-Q1	2964	69505.80
2	1999-Q2	6314	148063.30
3	1999-Q3	5122	120110.90
4	1999-Q4	3800	89110.00

Page Items: Product Name: AB-2500

Quarter		Ship Qty SUM	Selling Price SUM
1999-Q1		2964	69505.80
1999-Q2		6314	148063.30
1999-Q3		5122	120110.90
1999-Q4		3800	89110.00

While most of the analysis techniques in this chapter can be demonstrated using the two queries above, some cannot. Whenever we encounter a technique that cannot be shown with the above queries, we will include a more suitable example.

NOTE
Did you remember the two reasons for using Page Items (moving items to the page axis)? You either place items there when you want to see multiple pages of data, or when you have items that would display the same data in every row. In the two queries above, you can see that we have moved the product to the page axis. This is because we didn't define any condition on the product and wanted to be able to see the quarterly results for other products by clicking on the drop-down arrow.

Description of the Analysis Tools Available

In Chapters 4 and 5, you were shown the Discoverer tools available to you as part of the Workbook Wizard. We also showed you how to access these tools through the Edit Sheet dialog box. But you will recall that in Discoverer 3.1, the Edit Sheet dialog box only gives you access to some of the tools, and should only be used when you want to edit several worksheet definitions at once. All of the tools are available in the Edit Sheet dialog box of 3*i*, so you can use it if you wish.

Anyone familiar with computer software knows that there are at least three ways to do anything! Discoverer is no exception. There are two more ways to access the Discoverer tools: from the menu bar and through smart menus. When you access the tools using these methods, they open as stand-alone dialog boxes, and not as the multitabbed Edit Sheet dialog box; therefore, you can only edit a particular tool.

The process you follow for using these tools is virtually identical in every case. You can decide to turn on a tool to analyze the data, turn off the tool to return the data to its previous state, edit the definition to change the analysis being performed, create additional definitions, and apply the analysis tool to one or more data items. All of these options are under your control (refer to Chapters 4 and 5 for instructions on using these tools and Chapters 10, 11, and 12 for advanced techniques).

There is one additional tool available and that is the tool to find exceptions. Exceptions highlight data that falls outside of an established "norm." For example, maybe you want to highlight in red any product that has a markup of less than 33 percent. You can create an exception that will do just that. Exceptions will be covered later in the chapter.

Turning a Tool On and Off

In both versions of Discoverer, you can activate a tool from the menu bar. Clicking Tools displays the following drop-down menu.

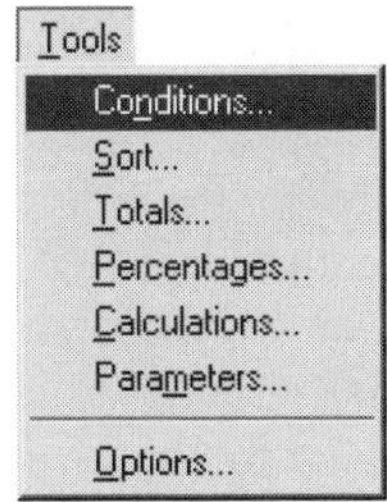

You can see that this menu has the following seven options: Conditions, Sort, Totals, Percentages, Calculations, Parameters, and Options. In this chapter, we are concerned with:

- Conditions
- Sort
- Totals
- Percentages
- Calculations

We have excluded the Parameters option because these are a specialized form of condition and will be covered in Chapters 11 and 12. The final menu item, Options, also has nothing to do with analysis and so is not discussed here. This menu item is explained in detail in Chapter 14.

The final way to access the tools is through smart menus. After a tool has been used to create an analysis definition, right-clicking in the column where it has been used will give you a smart menu offering a selection to edit the item definition.

Whichever method you choose to launch an analysis tool, a dialog box appears. This box shows any analysis definitions that you have already created and whether they are currently in use or not. In front of each definition is a check box. You can turn a definition on and off by checking and unchecking this box.

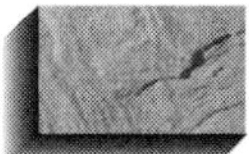

NOTE
After you have created analysis definitions, do not be too hasty to delete them. If you have decided that a definition is no longer required, simply uncheck it for now. This leaves the definition intact but does not apply that definition to the current query. Adopting this method of working will allow you to come back later and reuse the definition if required.

The Discoverer 3*i* Analysis Area

Unfortunately, the current release of Discoverer 3*i* does not have an analysis bar, although it does have buttons that take you to the relevant dialog box. As we explained earlier in the book, Discoverer 3*i* will display almost everything that Discoverer 3.1 can build—it just cannot be used itself to create a complete analysis.

While Discoverer 3*i* does not have an analysis bar, it does provide a section on the tool bar that we call the analysis area. This area has five buttons, and is separated by lines from the rest of the toolbar. Clicking on one of the buttons opens the corresponding tab in the Edit Worksheet dialog box. The following shows the analysis area of the toolbar.

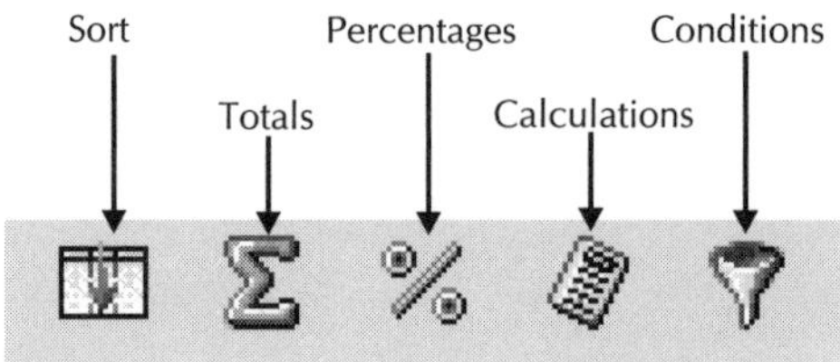

The Discoverer 3.1 Analysis Bar

Remember, in Chapters 4 and 5, that we recommended you do not create calculations, percentages, or totals in the Workbook Wizard? In this section we will show you another good reason why. It is called the analysis bar. As you will see, this bar provides shortcuts that allow you to create calculations, percentages, and totals by a single click of your mouse. The authors think that analysis of your data will become easier than you have ever experienced when you learn to use this powerful tool.

While most of Discoverer's analysis functions can be accessed from either the Tools drop-down menu or the Edit Sheet dialog box, Discoverer 3.1 also provides an analysis bar. We have found that performing analysis is very easy with this bar activated, and recommend that you always have it enabled.

NOTE

If you cannot see the analysis bar on your screen, activate it from the menu bar by clicking on View | Analysis Bar.

The analysis bar itself, shown below, has a number of buttons and is broken up into four main areas, each divided from the next by a line.

- **Totals area** This area contains five buttons, one each for the functions for sum, count, average, min, and max.
- **Percentage area** This area contains a single button. After you have highlighted a column of data, click this button to create a percentage.
- **Operator area** This part of the bar contains buttons for the four basic mathematical operators (plus, minus, multiply, and subtract), along with a button to launch the Calculations dialog box.
- **Conditions area** This area contains seven buttons that allow you to create conditions based on equality, nonequality, less than, less than or equal to, greater than, and greater than or equal to, and a button to launch the Condition dialog box itself.

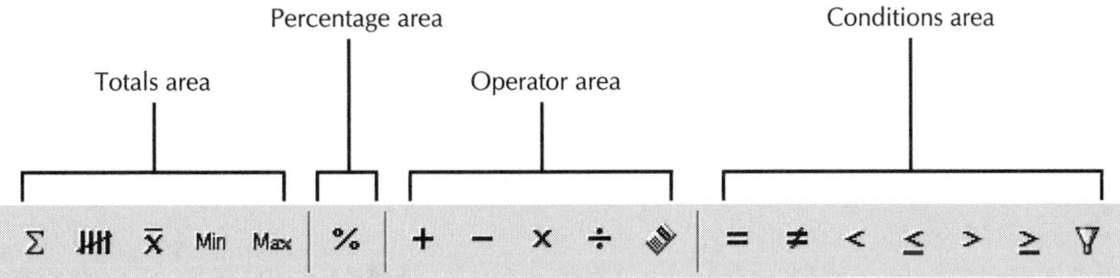

We will describe each area in turn and tell you what each button does. Many of the buttons on the analysis bar are mathematical and will only work if you include numerical data in your query. Having created a query, you now simply highlight the column or columns containing the data you want to analyze, and click the button for the operation you want Discoverer to perform. It really is that easy!

NOTE
After you highlight a column, moving the cursor along the analysis bar causes Discoverer 3.1 to highlight, in a bigger font, those analysis features that are available to you. Any function that does not display in this bigger font cannot be applied to the data you have selected.

Totals Area

The first part of the analysis bar, which we call the totals area, provides five buttons, one each for the functions sum, count, average, min, and max. Unless you highlight a column of data (remember, to highlight a column of data, place your cursor on the column heading and press the mouse button), these buttons will be inactive.

You cannot highlight multiple data points and expect Discoverer to insert totals for all of these columns. You may think that it should, and to be fair with you, so did we, but it doesn't. When you select multiple data points, all of the buttons in the totals area will be inactive.

Tables Are Complicated to Analyze

Before we get too far into this section, we would like to remind you one more time that we strongly recommend you analyze using crosstabs whenever possible.

The following example may help convince you that analyzing in a table is unpredictable. First of all, we clicked on the heading for the quarter. You can see below that Discoverer has highlighted all of the quarters and enabled all of the buttons in the totals area.

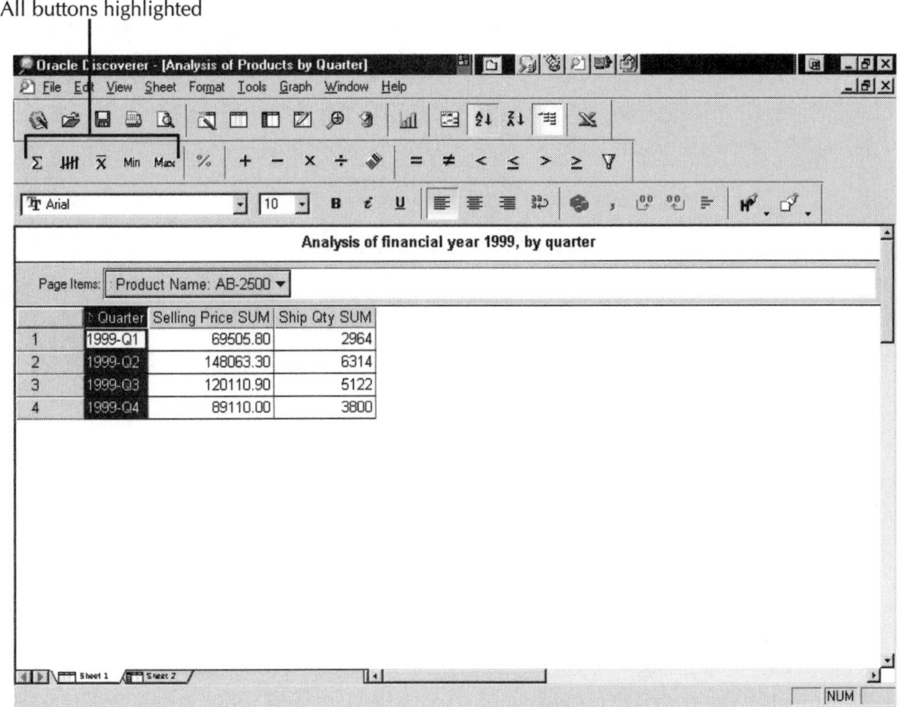

We then clicked on each of the five buttons in turn and, as you can see below, Discoverer inserted the same, identical subtotal for each function, for each of the data points. Not only that, but the subtotals that we got when we clicked on the Count and Average buttons were both created using the sum function!

While the authors understand why the same result is being applied in this example, it would have been better if Discoverer had allowed us to click on the Sum button only.

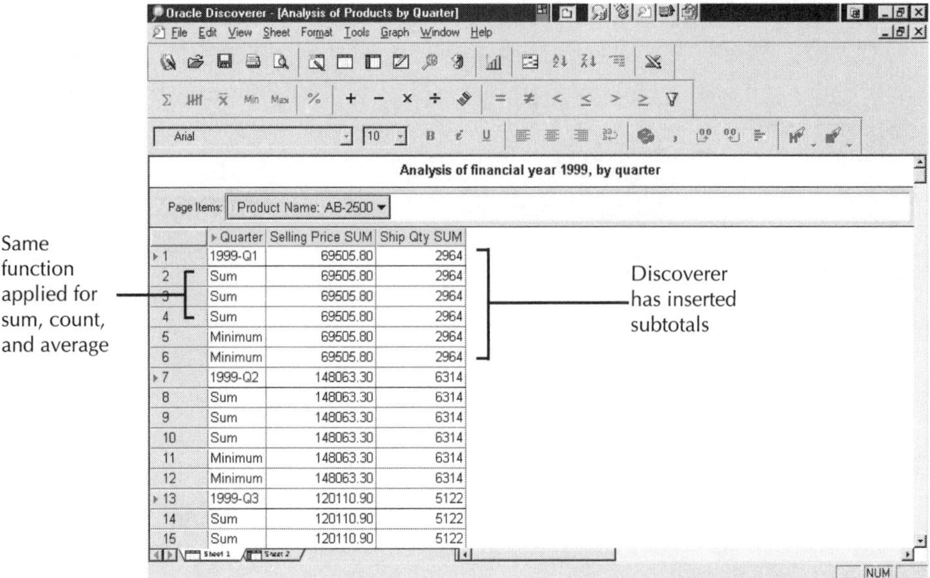

	Quarter	Selling Price SUM	Ship Qty SUM
1	1999-Q1	69505.80	2964
2	Sum	69505.80	2964
3	Sum	69505.80	2964
4	Sum	69505.80	2964
5	Minimum	69505.80	2964
6	Minimum	69505.80	2964
7	1999-Q2	148063.30	6314
8	Sum	148063.30	6314
9	Sum	148063.30	6314
10	Sum	148063.30	6314
11	Minimum	148063.30	6314
12	Minimum	148063.30	6314
13	1999-Q3	120110.90	5122
14	Sum	120110.90	5122
15	Sum	120110.90	5122

Next we took our base table, moved the product into the top axis, and the quarter into the page axis. This time, as you can see, when we clicked on the product heading, the Sum and Average buttons were inactive.

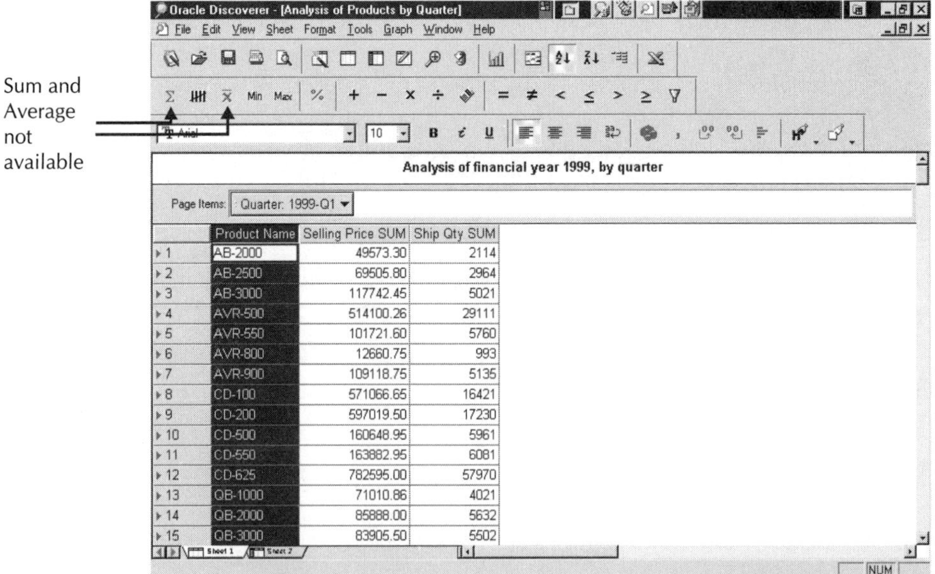

	Product Name	Selling Price SUM	Ship Qty SUM
1	AB-2000	49573.30	2114
2	AB-2500	69505.80	2964
3	AB-3000	117742.45	5021
4	AVR-500	514100.26	29111
5	AVR-550	101721.60	5760
6	AVR-800	12660.75	993
7	AVR-900	109118.75	5135
8	CD-100	571066.65	16421
9	CD-200	597019.50	17230
10	CD-500	160648.95	5961
11	CD-550	163882.95	6081
12	CD-625	782595.00	57970
13	QB-1000	71010.86	4021
14	QB-2000	85888.00	5632
15	QB-3000	83905.50	5502

Furthermore, as you can see in the following illustration, when we clicked on the available buttons, Discoverer inserted a grand total at the bottom and not a subtotal as it did when we had the quarter in the top axis. Discoverer also inserted the count, minimum, and maximum values for our product names, and not the data points as we were expecting. Why this should be so is not so obvious, but only underlines our recommendation not to use tables, especially with the analysis bar.

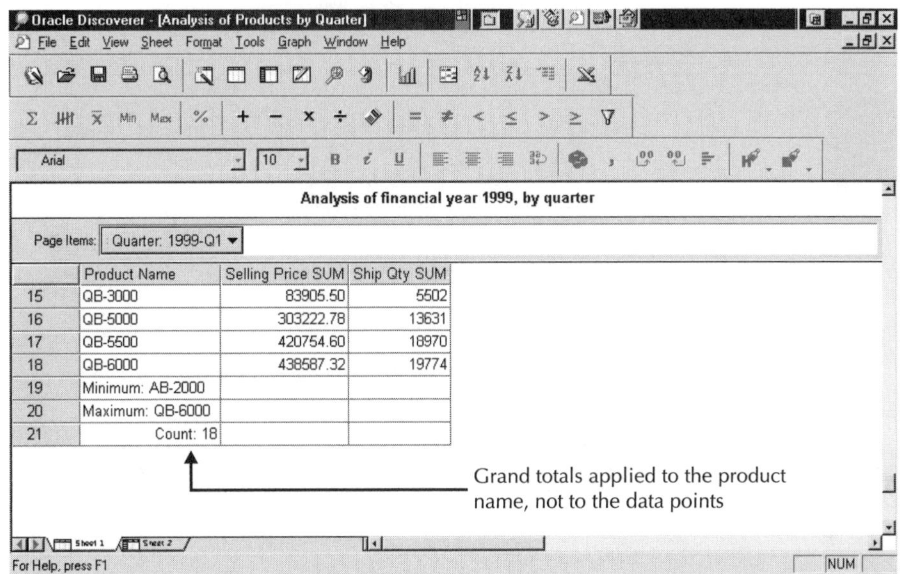

Crosstabs Are Great to Analyze

Before we get into explaining what the different buttons can do, we wanted to show you why analyzing a crosstab is simpler and easier to understand when compared to a table. The biggest advantage is that you can apply any of the functions in the totals area to all of the data points at the same time. You do this by clicking on the heading for one of the side axis items, then clicking one of the buttons in the totals area of the analysis bar.

For example, here we have highlighted the quarter heading. As expected, all of the buttons in the totals area are now active.

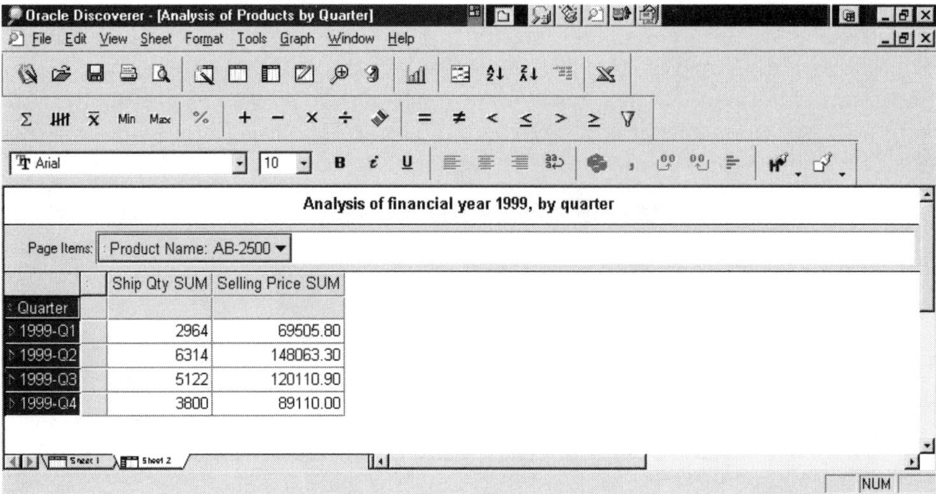

The illustration that follows shows the result of applying the sum function. You can see that Discoverer inserted a grand total for all of the data points.

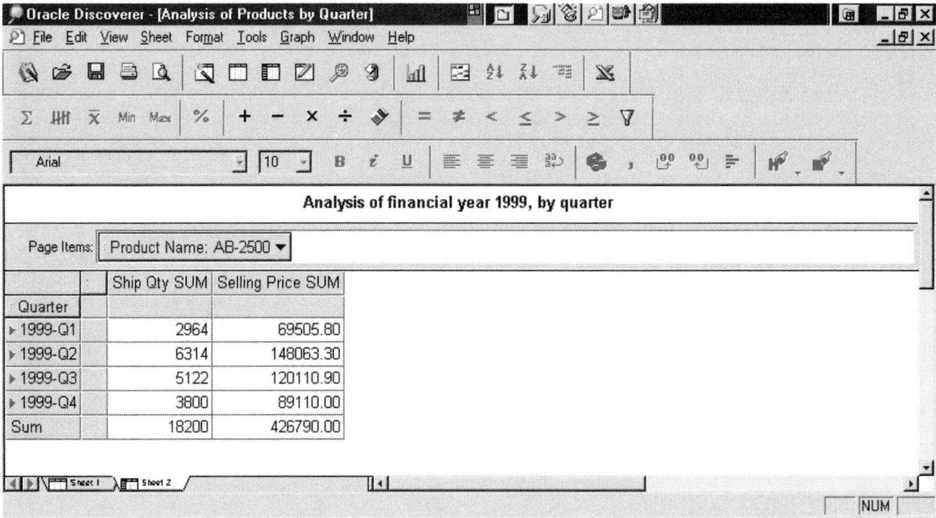

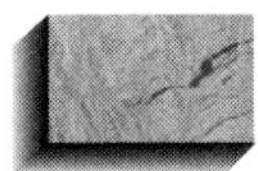

NOTE

The format applied to any of the functions in the totals area is the default format as specified on the Format tab of the Tools | Options dialog box. Also note that you can only apply a total to a numeric column of data.

Using Totals with Sorts

As we said earlier, Discoverer offers increased flexibility when you are using group sorts, especially in a crosstab. In the examples shown next, we have taken our base queries and moved the product out of the Page Items area, thereby allowing us to see all of the data for each product grouped together.

For the following table, the product has been placed in front of the quarter. We then defined a group sort on the product, and placed a standard high-to-low sort on the quarter.

Analysis of financial year 1999, by quarter

Page Items:

	Product Name	Quarter	Ship Qty SUM	Selling Price SUM
1	AB-2000	1999-Q1	2114	49573.30
2		1999-Q2	12576	295751.40
3		1999-Q3	3912	91736.40
4		1999-Q4	400	9380.00
5	AB-2500	1999-Q1	2964	69505.80
6		1999-Q2	6314	148063.30
7		1999-Q3	5122	120110.90
8		1999-Q4	3800	89110.00
9	AB-3000	1999-Q1	5021	117742.45
10		1999-Q2	12627	296103.15
11		1999-Q3	5609	132000.05
12		1999-Q4	750	17587.50
13	AVR-500	1999-Q1	29111	514100.26
14		1999-Q2	9497	167717.02
15		1999-Q3	5678	104511.88

Sheet 1 | Sheet 2

NUM

For the crosstab shown here, the product has been moved to become an axis point. As you can see, Discoverer automatically inserted a subtotal by product.

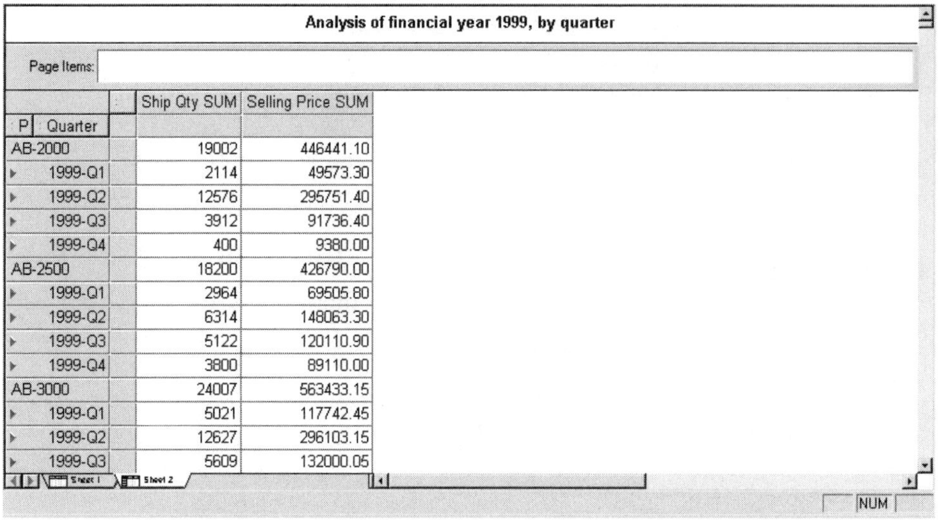

Analysis of financial year 1999, by quarter

Page Items:

P	Quarter	Ship Qty SUM	Selling Price SUM
AB-2000		19002	446441.10
	1999-Q1	2114	49573.30
	1999-Q2	12576	295751.40
	1999-Q3	3912	91736.40
	1999-Q4	400	9380.00
AB-2500		18200	426790.00
	1999-Q1	2964	69505.80
	1999-Q2	6314	148063.30
	1999-Q3	5122	120110.90
	1999-Q4	3800	89110.00
AB-3000		24007	563433.15
	1999-Q1	5021	117742.45
	1999-Q2	12627	296103.15
	1999-Q3	5609	132000.05

No matter which of the two queries we now work on, clicking the heading for any of the data points, and then clicking on any of the buttons in the totals area, works the same as for a nonsorted query. Discoverer simply inserts a grand total on that item. However, clicking on one of the sorted items causes Discoverer to insert a subtotal.

Sum Button

To show you how easy it is to create a sum using the analysis bar, we highlighted the Quantity Shipped column and clicked on the Sum button. As you can see, Discoverer automatically inserted a grand total of the quantity shipped. Defining a total this way produces the same result as creating a total in the Totals dialog box, based on the sum function.

The illustration that follows shows a grand total applied to a table.

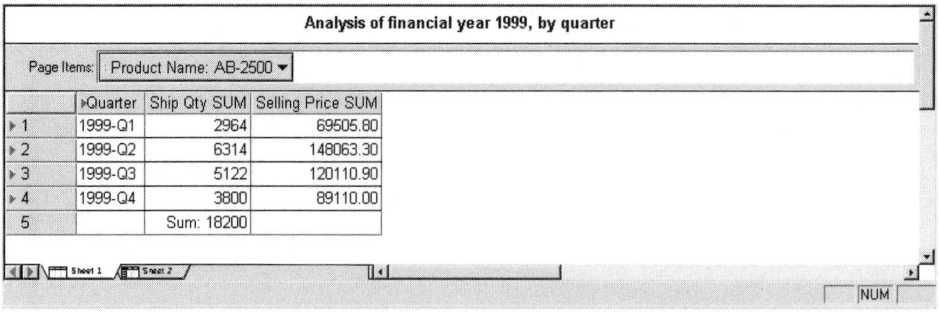

Analysis of financial year 1999, by quarter

Page Items: Product Name: AB-2500

	Quarter	Ship Qty SUM	Selling Price SUM
1	1999-Q1	2964	69505.80
2	1999-Q2	6314	148063.30
3	1999-Q3	5122	120110.90
4	1999-Q4	3800	89110.00
5		Sum: 18200	

The next illustration shows a grand total applied to a crosstab.

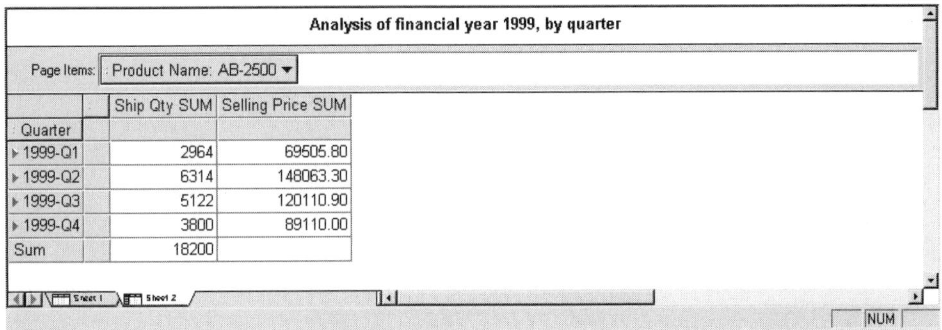
Analysis of financial year 1999, by quarter

Page Items: Product Name: AB-2500

Quarter	Ship Qty SUM	Selling Price SUM
1999-Q1	2964	69505.80
1999-Q2	6314	148063.30
1999-Q3	5122	120110.90
1999-Q4	3800	89110.00
Sum	18200	

If you are working with a crosstab and you want to insert a grand total for all data points, there are three ways to correct the situation.

Edit the Existing Total Definition To insert a grand total by editing the definition for the existing total, use the following workflow:

1. Right-click on the axis label for the total. This displays a drop-down list of options.
2. Select Edit Total from the list. This opens the following Total dialog box.

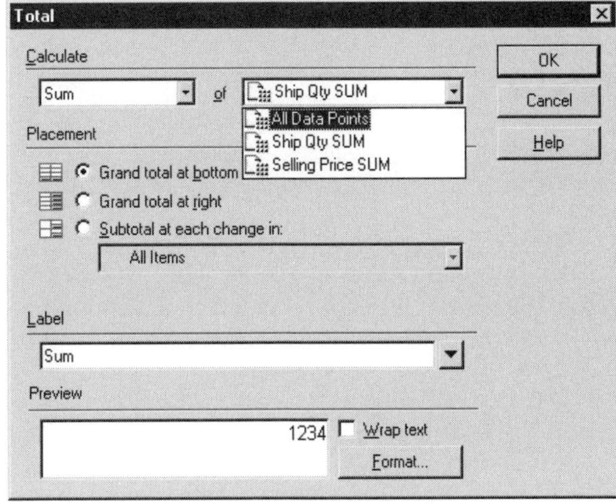

3. Click on the down arrow beside the item currently being totaled, and change the drop-down selection to All Data Points.
4. Click OK. The results are shown next.

Analysis of financial year 1999, by quarter

Page Items: Product Name: AB-2500

Quarter	Ship Qty SUM	Selling Price SUM
1999-Q1	2964	69505.80
1999-Q2	6314	148063.30
1999-Q3	5122	120110.90
1999-Q4	3800	89110.00
Sum	18200	426790.00

Create a Grand Total for All Data Points To create a grand total for all data points, use the following workflow:

1. Click on the axis label. This highlights all of the time periods in the axis.

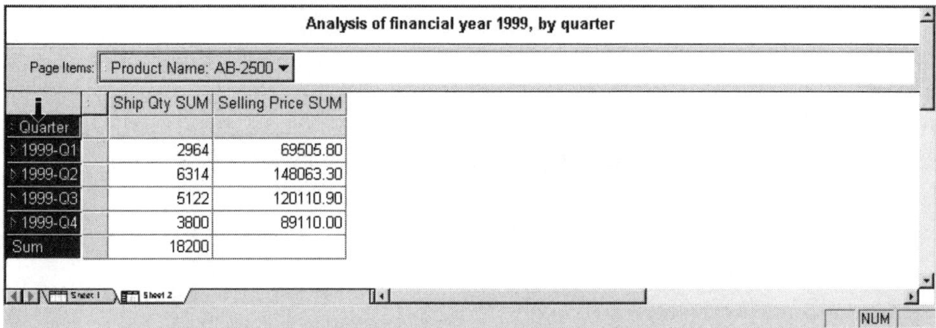

Analysis of financial year 1999, by quarter

Page Items: Product Name: AB-2500

Quarter	Ship Qty SUM	Selling Price SUM
1999-Q1	2964	69505.80
1999-Q2	6314	148063.30
1999-Q3	5122	120110.90
1999-Q4	3800	89110.00
Sum	18200	

2. Click the Total button on the analysis bar. Discoverer inserts a grand total at the bottom. However, Discoverer is not smart enough to use the existing definition and inserts a new row, as shown next.

Analysis of financial year 1999, by quarter

Page Items: Product Name: AB-2500

Quarter	Ship Qty SUM	Selling Price SUM
1999-Q1	2964	69505.80
1999-Q2	6314	148063.30
1999-Q3	5122	120110.90
1999-Q4	3800	89110.00
Sum	18200	
Sum	18200	426790.00

3. Click on the axis label for the old total. This highlights the label.
4. Press the DEL key on your keyboard. The row and the definition will be removed.

Create New Definitions for the Other Data Points The third way to correct the situation is to add individual totals to the data points that are currently not totaled. Highlight, in turn, each data point label you wish to be totaled, and press the Total button. When we did that in our example, Discoverer added the word "Sum" in front of each total, as shown next.

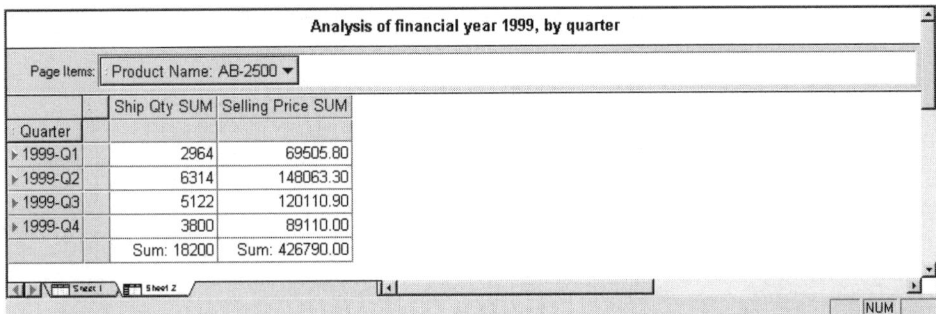

Analysis of financial year 1999, by quarter

Page Items: Product Name: AB-2500

Quarter	Ship Qty SUM	Selling Price SUM
1999-Q1	2964	69505.80
1999-Q2	6314	148063.30
1999-Q3	5122	120110.90
1999-Q4	3800	89110.00
	Sum: 18200	Sum: 426790.00

NOTE
If you decide that you want to have the word "Sum" appear only once, you should create a new total using the axis label, as described in the previous paragraph. However, when you press the DEL *key, Discoverer does not always delete both of the totals containing the word "Sum". Rather, the Totals dialog box is launched, and you will have to delete the totals individually.*

Count Button Highlighting a column of data and clicking this button inserts a count of the number of rows in the query. Let us assume that we want to know how many sales orders shipped in January. Using our example query, highlighting the Sales Order column, and clicking on Count caused Discoverer to insert the count.

	Month	Order Number	Ship Qty SUM
275	JAN-00	2569	4800
276	JAN-00	2570	4800
277	JAN-00	2571	1200
278	JAN-00	2572	1200
279	JAN-00	2573	2400
280	JAN-00	2574	2400
281	JAN-00	2575	24
282	JAN-00	2577	8
283		Count: 282	Sum: 418058

NOTE
You will notice that Discoverer has placed the count of sales orders on the same row as the total number of items shipped. Earlier versions of Discoverer do not do this, and will display the two figures on separate rows.

Average Button Highlighting a column of data and clicking this button inserts a calculation of the average of the data items in the row or rows highlighted. Let us assume that we want to know the average number of items shipped on each sales order. Using our example query again, highlighting the Shipped Quantity column and clicking on Average caused Discoverer to insert the average of 1,482.

	▸Month	Order Number	Ship Qty SUM
▸ 275	JAN-00	2569	4800
▸ 276	JAN-00	2570	4800
▸ 277	JAN-00	2571	1200
▸ 278	JAN-00	2572	1200
▸ 279	JAN-00	2573	2400
▸ 280	JAN-00	2574	2400
▸ 281	JAN-00	2575	24
▸ 282	JAN-00	2577	8
283		Count: 282	Sum: 418058
284			Average: 1482

Min Button Highlighting a column or columns of data and clicking this button inserts a calculation of the lowest-valued item in the column(s). For example, assume we want to know the minimum number of items that we shipped on any one sales order. Using our query, highlighting the Shipped Quantity column and clicking on Min caused Discoverer to insert the minimum value in the column.

	▸Month	Order Number	Ship Qty SUM
▸ 275	JAN-00	2569	4800
▸ 276	JAN-00	2570	4800
▸ 277	JAN-00	2571	1200
▸ 278	JAN-00	2572	1200
▸ 279	JAN-00	2573	2400
▸ 280	JAN-00	2574	2400
▸ 281	JAN-00	2575	24
▸ 282	JAN-00	2577	8
283		Count: 282	Sum: 418058
284			Average: 1482
285			Minimum: 1

Max Button Highlighting a column or columns of data and clicking this button inserts a calculation of the highest valued item in the column(s). For example, assume we want to know the maximum number of items that we shipped on any one sales order. Using our query, highlighting the Shipped Quantity column and clicking on Max causes Discoverer to insert the maximum value in the column.

	▸Month	Order Number	Ship Qty SUM
▸ 275	JAN-00	2569	4800
▸ 276	JAN-00	2570	4800
▸ 277	JAN-00	2571	1200
▸ 278	JAN-00	2572	1200
▸ 279	JAN-00	2573	2400
▸ 280	JAN-00	2574	2400
▸ 281	JAN-00	2575	24
▸ 282	JAN-00	2577	8
283		Count: 282	Sum: 418058
284			Average: 1482
285			Minimum: 1
286			Maximum: 26400

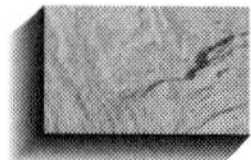

NOTE
Min and max can be applied to dates and strings just as easily as to numbers. If we had highlighted the Date Shipped column and clicked first on Min and then on Max, Discoverer would have inserted the first and last dates in January that we shipped the displayed product.

Percentage Area

The second part of the analysis bar, which we call the percentage area, provides a single button for creating percentages. Highlighting any column of numeric data activates this button. When you create a percentage this way, Discoverer creates a new column displaying a percentage based on the grand total, for each row. It names the column by prefixing the word "Percent" in front of the source column name. For example, if the source column is named Selling Price, the new column will be called Percent Selling Price.

To change the percentage definition use the following workflow:

1. Right click on the column heading and select Edit Percentage from the drop-down list, or from the menu bar select Tools | Percentages.
2. Change the percentage definition (refer to Chapter 5 for explanation of percentage definitions).
3. Click OK.

Operators Area

The third part of the analysis bar contains buttons for the four main mathematical operators Add (+), Subtract (-), Multiply (*) and Divide (/), along with a button to launch the Calculations dialog box.

Add (+), Subtract (-), Multiply (*) and Divide (/) Buttons

These four buttons work in exactly the same way, and usually require you to highlight two columns of numeric data before you click one of the buttons. We say usually because Discoverer will allow you to highlight non-numerical columns before clicking on the Add button. Doing this causes Discoverer to concatenate the two columns of data together.

Follow this simple workflow to create new calculations based on these four operators:

1. Highlight a column of data.
2. Hold down the CTRL key and highlight a second column of data.
3. Click one of the four operators.

Discoverer launches the appropriate dialog box. As all of the dialog boxes look the same, we will only describe the Subtract dialog box.

As you can see in the following bullet points, the Subtract dialog box contains the following six areas:

- **Name** The name typed here will appear as the column heading for the calculation.
- **Defined as** These two boxes contain the names of the two columns upon which the calculation is based.
- **Advanced** Click this to launch an advanced dialog box for the appropriate calculation.
- **OK** Clicking OK completes the calculation, closes the dialog box, and displays the results in a column of their own.
- **Cancel** Clicking Cancel abandons the calculation and returns you to the original query.
- **Help** Clicking Help launches the standard Discoverer help system.

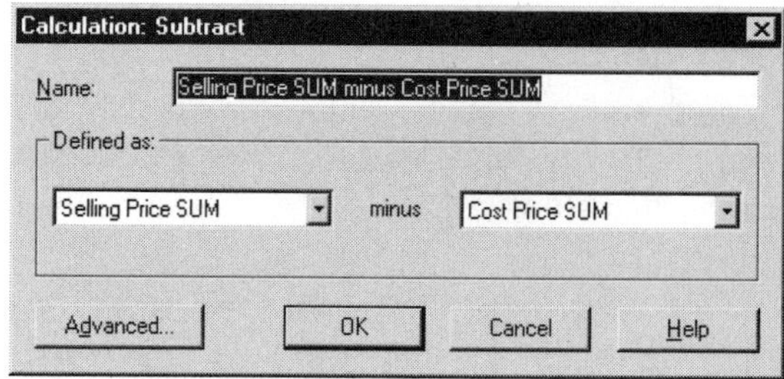

When you use the add and multiply functions, it makes no difference which column you highlight first. However, when you use the subtract and divide functions, the order is vitally important. The data in the second column will be subtracted from or divided into the data in the first column. If you have highlighted the columns in the wrong order, don't worry—clicking on the down arrow beside each of the columns in the dialog box allows you to change the columns being used.

Calculation Button

Clicking this button launches the Edit Calculations dialog box. This button is always active.

Conditions Area

The final part of the analysis bar is the conditions area. This area contains seven buttons, one each that allow you to create conditions based on equality (=), non equality (<>), less than (<), less than or equal to (<=), greater than (>), greater than or equal to (>=), and a button to launch the Edit Condition dialog box itself. This final button is always active.

The first six buttons can save you time and effort in creating conditions based on the data that has been returned by your query. For example, assume that you have a query that has returned the total quantity sold by product. If you want to see the query conditioned to display only the quantity from product CD-100 and higher, use the following workflow:

1. Click in the cell containing the data item CD-100.
2. Click the >= button. This opens the New Condition dialog box, with the item, condition, and value prefilled.
3. Click OK. This completes and applies the condition to the query. Discoverer does not re-run the query because the condition specified constrains the data to a subset of the data that you originally selected.

Finding Exceptions

As we mentioned earlier in the chapter, exceptions highlight data that falls outside of an established norm. You can create many exceptions concerning the same data items. The example above, for example, has two exceptions for Profit SUM. If both exceptions are turned on at the same time, they will conflict because one exception is for all values over 10,000 and the other is for only values between 40,000 and 60,000. If you inadvertently select two or more conflicting exceptions, a message asks you to reselect the exception so they don't conflict.

When working with exceptions, to use them effectively you need to bear in mind the following criteria:

Define the exception itself, such as "is greater than 10,000" or "is less than 25%" or "is between 10,000 and 50,000".

- Define the format of the data that the exception will be applied to, so you can see it easily among the rest of the data.

To create exceptions use the following workflow:

1. Select Format | Exceptions from the toolbar, or click on a column of data and select Format Exception from the drop-down menu displayed. This opens the Format Exceptions dialog box shown next. The functionality of this dialog box is the same as the other tools.

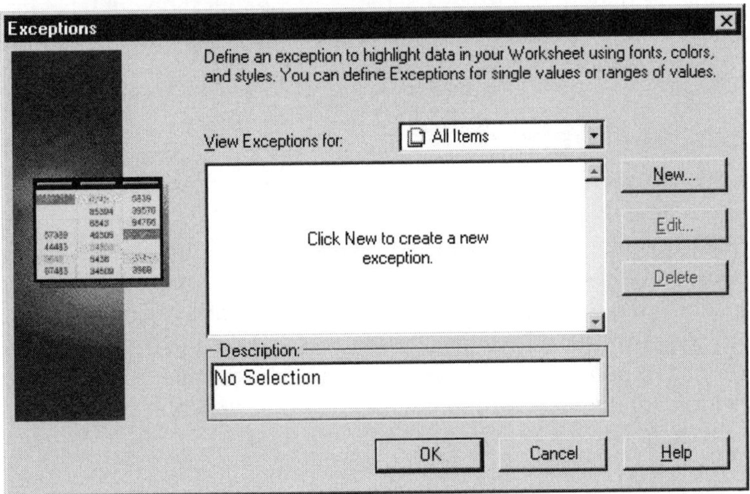

2. Click New. This opens the Exception dialog box. We will not explain its use until further on in this section.

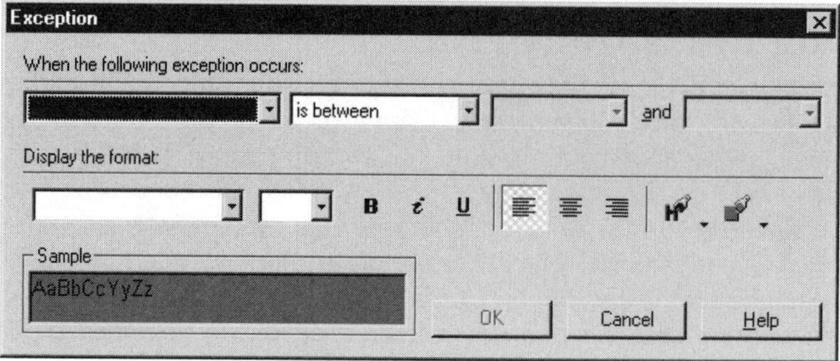

3. Define the exception.
4. Click OK. This will close the Exception dialog box.
5. Click OK in the Exceptions dialog box (yes, we know the names of the boxes are the same except for the "s" on the end).

It is quite easy and intuitive to create an exception in Discoverer.

How to Build the Example Queries

In the section of this chapter dealing with the different types of analysis, we showed you the results of queries to display examples of the four different types. This section shows you how we went about building those queries, and highlights which analysis tools were used.

Statistical Analysis

If you recall, this query was quite simple and was a crosstab built using the year, region, and selling price sum. The year was placed on the top axis because we didn't want to display the same data item in every row. The region was placed in the side axis, while the selling price sum was left on the top axis.

But just how did we display the region without pulling in anything from the customer, city, or district? To tell you the truth, we didn't. In order to get to the region, we had to pull in the other items because there was no join between the sales order folder and the region folder. Our original selections, therefore, looked as in the illustration that follows.

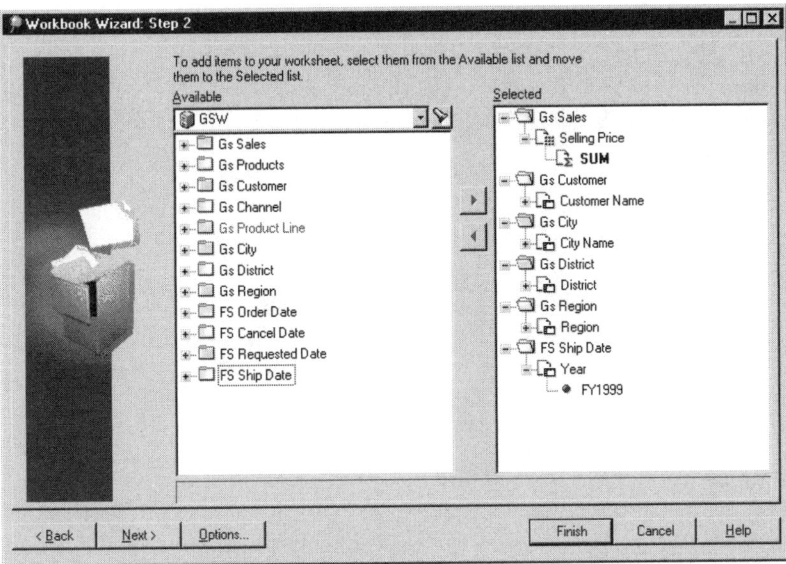

We then clicked on each of the items that we did not want—those being the customer name, city, and district—and removed them from the query. Discoverer, as you can see in the following illustration, remembers the join between sales orders and regions and is quite happy to run this query.

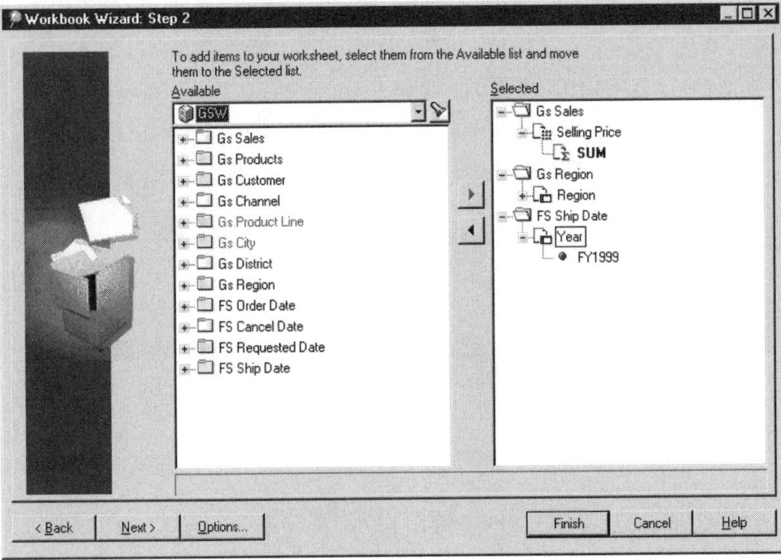

Having selected the items that we wanted, we used the next step of the Workbook Wizard to open the page items and move the year to the page axis. We then moved the region to the side axis, and we clicked on Finish. Discoverer ran the query, following which we added a simple title. This gave us the results shown here.

Page Items: Year: FY1999

Region	Selling Price SUM
EUROPE	3303568.77
FAR EAST	1197140.00
NORTH AMERICA	4932897.65
SOUTH AMERICA	716382.15

To complete the query, in Discoverer 3.1 we just clicked on the label entitled Selling Price SUM and then on the Percentage button on the analysis bar. In Discoverer 3*i*, because there is no bar, we selected Tools | Percentages from the menu bar, and created the new percentage as shown next.

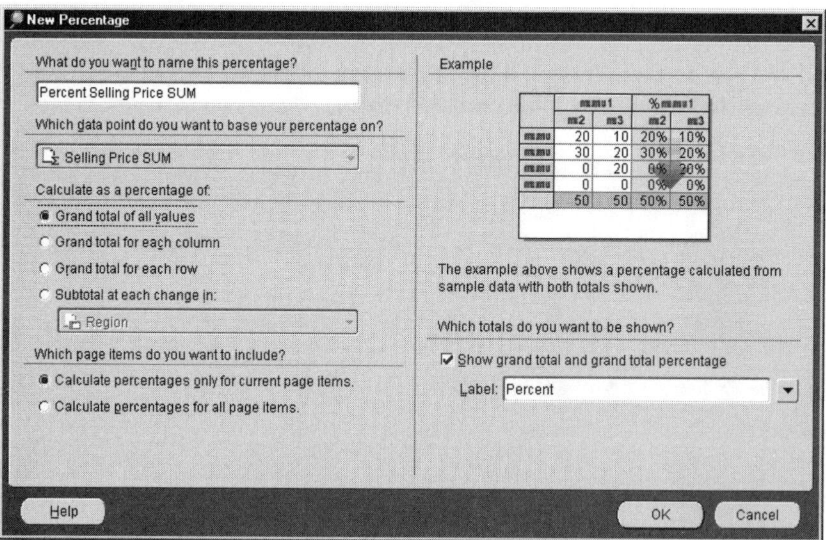

The completed query can be seen in Figure 9-1.

Classification Analysis

This query is, once again, a crosstab. This one selects the cost price, selling price, profit, product name, product line, and quarter, with a condition that the quarters are all for 1999. We did not apply a condition on the product line, but we did move it to the page axis in order to be able to select one product line at a time. After moving the product name and quarter to the side axis, the resulting output is as in Figure 9-2.

So far so good. But just how did we end up with the result shown in Figure 9-3? First of all, despite how it may look, we have to tell you that it really is the same query. We did not edit any of the selections, nor did we change any of the conditions. Moving the items between the various axes did everything.

The first thing we did was to move the data point items from the top axis to the page axis. It doesn't matter which data point you pick because, if you select and move one, Discoverer actually moves them all. For the record, we clicked on the cost price and dragged it to the page axis. Upon releasing the mouse button, Discoverer moved all three items and built a drop-down box, as you can see next, with the cost price as the default.

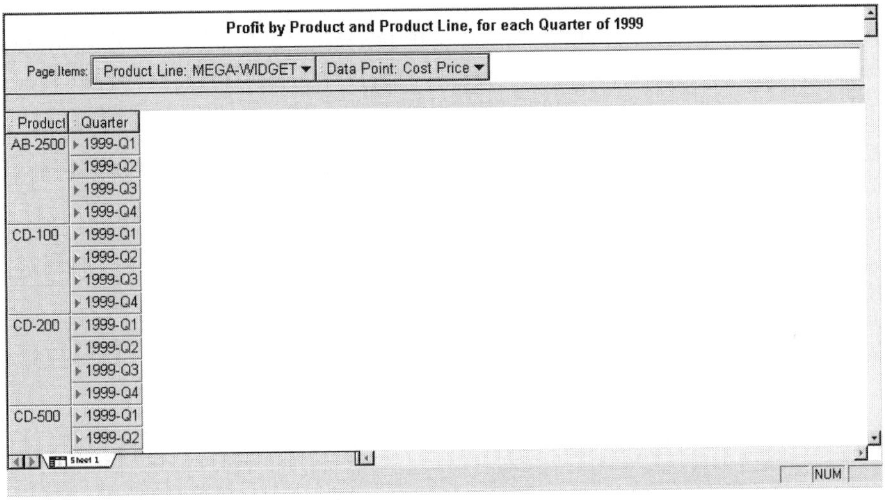

Profit by Product and Product Line, for each Quarter of 1999

Page Items: Product Line: MEGA-WIDGET ▾ Data Point: Cost Price ▾

Product	Quarter
AB-2500	1999-Q1
	1999-Q2
	1999-Q3
	1999-Q4
CD-100	1999-Q1
	1999-Q2
	1999-Q3
	1999-Q4
CD-200	1999-Q1
	1999-Q2
	1999-Q3
	1999-Q4
CD-500	1999-Q1
	1999-Q2

Sheet 1 NUM

In order to make some costs display, we have to move something to the top axis. So, we dragged the quarter there, which immediately caused Discoverer to display the cost price for each quarter, as shown here.

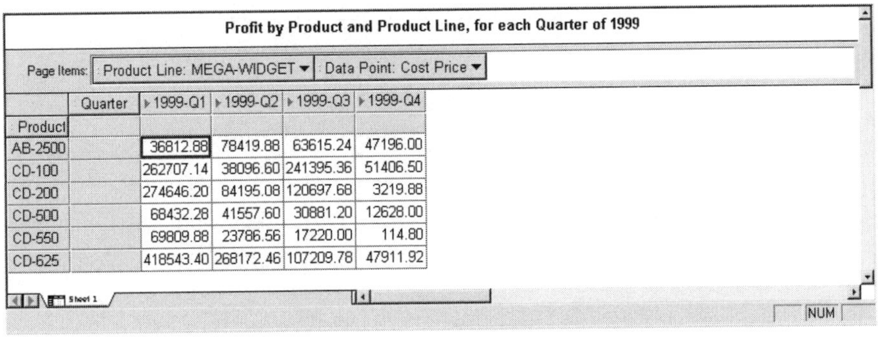

Profit by Product and Product Line, for each Quarter of 1999

Page Items: Product Line: MEGA-WIDGET ▾ Data Point: Cost Price ▾

Product	Quarter	1999-Q1	1999-Q2	1999-Q3	1999-Q4
AB-2500		36812.88	78419.88	63615.24	47196.00
CD-100		262707.14	38096.60	241395.36	51406.50
CD-200		274646.20	84195.08	120697.68	3219.88
CD-500		68432.28	41557.60	30881.20	12628.00
CD-550		69809.88	23786.56	17220.00	114.80
CD-625		418543.40	268172.46	107209.78	47911.92

Sheet 1 NUM

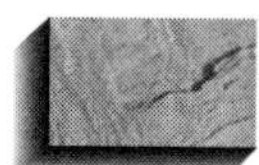

NOTE
There are no costs displayed in the main body of the uppermost report previously shown because there is no item in the top axis. This is one of the most common reasons why users complain that they can see no output from a query of this type. In any query, you must have at least one item in the top axis.

You can see from the above illustrations that the output has changed, yet we can assure you that Discoverer did not requery the database. This is one of the wonderful features of Discoverer that will be covered in more depth when we discuss advanced queries in a later chapter.

Having moved the quarter to the top axis, the next thing we did was to click on the product line and move it to the side axis. The first illustration shows this step completed, with the product line having been placed before the product name. You can see that Discoverer automatically does a group sort in this situation.

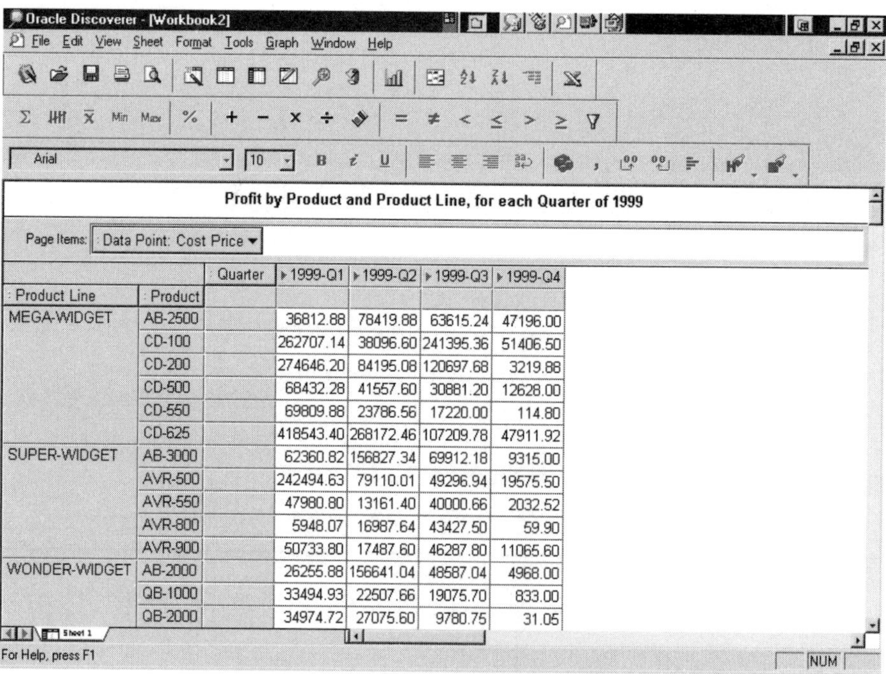

Product Line	Product	Quarter	1999-Q1	1999-Q2	1999-Q3	1999-Q4
MEGA-WIDGET	AB-2500		36812.88	78419.88	63615.24	47196.00
	CD-100		262707.14	38096.60	241395.36	51406.50
	CD-200		274646.20	84195.08	120697.68	3219.88
	CD-500		68432.28	41557.60	30881.20	12628.00
	CD-550		69809.88	23786.56	17220.00	114.80
	CD-625		418543.40	268172.46	107209.78	47911.92
SUPER-WIDGET	AB-3000		62360.82	156827.34	69912.18	9315.00
	AVR-500		242494.63	79110.01	49296.94	19575.50
	AVR-550		47980.80	13161.40	40000.66	2032.52
	AVR-800		5948.07	16987.64	43427.50	59.90
	AVR-900		50733.80	17487.60	46287.80	11065.60
WONDER-WIDGET	AB-2000		26255.88	156641.04	48587.04	4968.00
	QB-1000		33494.93	22507.66	19075.70	833.00
	QB-2000		34974.72	27075.60	9780.75	31.05

Finally, as you can see in the next illustration, we clicked on the drop-down arrow alongside the cost price.

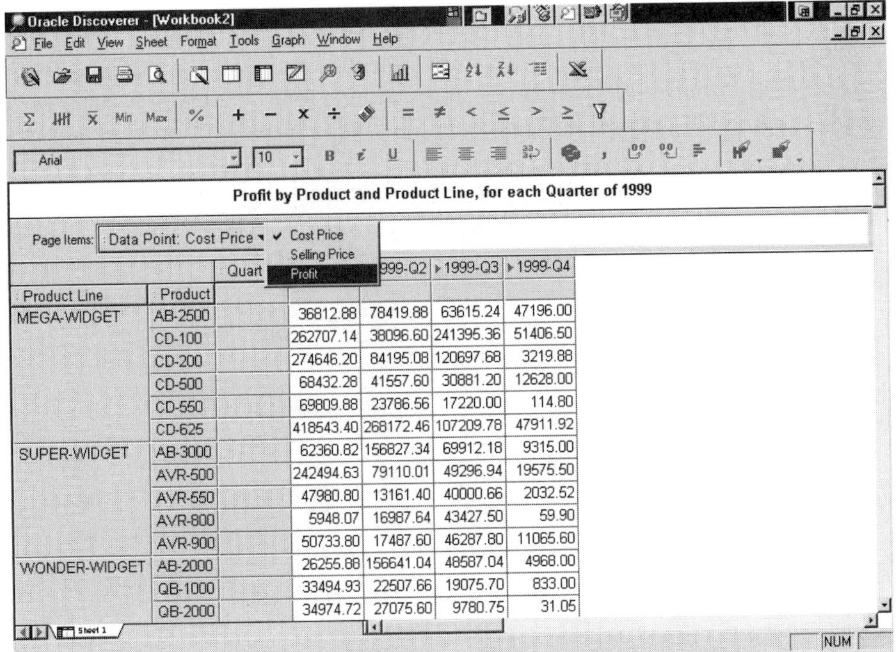

Product Line	Product	Quart		999-Q2	1999-Q3	1999-Q4
MEGA-WIDGET	AB-2500		36812.88	78419.88	63615.24	47196.00
	CD-100		262707.14	38096.60	241395.36	51406.50
	CD-200		274646.20	84195.08	120697.68	3219.88
	CD-500		68432.28	41557.60	30881.20	12628.00
	CD-550		69809.88	23786.56	17220.00	114.80
	CD-625		418543.40	268172.46	107209.78	47911.92
SUPER-WIDGET	AB-3000		62360.82	156827.34	69912.18	9315.00
	AVR-500		242494.63	79110.01	49296.94	19575.50
	AVR-550		47980.80	13161.40	40000.66	2032.52
	AVR-800		5948.07	16987.64	43427.50	59.90
	AVR-900		50733.80	17487.60	46287.80	11065.60
WONDER-WIDGET	AB-2000		26255.88	156641.04	48587.04	4968.00
	QB-1000		33494.93	22507.66	19075.70	833.00
	QB-2000		34974.72	27075.60	9780.75	31.05

From the drop-down list provided, we selected the profit, which resulted in the output you saw previously in Figure 9-3.

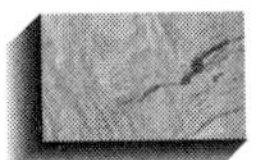

NOTE

By the way, if you are wondering how we got the side axis items to line up as they do, you can do this from Tools | Options off the menu bar. Select the Crosstab tab and then make sure that Axis Labels and Axis Gridlines are checked, with the Gridline Style set to 3D, and the Style set to Inline.

Deviation Analysis

This query is a little more complex than the other examples, but you should be able to easily follow how we did it. We used a crosstab, of course, because we couldn't have performed the manipulations that we wanted had we chosen a table.

The selections were very easy. We took the order quantity and the status from the sales folder, the product name from the product folder, and the channel. Before we left the Workbook Wizard, we moved the channel and product name to the side axis, and then defined the following condition on the product name: Product Name like 'QB%' This condition will constrain our selection to just those products that begin with QB. After running the query and adding a total, the result is as shown next. Notice how Discoverer has automatically built a group sort on the channel.

Total sales by Channel and Product

		Status	Order Qty SUM CANCELLED	HOLD	OPEN	SHIPPED
Channel	Product					
EXTERNAL	QB-1000		7812	2	2375	48025
	QB-2000		5000	0	1264	32963
	QB-3000		2420	0	27775	53144
	QB-5000		7580	600	50303	144069
	QB-5500		1410	0	9612	149724
	QB-6000		13680	400	16665	156817
INTERNET	QB-1000		6000	0	6622	8260
	QB-2000		0	172	22300	31170
	QB-3000		9300	0	2481	7238
	QB-5000		1220	1	45501	18422
	QB-5500		2401	100	14179	29678
	QB-6000		100	1	43017	21274

Sheet 1

Next, we clicked the side axis label for the product and then clicked the Sum button on the analysis bar. This gives us the result shown next.

NOTE
If we had clicked on the side axis label for the channel, we would have finished up with subtotals by channel, not the grand total that this type of analysis requires.

Total sales by Channel and Product

		Status	Order Qty SUM CANCELLED	HOLD	OPEN	SHIPPED
Channel	Product					
EXTERNAL	QB-1000		7812	2	2375	48025
	QB-2000		5000	0	1264	32963
	QB-3000		2420	0	27775	53144
	QB-5000		7580	600	50303	144069
	QB-5500		1410	0	9612	149724
	QB-6000		13680	400	16665	156817
INTERNET	QB-1000		6000	0	6622	8260
	QB-2000		0	172	22300	31170
	QB-3000		9300	0	2481	7238
	QB-5000		1220	1	45501	18422
	QB-5500		2401	100	14179	29678
	QB-6000		100	1	43017	21274
Sum			56923	1276	242094	700784

Sheet 1

The next part is straightforward, and just requires us to create percentages. We clicked on the label for the top axis item called Order Qty SUM, and clicked the Percentage button. This simple task results in the output as seen next.

Total sales by Channel and Product

		Percent Order Qty SUM			
	Status	CANCELLED	HOLD	OPEN	SHIPPED
Channel	Product				
EXTERNAL	QB-1000	1%	0%	0%	5%
	QB-2000	0%	0	0%	3%
	QB-3000	0%	0	3%	5%
	QB-5000	1%	0%	5%	14%
	QB-5500	0%	0	1%	15%
	QB-6000	1%	0%	2%	16%
INTERNET	QB-1000	1%	0	1%	1%
	QB-2000	0	0%	2%	3%
	QB-3000	1%	0	0%	1%
	QB-5000	0%	0%	5%	2%
	QB-5500	0%	0%	1%	3%
	QB-6000	0%	0%	4%	2%
Sum					

Sheet 1

Following that, we right-clicked on the label called Percent Order Qty SUM and selected Edit Percentage from the drop-down list. This displayed the Edit Percentage dialog box, in which we changed the percentage to "Grand total for each row," and clicked OK. We then clicked in any of the percentage cells and increased the decimals to three places. The end result of this can be seen next.

Total sales by Channel and Product

		Percent Order Qty SUM			
	Status	CANCELLED	HOLD	OPEN	SHIPPED
Channel	Product				
EXTERNAL	QB-1000	13.419%	0.003%	4.080%	82.497%
	QB-2000	12.746%	0.000%	3.222%	84.031%
	QB-3000	2.904%	0.000%	33.328%	63.768%
	QB-5000	3.742%	0.296%	24.835%	71.127%
	QB-5500	0.877%	0.000%	5.980%	93.143%
	QB-6000	7.294%	0.213%	8.885%	83.608%
INTERNET	QB-1000	28.733%	0.000%	31.712%	39.556%
	QB-2000	0.000%	0.321%	41.572%	58.107%
	QB-3000	48.898%	0.000%	13.045%	38.057%
	QB-5000	1.873%	0.002%	69.847%	28.279%
	QB-5500	5.179%	0.216%	30.586%	64.019%
	QB-6000	0.155%	0.002%	66.805%	33.038%
Sum					

Sheet 1

Almost done, apart from adding the exceptions so that we can easily view the deviation. To do this, we again right-clicked on Percent Order Qty SUM, but this time selected Format Exceptions. In the dialog box that was displayed, we added two exceptions based on the percentage. The first exception was formatted with a background color of light yellow when the percentage was greater than 60. The second exception was formatted in light blue when the percentage was between 25 and 49. Finally, we adjusted the column widths and scrolled the data to the left until only the percentages were showing. The final result is as you saw it in Figure 9-4.

Trend Analysis

Yet another crosstab! If you recall, this query displays the percentage of sales for each district for all of the quarters that the company has been in operation. We started by selecting the ship quantity, the quarter, and the district. As in the example for statistical analysis, we need to use the district without displaying the customer or the city. If you remember, we initially selected the customer name and the city in order to select the district. Then, we simply put back the customer name and the city, because Discoverer will remember the links.

Having selected our data, we placed the district in the side axis, and the quarter in the top axis, moving the quarter above the ship quantity. The following illustration shows step 3 of the Workbook Wizard, after we have placed the items in their correct positions.

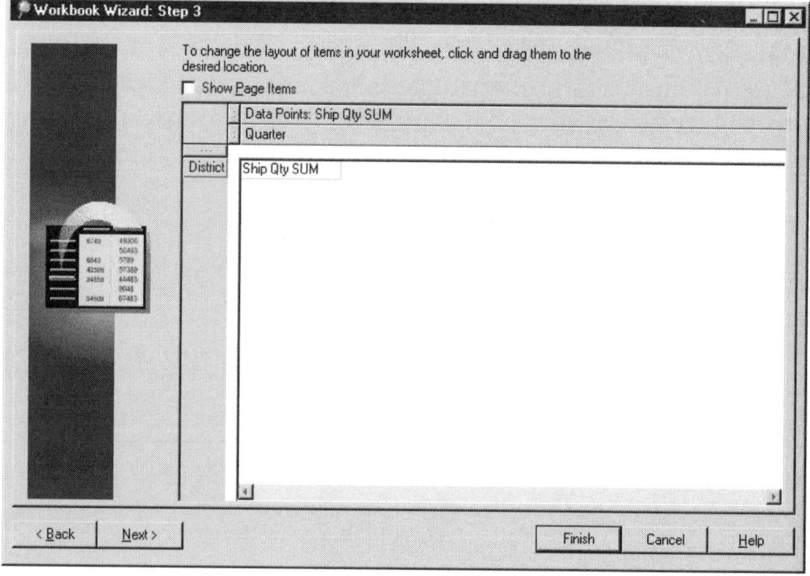

After clicking Finish, we added a suitable title and inserted a grand total of all data points. This resulted in the output shown next.

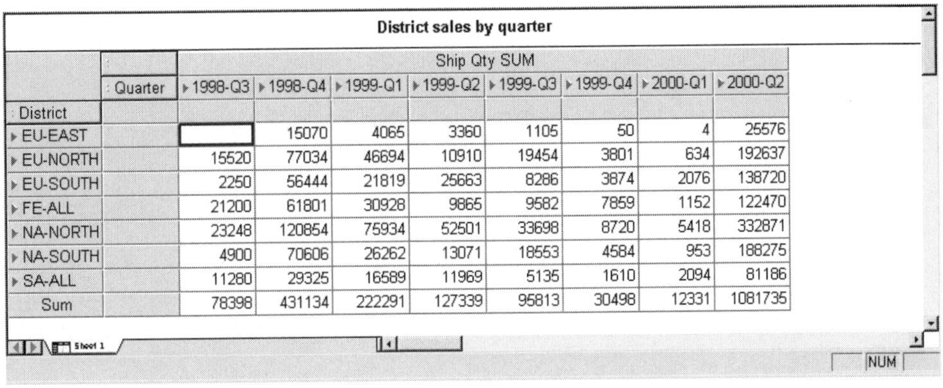

District sales by quarter

		Ship Qty SUM							
	Quarter	1998-Q3	1998-Q4	1999-Q1	1999-Q2	1999-Q3	1999-Q4	2000-Q1	2000-Q2
District									
EU-EAST			15070	4065	3360	1105	50	4	25576
EU-NORTH		15520	77034	46694	10910	19454	3801	634	192637
EU-SOUTH		2250	56444	21819	25663	8286	3874	2076	138720
FE-ALL		21200	61801	30928	9865	9582	7859	1152	122470
NA-NORTH		23248	120854	75934	52501	33698	8720	5418	332871
NA-SOUTH		4900	70606	26262	13071	18553	4584	953	188275
SA-ALL		11280	29325	16589	11969	5135	1610	2094	81186
Sum		78398	431134	222291	127339	95813	30498	12331	1081735

Sheet 1 NUM

To complete the query, we clicked on the top axis label called Ship Qty SUM, then clicked the Percentage button on the analysis bar. This produced a percentage that totaled 100 percent, derived by adding the percentages in each cell. This is not quite what we wanted, but we are almost there. All we did to complete the query was to right-click on the top axis label for the percentage, selected Edit Percentage from the drop-down menu, and changed the percentage to based on "Grand total for each column." The final result is shown in Figure 9-5.

Summary

Once we have a large amount of data, this should provide the basis and sufficient information to drive and push you to seek additional knowledge. Since large amounts of data are required, processing efficiency is essential—that is, we must have a means to effectively filter out unwanted data. A tool like Discoverer that provides these techniques at the click of a button is highly desirable. Accuracy is then required to ensure that whatever information is obtained, the knowledge gleaned from that information is valid. The results should be presented in a manner that is both understandable and interesting—that is, it must have potential value to the readers of the report.

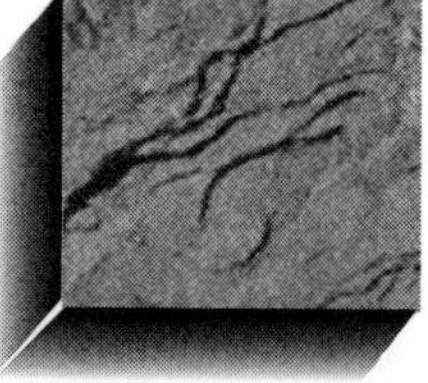

PART III

Advanced Discoverer Techniques

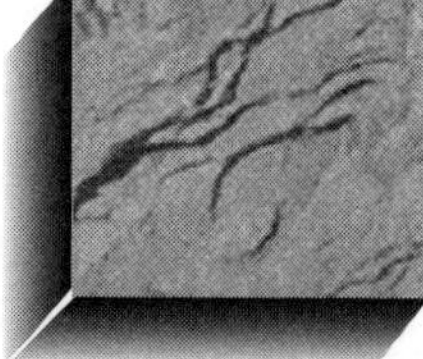

CHAPTER 10

Refining Items and Drilling

During the first nine chapters of this book, we have taught you how to create queries using the Workbook Wizard, how to analyze your data, and how to convert your queries into reports.

Most queries are not usually very efficient when first built. You run them to make sure that they at least work. Having avoided "The Query from the Twilight Zone" and decided that a query is worth keeping, you may have followed the steps in Chapter 9 and converted it into a report. Later, however, when working on a completely different problem, you may realize that a previous query satisfies most of the requirements. With a little tweaking and manipulation, you can modify or refine one query and turn it into another.

In this and the following two chapters, we will show you how to refine an existing query, how to fine-tune it, how to make it work more efficiently, or how to convert it into another query.

This chapter deals with refining the query items and drilling data.

Refining Query Items

Perhaps the most frequent task you will perform in Discoverer is refining the items in a query. Refining can be as simple as adding or removing an item, but even this can have its pitfalls, as you will see in the next section. The real fun comes when you start pivoting and drilling. These techniques allow a much more sophisticated method of refining a query. It actually takes a little time to understand the full implications of what is involved, so let's begin with the simplest: adding and removing items.

Adding or Removing Items

By far the simplest and most common way of refining a query is to select a new item, or take an item away. Refining a query using these techniques sounds so easy—you take away an item, or add a new item, and that's it, you have a new query. If only it really were this simple!

Unfortunately, these techniques are also one of the easiest ways to run into problems. Later in this section, we will detail some of the most common errors that you may encounter.

Adding a New Item

This is the simplest way to refine a query, but can still be somewhat tricky. We will introduce you to a workflow, plus give you an example of the most complicated way to add data by adding an item using an intermediate folder.

Adding a New Item To add a new item to an existing query, use the following workflow:

1. Decide what item needs to be added.
2. Open the Edit Sheet dialog box.
3. Examine Discoverer's open folders and see if the item you want is in a folder that you are already using. If the item you want is in one of the folders you are already using, proceed directly to step 7 of this workflow.
4. If the item you want is not in one of the folders that are currently in use, is it in a folder that is available? By this, we mean, is the folder containing the item you want, an active folder, or is it currently deactivated? If the item you want is in an active folder, proceed to step 7 of this workflow.

NOTE
Remember, a folder that is active has its name highlighted, while a folder that is inactive has its name grayed out.

5. If the item you want is not in one of the active folders, can the folder be activated by applying a join or joins through one or more intermediate folders? If the folder you want to get to cannot be accessed this way, you will not be able to add the desired item to your current query. Unfortunately, you will have to build a new query.

NOETIX
To determine if there is an intermediate folder, look in your system's help file. If you are using Noetix Views, look in the Noetix help file and examine the Z$ items. These are joins to other folders. Refer to Appendix B for a full explanation.

6. The item that you want is in a folder that can be accessed by joining through an intermediate folder. You will need to open the intermediate folder, then select any item from it. This should now make available the folder that contains the item that you want to add.

NOTE
You can use multiple intermediate folders to get to the folder that contains the item you require. Repeat step 6, as many times as required, until the item you need becomes available.

7. Open the folder containing the item that you want, and add the item to your query.

8. If you used any intermediate folders to join to the folder containing the item you just added, you should remove those folders now. Don't worry about removing these folders, because Discoverer will remember exactly how to join to the folder containing the item that you want.
9. Before you leave the Edit Sheet dialog box, revise the table layout, conditions, sort order, and calculations. In 3*i*, you can also revise the totals, parameters, and percentages.
10. Click OK, Discoverer now reruns the query and includes the item that you want.
11. Apply any formatting you require.
12. Save the query. Remember to save it under a new name if you want to also keep a copy of the original.

Adding items that are located inside folders that are either already in use or already active are simple tasks that do not need an example. However, adding an item by joining through an intermediate folder does need an example.

Adding an Item Using an Intermediate Folder Let us start from the following completed query and walk through all of the steps in the workflow. As you can see below, this simple query displays the total quantity ordered and the cost price for all customers.

	Customer Name	Order Qty SUM	Cost Price SUM
1	ABC WIDGET CO	80337	818386.77
2	ACE MANUFACTURING	60987	654151.82
3	BIG RIVER WIDGETS	35389	343241.26
4	BRIDGE THINGS	44049	475445.40
5	CASA DE WIDGETS	150651	1544599.53
6	CEBU WIDGET CO	137167	1311104.11
7	HONG KONG WIDGETS	90431	907242.29
8	LAC WIDGETS SA	98063	1084922.10
9	LAST RAILWAY WIDGETS	82183	926450.44
10	LONDON WIDGETS LTD.	88636	967561.39
11	LOTS OF WIDGETS	102522	956452.03
12	MOUNTAIN WIDGETS	83725	875412.89
13	MUM'S WIDGET CO.	137517	1460395.12
14	OXFORD WIDGETS	83706	858140.68
15	PALMELA WIDGETS	50819	504187.72
16	PATRIOT'S WIDGET CO.	105630	894759.96
17	REPUBLIC WIDGETS	61642	658400.92
18	RIO WIDGETS	46811	477540.84

Let us assume that we have been asked to change this query—to now display the totals by product line as well as by customer. Step 1 is complete, and as step 2 requires us to open the Edit Sheet dialog box, we did just that. In steps 3 and 4, we examined the currently used and active folders, and determined that the product line was not in any of those. As you can see here, the Product Line folder is inactive.

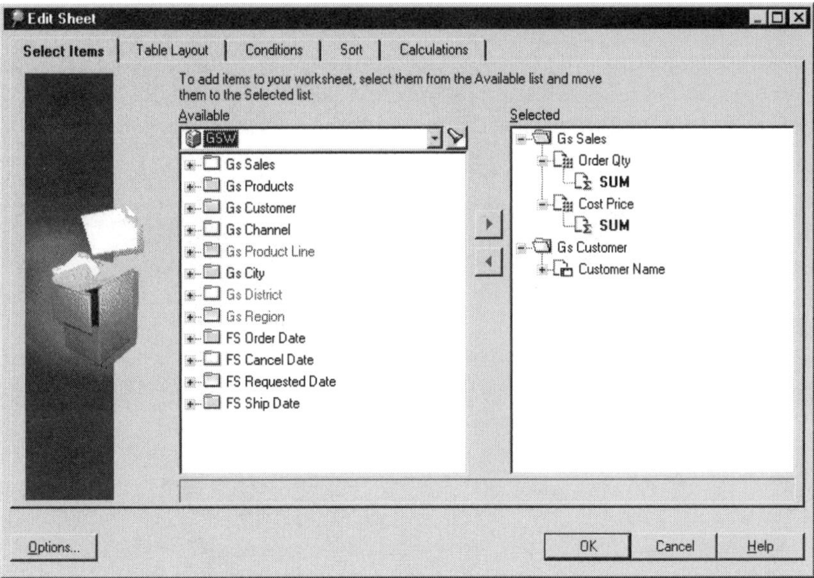

Step 5 of the workflow requires us to check whether any intermediate folder exists that can be joined to one of our in-use folders. After careful examination of our database (refer to Appendix D for a full data model of our database), we saw that there is indeed a join between the Products folder and the Product Line folder. Therefore, as required by step 6, we opened the Products folder and selected the product name. As you can see, these actions activated the Product Line folder.

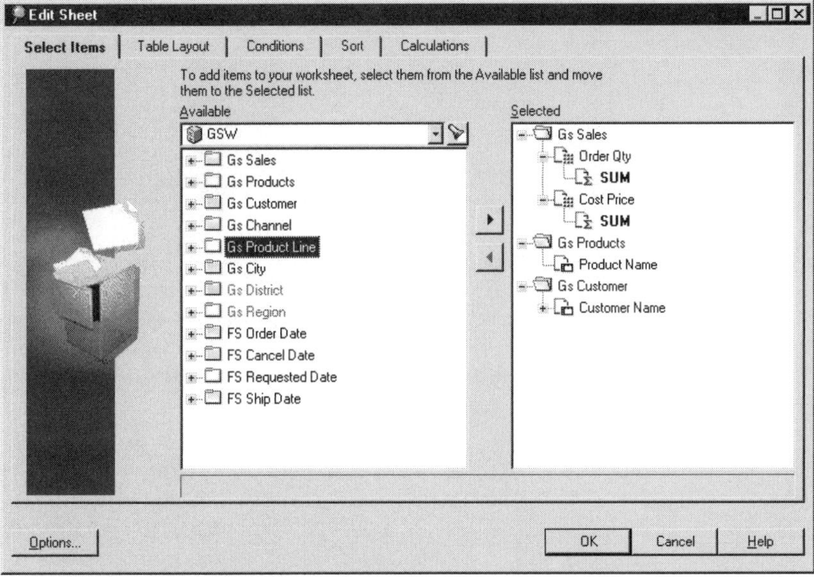

Adhering to step 7 of the workflow, we now were able to open the Product Line folder and added the product line item to our query. Removing the Products folder from our list of completed items thereby completed step 8. As you can see, even though we decided not to include anything from the Products folder, that folder enabled us to select the product line.

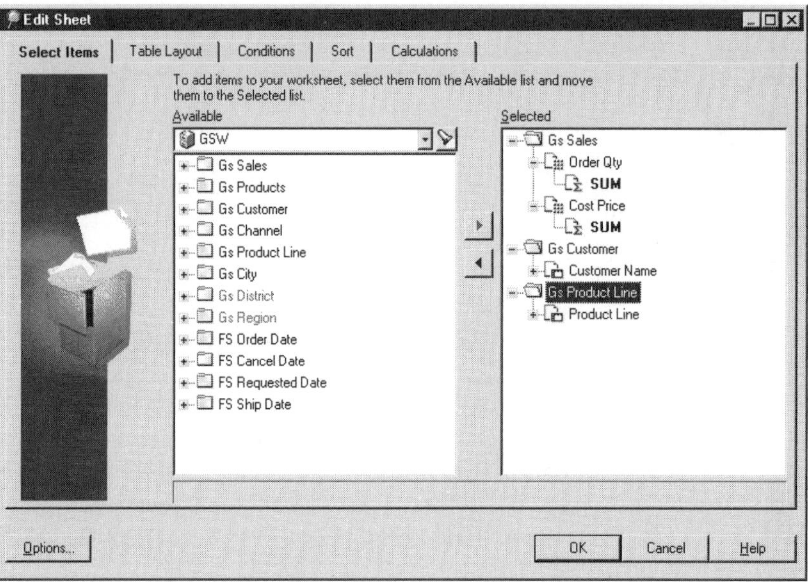

Finally, we completed the remaining steps of the workflow. We moved the product line alongside the customer name, applied a group sort on the customer, and a normal lo-to-hi sort on the product line.

	Customer Name	Product Line	Order Qty SUM	Cost Price SUM
1	ABC WIDGET CO	MEGA-WIDGET	31037	397825.06
2		SUPER-WIDGET	31138	258918.24
3		WONDER-WIDGET	18162	161643.47
4	ACE MANUFACTURING	MEGA-WIDGET	25917	323342.58
5		SUPER-WIDGET	19523	180997.30
6		WONDER-WIDGET	15547	149811.94
7	BIG RIVER WIDGETS	MEGA-WIDGET	10076	103701.16
8		SUPER-WIDGET	6822	57953.16
9		WONDER-WIDGET	18491	181586.94
10	BRIDGE THINGS	MEGA-WIDGET	26580	304312.00
11		SUPER-WIDGET	7959	84110.20
12		WONDER-WIDGET	9510	87023.20
13	CASA DE WIDGETS	MEGA-WIDGET	27169	330303.38
14		SUPER-WIDGET	59694	547912.59
15		WONDER-WIDGET	63788	666383.56
16	CEBU WIDGET CO	MEGA-WIDGET	40241	371376.08
17		SUPER-WIDGET	41612	359332.04
18		WONDER-WIDGET	55314	580395.99

The final result, as shown above, has effectively demonstrated how to add an item to a query using an intermediate folder. By adhering to the workflow outlined, we completed adding the product line without any difficulty.

NOTE
You can also add new items to a worksheet by using Discoverer's drilling capabilities. These are explained in detail later in this chapter in the section entitled "Drilling Into and Out of Data."

Removing an Item from Your Query

Removing a single item from a query is straightforward and easy to do. Of course, you can remove an item by launching the Edit Sheet dialog box and removing the item from the selections, but did you know you could just highlight the item and delete it by pressing the DELETE key? Refer to Chapter 6 for more information on removing items from queries.

Common Problems Associated with Adding or Removing Items

The most common problems users encounter when attempting to add or remove items are:

- Attempting to join multiple business areas
- Attempting to combine aggregate and detail data
- Attempting to join to the same child folder from multiple parent folders
- Multiple join methods from a child folder to a parent folder
- Missing joins
- Fan traps
- Lack of documentation

Attempting to Join Multiple Business Areas

Unless your Discoverer administrator has made it possible for you to link business areas together, you will usually not be able to select items from multiple business areas at the same time.

In the following example, we already have a query that selects the order quantity and cost price by product. After editing the sheet, we tried to select from another business area. As you can see in the following illustration, all of the folders in the other business area are deactivated.

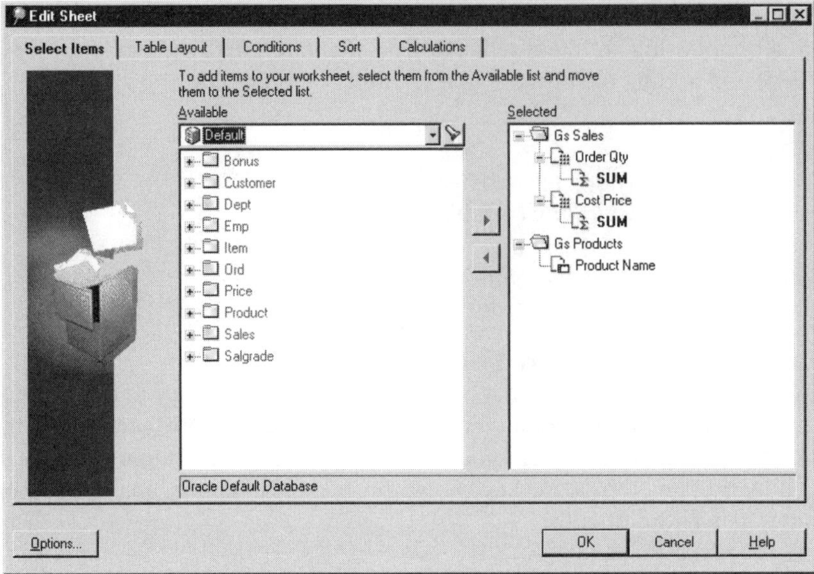

Attempting to Combine Aggregate and Detail Data

Another common error users make when adding new items to an existing query is to not define the new item to be at the same level of aggregation as the existing items.

In the following example, we have an existing query that selects the total quantity ordered by sales channel for the fiscal month of February 2000. We opened the Edit Sheet dialog box and attempted to add the ordered quantity detail to the same query. As you can see, Discoverer gave us the following warning.

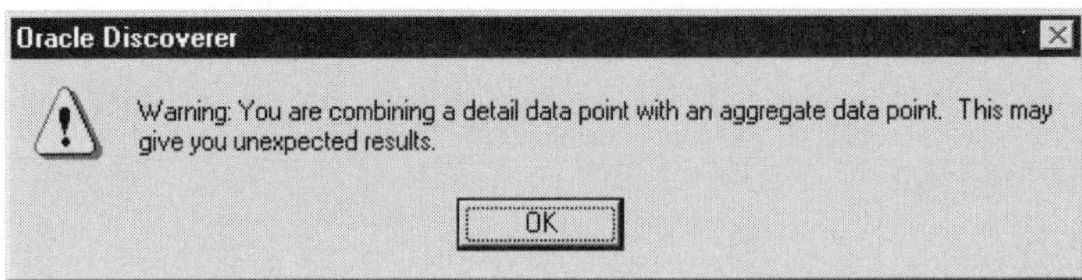

While Discoverer will not prevent you from mixing aggregate and detail data in the same query, be warned—your results may be incorrect. We ignored the warning that Discoverer gave us and ran the query anyway. This produced a very interesting result. As you can see, we placed a group sort on the channel and then subtotaled by channel. You might expect the subtotal for order quantity sum and order quantity total to be the same, but they are not! The correct answer is the one for the subtotal based on the order quantity sum, but if you did not know this, you could easily quote the wrong total to your manager or, worse still, to a customer or your shareholders, and understate the quantity booked by almost 200,000 items!

Page Items: Month: FEB-00

	Channel	Order Qty SUM	Order Qty
35		10000	5000
36		43200	4800
37		4000	4000
38		3800	3800
39		28800	3600
40		60000	2400
41		2000	2000
42		1800	1800
43		1600	1600
44	Sum	246735	47019
45	INTERNET	4	1
46		2	2
47		5	5
48		20	10
49		15	15
50		72	24

Attempting to Join to the Same Child Folder from Multiple Parent Folders

Pay particular attention when combining aggregate data with detail data, because this can give you problems. Data warehouses, for example, are usually built around a star schema with one or more fact tables and multiple dimensions. When multiple fact tables are employed, one of them usually contains only aggregated data, while the other(s) contain varying amounts of detail. If you have a query that pulls data from the aggregated folder, and then refine that query to also pull from the detail folder, you will have problems. Not only will Discoverer be trying to mix this data in the same row, but Discoverer will not be able to correctly identify which fact folder to use when joining to the remaining dimension folders.

As you can see in the following illustration, Discoverer states that you have an invalid join configuration. Unless you have the 3.1.41 version of Discoverer, you will not be able to continue.

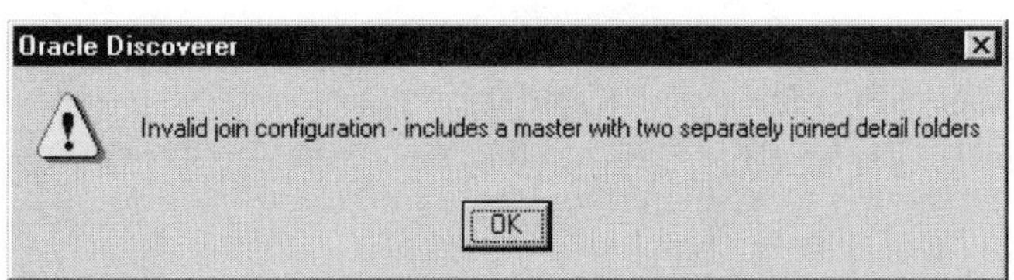

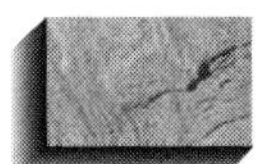

NOTE

*For an explanation of star schema terminology, please refer to Appendix B. The previous example has been corrected in 3.1.41, and will soon be corrected in 3*i *by Oracle's clever solution for fan trap problems. See the section in this chapter on fan traps for a full explanation.*

Multiple Join Methods from a Child Folder to a Parent Folder

Another easy-to-make mistake relates to incorrectly joining a child folder to a parent folder. The most common mistake that we have seen relates to users misunderstanding their company's use of foreign currencies and multicurrencies.

In the modern era, many companies use multiple currencies from around the world. Within the Sales Order folder, there could be amounts stored in the local, regional, and corporate currencies. A local currency is the currency of the transaction (USD, GBP, TWD, CHF and so on). A regional currency is the currency in which a region aggregates its amounts (for example, the European region could decide to aggregate using the Euro). A corporate currency is the currency in which the company decides to report its quarterly and annual returns.

However, most systems will probably have only one currency folder, containing the currency code and currency description for all currencies in use, probably using the ISO (International Standards Organization) set of currency codes. When users attempt to add currency codes into a query that is using multiple currencies, they need to be very careful to choose the correct link; otherwise, they could display the EURO code alongside the local amounts.

NOTE

While Discoverer will prompt for which join to make, it is down to the user to make the correct choice. Making a wrong join at this stage could cause the query to produce the entirely wrong result. You will have no choice but to rebuild the query, because once you have chosen a join, there is no going back.

For example, using our currency code model outlined above, suppose you have a query that reports by both regional and local currencies. Next, we want to add the currency code for the local currency. When you try to add this item, Discoverer recognizes that there is more than one way to join to this folder and opens the following Join Folders dialog box.

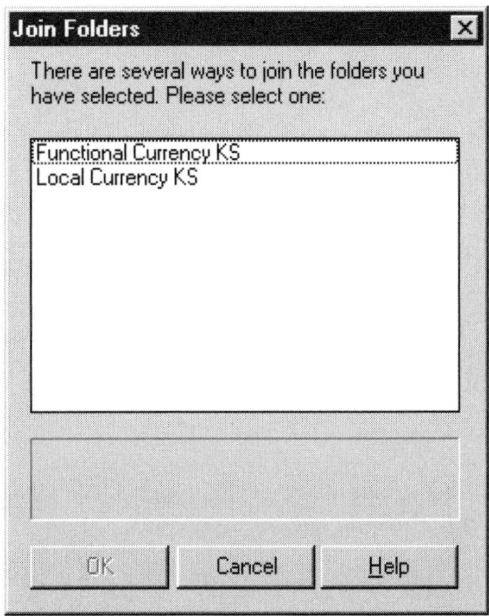

As you can see above, Discoverer tells you that there is more than one way of joining the folders you have selected. You should select the join that you want to use and click OK.

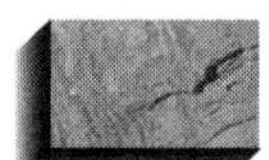

NOTE
This is a perfect example of why you need to take time to understand your data model. It is the responsibility of your Discoverer administrator to display this model in terms that are meaningful to your job. Discoverer prompts you with the names of the joins. It is a poor implementation if your Discoverer administrator chooses to display the primary- and foreign-key names, names that will probably be meaningless to you. It is your responsibility to know which join you need. A description of each join is displayed when selected to give you more information. If you have any doubt as to which one you should select, contact your Discoverer administrator.

To summarize this section, when adding or removing items from a query with multiple join capabilities between the folders, you need to take extra special care.

You need to make sure that you are fully aware of what joins are already being employed within the query.

Missing Joins

When you are attempting to add an item to your query, you may find that there is no join to the folder containing the item that you want. With many databases, there is usually more than one way to join folders together. First, you should see if there is a way to open up the folder you want by linking via an intermediate folder. If you cannot find a way to join to the folder that you want, you need to talk to your Discoverer administrator.

The two most common reasons that you cannot join folders together are as follows:

1. The Discoverer administrator did not expect this type of query to be used, and has not made the join available to you.
2. The Discoverer administrator purposely did not make the join available to you, because it would result in incorrect aggregation or expose sensitive data.

In either of the above cases, you should discuss your requirements with your Discoverer administrator. He or she may be able to define a new join that will allow you to select the items that you need.

Fan Traps

The fan trap problem has plagued administrators for a very long time, and until the recent launch of the 3.1.41 version of Discoverer, the fan trap was one of the most feared situations that could arise. Prior to the release of 3.1.41, all Discoverer could do was detect that a fan trap had occurred and then prevent the query from running.

In order to protect against the fan trap occurring, Discoverer has, as the default, an option to prevent you from building a query that contains fan traps. In the following illustration, activated from Tools | Options | Advanced, you can see in the center that Discoverer has an option to disable fan trap detection.

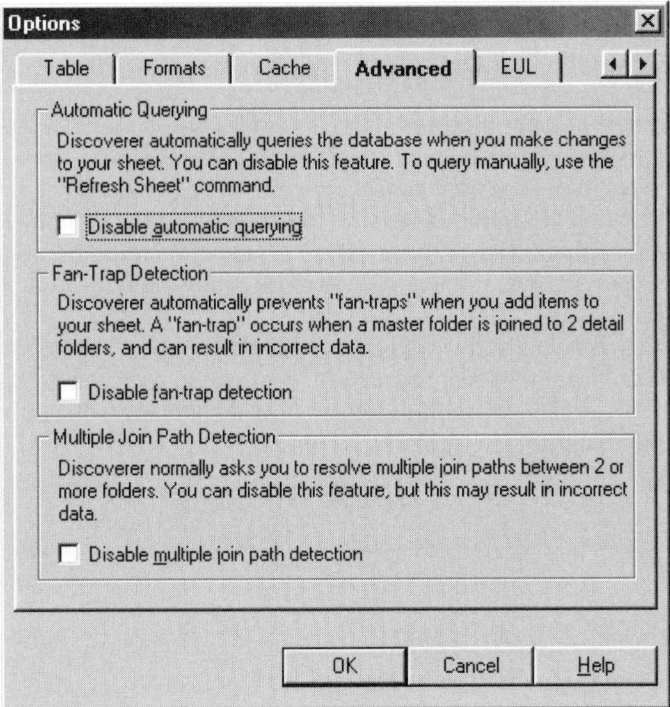

NOTE
Unless you are very proficient at writing queries and know how to control fan traps, or you have 3.1.41 installed, we strongly advise you not to disable this protection.

Oracle states that "*Discoverer 3.1.41 is the only product on the market that detects a fan trap, rewrites the query and executes the query on the server.*" While, at the time of writing, the solution is only available in the Windows product, Oracle hopes to make it available on the Web soon for both 3*i* and the Discoverer Viewer products.

But what is a fan trap? The following quotation is taken from the Oracle Technical White Paper "*Oracle Discoverer's Fan Trap Resolution – Correct Results*

Every Time," which was published in April 2000. The extracts reproduced in this section are given with the kind permission of Oracle Corporation.

Put very simply, a fan trap is a SQL query that generates unexpected results. The most common manifestation occurs when a master table is joined to two detail tables separately and results in incorrectly aggregated measures. To the end user the definition is meaningless, yet the consequences can be catastrophic.

Let us give you an example of what we mean by a fan trap. We have created a new business area that contains three folders: a Department folder, a Budget folder, and an Expense folder. The following three illustrations show the contents of each of these folders.

The illustration below shows all of the data in the Department folder. As you can see, there are just five departments. We want you to concentrate on department 10, the Sales department. We will show you how the fan trap will cause this department's amounts to be calculated incorrectly.

	Dept Number	Department
1	10	SALES
2	20	HR
3	30	MIS
4	40	MARKETING
5	50	TRAINING

The following illustration shows the data in the Budget folder. For each department, there is an allotted budget for the categories Equipment and Travel, along with the date the budget was set. We again draw your attention to the rows for department 10, the Sales department. As you can see, this department's budget for Equipment is 5,000, while for Travel their budget is 40,000.

	Dept Number	Budget Date	Budget Reason	Budget Amount SUM
1	10	24-JUL-2000	EQUIPMENT	5000.00
2	10	24-JUL-2000	TRAVEL	40000.00
3	20	25-JUL-2000	EQUIPMENT	2000.00
4	20	25-JUL-2000	TRAVEL	200.00
5	30	19-AUG-2000	EQUIPMENT	25500.00
6	30	19-AUG-2000	TRAVEL	10000.00
7	40	30-JUN-2000	EQUIPMENT	4250.00
8	40	30-JUN-2000	TRAVEL	25000.00
9	50	30-JUN-2000	EQUIPMENT	2090.00
10	50	30-JUN-2000	TRAVEL	200.00

The next illustration shows the data in the Expense folder. For some departments, there have been some expenses recorded. As you can see, for the

Sales department, number 10, we have recorded their expenses so far, for a total amount of 1,400.

	Dept Number	Expense Date	Expense Amount SUM
1	10	01-AUG-2000	150.00
2	10	20-AUG-2000	250.00
3	10	01-SEP-2000	1000.00
4	20	16-AUG-2000	1025.00
5	30	01-SEP-2000	12000.00
6	40	30-AUG-2000	2750.00

Our intention is to build a query by pulling data from all three folders, with the notion of showing the total amount of budget and expenses incurred to date. For our sales department, we know that the total budget is 45,000, and the total expenses so far are 1,400.

First of all, we attempted to build the query with Discoverer's fan trap detection in place. In the following illustration, you can see that we have almost completed building the query. We have already selected the items that we want from the Department and Budget folders, and are about to select an item from the Expense folder. This is the fan trap scenario.

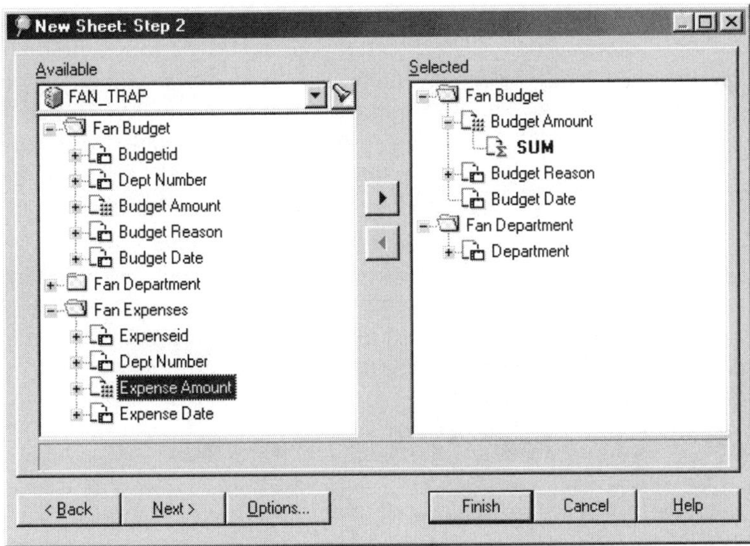

As expected, Discoverer will not allow this, and displayed the following error message.

Next we disabled the fan trap protection. We were able to build and run the query, but the results were totally incorrect. Look at the following illustration closely.

	Department	Budget Reason	Budget Date	Budget Amount SUM	Expense Date	Expense Amount SUM
1	HR	EQUIPMENT	25-JUL-2000	2000.00	16-AUG-2000	1025.00
2		TRAVEL	25-JUL-2000	200.00	16-AUG-2000	1025.00
3	MARKETING	EQUIPMENT	30-JUN-2000	4250.00	30-AUG-2000	2750.00
4		TRAVEL	30-JUN-2000	25000.00	30-AUG-2000	2750.00
5	MIS	EQUIPMENT	19-AUG-2000	25500.00	01-SEP-2000	12000.00
6		TRAVEL	19-AUG-2000	10000.00	01-SEP-2000	12000.00
7	SALES	EQUIPMENT	24-JUL-2000	5000.00	01-AUG-2000	150.00
8			24-JUL-2000	5000.00	20-AUG-2000	250.00
9			24-JUL-2000	5000.00	01-SEP-2000	1000.00
10		TRAVEL	24-JUL-2000	40000.00	01-AUG-2000	150.00
11			24-JUL-2000	40000.00	20-AUG-2000	250.00
12			24-JUL-2000	40000.00	01-SEP-2000	1000.00

As you can see, we do indeed have all of the items in the query, but the answer we got for the Sales department is incorrect. If you add up the total amount budgeted, you will see that this comes to 135,000 (three times more than expected), while for expenses, the amount is 2,800 (twice more than expected). The reason that this has happened is that Discoverer has built a temporary table and made joins in the data for every occurrence of budget and expense (the detail folder), by department (the master folder). Budget is overstated threefold because there are three expense items. Expenses are overstated by double because there are two budget reasons.

The following illustration shows the aggregated totals from the above query using version 3.1.36 of Discoverer. As you can see, the amounts are considerably overstated and Discoverer does not even include a row for the Training department. This is because there are no expenses for training, and therefore the null value causes the entire row to be omitted.

Workbook1

	Code	Expense	Budget
1	HR	2200.00	2200.00
2	MIS	24000.00	35500.00
3	SALES	2800.00	135000.00
4	MARKETING	5500.00	29250.00

Sheet 1

Unless you upgrade to Discoverer 3.1.41, you will have difficulty building a query that correctly returns the answer that you want. We say difficult because it is possible for your Discoverer administrator to build a new view of the database eliminating the fan trap. This sort of customization, though, is something that your company will probably try to avoid.

3*i* NOTE

*For those of you running Discoverer 3*i*, you will be pleased to know that the automatic rewrite feature that resolves fan traps will be implemented in 3*i*. At the time of going to press, the exact release date of this version is not known.*

Taking the exact same query that was written to show the incorrect aggregates obtained from 3.1.36, we upgraded our database to 3.1.41. Using the identical steps that we used earlier, this time the results were correct. Discoverer automatically rewrote the query to produce the correct results. No alert was given during this process, and the illustration below shows the results of running the query. As you can see, the totals for both budget and expenses are correct.

Workbook1

	Department	Expense Amount	Budget Amount
1	TRAINING	0.00	2290.00
2	HR	1025.00	2200.00
3	MIS	12000.00	35500.00
4	SALES	1400.00	45000.00
5	MARKETING	2750.00	29250.00

Sheet 1

Guaranteeing the Correct Results The following extracts are also quotations from the Oracle white paper.

Every query generated by Discoverer is interrogated. Discoverer will detect a fan trap and rewrite the query to ensure that the aggregation is done at the correct level.

Not only does it (Discoverer) leverage the database engine to completely derive the result set but Discoverer's fan trap solution extends to other fan trap scenarios.

The second type of fan trap involves aggregation at different levels within a hierarchy that spans multiple tables. For example, Customer-Order-Order Detail. A customer's order can contain many order lines – but the order table may hold its own totals and a query may try to aggregate both from the order table and the orderline table. Discoverer rewrites the query similar to the example above by aggregating first and then joining the results together through the use of inline views.

Zero Administration and Zero Training Required

Discoverer's solution requires no data model changes or semantic layer modifications to implement. Once installed, user's queries will automatically be rewritten. Even saved queries containing a fan trap will automatically be rewritten.

We commend Oracle for finding a solution to this problem. To take advantage of Oracle's fan trap solution, your company will need to upgrade to Discoverer version 3.1.41.

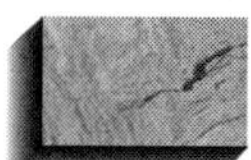

NOTE

If you upgrade to Discoverer 3.1.41, your company will need to allow time for the upgrade to take place. Discoverer requires that the EUL be updated and this can take from minutes to several hours, depending on the size and complexity of your database. During this time, there should be no one running queries using Discoverer. The good news is that you do not need to upgrade all of your local copies of Discoverer at the same time. Discoverer is perfectly happy for your EUL to be in version 3.1.41, with your client machines running 3.1.36 or above. You can then upgrade the client copies at leisure, although users will not be able to take advantage of the fan trap correction until this has happened.

Lack of Documentation

Probably the one thing that will put you at the biggest disadvantage is a lack of adequate documentation. It is essential that you, and preferably your company, keep documentation about queries. It is very common to find users building queries, saving them, using them for a while, then forgetting all about them.

At some point in the future there is a change requirement. Perhaps the person who created the query is no longer with the company, or you find a batch of queries sitting in a folder on your network and you have no idea who created them. So what do you do? What usually happens is that someone reinvents the wheel—sits down in his or her cubicle for several weeks and produces a complete new batch of queries.

Adequate documentation could have avoided some of this work. At least recording who did what and why, along with a specimen printout and a list of items and conditions, could have circumvented the need to draft up a new batch of queries. If your company has not yet recognized the need for documenting Discoverer queries, that time will come.

When all is said and done, prevention is better than the cure. What a wonderful feeling you will have when you can sit back and relax while your coworkers document their queries, safe in the knowledge that your queries were all documented a long time ago.

Pivoting and Drilling

Pivoting and drilling are two of the real "nice to use" features of Discoverer. In an experienced user's hands, the tools can be made to manipulate data in ways that were undreamed of only a couple of years ago.

Pivoting Data

During the previous chapter on analysis, we showed you how to move items between the various axes. If you recall, there are three of these: the top axis, side axis, and page axis. Simple tables and crosstabs have both a side and top axis, although the side axis on a table is only being used to display row numbers. Turning on Page Items opens up the third axis, the page axis.

The term given to moving data between these axes is called "pivoting." Using this technique, you can rearrange your data to reveal relationships that may not be apparent.

Duplicating Tables and Crosstabs as New Worksheets

There are times when you will build a query that you think is just right and you don't want to touch it for fear of messing it up. However, you can see that with a few changes it will serve another purpose. You have two choices: you can save the workbook as a new file, leaving the original workbook intact, or duplicate the query within the workbook. It is a good idea to keep queries with a similar purpose together as a means of data management. Discoverer has made it very easy to duplicate queries as new worksheets within the same workbook.

Duplicating a Worksheet as a Table

You can duplicate either a crosstab or a table as a table. You do this through the Duplicate as Table dialog box.

You have three methods of opening the Duplicate as Table dialog box:

- From the menu bar by clicking on Sheet | Duplicate as Table.
- From the toolbar by clicking the Duplicate as Table button as seen here:

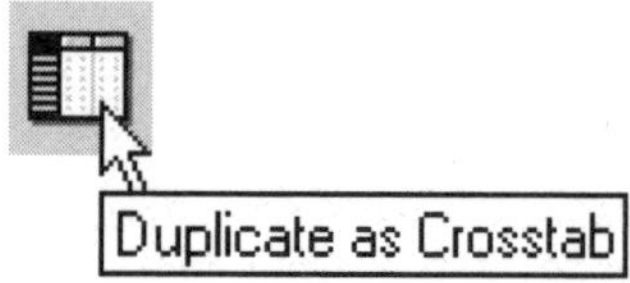

- From a pop-up list, which you access by right-clicking on the Sheet tab at the lower-left corner of the worksheet and clicking Duplicate as Table. This is shown here:

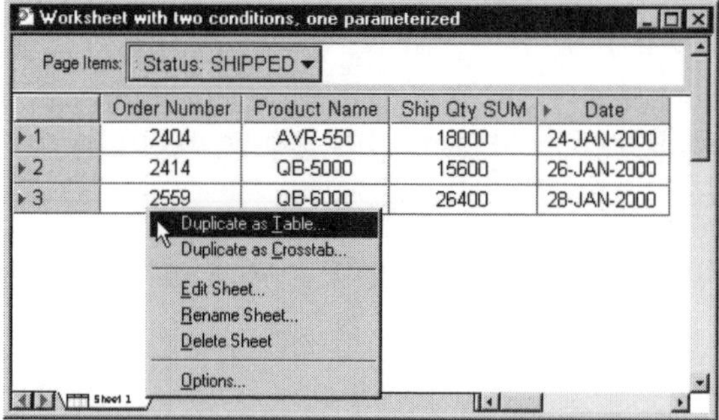

The Duplicate as Table dialog box is identical to the Edit Sheet dialog box; however, when you finish making your refinements and click OK, you will have a new worksheet in your workbook. In 3.1, you could simply click OK and go to the sheet directly for modification. In 3*i*, on the other hand, you should make as many of the desired adjustments as possible before running the new query.

Duplicating a Worksheet as a Crosstab

The method for duplicating a worksheet as a crosstab is virtually identical to that of a table. The only differences are:

- From the menu bar, select Sheet | Duplicate as Crosstab.
- From the toolbar, click the Duplicate as Crosstab button, shown in the following illustration.

- From a pop-up list, which you access by right-clicking on the Sheet tab at the lower-left corner of the worksheet and clicking Duplicate as Crosstab.

Either of the above three methods will open the Duplicate as Crosstab dialog box. Again, this dialog box has the same functionality as the Edit Sheet dialog box. The Duplicate as Crosstab dialog box opens with the data set up to be pivoted into the format that you want. You can make your modifications here, or directly in the worksheet in 3.1, but you should do as much as possible before running the new query in 3*i*.

Renaming Worksheets

If you are going to have multiple worksheets in a workbook, it is a good idea to give them meaningful names. Discoverer gives them the default names of Sheet 1, Sheet

2, and so on. It is a simple task to rename the sheets, and it will help to keep you organized within the workbook. We like meaningful names, and Discoverer will allow you to give the sheets very long names. However, just like with filenames, don't get carried away, because if you use too long a sheet name, you will not be able to see the tabs of the other sheets without using a set of navigation arrows in the lower left of the workbook.

Renaming Worksheets in Discoverer 3.1

You can access the Rename Sheet dialog box in the following three ways:

- From the menu bar, by clicking on Sheet | Rename Sheet.
- From the pop-up list, which you access by right-clicking on the Sheet tab at the lower-left corner of the worksheet and clicking Rename Sheet.
- By double-clicking the Sheet tab at the lower-left corner of the worksheet.

To rename a worksheet, use the following workflow:

1. Use one of the methods above to open the Rename Sheet dialog box.
2. Type in the new worksheet name.
3. Click OK.

Renaming Worksheets in Discoverer 3*i*

To rename a worksheet in Discoverer 3*i*, use the following workflow:

1. Double-click the Sheet tab at the lower-left corner of the worksheet. This opens the Rename Sheet dialog box.
2. Type in the new worksheet name.
3. Click OK.

Drilling Into and Out of Data

Drilling into and out of data is a technique that enables you to view more data on a related item. Drilling is also a shortcut for adding another item to your query. For example, suppose you have a query that shows all votes cast for each person in a presidential election and you want to see how those votes were cast in each state. Discoverer will allow you to view this data with a few clicks of the mouse, without having to rebuild the query. Drilling is done from the Drill dialog box or directly in your result set.

Drilling is currently limited to up or down a predefined hierarchy in Discoverer 3*i*. In a future release, all the drill features described below will be available.

As shown in Figure 10-1, the Drill dialog box consists of the following features:

- **Drill Up/Down** Click this radio button to drill to an item in the "Where do you want to drill to?" selection box. If there are no items available in the selection box, the OK button will be disabled. This option allows you to drill to items that belong to a predefined hierarchy, such as City to Region to District.
- **Drill to a Related Item** Click this radio button to drill up or down to an aggregate level to data that is related but is not part of a predefined hierarchy, such as Status to State or City Name to Address.
- **Drill to Detail in another Sheet** Click this radio button to drill to data that is in the workbook, but is not in the data's hierarchy. Another sheet is created to show these details.
- **Where do you want to drill from?** The row or column that you were in when you opened the dialog box will appear as the default. To change the item to be drilled from, click on the down arrow for a drop-down list of available items. Depending upon whether the item now selected is part of a predefined hierarchy; the content of some of the other boxes may change.
- **Where do you want to drill to?** This is list of available items. The content of the list varies, depending upon other selections you make within the dialog box. For example, if you check the Drill Up/Down box and select to drill from an item that is part of a predefined hierarchy, this box will contain a list of the items in the hierarchy. Beside each item will be an arrow, indicating whether you can drill up or down to that item. If you opt to drill to a related item, this box will give you a list of the remaining items in the folders used in the current worksheet. Use this to add single items to your worksheet. If you opted to drill to detail in another sheet, this box contains "Show component rows of selected values" as the only option.
- **Options** Clicking this button opens the Drill Options dialog box, which we will discuss later.

To drill within a worksheet, use the following workflow:

1. Click in the cell, row, or column containing the data you want to drill from.
2. Right click and select Drill from the drop-down list, or select Sheet | Drill from the menu bar. This opens the Drill dialog box, as seen in Figure 10-1.

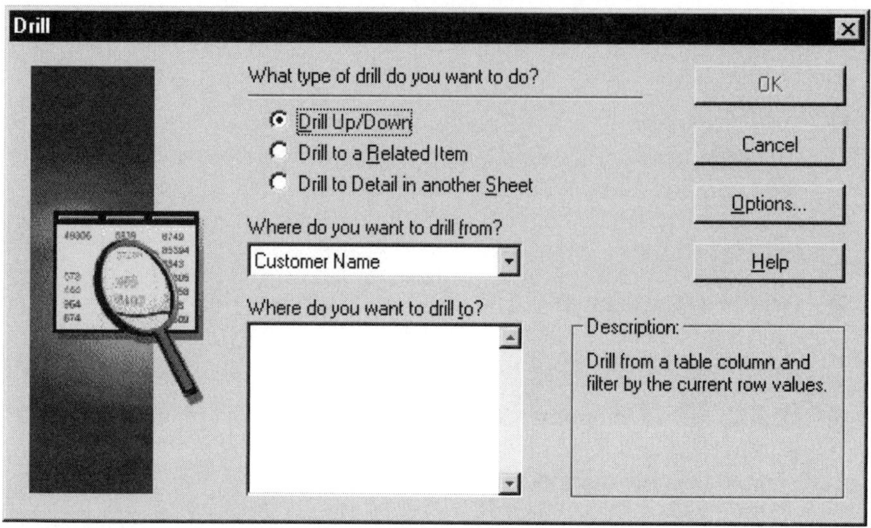

FIGURE 10-1. *Drill dialog box*

3. Make the desired selections.
4. Click OK.

Drill Options Dialog Box

The Drill Options dialog box allows you to customize the drill results. As shown in Figure 10-2, this dialog box consists of the following features:

- **When drilling to a new item, current item is** This area allows you to either expand the query to include the new item or replace the current item with the new item.
- **Place drill results in** Here, you decide whether you want the drill results to be displayed in the current worksheet or in a new worksheet.
- **Display results as** If you want to display the results in a new worksheet, in this area you can decide whether to display them as a table or a crosstab.

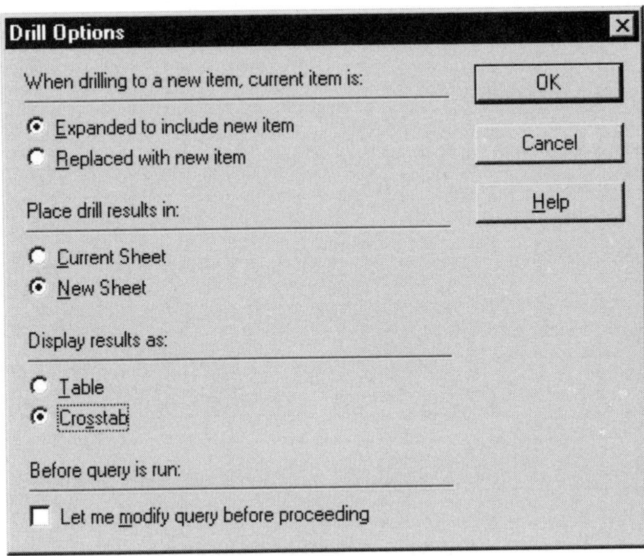

FIGURE 10-2. *Drill Options dialog box*

- **Before query is run** Tick this box if you want to modify the new worksheet before it runs. When you complete the drill by clicking OK in the Drill dialog box, Discoverer opens the New Sheet dialog box. This box is identical to the Edit Sheet dialog box and allows you to make any edits and modifications you want before the query runs.

STICKY FEATURE

Discoverer remembers the settings you make in the Drill Options dialog box, and uses these as the default each time you drill. Even if you don't open the Drill Options dialog box, those options will still be applied.

Let us use the Global Widgets database to show you how easy it is to drill within Discoverer. The following illustration shows a query that has customer name, city, order status, quantity shipped, and selling price. As you can see, this is a very simple query and one that could easily form the basis for many other queries.

	Customer Name	City Name	Status	Qty Shipped	Selling Price
1	ABC WIDGET CO	SEOUL	CANCELLED	1,900	139,230.00
2		SEOUL	OPEN	0	206,415.59
3		SEOUL	SHIPPED	61,733	1,398,638.34
4	ACE MANUFACTURING	LISBON	CANCELLED	300	8,830.00
5		LISBON	OPEN	0	454,309.33
6		LISBON	SHIPPED	42,187	897,862.56
7	BIG RIVER WIDGETS	DALLAS	CANCELLED	176	162,089.50
8		DALLAS	OPEN	0	172,600.90
9		DALLAS	SHIPPED	17,179	382,312.41
10	BRIDGE THINGS	SAN FRANCISCO	CANCELLED	3,400	77,400.00
11		SAN FRANCISCO	OPEN	0	41,854.45
12		SAN FRANCISCO	SHIPPED	35,998	884,843.44
13	CASA DE WIDGETS	MADRID	CANCELLED	0	522,513.63
14		MADRID	OPEN	0	786,971.22
15		MADRID	SHIPPED	86,544	1,880,475.54
16	CEBU WIDGET CO	MANILLA	CANCELLED	0	30,131.80
17		MANILLA	OPEN	0	609,415.50
18		MANILLA	SHIPPED	103,483	2,080,474.79

We will now show you how easy it is to drill into more data from this query. First of all, we will drill to see all of the remaining items about one of our customers, Ace Manufacturing. To do this, you would use the following workflow:

1. Click in the cell containing the customer name.
2. Right-click and select Drill from the drop-down list, or select Sheet | Drill from the menu bar. This opens the Drill dialog box as seen in Figure 10-1.
3. Complete the drill dialog box and then select "Drill to Detail in another Sheet."
4. Double-click on the folder you want to drill to.
5. If you opted to select "Let me modify the query before proceeding," Discoverer will open the workbook with it. Make any modifications you need, then click Finish. Discoverer will now run the new query.

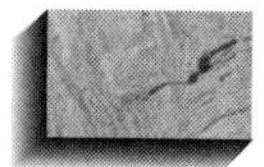

NOTE
Using this method, you can only drill when the item you are drilling to is in a folder that you do not currently have open.

Drilling into Data from a Graph

Discoverer allows you to drill into data from a graph. This is a clever feature for those of us who are visual in the way that we work.

To drill into data from a graph, use the following workflow:

1. From the graph that you have created, double-click on the item that you want to drill from. This opens the Drill dialog box.
2. Determine the type of drill that you want to do.
3. Click the Options button to define whether you want to add items in a new sheet.
4. If you are going to use a new sheet, in the New Sheet dialog box, remove any items that are not required and define any other criteria that you want to use.
5. Click OK.

For example, we have a pie graph (see the following illustration) showing the status of all of our sales for Q1 of 2000.

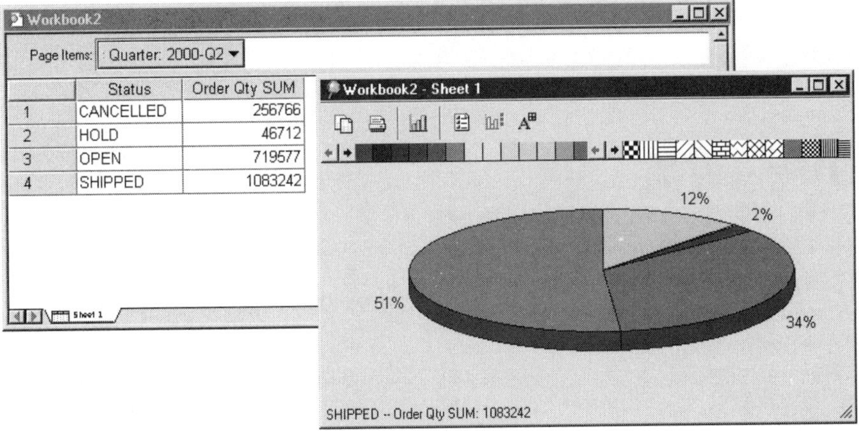

We can see instantly that the cancellations for that quarter are extremely high. When compared to the other totals, cancellations make up the third largest order quantity. Looking then at the third largest piece of the pie graph, it is evident that cancellations are making up 12 percent of the total. We want to know why this is so, and will use Discoverer's drill capability to find out. The process for doing this is simple. Because you are already familiar with the Drill dialog box, we will not explain it again here. However, we will show you the end result of drilling into data from a graph.

First, we double clicked in the graph on the Cancellations wedge in the pie. This opened the Drill dialog box. Because we wanted to see more of the detail associated with the cancellations, we opted to display the results in a new sheet. As we believe that analysis is easier in a crosstab, this is the type of worksheet that we selected. Before we completed the drill, we edited the new worksheet and removed the items that did not appear to be of interest. The resulting crosstab is shown next.

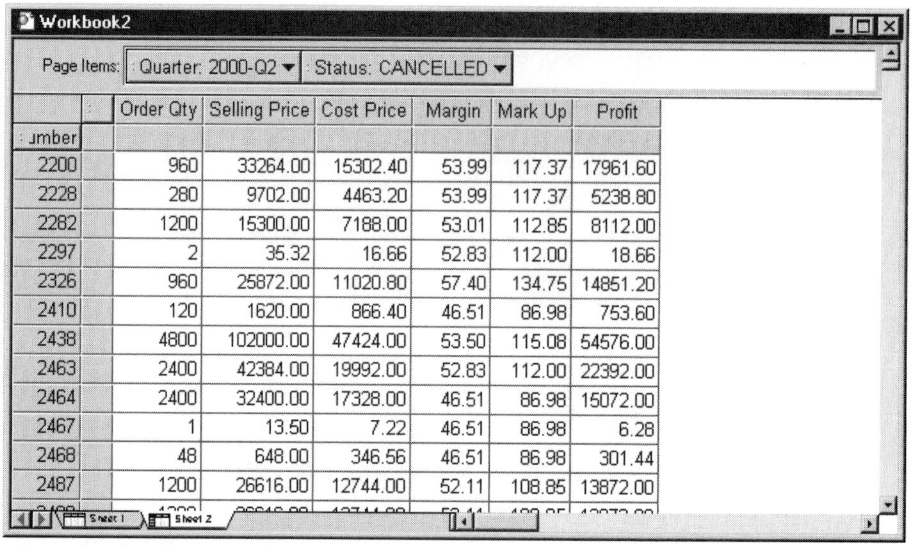

Workbook2

Page Items: Quarter: 2000-Q2 | Status: CANCELLED

umber	Order Qty	Selling Price	Cost Price	Margin	Mark Up	Profit
2200	960	33264.00	15302.40	53.99	117.37	17961.60
2228	280	9702.00	4463.20	53.99	117.37	5238.80
2282	1200	15300.00	7188.00	53.01	112.85	8112.00
2297	2	35.32	16.66	52.83	112.00	18.66
2326	960	25872.00	11020.80	57.40	134.75	14851.20
2410	120	1620.00	866.40	46.51	86.98	753.60
2438	4800	102000.00	47424.00	53.50	115.08	54576.00
2463	2400	42384.00	19992.00	52.83	112.00	22392.00
2464	2400	32400.00	17328.00	46.51	86.98	15072.00
2467	1	13.50	7.22	46.51	86.98	6.28
2468	48	648.00	346.56	46.51	86.98	301.44
2487	1200	26616.00	12744.00	52.11	108.85	13872.00

Sheet 1 | Sheet 2

Summary

In this chapter you have been shown how to further manipulate your queries to make them more powerful. You have been shown how to add and remove items from your queries and the most common problems associated with it. We have also shown you the fan trap and how to avoid it, as well as possible solutions to this problem.

You have been taught how pivoting data items between axes allows you to view the same data in different ways. You were also shown how sometimes when pivoting the data items there are no data points displayed at all. It happens to us all, so work with it and become more expert; then, your queries can become more meaningful.

We showed you how to duplicate tables and crosstabs. This is a simple process, and because so many queries can be created using almost the same data, you should give it a try. This will keep you from creating almost the same workbook over and over and help you to organize your work. Another method of organization is renaming workbooks within worksheets. You have been taught how a few simple steps will save you time and possible frustration in the future.

Finally, you were shown how to drill into data to "dig deeper" into a data item. Drilling is an excellent way to get a closer look at a particular piece of the data. You also learned how easy it is to drill from a graph. Using the visual approach can sometimes keep you from missing something that would not jump out at you if it were viewed only as numbers or text.

In the next chapter, you will learn the power of creating conditions, from the simple to the complex.

CHAPTER 11

Building Effective Conditions

fter refining the query items, and pivoting the data, perhaps the next most common way to refine a query is to refine the conditions. The ability to add, edit, or remove conditions is one of the things you need to master in order to become an expert in Discoverer.

In Chapter 4, we introduced you to the Workbook Wizard. One of the essential steps that you were shown was setting user-defined conditions. However, in that chapter, we advised you to only create enough conditions to avoid "The Query from the Twilight Zone." Those conditions were very simple. In this section, we will show you how to build effective conditions and explain all of the options that are available to you.

Adding Conditions

The most frequently used way of adding conditions is to use the Conditions dialog box, but, as you will see in this section, this is not the only way.

There are, in fact, three ways to add conditions to a Discoverer query. These are as follows:

- Using Show Values from a drop-down list
- Using the conditions area buttons on the analysis bar
- Clicking New in the Conditions dialog box

Using Show Values to Add a Condition

This menu item is probably one of the least known yet, at the same time, one of the best features of Discoverer. It is also one of the easiest ways to create new conditions.

NOTE
Conditions can only be created, using Show Values, for items that have a list of values. If you have a data item that does not have a list of values, you should ask your Discoverer administrator if it is possible to have such a list made available.

Whenever you add conditions using this method, Discoverer opens the Values dialog box. As shown in Figure 11-1, this dialog box consists of the following features:

- **Select values for** Discoverer displays the full list of values for the item concerned, along with a check box indicating whether the item is already being used in the query. If there is no active condition currently in use for the item concerned, Discoverer automatically checks all of the boxes. If there is a condition on the item, Discoverer checks only those items that are constrained by the current condition. Discoverer then allows you to manually check and uncheck items using the mouse.
- **Select All** Check this box if you want Discoverer to include all values for the item in your query.
- **Select None** Check this box if you want Discoverer to include no values at all for the item in your query. Doing this and clicking OK causes Discoverer to return nothing. This option should only be used as a means of clearing the current selections, before manually selecting the items that you want.

To use Show Values to add a new condition to a query, use the following workflow:

1. Right-click on the heading for any axis item that has a list of values.
2. From the drop-down menu, select Show Values. This opens the Values dialog box as displayed in Figure 11-1.

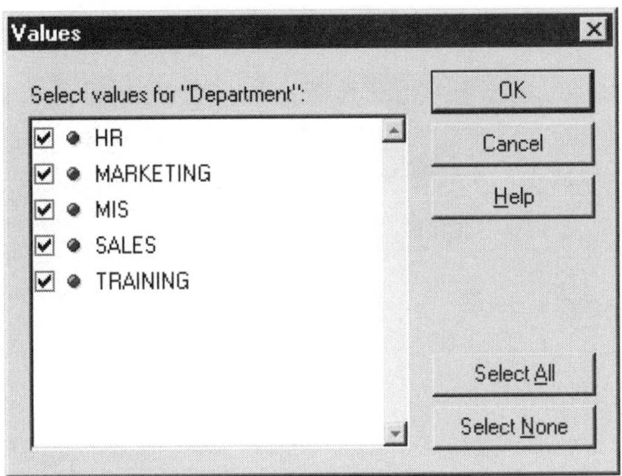

FIGURE 11-1. *Values dialog box*

3. Make the desired selections.
4. Click OK. Discoverer will now create a condition based upon your selections and then rerun the query.

Let's show you how quickly you can modify a query and add new conditions using Show Values. We have started out with a very simple query containing just the department name, department number, expense amount and expense date, and no conditions. This caused Discoverer to display a list of all expenses currently on file. There are only six of these and you can see below that this is a very simple query.

	Dept Number	Department	Expenses SUM	Exp Date
1	10	SALES	150.00	01-AUG-2000
2	10	SALES	250.00	20-AUG-2000
3	10	SALES	1000.00	01-SEP-2000
4	20	HR	1025.00	16-AUG-2000
5	30	MIS	12000.00	01-SEP-2000
6	40	MARKETING	2750.00	30-AUG-2000

To demonstrate how easy it is to add a condition using Show Values, we right-clicked on the heading for the department name and selected Show Values from the drop-down list. This opened the Values dialog box. Examining the contents of the box, you can see (in Figure 11-1) that all of the departments, as we would expect, are checked.

Next, we unchecked the box alongside the MIS department.

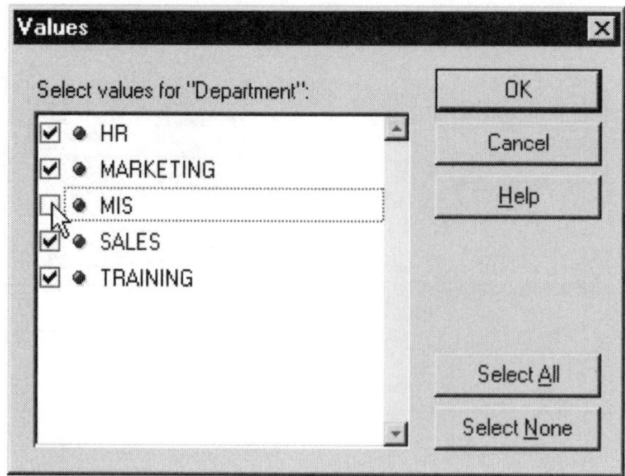

After clicking OK, Discoverer reran the revised query, omitting the MIS department from the result. Opening the Conditions dialog box, you can see that Discoverer has indeed created a new condition for us using the IN expression.

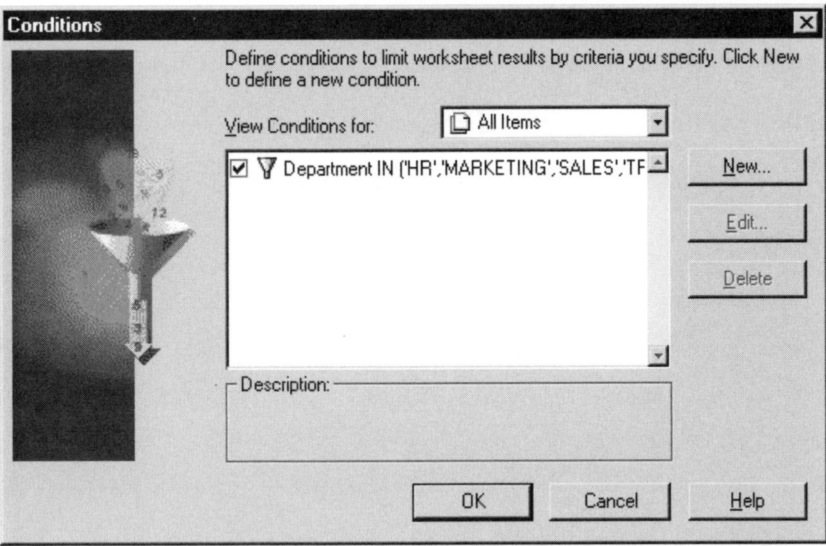

Let us now revise the query again, by once more opening the Values dialog box and changing the criteria for the department. This time we will check the MIS department, but uncheck both Marketing and Training. Taking a close look at the Conditions dialog box that follows, you can see that Discoverer did not amend the original condition. Instead, Discoverer created a new condition and deactivated the original one.

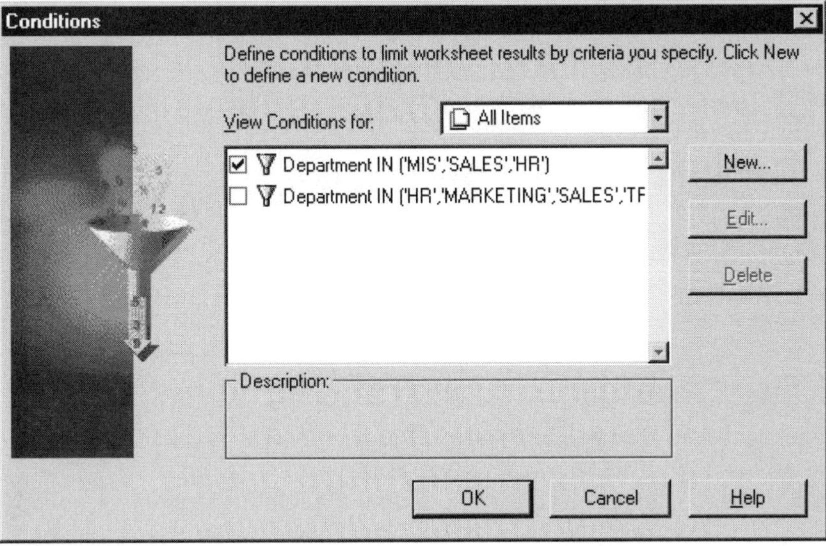

To make the situation even more complicated, we reopened the Values dialog box, and re-created the situation as it was a few steps ago. That is, we checked all departments except MIS. Looking at the following illustration, you can see that Discoverer has created a third condition, and deactivated the second one.

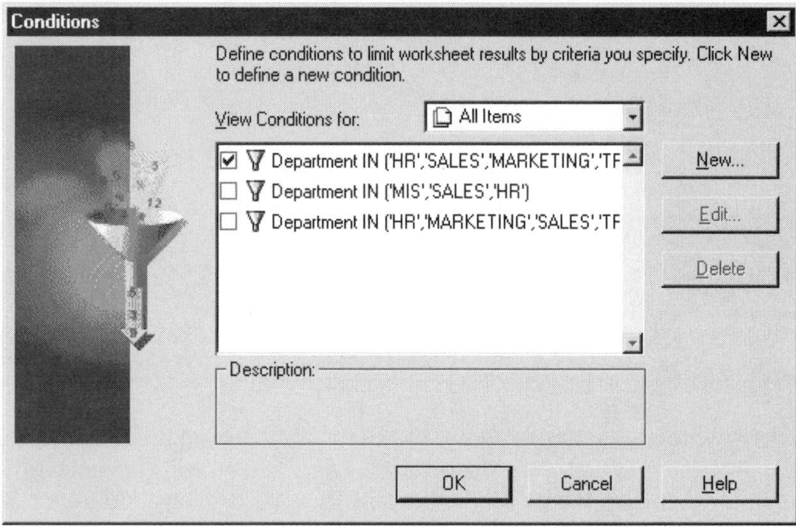

This new condition has exactly the same constraint set as the first condition that we created, yet Discoverer did not recognize this. This fault of Discoverer—to not be able to detect that a condition already exists—is the only drawback that we can see to stop us recommending that you always create conditions using Show Values.

Be aware when using Show Values, that these conditions are created when using the IN expression. When using IN, you are restricted to using 254 items. If you have more than 254 items, Discoverer will report an error. You will have to use a different construct, perhaps using a complex condition.

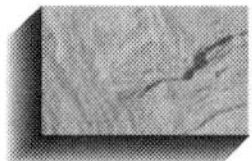

3*i* NOTE

*Unfortunately, the current 3*i *version of Discoverer does not support the right mouse click and you will be unable to create a condition using this method.*

Adding Conditions Using the Analysis Bar

The analysis bar in Discoverer 3.1 offers you another way to create conditions. As we explained in Chapter 9, Discoverer's analysis bar has four areas. The fourth area, highlighted in Figure 11-2, is what we call the "conditions area." Chapter 9 introduced you to the analysis bar and gave a brief description of each of the four areas.

FIGURE 11-2. *Conditions area of the analysis bar*

3*i* NOTE
*Discoverer 3*i *does not have an analysis bar, although it does have an analysis area. None of the functionality that is described in this section is currently available from the 3*i *analysis area. The only way to refine conditions in 3*i *is by opening the Conditions dialog box.*

As you can see in Figure 11-2, the conditions area has seven buttons, one each that allows you to create conditions based on equality(=), nonequality(<>), less than(<), less than or equal to(<=), greater than(>), greater than or equal to(>=), and a button to launch the Conditions dialog box itself. While the first six buttons are only active when a column, row, or cell is highlighted, this final button is always active.

NOTE
Clicking one of the first six condition buttons opens the New Condition dialog box, which is described later in the chapter. When you enter the box, as a result of clicking one of the bottons, all three of the basic components of a condition (the item, the expression, and the value) are complete. All that is required to complete the condition is to click OK.

Using the Buttons to Create a New Condition

As we explained above, clicking in a data cell, or column or row heading, activates the main conditions buttons on the analysis bar. We gave you a simple example of its use in Chapter 9, but to save you having to go back to that section we will give you the workflow once again for using the conditions area:

1. Click on either a column or row heading, or in any cell.
2. Click the button for the condition you want to apply. Discoverer opens the New Condition dialog box, and fills in as much information as it can.

3. Amend the condition if required.
4. Click OK. Discoverer now creates the condition and executes the query.

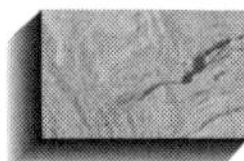

NOTE
If you want to make other changes to the query, you must cancel the running of the query. To do this, click Cancel while the query is running. When prompted to return the query to the original state, click No.

Let us give you an example. We built the following crosstab of total quantity ordered, by product by order status. As you can see, all of the buttons in the conditions area of the analysis bar, except the Conditions button itself, are inactive.

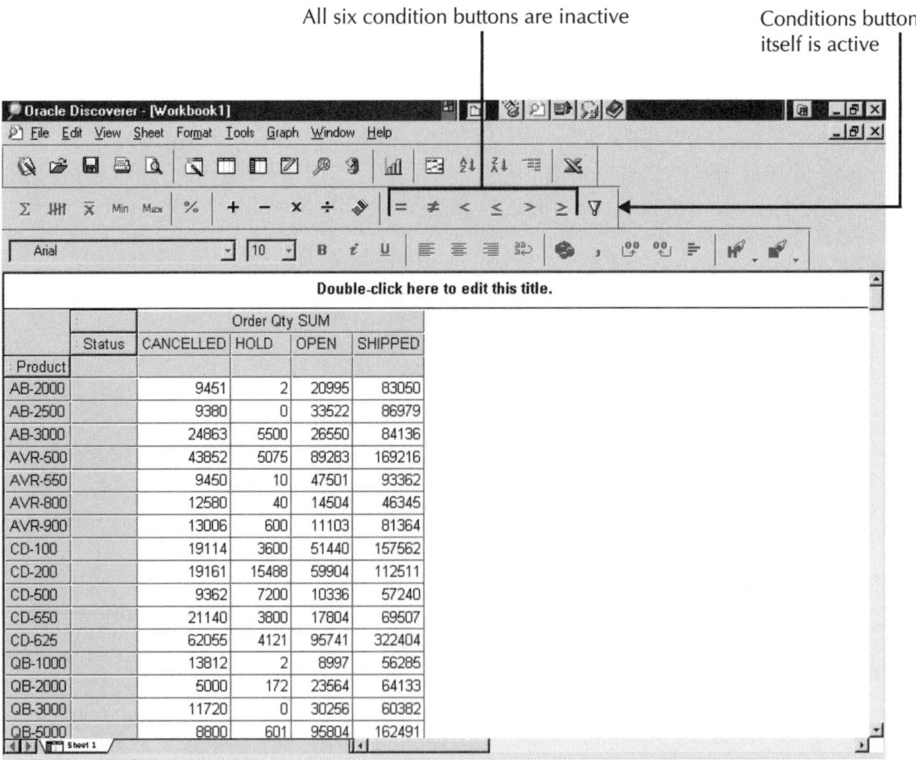

	Order Qty SUM			
Status	CANCELLED	HOLD	OPEN	SHIPPED
Product				
AB-2000	9451	2	20995	83050
AB-2500	9380	0	33522	86979
AB-3000	24863	5500	26550	84136
AVR-500	43852	5075	89283	169216
AVR-550	9450	10	47501	93362
AVR-800	12580	40	14504	46345
AVR-900	13006	600	11103	81364
CD-100	19114	3600	51440	157562
CD-200	19161	15488	59904	112511
CD-500	9362	7200	10336	57240
CD-550	21140	3800	17804	69507
CD-625	62055	4121	95741	322404
QB-1000	13812	2	8997	56285
QB-2000	5000	172	23564	64133
QB-3000	11720	0	30256	60382
QB-5000	8800	601	95804	162491

Let's assume that we wanted to print the order quantities for what is currently open. We need to have a condition where the status = OPEN. This is a very simple condition to build. Following our workflow outlined earlier:

1. We clicked on the cell containing the status OPEN. This caused Discoverer to activate the conditions buttons.
2. We next clicked on the = button. This opened the New Condition dialog box. As you can see below, Discoverer correctly populated the Item, Condition, and Value(s) boxes for us.

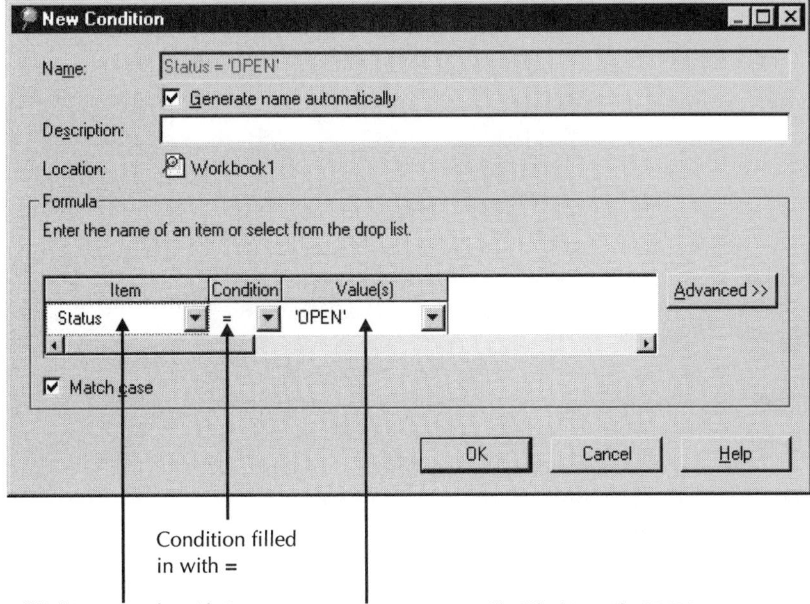

Condition filled in with =

Item filled in correctly with Status

Value automatically filled in with OPEN

3. There is nothing to amend because Discoverer has created everything that we need.
4. To complete the condition, we clicked OK. As you can see, Discoverer adjusted the query for us and created a list of only the open order quantities. We could now send this list to our planning department, who would ensure that we had enough purchase orders to satisfy the demand.

		Order Qty SUM
	Status	OPEN
Product		
AB-2000		20995
AB-2500		33522
AB-3000		26550
AVR-500		89283
AVR-550		47501
AVR-800		14504
AVR-900		11103
CD-100		51440
CD-200		59904
CD-500		10336
CD-550		17804
CD-625		95741
QB-1000		8997
QB-2000		23564
QB-3000		30256
QB-5000		95804

NOTE
One word of caution when using the conditions buttons. As for Show Values, Discoverer is not smart enough to recognize that a condition already exists. If we repeat the above exercise, clicking on 'Open', followed by the = symbol, Discoverer will create another condition identical to the first.

Using the Conditions Dialog Box to Add a Condition

The third way to add new conditions to your query is via the Conditions dialog box. Advanced conditions can only be created using the Conditions dialog box. There are three ways to open this box:

- Click the Conditions button from the analysis bar (recommended for 3.1).
- From the menu bar, select Tools | Conditions (recommended for 3*i*).
- From the Conditions tab on the Edit Sheet dialog box.

Creating a Condition Using the Conditions Dialog Box

When creating conditions, you should use the following workflow:

1. If you know the item on which you want to build the condition, from the "View Conditions for" drop-down list of the Conditions dialog box, select the item you want to apply the condition to. If you do not yet know the item or want to choose an item that is not being used within the worksheet, proceed to the next step.
2. Click New. This opens the New Condition dialog box, as shown in Figures 11-3 and 11-4. Discoverer automatically inserts the item you selected in step 1 into the Item field of the formula area. If this is not the item that you want, or if there is no item shown, select one now from the drop-down list. A detailed explanation of the choices available to you at this point is given later in this chapter when we deal with the basic components of a condition.
3. From the Condition drop-down list, select the expression you want to apply to the item. By default, Discoverer inserts the expression =. The available expressions are explained later in this chapter when we deal with the basic components of a condition.
4. In the Values box, type in the value(s) you want Discoverer to constrain the item on, or from the drop-down list select one or more values. This drop-down list, in addition to a list of values, also contains options to select multiple values, create a calculation, select an item, create a new parameter, and create a new subquery. These options are explained in detail when we explain the basic components of a condition, later in this chapter.
5. Make sure the box entitled "Match case" is checked. The reason for this is explained later in this chapter when we explain the New Condition dialog box.
6. If you want to define an advanced condition, click the Advanced button. The advanced features are discussed later in this chapter.
7. If the name that Discoverer has generated for you is not to your liking, uncheck the box entitled "Generate name automatically" and type a suitable name for the condition into the Name box.

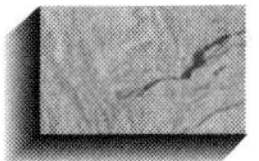

3*i* NOTE

In Discoverer 3i, Oracle has renamed the Name box to "What would you like to name your condition?"

8. Enter a description, if desired. This is optional.
9. Click OK to close the New Condition dialog box and return to the Conditions dialog box. You will see your condition highlighted at the top of the list of conditions.
10. Click OK to finish.

The New Condition Dialog Box

The New Condition dialog box is shown in Figures 11-3 and 11-4. This box consists of the following features:

- **Name** Discoverer automatically generates a name for your condition based on the criteria that you use to build the condition. Normally, the name given by Discoverer will suffice. However, Discoverer will allow you to create your own name, but only if you uncheck the box described next.
- **Generate name automatically** By default, Discoverer names conditions for you, and does it very well. Uncheck this box only if you want to name the condition yourself, then go back to the Name box and type in your own name.
- **Description** For simple queries, the name generated by Discoverer is more than adequate for identifying what will happen when a condition is selected. There are occasions, however, when using complex conditions, that the name alone will not be sufficient. When the name generated by Discoverer does not accurately convey what will happen when the condition is selected, you should type in a description here.
- **Location** In case you have forgotten in which workbook you are working, Discoverer inserts the current workbook name here.
- **Item** A drop-down list of available items, upon which you can base the condition. You must select something here; otherwise, Discoverer will be unable to create your condition. A full explanation of the options open to you is given in the next section. An example of an item is the ship date.
- **Condition** A drop-down list of expressions, from which you have to select one. A full list of all available expressions is given in the next section. An example of an expression is the = symbol, such that the condition now looks like ship date =.
- **Value(s)** Another drop-down list. This time there is a list of values, from which you must select one or more in order to complete the condition. For example, we could enter the date 01-AUG-2000, thus completing our condition to be ship date = 01-AUG-2000. A full explanation of all available values is given in the next section.

NOTE
The previous three components are the three required elements of any Discoverer condition. The next section explains each of these in detail.

NOTE
When you enter values that are dates or text, you must enter them inside single quotes.

- **Match case** Uncheck this box only if you do not want Discoverer to match the case values in your query. Normally, you would not want to uncheck this, especially if you have selected from a list of values to begin with.

NOTE
Queries will take much longer if you uncheck this box. In the authors' experience, it is not uncommon to find query times increasing by 200 percent or more. This is because Discoverer is doing exactly as instructed, by ignoring match case, and therefore searching for all possible combinations of the value. For example, say we were searching for the name 'Michael' in our condition but did not check the "Match case" box. Discoverer would scan for 'Michael', 'michael', MICHAEL', and all combinations of the uppercase and lowercase values of the seven letters in the name! You can see how long this would take and how much of an impact this would have on your own queries.

- **Advanced** Click this button if you want to access the advanced features associated with creating conditions. These are explained in detail later in this chapter.

Building a Simple Condition Using the Workflow

Following the previous workflow, we will show you how to create a simple condition using the Conditions dialog box. We will follow each step exactly as specified.

We have a query that reports, for all products and statuses, the total quantity shipped and the margin. There are no conditions in this query so far, but we want to add one that only shows the margin when the product has shipped.

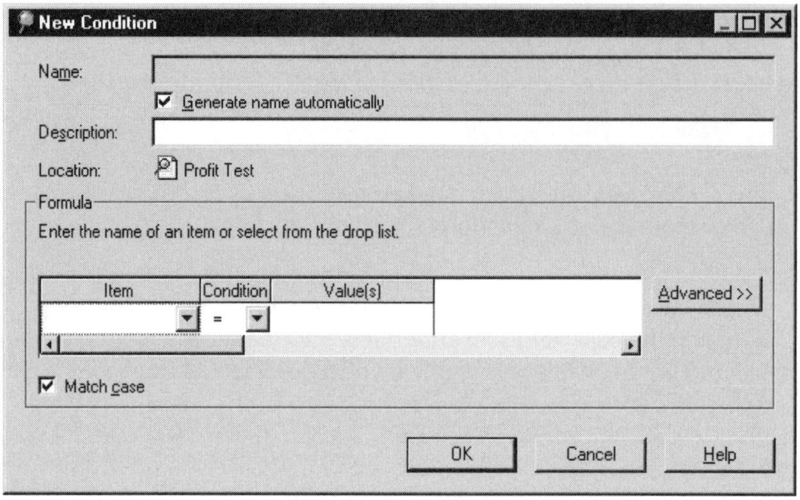

FIGURE 11-3. *Discoverer 3.1 New Condition dialog box*

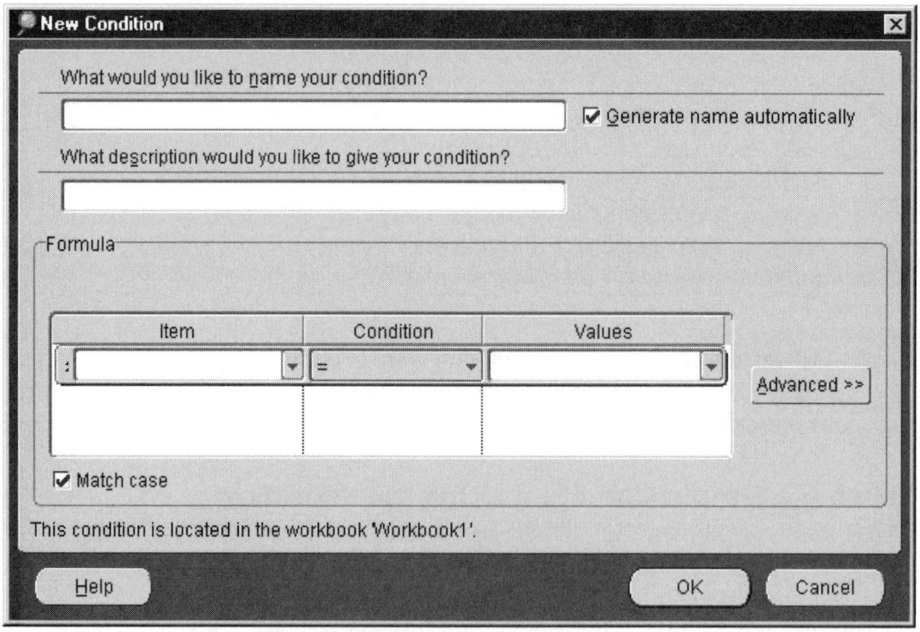

FIGURE 11-4. *Discoverer 3i New Condition dialog box*

Step 1 of the workflow requires us, where possible, to select the item we want to place the condition on. In this example, we want the condition to be on the status. The following illustration shows the drop-down list in the View Conditions dialog list with Status highlighted.

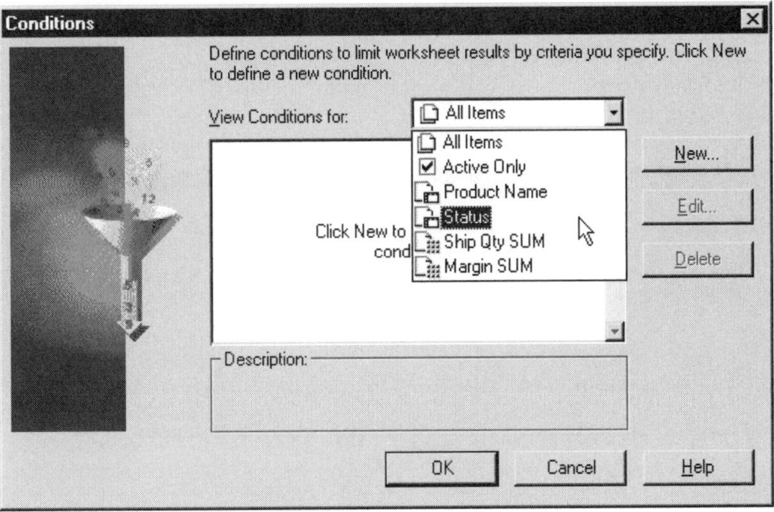

Step 2 says that we should click New and that Discoverer will open the New Condition dialog box with the item we selected already populated. As you can see below, Discoverer did just that.

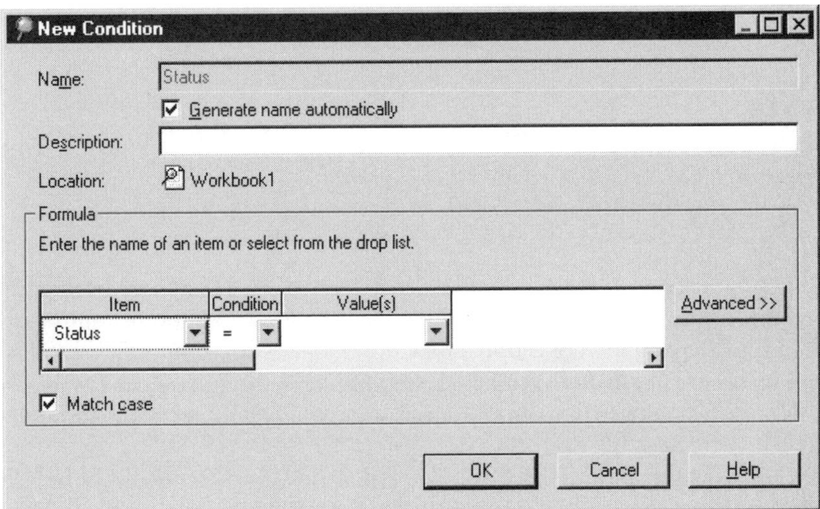

Step 3 of the workflow is where we set the expression. As Discoverer has already inserted the default of =, there is no need for us to pick an expression, so we will proceed directly to step 4.

In step 4, we have to open the drop-down list and select the value that we want to constrain the status on. As we are not building a complex condition, only a simple condition, we will just select the status SHIPPED from the list of values. As you can see in the following illustration, when we opened the drop-down list, we were presented with a number of options, below which is the list of values from which we selected SHIPPED.

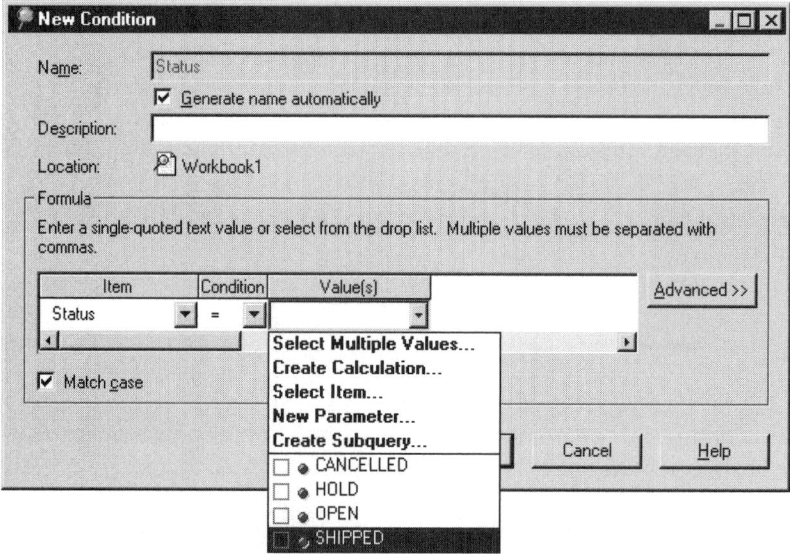

NOTE

For an explanation of all of the options in the drop-down list, please read ahead to the section that explains the basic components of a condition.

Step 5 requires us to make sure that "Match case" is checked. By default, it is checked. The next three steps—for creating advanced conditions, naming the condition, and giving the condition a description—are not required. Therefore, we will proceed directly to finishing the condition. All that remains now is for us to click OK. At this point, Discoverer will rerun the query and apply the condition that we have just created.

If you follow the above workflow, you will quickly master the art of building simple conditions. Advanced conditions are more difficult, and are dealt with later in this chapter.

The Basic Components of a Condition

As stated in the previous section, three basic components must be supplied for all Discoverer conditions. Without these components, Discoverer will be unable to build your condition. The three components are as follows:

- The item upon which the condition is based
- The expression being applied to the item
- A value (not always required)

In this section, we will take an in-depth look at these three basic components.

Basic Component 1 – The Item

When building a condition, you must specify the item you want Discoverer to use. You do this in one of two ways:

- Outside the New Condition dialog box
- Inside the New Condition dialog box

Specifying an Item Outside the New Condition Dialog Box

To specify the item that Discoverer must build the condition on from outside of the New Condition dialog box, you must select the item from the drop-down list of the Conditions dialog box. After that, you should click New. Discoverer will then open the New Conditions dialog box, and populate the Item field with whatever item you chose. We showed you how to do this in the previous section.

NOTE
The drop-down list of items in the Conditions dialog box contains only the items that are used within the worksheet. However, in the drop-down list of items in the New Conditions dialog box, you can select from all of the items contained in the folders used in the worksheet.

Specifying an Item Inside the New Condition Dialog Box

Specifying the item inside the New Condition dialog box gives you more flexibility. This method should be used when:

- You are not 100 percent sure which item you want to use in your condition.

- You want to build the condition on an item that is not currently used within the worksheet.
- You want the item to be a calculation (advanced condition).
- You want the item to be a predefined or user-defined condition (advanced condition).

To build conditions based on the above types, use the drop-down list inside the New Condition dialog box. Doing this, you will always see at the top of the list an option to create a calculation. If you have other conditions available, whether they be predefined or user-defined, you will also see an option to use these. The list will also contain all of the available items in the query, whether or not you have included them in your worksheet selections.

For example, suppose you have a folder containing ten items, and you include five of these in your worksheet. Opening the drop-down list of items inside the New Condition dialog box will display all ten items.

Building conditions based on other conditions or calculations will be explained later in this chapter when we discuss advanced conditions.

Basic Component 2 – The Expression

The second basic component that you must supply, when building a condition, is the expression. Table 11-1 is a list of all of the available expressions:

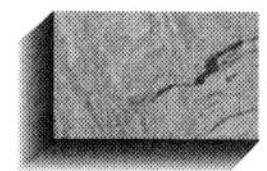

NOTE

The expressions IS NULL and IS NOT NULL do not require a value. The Value field is removed when you select one of these expressions.

Discoverer will automatically change the expression if the value you subsequently pick is incompatible with the current expression. For example, if you select = and then select two or more items from the list of values, Discoverer will change the expression to IN. This is because = takes only a single value, whereas IN can take single and multiple values.

Basic Component 3 – The Value

The third basic component of a condition is the value. As you have seen in the previous section, most, but not all, conditions take a value. If you select the expression BETWEEN, Discoverer will expect you to provide two values, a lower or start value and a higher or end value. It is up to you to ensure that the end value is indeed higher than the start value, because Discoverer will not validate your condition.

Symbol	Description	Examples
=	The item must equal the value.	Ship Qty = 15000
<>	The item must not equal the value.	Ship Qty <> 15000
>	The item must be greater than the value.	Ship Qty > 15000
<	The item must be less than the value.	Ship Qty < 15000
<=	The item must be less than or equal to the value.	Ship Qty <= 15000
>=	The item must be greater than or equal to the value.	Ship Qty >= 15000
LIKE	The item must match the value. You can use wildcards to find like values. The value must be enclosed in single quotes. Wildcards can only be used with text strings.	
	In Oracle, the % sign indicates that everything after this is ignored. For those familiar with Microsoft, the % sign equates to the asterisk (*).	City Name LIKE 'D%' This will return both Dallas and Denver.
	In Oracle, the _ (underscore symbol) matches a single character.	Product LIKE 'B_t' This will return both Bat and Bit.
IN	Contains one or more values separated by commas and enclosed in brackets.	City IN ('Madrid','San Francisco','Tokyo') This will find data that is for at least one of the cities.
IS NULL	This expression returns values only when the named item is null (no value whatsoever, not even zero).	Cancel Date IS NULL This means the item is not cancelled.
IS NOT NULL	This expression returns values only when the named item is not null.	Ship Qty IS NOT NULL This means there is a ship quantity.

TABLE 11-1. *Table of Expressions*

Symbol	Description	Examples
NOT IN	Returns data that is not contained in one or more values.	City NOT IN ('Madrid','San Francisco','Tokyo') This will find data for all cities except the ones above.
BETWEEN	Returns all data between two values.	Ship Date BETWEEN '01-JUN-2000' and '30-JUN-2000' This will find all shipments in the month of June, both start and end values are included.
NOT BETWEEN	Returns data that is outside of two values.	Ship Date NOT BETWEEN '01-JUN-2000' and '30-JUN-2000' This will find all shipments excluding those shipped in the month of June.
NOT LIKE	The item must not match the value. You can use wildcards to omit like values. The value must be enclosed in single quotes. Wildcards can only be used with text strings.	City Name NOT LIKE 'D%' This will exclude both Dallas and Denver
!=	Identical to <>.	These work the same as <> but because some versions of SQL don't support <>, Discoverer offers you these alternatives. Always use <> if available.
^=		

TABLE 11-1. *Table of Expressions* (continued)

Having selected the item on which to build a condition, and the expression, you should click in the Value field. Unless you created the condition using one of the condition buttons on the analysis bar, the Value field will be blank.

If you know the value that you want, you can type it in; otherwise, open the drop-down list. Depending on whether the data item has a list of values, the drop-down list does not always give the same options. When there is no list of values, the options are as follows:

- Create Calculation…
- Select Item…
- New Parameter…
- Create Subquery…

When there is a list of values, the above options are supplemented by:

- Select Multiple Values…
- The list of values

NOTE
Until you have selected an item upon which to base the condition, you will not be able to see the drop-down list options for values. This is because Discoverer needs to ascertain whether a list of values is associated with the item.

Create Calculation

This option opens the Edit Calculation dialog. This box is identical to the New Calculation dialog box that was described in Chapter 5. Creating calculations as part of a condition is described later in this chapter, while stand-alone calculations will be dealt with when we show you how to refine calculations in Chapter 12.

Select Item…

This option opens the Items dialog box. This box lists all of the items in the folders used in the worksheet. You could reverse the contents of the Item and the Value fields, by inserting, for example, 'SHIPPED' in the item, and selecting 'STATUS' from the list of items. You can also create conditions that use two items, such as shipped date equals ordered date, so that you can analyze all of the orders that shipped the same day that they were ordered.

New Parameter...

This option opens the New Parameter dialog box. Use this box to convert a condition into a parameter, or define a new parameter for your worksheet. Defining parameters from the Workbook Wizard was covered in Chapter 5, while converting conditions into parameters will be covered in Chapter 12.

NOTE

The New Parameter option cannot be used unless you have chosen an item from a folder. If you have typed in a value, such as SHIPPED, into the item field, Discoverer will not allow you to create a parameter based on this.

Create Subquery...

This option opens the Create Subquery dialog box. Use this box to apply a condition on an item or value in another worksheet. Discoverer lets you associate a condition with an item in an existing worksheet, or it will allow you to create a new worksheet.

The use of subqueries is an advanced form of condition, and is covered later in this chapter.

Select Multiple Values...

This option, only available if a list of values has been defined for the item, opens up the Values dialog box, as seen in Figure 11-1. Use of this dialog box was covered in the first part of this chapter when we explained creating conditions using Show Values. The difference between opening the Values dialog box using Show Values and Select Multiple Values, is that Show Values checks the items that are currently in use, whereas Select Multiple Values displays all values unchecked.

The exception to this is, if you have selected items from the list of values, then click on Select Multiple Values—the values previously selected will be checked. For example, we have selected from the list of values the status SHIPPED. We then clicked on Select Multiple Values and, as you can see in the following illustration, SHIPPED is checked.

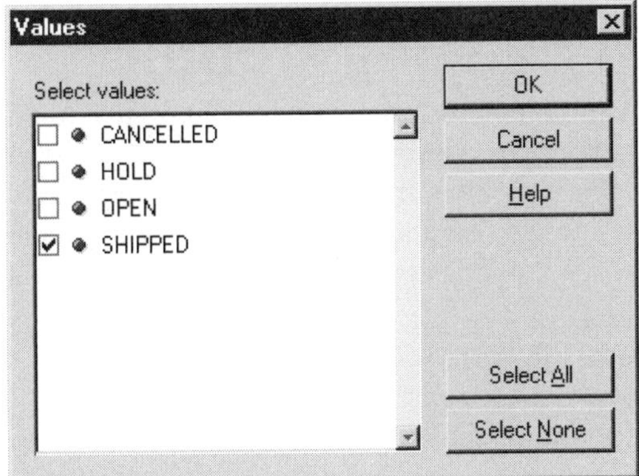

The List of Values

When an item has a list of values, Discoverer displays all of the items, as you can see below.

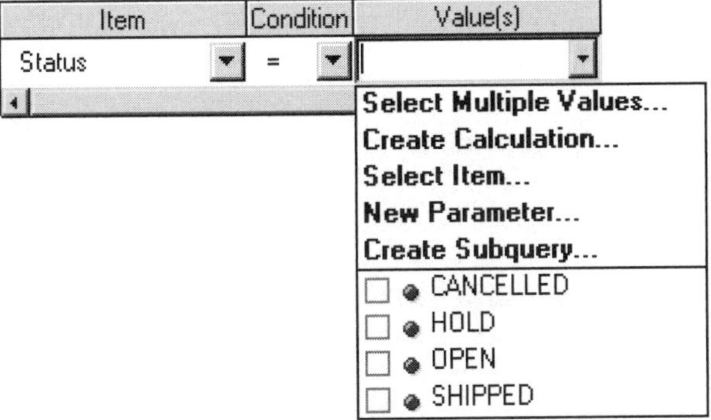

NOTE

Remember, when you are using the Between expression, you must provide two values, a lower or start value, and a higher, end value. Discoverer does not check the validity of the start and end values. If you enter an end value that is lower than the start value, Discoverer will accept the condition, but will return no data.

Editing an Existing Condition

Another technique commonly used when refining queries, is to edit an existing condition. In this situation, you are neither adding nor removing existing conditions, just changing an existing definition. If you find that the same query constantly needs modifying just to edit a single condition, we recommend you change that condition into a parameter. Changing conditions into parameters is dealt with in detail in Chapter 12.

To edit an existing condition, use the following workflow:

1. Open the Conditions dialog box.
2. From the list of conditions displayed, highlight the condition you want to edit.
3. Click the Edit button. This opens the Edit Condition dialog box.
4. Change the condition as required.
5. Click OK once to exit from the Edit Condition dialog box, then again to exit from the Conditions dialog box.

When you have completed editing the condition, Discoverer will execute the query and display the new results.

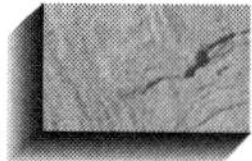

NOTE
As stated earlier, if you realize at this point that you have made a mistake and edited the wrong condition or changed it incorrectly, you can reverse the changes by clicking on Edit | Undo Conditions or pressing CTRL-Z.

Using Advanced Conditions

Probably the most daunting aspect of crediting or editing conditions is knowing how to use advanced conditions effectively. Following the workflow given earlier in this chapter, it is very easy to create simple conditions. To fully master Discoverer, you need to spend time learning how Discoverer handles complex, advanced conditions.

Using Discoverer, we have identified the following four types of advanced conditions:

- Conditions based on calculations
- Conditions based on other conditions

- Conditions using Boolean operators
- Conditions using subqueries

Creating Conditions Based on Calculations

As you saw earlier in this chapter, when we discussed the three basic components of a condition, both the Item and the Value drop-down boxes have options to create calculations. In this section we will show you how this is done.

There are two ways of creating conditions based on calculations. These are:

- Using an existing calculation
- Creating a new calculation as part of the condition

There, in a nutshell, is the reason why Discoverer allows you to create two types of conditions based on calculations.

Using an Existing Calculation

Existing calculations will appear in the list of items, even if they are not being displayed in the final output. If you base a condition on an existing calculation, and then delete the calculation from the worksheet by deleting the column, the condition can still use the calculation. You can even create a new condition based on the calculation.

However, if you delete a calculation from the Calculations dialog box, it can no longer be used. Any conditions that used that calculation are also deleted. Conditions based on existing calculations are therefore vulnerable because the calculation could accidentally be deleted, unaware that it is used in a condition. Discoverer will not warn you that you are deleting a needed calculation. Once the damage is done, you have to start over!

To use an existing calculation within a condition, use the following workflow:

1. Open the New Condition dialog box.
2. In the Item field, open the drop-down list.
3. From the options provided, select the calculation.
4. Set the expression and value you require.
5. Click OK.

Let us give you an example. We built a query of shipments, showing order number and quantity shipped, sorted by order number. We next added a profit calculation, being defined as the sum of the selling price minus the sum of the cost price. The following illustration shows how this looks.

	Order Number	Ship Qty SUM	Profit
1	1059	10000	113700.00
2	1060	1200	10848.00
3	1061	1000	9040.00
4	1062	1920	29702.40
5	1063	1920	29702.40
6	1064	48	301.44
7	1065	50	338.00
8	1066	10000	113700.00
9	1067	1600	18496.00
10	1068	8400	97104.00
11	1069	10000	115600.00
12	1070	15000	280650.00
13	1071	200	3742.00
14	1072	1200	11196.00
15	1073	1200	11196.00
16	1074	1200	13236.00

Next, we opened the New Condition dialog box. From the drop-down list of items we selected the profit, as you can see here:

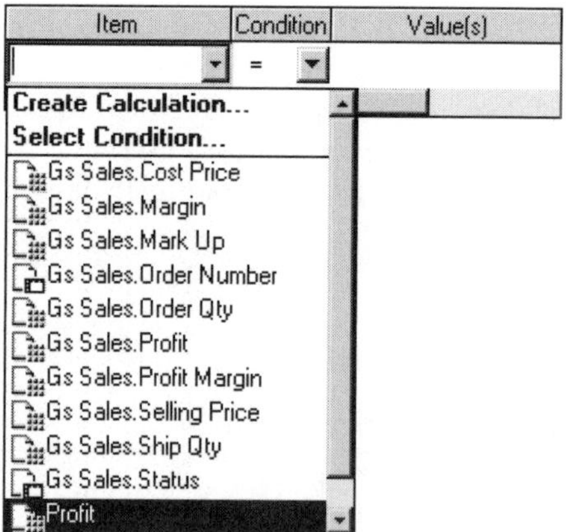

Finally, as shown in the following illustration, we selected the expression > and entered a value of **20000**.

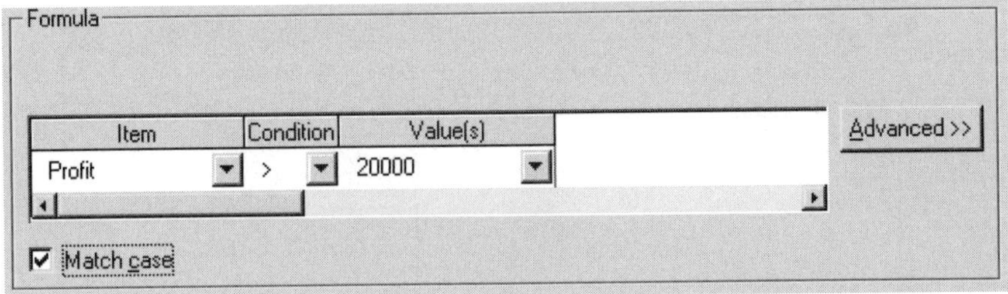

After clicking OK, Discoverer ran the query using the condition just created, and the query was constrained to show only orders with a profit greater than 20,000.

Creating a New Calculation as Part of the Condition

Calculations created as part of a condition will not appear in the list of items, nor will they be listed in the Calculations dialog box. They exist only as part of the condition and cannot be manipulated outside of the condition. Calculations created this way will only be used internally by the condition, they cannot be displayed as a column of the worksheet, nor can they be used in other conditions. If you delete the condition, the calculation is also deleted.

Because these calculations are created as part of the condition, they are not vulnerable to being accidentally deleted.

To build a condition, with a calculation created as part of it, use the following workflow:

1. Open the New Condition dialog box.
2. From the options provided, select Create Calculation. This opens the Edit Calculation dialog box.
3. Create the calculation.
4. Click OK. This returns you to the New Condition dialog box.
5. Set the expression and value you require.
6. Click OK.

Using the same query of shipments we used in the example for creating conditions based on an existing calculation, we will show you how to create the same condition. However, this time, we will create the calculation from within the New Condition dialog box.

After opening the New Condition dialog box, we selected Create Calculation from the Item drop-down list. This opened the following Edit Calculation dialog box.

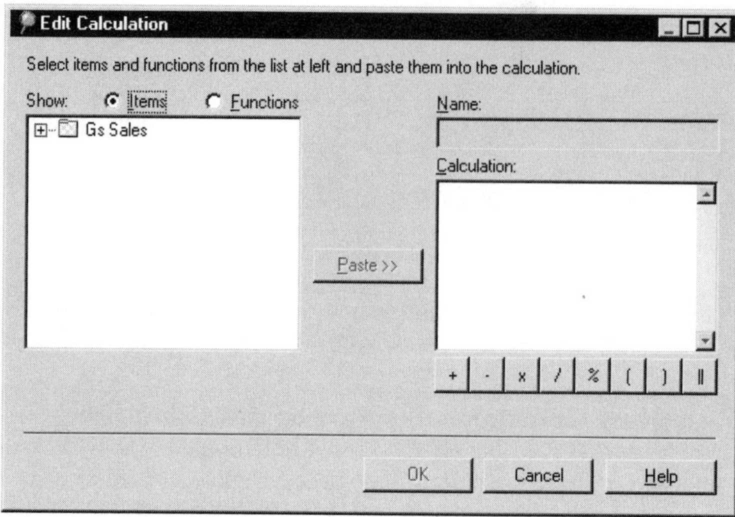

Looking at the preceding illustration, you will notice that this box looks identical to the New Calculation dialog box. However, if you look closely, you will notice that the Name field is deactivated. This is because the calculation belongs to the condition that created it. It cannot be used in any other context and, therefore, needs no name.

3*i* NOTE
*In Discoverer 3*i*, the Name field is not even displayed.*

Next, we will create the profit calculation. This is the sum of the selling price minus the sum of the cost price. As you can see in the following illustration, we have used the SUM function to build the calculation.

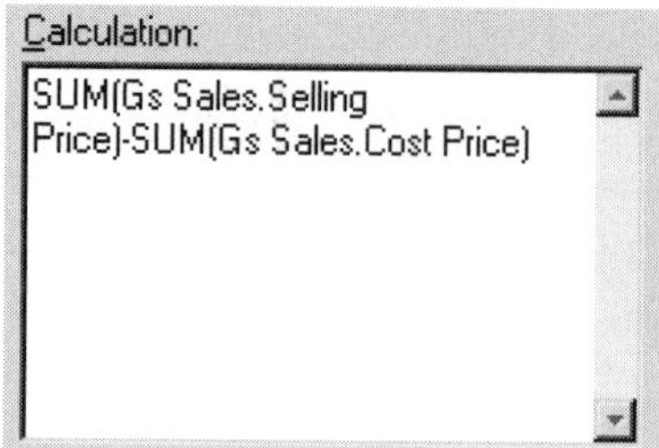

After clicking OK, we were returned to the New Condition dialog box. In here, we entered the expression > and a value of **20000**. In the completed condition, the calculation displays in its entirety in the Item field, obviating the need to name the calculation, shown here:

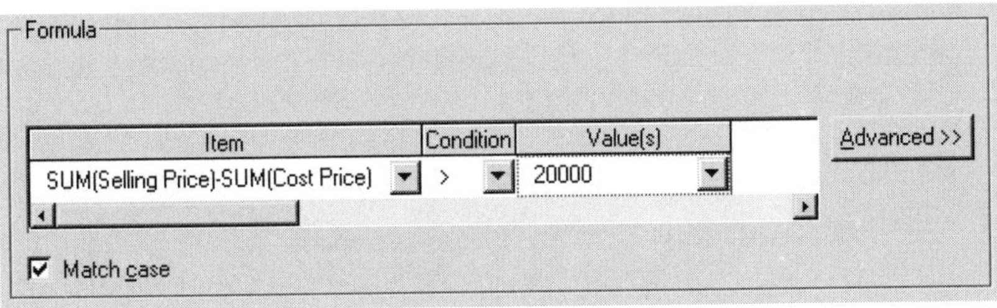

After clicking OK, Discoverer ran the query using the condition just created, and the query was constrained to show only orders with a profit greater than 20,000.

Creating Conditions Based on Conditions

The second of the advanced types of conditions is to create a condition based on an existing condition. Whether these existing conditions are administrator- or user-defined is irrelevant. The important thing you need to know is that Discoverer allows you to create these conditions. Extending your skill set to include creating conditions based on conditions will greatly enhance your expertise in Discoverer.

Perhaps the simplest way to explain why you would even bother to build a condition based on another is as follows. If you have created, or have available to you, multiple existing conditions, and are using more than one of them at the same time, Discoverer will apply an AND between each one.

For example, let's say you have two conditions in your worksheet, an administrator-defined one, which constrains the order quantity to be greater than 15,000, and a user-defined condition limiting the status to just SHIPPED. In the Conditions dialog box, you can only decide whether to use or not use these conditions. If you check both of them, Discoverer will only select data when both of the conditions are true. However, what if you want your query to return data when one or the other condition is true, such as, order quantity > 15000 OR status = 'SHIPPED'? The only way to do this is to create a new condition, based on both of these conditions, combining them with the Boolean operator OR.

As you have seen in the Item drop-down list, one of the options is to use Select Condition. To build a condition based on another condition, use the following workflow:

1. Open the New Condition dialog box.
2. From the options provided, choose Select Condition. This opens a dialog box entitled Conditions. Don't confuse this dialog box with the Conditions dialog box. The box that has been opened here merely contains a list of the available conditions upon which you can base another condition.

3. From the list, select the condition you want to use.
4. Click OK. This returns you to the New Condition dialog box, with both the Expression and Value fields removed. At this stage, you could click OK, but all this will do is create another condition with the identical functionality to the original. What you should do instead is use Discoverer's advanced features and use Boolean logic to combine the existing condition with something else.
5. Click Advanced. This opens an extended version of the Edit Condition dialog box, in which you should create a Boolean condition (see the next section for details on how to do this).
6. When you have finished creating the Boolean condition, click OK.

Using the example outlined above, the following illustration shows a worksheet with the two existing conditions, order quantity > 15000 and status = 'SHIPPED'. With both conditions checked, we would see only three rows of data. Discoverer has applied the Boolean operator AND between the two conditions.

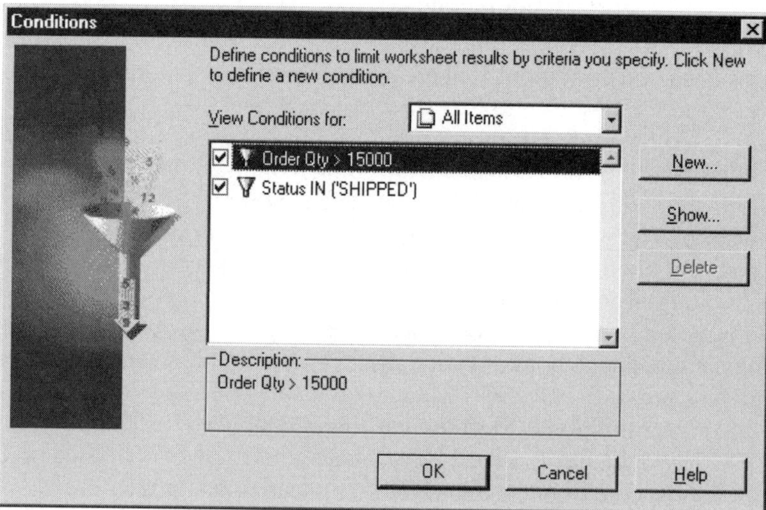

However, we don't want to see only the rows that satisfy both conditions—we want to see all orders with an order quantity > 15000 OR a status of SHIPPED. By creating a new condition that combines both of the existing conditions, we can do just that.

Therefore, we will open the New Condition dialog box and from the Item drop-down list we will take the option Select Condition. This opened the Conditions dialog box shown in the illustration that follows. As you can see, both of our existing conditions are available to use.

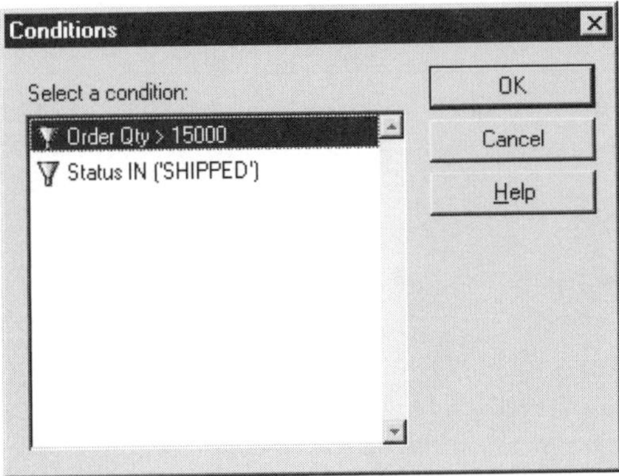

We selected the first condition and clicked OK. As you can see below, this inserted the condition into the New Condition dialog box, and removed both the Expression and Value fields.

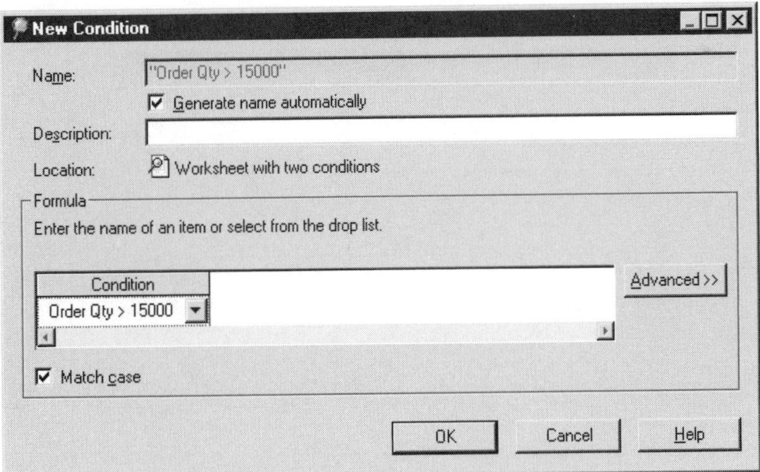

Next, we clicked Advanced. This opened the extended New Condition dialog box, as seen in the following illustration. This box, and all its functionality, will be explained in the next section when we deal with Boolean conditions.

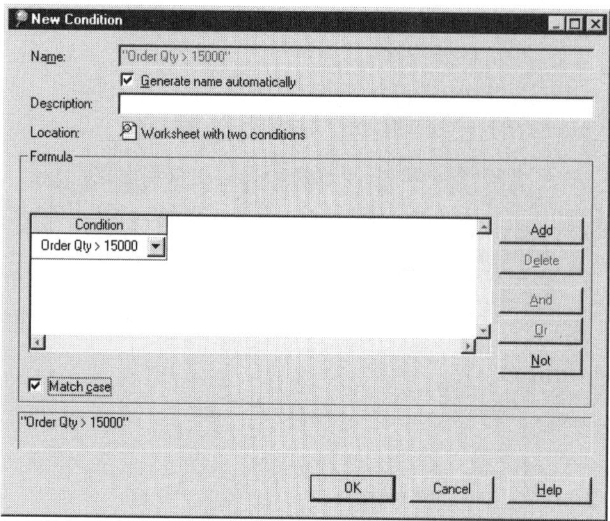

In order to combine the two existing conditions, we need to add the second condition to the one that is already selected. To do this, we clicked Add. This changed the display of the dialog box, and inserted another set of the three basic components of a condition, as you can see in the following illustration.

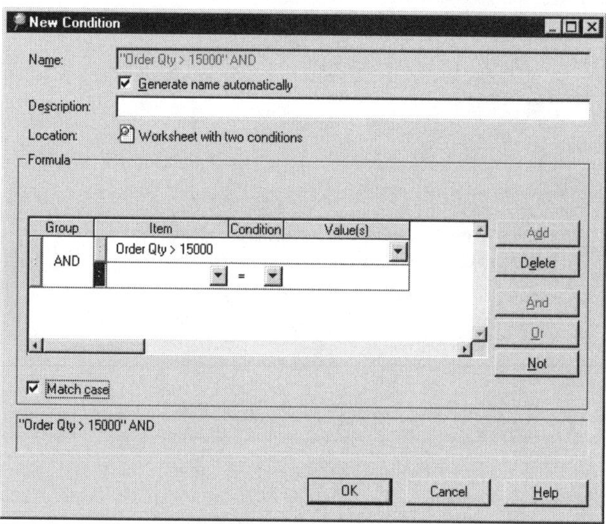

Not quite done. To add the second condition, from the new Item drop-down list we again chose Select Condition. From the list of available conditions, we selected the second one and clicked OK. This resulted in the following illustration. As you can see, Discoverer has now combined the two conditions into one, using the Boolean operator AND.

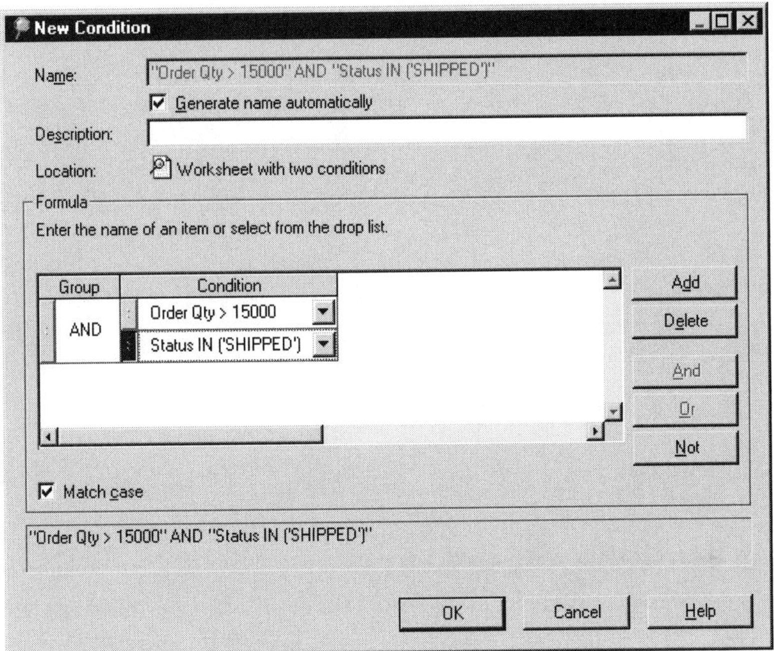

Almost there! We now have to change the Boolean operator to OR. To do this, we clicked on the AND joining the two conditions, then clicked the Or button. We then clicked OK to save this new condition. This returned us to the Conditions dialog box. The last step we took was to deselect the two existing conditions, then clicked OK. As you can see in the next illustration, the result of running with this condition is quite different from the three rows that we started with.

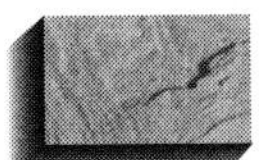

NOTE
Don't forget to deselect the existing conditions upon which you have created the new condition. If you forget this, Discoverer will give you a result based on the original conditions.

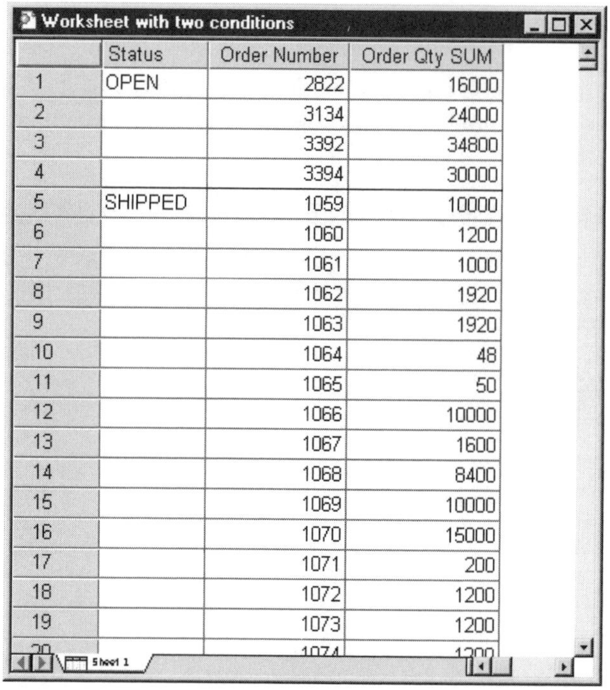

Worksheet with two conditions

	Status	Order Number	Order Qty SUM
1	OPEN	2822	16000
2		3134	24000
3		3392	34800
4		3394	30000
5	SHIPPED	1059	10000
6		1060	1200
7		1061	1000
8		1062	1920
9		1063	1920
10		1064	48
11		1065	50
12		1066	10000
13		1067	1600
14		1068	8400
15		1069	10000
16		1070	15000
17		1071	200
18		1072	1200
19		1073	1200
20		1074	1200

Sheet 1

Using Boolean Operators

The third of Discoverer's advanced types of conditions uses Boolean operators. We touched on this subject in the previous section, when we showed you how to combine conditions using Boolean operators. In this section, we will explore the whole gamut of Boolean operators and show you how to make effective use of them.

Firstly, if you are not familiar with Boolean operators, we will give you a brief explanation. Boolean algebra, a system of symbolic logic dealing with operands, was devised by G. Boole (1815-1864), an English mathematician. This system is any logical operation in which each of the operands and the result take one of the two values, True or False. These operations form the basis of logic gates in computers.

Within Discoverer there are operands and operators. An operand is anything that equates to a true or false value, such as status=shipped, or quantity > 15000.

An operator is a symbol that allows you to make a connection between operands, such as status=shipped AND quantity > 15000. Discoverer allows you to use the operators AND, OR, and NOT.

Now that you understand the concept of Boolean operators, it is a straightforward task to convert these into conditions. We will show you how to build both simple and complex Boolean conditions. Before you start building complex conditions, you should check that there are no existing conditions that will satisfy what you are trying to do.

Creating Boolean Conditions

When creating Boolean conditions, use the following workflow:

1. Open the New Condition dialog box.
2. Because you know you will be creating a Boolean condition, click Advanced. This opens the Extended New Condition dialog box as shown in Figure 11-5.
3. Create a condition, or use the Item drop-down list to create a new calculation or select an existing condition. This step creates the first part of the Boolean condition.
4. Click Add to create or insert another condition.
5. Set the Boolean operator you want to be applied between the conditions.
6. Repeat steps 4 and 5, adding new conditions and operators, until you have created the desired complex condition.
7. Click OK.

The Extended New Condition Dialog Box

Whenever you are creating complex conditions, Discoverer opens the Extended New Condition dialog box. This dialog box has all of the fields from the New Condition dialog box, as seen in Figures 11-3, and 11-4, but in addition, it also has several more. As shown in figure 11-5, this extended dialog box consists of the following additional features.

- **Group** An area containing the Boolean operators being used to join the elements of the complex condition together. Clicking on one of the operators in this area highlights it. You can then click on one of the Boolean operator buttons to change the join operator.
- **Row Selection button** Click this button to highlight a condition that is to become part of a sublevel.

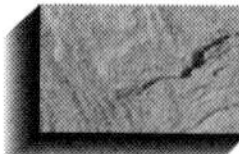

NOTE
Sublevels are used to group together conditions that are to have different Boolean operators to the main conditions. This allows you to create complex conditions such as A = 1 or (A = 2 and B = 4), where conditions A = 2 and B = 4 are combined together in a sublevel using the AND operator, as compared to A = 1, which is joined to the sublevel using the OR operator. In essence, this query returns all rows where A = 1, or where A = 2 and B = 4.

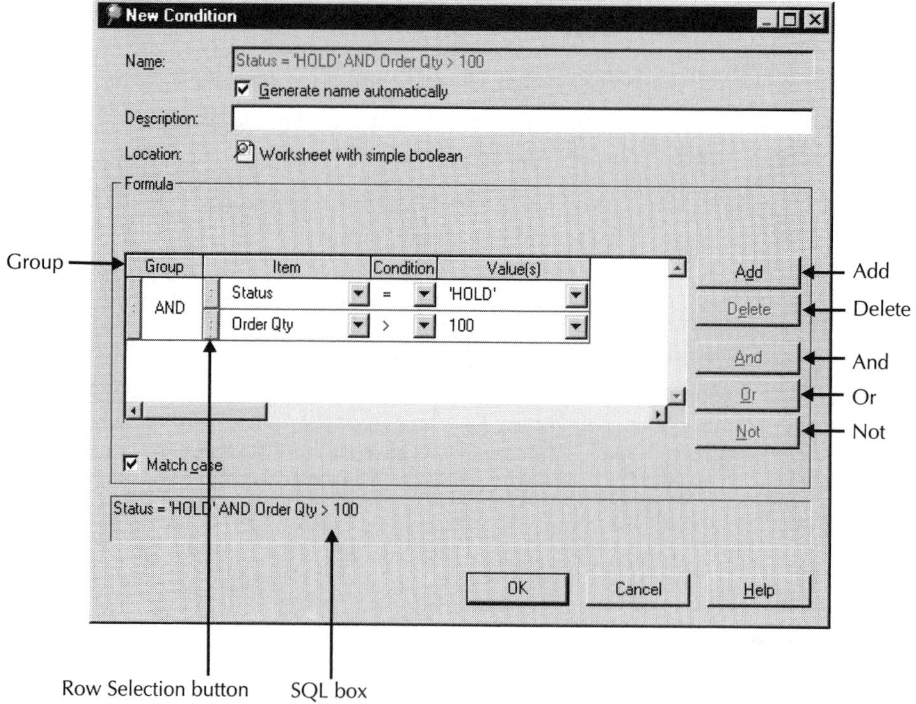

FIGURE 11-5. *Extended New Condition dialog box*

- **Add** When active, click this button to add a new condition to the complex condition you are creating or editing.
- **Delete** When active, click this button to delete a highlighted condition from the complex condition.
- **And** When active, click this button to change the join operator between two elements of the complex condition to the AND operator.
- **Or** When active, click this button to change the join operator between two elements of the complex condition to the OR operator.
- **Not** When active, click this button to negate the current highlighted item in the dialog box. With a join operator highlighted, Discoverer adds the word NOT as a prefix to the current join operator. Clicking Not a second time returns the join operator to its original state. With an expression highlighted, Discoverer negates that expression. For example, IN would become NOT IN, and >= (greater than or equal to) would become <(less than).
- **SQL box** As you create the condition formula, a box at the bottom of the dialog box displays the SQL syntax for the condition that you are entering. If you know SQL very well, you can use this box to validate that Discoverer is defining the condition as you would like it.

When you enter the Extended New Condition dialog box for the first time, all of the Boolean operator buttons, apart from Not, are deactivated. This is because Add, Delete, And, and Or cannot be used until you have created at least one condition. Clicking Not would change the default condition to <>.

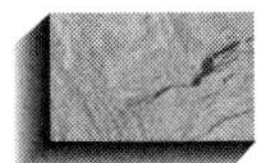

NOTE
Do not click OK until you have built at least one condition. If you click OK too early, Discoverer will give you the following error message.

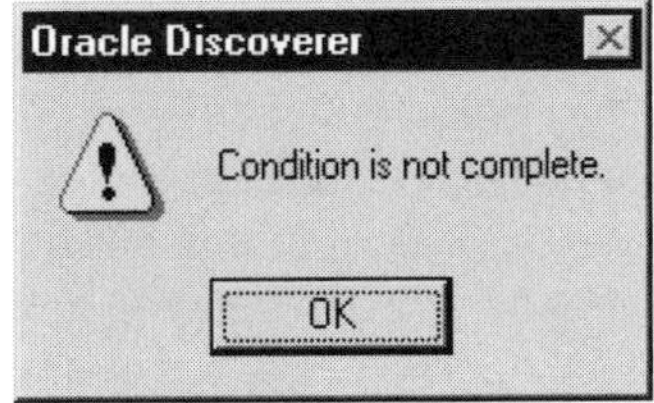

Building a Simple Boolean Condition

Before building a Boolean condition, you need to work out in advance what you want to know and convert that into simple Boolean algebra.

For example, let's build a condition that constrains a query to orders that are on hold and have a quantity ordered in excess of 1,000. First of all, the Boolean algebra for this is as follows:

Order Status = HOLD AND Quantity Ordered > 1000

Having ascertained that there are no existing conditions that will satisfy what we want, we opened the New Condition dialog box and clicked Advanced. This opened the Extended New Condition dialog box as seen in Figure 11-5.

Using the status to constrain the worksheet to only those orders that are on hold, we will now build the first condition. There are no illustrations for any of these steps, because by now you should know how to do this. Having created the first condition, all of the Boolean operator buttons are now activated.

Next, we clicked Add, opened another row of basic components, and built the second condition. The final complex condition is shown in Figure 11-5.

Building a Complex Boolean Condition

Once you know how to build simple Boolean conditions, building complex ones is straightforward. A complex Boolean condition takes three or more separate conditions and uses Boolean operators to join them together. Many people have asked the authors if it is possible to combine different Boolean operators in the same condition. The answer is yes and, in this section, we will show you how.

First of all, as always, we need to think out in advance what it is that we are trying to do. The complex Boolean that we are going to build uses the following logic to analyze our query of sales orders and quantities:

Order quantity > 15000 OR (order quantity between 7000 and 8000,
AND the status is OPEN)

The portion in brackets is to be considered a single condition, such that our result will display all orders that have an order quantity in excess of 15,000, along with all open orders that have a quantity between 7,000 and 8,000.

So, where do we begin? As always with complex conditions, we need to proceed directly to the Extended New Condition dialog box, by clicking Advanced in the normal New Condition box. By examining our documentation of the system, we discovered that there is already an administrator-defined condition for the order quantity being in excess of 15,000. Therefore, we opened the Item drop-down list and took the option to Select Condition. Doing this opened the following Conditions dialog box. As you can see in the next illustration, the condition we want already exists and, as it is the only condition available to use, it has been automatically highlighted.

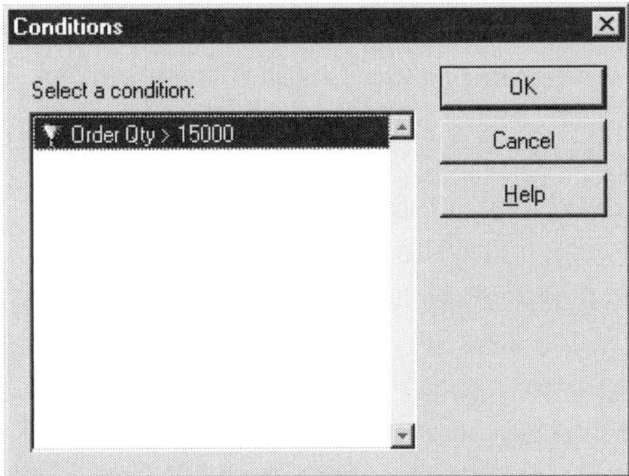

Clicking OK returned us to the Extended New Condition dialog box, placing the condition we just selected in the first row. Next, we clicked Add to add the second part of our complex condition, the order quantity between 7,000 and 8,000. When we opened the Item drop-down list this time, Discoverer had added another option to the list, the chance to Copy Condition.

As the second part of our condition uses the same item as the first part, so that we cannot possibly select the wrong item in error, we will copy the first condition and then change it. Taking the option Copy Condition reopens the Conditions dialog box, from where we once again selected the administrator-defined condition. This resulted in the following:

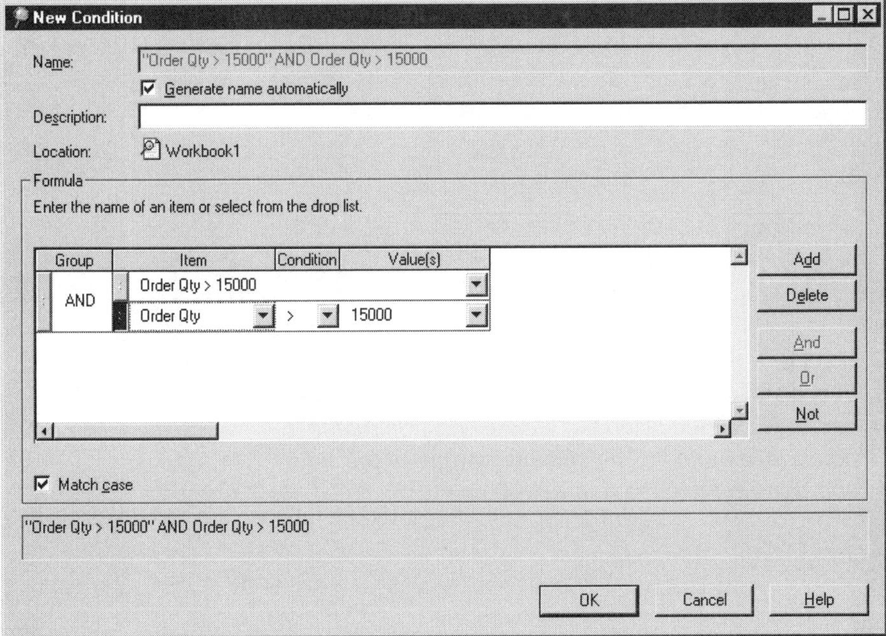

As you can see in the preceding illustration, Discoverer has added the condition a second time, but this time has made it available for editing.

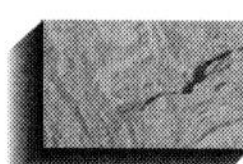

NOTE
Remember you cannot edit administrator-defined conditions. By copying them, you are in effect creating a new condition, a condition that you can edit.

We edited this second condition and changed it so that it now selected quantities between 7,000 and 8,000, as shown here:

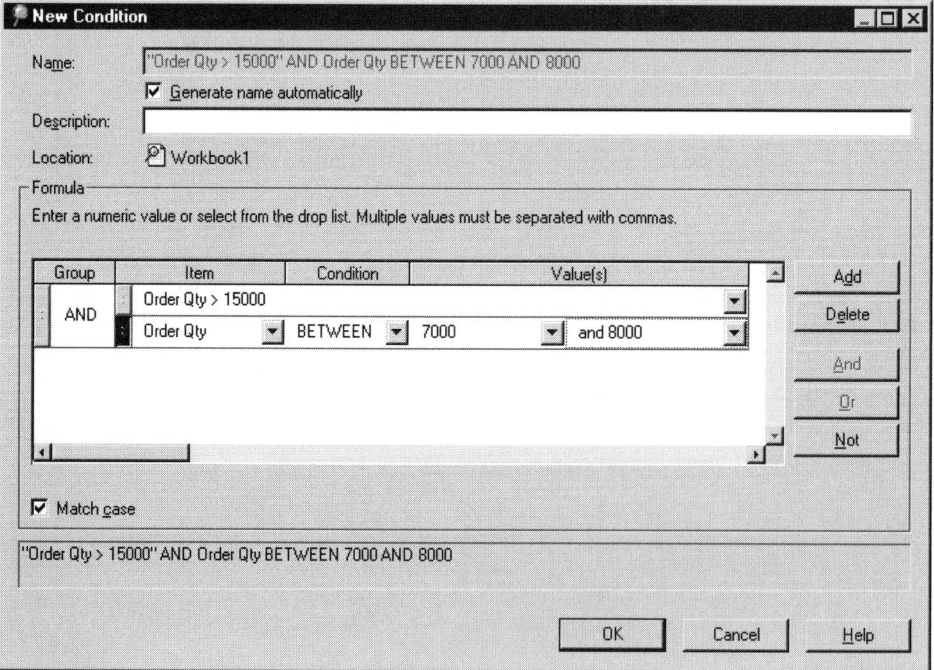

NOTE
In order to show you the preceding illustration, we had to widen the Extended New Condition dialog box. You can do this by clicking on one of the sides and dragging it to the required size.

As you can see from the previous illustration, the two parts of this condition are out of sync with each other. It is not possible to select order quantities in excess of 15,000 when the quantity is set between 7,000 and 8,000. Discoverer will allow you to complete this condition, but the query will return no data.

We now have to add the third component of this complex condition, the bit that constrains the status to only orders that are on hold. We clicked on Add, then added the third condition, so that our complex condition now looks as shown here:

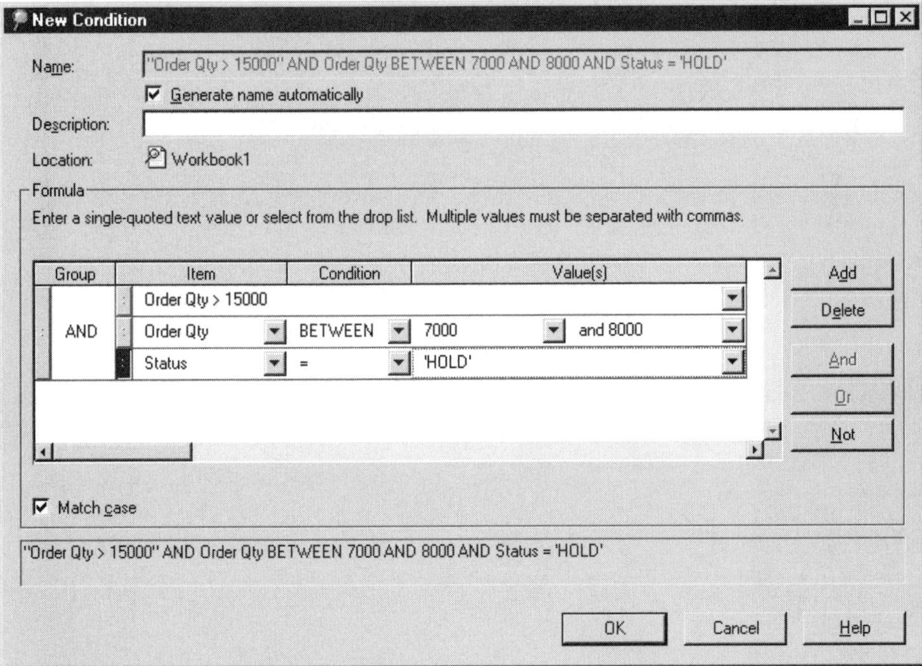

Finally, we need to convert the structure of our condition, such that it satisfies our original request for Order quantity > 15000 'OR' (order quantity between 7000 and 8000, 'AND' the status is open).

In order to accomplish this, we need to create a sublevel within our condition based on the items that are in brackets. To create a sublevel in a complex condition, use this workflow:

1. Determine which items need to be part of the sublevel.
2. Click on the Row Selection button to the left of the first item that needs to be part of the sublevel. This highlights the Row Selection button (see Figure 11-5).

3. Hold down the CTRL key and click on the row selection button for the next condition that needs to be part of the sublevel.
4. Click on the Boolean operator button that you want to apply to the two conditions selected. Discoverer will now create a new sublevel to your condition.
5. Check that the Boolean operator linking the new sublevel to the remainder of the complex condition is correct. If not, click on it and change it.
6. Repeat steps 2 through 5 as many times as needed, creating as many sublevels as is necessary.
7. When you have finished creating sublevels, click OK.

Using the above workflow, we clicked on the Row Selection button for the second order quantity condition (between 7,000 and 8,000), held down the CTRL key, clicked on the Row Selection button for the status condition, then finally clicked on AND. You can see in the following illustration how our complex condition now contains a sublevel.

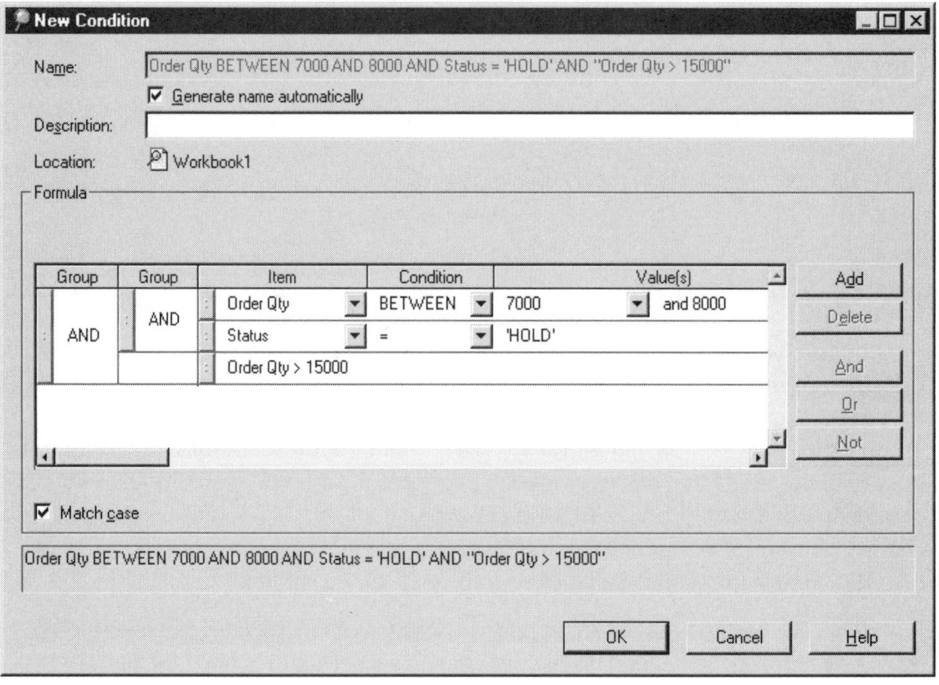

The final step to creating the correct condition that was originally specified requires us to change the join operator between the sublevel and the administrator-defined condition to an OR. To do this, we clicked on the AND operator in the Group area, then clicked on the Or button. This gave us the correct complex condition as seen below. In particular, notice how Discoverer has defined the SQL syntax.

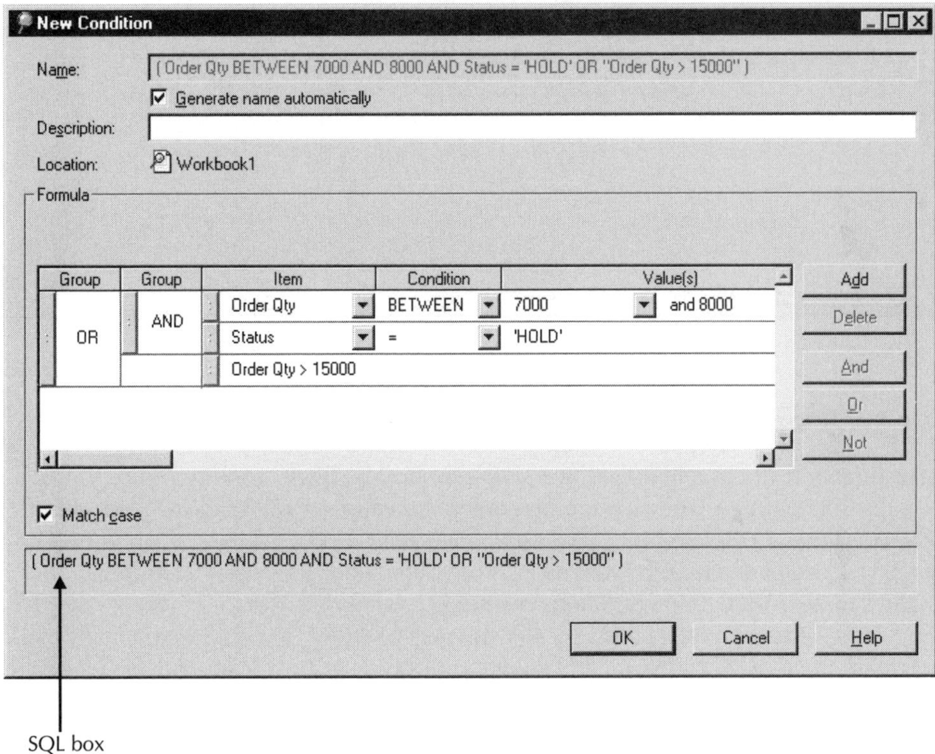

Finally, when we clicked OK to complete the condition, Discoverer ran the query again and gave us the following result. As you can see in the next illustration, we do indeed have both conditions satisfied. We have a row containing an on-hold order with a quantity between 7,000 and 8,000, while at the same time we have several other rows containing quantities in excess of 15,000.

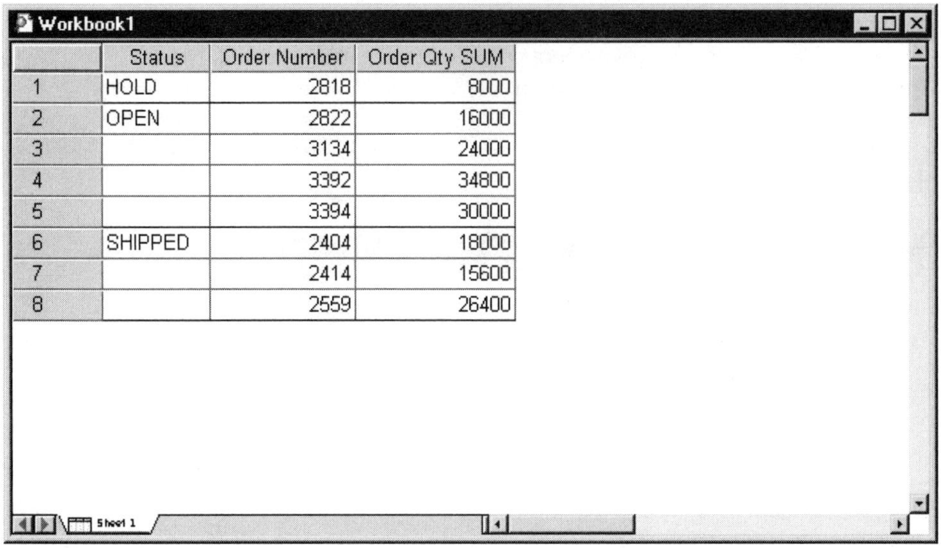

Workbook1

	Status	Order Number	Order Qty SUM
1	HOLD	2818	8000
2	OPEN	2822	16000
3		3134	24000
4		3392	34800
5		3394	30000
6	SHIPPED	2404	18000
7		2414	15600
8		2559	26400

Sheet 1

Using Subqueries

The final type of complex condition uses subqueries. These conditions use the results from another worksheet to determine the value or values to be used within the conditions. You can build very complex queries using this type of condition. In fact, you can even combine the results from different worksheets to be applied as values to be used within conditions of your current worksheet.

These types of queries are very easy to use and build, but can dramatically increase the length of time it will take for your query to run. Many queries using subqueries could be rewritten as Boolean conditions. You should, therefore, only use subqueries when it is impossible to build a condition or conditions within the main query that would give you the result you are looking for.

There are two types of subquery conditions. These are:

- Subqueries using single items
- Subqueries using correlated items

Whichever type of subquery condition you decide to build, you will use the Create Subquery dialog box.

Create Subquery Dialog Box

The only way to create a condition based on a subquery is to use the Create Subquery dialog box. This box, as seen in Figure 11-6, has the following features:

- **Subquery sheet selection** An area where you can type in or use the associated drop-down list to tell Discoverer which sheet to use.
- **Item Match** An area where you can type in or use the associated drop-down list to tell Discoverer which item to use in the sheet being linked to.
- **New** Click this button to create a new worksheet, in which you intend to build constraints to define the item you want your main query to link to.
- **Add** Click this button to add a pair of correlated items to the subquery.
- **Remove** Click this button to remove a pair of correlated items from the subquery.

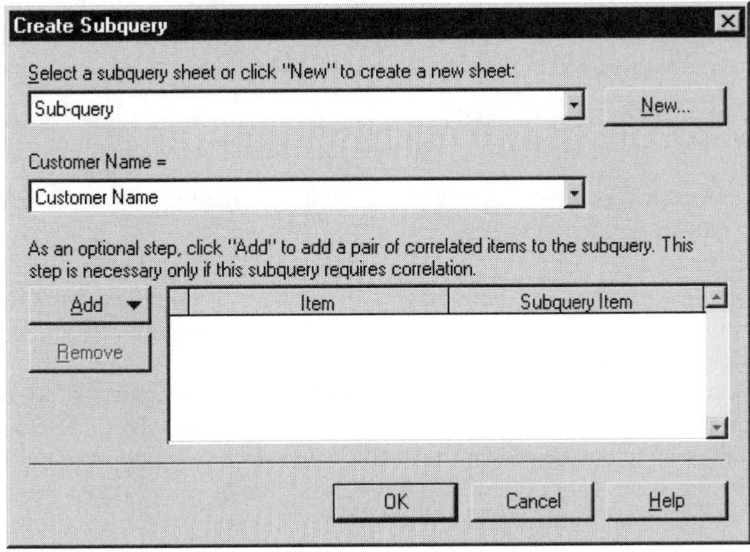

FIGURE 11-6. *Create Subquery dialog box*

Building a Condition Using a Subquery

Whether you decide to build a condition using a single value from a subquery or using correlated items, the way that you build the condition is the same.

To build a condition based on a subquery, use the following workflow:

1. Open the New Condition dialog box.
2. Select the item you want to use to link to the subquery, then select an expression.
3. From the Values drop-down list, choose Create Subquery. This opens the Create Subquery dialog box shown in Figure 11-6.
4. Discoverer tries to find a link to the item you chose in step 2 within an existing worksheet in the workbook. If a link can be found, Discoverer inserts both the sheet and item names into the dialog box. If multiple sheets exist, and the one you want is not the one Discoverer has defaulted to, use the drop-down list of worksheets to locate the worksheet that you want, then use the drop-down list of items to locate the item.
5. If the worksheet does not exist, use the New button to create a new worksheet. This opens the Workbook Wizard, ready for you to build the new worksheet. After you have specified the new worksheet, Discoverer will return you to the Create Subquery dialog box.
6. If you are using correlated items, Discoverer will only allow you to link to an item in the same worksheet that you based the initial Subquery on.
7. Click OK. Discoverer applies the condition, creating any new worksheet that was defined in step 5.

The above workflow, while not having many steps, is complex. Take your time learning this workflow. Steps 4, 5, and 6, in particular, involve much more than the mere clicking of a button.

Please take it easy when building conditions based on subqueries, because the time taken to run the query could be very long. This is especially true if you are scanning the whole database against several values in a subquery. We have found that basing the subquery on items that have small lists of values, like sales channels, statuses, codes, or customer names, will improve the performance of these types of conditions. Using items that have large lists of values, such as sales order numbers, quantities, amounts, and dates, will take much longer.

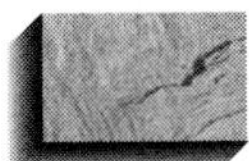

NOTE
If you edit a subquery and cause the values to change, Discoverer will not recognize that the values being linked to have changed, even if you manually make Discoverer rerun the original query. This limitation prevents us from building template queries that automatically work out, using subqueries, new sets of values based on time. The only way to make Discoverer refresh a link to a subquery is to edit the subquery condition itself. For details on how to force Discoverer to use the latest subquery data, refer to the section "Editing a Sub-query" later in this chapter.

Subqueries Without Correlated Items

These are the simplest type of subquery condition to build and understand. Whether you build the subquery first or build it from within the main worksheet makes no difference to Discoverer. However, if the subquery requires some manipulations or extremely complicated mathematical computations, we advise you to create the subquery first. Spending time refining subqueries to make them efficient in terms of indexes and items being selected will prove to be time well spent.

A good example, and the one that we will show you here, makes sheet 1 (the subquery) return a list of all customers who have had a cancellation in the current month, then using that list, make the current query return a list of those customers who also have outstanding orders not yet shipped. You might want to have a heads up and be aware that these orders could be in risk of being cancelled as well. At the very least, you should have the salesperson call the customer and make sure the outstanding orders are still required.

The above query could be created both ways, building either the subquery first or building the main query, and then building the subquery as part of the condition. We will show you both ways.

Example Subquery, Building Subquery First First of all, we built the query that is destined to become the subquery. In this example, we selected the customer name, the fiscal cancellation month of January 2000, and the total quantity ordered. We don't need to use the status in this query because orders with a cancellation date are cancelled! When we ran this query, as you can see in the next illustration, it returned a list of the nine customers who had cancelled an order in January.

To make this example easier to follow, we have named this sheet "Sub-query".

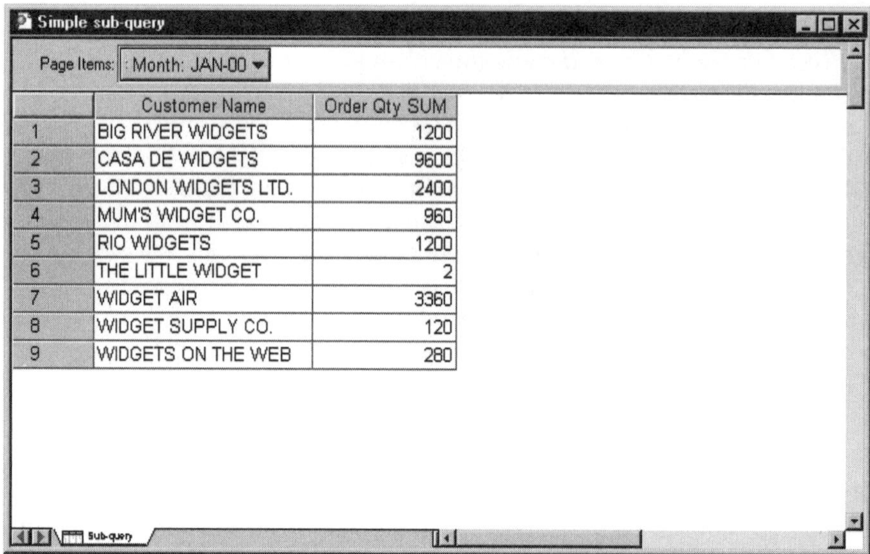
Simple sub-query

Page Items: Month: JAN-00

	Customer Name	Order Qty SUM
1	BIG RIVER WIDGETS	1200
2	CASA DE WIDGETS	9600
3	LONDON WIDGETS LTD.	2400
4	MUM'S WIDGET CO.	960
5	RIO WIDGETS	1200
6	THE LITTLE WIDGET	2
7	WIDGET AIR	3360
8	WIDGET SUPPLY CO.	120
9	WIDGETS ON THE WEB	280

Sub-query

Next, we opened a new sheet in the workbook (Sheet | New Sheet from the menu bar). In this sheet, we selected customer name (for the link), the fiscal order month of January 2000, the status OPEN, and the total quantity ordered. The status is required this time because we need to identify which orders are not shipped. When we ran this query, as you can see below, it returned a list of 20 customers with open orders.

Simple sub-query

Page Items: Month: JAN-00 Status: OPEN

	Customer Name	Order Qty SUM
1	ABC WIDGET CO	1
2	ACE MANUFACTURING	50
3	CASA DE WIDGETS	1202
4	CEBU WIDGET CO	6266
5	HONG KONG WIDGETS	4800
6	LOTS OF WIDGETS	3
7	MOUNTAIN WIDGETS	1
8	PATRIOT'S WIDGET CO.	1
9	THING'S	50
10	TRICOLOR WIDGETS	202
11	WARSAW WIDGETS	1201
12	WE'VE GOT WIDGETS	3600
13	WIDGET O THE MERSEY	600
14	WIDGETS BY THE BAY	3600
15	WIDGETS DE MEXICO	1202
16	WIDGETS MARKET	1
17	WIDGETS ON THE WEB	300
18	WIDGETS R US	3
19	WONDER WIDGETS	11766
20	YAMATA WIDGET LTD.	1201

Subquery | Master Sheet

We now need to build a new condition restricting the main sheet to only the customers from sheet 1. In order to do this, we will follow the workflow that we gave you earlier.

First, we opened the New Condition dialog box, then from the drop-down list of items we selected the customer name, set the expression to be =, and the value to be Create Subquery. As you can see in the next illustration, this opened the Create Subquery dialog box. Discoverer has already found another sheet in our query, the sheet entitled "Sub-query", and has also scanned all of the items in that sheet, locating an item called Customer Name. These values have automatically been inserted into the Create Subquery dialog box.

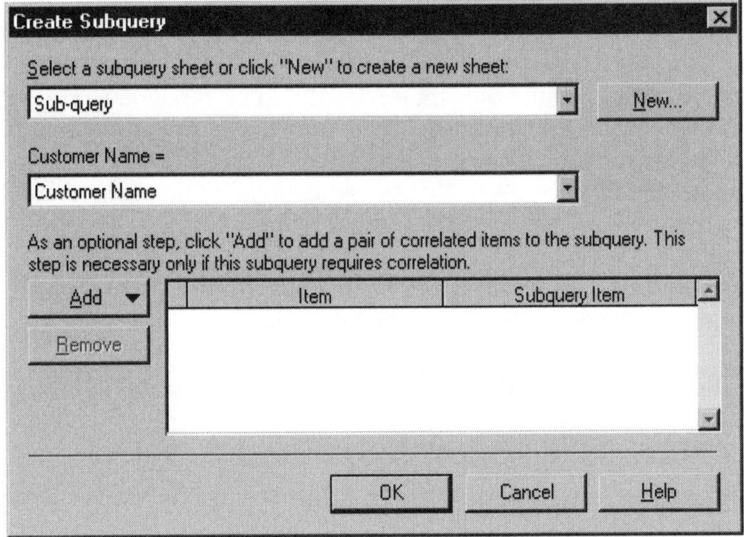

As all required items within the Create Subquery box are complete, we clicked OK. Discoverer returned us to the New Condition dialog box, where we could see the resulting condition was Customer Name = Sub-query. Clicking OK this time caused Discoverer to rerun the query using the condition that we have just defined, returning only those customers with current orders who also had a cancellation in January 2000.

Example Subquery, Building Main Query First This time we built the main query first, then opened the New Condition dialog box. We will not show you any illustrations, because these are the same as in the preceding example. We again selected the Customer Name from the Item drop-down list, set the expression to be =, and the value to be Create Subquery. This time when we entered the Create Subquery dialog box (see Figure 11-6), Discoverer was unable to populate any of its fields because there is no subquery within the workbook.

We therefore need to add a new sheet. Clicking Add launched the Workbook Wizard. In there, we created a new query using the customer name and quantity ordered for January 2000. When we clicked Finish to complete this query, rather than running it, Discoverer returned us to the Create Subquery dialog box. As the subquery is now complete, we clicked OK and completed the condition.

Subqueries Using Correlated Items

Queries using correlated items are simply queries that link to more than one item in the subquery. For example, suppose you had a subquery that returned the average unit selling price for each product sold in the past month. Using correlated items, you could analyze the selling price of the same products by customer, returning a list of customers who had paid more than the average selling price for their goods. Obviously, last month these customers were willing to pay more than the average price for these items. Therefore, if you want to quickly increase your profits for the current month, all you need do is have a salesperson contact these customers and see if they are willing to buy some more. You could even offer them a discount, yet still sell to them at above the average selling price!

We will show you how to create this query. We have chosen to build the subquery first, although we could just as easily have opted to build the main query first.

For the subquery, we selected the product name, average selling price, and average quantity shipped for January 2000. We then created a calculation to derive the average unit price, by dividing the average quantity shipped into the average selling price. This produced the list as shown here:

Workbook1

Page Items: Month: JAN-00

	Product Name	Selling Price AVG	Order Qty AVG	Unit Price
1	AB-2000	25226.33	1076	23.45
2	AB-2500	30400.58	1296	23.45
3	AB-3000	30922.73	1319	23.45
4	AVR-500	18146.00	1028	17.66
5	AVR-550	33683.50	1907	17.66
6	AVR-800	12193.63	956	12.75
7	AVR-900	32416.16	1525	21.25
8	CD-100	25387.62	733	34.65
9	CD-200	22374.00	646	34.65
10	CD-500	24928.75	925	26.95
11	CD-550	38538.50	1430	26.95
12	CD-625	16295.00	1207	13.50
13	QB-1000	31689.88	1794	17.66
14	QB-2000	37806.13	2479	15.25
15	QB-3000	11915.33	781	15.25
16	QB-5000	56874.73	2564	22.18
17	QB-5500	62710.68	2827	22.18
18	QB-6000	55520.45	2503	22.18

Sheet 1

For the main query, we selected the customer name, average selling price, average quantity shipped, and product name for the same month. We also calculated the customer's unit price, then launched the New Condition dialog box. Here, we created a new condition where the customer's unit price was greater than the unit price in the subquery, then clicked Add in the Create Subquery dialog box to add a correlated item.

In the following illustration, you can see both the New Condition and Create Subquery dialog boxes. In the New Condition dialog box, we selected the Cust Unit Price from the Item drop-down box, changed the expression to >, then selected Create Subquery from the Values drop-down list. This opened the Create Subquery dialog box, in which Discoverer detected the existence of an existing sheet, but was unable to detect a field called Cust Unit Price. We had to select the Unit Price from the drop-down list. After clicking Add to add a correlated item, from the drop-down list we selected Product Name. Discoverer, finding a matching item in sheet 1, automatically made the correlation.

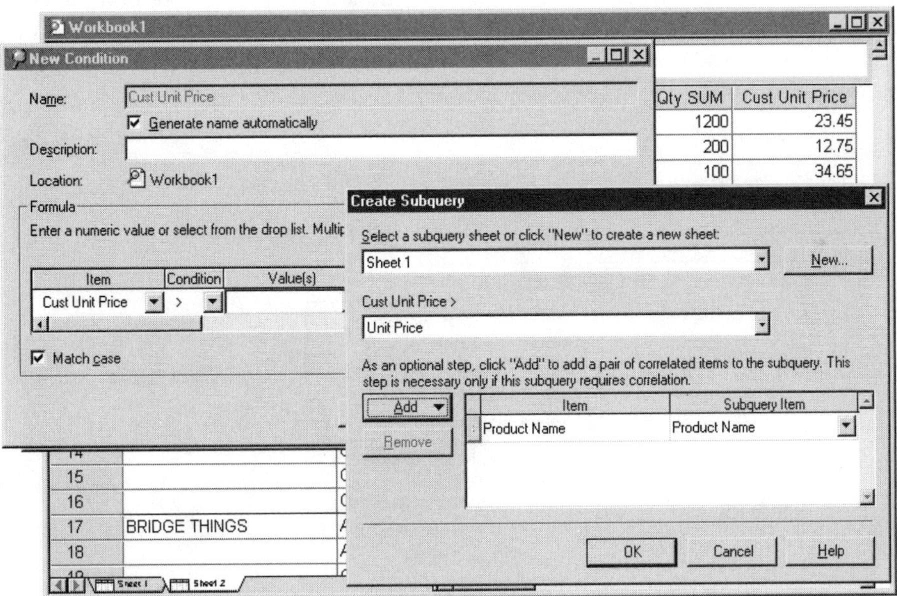

Editing a Subquery

Unfortunately, as previously mentioned, Discoverer will not detect that the data being returned in a subquery has changed. Therefore, changing a subquery will have no impact on the main query that it is referenced by. This will produce totally unexpected results when comparing the output of the worksheets.

In the preceding example, when we showed you how to build a subquery excluding correlated items, we constrained the subquery to return a list of customers who had cancellations in January 2000. Editing the subquery by adding a new condition to show only those customers who had total cancellations with a quantity in excess of 3,000 will result in a smaller list of customers. This will cause the subquery result to change, but not the main query. Even if you refresh the main sheet, it will not recognize the new list and will continue to be constrained on the original subquery.

To compound the problem, if we share this query with someone who is not very proficient in Discoverer, they will look at the conditions for the subquery and assume that the main query result is correct, totally unaware that there is a mismatch.

The only way to correct this is to edit the subquery condition. This causes Discoverer to recognize that the subquery has changed. To show you how this works, we added a new condition to the subquery, where the order quantity is greater than 3,000. When we ran the query in the master sheet, as expected, Discoverer did not warn us that the subquery had changed.

As we are aware of the situation, we launched the Conditions dialog box, highlighted the Customer Name IN Sub-query condition, then clicked on the Edit button. In the Edit Condition dialog box, we opened the drop-down list in the Value field. As you can see here, Discoverer had added another option to the list, an option to Edit Subquery.

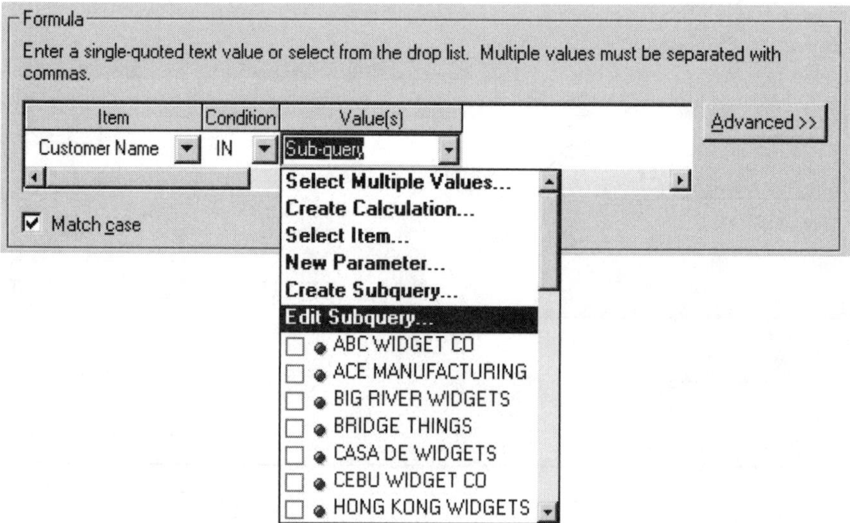

Taking the option Edit Subquery caused Discoverer to at last recognize that the subquery had changed. As you can see in the next illustration, we were given the following warning that the subquery had changed. We clicked Yes, then clicked OK in the Edit Subquery box, and completed the condition. This caused Discoverer to rerun the query correctly.

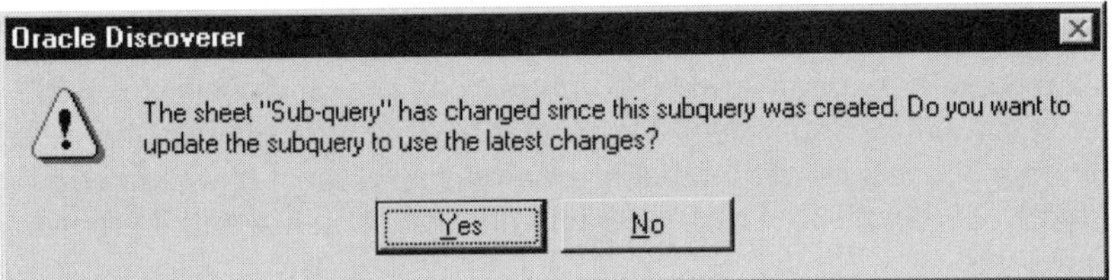

Removing Conditions

There are three very good reasons why you may want to remove a condition. These are:

- To return a query to its original state following analysis or printing
- Because you made a mistake and created an incorrect condition
- Because you avoided "The Query from the Twilight Zone" and now wish to open up the query to produce some more meaningful results

There are two ways to permanently remove a condition from a query, and one way to deactivate a condition yet still leave it in situ in case of a future requirement.

Permanently Removing Conditions

As stated above, there are two methods of permanently removing a condition from a query. These are:

- Undo the last condition.
- Delete the condition from the query.

Permanently Removing a Condition by Undoing the Last Condition

If you made a mistake and created an incorrect condition, you can return your query to its original state very easily by either pressing CTRL-Z, or from the menu bar selecting Edit | Undo Conditions.

Either of these methods causes Discoverer to automatically undo the condition that you just created. In fact, Discoverer actually deletes the condition.

NOTE
You can only use undo immediately following the creation of a condition, although it does not matter which method you used to create the condition.

Deleting a Condition from a Workbook

Deleting a condition from a workbook removes it from all worksheets in the workbook. If you have multiple worksheets in your workbook, you should be very careful not to delete a condition that is used by a worksheet other than the one you are currently working with. Discoverer will not warn you nor will it prevent you from doing this.

To delete a condition from a workbook you should use the following workflow:

1. Open the Conditions dialog box.
2. From the list of conditions displayed, highlight the condition you want to delete.
3. Click the Delete button.
4. Click OK.

Deactivating a Condition

Deactivating a condition does not delete a condition from a workbook. In fact, unless you are certain that you no longer require a condition, you would be better advised to deactivate it. This recommendation has even more merit when there are multiple worksheets in the workbook.

To deactivate a condition, use the following workflow:

1. Open the Conditions dialog box.
2. From the list of conditions displayed, uncheck the condition you want to deactivate.
3. Click OK.

Removing Columns Upon Which Conditions Are Based

At first sight, this may seem a rather dangerous thing to do. However, the ability to remove a column from the display, without impacting any condition based upon that column, is another of Discoverer's really useful features. Discoverer will remember the item and will continue using it. There are two types of column that you can remove. These are:

- Columns based on data items from the database
- Columns based on calculations

Removing a Database Item Used in Conditions

You are quite safe removing a database item from a query, even if that item is used in one or more conditions. This is because the item, being in the database, is still accessible. Discoverer will continue being able to apply conditions on that item, even if you no longer wish to display the item in the final results set.

Removing Calculations Used in Conditions

You can even remove calculated columns from the results set and Discoverer will continue using those calculations within conditions. This is because when you remove a calculated column, Discoverer does not delete the calculation. Instead, Discoverer leaves the calculation in the workbook but marks it as being inactive. There are two ways to deactivate a calculation, yet still allow Discoverer to use that calculation in a condition. These are as follows:

- Deactivate the calculation in the Calculations dialog box by removing the check mark alongside the calculation.
- In 3.1 only, highlight the column heading, then press the DELETE key on your keyboard. This does not delete the calculation from the worksheet. The calculation is deactivated just as if you had unchecked it in the Calculations dialog box.

Deleting Calculations Used in Conditions

Take care when deleting calculations from worksheets if those calculations are used in a condition. If you delete a calculation from a worksheet, and that calculation is used in a condition, Discoverer also deletes the condition. You will not be warned that there is a condition dependent upon the calculation you are about to delete. The query will be rerun automatically, and the results you see will be minus both the calculation and the condition.

Summary

In this chapter, we have shown you how to build effective conditions, and how learning this skill will allow you to unleash the power of Discoverer. You have learned to add a condition using the analysis bar buttons to create a new condition. You have been shown how to use the Conditions dialog box to add a condition. We have introduced you to a workflow to create a condition and shown you how to effectively use the New Condition dialog box.

You were also shown, in this chapter, how to put into practice the skills learned in the early part of the chapter, building skill by skill. We showed you real-world examples of building conditions using the workflow.

Next, you were taught the basic components of a condition: the item, the expression, and the value. Using these basic components, you learned to edit an existing condition. We also showed you how to take it a step further by using the Advanced button. This allows you to create conditions based on other conditions, conditions based on calculations, conditions using Boolean operators, and conditions using subqueries. We taught you how to create conditions using correlated items and how to edit a subquery.

Finally, We showed you how to remove conditions temporarily and permanently, as well as how to undo a condition. You learned how to delete a condition from a workbook, and deactivate a condition. We also explained how you can remove items from a worksheet, while still allowing Discoverer to use those items in conditions.

In the next chapter, you will continue to learn important advanced techniques that will allow you greater and greater control of this powerful product.

CHAPTER 12

Refining Parameters, Calculations, Sorting, and Percentages

his, the third chapter in the advanced techniques section of the book, will deal with parameters, calculations, sorting, and percentages. As you become more proficient in Discoverer, your queries will become more complex. A change in one data item could bring about the need to change a variety of query definitions. Chapter 11 took an in-depth look at conditions. By changing a condition, you may find yourself needing to reevaluate one or more of the following items: parameters, conditions, sorts, and percentages.

In this chapter, you will learn to change a condition to a parameter, edit parameters, and rearrange the order of parameters. We will also show you how to refine calculations by defining the main components of a calculation and how to define the calculation in advance. You will learn how to convert an algorithm into a Discoverer script as well as how to avoid division by zero errors.

We will show you housekeeping techniques to use after editing a condition by reviewing conditions based on calculations, and reviewing the data items used in the edited calculation. We will explain how to use standard functions and show you how to define calculations for standard margin and markup. You will be taught how to place a final refinement on the sort order, as well as how to remove an item from the sort order. Finally we will show you techniques for refining percentages, including how to change and how to remove them.

Refining Parameters

After dealing with conditions, as we did in Chapter 11, the next most common way to refine a query is to refine or define parameters. The ability to convert conditions into parameters is essential if you are going to build queries on behalf of your department.

Parameters can be considered as placeholders that are used instead of hard-coded values in the definition of a condition. Unlike normal conditions, that always return the same results each time the worksheet is executed, parameters offer you the chance to enter a value before the worksheet is executed. The value entered is then fed to the condition, with the net result being that the same worksheet can produce a variety of results.

Parameters are particularly useful if many people have access to the same worksheet. Discoverer will then produce a result that is only of interest to a particular person or department. As you can see, the use of parameters can save time and money, allowing you the freedom to move on to other tasks. Later, when a change is required to this query, you only have one worksheet to worry about. If, however, you had built one workbook per user, you would have many queries to refine.

Chapter 5 has detailed instructions on creating parameters, and explains the difference between parameters and conditions. We also showed you how to build a parameter. However, we did not show you how to convert a condition into a parameter. In this section on refining parameters, we will show you how to convert a condition into a parameter as well how to edit a parameter.

Changing a Condition to a Parameter

In Chapter 4, we advised you to avoid "The Query from the Twilight Zone" by applying strict conditions. Those hard-coded conditions need to be either replaced or converted into parameters to make the query more useful and flexible.

Converting a Condition into a Parameter

To change a condition to a parameter, use the following workflow:

1. Open the Edit Condition dialog box and make any changes to the condition that may be required.

NOTE
If you want your users to be able to use wildcard characters in the Parameter Wizard, you must ensure that you build the condition using the LIKE expression. Creating conditions using expressions such as = and < will return no data and need changing.

2. From the Values drop-down list, select New Parameter. This opens the New Parameter dialog box, as seen in Figure 12-1. Refer to Chapter 5 if you are unsure how to use this box.

FIGURE 12-1. *New Parameter dialog box for converting a condition into a parameter*

3. Enter a meaningful name if you so choose. This is not a required field, but if you do add your own name, we recommend that you include the word "Parameter" somewhere in the name. Later, when you are editing your conditions, this will help you to differentiate between hard-coded conditions and parameters.
4. Enter a helpful prompt for the end user. This needs to be text that will be easily understood by the end user. It may not be obvious what the choices for the parameter are.
5. Enter a description if you choose. This is not a required field. However, this is an excellent extension of the prompt, and can actually contain the list of values that the end user may choose from.
6. Check the box for multiple values if you want the end user to be able to select multiple values for the parameter.
7. Enter a default value if you choose. If a drop-down list is available, you should select the default from that list. This is not a required field.
8. Click OK and complete editing the condition.

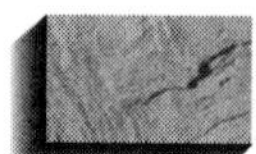

NOTE
The workflow outlined above is different from the workflow given in Chapter 5. This workflow is based on an existing condition, which means the data item and operator are already selected for you. You cannot change them.

Converting a Condition into a Parameter Using the Workflow

In our database, we have an existing query that has multiple conditions and no parameters. Following the above workflow, we will show you how to change one of the conditions to a parameter. Once you have learned this skill, you will be able to convert any condition into a parameter.

Our example query displays the order number, product name, ship quantity, ship date, and status. The status is located on the page axis. We currently have two conditions:

- Order Qty > 15000 (an administrator defined condition)
- Status = 'SHIPPED'

As the first condition was defined by the administrator, we cannot change it to a parameter. We will therefore show you how to convert the second condition so that the same query is capable of showing results for different statuses.

Following the workflow, we opened the Edit Condition dialog box for the condition concerned, then from the Values drop-down list we selected New Parameter. This opened the New Parameter dialog box, as seen in Figure 12-1.

As you can see in the following illustration, we have completed the dialog box. We chose not to add our own name, as Discoverer will create one for us. The rest of the fields are self-explanatory. By adding a default of 'SHIPPED', the parameter duplicates the original condition, thereby allowing the end user to run the query as it was originally built.

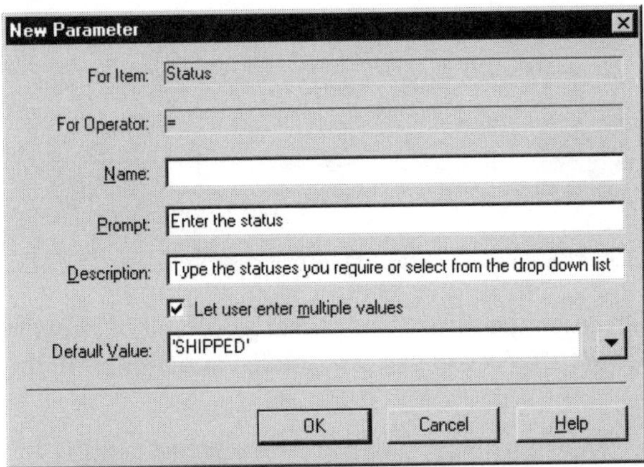

As the parameter is now complete, we clicked OK. This returned us to the Edit Condition dialog box shown below. As you can now see, Discoverer has changed the condition value to be the name of the parameter prefixed by a colon.

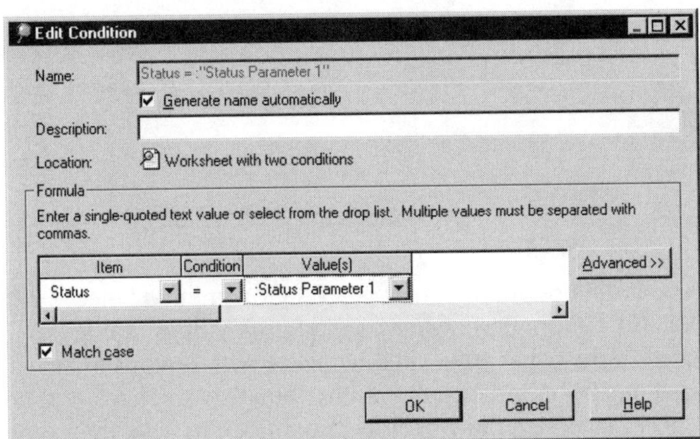

The condition is now complete, and we clicked OK to complete the condition. Discoverer now ran the query and presented us with the following Parameter Wizard entry screen. As you can see, Discoverer has inserted the default and description that we specified. Because we checked the box to allow a user to select multiple values, you can see that Discoverer has also added a drop-down arrow alongside the default.

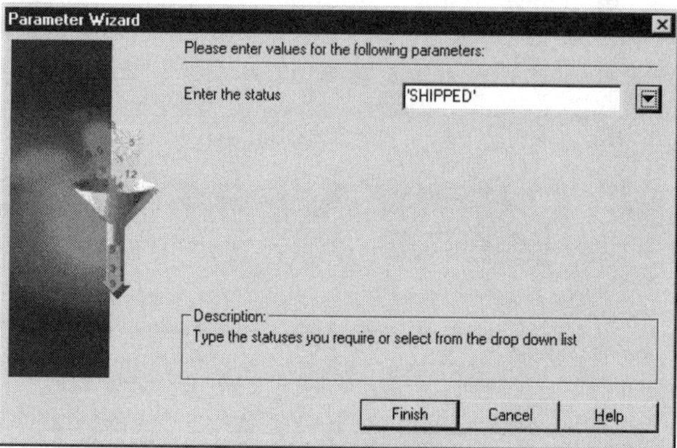

When we clicked on the arrow alongside the default, Discoverer gave us the following drop-down list. As you can see, the list contains all of the values for the Status item.

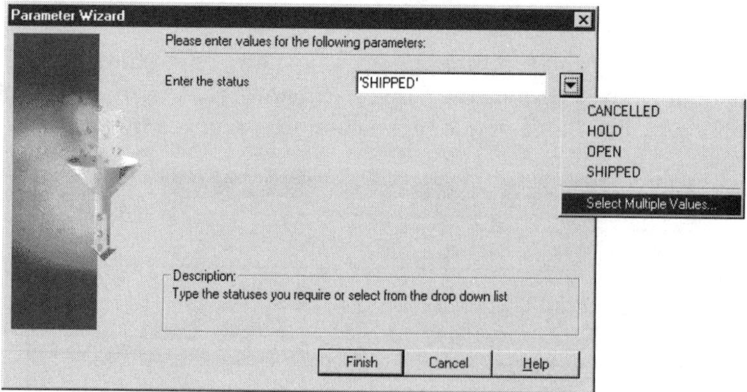

In addition, at the bottom of the list is an option entitled Select Multiple Values. When we took this option, Discoverer opened up a Values dialog box. This box displays all of the values that are available, along with buttons to Select All or Select None. Between these buttons, and the ability for a user to check and uncheck items, the user can now customize the worksheet parameter to view the results they desire.

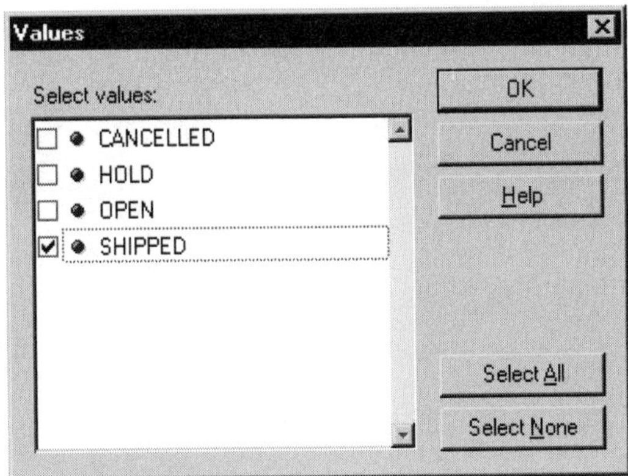

Clicking OK in the Values dialog box returns the user to the Parameter Wizard. Clicking Finish in here causes Discoverer to run the query using the parameters entered.

NOTE
By the careful use of default values in parameters, you can force the query to run as it was originally built. If a user clicks Finish when prompted in the Parameter Wizard, without changing the default, the query will return exactly the same result as if there was still a hard-coded condition.

Editing Parameters

Perhaps you want to add a bitmap to the Parameter Wizard entry screen. Maybe you want to place this new parameter at the top of the Parameter list. Neither of these can be done during the creation of a parameter based on a condition. You will have to edit the parameter if you want to make changes like these.

Remember that parameters and conditions work together. When a parameter is created, it will be added to the Conditions list in the Conditions dialog box. If you allowed Discoverer to name the parameter, the name will contain the word "Parameter". If you named the parameter yourself, and you followed our recommendation, your name will also contain the word "Parameter".

If you want to edit a parameter that has been based on a condition, you have to amend the parameter definition in the Edit Parameter dialog box, and the condition itself in the Edit Condition dialog box. This dual process can seem somewhat irritating at first but, in our experience, you will soon learn to handle this. We hope that in a future release, Oracle will make the link between these more intuitive.

Editing a Parameter

To edit an existing parameter, use the following workflow:

1. From the menu bar, select Tools | Parameters, or in Discoverer 3*i* you can also click the Parameters tab on the Edit Sheet dialog box. This will open the Parameters dialog box.
2. Highlight the parameters you want to edit.
3. Click the Edit button. This opens the Edit Parameter dialog box.
4. Change the parameter as required.
5. Click OK.
6. If required, adjust the ordering of the parameters.
7. If required, you can add your company logo by clicking Bitmap. This opens a drop-down list. From the list, select Set Bitmap, then browse to the bitmap you desire and click Open. This displays the logo to the left of the available parameters. It will also display on the Parameter Wizard.
8. Click OK.

Rearranging the Order of Parameters

After adding a parameter based on a condition, or following an edit of an existing parameter, you should review the order in which they will be presented to the end user. The section entitled "Rearranging the Parameter Order" in Chapter 5 explains how to do this. We recommend that you position the most important parameters at the top of the list.

For example, in the following illustration you can see that we have created a worksheet with four parameters. When a user runs this worksheet, the Parameter Wizard opens and displays the first three parameters. The user selects the required criteria for each parameter and then should click Next to add the criteria for the final parameter.

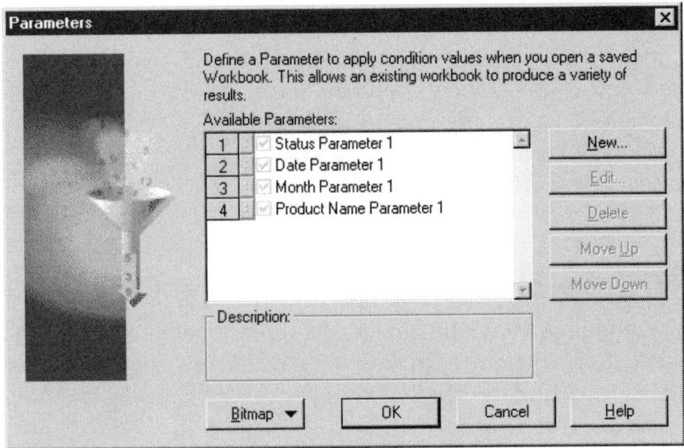

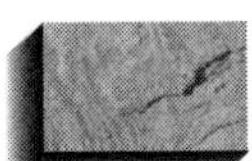

STICKY FEATURE
Discoverer remembers the last set of criteria that you entered into the Parameter Wizard, and will insert these as the default the next time that the worksheet is run.

When the user runs this query, Discoverer opens the following Parameter Wizard. As you can see in the following illustration, the parameters are presented to us in the order in which they appear in the Parameters dialog box. Because there are more than three parameters, the Next button is active.

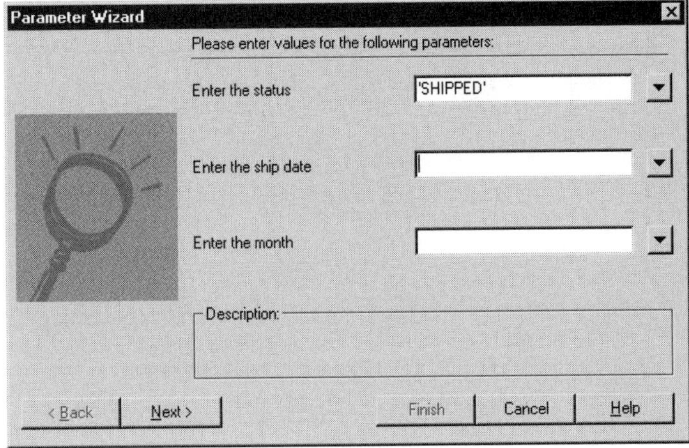

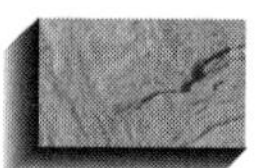

NOTE
The Parameter Wizard will only show three parameters per screen. If there are more than three parameters, Discoverer creates multiple entry screens. Users can navigate between these screens using the Next and Back buttons.

Refining Calculations

After dealing with parameters, the next most common way to refine a query is to refine the calculations. The ability to manipulate data by the use of both simple and complex calculations, and the ability to create new items using calculations, are very useful skills to master.

Main Components of a Calculation

Before we get too deep into the complexities of calculations, we feel it would be appropriate to remind you of the main components of a calculation. Whether you are creating or editing a calculation, Discoverer opens the Edit Calculation dialog box shown in Figure 12-2. This box allows you to give your calculation a meaningful name, and to build your calculation using a combination of items from the database,

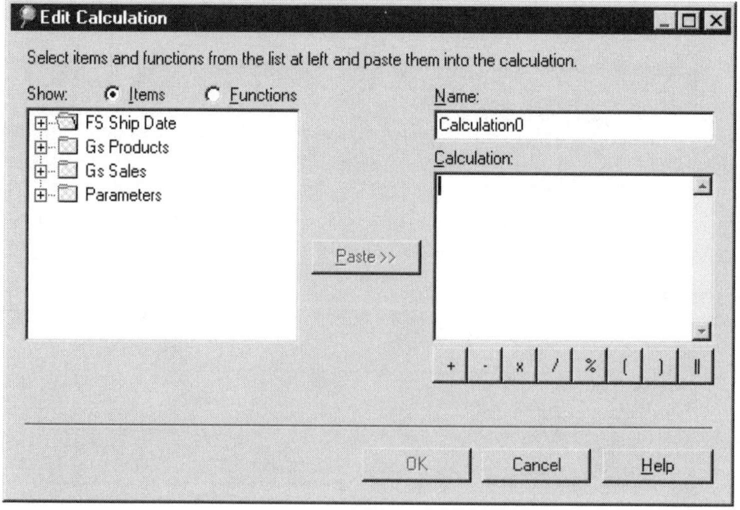

FIGURE 12-2. *Edit Calculation dialog box*

functions, and operators. In Chapter 5, we introduced you to calculations using the Workbook Wizard. Appendix A contains a full list of all the functions used within Discoverer, and we strongly recommend that you spend some time learning how to use these functions.

Define the Calculation in Advance

As with just about everything that we have taught you so far, once again we want to impress upon you the need to think ahead. Unless the calculation is very simple and can be obtained by adding one column to another, or something equally straightforward, we recommend that you work out the calculation in advance.

In our experience, even the simplest of algorithms can prove difficult to translate into a script that Discoverer can understand. In this section, we will outline a few fundamentals to bear in mind, which may help you when dealing with calculations. These are as follows:

- How to convert an algorithm into a Discoverer script
- How to avoid division by zero errors
- How to choose the correct level of aggregation for a calculation

How to Convert an Algorithm into a Discoverer Script

Converting an algorithm into a Discoverer script need not be daunting, yet many people make it so. This is because they don't remember, or don't know, that the basic language of all computers is a series of zeros and ones. When working with a computer, you need to break everything down into its simplest form, and the same applies to Discoverer.

You need to remember that there is a hierarchy when dealing with Discoverer's mathematical operators. Put simply, this mathematical hierarchy is as follows:

1. Powers and square roots
2. Multiplication and division
3. Addition and subtraction

Normally, Discoverer will work out a calculation from left to right—exactly as you key it in, providing all of your operators are at the same level. If you have operators from mixed levels, Discoverer will evaluate the operators from the highest level first, again left to right, then the next level down, and so on. If you are not careful with your operators, you will end up with an incorrect calculation.

For example, look at the following algorithm:

5-2*6+10/2

How do you think Discoverer will evaluate this?

In fact, the answer given by Discoverer is –2, because Discoverer evaluated the multiplication and division parts first, then the subtraction and the addition. Inserting parentheses into the formula may help you understand what Discoverer did:

5-(2*6)+(10/2), which then evaluates to 5-12+5

If you want to force Discoverer to evaluate an expression differently than its hierarchy, you have to use parentheses.

For example, suppose we wanted the expression above to be calculated exactly as written, that is: five minus 2, multiplied by 6, add 10, and finally divide by 2. Inserting parentheses as follows:

(((5-2)*6)+10)/2

evaluates to 14 as required.

How to Avoid Division by Zero Errors

As with all things computational, you cannot divide by zero in Discoverer. You must be very careful defining expressions using division, to ensure that the divisor does not evaluate to zero. A calculation that has worked for the last six months may suddenly stop working because a divisor has now evaluated to zero.

We think that it is folly to assume that a divisor will never be zero. Even the best-designed systems occasionally have glitches that cause erroneous data to get onto the database. Perhaps an upload mechanism that was designed to add the cost price for new products did not run when it was supposed to, leaving those costs at zero!

There may also be valid zero values on the database. Sales orders that have not yet shipped will have an invoiced amount of zero.

So, if you cannot guarantee that the divisor will never be zero, what can you do? There are two ways to overcome the divide by zero error. These are:

- Using a condition to omit zero values
- Using the decode function

Using a Condition to Omit Zero Values This is the simplest way to avoid divide by zero errors. If you are going to use this method, you must ensure that the item you are going to place the condition on is in fact the same item that Discoverer is using within the calculation.

Sounds obvious, doesn't it? At first sight, we expect that you will say something like "That's obvious", and so it is—yet many users make the mistake of pulling the wrong item into the condition. For example, using our test database, we built a query that showed the total quantity shipped and the selling price by month for the fourth quarter of 1998, then calculated the unit price by dividing the price by the quantity. As you can see below, there are no zero values. But is this the right answer?

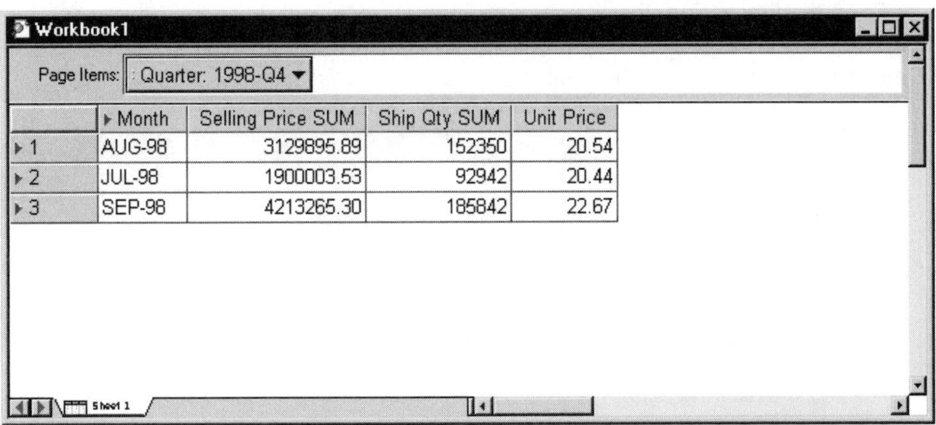

	Month	Selling Price SUM	Ship Qty SUM	Unit Price
1	AUG-98	3129895.89	152350	20.54
2	JUL-98	1900003.53	92942	20.44
3	SEP-98	4213265.30	185842	22.67

Without investigating further, it would be very easy to take the answer at face value and assume that the unit price is correct. In fact, as we will show you, the answer is not correct. We first noticed we had a problem when we drilled into the data for August 1998 and opted to view all the details for that month from the Sales Order folder. Looking at the drilled-down data that follows, you can see that we have a divide by zero error.

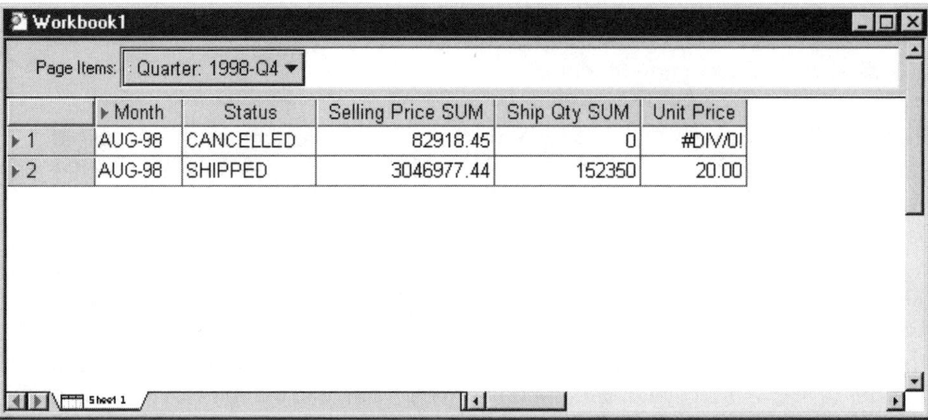

From the illustration, the logical condition to apply would seem to be to set the Ship Qty SUM not equal to zero. This would at least solve the divide by zero error. Doing just that resulted in the output you see next.

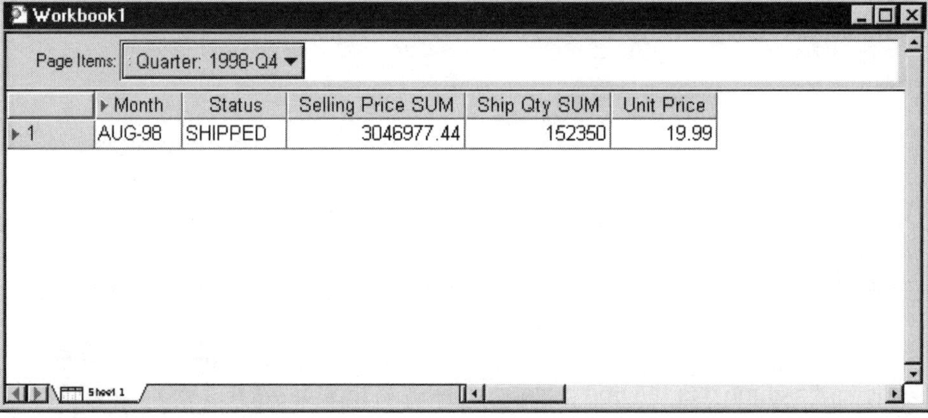

So far, so good. Having avoided our divide by zero error, we glanced at the unit price and wondered why this was lower than in our query before we began drilling. Leaving the condition in place, we used Show Values on the Month heading to get back to the original selections. As you can see next, the result is identical to the result we had when we first started out.

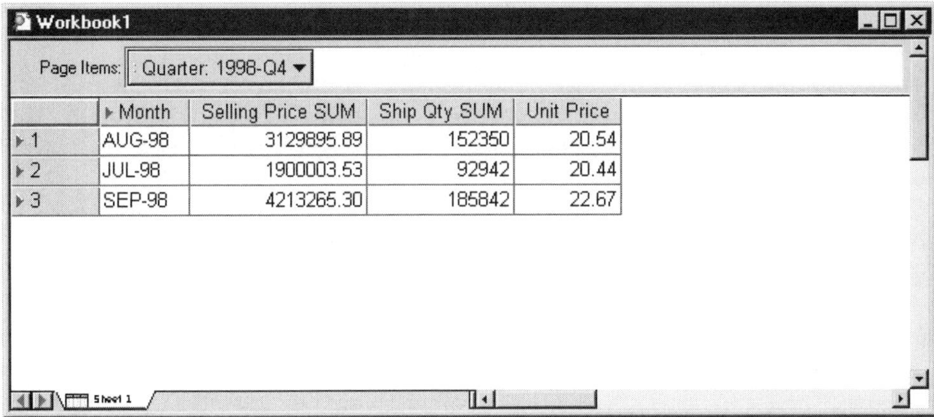

	Month	Selling Price SUM	Ship Qty SUM	Unit Price
1	AUG-98	3129895.89	152350	20.54
2	JUL-98	1900003.53	92942	20.44
3	SEP-98	4213265.30	185842	22.67

Have you spotted the error yet?

By applying the condition to be on the Ship Qty SUM, as opposed to applying it on the Ship Qty itself, not being equal to zero, we have uncovered a fundamental flaw in our query. In fact, we should be excluding all items that have a ship quantity of zero because these items are causing our item cost calculation to be too high. We have been adding the selling price for items that have not shipped. After we refined the condition, the result looked as in the next illustration. Notice how the unit price for August is now the same as what we had when we drilled into the data a few steps back!

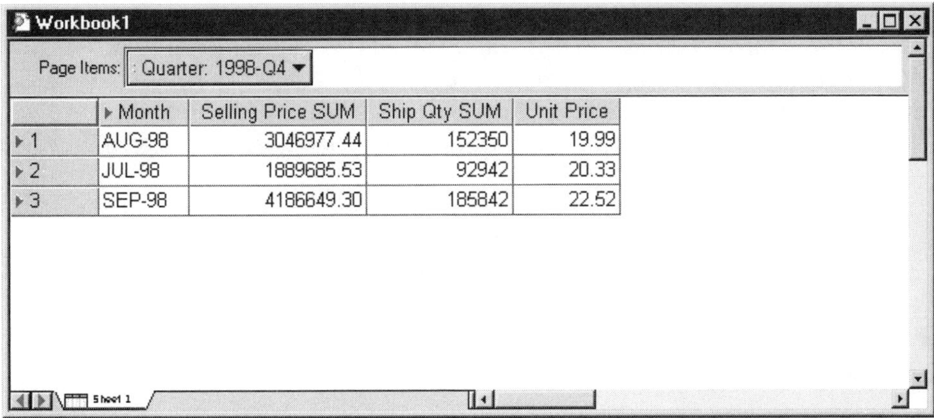

	Month	Selling Price SUM	Ship Qty SUM	Unit Price
1	AUG-98	3046977.44	152350	19.99
2	JUL-98	1889685.53	92942	20.33
3	SEP-98	4186649.30	185842	22.52

We hope the above example has shown you how critical it is to place the condition on the right item when trying to avoid the divide by zero error. At first glance, it appeared as though the condition should have been on the Ship Qty SUM, whereas in fact the correct condition needed to be applied to the Ship Qty itself.

Do not be drawn into believing that all divide by zero errors can be solved by placing the condition on the item, as opposed to the SUM, because they cannot. Databases that use negative values to store amounts and quantities to represent returns may require that the condition be placed on the SUM. For example, suppose you have a sales database where positive values are used to represent actual shipments, and negative values are used to store customer returns. You may not have any zero values in the individual items, yet still end up with zero values in the result. This is caused by the total amount for the returns exactly counteracting the amount of real shipments. If you place a condition on the individual items not being zero, the total amount will still be zero.

For example, suppose you had total shipments of 8,000 items to various customers during August 2000, then received a single return from a major customer, also for 8,000 items. As you can see, adding the two together, you will get a total stock movement of zero. You would be wrong to place a condition on the SUM because the answer is correct and this row should be included in the result. The only way to overcome this situation is to use the Decode function as described in the next section.

Using the Decode Function to Avoid Divide by Zero Errors As we showed you in the previous section, there are times when a zero value belongs in a column that will be used as a divisor. In these cases, you cannot use a condition to omit the item because the end result will be wrong. Perhaps the calculation is only a small portion of the overall report. In order to avoid the divide by zero error and yet leave zero values in the divisor column, you must use the Decode function.

What is the Decode function? The Decode function equates directly to the @IF functions used in Excel and 1-2-3 spreadsheets, and to the IF...THEN...ELSE constructs used in traditional programming languages.

To avoid the divide by zero error, we therefore need to tell the computer:

IF the column being used as the divisor equals zero
THEN place a zero in the calculated column
ELSE perform the calculation

In simple syntax the above could be written as:

IF A=B
THEN C
ELSE D

In Discoverer, these would be written as:

DECODE(column being used,0,0,calculation),
or DECODE(A,B,C,D)

Refer to Appendix A for a full description of the syntax of the Decode function, and see the section entitled "Using Standard Functions in a Query" later in this chapter for a basic overview of how to use functions in your worksheet.

Choosing the Correct Level of Aggregation for a Calculation

Similar to our advice to use care when applying conditions to avoid the divide by zero error, you must be careful when selecting items that will be used inside calculations. Be sure to select the data item that is being used within a column, rather than the data item that is within the database.

For example, we have a worksheet in which we created two calculations, both subtracting the value in one column from another. The following illustration shows the end result, with both the correct and incorrect calculations, plus a column showing the factor of incorrectness. Looking at the factor for the first row of data, you can see that the incorrect calculation is seven times higher than the correct calculation. This is because there are seven sales orders on the system that have a selling price of 1,172.50 and a cost price of 621.00.

Workbook1

	Selling Price	Cost Price	Correct Calc	Incorrect Calc	Factor
1	1172.50	621.00	551.50	3860.50	7.00
2	1161.00	620.92	540.08	540.08	1.00
3	1149.05	608.58	540.47	540.47	1.00
4	1134.00	606.48	527.52	1055.04	2.00
5	1125.60	596.16	529.44	2647.20	5.00
6	1109.00	531.00	578.00	6358.00	11.00
7	1108.80	510.08	598.72	598.72	1.00
8	1098.00	447.12	650.88	650.88	1.00
9	1080.00	577.60	502.40	2512.00	5.00
10	1078.00	459.20	618.80	2475.20	4.00
11	1071.00	503.16	567.84	567.84	1.00
12	1064.64	509.76	554.88	4993.92	9.00
13	1062.50	494.00	568.50	1137.00	2.00
14	1059.60	499.80	559.80	1119.60	2.00
15	1039.50	478.20	561.30	2806.50	5.00
16	1024.28	483.14	541.14	541.14	1.00
17	1020.00	479.20	540.80	540.80	1.00

Sheet 1

As you can see in the following illustration, the correct calculation uses the data without any aggregation, in that we subtracted the cost price from the selling price, not the SUM of these.

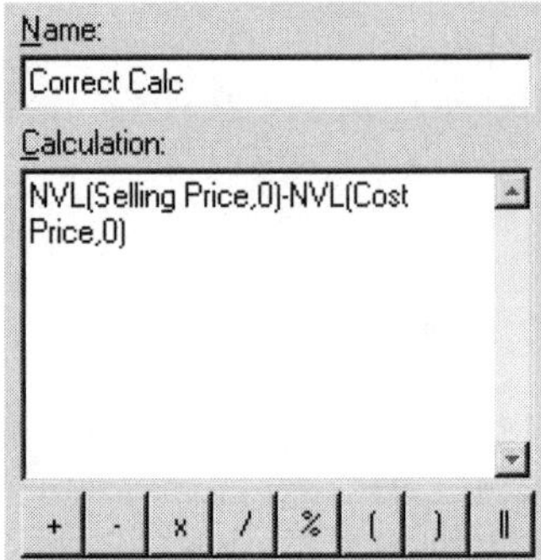

The incorrect calculation, shown next, used the SUM aggregation. This caused Discoverer to add all instances where the selling price is the same and the cost price is the same.

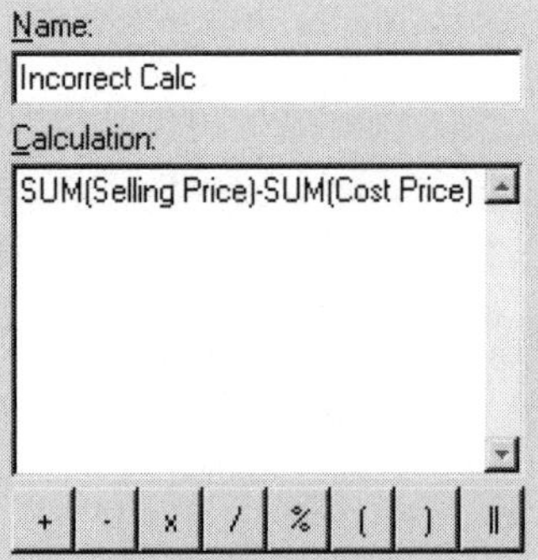

During the construction of the incorrect calculation, Discoverer recognized that there was a potential problem by giving us the following warning:

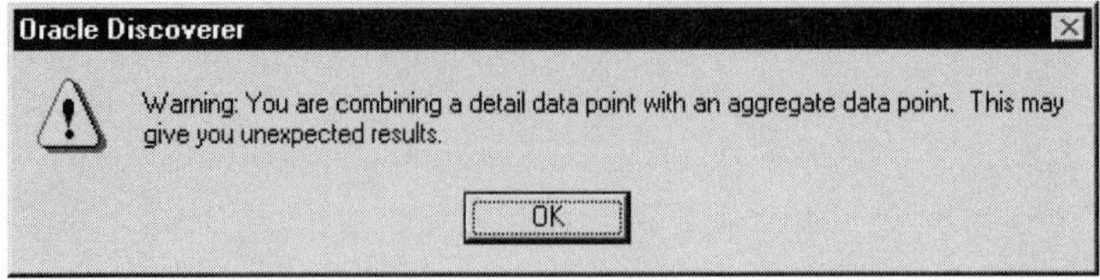

Ignore these warnings at your peril, because there is always a good reason why Discoverer issues warnings like these.

Housekeeping After Editing a Calculation

After you have edited a calculation, you should undertake some housekeeping measures to maintain the efficiency of the worksheet. There are two steps to take after editing a calculation. These are:

- Review any conditions based on the edited calculation
- Review the data items used in the edited calculation

Review Conditions Based on Calculations

As we showed you in Chapter 11, one of the advanced condition types that Discoverer allows is to build a condition based on a calculation. If you create a condition based on a calculation, and subsequently edit that calculation, you should evaluate whether the condition is still valid. Discoverer will automatically use the new calculation; however, the condition may no longer do what you wanted.

Review the Data Items Used in the Edited Calculation

After editing a calculation in which you have changed data items, you should check to see if the original data items are still needed in the worksheet. If they are no longer needed, delete them. If you have used additional items, you may need to add them. This will add to the integrity of the workbook as well as keep the query running efficiently.

For example, suppose you have a worksheet in which you are calculating the unit cost price for each sales order by dividing the order quantity into the cost price sum. For clarity, the worksheet will probably include both source items. If you now edit the calculation to base the unit price on the selling price, without changing the items displayed in the result, you could confuse the recipient of your report.

The following illustration perfectly demonstrates this situation. We have a query where the unit price was based on the cost price. The calculation has been changed and the unit price is now based on the selling price. As you can see, you could easily be led into believing that the unit price is still based on the cost price. You should edit the worksheet, remove the cost price, and insert the selling price in its place.

Workbook1

	Order Number	Order Qty SUM	Cost Price SUM	Unit Price
1	1059	10000	98800.00	21.25
2	1060	1200	7452.00	15.25
3	1061	1000	6210.00	15.25
4	1062	1920	22041.60	26.95
5	1063	1920	22041.60	26.95
6	1064	48	346.56	13.50
7	1065	50	299.50	12.75
8	1066	10000	98800.00	21.25
9	1067	1600	16992.00	22.18
10	1068	8400	89208.00	22.18
11	1069	10000	106200.00	22.18
12	1070	15000	239100.00	34.65
13	1071	200	3188.00	34.65
14	1072	1200	9996.00	17.66
15	1073	1200	9996.00	17.66
16	1074	1200	14904.00	23.45
17	1075	1200	14904.00	23.45

Sheet 1

Using Standard Functions in a Query

Perhaps the most difficult part about using calculations in Discoverer is learning how to use the functions that are available to you. When you open the Edit Calculation dialog box (see Figure 12-2) and click the Functions button, Discoverer displays the folders shown here:

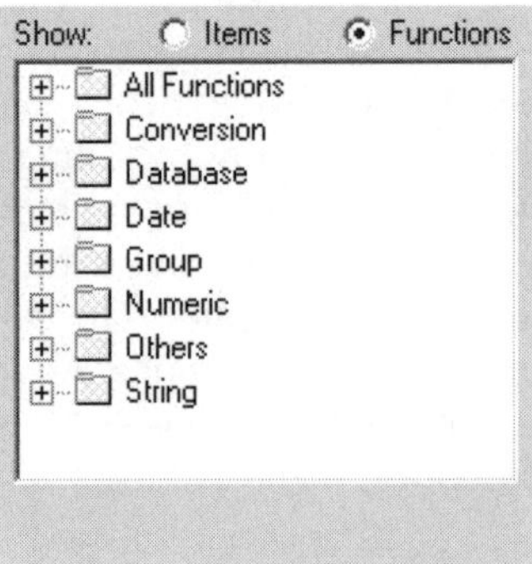

There are eight folders of functions available to you. These are:

- **All Functions** Opening this folder displays all of the functions available to you. They are listed in the order in which they are displayed in the other six folders.
- **Conversion** This folder contains functions relating to converting data from one format into another. There are functions to convert strings into dates, dates into strings, and so on.
- **Database** This folder contains user-defined functions that are specific to the database you are currently using. This folder will be empty unless your Discoverer administrator has created some functions for you.
- **Date** This folder contains functions that manipulate dates. There are functions to generate the system date and time, functions to truncate the time, and so on.
- **Group** This folder contains functions that work on groups of data. These functions include SUM, MAX, MIN, and so on.
- **Numeric** This folder contains functions that are used in mathematical computations, such as +, -, *, /, and so on.
- **Others** This folder contains functions that cannot be categorized into one of the other folders. Examples of these include NVL, DECODE, and so on.
- **String** This folder contains functions that manipulate strings. Examples of these include UPPER, LENGTH, CONCAT, and so on.

In the remainder of this section, we will demonstrate the use of some of the more common functions available to you in Discoverer. In particular, we will show you the following:

- Advanced use of the Decode statement
- Manipulation of dates
- Using TO_CHAR with the number format mask

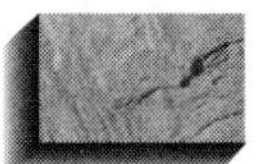

NOTE
A full explanation of all the functions used in Discoverer can be found in Appendix A, along with many examples. Appendix A also contains a full listing of the format masks available to you.

Advanced Use of the Decode Statement

Not a lot of people have harnessed the power of the Decode function, yet its use is one of the most powerful features of Discoverer. Two of the best uses of this function are:

- Defining a list of new values
- Creating calculations based on data subsets

Defining a New List of Values Few people understand that you can use the Decode function to change a list of values as defined in your database to one that is more meaningful. For example, in many Oracle tables you will notice that Oracle uses the character 'Y' for Yes and a null value for No. To make a report more meaningful and user friendly, you might want to display the words Yes and No instead of Y and null. You can intercept the Oracle list of values and replace it with your own by using the following code:

```
DECODE(Oracle field name, 'Y', 'Yes', 'No')
```

Using our example database, we will now show you how to replace one list of values with another. As you have seen in our test database, the original list of values for Status is:

- CANCELLED
- HOLD
- OPEN
- SHIPPED

We have decided that we want to use the value Pending instead of OPEN in our Status list of values. Also, we want the remaining values to appear with the first letter capitalized and the rest in lowercase. In the following illustration, we have used a DECODE statement to give us the desired result.

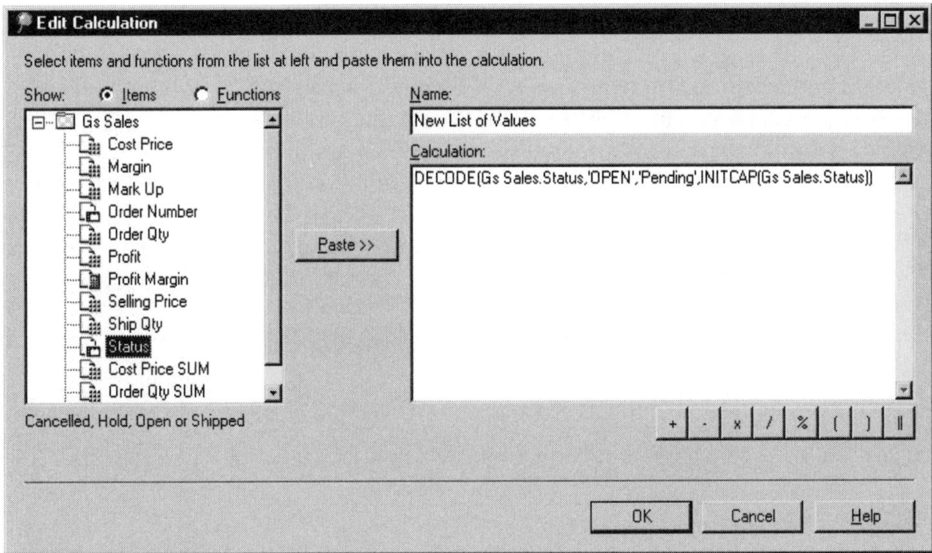

Running this calculation would produce the following list of values:

- Cancelled
- Hold
- Pending
- Shipped

Calculations and conditions can use either the original or amended list of values, but our report will always display the new list.

NOTE

When the current data cannot be sorted into the order that you desire, creating a sort using a new list of values will do the trick. This technique, very common in programming circles, is a very clever use of calculations. In the previous example, we created a new list of values. However, in our final report we want them sorted Shipped, Hold, Pending, then Cancelled. By prefixing the items using A-, B-, and so on, you can reorder any list of values in any arrangement.

Creating a Calculation on the Subset of an Item The second advanced use of the Decode function is a bit more tricky. Let's say you have two sales channels: external and Internet. Discoverer normally sees these as a subset of the channel and will not allow you to apply a calculation to one without it being applied to the other. For example, suppose you want to see a retail unit price for the external channel only. Defining a calculation as we have done previously causes Discoverer to show the unit price for both channels.

However, let's suppose you want to see the following output, in which we have displayed the correct unit price for the external channel, and N.A. for the Internet.

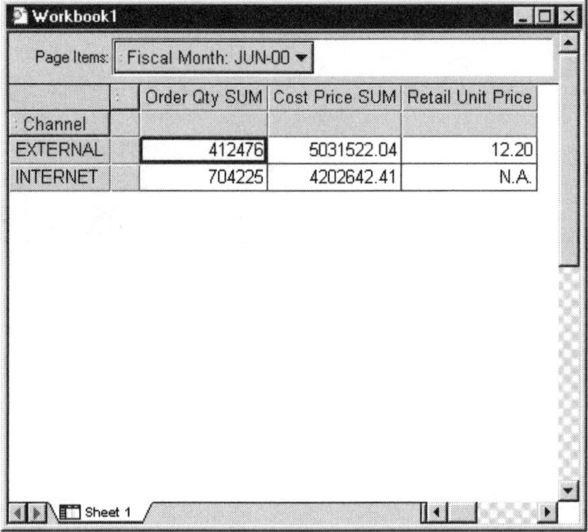

Channel	Order Qty SUM	Cost Price SUM	Retail Unit Price
EXTERNAL	412476	5031522.04	12.20
INTERNET	704225	4202642.41	N.A.

The only way to do this is to use DECODE. The code below shows exactly how to create this:

```
DECODE(Channel, 'INTERNAL', NULL, Cost Price / Ship Qty)
```

To complete the report, we made Discoverer display N.A. instead of the null value. This was done in Tool | Options. Refer to Chapter 14 for a full explanation of how to manipulate null values.

Manipulating Dates

There are many date functions available to you in Discoverer, and the skilled application of these coupled with other functions can greatly enhance your skill set. The ability to effectively manipulate and understand date logic is vitally important to you becoming proficient in Discoverer.

Manipulating the Current Date Current date manipulation lies at the heart of all date manipulations. Once mastered, you can apply the same techniques to other dates, creating more and more powerful queries as you advance your knowledge.

The SYSDATE function returns the current date *and* time. We have italicized the word "and" to draw your attention to the fact that this function returns the time as well as the date. The TRUNC(SYSDATE) function returns the current date alone, with the time portion truncated. It is vitally important that you remember these two functions.

The addition of the time to the date means that you can apply both time and date formats to the SYSDATE, but you should not use it alone in calculations or conditions. To demonstrate this, look at the following illustration. In it we have a single item, the SYSDATE, which has been formatted to show the current date and time in the 24-hour-clock format.

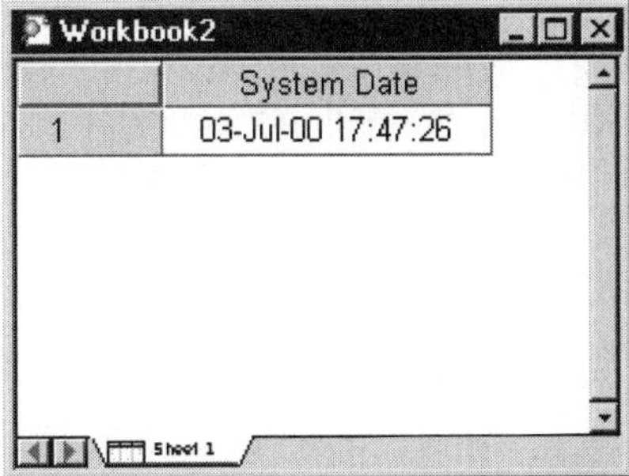

As you can see, if you attempt to find all shipments using this date, you would only find shipments that took place at precisely 17:46 and 26 seconds! An unlikely scenario, we think you will agree. You might be lucky, but probably not.

To use the current date in calculations and conditions, you must apply the TRUNC function to all dates that you use. This will truncate the time portion from the date and allow you to do comparisons and computations safe in the knowledge that you are comparing apples with apples.

To find all shipments that have taken place today, you should use this construct:

```
TRUNC(SYSDATE)=TRUNC(Ship Date)
```

NOTE
Unless you apply formatting criteria to the results of your calculation, the result of a date calculation will always be displayed in the default date format as specified by your Discoverer administrator. Most Oracle systems display the date as either DD-MON-YY or DD-MON-YYYY, meaning that 25 December, 2000 will display either as 25-DEC-00, or 25-DEC-2000.

Common Problems Associated with not Using TRUNC As the correct manipulation of the current date requires the application of the TRUNC function to all dates used when comparing one date with another, it is not surprising to find that users frequently run into problems with this. The most common errors encountered when users try to use this function are as follows:

- A condition such as Current Date = Ship Date returns no data. This is because one or both of the dates have a time portion associated with them. Some databases—data warehouses, for example—may be stored with dates already truncated, so you would only need to apply the TRUNC to the SYSDATE.
- A condition such as Ship Date < Current Date may return incorrect results by including some of the current day's shipments in the result. Suppose the current time is 4:30 P.M., and you last made a shipment at 4:00 P.M. This last shipment would be included in the result because the date and time combination on the shipment is prior to the current date and time combination.
- Ship Date <= Current Date returns data but Ship Date = Current Date does not. We have seen this happen in data warehouse applications when the ship date has been truncated, but the user forgot to truncate the current date.

Manipulating Other Dates We will conclude this section with two more examples on manipulating dates. Suppose you wanted to find the date an item first shipped. A combination of the DECODE, SUM, and MIN functions will give you the answer you are looking for, using this construct:

```
DECODE(SUM(Qty Shipped), 0, NULL, MIN(Ship Date))
```

If we take a closer look at this construct and break it down into plain English, you will be able to follow what is happening. Translating this into words, we get:

> If the sum of the quantity shipped in 0 then return a null value, otherwise return the earliest ship date on file. You may think that the MIN(Ship Date) alone would return the answer you are looking for, but it will not.

The following example will explain why not. Imagine that product A has three sales orders: one has not shipped, one shipped last month, and one shipped this month. The MIN(Ship Date) will return a null value because it encountered a null value in the ship date. Null values anywhere in the set of results will cause the whole result to be null—therefore we need to eliminate them.

Lastly, to find yesterday's date, the function TRUNC(SYSDATE)-1 can be used irrespective of the current date. Some Discoverer administrators supply a prebuilt condition for their users in tables that require a lot of reporting on data from yesterday.

Using TO_CHAR with the Number Format Mask

There are three ways to use the TO_CHAR function in Discoverer: with dates, with numbers, and with labels. In this section, we will show you a practical use of the TO_CHAR function being applied to numbers.

We have frequently been asked if there is a way to make Discoverer apply a grand total to a select number of columns in a single statement. The answer, as you will by now have realized, is no. You can either define individual totals to the columns you want to total, or you can apply the total to all of the data points. There is no middle ground; however, there is a workaround using the TO_CHAR function.

Let's assume you have three columns of data: one for quantity shipped, one for the local currency amount, and one for the regional currency amount. If you are using multiple currencies, you cannot apply a total to the local currency amount. However, you also do not want to create individual totals for the remaining columns, each with their own label. What you want is a way to apply the grand total to all of the data points—except the local currency—with a single label of "Grand Total".

The answer is simple. Well, simple if you know how! You create a new calculation, using TO_CHAR, based on the column or columns that you do not want to include in the grand total. For example, the syntax for converting the local currency amount into a string is 'TO_CHAR(local currency amount)'. However, on its own, the TO_CHAR function will not retain any formatting that you applied to the original number. To do this, you must add a format mask to the calculation. Let's use the same example and assume you want the local currency to be formatted with leading zeros and two decimal places. The following is the revised syntax: 'TO_CHAR(local currency amount,'999990D99')'. For a full description of all of the format masks available to you, refer to Appendix A.

Calculating Standard Margin and Markup

These two mathematical formulae are arguably the two most used formulas within Discoverer queries. The ability to be able to know how to create calculations for these is fundamental to becoming a master of Discoverer.

There is a marked difference between margin and markup. Confusing the two may cause you to create an incorrect calculation or compute a quotation that is too low. Margin is defined as the percentage of the selling price represented by the gross profit. Markup is the amount (usually stated as a percentage of cost) that has to be added to the cost to achieve the selling price.

Standard Margin

Using the definition outlined above, the calculation for standard margin is therefore calculated by taking the difference between the selling price and the cost price, dividing that by the selling price, and finally multiplying by 100.

In order to transform this into Discoverer format, we need to place in brackets the subtraction portion of this definition so that it now becomes:

(selling price – cost price) / selling price * 100

Taking a selling price of 10 and a cost price of 5, and inserting these into the algorithm, we get:

Margin = (10 – 5) / 10*100

which works out to be 50 percent.

As you can see in the following illustration, we used our test database to show you how this translates into a Discoverer calculation.

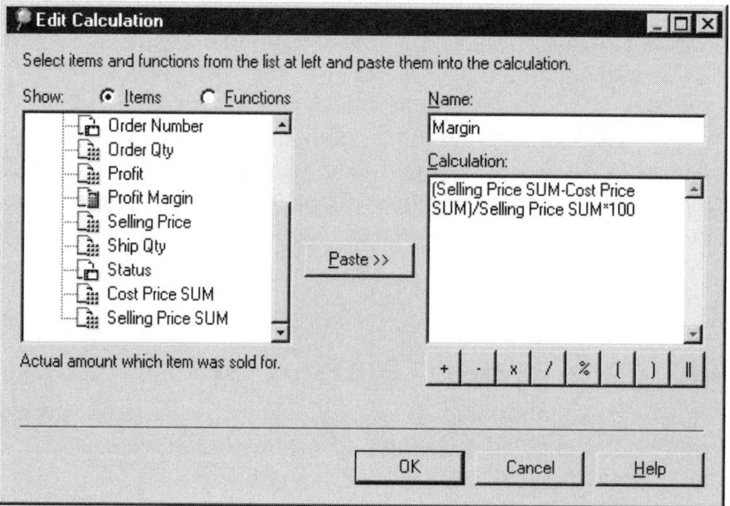

Standard Markup

Using the definition outlined in the previous section, the calculation for standard markup is therefore calculated by taking the difference between the selling price and the cost price, dividing that by the cost price, and finally multiplying by 100.

Again, in order to transform this into Discoverer format, we need to place in brackets the subtraction portion of this definition so that it now becomes:

(selling price – cost price) / cost price*100

Taking a selling price of 10 and a cost price of 5, and inserting these into the algorithm, we get:

Markup = (10 – 5) / 5 *100

which works out to be 100 percent.

As you can see in the following illustration, we used our test database to show you how this translates into a Discoverer calculation.

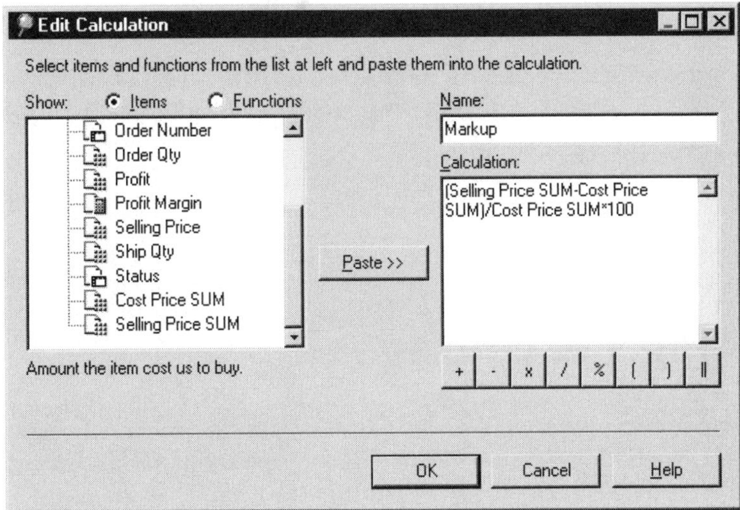

Refining the Sort Order

After you have refined conditions, parameters, and especially calculations, the next logical step is to refine the sort order. Perhaps the addition of a new calculation has added a new column. Maybe the calculation was created specifically for the purpose of defining a new list of values. It is also likely that an erroneous data item was removed from the worksheet when you refined your calculations.

Therefore, after you have refined calculations, you will need to revisit sorting if one of the following is true:

- You deleted a column upon which a sort had been created.
- You added a new item that needs to be part of a sort.
- You added a new list of values and a sort exists on the old list.
- The new items that have been added to the worksheet fundamentally changed the essence and meaning.

In Chapter 5, we explained in detail how to sort, add group sorts, add multiple sorts, and rearrange the sort order. If you are not sure how these are done, you should go back and read the section on sorting in Chapter 5 again.

Removing an Item from the Sort Order

If you have decided that an item no longer needs to be included in the sort order, you can remove it by using the following workflow:

1. From the menu bar, select Tools | Sort, or you can also click the Sort tab on the Edit Sheet dialog box. This will open the Sort Table dialog box.
2. Highlight the sort you want to remove.
3. Click the Delete button.
4. Click OK.

Refining Percentages

Finally, the last component to refining a worksheet is refining percentages. Very little of the previous refinements will have had any significant impact on the percentages, which is why we have left this section till last. However, you may have changed the definition of a calculation that was used in a percentage. That change may now require you to either amend or remove the percentage definition.

In Chapter 5, we explained in great detail how to create percentages. We also gave you examples of all of the different types of percentage that you can create in Discoverer. In Chapter 9, we showed you many examples of percentages being used to analyze data. In this chapter, we will give you workflows for editing a percentage and for removing an unwanted percentage.

Changing a Percentage

To change a percentage definition, use the following workflow:

1. From the menu bar, select Tools | Percentages, or in 3*i* click the Percentage button on the toolbar. Either one of these methods opens the Percentages dialog box.

NOTE
Clicking the Percentage button on the analysis bar in 3.1 does not open the Percentages tool. This button creates a percentage based on the column currently highlighted.

2. Highlight the percentage you want to change, then click Edit, or in 3.1 click on the column heading and select Edit Percentage from the drop-down list. Either of these methods opens the Percentage dialog box.
3. Change the percentage definition (refer to Chapter 5 for explanation of percentage definitions).
4. Click OK.

Removing a Percentage

To change a percentage definition, use the following workflow:

1. From the menu bar select Tools | Percentages, or in 3*i* click the Percentage button on the toolbar. Either one of these methods opens the Percentages dialog box.
2. Highlight the percentage you want to remove, then click Delete.
3. Click OK.

Summary

In this chapter, you have learned to change a condition to a parameter, edit parameters, and rearrange the order of parameters. We have also shown you how to refine calculations by defining the main components of a calculation and how to define the calculation in advance. We have taught you how to convert an algorithm into a Discoverer script as well as how to avoid division by zero errors. We have shown you how to use DECODE to overcome divide by zero errors, as well as how to create custom lists of values. We have shown you to how review conditions based on calculations and review the data items used in the edited calculation. We have shown you how to use standard functions to define calculations for standard margin and markup.

We taught you how to refine the sort order, as well as how to remove an item from the sort order. And, finally, we gave you workflows for refining percentages, including how to change and how to remove them.

In the following chapter, we will teach you techniques for managing queries, including sharing, security, and understanding your access to the queries of others.

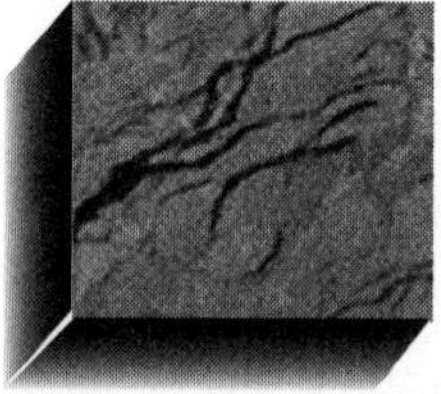

CHAPTER 13

Query Management

nce a query has been formatted into a valuable report, the decision needs to be made about who will have access to it. Will it be distributed in print only, or will others have access to it through Discoverer? Will it be emailed to your manager, or even become a company-wide report used by many people every day?

In this chapter, you will learn the role of the Discoverer administrator, and how he or she is an important part of report management. You will need to know what access you have to any given report. A good relationship with your Discoverer administrator plays an important role in that access. You might be given access to a report that has been developed by another person, perhaps a superuser. The access you are given might be limited and you will only be allowed to view the report, but not make any changes to it.

We will show you how to share queries that you have created as well as how to open queries that have been shared with you. You will learn the benefits of sharing queries as well as the involvement of superusers in the management of shared queries. We will teach you how to use and edit shared queries.

Deleting reports from the database is another important part of report management. An equally important issue is changing the properties of a report. This chapter will teach you how to perform these functions as well as why caution should be used. We will explain how security is set up to protect sensitive company data and how that affects you.

Use of the Query Scheduler will be covered, as well as the benefits to you of running your queries at a scheduled time. You will learn how to schedule a workbook, and how to view the results and unschedule a workbook. We will show you the added flexibility that using a third-party scheduler provides by using the command line.

We have also added a section on command-line features that gives additional power to the end user. An overview has been provided to give you the syntax of all command-line functions.

Another topic to be covered in this chapter is the management of SQL code: importing, exporting, and the use of structured SQL. You will also be shown how to send reports to others via email.

The System Administrator and the End User

Before you can begin to work with Discoverer, your Discoverer administrator needs to have granted or arranged for you to have various rights and privileges. The most important of these is the creation of a user account for the database(s) that you will be accessing. This setup will assign you a user ID and password, and will create the basic database privileges that you will need. Your Discoverer administrator will convey these to you, probably in an email.

Having set up an account for you, your Discoverer administrator will now grant you access to one or more business areas as well as setting your end-user privileges. The rights that you are assigned at this stage dictate whether you have the power to grant access for other people to share your queries, whether you have the power to save and delete queries on the database, and whether you have the power to schedule queries.

Sharing Queries with Other Users

Sharing workbooks allows you to grant other people rights to run your queries. These other users will be allowed to view, analyze, and print the results from your query, but they will not be allowed to save any changes to your query. Users who are running shared queries will see that the Save option on the menu bar is disabled. However, users will be allowed to save the file under their own name, leaving the original intact.

Apart from the convenience of having the ability to share your queries with other users, there are a number of other benefits to sharing queries. Sharing gives users without the right to create queries the ability to run them and perform analysis on the data.

Another key benefit of sharing queries is the all-important matter of saving resources. There is nothing more frustrating to a manager than to find that two of their staff have used time and effort creating virtually the same report. Communication among the Discoverer users in a department will keep staff members from "reinventing the wheel." Even when the reporting needs of two separate users are different, the same query may satisfy both needs as the foundation to build upon.

There is no difference between 3.1 and 3*i* with respect to sharing workbooks. You can do it in both.

Superuser Involvement with Shared Queries

One of the real pluses of having a superuser is the ability to appoint him or her as your departmental query master. Having a single person in this position can be extremely advantageous. Involvement with shared queries could then be the responsibility of the superuser in the following three ways:

- **For development of shared queries** Given that your superuser has increased knowledge of the database, he or she could be tasked with query development. These queries, once written, could then be shared with other members of your department or even company wide.

- **For support of shared queries** If you have a superuser who has taken on the responsibility for creating your department's queries, the same person should be tasked with supporting those queries. They would become the first line of support.
- **For maintaining documentation** When shared queries are used, it is vitally important that documentation is provided about those queries. It is natural that the person who creates the queries also creates and maintains that documentation.

How to Share a Query

In order to share a query, you need to have been granted the appropriate rights. If you do not have the correct privileges, both at the database and end-user layer levels, you will not be able to share a query. The privileges are set by the Discoverer administrator, and you will need to submit a request to have these set up for you.

You can share workbooks in one of two ways:

- You can allow one or more users to share one of your workbooks.
- You can allow one or more workbooks to be shared by one user.

Sharing a Query with Another User

To share a workbook in either Discoverer 3.1 or 3*i*, use the following workflow:

1. To share a workbook with another user, from the menu bar select File | Manage Workbooks | Sharing. This opens the Share Workbooks dialog box, as seen in Figure 13-1. As you can see, the Share Workbooks dialog box has two tabs: one for Workbook > User, and one for User > Workbook.
2. Select the tab Workbook > User.
3. The Workbook drop-down list displays all of the queries that you have created. From the Workbook drop-down list, select the workbook that you want to share.
4. The user list displays all of the users that have access to the same database as yourself, although they may not have access to the business area that the query is using. From the list of available users, click the user you want to share the query with.

NOTE
To highlight more than one user, hold down the CTRL *key while clicking on the user names. This allows you to share the query with multiple users at the same time.*

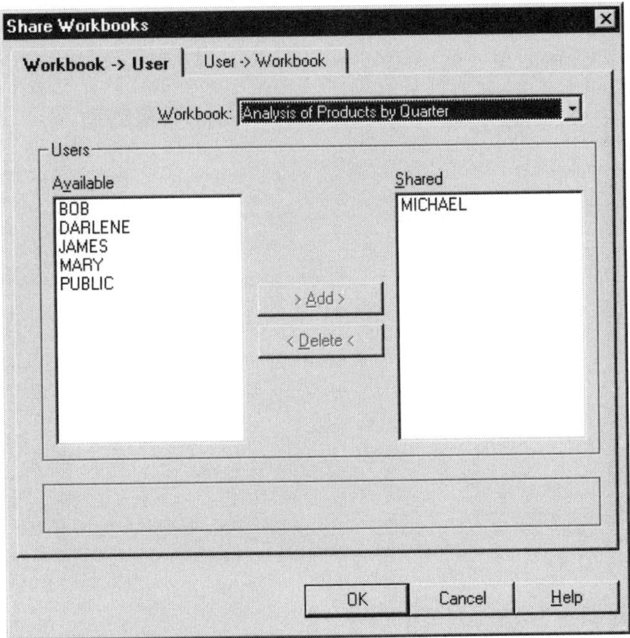

FIGURE 13-1. *Share Workbooks dialog box*

5. Click Add. This moves the users over into the Shared box.
6. Click OK. This closes the Share Workbooks dialog box and completes the sharing of the workbook with the user(s) concerned.

Using a Shared Query

If you have been granted permission to share a query, there are a number of things that you need to be able to do, including the following:

- How to recognize a shared query
- How to open a shared query
- How to manage missing items
- How to edit and save a shared query

How to Recognize a Shared Query

When you log on to Discoverer to open an existing query, Discoverer prefixes shared queries with the name of the owner. In the following illustration, you can see that this user has three workbooks available from the database. The first two in the list are the user's own queries, and the last one has been shared by the user oot_sch. Shared queries always appear at the bottom of the list of available queries.

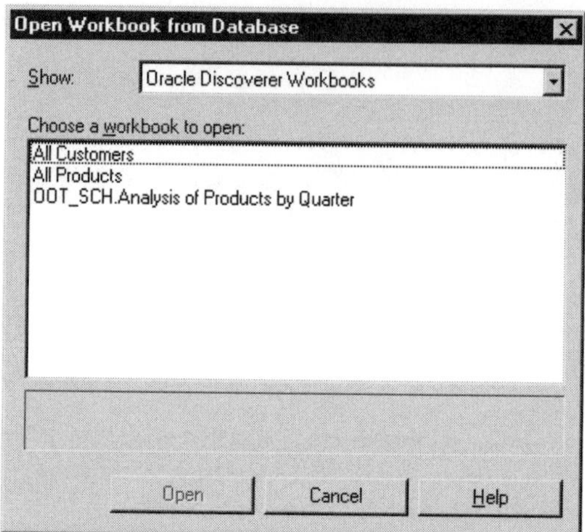

How to Open a Shared Query

When you click on a shared query, then click Open, Discoverer prompts you with the following Workbook in Other Database Account dialog box.

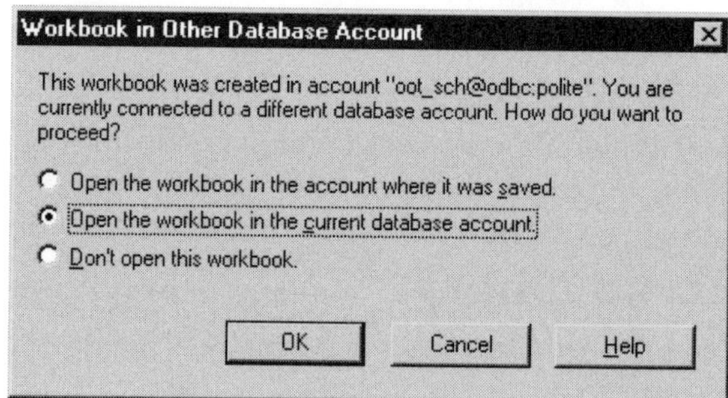

In the preceding box, you can see that you have three options:

- **Open the workbook in the account where it was saved** Clicking this button, then clicking OK, closes your current database connection. You will then be prompted to type in the password for the owner of the query. If you enter the correct password, Discoverer will launch the query and ask whether you want to run the sheet.

- **Open the workbook in the current database account** Clicking this button (the default), then clicking OK, launches the query. Discoverer validates whether you have access to the required business area, then asks whether you want to run the sheet. If you do not have rights to the business area used by the workbook, you will be unable to open the workbook. See the following section "How to Manage Missing Items."
- **Do not open the workbook** This option does just as it says and returns you to the workbook selection list, from where you should select another workbook.

How to Manage Missing Items

When opening a workbook that has been shared with you by another user, Discoverer validates that you have the rights to the business area used by the workbook. If this validation fails, you will see the following Missing Item or Condition dialog box. Unless you successfully manage these missing items, you will not be able to run the query that has been shared with you.

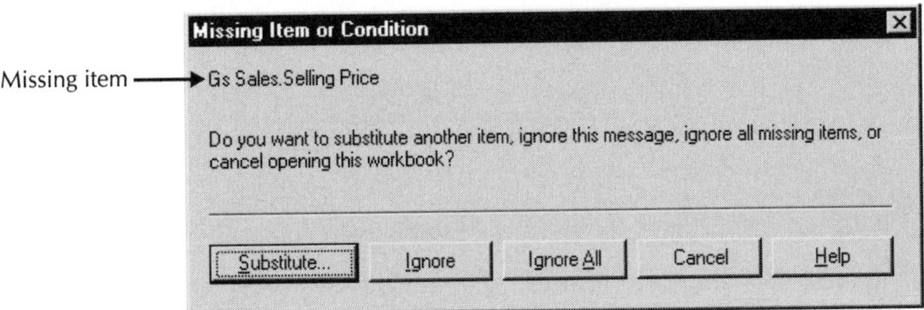

As you can see in the preceding illustration, this dialog box has a number of buttons. The first item that Discoverer is unable to find will be displayed in the box. You will be informed of the name of the folder and the name of the item. At this point, you have the following options:

- **Substitute** Clicking this button opens the following Substitute Item dialog box. In this box, Discoverer will once again display the item that you do not have access to, along with all of the business areas and folders that you do have access to. You should select another item that will be substituted for the missing item.

For example, many companies have business areas that are broken down by region or department. If you have been granted access to a workbook that was created using the European region and you only have access to the Middle East region, you should open the Middle East business area, locate the matching folder and item, then substitute it. When done, click OK.

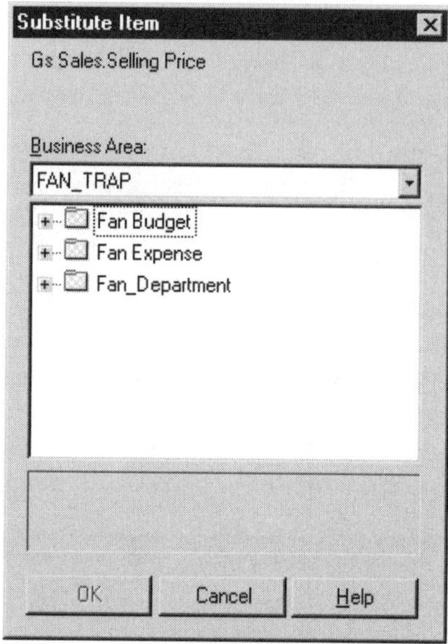

- **Ignore** Clicking this button ignores the current item and displays the next item that Discoverer could not validate.
- **Ignore All** Clicking this button causes Discoverer to ignore all invalid items.
- **Cancel** Clicking this button cancels the opening of the workbook.
- **Help** Clicking this button opens Discoverer's help system.

When you have completed substituting items, Discoverer either runs the query or displays the following "Item dependency" error message. This message means that you did not successfully substitute a new item for every item that was missing.

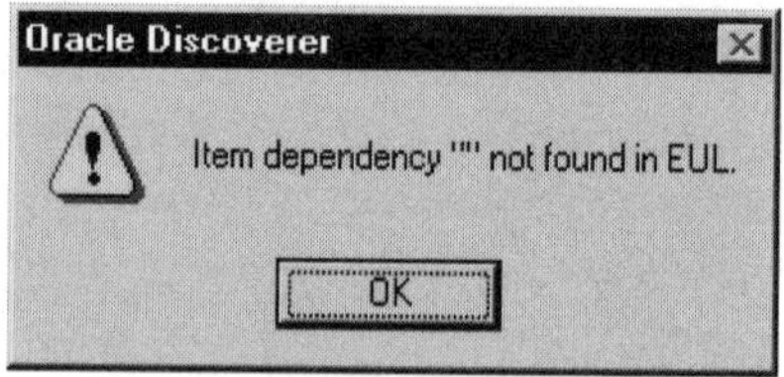

Clicking OK in the Item Dependency error box causes Discoverer to display the "failed workbook" error message. You will not be able to continue opening this workbook.

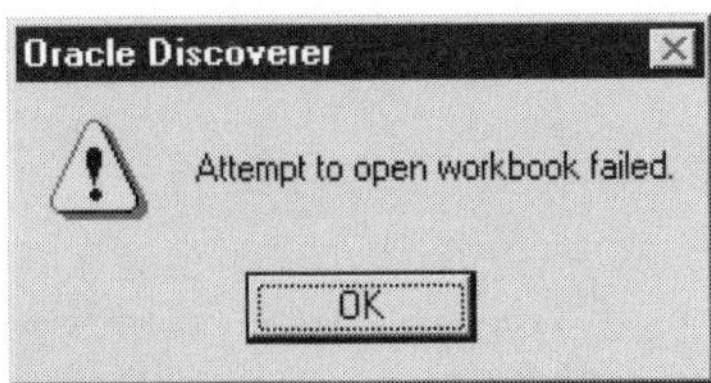

At this stage, you now have two options available to you. The first option is to speak with the person who owns the query. The owner may be able to share another query with you that does use a business area to which you have access. The second option is to speak with your Discoverer administrator. He or she may be able to grant you access to the business area that this workbook tried to open.

How to Edit and Save a Shared Query

As mentioned earlier in this chapter, you are not permitted to make permanent changes to workbooks that are owned by someone else. Therefore, you will notice that some of the menu items are deactivated. You will not be able to save or schedule, nor will you be able to turn Page Items on or off.

If you do want to make permanent changes to this workbook, you will have to save the workbook to your own database account using the Save As option. However, if you have spotted an error in the workbook—perhaps an incorrect calculation or a missing condition, for example—the correct approach would be to report this back to the owner of the query.

NOTE

Do not try sharing a workbook that has been shared with you. You are not the owner, and you do not have the required sharing privileges. Discoverer will therefore not allow you to share that workbook with anyone else.

Deleting Queries from the Database

The most important thing to say about deleting queries from the database is that caution should always be used, especially when deleting shared queries. Discoverer will not warn you if you are about to delete a query that is being shared with someone else.

Let's say you have created a query, but no longer use it. Because you are conscientious and care about not wasting space on the database, your inclination is to delete it. However, before you do so, please check whether you have shared that query with someone else. That person may be using your query on a regular basis, and deleting it could be devastating.

How to Delete a Query from the Database

To delete a query from the database, use the following workflow:

1. From the menu bar, click File | Manage Workbooks | Delete.
2. The Delete Workbook from Database dialog box will open as shown here:

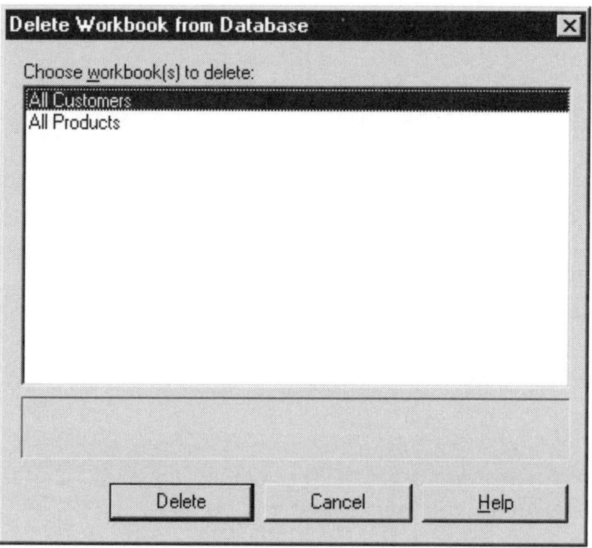

3. Select the workbook you wish to delete.
4. Click Delete.

NOTE

Be sure you really want to delete a query from the database. Because Discoverer will delete it without any further prompting, it will be gone for good!

Query Properties (Adding a Description)

For those of us that affectionately remember the DOS days with naming conventions that limited us to eight-character filenames with three-character extensions, long filenames are a real blessing. We have, however, gotten over our giddiness now and tend to be fairly utilitarian in the naming of our files. Discoverer gives you the added option of giving a description to your files that will help you keep track of queries and the purpose they serve.

Adding Descriptions to Your Queries

To add a description to a query, use the following workflow:

1. From the menu bar, click File | Manage Workbooks | Properties.
2. This opens the Workbook Properties dialog box, shown in the following illustration.

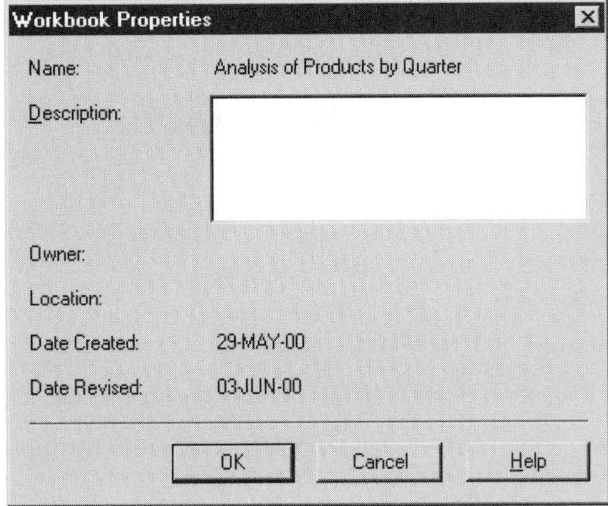

3. Enter the workbook description in the Description field.
4. Click OK.

Scheduling Queries

Scheduling queries is a way to run a report at a set time. These reports will probably not be the ones you use on a daily basis for analysis purposes. Scheduled reports are the ones that you want, for example, to run monthly. Good candidates for scheduled reports might be monthly profits or weekly sales.

Another reason to schedule a report is time. Some queries are complex and take a long time to run. A query of this type may take so long to run, in fact, that the time it takes exceeds the time your Discoverer administrator has allotted for you to run queries. Scheduling a query of this nature allows the query to run in the background during "off-peak" hours, and you are not under the same time constraints. Another advantage to scheduling is that you can schedule a query to run on the server, and don't even need to leave your PC on.

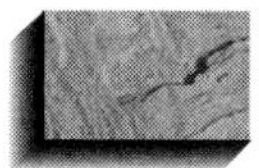

STICKY FEATURE
*Reports cannot be scheduled in 3*i*. You will need to create the schedule in 3.1, then 3*i *can be used to view results.*

Discoverer's Scheduling Wizard is intuitive and easy to use; however, it does have some limitations. We have included a piece at the end of this section addressing some third-party scheduling applications and their use.

The Benefit of Scheduling Queries

There are a number of benefits to scheduling queries. The five main benefits of scheduling queries are as follows:

- The user does not need to be logged on to Discoverer while their queries run.
- Eases network congestion at peak times.
- Allows the user to run key reports prior to the working day at off-peak hours.
- The user can run queries that normally exceed the time they are allowed by the Discoverer administrator.
- The user can schedule special reports to run, such as weekly or monthly reports that will run automatically without user intervention.

How to Schedule a Query

In order to schedule a query, you need to have been granted the appropriate rights. If you do not have the correct privileges, both at the database and end-user layer levels, you will not be able to schedule a query. The privileges are set by the Discoverer administrator, and you will need to submit a request to have these set up for you.

Using the Schedule Workbook Wizard

To schedule a workbook in Discoverer 3.1 using the Scheduler Wizard, use the following workflow:

1. If the workbook that you want to schedule is the one in active memory, from the menu bar select File | Schedule. This automatically opens the first part of the Schedule Workbook Wizard, as seen in Figure 13-2. Proceed to step 6 of this workflow.

   To schedule any other workbook, from the menu bar select File | Manage Workbooks | Scheduling Manager. This opens the Scheduling Manager dialog box.

2. Click Schedule. This opens the following Schedule Workbook dialog box. This box, as you can see, has two selection buttons, one for My Computer, the other for Database.

3. Select the location where the Discoverer workbook has been saved.
4. Click Schedule. This opens the Open dialog box.
5. From within the Open dialog box, locate the query that you want to schedule. Discoverer opens the first part of the Schedule Workbook Wizard, as seen in Figure 13-2.
6. Define which sheet or sheets are to be scheduled by clicking in the check box to the left of the worksheet name(s). Click Select All to include all of this workbook's worksheets. Click Select None to deselect all of the worksheets. Once all worksheets have been deselected, you should check the individual sheets that you want.

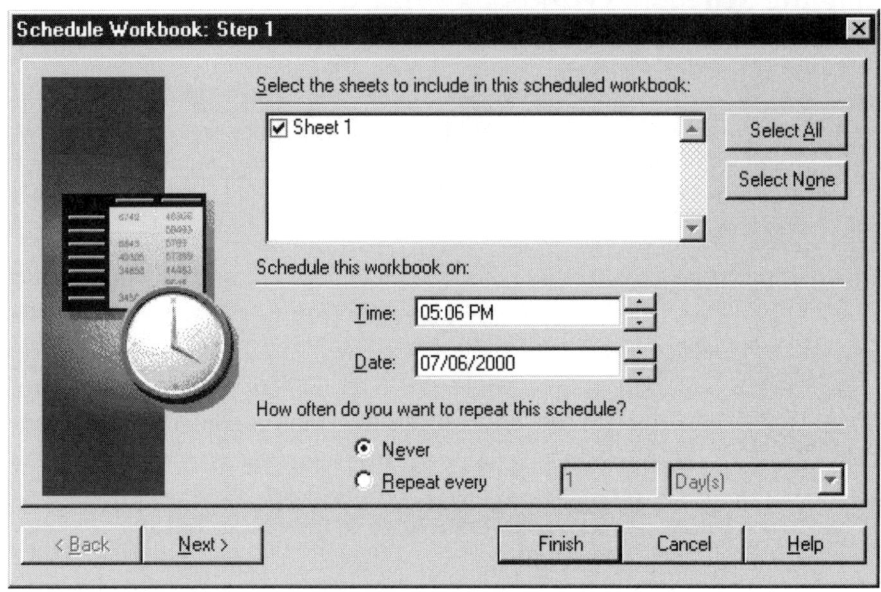

FIGURE 13-2. *Schedule Workbook Wizard: Step 1*

NOTE
All worksheets in the workbook will be listed by their name. This is another reason we recommend giving your worksheets meaningful names, because Sheet1, Sheet2, and so on might not be obvious.

7. Set the date and time you want the query to run.
8. Define a repeat schedule, if required. Under the prompt, "How often do you want to repeat this schedule?", there are two radio buttons, Never and Repeat Every. This is your opportunity to set this schedule up to run periodically, daily, weekly, or however often you choose. To do this, click Repeat Every, type in a number, then select a time period from the

drop-down list illustrated next. The default is Never, which will run the scheduled query only once.

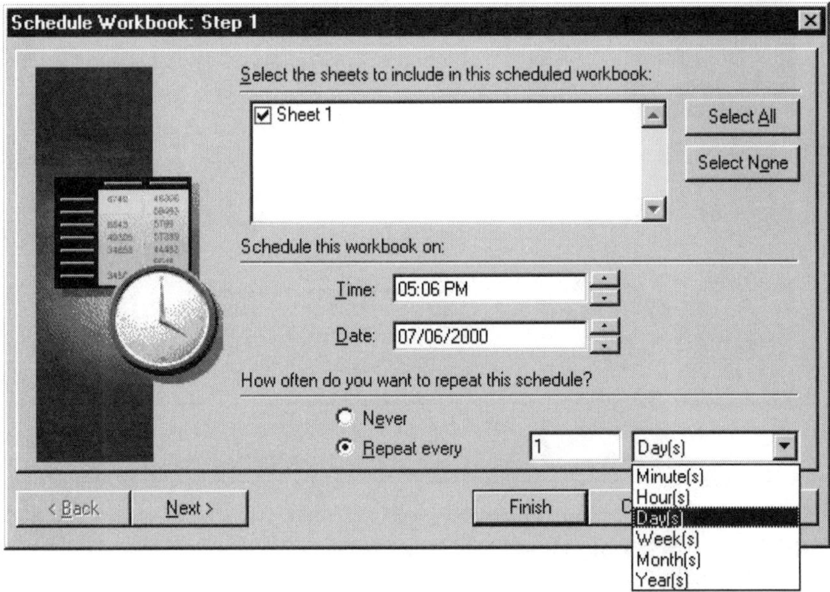

9. Having completed step 1 of the Schedule Workbook Wizard, click Next. Discoverer opens step 2 of the wizard, as seen in Figure 13-3.

10. Enter a unique name for the workbook that you are scheduling. This is an optional step, as Discoverer will automatically give your workbook a unique name; however, we recommend that you give it a name that is meaningful to you.

11. Enter a description for the workbook that you are scheduling. This is another optional step; however, again, we recommend that you take some time to give your scheduled workbook a description. This may seem like extra work, but we feel it is worth the effort. A description might include why you have scheduled the worksheet, and what is to be done with it after it has run. The description you enter will be displayed at the bottom of the Scheduling Manager dialog box seen in Figure 13-4.

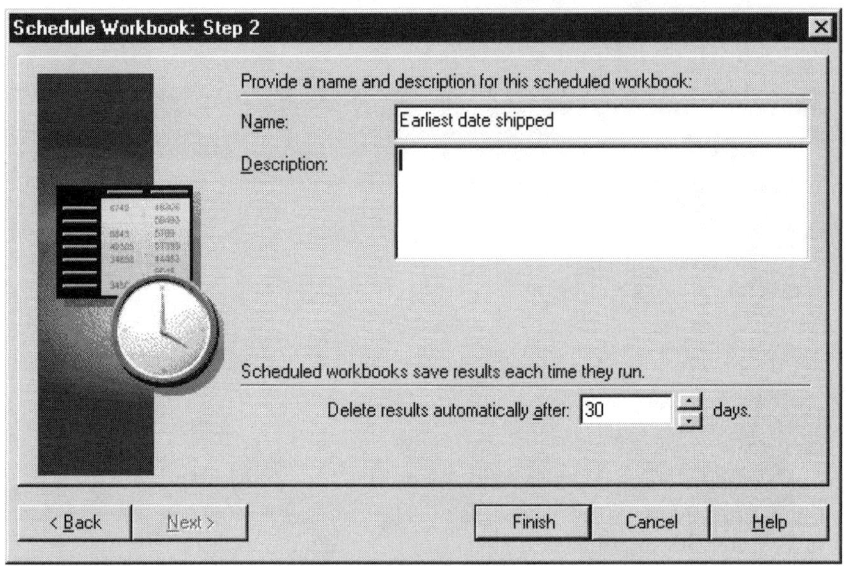

FIGURE 13-3. *Schedule Workbook Wizard: Step 2*

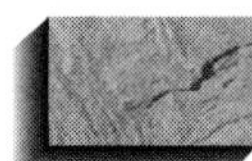

NOTE
Discoverer will automatically give your scheduled workbook a description, based on the original query name, the name you have given the scheduled query, and the date upon which the query is to run.

12. Define the delete criteria. Discoverer automatically deletes the results after 30 days.
13. Having completed step 2 of the wizard, click Finish.
14. If you did not give your scheduled workbook a unique name, Discoverer issues the warning shown in the following illustration. Click Yes to force Discoverer to assign a unique name, or No to return to step 2 of the wizard to enter your own unique name.

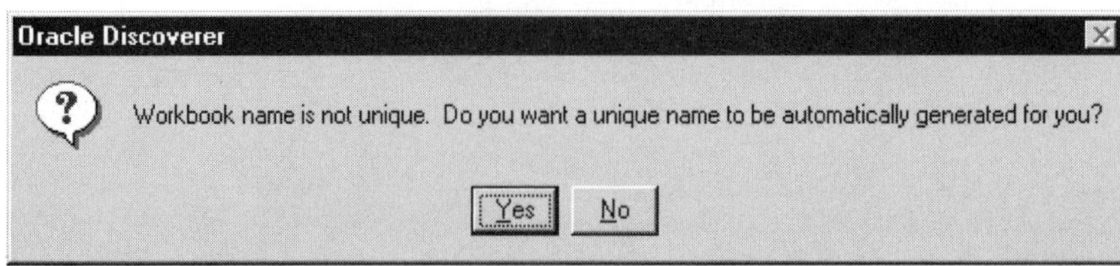

15. If there are any parameters in the worksheets within the workbook, Discoverer will now prompt you for those parameters. The following illustration shows the sheet prompt. Enter the parameters that you want.

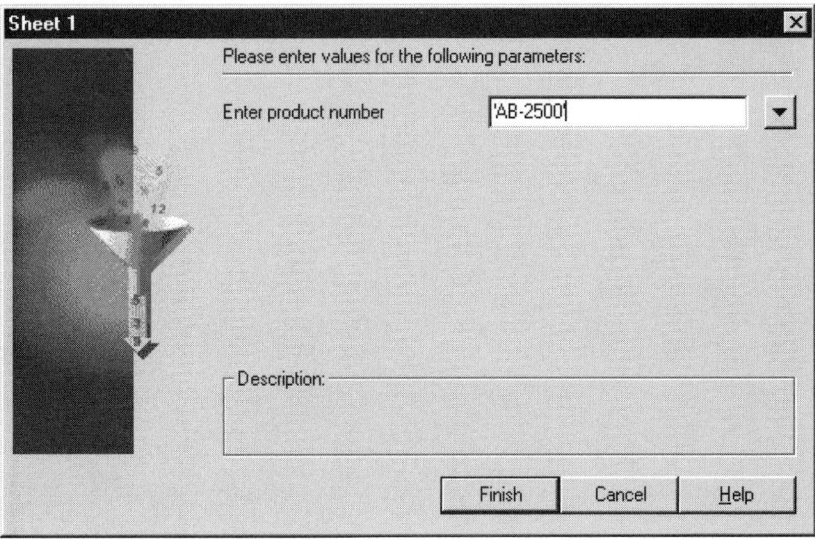

16. Click Finish.

The worksheets that you have just scheduled will be run on the date and time that you specified.

The Scheduling Manager Dialog Box

The Scheduling Manager dialog box, as seen in Figure 13-4, has the following features:

- **Scheduled workbooks area** In this area, Discoverer displays details about all of your scheduled queries. This includes those scheduled to run, those that are running, and those that have already run. The Status column will tell you whether the query is scheduled, running (Running query), expired, completed (Report ready), or has encountered an error. It is also possible for you to see a status that your Discoverer administrator has unscheduled your workbook.

  In addition to the Status column, there are columns for the date and time that the query is scheduled to run, and how long the query took to run. To the left of the workbook name are icons indicating the status of the query.

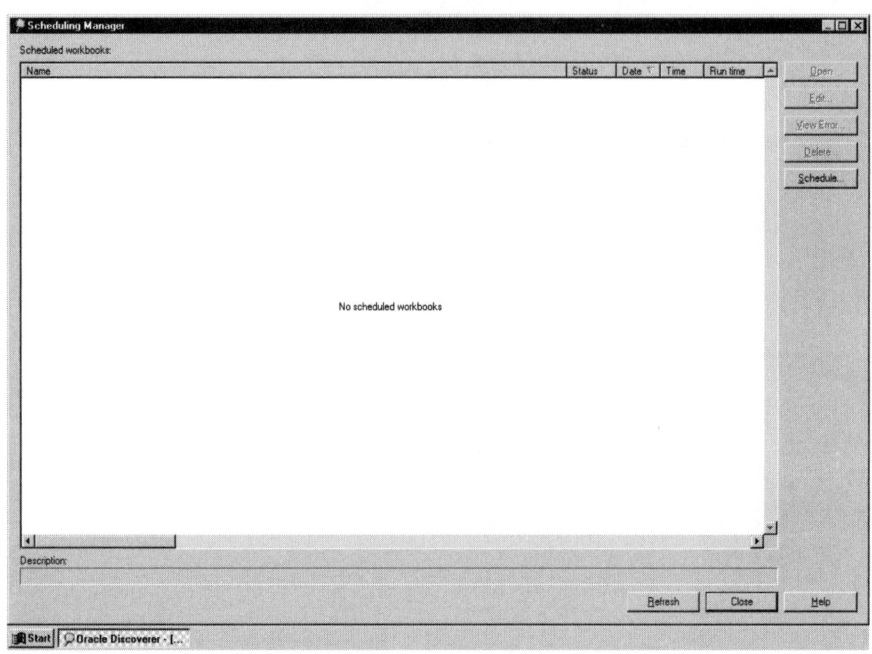

FIGURE 13-4. *Scheduling Manager dialog box*

The Clock icon indicates that the query is scheduled to run or is running. The icon without a clock indicates that the query has run and that the report is ready for viewing.

- **Open** If your query has the status "Report ready", this means that the query has run and that the results are ready to be viewed. Click this button or double-click the query name to view the results.
- **Edit** Click this button to edit a report's schedule. Discoverer reopens the Schedule Workbook Wizard.
- **View Error** If your query is showing an error status, click this button to view the details. Viewing errors might be frustrating, because these generally describe database conditions, and these error messages can be difficult to understand. If you encounter errors with your scheduled queries, see your Discoverer administrator.

- **Delete** Click this button to delete the output from a completed scheduled query. If the query was scheduled not to repeat, this also causes the scheduled query itself to be deleted.

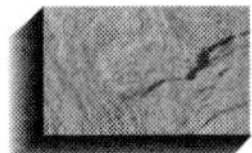

NOTE
The original query is still intact because Discoverer uses a copy of the workbook within the scheduler. It is important for you to remember this when you change the original. It has changed, but the scheduled one has not. If you want the scheduled query to reflect the changes to the original, you will need to delete and reschedule the query.

- **Schedule** Click this button to schedule a new workbook.
- **Refresh** Click this button to refresh the status of all scheduled workbooks. Discoverer will not automatically refresh the statuses while you are in the dialog box. Therefore, if the status is "Running query," and you are waiting for the query to complete, keep clicking Refresh until the status changes to "Report ready."
- **Close** Click this button to exit from the Scheduling Manager dialog box.
- **Description** This area displays the description you typed in when you first scheduled the query.

Viewing Results

There are two ways of viewing the results of a scheduled query that has run. These are:

- From the Open File dialog box, in both 3.1 and 3*i*.
- From the Scheduling Manager in 3.1 only.

Viewing Results from the Open File Dialog Box

In both 3.1 and 3*i*, to view the results of a scheduled query from the Open File dialog box, use the following workflow:

1. From the menu bar, select File | Open. This launches the Open File dialog boxes as seen in Figures 13-5 and 13-6.

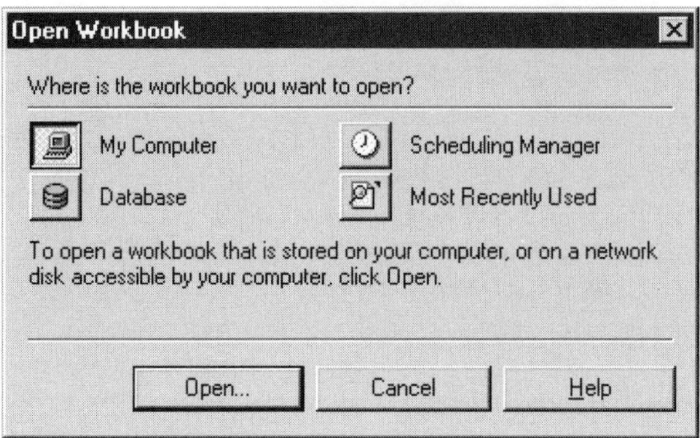

FIGURE 13-5. *3.1 Open File dialog box*

NOTE
The dialog box in 3.1 has two extra options not on the dialog box in 3i.

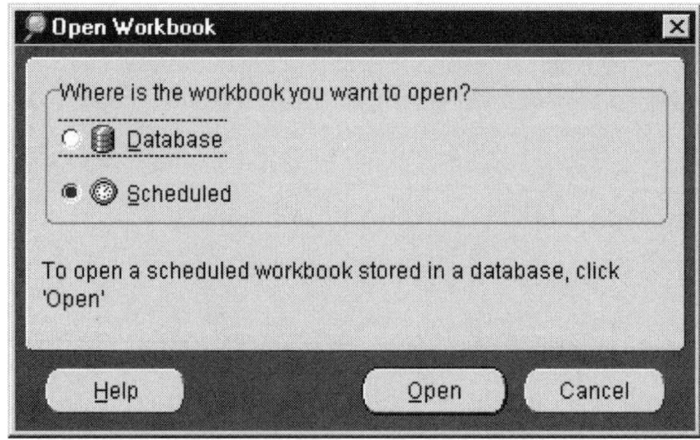

FIGURE 13-6. 3i *Open File dialog box*

2. Select the option to open scheduled workbooks. This opens the Open Scheduled Workbook dialog box. As the dialog boxes in 3.1 and 3*i* are identical, we will show you just the 3.1 dialog box, shown here:

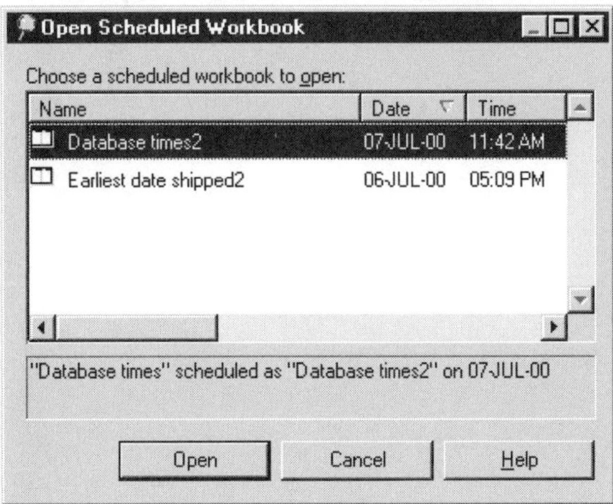

3. Continue with step 3 of the workflow in the following section.

Viewing Results from the Scheduling Manager Dialog Box

In Discoverer 3.1 only, to view the results of a scheduled query from the Scheduling Manager dialog box, use the following workflow:

1. From the menu bar, select File | Manage Workbooks | Scheduling Manager. This opens the Scheduling Manager dialog box as seen in Figure 13-7.
2. Highlight the query that has been run.
3. Click Open, or double-click the query. This causes Discoverer to ask, as displayed in the following illustration, whether you want to open the results for the sheet.

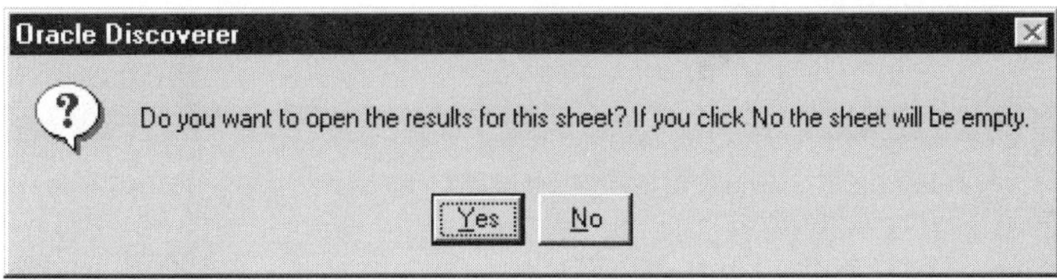

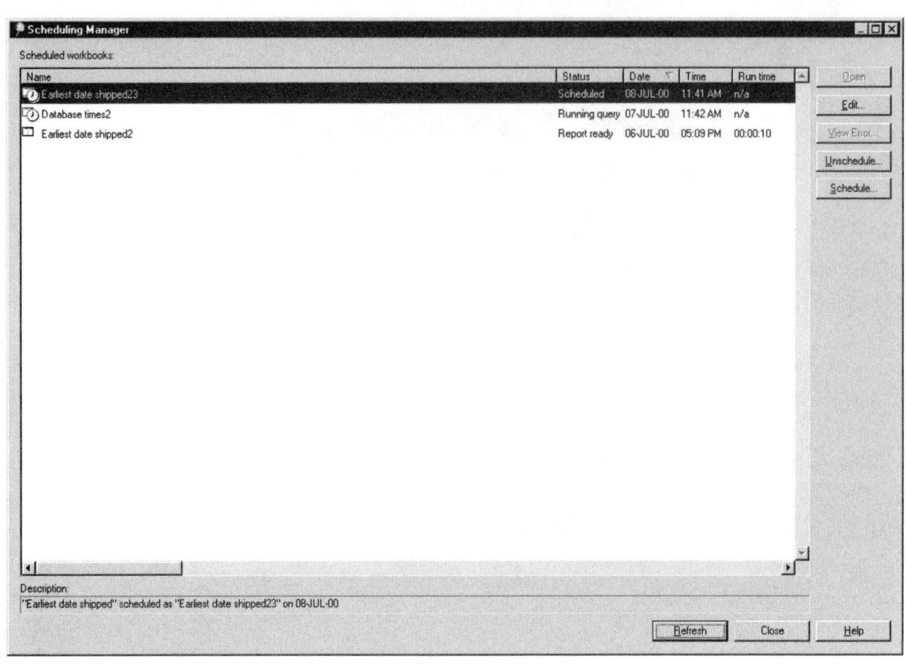

FIGURE 13-7. *Scheduling Manager dialog box with scheduled query highlighted*

4. Clicking Yes causes Discoverer to open the workbook and display the results. Clicking No still opens the workbook but leaves the display empty.
5. If you selected No, and you later decide that you want to refresh the data in the sheet, clicking the Refresh button causes Discoverer to display the warning illustrated next. Clicking Yes requeries the database and displays the results using the latest data. Clicking No displays the results from the scheduled workbook.

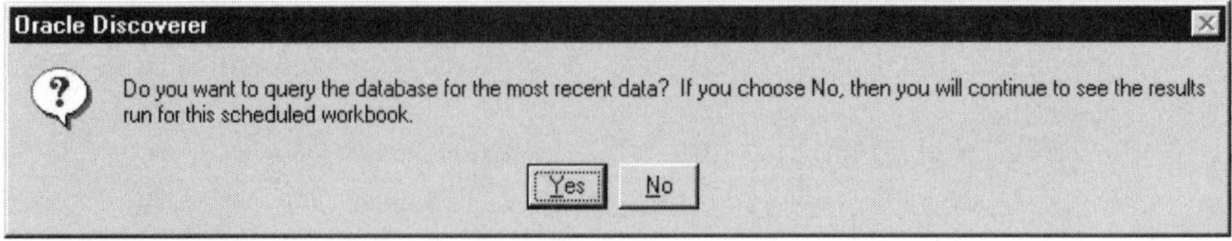

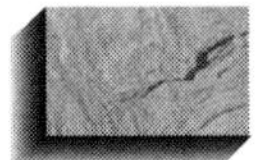

NOTE
Discoverer will always keep the results of a scheduled query until you either refresh the data from the database or delete the output. Careful management of the results of scheduled queries will allow you to retain important results virtually indefinitely. We do not recommend that you keep results forever; however, retaining them for a couple of months should satisfy your need for the output. This is especially true if you want to manipulate the results in the future.

Unscheduling a Scheduled Workbook

Unscheduling can only be done in Discoverer 3.1. To unschedule a scheduled workbook that has not yet run, use the following workflow:

1. Open the Scheduling Manager dialog box as seen in Figure 13-7.
2. Highlight the scheduled workbook.
3. Click Unschedule. This opens the following Confirm Unschedule dialog box.

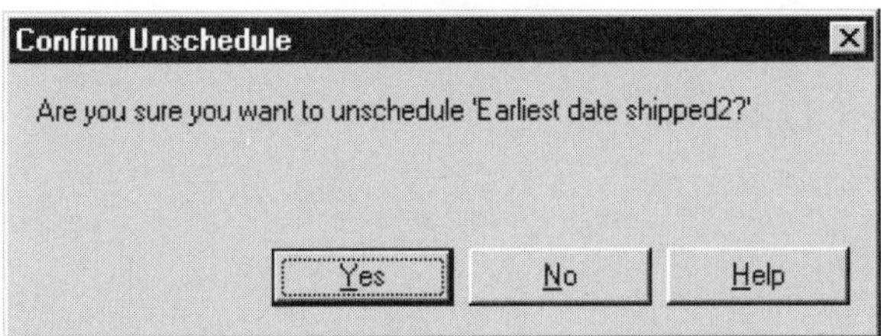

4. Click Yes to unschedule.
5. Close the Scheduling Manager dialog box.

Editing a Scheduled Workbook

Editing can only be done in Discoverer 3.1. To edit a scheduled workbook that has not yet run, use the following workflow:

1. Open the Scheduling Manager dialog box as seen in Figure 13-7.
2. Highlight the scheduled workbook.

3. Click Edit. This opens the following Schedule Workbook dialog box. This box has two tabs: Schedule and General.

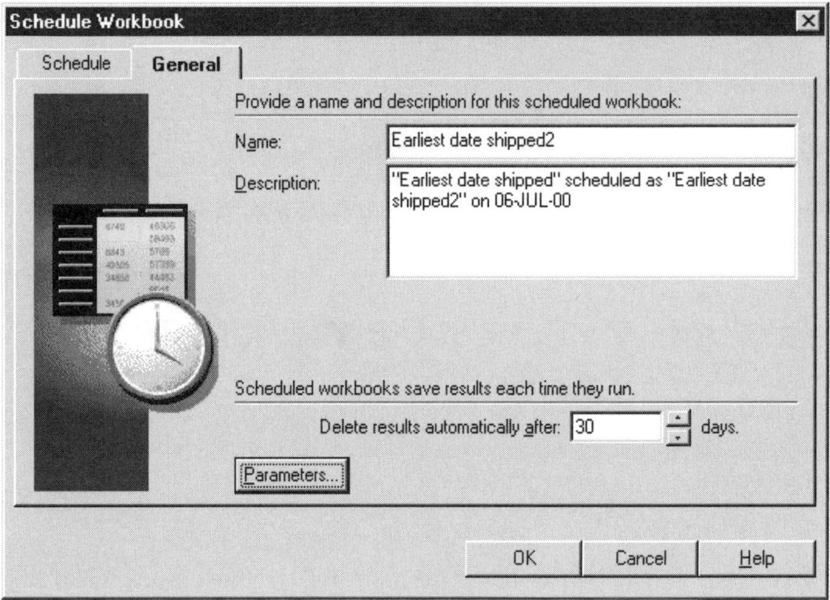

NOTE
The preceding dialog box is almost the same as the Schedule Workbook Wizard that we showed you earlier in this chapter. It differs in that the dialog box has tabs instead of the Back and Next buttons that you saw earlier. There is also an additional button on the General tab for parameters.

4. From the two tabbed forms, make any edits that you require.
5. If you need to edit the parameters for the workbook, click the Parameters button. Follow the instructions given earlier in this chapter for setting parameters in a scheduled workbook.
6. When you have finished editing, click OK.

Security

In order for a user to be able to schedule a query, the Discoverer administrator must grant scheduling privileges to that user. The following illustration comes from the

Discoverer Admin Edition, and shows the security privileges that are controlled by the Discoverer administrator.

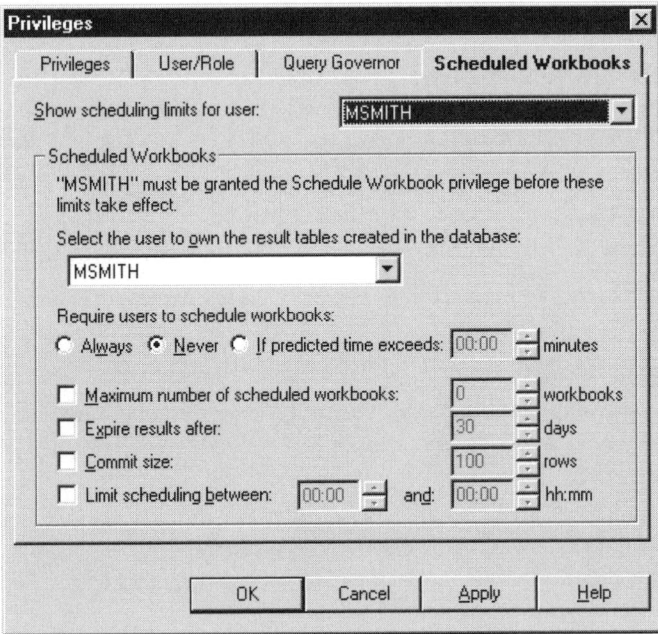

Amongst the privileges that are controlled are the following:

- **Owner of the results** The Discoverer administrator dictates who owns the results of scheduled queries that you create. Normally, this is yourself; however, you may agree to transfer your viewing rights to a colleague. When your Discoverer administrator deems that the database privileges required to schedule queries is beyond the level they wish you to possess, he or she can grant these privileges to another database user. This will enable you to still schedule and view reports as if the results were owned by you. This is different than allowing another user the ability to read the scheduled report.

NOTE

In a future release of Discoverer, Oracle will leverage the Oracle Reports scheduling facility. This will provide a richer scheduling and viewing option for end users within the Oracle Reports security mechanism.

- **Maximum number of scheduled workbooks** Your Discoverer administrator can restrict the number of workbooks that you are allowed to schedule. If you think you should have more, you must discuss this with your Discoverer administrator.
- **Limits on scheduling time** Your Discoverer administrator can limit the times between which you are allowed to schedule workbooks. Perhaps the peak hours will be off-limits, maybe during system backup and so on.

Limitations of the Discoverer Scheduler

There are three major limitations of the Discoverer scheduler. These are as follows:

- Scheduled reports can only be viewed by the owner.
- There is no export feature within the Discoverer scheduler.
- There is no email feature within the Discoverer scheduler.

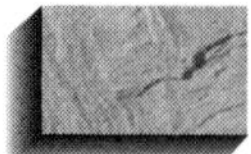

NOTE
Oracle plans to review the entire scheduling functionality of Discoverer. Therefore, in a future release this could change.

Scheduled Reports Can Only be Viewed by the Owner A weekly sales report that you have created may need to be viewed by the entire sales staff. However, with the Discoverer scheduler, the owner will need to open the report, then distribute it by whatever means he or she chooses. We see this as a serious disadvantage and hope Oracle changes it in a future release.

There Is No Export Feature Within the Discoverer Scheduler Using the previous weekly sales report scenario, you would love for the Discoverer scheduler to automatically export the results in a specified format into a specific folder. Then, your email system could scan the folder, pick up the contents, and email them to the sales force. The sales force would not even need to have access to Discoverer; instead, they would receive the reports via email. Alas, Discoverer cannot do this. You will either need to do this manually or use a third-party scheduler.

There Is No Email Feature Within the Discoverer Scheduler For those of you who are used to scheduling jobs overnight and emailing the results to company managers, customers, vendors, and so on, you will be disappointed in Discoverer's scheduler. We know that there are many companies who have old legacy systems that allow this sort of scheduling, and have heard complaints that Oracle's system does not allow this directly from within the scheduler.

All is not lost, though, as there are two ways of getting around this problem. The first is to use a third-party scheduler to export the results into a specified folder, then use an agent on the email application to pick up the file and send it to a designated recipient. Lotus Notes, for example, can be set up very easily to do just this.

The second workaround is to export the query into an Oracle Report format and then get Oracle's Report scheduler to do the rest. To do this, you would export the file as an RDF file, then manually submit the file to the Reports server, from where the report can be run and the results emailed.

Third-Party Scheduling

As you now know, Discoverer's own scheduler cannot output your data to a file, nor can the results be made available to other users. However, using the command-line interface, you can use third-party schedulers to run queries, and create output automatically, without the intervention of the human hand.

The use of third-party schedulers can be advantageous because they offer more flexibility and allow users to open reports in formats like HTML without the need to have Discoverer installed. There are many scheduling products on the market, including the following:

- **Winat.exe** The Windows NT native scheduler.
- **Task Scheduler** The Windows 98 native scheduler.
- **Norton Program Scheduler** The Norton Utilities scheduler.
- **JIT Scheduler** A freeware utility available from the Web.

Running Discoverer from the Command Line

Perhaps one of the lesser-known capabilities of Discoverer is the ability to specify many of its functions directly from the command line. Using this command-line interface, you can, without opening Discoverer itself, run queries, automate printing, and export the results. You can also use third-party schedulers to control the running of queries outside of normal hours.

Running Discoverer from the Command Line

To run Discoverer from the command line, use the following workflow:

1. From the Windows Start button, select Run. This opens the Run dialog box as shown here:

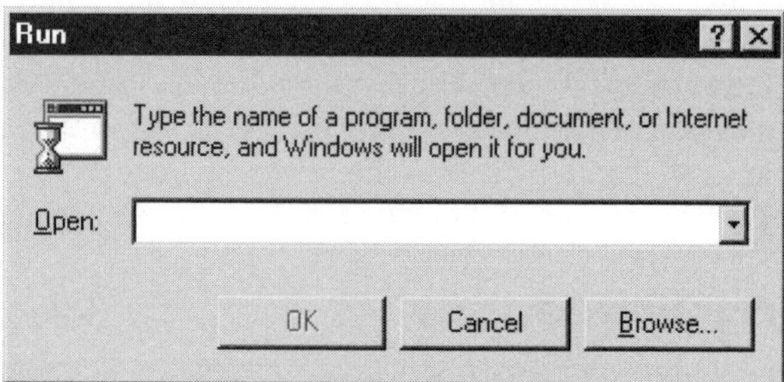

2. Click Browse. This opens the following Browse dialog box:

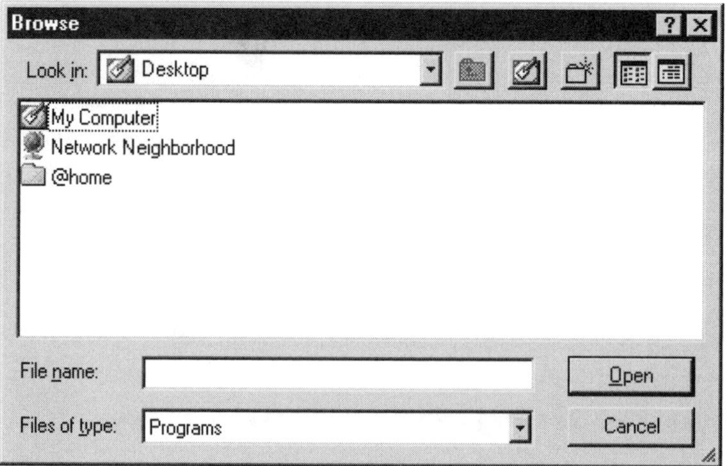

3. Locate the Discoverer end-user runtime program, dis31usr.exe, then click Open. As shown here, Windows now inserts the path and location of Discoverer into the Run dialog box.

4. Add the options that you require to pass to Discoverer, which will be explained in the following section.
5. Click OK. Windows now performs the command-line instructions, opening and running Discoverer.

Optional Command-Line Parameters

To increase the efficiency of the command-line interface, Discoverer will accept various parameters when launched this way. Each option begins with the forward slash character /, and is preceded and followed by a space. The command-line options are as follows:

- **/batch** This causes Discoverer to run in batch mode. This mode does not wait for user interaction and will process one workbook after another, even if an earlier one fails. This mode is mandatory if you are scheduling queries using a third-party scheduler. When using this command, you must also include either an export or a print command; otherwise, you will get an error.
- **/cmdfile <file>** This causes Discoverer to open the text file named in the command, and execute it. Inside the text file, you should place all of the parameters that you need to run one job. To run multiple jobs one after the other, use DOS batch files.
- **/connect userid/password@connect** This is a means for you to pass your login information to Discoverer. If the information that you specify is correct, in that you have provided a valid user ID, password, and database connect string, Discoverer will bypass the login screen and log you in.

For example, if your user ID is 'Michael', your password is 'happy', and the database you want to connect to is 'odbc:polite', the following command-line option will log you in automatically:

/connect Michael/happy@odbc:polite

- **/export <format><export file name>** This exports the results to the file named, in the format specified. If you did not specify a sheet on the command line, Discoverer exports the results from the active sheet. If you nominate all sheets on the command line, Discoverer names the output files as <file><sheet-name>.<ext>, identical to the behavior of the Export Data command.
- **/open <file>** This opens a Discoverer file (.DIS) from My Computer. You need to specify the full path and location of the file, and need to combine this with a valid connect parameter.
- **/opendb <file>** This opens the named file from the database.
- **/p<file>** This opens, runs, and prints a file located in My Computer to the default printer.
- **/pt <file><printer><driver><port>** This opens, runs, and prints a file located in My Computer to a specified printer, with specified printer driver and port.
- **/parameter <parameter name><parameter-value>** This option is a means for you to pass a value to a parameter in a worksheet. If you do not pass a parameter value, Discoverer will use the default value. If you are running in batch mode, Discoverer will run the query using the defaults; otherwise, it will prompt you when Discoverer opens.
- **/savedb <file>** This saves a file from My Computer to the database. Again, you need to specify the full path and location of the file, and must have supplied a valid connect parameter.
- **/sheet ALL** This forces Discoverer to open and run all sheets in the query.
- **/sheet <sheet-name>** This forces Discoverer to open and run the sheet specified by the sheet name.
- **/sheet <sheet-number>** This forces Discoverer to open and run the sheet specified by the sheet number.

- **/?** This option displays the following Command Line Help dialog box.

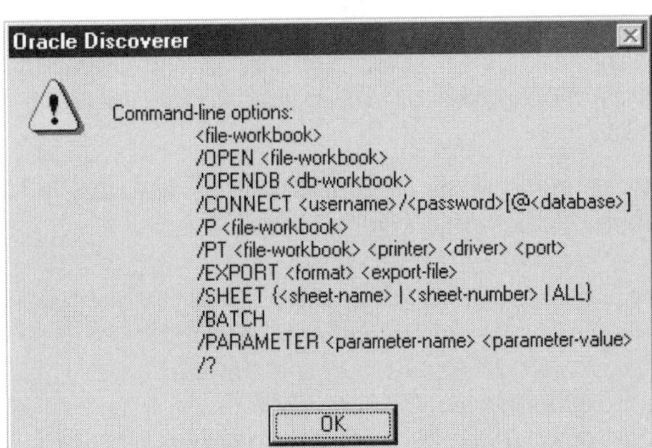

Command-Line Examples

The following is a list of command-line examples. Most of the commands can be mixed together, and Discoverer allows you to place them in any order.

- **c:\orawin95\DISCVR31\Dis31usr.exe /connect bob/apple@report**

This example logs the user bob, using the password apple, into the report database. The logon screen is bypassed and Discoverer launches with the screen that asks whether the user should open an existing report or create a new one.

- **c:\orawin95\DISCVR31\Dis31usr.exe /connect john@odbc:polite /opendb query5 /sheet 1**

This example connects john to an Oracle Lite database polite, using ODBC connectivity. It opens the file query5 from the database, and runs sheet 1. As this user has no password, the password component has been omitted.

- **c:\orawin95\DISCVR31\Dis31usr.exe /connect john@odbc:polite /opendb paramtest /sheet 1 /parameter param1 AB-2000**

This example, an extension of the previous one, names a parameter and supplies a value to it. This time, Discoverer runs the query without prompting us for input. The parameter name that you specify must match exactly with the name you gave the parameter when you created the query. If you recall, we recommended giving your parameters meaningful names. This is one of the reasons why.

- **c:\orawin95\DISCVR31\Dis31usr.exe /connect john@odbc:polite /opendb paramtest /sheet 1 /parameter param1 AB-2000 /batch /export HTML test2**

This example, building on the previous one, runs the query in batch mode and exports the result in HTML format to the file test2.

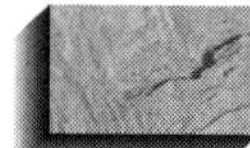

NOTE
Discoverer recognizes the following format options in the command line; XLS for an Excel spreadsheet, WKS for a Lotus spreadsheet, TEXT for a text file, CSV for a comma-separated file, HTML for a file in htm format, SYLK for a symbolic link file, FIXED for a PRN file, DIF for a data interchange file, and RDF for an Oracle Report format file.

- **c:\orawin95\DISCVR31\Dis31usr.exe /connect bob/apple@report /opendb "bob's report" /sheet ALL**

This example opens the file "bob's report" from the database and runs all sheets. Notice how we have enclosed the file name in double quotes. This is because the file name contains spaces.

- **c:\orawin95\DISCVR31\Dis31usr.exe /connect oot_sch@odbc:polite /open c:\examples\paramtest /sheet 1 /parameter param1 AB-2500,AB-2000**

This example shows you how to pass multiple values to a parameter and open a file from your hard disk. In this case, because we have not specified batch mode, the query will run online with the output being visible onscreen. When passing multiple values to a parameter, separate each value by a comma, with no spaces. We have seen reports that Discoverer wants the parameters to be enclosed in double quotes, but we have not needed to do this with our system.

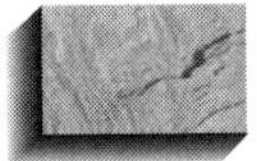

NOTE
When exporting results, you can either export one sheet or all sheets. If you want to export more than one sheet, but not all of them, you will have to create batch files for each sheet that you want to export.

Known Command-Line Problems

There are a number of known problems with the command line, two of which are:

- Giving a parameter the name "prompt"
- Defining the parameter prompt to be the same as the parameter name

Giving a Parameter the Name "Prompt" While you may think of this as being obvious, Discoverer itself does not have a problem with this construct. However, running this from the command line results in either a Dr. Watson error or the following illegal operation error.

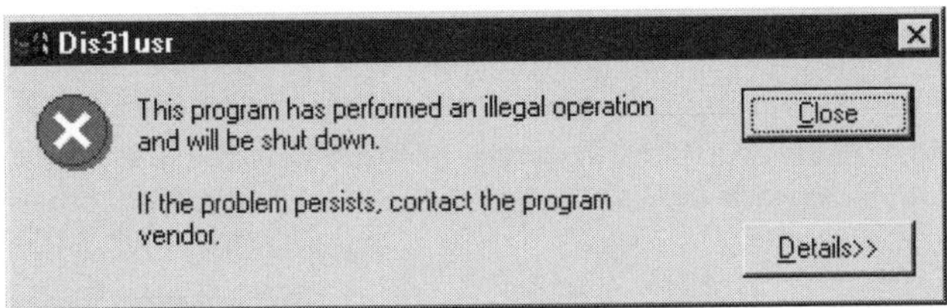

The only remedy for this is not to give parameters the name "Prompt".

Defining the Parameter Prompt to be the Same as the Parameter Name
The illegal operation error message can also be caused when you have this combination of events:

1. You have defined the parameter prompt to be the same as the parameter name itself.
2. You have not associated the parameter with any particular item.
3. You have placed a condition on the parameter.

The following illustration shows you what we mean.

First, here is a parameter definition in which we defined the parameter prompt to be the same as the parameter name itself. Notice how we have chosen the value <NONE> for the item to associate the parameter with.

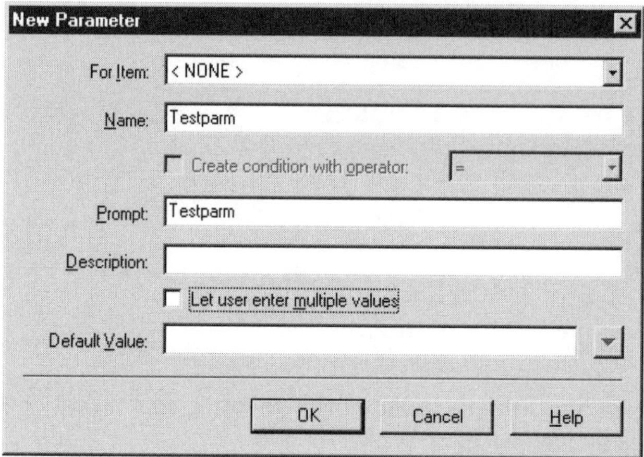

Next, we created the following condition. As you can see, we have now associated the input from the parameter with the product name. Running this from within Discoverer itself produces no error, but running this from the command line does.

To remedy this, change the prompt for the parameter to anything other than the name of the parameter itself.

SQL Management

As we stated earlier in the book, when Discoverer runs a query, it converts it into SQL. This SQL is then submitted to the database. If you want to see what the SQL being used in your query looks like, from the menu bar select View | SQL Inspector. Discoverer now opens a dialog box in which you can see the SQL code.

Discoverer allows you to both export and import SQL.

Exporting SQL

To export the SQL code from your query, use the following workflow:

1. From the menu bar, select View | SQL Inspector. This opens the following SQL Inspector dialog box.

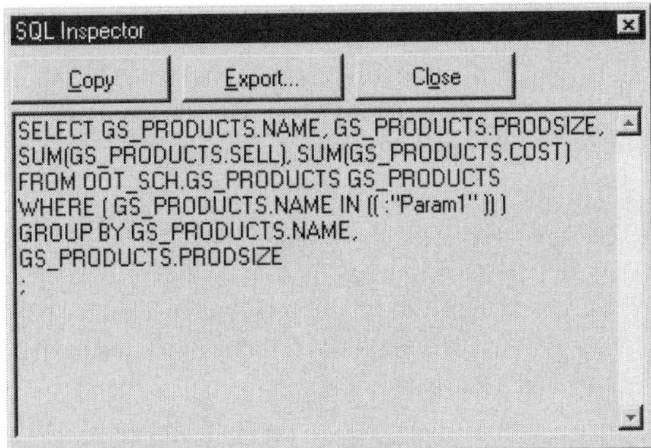

2. Click Export. This opens the Save As dialog box.
3. Select the location to where the code should be saved.
4. Give the export file a name.
5. Click Save.

Importing SQL

To import SQL code into a worksheet, use the following workflow:

1. From the menu bar, select File | Import SQL. This launches the Open dialog box.
2. Locate the SQL file you want to import.

3. Click Open. Discoverer imports the code into a new worksheet.
4. If the code has parameters, Discoverer opens the Parameter Wizard dialog box. Enter the parameters. When you have entered all of the parameters, click Finish.

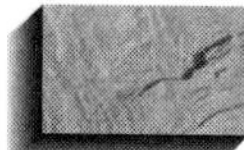

NOTE
Discoverer deactivates the Finish button until you have entered all of the parameters. When Discoverer imports code with parameters, it gives each prompt the same name as the name of the parameter. You will need to edit each parameter and give it a correct and meaningful prompt.

Structured SQL

For those of you unfamiliar with SQL, looking at the code in the SQL Inspector dialog box might be daunting. No matter how complex and involved the SQL code appears, there are in fact only four basic components of an SQL query. These are:

- **Select** This command begins all SQL queries. Following it is a list of all of the items that are to be displayed in the final result of the query. Each item is usually prefixed by the name of the table or folder in which the item resides. Multiple items are separated from each other by a comma. There is no comma after the last item.
- **From** This command follows the last selected item and starts on a new line. Following this command is a list of all of the tables and folders used in the query. Each folder or table is normally prefixed by the name of the owner of the object. Multiple entries are separated from each other by a comma. There is no comma following the last table or folder.
- **Where** This command follows the last table or folder and again starts on a new line. In this section of the query, you will see the joins, conditions, and parameters. However, as Discoverer usually protects you from knowing the joins between folders, you will probably only see conditions and parameters in here. If there are multiple statements, each will be separated from the next by the word "AND."
- **Group By** If used, this statement follows the last join, condition, or parameter. These are the sort criteria being used within the query.

In the following illustration is the example of SQL code that was exported from our database earlier in this section. As you can see, each of the four basic components starts on a new line.

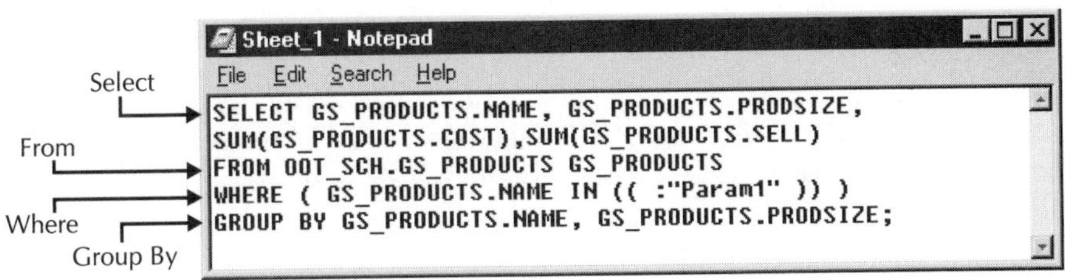

While not pretending to even begin teaching you all about SQL, we hope this small section on the basic components of a SQL query will be of some help.

Emailing Queries and Reports

An excellent way of sharing the results of queries and reports is by email. This feature can only be used if your email system supports this kind of linking. If you do not see the email option on your menu bar, your email application does not support this feature.

Discoverer can send a workbook in a variety of formats including the following:

- Discoverer Workbook
- Excel Workbook
- HTML
- Text File (Tab Delimited)
- CSV (Comma Delimited)
- Formatted Text (Space Delimited)
- Oracle Report Definition File
- DCS (Express Format)
- DIF (Data Interchange Format)
- SYLK (Symbolic Link)
- Lotus 1-2-3

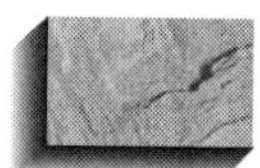

NOTE
Depending upon what software has been installed on your system, you may also see options to send workbooks in PDF and RDF formats.

You can send the above files as an attachment to an email. Or, message text can be sent directly in the body of the email. This would only be the recommended method if the email system you or the recipient uses does not support attachments. The following three formats can be sent as message text.

- Text File (Tab Delimited)
- CSV (Comma Delimited)
- Formatted Text (Space Delimited)

To Send a Discoverer Workbook via Email

To send a Discoverer workbook or results via email use the following workflow:

1. From the menu bar, Click File | Send.
2. This opens the Prepare Mail dialog box, shown here:

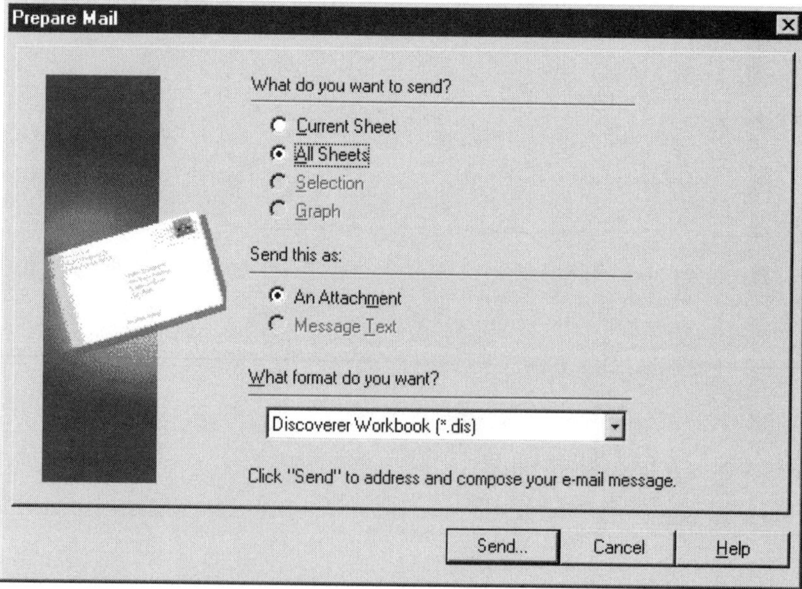

3. Tell Discoverer what you want to send. Will you send the Current Sheet, All Sheets, Selection, or Graph? Graph will be inactive if there is no graph in the workbook you want to send.

NOTE
To send a selection, you need to highlight the rows and columns you want to send before you launch the dialog box.

4. Choose whether you will send it as an Attachment or as Message Text.
5. Select the file type, the format, in which you will send the workbook or the results. If you select the type htm, and you are sending the results from only one worksheet, Discoverer inserts the html code directly into the email as message text, irrespective of whether you chose to send it as an attachment or not.

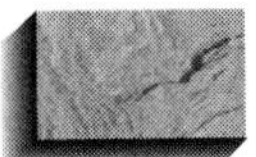

NOTE
The drop-down menu is not available for graphs, as graphs are always sent as a WMF (Windows Meta File). This format is the recognized format for sending a graph. Do not worry if you have not exported a document in the format in which you want to send the attachment. Discoverer will create this for you when it sends the email.

6. Click Send. Your email application system will open. Based on the selections that you made in the Prepare Mail dialog box, the worksheet or workbook will appear either as an attachment or in the message body itself.

NOTE
If you are emailing all sheets or a sheet that you have not yet run, Discoverer will prompt you to run those sheets before you email the results.

7. Using your normal email system, address the message and send the email. In the following illustration you can see that Discoverer has opened our

email application, inserted the workbook name as the subject, and inserted the attachments that we specified.

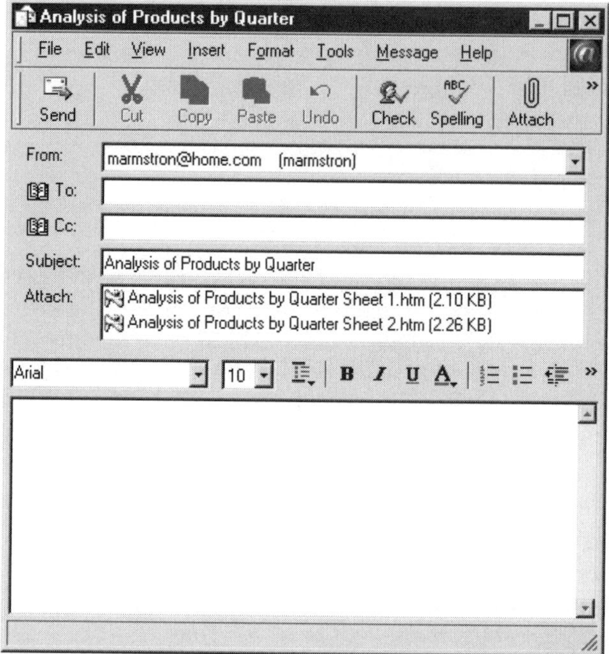

Known Problem with Emailing from Within Discoverer

Some email systems are unable to decipher graph documents. If you see the following error message when attempting to send a graph, this means that your email application is unable to handle files sent as a WMF (Windows Meta File).

Summary

In this chapter, we have shown you the importance of the system administrator and their relationship with the end user. You have learned the security issues of access rights, sharing rights, and scheduling privileges, all of which are established by the Discoverer administrator.

You have learned the benefits of sharing queries with other users and the importance of superuser involvement with shared queries. We have taught you how to share a query and a workflow for sharing a query with another user. You have learned how to use a shared query, and how to recognizing a shared query. We have shown you how to open, edit, and save a shared query.

In this chapter, we taught you about deleting queries from the database, including how to delete a query from the database and the caution that should be used. We taught you how to add a description to the query properties.

You have been taught the power of scheduling queries, the benefit of scheduling queries, and how to schedule a query. We have taught you how to view the results of a scheduled query, and how to unschedule a scheduled workbook. You have been taught how to edit a scheduled workbook, and the security issues surrounding a scheduled workbook. You were introduced to the benefits of third-party scheduling, and using the command line in scheduling. We taught you how to run Discoverer from the command line and known command-line problems.

In this chapter, we taught you how to manage SQL code. We taught you about exporting importing and structured SQL. And finally, we showed you how to email queries and reports, how to send a Discoverer workbook via email, and known problems with emailing from within Discoverer.

In the next chapter, you will learn about some of your options in setting up user preferences. You will learn to customize some of Discoverer's features and establish defaults for some common formatting issues. We will also give you a more in-depth look at the Discoverer administrator.

CHAPTER 14

User Preferences, the Toolbar, and the Discoverer Administrator

There are a variety of user preferences that you can set up within Discoverer. Most of these are done using the Options dialog box. In this chapter, we will show you the various settings available to you for customizing Discoverer to suit your particular needs. Because Discoverer 3.1 and 3*i* have enough differences, we will show you the Options dialog box in both versions.

In this chapter, we will also give you a quick reference guide to the Discoverer 3.1 and 3*i* toolbars. We will describe each buttons' functionality and its location on the toolbar.

You will also learn more about your Discoverer administrator, and his or her role in your successful use of Discoverer. We will teach you about the various tasks a Discoverer administrator needs to perform as well as what he or she can do for you.

Discoverer allows you to customize many of the day-to-day features you will be using. These features include setting file locations, how queries run by default, how your reports are set up, and many more. This customization is done using the Options dialog box. You have already been introduced to this dialog box in relation to creating reports and formatting queries, as well as in how your queries run. We want to be sure nothing is missed and so will take you through each section of the Options dialog boxes for both 3.1 and 3*i*.

The Options dialog box is accessed through the Tools menu on the menu bar. To open the Options dialog box, use the following workflow:

- Select Tools | Options from the menu bar.

NOTE
The Options dialog box can also be accessed from a button in the Workbook Wizard. This button is active in all steps of the Workbook Wizard except step 1. Before the button can be activated, you need to have chosen a table or crosstab layout. If you click Options in the Workbook Wizard, only the Query Governor, Sheet Format, and Default Format tabs are available.

3.1 Options

The 3.1 Options dialog box consists of seven tabs, however, only five of them can be seen at the same time. There are left and right arrows in the upper-right corner that give you access to the additional tabs. The seven tabs are as follows:

- General
- Query Governor

- Sheet Format (Table or Crosstab)
- Default Formats
- Cache Settings
- Advanced
- EUL

Our tutorial on the Options dialog box will begin with the General tab.

General

The General tab in 3.1, as seen in Figure 14-1, is divided into three areas.

The first area, called Viewers, concerns how you want to view multimedia files. If the Discoverer workbook contains video, images, or sound items, click these boxes to have Discoverer's built-in viewers open and play these files.

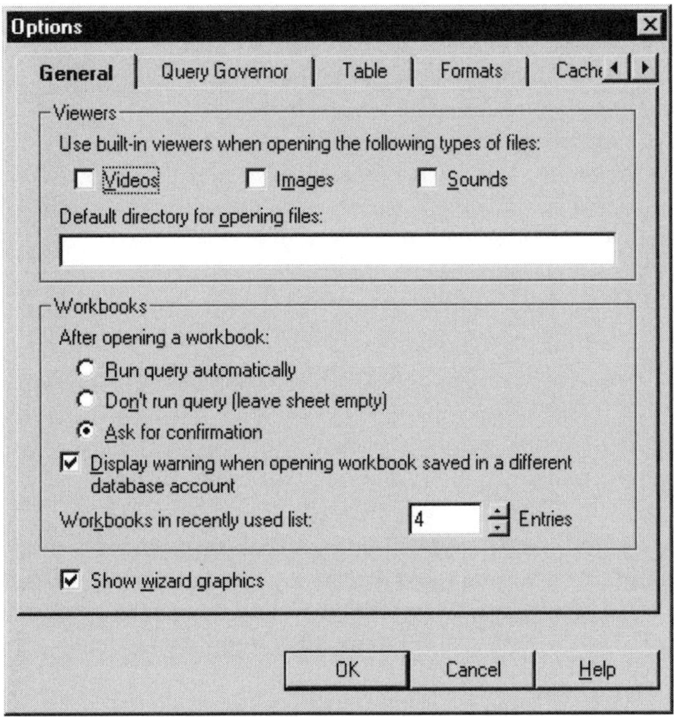

FIGURE 14-1. *The 3.1 Options dialog box, General tab*

The second area, called Workbooks, is for setting up preferences for how and when your workbooks run. As you can see in Figure 14-1, there are three radio buttons to choose from, a check box, and an input box. The radio buttons are as follows:

- **Run query automatically** When you open a workbook, Discoverer will automatically run the active worksheet if you select this option. Discoverer will not run any of the other worksheets until you click on the corresponding worksheet tab.
- **Don't run query (leave sheet empty)** When you open a workbook, Discoverer will not run any of the worksheets if you select this option. You will, however, be in the active worksheet with no data displayed.
- **Ask for confirmation** When you open a workbook, Discoverer will ask for confirmation that you want to run the active worksheet. Clicking Yes will run the worksheet, and clicking No will not.

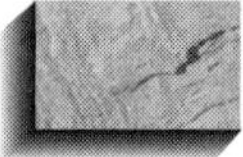

NOTE
Because Discoverer has sticky features, it remembers the last worksheet that was opened in the workbook. This worksheet is called the active worksheet. We think the best option to choose is "Ask for confirmation." If you are anything like us, you don't remember which worksheet you last had open. By selecting this option, you have the chance to choose whether Discoverer runs the active worksheet. If you are not sure what the active worksheet does, click No when prompted, then open the Edit Sheet dialog box and check it out. With the other options, you could be waiting for a query to run when it is not even the one you need.

The remaining options in the Workbook area are as follows:

- **Display warning when opening workbook saved in a different database account** Check this box to display a warning if you are about to open a workbook that has been saved in a different database account. This is checked by default, and we think it is a good idea to leave it that way.

- **Workbooks in recently used list** This is a selection box to the right, near the bottom of this area. In this box, enter how many files you want to see in the recently used file list. The default is four, but you can select up to nine.

The last area in the General tab is a check box for showing graphics in the Workbook Wizard. Graphics use a tremendous amount of system resources and can seriously decrease performance. If you have a slow-running computer, or are querying over long distances, we recommend you deselect this option.

Query Governor

The Query Governor tab gives you options for how you want large queries to run. Figure 14-2 shows the Query Governor tab.

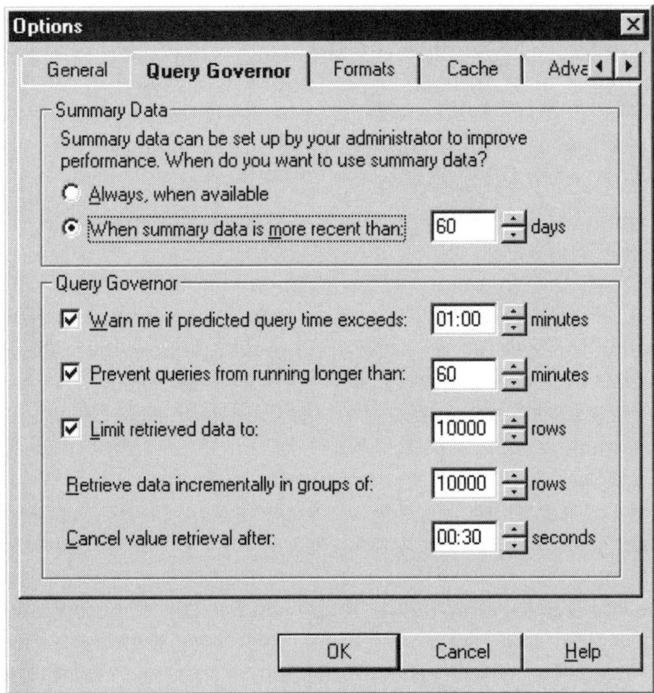

FIGURE 14-2. *The 3.1 Options dialog box, Query Governor tab*

The Query Governor has two areas, one called Summary Data and one called Query Governor.

The Summary Data area has two radio buttons. These are as follows:

- **Always, when available** Select this option if you want to force Discoverer to always use summary data.
- **When summary data is more recent than** Select this option if you want to force Discoverer to only use summary data when the data is more recent than the number of days specified.

Later in this chapter, we will teach you about summary data and how it can be set up by your Discoverer administrator.

The second area of the Query Governor tab allows you to customize the following five query options:

- **Warn me if predicted query time exceeds** This option allows you to ask Discoverer for a warning if the query will take more than a designated time to run. Select from one minute to 99 hours and 59 minutes. Your Discoverer administrator can set a maximum default time. If this has happened, you can only set lower time limits.

  This option is only relevant if your company's Discoverer administrator has not disabled Discoverer's query predictor. Discoverer's query predictor is a clever feature that predicts approximately how long a query will take to run. To do this, Discoverer needs certain database settings to have been made by the DBA. When set correctly, Discoverer will maintain a log of past queries and compare your query with those results. If your query uses items that have been queried before, Discoverer will be able to give you an approximation of how long it will take this time. Unfortunately, the settings that Discoverer's query predictor needs are incompatible with Oracle Applications prior to 11*i*. If your Discoverer administrator has not disabled the query predictor, your queries will take much longer to run.

- **Prevent queries from running longer than** This option allows you to create a time limit for your queries. Worksheets that reach this deadline are terminated. The Discoverer administrator can set a default time period. If this has happened, you can only set a lower time limit.
- **Limit retrieved data to** Here you can designate the maximum number of rows of data you want a query to retrieve. If your Discoverer administrator has set a maximum value, you cannot set a limit that is higher. When querying, if the maximum has been reached and your query has not

completed, Discoverer will give you a warning that not all data has been retrieved. This warning is shown here:

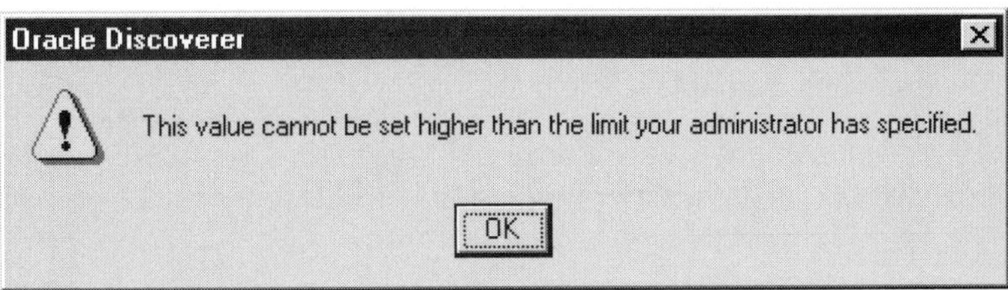

- **Retrieve data incrementally in groups of** Here you can select the number of rows of data you want Discoverer to retrieve at one time. The default is 100 rows. As each group of data is retrieved, Discoverer displays what has been retrieved so far. Assuming the data is good, you can continue by retrieving the next group.
- **Cancel value retrieval after** This setting is used by Discoverer when displaying lists of values. In order to display a list of values, Discoverer queries the databases to find a unique list. These queries can take a long time. If the search for a list of values exceeds the time allotted, Discoverer will abandon the search.

Table/Crosstab

The third tab in the Options dialog box is the Table or Crosstab tab. Depending upon the worksheet format you have chosen, this tab will be labeled either Table or Crosstab. In this tab, you can determine how the worksheet will be seen on the screen, and how it will look when printed. Most of the options for the Table and Crosstab are the same. When there is a difference we will bring this to your attention. The tab for a Table is shown in Figure 14-3, while the tab for a Crosstab can be seen in Figure 14-4.

The options for the Table and Crosstab tabs are as follows:

- **Title** Here you can turn on or turn off the title display of your worksheets. When checked, the worksheet title will be displayed.
- **Default Title** Click this button to open the Edit Title dialog box. We covered the functionality of this box in Chapter 6, so we will not do so again here. When you create a title using the Default Title button, the title you create will become the default for all future workbooks. It will not, however, apply to any of the titles in the current workbook.

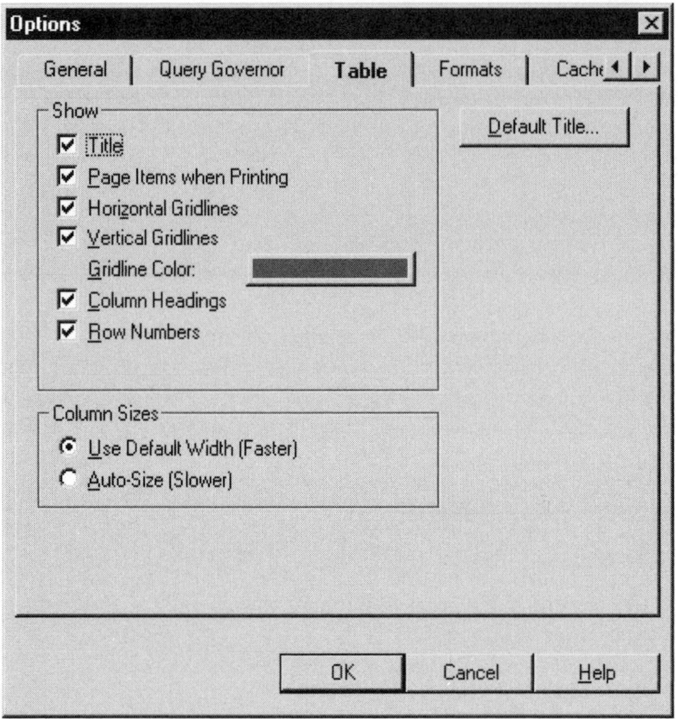

FIGURE 14-3. *The 3.1 Options dialog box, Table tab*

- **Page Items when Printing** This option allows you to turn on or turn off the printing of Page Items. When checked, the Page Items will be printed.
- **Horizontal Gridlines** This option allows you to turn on or turn off the horizontal gridlines. When checked, the horizontal gridlines will be displayed.
- **Vertical Gridlines** This option allows you to turn on or turn off the vertical gridlines. When checked, the vertical gridlines will be displayed.
- **Gridline Color** This button allows you to change the color of the gridlines in your worksheet. Click the button to open the color box, then select the color you desire.

- **Column Headings (table only)** This option allows you to turn on or turn off the column headings. When checked, the column headings will be displayed.
- **Row Numbers (table only)** This option allows you to turn on or turn off the row numbers. When checked, the row numbers will be displayed.
- **Column Sizes (table only)** This area has two radio buttons. You can choose between Use Default Width (Faster) and Auto-Size (Slower). We have tried both settings, and have seen no appreciable difference in speed. However, if you are concerned about performance, you should use the default width as recommended by Oracle.
- **Axis Labels (crosstab only)** This option allows you to turn on or turn off the side axis labels. When checked, the axis labels will be displayed.

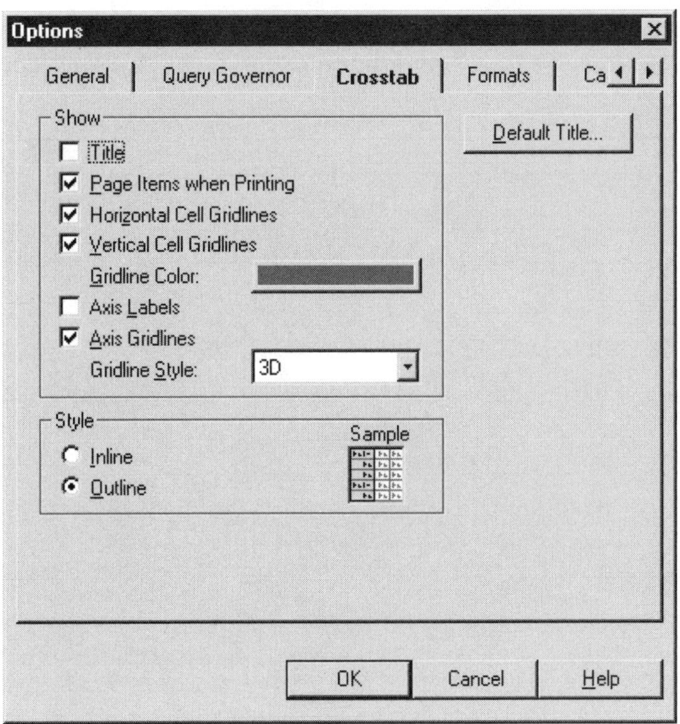

FIGURE 14-4. *The 3.1 Options dialog box, Crosstab tab*

NOTE
There is no option for turning off the column labels in a crosstab. These are always displayed.

- **Axis Gridlines (crosstab only)** This option allows you to turn on or turn off the axis gridlines. When checked, the axis gridlines will be displayed.
- **Gridline Style (crosstab only)** This box contains two choices, 3D and Normal. 3D is the default setting. Selecting Normal will give a flat appearance to the axis gridlines. We don't see any performance issues either way. This is simply a user preference issue.
- **Style (crosstab only)** This area gives you two radio buttons to choose from. The first, Inline, will layout the Y axis labels (the side axis) side by side, as seen in Figure 14-5. This is the default for a crosstab style.

The second radio button is for an outline style crosstab. This style of crosstab places the first side axis item above the second side axis item, and so on. It also creates a subtotal on the data items for the topmost side axis item. Figure 14-6

Customer Name	Quarter	Sales
ABC WIDGET CO	1998-Q3	$28,140
	1998-Q4	$397,868
	1999-Q1	$50,014
	1999-Q2	$122,210
	1999-Q3	$70,762
	1999-Q4	$31,274
	2000-Q1	$7,009
	2000-Q2	$752,562
ACE MANUFACTURING	1998-Q3	$21,192
	1998-Q4	$225,247
	1999-Q1	$67,393
	1999-Q2	$33,821
	1999-Q3	$60,318
	1999-Q4	$29,225
	2000-Q1	$575
	2000-Q2	$468,922
BIG RIVER WIDGETS	1998-Q3	$21,192
	1998-Q4	$49,859
	1999-Q1	$47,852

Sheet 1 | Sheet 2

FIGURE 14-5. *An inline crosstab in Discoverer 3.1*

shows the same table seen in Figure 14-5, but this time as an outline crosstab. Notice how each item is indented from the previous one.

Formats

The fourth tab in the Options dialog box is the Formats tab. This tab allows you to view the currently defined formats for five of the most common worksheet options, and for determining what Discoverer will display when null values are returned in your query. The Formats tab is shown in Figure 14-7.

If you want to amend the current default format of one of the five options described next, select the format you want to amend and click the Change button. This opens the relevant Edit dialog box. These were described in detail in Chapter 6.

To reset an option back to Discoverer's default, select the format you want to change, and click the Reset button.

These five default options you can set are as follows:

- **Data** Setting this controls how your data will look onscreen. You can set font, alignment, and background color. The Discoverer default is Arial 10 point, in a regular typeface, left justified, using black text on a white background.

C : Quarter	Sales
ABC WIDGET CO	$1,459,838
1998-Q3	$28,140
1998-Q4	$397,868
1999-Q1	$50,014
1999-Q2	$122,210
1999-Q3	$70,762
1999-Q4	$31,274
2000-Q1	$7,009
2000-Q2	$752,562
ACE MANUFACTURING	$906,693
1998-Q3	$21,192
1998-Q4	$225,247
1999-Q1	$67,393
1999-Q2	$33,821
1999-Q3	$60,318
1999-Q4	$29,225
2000-Q1	$575
2000-Q2	$468,922
BIG RIVER WIDGETS	$411,758

Sheet 1 | Sheet 2

FIGURE 14-6. *An outline crosstab in Discoverer 3.1*

- **Headings** Setting this controls how your column headings will look on screen. You can set font, alignment, and background color. The Discoverer default is Arial 10 point, in a regular typeface, center justified, using black text on a light-gray background.
- **Sheet Titles** Setting this controls how your sheet titles will look onscreen. You can set font and background color. The Discoverer default is Arial 10 point, in a bold typeface, center justified, on a white background.
- **Totals** Setting this controls how your totals will look onscreen. You can set font and background color. The Discoverer default is the same as for the data option (Arial 10 point, in a regular typeface, left justified, on a white background).
- **Exceptions** Setting this controls how your exceptions will look onscreen. You can set font and background color. The Discoverer default is Arial 10 point, in a regular typeface, left justified, on a red background.

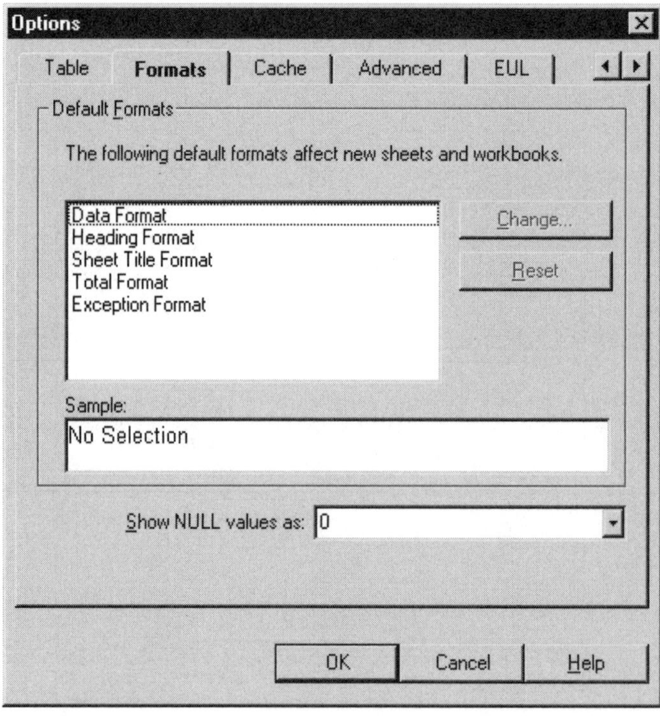

FIGURE 14-7. *The 3.1 Options dialog box, Formats tab*

The last option on the Formats tab, as shown in Figure 14-7, is for formatting null values. In the field entitled "Show NULL values as", you can either select from the drop-down list or type in your default. Normally a null value displays as nothing, but you can change this to any text value, number, or date that you want to see.

Cache Settings

The Cache tab is where you set the options for memory and disk caching. On the tab shown in the illustration that follows, Discoverer allows you to set various caching options. You should not change any of these settings without the approval of your Discoverer administrator.

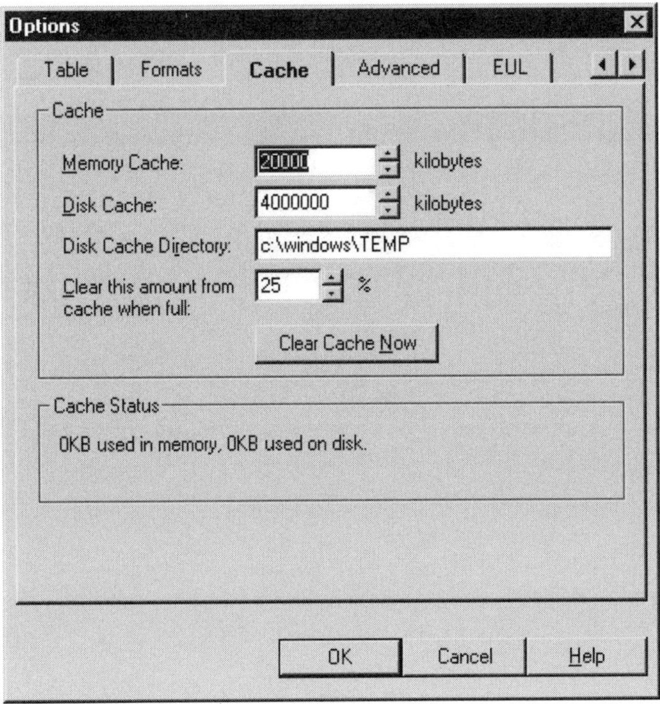

If you encounter errors such as "Cannot create virtual memory swap file" or "No data can be retrieved because the disk is full," your settings may need changing. However, as stated above, do not attempt to make these changes without consulting your Discoverer administrator.

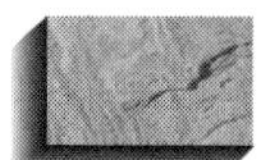

NOTE
If you are still using Discoverer 3.0.7, this version does not have a Refresh Sheet button on the toolbar. You either have to exit the worksheet and reopen it or clear the cache using the Clear Cache Now button on the Cache tab.

Advanced

On the Advanced tab, as shown in Figure 14-8, Discoverer allows you to turn on or turn off automatic querying and the trapping of join errors.

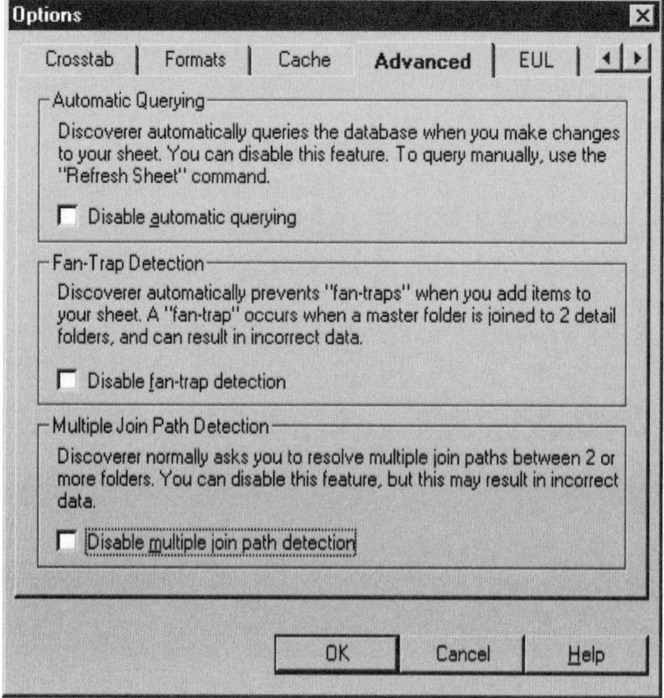

FIGURE 14-8. *The 3.1 Options dialog box, Advanced tab*

The options for the Advanced tab are as follows:

- **Disable automatic querying** Check this box if you want to prevent Discoverer from automatically requerying the database after you have made changes to the worksheet. With this box checked, you will need to manually refresh the worksheet. We do not recommend that you check this box without approval from your Discoverer administrator.
- **Disable fan-trap detection** Check this box if you want to prevent Discoverer from detecting fan traps. Fan traps were covered in detail in Chapter 10. Unless you are using Discoverer version 3.1.41 or above, we do not recommend you check this box. In any case, you should not check this without approval from your Discoverer administrator.
- **Disable multiple join path detection** Check this box if you want to prevent Discoverer from detecting multiple join paths. This topic was also discussed in detail in Chapter 10. Do not check this box without approval from your Discoverer administrator.

EUL

On the EUL tab, as shown in Figure 14-9, Discoverer allows you to change the end-user layer you are using. This feature is primarily used by the Discoverer administrator who needs access to both a development and production Discoverer end-user layer. Unless you are a very experienced user, you should not attempt to change the default setting. If you are unsure about what EUL should be the default, check with your Discoverer administrator.

3*i* Options

The 3*i* Options dialog box has six tabs. The six tabs are as follows:

- General
- Query Governor
- Sheet Format
- Default Formats
- Advanced
- EUL

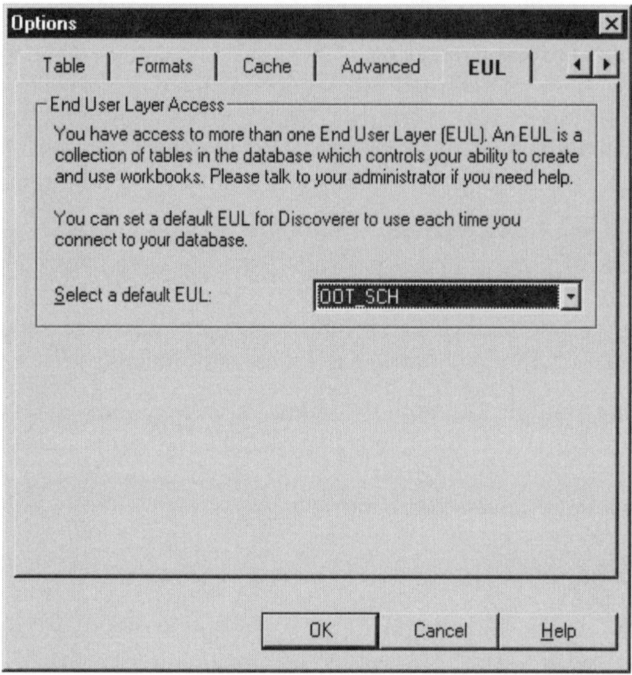

FIGURE 14-9. *The 3.1 Options dialog box, EUL tab*

Our tutorial on the 3*i* Options dialog box will begin with the General tab.

General

The General tab is for setting up preferences for how and when your workbooks run. The General tab in 3*i* is seen in Figure 14-10.

As you can see in Figure 14-10, there are three radio buttons to choose from. They are as follows:

- **Run query automatically** When you open a workbook, Discoverer will automatically run the active worksheet if you select this option. Discoverer will not run any of the other worksheets until you click on the corresponding worksheet tab.
- **Don't run query (leave sheet empty)** When you open a workbook, Discoverer will not run any of the worksheets if you select this option. You will, however, be in the active worksheet with no data displayed.

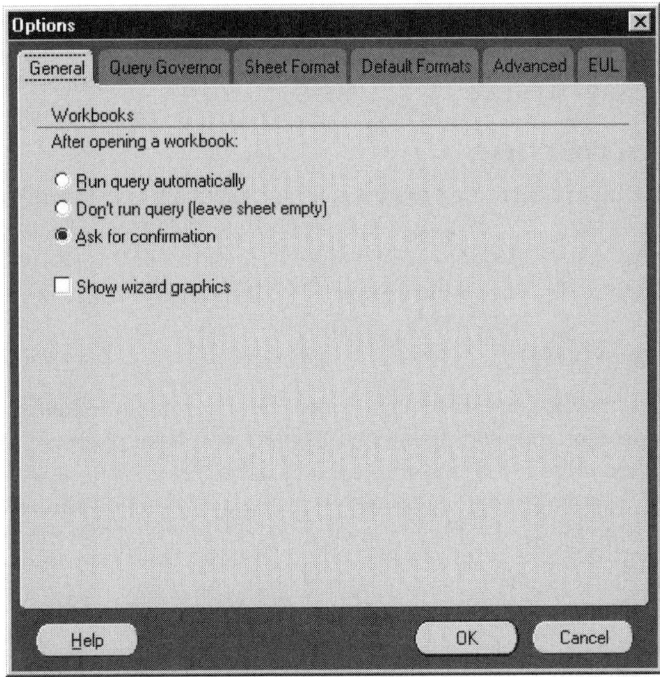

FIGURE 14-10. *The 3i Options dialog box, General tab*

- **Ask for confirmation** When you open a workbook, Discoverer will ask for confirmation that you want to run the active worksheet. Clicking Yes will run the worksheet, clicking No will not.

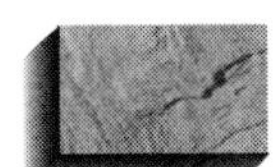

NOTE
Because Discoverer has sticky features, it remembers the last worksheet that was opened in the workbook. This worksheet is called the active worksheet. We think the best option to choose is "Ask for confirmation." If you are anything like us, you don't remember which worksheet you last had open. By selecting this option, you have the chance to choose whether Discoverer runs the active worksheet. If you are not sure what the active worksheet does, click No when prompted, then open the Edit Sheet dialog box and check it out. With the other options, you could be waiting for a query to run when it is not even the one you need.

The last area in the General tab is a check box for showing graphics in the Workbook Wizard. Graphics use a tremendous amount of system resources and can seriously decrease performance. If you have a slow-running computer, or are querying over long distances, we recommend you deselect this option.

Query Governor

The second of the 3*i* tabs is the Query Governor tab. This tab is identical to the Query Governor tab in 3.1 in appearance and functionality. For details on the 3.1 tab, please refer to the 3.1 query governor section earlier in this chapter. You should also refer to Figure 14-2 to see the Query Governor tab.

Sheet Format

The third tab in the Options dialog box is the Sheet Format tab. There are some differences in this tab, depending if the worksheet you have open is a table or if it is a crosstab. When there is a difference, we will bring this to your attention. This tab is also used to determine what Discoverer will display when null values are returned in your query. The tab for a table is shown in Figure 14-11, while the tab for a Crosstab can be seen in Figure 14-12.

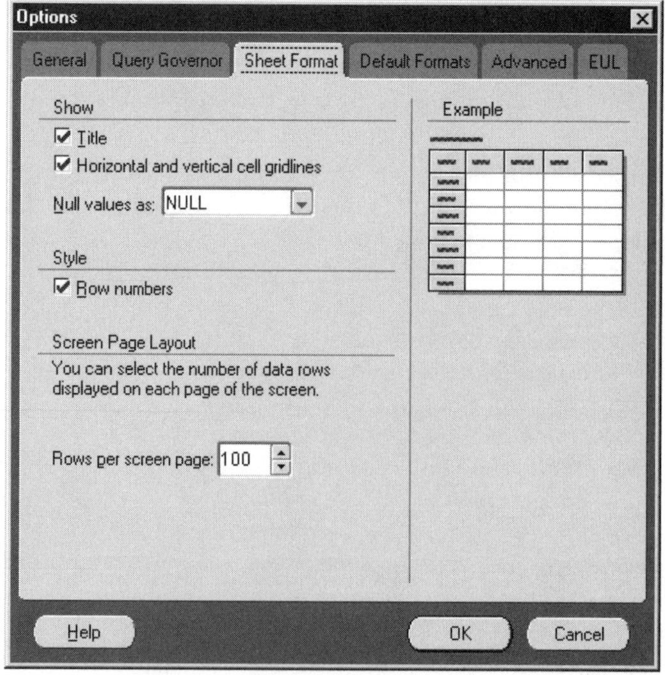

FIGURE 14-11. *The 3i Options dialog box, Table Sheet Format tab*

The options for the Table and Crosstab tabs are as follows:

- **Title** Here you can turn on or turn off the title display of your worksheets. When checked, the worksheet title will be displayed.
- **Horizontal and vertical cell gridlines** This option allows you to turn on or turn off the horizontal and vertical cell gridlines. When checked, the horizontal and vertical cell gridlines will be displayed.
- **Null values** This option allows you to either select from the drop-down list or type in your default. Normally, a null value displays as nothing, but you can change this to any text value, number, or date that you want to see.
- **Row numbers (table only)** This option allows you to turn on or turn off the row numbers. When checked, the row numbers will be displayed.
- **Screen Page Layout** This option allows you to choose how many rows of data will be displayed per page. Type in the number of rows you want to display, or use the up and down arrows to make your selection.

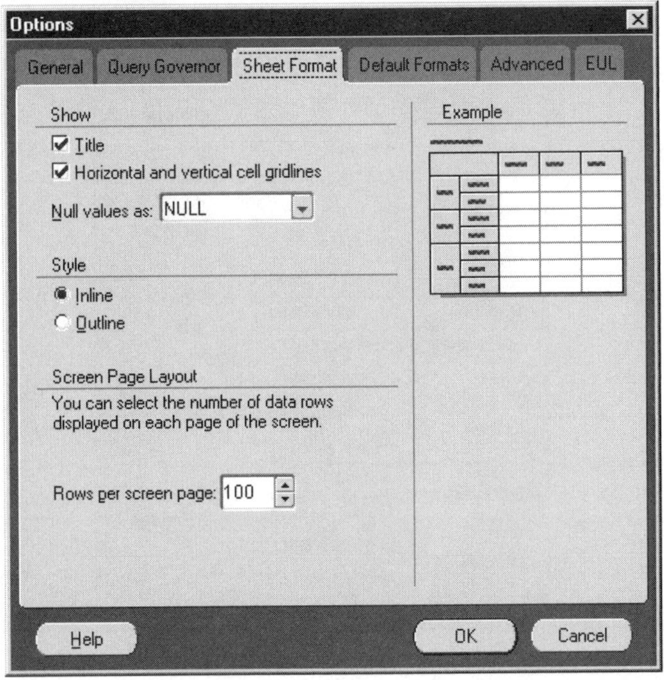

FIGURE 14-12. *The 3*i *Options dialog box, Crosstab Sheet Format tab*

- **Style (crosstab only)** This area gives you two radio buttons to choose from. Both styles will lay out the Y axis labels (the side axis) side by side. The difference between the two styles is that the outline type inserts subtotals. An example of an inline style, the default style, can be seen in Figure 14-13, while an example of an outline crosstab can be seen in Figure 14-14.

Default Formats

The fourth tab in the Options dialog box is the Default Formats tab. This tab allows you to view the currently defined formats for three of the most common worksheet options. The Formats tab is shown in Figure 14-15.

If you want to amend the current format of one of the five options described next, click the Change button. To reset the option back to Discoverer's default, click the Reset button.

The three default options you can set are as follows:

- **Data** Setting this controls how your data will look onscreen. You can set font, alignment, and background color. The Discoverer default is Arial 10 point, in a regular typeface, left justified, using black text on a white background.

		Ship Qty SUM
City Name	Customer Name	
ATLANTA	LAST RAILWAY WIDGETS	48441
DALLAS	BIG RIVER WIDGETS	17355
DENVER	MOUNTAIN WIDGETS	66164
	THE LITTLE WIDGET	60516
GENEVA	LAC WIDGETS SA	53963
HONG KONG	HONG KONG WIDGETS	49817
LIMA	REPUBLIC WIDGETS	46740
LISBON	ACE MANUFACTURING	42487
	PALMELA WIDGETS	41369
LIVERPOOL	MUM'S WIDGET CO.	74688
	WIDGET O THE MERSEY	65054
LONDON	LONDON WIDGETS LTD.	42439
	OXFORD WIDGETS	73894

FIGURE 14-13. *An inline crosstab in Discoverer 3*i

		Ship Qty SUM
▸ City Name	Customer Name	
▸ ATLANTA		48441
	LAST RAILWAY WIDGETS	48441
▸ DALLAS		17355
	BIG RIVER WIDGETS	17355
▸ DENVER		126680
	MOUNTAIN WIDGETS	66164
	THE LITTLE WIDGET	60516
▸ GENEVA		53963
	LAC WIDGETS SA	53963
▸ HONG KONG		49817
	HONG KONG WIDGETS	49817
▸ LIMA		46740
	REPUBLIC WIDGETS	46740

FIGURE 14-14. *An outline crosstab in Discoverer 3*i

- **Headings** Setting this controls how your column headings will look onscreen. You can set font, alignment, and background color. The Discoverer default is Arial 10 point, in a regular typeface, center justified, using black text on a light-gray background.
- **Totals** Setting this controls how your totals will look onscreen. You can set font and background color. The Discoverer default is the same as for the data option (Arial 10 point, in a regular typeface, left justified, on a white background).

NOTE

If you are still using Discoverer 3.0.7, this version does not have a Refresh Sheet button on the toolbar. You either have to exit the worksheet and reopen it or clear the cache using the Clear Cache Now button on the Cache tab.

Advanced

The Advanced tab in 3*i* is identical to the Advanced tab in 3.1 in both appearance and functionality. For details on this tab, please refer to the 3.1 advanced section earlier in this chapter. Also refer to Figure 14-8 to see the Advanced tab.

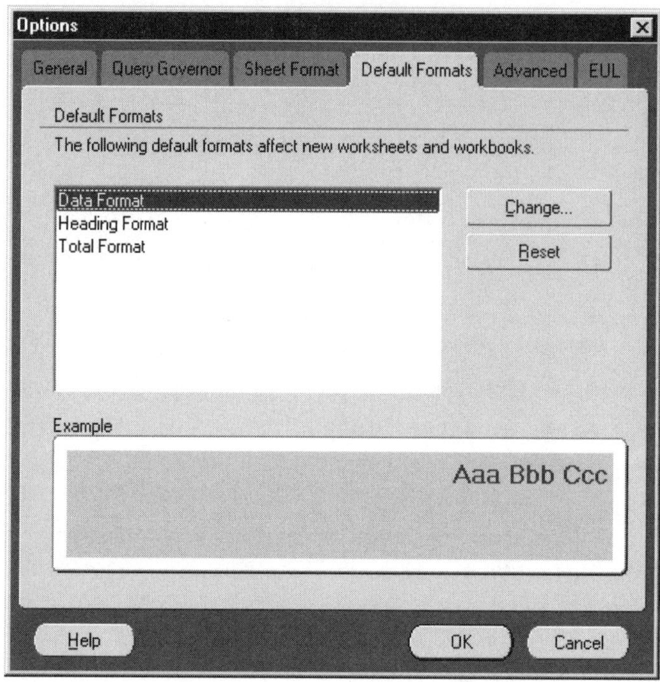

FIGURE 14-15. *The 3i Options dialog box, Default Formats tab*

EUL

The EUL tab in 3*i* is identical to the EUL tab in 3.1 in both appearance and functionality. For details on this tab, please refer to the 3.1 EUL section earlier in this chapter. Also refer to Figure 14-9 to see the EUL tab.

The Toolbar

For the sake of not wanting to miss anything, we are adding this section on the toolbar. We are the types who, when we get new software, point at all of the buttons on the toolbar to see what they are for. If you are used to working in a Windows environment, you may have done the same. For those of you who are not as familiar with Windows, you might not be in the habit of "checking out" the toolbar.

Many of the buttons on the toolbar have been covered in the preceding chapters. However, we will show them all here as a reference guide.

The Discoverer 3.1 Toolbar

The Discoverer 3.1 toolbar buttons are grouped in a logical manner, and in a very similar order to other Windows programs. The toolbar has been divided into five sections, so we will show them to you by these sections.

Workbook Section of the 3.1 Toolbar

The first section of the toolbar is used for managing workbooks: opening, saving and printing. The following illustration shows the first section of the toolbar.

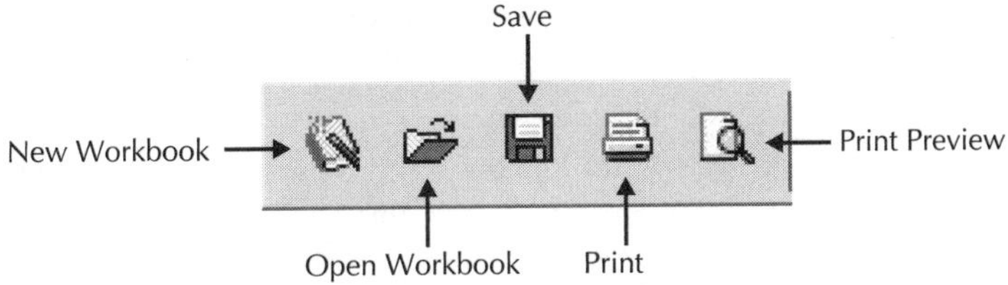

The workbook section of the 3.1 toolbar has the following five buttons:

- **New Workbook** Opens the Workbook Wizard.
- **Open Workbook** Opens the Open Workbook dialog box.
- **Save** Saves the workbook. If the workbook has not already been saved, the Save Workbook dialog box will open.
- **Print** Prints the workbook.
- **Print Preview** Displays how this workbook will print.

Worksheet Section of the 3.1 Toolbar

The second section of the toolbar is used for managing worksheets; creating new worksheets, editing, copying, drilling, and refreshing. The following illustration shows the worksheet section of the toolbar.

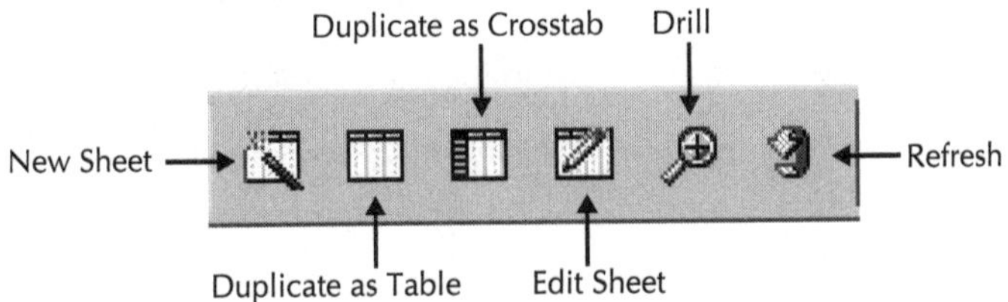

The worksheet section of the 3.1 toolbar has the following six buttons:

- **New Sheet** Opens the New Sheet Wizard.
- **Duplicate as Table** Opens the Duplicate as Table dialog box.
- **Duplicate as Crosstab** Opens the Duplicate as Crosstab dialog box.
- **Edit Sheet** Opens the Edit Sheet dialog box.
- **Drill** Drills to the data for the column selected.
- **Refresh** Refreshes the data in the worksheet.

Graph Section of the 3.1 Toolbar

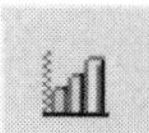

The third section of the toolbar has only one button, and is used for managing graphs. The first time you click this button, the Graph Wizard will open. Once a graph has been created, the button will open the graph. The illustration to the left shows the third section of the toolbar.

Sorting Section of the 3.1 Toolbar

The fourth section of the toolbar is used for formatting exceptions and sorting. The fourth section of the toolbar is shown here:

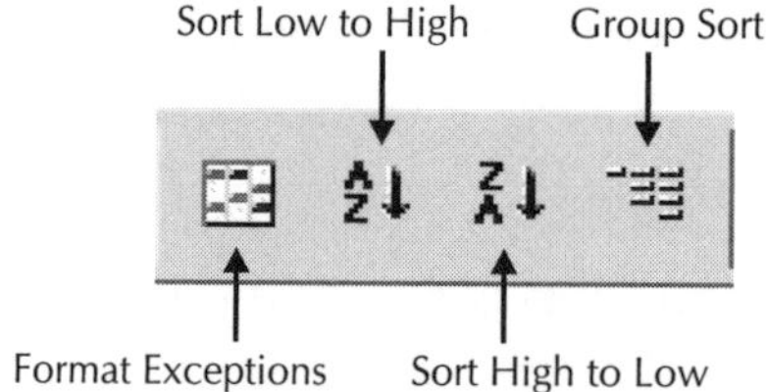

The sorting section of the 3.1 toolbar has the following four buttons:

- **Format Exceptions** Opens the Exceptions dialog box.
- **Sort Low to High** Sorts the data in the column selected in ascending order.
- **Sort High to Low** Sorts the data in the column selected in descending order.
- **Group Sort** Group sorts the data in the column selected.

Excel Section of the 3.1 Toolbar

The fifth section of the toolbar is used for exporting the data in the worksheet into an Excel worksheet. If there is more than one worksheet in a workbook, Discoverer will export the first sheet by the same name as the workbook. After the first worksheet has been exported, you will be prompted to name the additional worksheets to be exported. The fifth section of the toolbar is shown to the left.

The Discoverer 3*i* Toolbar

The Discoverer 3*i* toolbar buttons are grouped into five sections, much the same as the 3.1 toolbar. There are a few differences in the 3*i* toolbar because of differences in the functionality of the two products. Just like we did when we explained the 3.1 toolbar, we will show the 3*i* toolbar to you by sections.

Workbook Section of the 3*i* Toolbar

The first section of the toolbar is used for managing workbooks: opening, saving, and printing. There is no print preview in 3*i* because 3*i* is WYSIWYG. The illustration, as shown here, displays the first section of the toolbar.

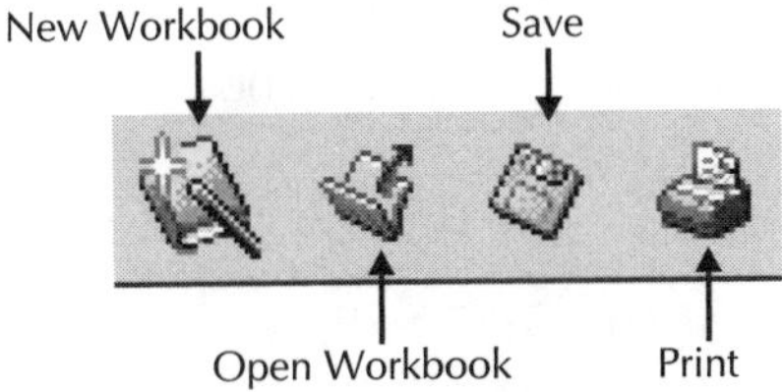

The workbook section of the 3*i* toolbar has the following four buttons:

- **New Workbook** Opens the Workbook Wizard.
- **Open Workbook** Opens the Open Workbook dialog box.
- **Save** Saves the workbook. If the workbook has not already been saved, the Save Workbook dialog box will open.
- **Print** Prints the workbook.

Worksheet Section of the 3*i* Toolbar

The second section of the toolbar has five buttons. These buttons are used for managing worksheets; creating new worksheets, editing, and copying. When compared to 3.1, you cannot drill from the toolbar in 3*i*, and the Refresh button has been moved into its own section. Oracle has also added an extra button to this section. This extra button opens the Table Layout dialog box. The worksheet section of the toolbar is shown here:

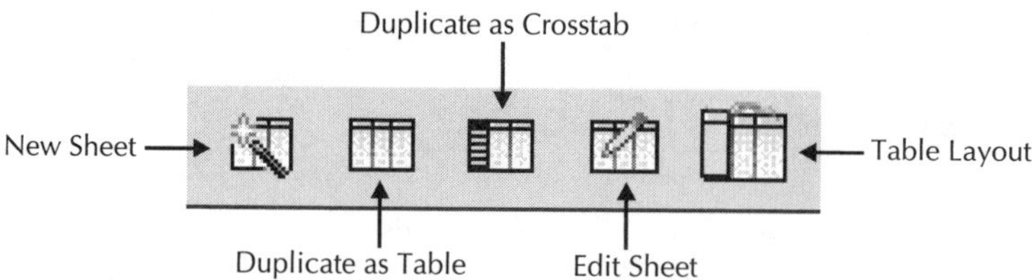

The worksheet section of the 3*i* toolbar has the following five buttons:

- **New Sheet** Opens the New Sheet Wizard.
- **Duplicate as Table** Opens the Duplicate as Table dialog box.
- **Duplicate as Crosstab** Opens the Duplicate as Crosstab dialog box.
- **Edit Sheet** Opens the Edit Sheet dialog box.
- **Table Layout** Opens the Table Layout dialog box.

Refresh Data Section of the 3*i* Toolbar

The third section of the toolbar has only one button, and it is used to refresh the data in the query.

Tools Section of the 3*i* Toolbar

The fourth section of the toolbar is used for opening five of the various tool dialog boxes. The following illustration shows the tools section of the toolbar.

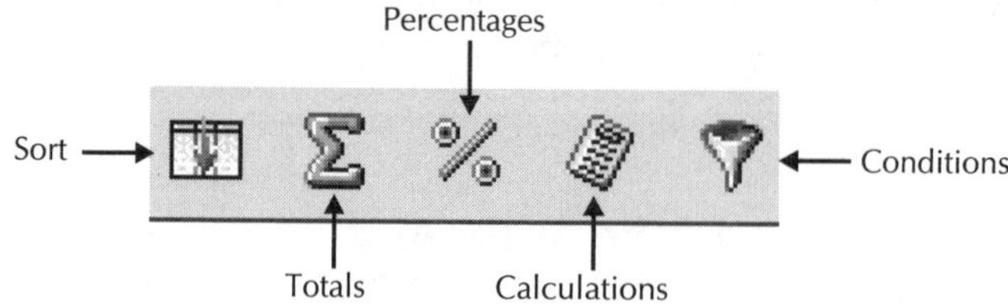

The tools section of the 3*i* toolbar has the following five buttons:

- **Sort** Opens the Sorting dialog box.
- **Totals** Opens the Totals dialog box.
- **Percentages** Opens the Percentages dialog box.
- **Calculations** Opens the Calculations dialog box.
- **Conditions** Opens the Conditions dialog box.

Excel Section of the 3*i* Toolbar

Like in Discoverer 3.1, the fifth section of the toolbar has a single button. Use this button to export the data in the worksheet into an Excel worksheet. The fifth section of the toolbar is shown to the left.

The Discoverer Administrator

We cannot tell you everything that the Discoverer administrator does, but in this section we will try to give you a brief glimpse behind the scenes. We hope this will give you a better understanding and insight into the job that this person does. Later in this section, we will outline just what the Discoverer administrator can do for you. Here, you will find a list of all of the things that your Discoverer administrator can change on your behalf.

The Discoverer Administrator's Role

As far as Discoverer is concerned, the most important person that you will come into contact with is your Discoverer administrator. Without this person, there will be no Discoverer. The role of the Discoverer administrator is a very specialized role indeed. Each company has at least one, and all of the users are thankful that he or she is there. The Discoverer administrator understands how to design business areas that support your company's way of doing things. At least one of the Discoverer administrators is also a database guru. This is the person who knows all there is about your company's databases—where they are located, how they are stored, and how the data is all linked together. It is not required that every Discoverer administrator be a database guru or even a DBA. The only prerequisite is that they understand the portion of data (tables, views, and joins) for which they are responsible. In addition, users who understand the data can share some of the responsibilities of administering the Discoverer end-user layer. For example, a user who understands the business terms used by the rest of the user community could be responsible for defining descriptions for folders and items.

Being able to design business areas and being a database guru are just two of the roles. The third role of the Discoverer administrator is somewhat more abstract than the other two, both of which are primarily technical. This third role requires good interpersonal skills and a really good sense of business acumen, something not usually associated with "techies." The Discoverer administrator knows the decision-makers within your company. He or she is able to talk with users at their level and in their language, omitting the jargon and techno-babble that is the domain of programmers. We feel strongly that this third role of the Discoverer administrator is the most important, and cannot be overemphasized. Having built a good rapport with the business management, the Discoverer administrator is in a perfect position to identify what data is needed within your business areas.

You Can Help Your Discoverer Administrator Identify the Data Needed

Before your company makes Discoverer available to you, the users, it is your Discoverer administrator's responsibility to identify the data that is needed. He or she does this by talking with you and your fellow coworkers.

If you are lucky enough to be selected as a key user during the analysis phase, you can help your Discoverer administrator by having answers to some of the following questions:

- What reports do you create today and who do you send them to?
- What is wrong with the data that you have today and how would you like to see it made better in the future?
- Do you know where the data is kept today? Is it kept in a database, or perhaps you use spreadsheets?
- Maybe you have an EDI system and you need Discoverer to take a feed from that?
- Are you able to define any corporate algorithms or calculations that you would like to see standardized?

Do not keep quiet at this point. If you do not understand something at this stage, be sure to ask. Waiting until you have access to Discoverer is far too late.

Once the data has been identified, your Discoverer administrator will design the business areas that you will eventually see inside Discoverer. These are designed on paper first and are refined many times before the Admin Edition is even touched! It is a very complex and expensive process to unbundle badly created business areas, even with a product as good as Discoverer. Time spent analyzing and designing will repay itself over and over again.

Once the business areas have been created and you have a working system, the fun really starts. No Discoverer system can ever be considered finished. It is your responsibility to ensure that the system delivers what you need. You must keep in touch with your Discoverer administrator and be aware what he or she can do for you.

What Can the Discoverer Administrator Do for You?

Perhaps the most interesting part of the interaction between yourself and your Discoverer administrator is knowing what he or she can do for you. Using this knowledge, you should be better able to make requests of your Discoverer administrator. He or she can then take your request, act on it, and make modifications on your behalf. These modifications will make your life easier and enable you to write more cost-effective queries.

The following is a list of all of the items that your Discoverer administrator has control over. Use this list to see what your Discoverer administrator can do for you.

- **Adding new users** The Discoverer administrator is responsible for adding new users to the system. Whether he or she does it, or whether the DBA is assigned the task, is irrelevant. Any request for access should initially be directed to the Discoverer administrator. If you are able to specify exactly what type of access is required, this will make the job that much easier.
- **Granting access to business areas** If you find that you do not have access to a business area that you need, you should raise a request to your Discoverer administrator to have that access granted. Perhaps you have changed your job, or maybe your responsibilities have been extended.
- **Granting privileges within the user edition** If you feel that your privileges are not sufficient, you should discuss this with your Discoverer administrator. On the Privileges tab of the Discoverer Admin Edition, your Discoverer administrator grants access to the User Edition. Having granted you access to run the User Edition, your Discoverer administrator also determines whether you can create or edit a query, whether you can drill, whether you can share or schedule workbooks, and whether you can save

workbooks to the database. The Discoverer administrator Privileges tab is shown here:

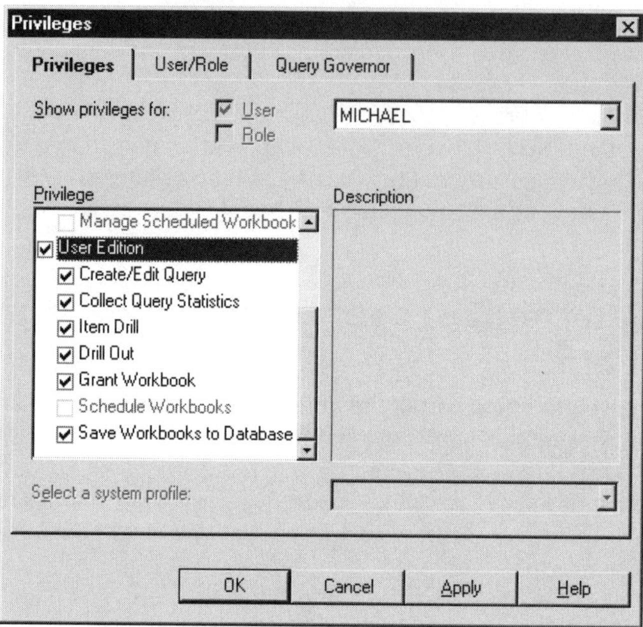

- **Adding meaningful descriptions to business areas, folders and data items** A very simple, yet very useful, means of helping you understand your data better is to add descriptions to the data objects. This adds no overhead to the processing of the system, yet it is incredible to us how many business areas and folders are not given meaningful descriptions. In the following illustration, you can see that a description has been created for the main business area of our tutorial database. Similar descriptions can be created for each folder, making it a lot easier for you to understand what the folder contains.

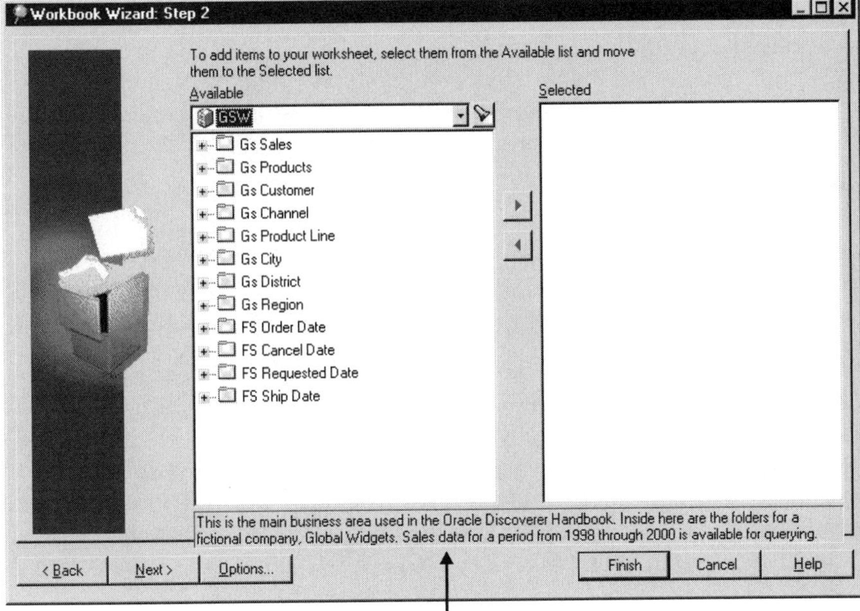

Business area description

- **Adding new items to folders** If you think that there is an item missing from a folder, you should talk to your Discoverer administrator. He or she is able to add new items to folders. Adding items to a data warehouse folder, however, could be a lengthy process. If the item already exists in your warehouse and your Discoverer administrator has determined that it does not contain sensitive information, then it only takes a few minutes for the administrator to make this item available.
- **Creating new folders** Your Discoverer administrator can create new folders within Discoverer. These folders can be based on SQL statements, extracts from the database, or even items contained in existing folders.

- **Creating joins between folders** There will be times when Discoverer deactivates folders. This is because there is no join between the items you have chosen and the deactivated folder containing the item that you want. It may be possible for your Discoverer administrator to create a join for you, thus enabling you to choose the item that you want.
- **Creating lists of values** Many users do not know that the lists of values that you see inside Discoverer have actually been created by the administrator. It is a misconception that these lists are created by the database—they are not. If you see a data item in a folder and you think that there should a list of values, contact your administrator and request that one be created.
- **Creating alternative sorts** Another way that your administrator can help you is by creating alternative sorts. An example of an alternative sort is sorting the months of the year into the order in which they occur. Month names are text values, and a text list would place 'January' after 'February'. Your Discoverer administrator can create a custom sort placing the months in the order in which they occur. You can even have the months sorted by fiscal year.
- **Creating new items based on calculations** If you have standardized calculations within your company, it makes sense to include these as items in Discoverer. Your administrator can create these custom calculations and add them as items to folders. You can then select these new items, saving you the step of creating the calculation in the query.
- **Creating new conditions** Another simple task for your Discoverer administrator is the creation of conditions. Perhaps you have a large list of part numbers, of which only a certain range of numbers are available for shipment to customers. The remainder could be components or for internal use only. Your Discoverer administrator can create a condition based on the part number, constraining the list to only those that are shippable. You would then be able to select this condition just as you would any item.
- **Creating drill hierarchies** One of the least-used features of Discoverer is the use of hierarchical drilling. This type of drill uses a predefined hierarchy of items, within which you can drill up or down by a click of the mouse. Typical hierarchies used are dates and geographic data, such as ZIP Code

drilling up to State, and State drilling up to Country, and so on. If you can define a drill of this type, your Discoverer administrator can build a hierarchy for you.

- **Modifying an item's type** A little-used function available to your Discoverer administrator is the ability to change an item's data type. If you always need to be able to manipulate a date—for example, as a string—you can ask your administrator to change the item's type.
- **Creating summary data** When reporting from transaction systems, you do not want to be querying from the detail tables if you can help it. This will cause long delays while querying, and can seriously reduce the performance of your OLTP system. Your Discoverer administrator can create summary folders that contain preaggregated data. If these have been created for you, your Discoverer administrator will advise you of the correct setting to make in the summary data section of the Query Governor tab of the Options dialog box. By default, summary administration is transparent to users and probably does not require any action.
- **Rearranging the order of items in a folder** When you are querying from a folder, you may notice that you are always scrolling down the list of items to get the one you want. You can ask your Discoverer administrator to change the ordering of the items within the folder. This has no impact on the system, yet can be a tremendous timesaver.
- **Changing refresh cycles** Many Discoverer systems are based on either a snapshot of the OLTP system, or are based on data warehouses. Both of these types of databases use a refresh mechanism to update. If you believe that the refresh schedule is insufficient, you can ask your Discoverer administrator to change it. Perhaps you would like an extra collection during the lunch period. It is possible that your Discoverer administrator will be able to accommodate you, if your justification is strong. Always remember that it doesn't hurt to ask, your Discoverer administrator can only say no!
- **Allowing scheduling of workbooks** Not all users are granted permission to schedule workbooks. Not all users need to schedule workbooks. If you believe that you should be given permission to schedule, you should bring that to the attention of your Discoverer administrator. You may be asked to

provide justification. The screen that your Discoverer administrator uses to control scheduling is shown here:

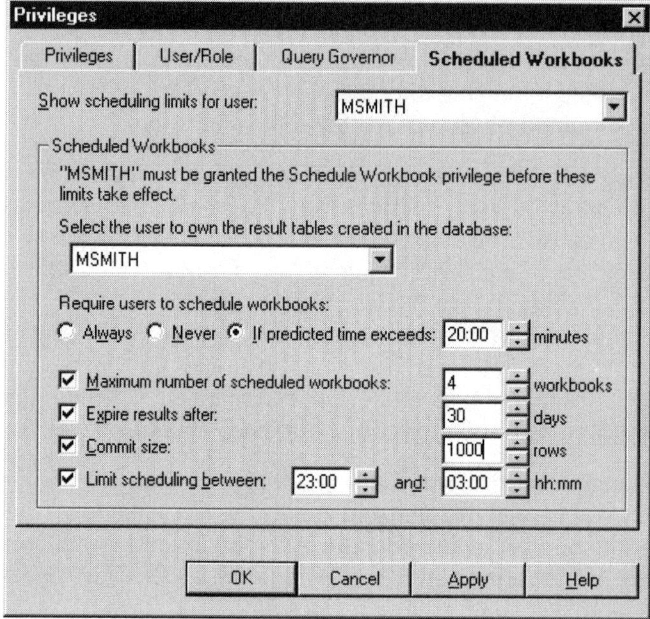

- **Creation of new functions** Discoverer already has a vast array of functions at your disposal. Refer to Appendix A for an alphabetical list of all of the functions. However, there may be times when you need a new function. Your Discoverer administrator has the ability to create new functions and make these available within the system. For those of you who are familiar with SQL, you will notice that not all SQL functions are available in Discoverer. If there is an SQL function that you would like to use, your Discoverer administrator might be able to add it.
- **Another source of help** Your Discoverer administrator is an expert in Discoverer, and you should treat him or her as a resource. If you are stuck with a tricky calculation or cannot define the right conditions, pick up the telephone.

Discoverer 3.1 Directory Structures

There are two important directories that must be set in order for Discoverer 3.1 to work correctly. Your Discoverer administrator is responsible for determining the location of these directories. The two vital directories are as follows:

- **Discoverer's default directory for opening files** On the General tab of the Discoverer 3.1 Options dialog box is a placeholder for entering the default directory for opening files. If this directory is located on a shared drive—such as on a network, on a terminal server, or on a shared PC—your Discoverer administrator will help you determine the correct entry for this placeholder. He or she is also responsible for ensuring that you have the correct read and write access to this directory. If the directory is to be located on your local PC, you should use a folder such as c:\temp.
- **Discoverer's cache directory** On the Cache tab of the Discoverer 3.1 Options dialog box is a placeholder for entering the default directory for disk caching. Unless advised by your Discoverer administrator, you should not change this directory.

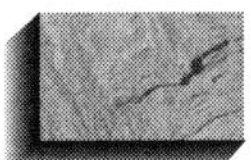

NOTE
If you have many users sharing drives, particularly when using terminal servers, you may want to consider not sharing the same cache drive between all users. The reasoning behind this is that no one can determine exactly when Discoverer will need the disk cache. If two users swap to disk at the same time, it is possible that the caching may get impacted, with the resulting crash of the system.

Terminal Server Directories

This section is only applicable if your company uses terminal servers for accessing Discoverer. When using these shared machines, your network administrator will not take kindly to you saving files all over his or her server. Your Discoverer administrator, therefore, will work with the network administrator to create directories into which you can save workbooks.

If you have been advised to use a certain directory for your files, please use it. It is not just out of courtesy that we say this, although this is certainly a consideration. The biggest concern we have is that your saved workbooks may get deleted if they are stored outside of the agreed area. Having spent a great deal of time making a query work, we are sure that the last thing you want right now is to start all over again!

Summary

In this chapter, you have learned how to use the Options dialog box in both versions of Discoverer. We have shown you the various settings you can select to create defaults to customize Discoverer to meet your needs. Included in these options, you have learned how to create default formats for some of the most common data types. You have been shown how to format tables and crosstabs to present your data better. We have taught you which of these settings to use care in setting and when to contact your Discoverer administrator for assistance.

You have been given a quick reference guide to the Discoverer 3.1 and 3*i* toolbars, with all of the functions. And, finally, you have learned about your Discoverer administrator. You have learned about the privileges you can be granted, and how the Discoverer administrator provides you with them. You have also been taught how you can help the Discoverer administrator to determine the kinds of data and business areas you will need to create your queries and reports. We have shown you how a directory structure is set up in Discoverer, and why it is important to save your workbooks to the correct directory folders.

PART IV

Appendixes

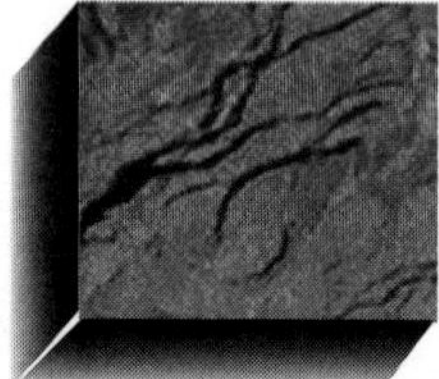

APPENDIX A

Functions

his appendix contains an alphabetic listing of all of the SQL functions available within Discoverer. Each function is listed with its correct syntax, an explanation of its purpose or use, and the Discoverer folder in which you will find the function. For most functions, we will give you examples. We also explain in depth how to use the wildcard characters used within Discoverer.

We are extremely pleased with the way that Oracle has implemented functions in Discoverer. If you know SQL, you will know that it can be very unforgiving—demanding that you get the syntax right. With Discoverer, most of the errors that you could make have been allowed for and will not cause your query to crash. Instead, the worst that can happen is that the function returns a null value.

This appendix is not designed to teach you all about SQL functions, only to explain in simple terms what each function does. If you want a complete understanding of Oracle's functions, we recommend you look at *Oracle8: The Complete Reference,* an Oracle Press book by George Koch and Kevin Loney.

Standards Used in the Listing

Within the listing of the functions, we refer to data types. Functions usually operate on one data type at a time, although some may be able to use more. The following are the data types referred to in this appendix:

- **Character** This data type consists of a single character. Examples of this data type are 'A', 'b', and '1'. Characters are entered into Discoverer surrounded by single quotes, as shown here, and can be in uppercase or lowercase.
- **Date** This data type represents a date, a date and time combination, or a data item that can be used like a date in an expression or calculation. Format masks can be applied to dates. A full listing of the date and time format masks can be found at the end of this appendix.
- **Integer** This data type represents whole numbers. These numbers can be positive or negative. Examples of this data type are –5, 0, and 50.
- **Number** This data type represents numbers with decimal places. These numbers can be positive or negative. Examples of this data type are –5.15, 0, and 47.775. Format masks can be applied to numbers. A full listing of the numeric format masks can be found at the end of this appendix.

- **String** This data type represents combinations of characters and is entered into Discoverer surrounded by single quotes. Strings can use any combination of uppercase and lowercase characters. Examples of strings are 'Hello', 'ZIP 55555' and 'CAP'.

Wildcards

Many of the Discoverer functions will allow you to enter wildcard characters into strings. The wildcard characters used within Discoverer are as follows:

- % The percent symbol is a wildcard character used to represent any number of characters in a string. It can be used in any position and any number of times within the string.
- _ The underscore character is a wildcard character used to represent a single character in a string. It can be used in any position and any number of times within the string.

Wildcard Examples

The following examples show how to use both of the wildcards in strings.

- **'AB%'** This would constrain the string to values beginning with the uppercase characters 'AB'. Valid examples of this are 'AB' and 'ABRACADABRA'.
- **'_b%'** This would constrain the string to values of any length, but where the second character is lowercase 'b'. Valid examples of this are 'Ab' and 'Ebony'.
- **'%m%'** This would constrain the string to values that contain the lowercase character 'm' anywhere within the string. Valid examples of this would be 'mountain' and 'America'.

NOTE
When using the % wildcard character, there do not need to be any characters in the position indicated by the % character. Hence, in the examples above, 'AB' is a valid match for the constraint 'AB%' and 'mountain' is a valid match for '%m%'.

Folders in Discoverer

When you open a calculation in Discoverer and click the Functions radio button, Discoverer displays a list of folders. Depending upon the database that you are using, you will see either seven or eight folders listed. As you can see in Figure A-1, our system has displayed seven. The folder that is missing from our display is called Database, although you will probably see this. This folder is used to store functions that have been created for you by your Discoverer administrator.

Alphabetical Listing of Functions

This section lists all of Discoverer's functions in alphabetical order.

+ (Addition)

Syntax: value1 + value2
Description: value1 + value2 means add together the two values to produce a new value of the same type. This function can be used with data types of date, integer, and number, and generally you can mix the data types, although you cannot add numbers to dates.

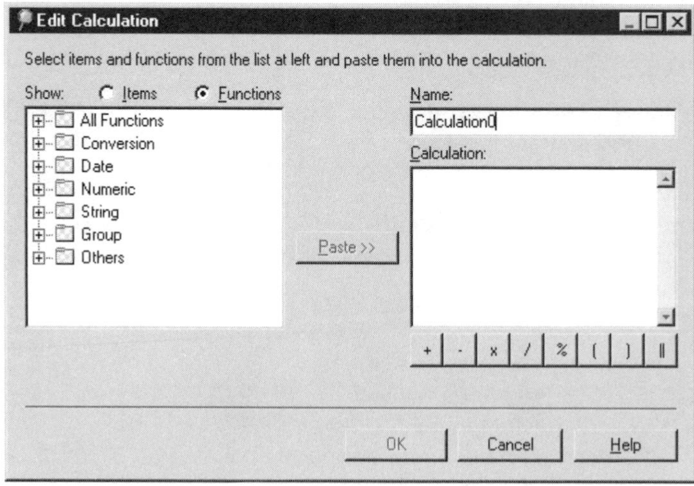

FIGURE A-1. *The folders containing functions*

Folder: Addition can be found in the Numeric folder, as seen in Figure A-2.
Examples:

- **Date** SYSDATE + 1 returns tomorrow's date.
- **Integer** 177 + 192 + 6 returns the answer 375.
- **Number** 10.55 + 8.00 returns the answer 18.55.
- **Mixed** 177 + 10.55 returns the number 187.55.

Notice how multiple additions can be applied at the same time. In the second example, we added three integers to get the answer we were looking for. Generally, you can mix the data types, although you cannot add numbers to dates.

– (Subtraction)

Syntax: value1 – value2
Description: value1 – value2 means subtract the second value from the first value to produce a new value. This function can be only used with data types of date, integer, and number.
Folder: Subtraction can be found in the Numeric folder, as seen in Figure A-2.
Examples:

- **Date** SYSDATE – 1 returns yesterday's date.
- **Integer** 200 – 192 – 8 returns the answer 0.
- **Number** 10.55 – 8.00 returns the answer 1.45.
- **Mixed** 200 – 10.55 returns the number 189.45.

Notice how multiple subtractions can be applied at the same time. In the second example, we subtracted three integers to get the answer we were looking for. Generally, you can mix the data types, although you cannot subtract numbers from dates.

* (Multiplication)

Syntax: value1 * value2
Description: value1 * value2 means multiply the first value by the second value to produce a new value. This function can be only used with data types of integer and number.
Folder: Multiplication can be found in the Numeric folder, as seen in Figure A-2.

/ (Division)

Syntax: value1 / value2
Description: value1 / value2 means divide the first value by the second value to produce a new value. This function can be only used with data types of integer and number. You need to be very careful when using division that you do not finish up dividing by zero; otherwise, Discoverer will return an error. See Chapter 12 for tips on how to avoid division by zero errors.
Folder: Division can be found in the Numeric folder, as seen in Figure A-2.

|| (Concatenation)

Syntax: value1 || value2
Description: value1 || value2 means append or concatenate the character or string with the value of value2 to the end of the character or string in value1. The result is always a string. This function is identical to the CONCAT function described later.
Folder: Concatenation can be found in the String folder (see Figure A-4 later in this appendix).
Examples:

- **Character** 'A' || 'B' returns the string 'AB'.
- **String** 'Apple' || 'Pie' returns 'Apple Pie'.

ABS (Absolute Value)

Syntax: ABS(value)
Description: This function returns the absolute value of the item in parentheses, as a positive number, whether the original item is positive or negative. The item must be a number, whether this be a literal number, a string containing only numbers, the name of a column containing a number, or the name of a string column containing only numbers.
Folder: ABS can be found in the Numeric folder as seen in Figure A-2.
Examples:

- ABS(-55) returns the value 55.
- ABS('18') returns the value 18.
- ABS(968.51) returns the value 968.51.

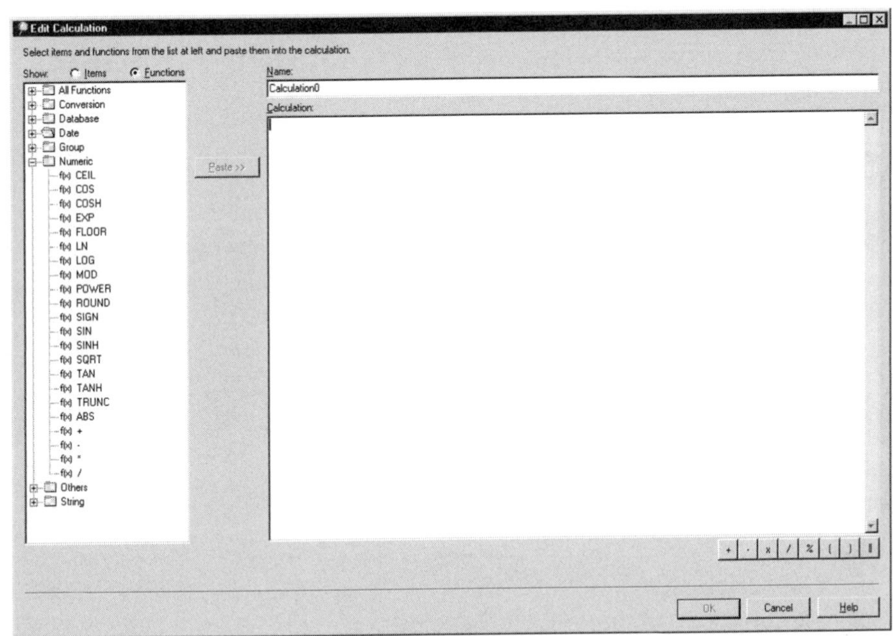

FIGURE A-2. *Discoverer's numeric functions*

ADD_MONTHS

Syntax: ADD_MONTHS(date, integer)
Description: This function adds the integer number of months to the date specified, returning a new date that is that number of months in the future. The date specified must be a valid date. If the date you want to check is not currently a valid date, you must convert it into a valid date first. The second parameter should be an integer. If you provide a negative value, the date returned will be in the past. If you provide a number with decimal places, Discoverer ignores the decimal part. If the date you provide is the null value, then the result will be null.
Folder: ADD_MONTHS can be found in the Date folder (see Figure A-3 later in this appendix).
Examples:

- ADD_MONTHS(SYSDATE, 1) returns the date one month from today.
- ADD_MONTHS(ship date, 2) returns the ship date plus 2 months.

- ADD_MONTHS(TO_DATE('20-JUL-00'),2 returns the date given as a string, plus 2 months, as a new date. You cannot supply a string directly to ADD_MONTHS because the date supplied *must* be a valid date in its own right.

ASCII

Syntax: ASCII(string)
Description: This function takes a string and returns the ASCII (American Standard Code for Information Interchange) value of the first character. The code is based on a series of numbers from 0 to 254, with 65 representing the character 'A', 66 representing 'B', and so on. The numbers 0 through 9 are represented by the ASCII values 48 through 57.

See the function CHR for the opposite function that converts a number to a character.
Folder: ASCII can be found in the String folder (see Figure A-4 later in this appendix).
Examples:

- ASCII('APPLE') returns the value 65.
- ASCII('BANANA') returns the value 66.
- ASCII('-15') returns the value 45, because the minus sign is number 45 in the ASCII list.

AVG (Average)

Syntax: AVG(value)
Description: This function returns the average. The value parameter can be any value, database item, or calculation. As Discoverer has this function available within the Workbook Wizard Step 2, we will not describe this function any further. Please note that null values are ignored by this function, which may affect your results.
Folder: AVG can be found in the Group folder (see Figure A-5 later in this appendix).

AVG_DISTINCT

Syntax: AVG_DISTINCT(value)
Description: This function returns the distinct average of all the unique items in the list. Please note that null values are ignored by this function, which may affect your results.
Folder: AVG_DISTINCT can be found in the Group folder as seen in Figure A-5.

Example:

- **AVG_DISTINCT(list)** When the list contains "null, 1, 1, 3, 5, 5, 5, 5, 7, 7, 7", the answer is 4. This is because Discoverer computes the average of the values 1, 3, 5, and 7. If we had used AVG on this same list, the answer would have been 4.6. Which one is correct depends upon your viewpoint and how you want to display the result.

CHARTOROWID

Syntax: CHARTOROWID(string)
Description: This function takes a string and makes it act like an internal Oracle row identifier. According to the information that we have gathered together, this function should never be needed. It apparently is used as a debugging tool, yet somehow has made its way into Discoverer. Your Discoverer administrator will be the one who uses this.
Folder: CHARTOROWID can be found in the Conversion folder (see Figure A-6 later in this appendix).

CEIL

Syntax: CEIL(value)
Description: This function takes the value given and returns the smallest integer larger than or equal to that value. Refer to FLOOR for the function that returns the highest integer. You cannot use the null value in this function. If you use the null value the result will be an error.
Folder: CEIL can be found in the Number folder, as seen in Figure A-2.
Examples:

- CEIL(7) returns the value 7.
- CEIL(-6.75) returns the value –6.
- CEIL(100.55) returns the value 101.

CHR

Syntax: CHR(integer)
Description: This function takes an integer and returns the ASCII (American Standard Code for Information Interchange) character that corresponds to the integer. The code is based on a series of numbers from 0 to 254, with 65

representing the character 'A', 66 representing 'B', and so on. The numbers 0 through 9 are represented by the ASCII values 48 through 57.

See the function ASCII for the opposite function that converts a character into a number.

Folder: CHR can be found in the String folder, as seen in Figure A-4.

Examples:

- CHR(45) returns the character that is the minus sign.
- CHR(65) returns the character 'A'.
- CHR(66) returns the character 'B'.

CONCAT

Syntax: CONCAT(value1, value2)

Description: CONCAT(value1, value2) means append or concatenate the character or string with the value of value2 to the end of the character or string in value1. The result is always a string. This function is identical to the | | function described earlier.

Folder: CONCAT can be found in the String folder, as seen in Figure A-4.

Examples:

- **Character** CONCAT('A', 'B') returns the string 'AB'.
- **String** CONCAT('Apple ', 'Pie') returns 'Apple Pie'.

CONVERT

Syntax: CONVERT(string, destination_set [, source_set]])

Description: This function takes a string and converts all the characters from one standard bit representation, or set, to another set. You would normally do this when the characters cannot be properly displayed on your screen or printed. To find out what character set is currently in use on your system, use the USERENV function.

Folder: CONVERT can be found in the Conversion folder, as seen in Figure A-6.

Example sets:

- **F7DEX** Digital's 7-bit ASCII for France
- **US7ASCII** The standard 7-bit ASCII set
- **WE8DEC** Digital's 8-bit ASCII set for Western Europe
- **WE8HP** Hewlett Packard's 8-bit ASCII set for Western Europe

- **WE8ISO8859P1** International Standards Organization's 8859-1 8-bit character set for Western Europe

COS (Cosine)

Syntax: COS(value)
Description: This function takes the value given and returns the trigonometric cosine of that value. The function returns an angle expressed in radians.
Folder: COS can be found in the Numeric folder, as seen in Figure A-2.
Examples:

- COS(-60) returns the value 0.5
- COS(0) returns the value 1.0
- COS(180) returns the value –1.0

COSH (Hyperbolic Cosine)

Syntax: COSH(value)
Description: This function returns the hyperbolic cosine of the given value. The function returns an angle expressed in radians.

For those of you who are mathematically oriented, the hyperbolic cosine is defined as $\cosh(x) = (e^{x} + e^{-x})/2$.
Folder: COSH can be found in the Numeric folder, as seen in Figure A-2.
Examples:

- COSH(0) returns the value 1.0.
- COSH(0.3) returns the value 1.04534.
- COSH(0.9) returns the value 1.43309.

COUNT

Syntax: COUNT(expression)
Description: This function returns a count of the number of non-null items in the given expression.
Folder: COUNT can be found in the Group folder, as seen in Figure A-5.

COUNT_DISTINCT

Syntax: COUNT_DISTINCT(expression)

Description: This function returns a count of the number of non-null, unique items in the given expression. Please note that null values are ignored by this function, which may affect your results.
Folder: COUNT_DISTINCT can be found in the Group folder, as seen in Figure A-5.
Example:

- **COUNT_DISTINCT(list)** When the list contains "null, 1, 1, 3 ,5, 5, 5, 5, 7, 7, 7", the answer is 4. This is because Discoverer only counts the items 1, 3, 5, and 7. If we had used COUNT on this same list, the answer would have been 10. Which one is correct depends upon your viewpoint and how you want to display the result.

DECODE

Syntax: DECODE(value, x, y, z) where this equates to the following:

IF value = x THEN y ELSE z

Description: This function is, in our opinion, the most powerful and useful of all of Discoverer's functions. Mastery of this function lies at the heart of unlocking the true power of Discoverer.

As stated in the syntax, the basic structure of this function is:

IF value = x (where value can be any expression, algorithm, data value, or literal)
THEN y
ELSE z – the default value

The DECODE statement can, and frequently does, check multiple values, culminating eventually with an ELSE, the default expression to be used when all else fails. You can also embed DECODE statements inside one another, which when mixed with other functions, makes for very powerful algorithms. If no default expression is specified, the result of DECODE will be the null value.

When using the DECODE statement, you might think that you always have to find a value that equates to equality. However, this is not the case, and Discoverer can be made to work with values greater than, equal to, and less than. To do this though, you will have to create special calculations using the SIGN function. The final example shows this construct.
Folder: DECODE can be found in the Others folder (see Figure A-4 later in this appendix).

Examples:

- **DECODE(requested date, SYSDATE, 'Y', 'N')** In this example, if the requested date equals the current date, then the function returns the value 'Y'; otherwise, the value 'N' is returned. This algorithm can be used to work out which orders are due for shipment.
- **DECODE(code value, 123, 'Classic', 456, 'Old Style', 'New Style')** In this example, if the code value is 123 the function returns the value 'Classic', but if the code value is 456 the function returns the value 'Old Style'. If code value is neither 123 nor 456, the function returns the value 'New Style'.
- **DECODE(customer, 'ABC', DECODE(SUM(owed), 0, 5000, 5000 – (SUM(owed) / 2)), 10000)** This more complicated example calculates customer credit limits. If the customer is 'ABC' and the total amount owed is zero, then the credit limit is set to 5000. However, if the total amount owed by 'ABC' is not zero, then we set their credit limit to be 5000 minus half the amount owed. Finally, for all other customers, the credit limit is set to 10000.
- **DECODE(SIGN(SUM(owed) / 15000), -1, 20000, 20000 – SUM(owed))** This is a clever combination of the SIGN and DECODE functions. Because SIGN returns a value of –1 for all numbers less than 1, if the amount owed by the customer is less than 15000, we will allow them to have a credit limit of 20000; otherwise, the credit limit is reduced by the amount owed.

DUMP

Syntax: DUMP(string [, format [, start [, number_to_dump]]])
Description: This function takes a string and displays it in a new format. The function optionally takes a start position and length. If these are provided, Discoverer dumps the string from the start position for the number of characters specified. The format can be 8 for octal, 10 for decimal, 16 for hex, and 17 for character.
Folder: DUMP can be found in the Others folder, as seen in Figure A-7.
Example:

- DUMP('michael', 16) returns 'Type=96 Len=7: 6d,69,63,68,61,65,6c' where each character of the string was dumped into hex.

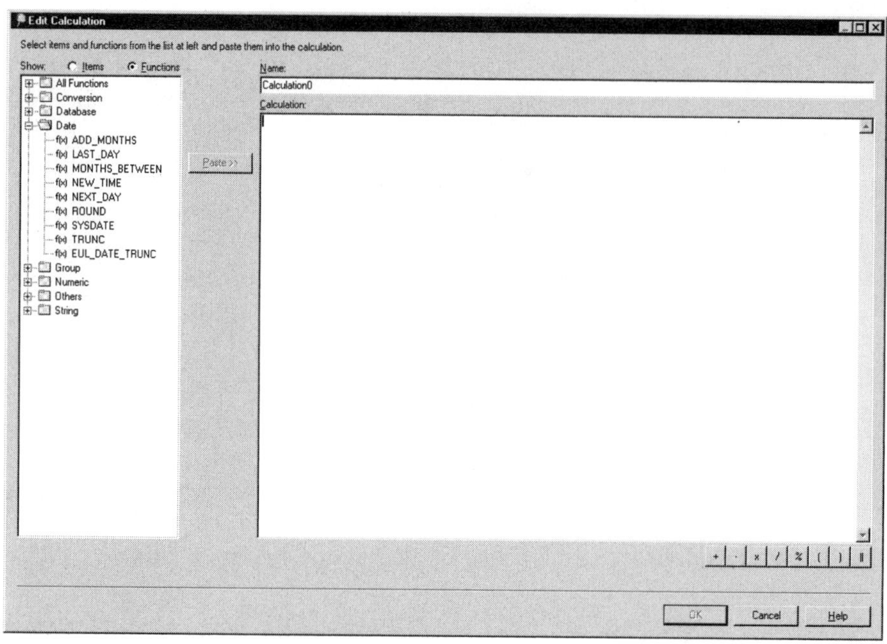

FIGURE A-3. *Discoverer's date functions*

EUL_DATE_TRUNC

Syntax: EUL_DATE_TRUNC(date, format)

Description: This function takes a date and a format mask and truncates the date based on the format mask. The date specified must be a valid date. If the date you want to check is not currently a valid date, you must convert it into a valid date first.

Folder: EUL_DATE_TRUNC can be found in the Date folder, as seen in Figure A-3.

Examples: In the following examples, suppose that the current date is 22-JUL-00.

- EUL_DATE_TRUNC(SYSDATE,'YY') returns '01-JAN-00'. Because we only specified the year within our format, Discoverer truncated the current date to the earliest date of the year.
- EUL_DATE_TRUNC(SYSDATE, 'MM') returns '01-JUL-00'. Because we specified just the month within our format, Discoverer truncated the current date to the earliest date of the current month.

- EUL_DATE_TRUNC(SYSDATE, 'DD') returns '22-JAN-00'. Because we specified just the day within our format, Discoverer truncated the current date to the earliest day of the year equal to the current day.

EXP (Exponential)

Syntax: EXP(*n*)
Description: This function returns *e* to the *n*th power, where *e* is the universal constant 2.718281828. It goes on forever repeating the numbers 1828, but for Discoverer usage, the number given here will suffice.

The opposite of EXP(*x*) is the natural logarithm LN(*x*), so that if you compute the exponential of the natural logarithm LN(*x*), you get *x* back. This works either way, as seen in the examples below.
Folder: EXP can be found in the Numeric folder, as seen in Figure A-2.
Examples:

- EXP(1) returns the universal constant, 2.718281828.
- EXP(4) returns the value 54.589150—that is, 2.718281828 to the power 4.
- EXP(LN(8)) returns the number 8.

FLOOR

Syntax: FLOOR(value)
Description: This function takes the value given and returns the highest integer smaller than or equal to that value. Refer to CEIL for the function that returns the largest integer.
Folder: FLOOR can be found in the Numeric folder, as seen in Figure A-2.
Examples:

- CEIL(7) returns the value 7.
- CEIL(-6.75) returns the value –7.
- CEIL(100.55) returns the value 100.

GLB

Syntax: GLB(label)
Description: This function is an operating system function and would not normally be used within Discoverer. It returns the greatest lower bound of a secure operating system label.
Folder: GLB can be found in the Group folder, as seen in Figure A-5.

GREATEST

Syntax: GREATEST(value1, value2, ...)
Description: This function returns the value that is the greatest of the given list of values. If one of the arguments in the list is the null value, the result will be null. You can use all of the data types with this function, although some unexpected results may occur if you are not careful. The number 27 is obviously greater than the number 7, but the string '7' is greater than the string '27'. The date 14-OCT-2000 is greater than 23-JUN-2000, but the string '23-JUN-2000' is greater than the string '14-OCT-2000'. Strings are compared using their ASCII number. You therefore must be careful when comparing strings. If you want to compare dates that are stored as strings, you must use the TO_DATE function. If you want to compare numbers that are stored as strings, you must use the TO_NUMBER function.
Folder: GREATEST can be found in the Others folder, as seen in Figure A-7.
Examples:

- GREATEST(9, 18, 5, 60) returns the value 60.
- GREATEST('23-JUN-00','14-OCT-00') returns the string '23-JUN-00'.
- GREATEST(TO_DATE('23-JUN-00'), TO_DATE('14-OCT-00')) returns the date 14-OCT-00.
- GREATEST(TO_NUMBER('2'), TO_NUMBER('14')) returns the number 14.

GREATEST_LB

Syntax: GREATEST_LB(label1 [label2] ...)
Description: This function is another of those operating system functions that would not normally be used within Discoverer. It returns the greatest lower bound of a list operating system labels.
Folder: GREATEST_LB can be found in the Others folder, as seen in Figure A-7.

HEXTORAW

Syntax: HEXTORAW(hex_string)
Description: This function changes a character string of hex numbers into binary.
Folder: HEXTORAW can be found in the Conversion folder, as seen in Figure A-6.

INITCAP

Syntax: INITCAP(string)

Description: This function takes a string and returns a new string with the first letter of each word capitalized. The function also recognizes the presence of punctuation, and uppercases the first letter following any punctuation. The punctuation symbols include the comma, period, colon, semicolon, hyphen, and so on.
Folder: INITCAP can be found in the String folder, as seen in Figure A-4.
Examples:

- INITCAP('armstrong-smith') returns 'Armstrong-Smith'.
- INITCAP('the cat is on the mat') returns 'The Cat Is On The Mat'.

INSTR

Syntax: INSTR(string1, string2 [, start [, n]])
Description: This function takes a string and finds the position of a second string in that string. The function will optionally begin the search at a given start position and return the position of the nth set. If you omit the start position, Discoverer will search from the beginning. If you use a negative number for the start, Discoverer begins the search at the end of the string and searches backwards. If you use zero for the start position, the answer will be zero.
Folder: INSTR can be found in the String folder, as seen in Figure A-4.
Examples:

- INSTR('San Francisco', 'an') returns 2.
- INSTR('San Francisco', 'an', 1, 2) returns 7.
- INSTR('San Francisco', 'an', -1, 2) returns 2.

INSTRB

Syntax: INSTRB(string, set [, start [, occurrence]])
Description: This function, like INSTR, takes a string and locates the position of a set of characters in that string. However, INSTRB locates the string you are looking for at the byte position. Within Discoverer, we recommend you use INSTR instead of this function.
Folder: INSTRB can be found in the String folder, as seen in Figure A-4.

LAST_DAY

Syntax: LAST_DAY(date)
Description: This function returns the date that is the last day of the month for a given date. The date specified must be a valid date. If the date you want to check

is not currently a valid date, you must convert it into a valid date first. If you supply a null date, then the result will also be null.
Folder: LAST_DAY can be found in the Date folder, as seen in Figure A-3.
Examples:

- LAST_DAY(TO_DATE('16-OCT-00')) returns 31-OCT-00.
- LAST_DAY(ship date) returns the last day of the month in which the item shipped.
- LAST_DAY(TO_DATE('')) returns null.

LEAST

Syntax: LEAST(value1, value2, ...)
Description: This function returns the value that is the least of the given list of values. If one of the arguments in the list is the null value, the result will be null. You can use all of the data types with this function, although some unexpected results may occur if you are not careful. The number 7 is obviously less than the number 27, but the string '7' is greater than the string '27'. The date 23-JUN-00 is prior to 14-OCT-00, but the string '23-JUN-00' is greater than the string '14-OCT-00'. Strings are compared using their ASCII number. You therefore must be careful when comparing strings. If you want to compare dates that are stored as strings, you must use the TO_DATE function. If you want to compare numbers that are stored as strings, you must use the TO_NUMBER function.
Folder: LEAST can be found in the Others folder, as seen in Figure A-7.
Examples:

- LEAST(9, 18, 5, 60) returns the value 5.
- LEAST('23-JUN-00','14-OCT-00') returns the string '14-OCT-00'.
- LEAST(TO_DATE('23-JUN-00'), TO_DATE('14-OCT-00')) returns the date 23-JUN-00.
- LEAST(TO_NUMBER('2'), TO_NUMBER('14')) returns the number 2.

LEAST_UB

Syntax: LEAST_UB(label1 [label2] ...)

Description: This function is another of those operating system functions that would not normally be used within Discoverer. It returns the least upper bound of a list of operating system labels.
Folder: LEAST_UB can be found in the Others folder, as seen in Figure A-7.

LENGTH

Syntax: LENGTH(string)
Description: This function returns the length of a string, number, date, or expression.
Folder: LENGTH can be found in the String folder, as seen in Figure A-4.

LENGTHB

Syntax: LENGTHB(string)
Description: This function takes a string and returns the length as a number of bytes, as opposed to a number of characters. Within Discoverer, we recommend you use LENGTH instead of this function.
Folder: LENGTHB can be found in the String folder, as seen in Figure A-4.

LN (Logarithm)

Syntax: LN(number)
Description: This function returns the natural, or base *e*, logarithm of a number, where *e* is the universal constant (see EXP for an explanation of *e*). If the number specified is the null value, the result will be null. The number or expression you provide must be positive; otherwise, you will encounter an error.

The opposite of LN(*x*) is EXP(*x*), so that if you compute the natural logarithm of EXP(*x*), you get *x* back. This works either way, as seen in the examples below.
Folder: LN can be found in the Numeric folder, as seen in Figure A-2.
Examples:

- LN(1) returns the value 0.
- LN(8) returns the value 2.079.
- LN(EXP(8)) returns the number 8.
- *x* / LN(*x*-1) returns the approximate number of prime numbers not exceeding the value *x*. This is included just for fun and is something you can experiment with yourself to show the usage of LN.

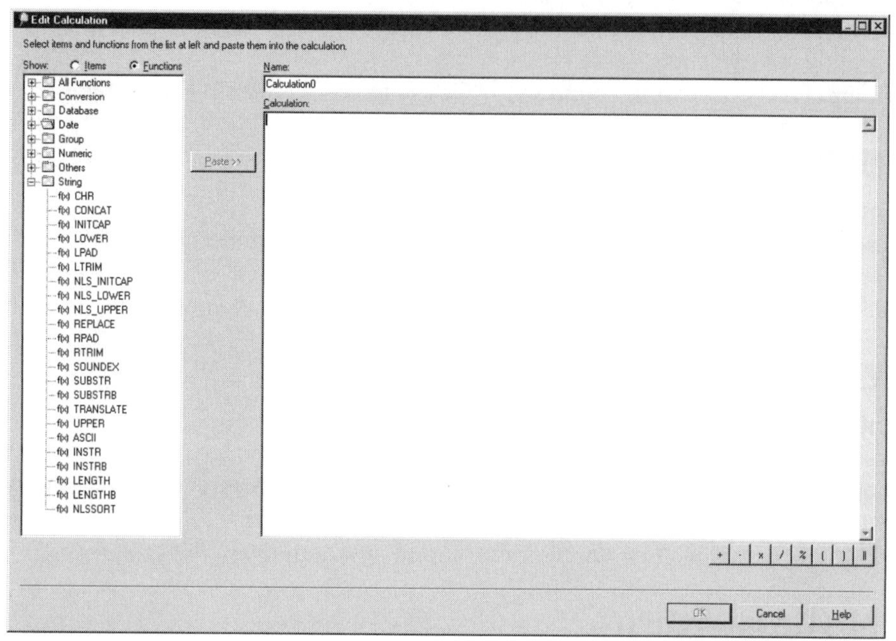

FIGURE A-4. *Discoverer's string functions*

LOG

Syntax: LOG(base, number)

Description: This function returns the power to which a number, called the base, must be raised in order to obtain a given positive number. Common logarithms use 10 as the base. Naperian (named after John Napier, the Scottish inventor of logarithms and, incidentally, the decimal point) logarithms use the number *e* (the universal constant) as the base.

Folder: LOG can be found in the Numeric folder, as seen in Figure A-2.

Examples:

- LOG(10,10) returns the number 1.
- LOG(10, 100) returns the number 2.
- LOG(EXP(1), 3) returns 1.0986, because $e^{1.0986}$ is 3. See the section on EXP for more details on the universal constant *e*.

LOWER

Syntax: LOWER(string)
Description: This function takes a string and returns a new string with every letter in lowercase.
Folder: LOWER can be found in the String folder, as seen in Figure A-4.
Example: LOWER('Armstrong-Smith') returns the string 'armstrong-smith'.

LPAD (Left Pad)

Syntax: LPAD(string, number [, characters])
Description: This function takes a string, a number, and optionally a set of characters, and pads the string to the length specified by the number. If the current length of the string is less than the number specified, Discoverer inserts as many sets of characters into the beginning of the string as it can, until the length is as required. If the current length of the string is greater than the number specified, Discoverer truncates the string, returning a new string with only that number of characters remaining—counting from the left. When padding, if no character set is specified, Discoverer pads out the string with spaces. If either the specified string or the character set is the null value, or the number is not positive, the overall result will be the null value. If the number specified is a decimal, Discoverer ignores the decimal portion, acting on the number before the decimal point.
Folder: LPAD can be found in the String folder, as seen in Figure A-4.
Examples:

- LPAD('Armstrong', 5) returns 'Armst', containing only the first five characters.
- LPAD('Smith', 15, 'Darlene') returns 'DarleneDarSmith'.
- LPAD('',5,'M') returns a null string because the initial string is empty.

LTRIM (Left Trim)

Syntax: LTRIM(string [, characters])
Description: This function takes a string, and optionally a set of characters, and returns a new string with all occurrences of those characters removed from the beginning of the original string. If no characters are specified, Discoverer removes all leading spaces. If either the specified string or the set of characters is the null value, the result will be the null value.
Folder: LTRIM can be found in the String folder, as seen in Figure A-4.

Examples:

- LTRIM('   Armstrong') returns 'Armstrong' with all leading spaces removed.
- LTRIM('Armstrong-Smith', 'Armstrong-') returns 'Smith'.
- LTRIM('', 'Jones') returns null.

LUB

Syntax: LUB(label)
Description: This function is another of those operating system functions that would not normally be used within Discoverer. It returns the least upper bound of an operating system label.
Folder: LUB can be found in the Group folder, as seen in Figure A-5.

MAX (Maximum)

Syntax: MAX(argument)
Description: From the argument, column, or set of values specified, this function returns the item that has the largest value. MAX ignores null values.
Folder: MAX can be found in the Group folder, as seen in the Figure A-5.
Example: MAX(ship date) returns the most recent ship date held on the system.

MAX_DISTINCT

Syntax: MAX_DISTINCT(argument)
Description: From the argument, column, or set of values specified, this function returns the item that has the largest value. MAX ignores null values. This function is identical to the MAX function.
Folder: MAX_DISTINCT can be found in the Group folder, as seen in the Figure A-5.

MIN (Minimum)

Syntax: MIN(argument)
Description: From the argument, column, or set of values specified, this function returns the item that has the lowest value. MIN ignores null values.
Folder: MIN can be found in the Group folder, as seen in the Figure A-5.
Example: MIN(ship date) returns the oldest ship date held on the system.

MIN_DISTINCT

Syntax: MIN_DISTINCT(argument)

Description: From the argument, column, or set of values specified, this function returns the item that has the lowest value. MIN_DISTINCT ignores null values. This function is identical to the MIN function.
Folder: MIN_DISTINCT can be found in the Group folder, as seen in the Figure A-5.

MOD

Syntax: MOD(value, divisor)
Description: This function divides the given value by the divisor, and returns the remainder. Both the value and the divisor can be any real number. If the divisor is zero, Discoverer returns the original value in the result.
Folder: MOD can be found in the Numeric folder, as seen in the Figure A-2.
Examples:

- MOD(7, 8) returns 7.
- MOD(8, 7) returns 1.
- MOD(-8,7) returns –1.
- MOD(8,0) returns 0.

MONTHS_BETWEEN

Syntax: MONTHS_BETWEEN(first_date, second_date)
Description: This function returns the number of months between the first_date and the second_date. Both dates specified must be valid dates. If either date you want to check is not currently a valid date, you must convert it into a valid date. If the first_date precedes the second_date, the result will be negative. In most databases, the result of this function will be a number with decimal places; however, if you are using Oracle Lite, the result will be an integer. If you want to compare a date prior to 01-JAN-2000 with a date after this, you must give the complete four-digit year.
Folder: MONTHS_BETWEEN can be found in the Date folder, as seen in Figure A-3.
Examples:

- MONTHS_BETWEEN(TO_DATE('01-DEC-1999'), TO_DATE('26-MAY-2000)) returns the value 5.80645.
- MONTHS_BETWEEN(TO_DATE('01-DEC-99'), TO_DATE('26-MAY-00)) returns the value –1194.19355.

NEW_TIME

Syntax: NEW_TIME(date, this_zone, destination_zone)
Description: This function returns the date and time for the destination_zone based on the specified date and time in this_zone. This is a very useful and clever function, and can be used to work out the current time in different parts of the world. Both this_zone and destination_zone must be supplied as three-letter abbreviations. A list of the valid time zones used within Discoverer can be found at the end of this appendix.

By the clever use of the TO_CHAR function, and knowing how many hours ahead or behind you are to other countries, you can work out the time anywhere in the world. To calculate the time in China, for example, we know that China is 15 hours ahead of California. Therefore, we need to add 15/24 to the current time.
Folder: NEW_TIME can be found in the Date folder, as seen in the Figure A-3.
Examples: In the following examples, suppose that the current time zone is PST (Pacific Standard Time).

- NEW_TIME(SYSDATE, 'PST', 'GMT') returns the date in London.
- TO_CHAR(NEW_TIME(SYSDATE, 'PST', 'GMT'),'HH24:MI') returns the time, based on the 24-hour clock, in London.
- TO_CHAR(NEW_TIME(SYSDATE + (15 / 24), 'PST', 'PST'),'DD-MON-YY HH24:MI') returns the date and time in China.

If you are in a part of the world that does not have a supported time zone, do not despair. The solution is very simple. You calculate the time difference between your offices, insert that instead of the word "diff" in the function below, then run the function. Make sure both of the quoted time zones are the same. We inserted 'GMT', but this works with all supported zones.

- TO_CHAR(NEW_TIME(SYSDATE + (diff / 24), 'GMT', 'GMT'),'DD-MON-YY HH24:MI') returns the date and time of your office.

NEXT_DAY

Syntax: NEXT_DAY(date, string)
Description: This function returns the date of the first weekday, named by string, which is later than the date given. The string must contain at least the first three letters of a day of the week.
Folder: NEXT_DAY can be found in the Date folder, as seen in Figure A-3.

Examples:

- NEXT_DAY(SYSDATE, 'Wednesday') returns the date for next Wednesday.
- NEXT_DAY(ship_date, 'FRI') returns the date for the Friday following the ship date.

NLS_INITCAP

Syntax: NLS_INITCAP(string [, nls_parameters])
Description: This function is identical to INITCAP, except that it takes an optional NLS (National Language Support) string of parameters. If provided, this string must take the form 'NLS_SORT = option' where option is a linguistic sort sequence. These sequences should be used whenever your Oracle database is not based on the English language. These rules are required in order for Discoverer to work out exactly how to initialize the given string.
Folder: NLS_INITCAP can be found in the String folder, as seen in Figure A-4.
Example: NLS_INITCAP('ijsland', 'NLS_SORT = Xdutch') returns 'IJsland'.

NLS_LOWER

Syntax: NLS_LOWER(string [, nls_parameters])
Description: This function is identical to LOWER, except that it takes an optional NLS (National Language Support) string of parameters. For an explanation of NLS, see the function NLS_INITCAP.
Folder: NLS_LOWER can be found in the String folder, as seen in Figure A-4.

NLS_UPPER

Syntax: NLS_UPPER(string [, nls_parameters])
Description: This function is identical to UPPER, except that it takes an optional NLS (National Language Support) string of parameters. For an explanation of NLS, see the function NLS_INITCAP.
Folder: NLS_UPPER can be found in the String folder, as seen in Figure A-4.

NLSSORT

Syntax: NLSSORT(string [, nls_parameters])
Description: This function gives the string of bytes used to sort a string.
Folder: NLSSORT can be found in the String folder, as seen in Figure A-4.

Examples:

- NLSSORT('DARLENE', 'NLS_SORT = Xdutch') returns the code 2314644B28552800010101010101.
- NLSSORT('mike','NLS_SORT = Xswiss) returns the code 503C46280002020202.

NVL

Syntax: NVL(expr1, expr2)
Description: If the first expression is null, Discoverer returns the second expression. If the first expression is not null, Discoverer returns that expression.
Folder: NVL can be found in the Others folder, as seen in figure A-7.
Examples:

- NVL(code, 'Y') returns the code if it is not null, otherwise the value 'Y'.
- NVL(ship quantity, 0) returns the ship quantity if there is one; otherwise, it returns zero.

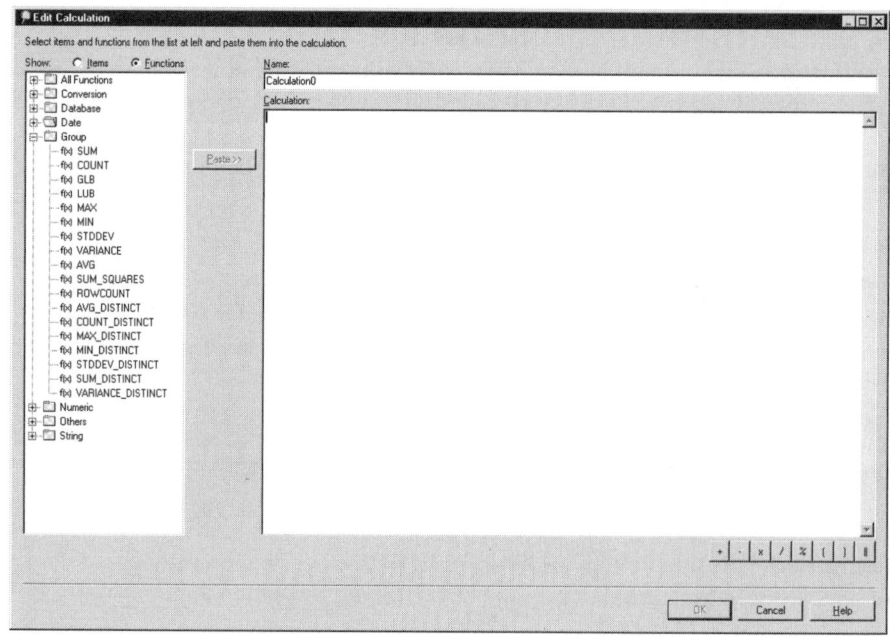

FIGURE A-5. *Discoverer's group functions*

POWER

Syntax: POWER(base number, *n*)
Description: This function raises the base number given to the nth power. The base and the exponent can be any numbers; however, if the base number is negative, the exponent must be an integer. A negative exponent means divide the answer into 1.
Folder: POWER can be found in the Numeric folder, as seen in Figure A-2.
Examples:

- POWER(2.5, 2) returns 6.25, which is 2.5 squared.
- POWER(2.5, -2) returns 0.16, which is 1 divided by 6.25.
- POWER(-3,-3) returns –0.37037037 and so on, which is 1 divided by –27.

RAWTOHEX

Syntax: RAWTOHEX(raw)
Description: This function takes a raw string of decimal numbers and converts it into a string of hexadecimal numbers.
Folder: RAWTOHEX can be found in the Conversion folder, as seen in Figure A-6.

REPLACE

Syntax: REPLACE(string, search_string [, replace_string])
Description: This function takes a string and returns a new string that has had every occurrence of the search_string replaced with the replace_string. If the replace_string is omitted or it is null, all occurrences of the search_string are removed. If the search_string is null, the original string is returned.
Folder: REPLACE can be found in the String folder, as seen in Figure A-4.
Examples:

- REPLACE('JACK and 'JUE', J', 'BL') returns 'BLACK and BLUE'.
- REPLACE('The Cat is at the Mat', 'at') returns 'The C is the M'.
- REPLACE('GEORGE', 'GE') returns 'OR'.

ROUND (for Dates)

Syntax: ROUND(date, format)
Description: This function rounds a date according to the format specified. When no format is specified, the date is rounded to noon tomorrow if the time is later than midday, or to noon today if the time is before midday. In either case, the resulting

time is set to noon. For a full list of the formats allowed, see the section at the end of this appendix.
Folder: ROUND can be found in the Date folder, as seen in Figure A-3.
Examples: All examples for this function can be found at the end of this appendix.

ROUND (for Numbers)

Syntax: ROUND(number, places)
Description: This function rounds a number to the number of decimal places specified. If the number of places is omitted, Discoverer rounds to zero decimal places. If a negative value is supplied for the number of places, Discoverer rounds the digits to the left of the decimal point. If any decimals are supplied in the number of places, these are ignored. This function is not the same as TRUNC. We have used the same examples in both functions to show you the difference.
Folder: ROUND can be found in the Numeric folder, as seen in Figure A-2.
Examples:

- ROUND(578.666, 2) returns 578.67.
- ROUND(578.666, 0) returns 579.00.
- ROUND(578.667, -1) returns 580.00.
- ROUND(578.667, -2) returns 600.00.

ROWCOUNT

Syntax: ROWCOUNT
Description: This function returns the total number of rows returned by the query. This total includes duplicates and null values.
Folder: ROWCOUNT can be found in the Group folder, as seen in Figure A-5.

ROWIDTOCHAR

Syntax: ROWIDTOCHAR(rowid)
Description: This function takes an internal row identifier, or rowid, and converts it into a string. According to the information that we have gathered together, this function should never be needed. It apparently is used as a debugging tool, yet somehow has made its way into Discoverer. Your Discoverer administrator will be the one who uses this. There does not seem to be a great use for this function in normal queries, and we advise you not to use it.

Folder: ROWIDTOCHAR can be found in the Conversion folder, as seen in Figure A-6.

ROWNUM

Syntax: ROWNUM
Description: This function returns a number indicating the order in which the row was selected by the query. The number is assigned before any sorting is done and gives you the true order in which the row was selected.
Folder: ROWNUM can be found in the Others folder, as seen in Figure A-7.

RPAD (Right Pad)

Syntax: RPAD(string, number [, character])
Description: This function takes a string, a number, and optionally a character, and appends the character defined as the third parameter as often as is needed to give the string the length specified in the second parameter. If no character set is specified, Discoverer pads out the string with spaces. If the specified string is the null value, the result will be the null value. If the specified number or character, if supplied, is the null value, Discoverer will report an error. If the length of the original string is already equal to or bigger than the number specified, Discoverer returns the original string.
Folder: RPAD can be found in the String folder, as seen in Figure A-4.
Examples:

- RPAD('Armstrong', 14) returns a new string 'Armstrong   ', now with a length of 14, with five space characters having been appended to the end.
- RPAD('Jones', 7, '-') returns 'Jones—'.

RTRIM (Right Trim)

Syntax: RTRIM(string [, characters])
Description: This function takes a string, and optionally a set of characters, and returns a new string with all occurrences of those characters removed from the end of the original string. If no second string is specified, Discoverer removes all trailing spaces. If either the specified string or the set of characters is the null value, the result will be the null value.
Folder: RTRIM can be found in the String folder, as seen in Figure A-4.

Examples:

- RTRIM('Armstrong   ') returns 'Armstrong' with all trailing spaces removed.
- RTRIM('Armstrong-Smith', '-Smith') returns 'Armstrong'.
- RTRIM('Michael','') returns the null value because the character set is null.

SIGN

Syntax: SIGN(numeric expression)
Description: This function returns three possible vales; -1, 0 and 1. These values are assigned depending upon whether the numeric expression evaluates to less than zero (-1), zero (0), or greater than zero (1). Using SIGN in conjunction with DECODE produces very effective if, then type expressions.
Folder: SIGN can be found in the Numeric folder, as seen in Figure A-2.
Examples:

- SIGN(133) returns 1.
- SIGN(-15) returns –1.
- SIGN(0) returns 0.

SIN

Syntax: SIN(value)
Description: This function takes the value given and returns the sine of that angle. The function returns a result expressed in radians.
Folder: SIN can be found in the Numeric folder, as seen in Figure A-2.
Examples:

- SIN(30) returns a value of 0.5.
- SIN(90) returns a value of 1.

SINH (Hyperbolic Sine)

Syntax: SINH(value)
Description: This function takes the value given and returns the hyperbolic sine of that value. The function returns an angle expressed in radians.
Folder: SINH can be found in the Numeric folder, as seen in Figure A-2.

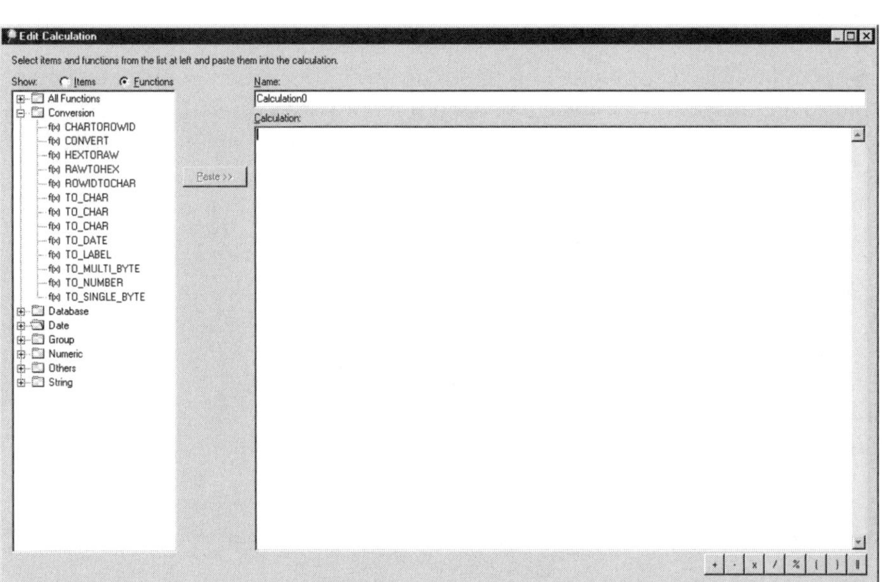

FIGURE A-6. *Discoverer's conversion functions*

SOUNDEX

Syntax: SOUNDEX(string)

Description: This function takes a string and returns the soundex code for that string. The function finds words that sound like an example. Using SOUNDEX in calculations and conditions can help you find words that sound like each other—perhaps similar sounding customer names, for example.

Folder: SOUNDEX can be found in the String folder, as seen in Figure A-4.

Examples:

- SOUNDEX('m') returns the value M000.
- SOUNDEX('michael') returns the value M240.

SQRT

Syntax: SQRT(number)

Description: This function takes a number and returns the square root of that number. You must take care to ensure that the number does not evaluate to a negative number; otherwise, Discoverer will return an error. The square roots of negative numbers are imaginary numbers and cannot be displayed in Discoverer.
Folder: SQRT can be found in the Numeric folder, as seen in Figure A-2.
Examples:

- SQRT(169) returns the value 13.
- SQRT(-7) returns the error #NUM.

STDDEV (Standard Deviation)

Syntax: STDDEV(value)
Description: This function gives the standard deviation from the norm of values in a group of rows. The function is applied to the set of values derived from the argument values by the elimination of null values.
Folder: STDDEV can be found in the Group folder, as seen in Figure A-5.

STDDEV_DISTINCT (Distinct Standard Deviation)

Syntax: STDDEV_DEVIATION(value)
Description: This function gives the standard deviation from the norm of values in a distinct group of rows. The function is applied to the set of values derived from the argument values by the elimination of null values and duplicates.
Folder: STDDEV_DEVIATION can be found in the Group folder, as seen in Figure A-5.

SUBSTR

Syntax: SUBSTR(string, start [' count])
Description: This function takes a string and returns a portion of that string, beginning at the start position, making the portion count characters long. If you omit the count or provide a count that is bigger than the length of the original string, Discoverer returns a new string with the start number of characters removed. If you provide a start number that is bigger than the length of the original string, the result will be an empty string.
Folder: SUBSTR can be found in the String folder, as seen in Figure A-4.

Examples:

- SUBSTR('Michael', 5) returns 'ael', with the first 5 characters of 'Michael' removed.
- SUBSTR('Michael', 2, 3) returns 'ich'.

SUBSTRB

Syntax: SUBSTRB(string, start [' count])
Description: This function takes a string and returns a substring of that string, beginning at the start byte position and going on for count number bytes.
Folder: SUBSTRB can be found in the String folder, as seen in Figure A-4.

SUM

Syntax: SUM(values)
Description: This function returns the sum of all the values in the expression or row.
Folder: SUM can be found in the Group folder, as seen in Figure A-5.
Example: SUM(ship quantity) returns the total quantity shipped.

SUM_DISTINCT

Syntax: SUM_DISTINCT(values)
Description: This function is similar to the SUM function, except that it returns the sum of all the unique values in the expression or row.
Folder: SUM_DISTINCT can be found in the Group folder, as seen in Figure A-5.

SUM_SQUARES

Syntax: SUM_SQUARES(number)
Description: This function returns the total of the square of the number given. If you select this function and then edit the calculation, you will notice that Discoverer changes the function to SUM(POWER(number, 2)).
Folder: SUM_SQUARES can be found in the Group folder, as seen in Figure A-5.
Example: SUM_SQUARES(3) returns 9, and Discoverer writes this as SUM(POWER(3,2)).

SYSDATE

Syntax: SYSDATE
Description: This function returns the current date and time. You can use this date inside many other functions, because it acts exactly like a DATE data type.
Folder: SYSDATE can be found in the Date folder, as seen in Figure A-3.

TAN (Tangent)

Syntax: TAN(value)
Description: This function takes the value given and returns the trigonometric tangent of that value. The function returns an angle expressed in radians.
Folder: TAN can be found in the Numeric folder, as seen in Figure A-2.
Examples:

- TAN(-60) returns a value of –1.73205.
- TAN(0) returns a value of 0.
- TAN(30) returns a value of 0.577350.

TANH (Hyperbolic Tangent)

Syntax: TANH(value)
Description: This function takes the value given and returns the hyperbolic tangent of that value. The function returns an angle expressed in radians.

For those of you who are mathematically oriented, the hyperbolic tangent is defined as

$$\tan(x) = (e^x - e^{-x}) / (e^x + e^{-x})$$

Folder: TANH can be found in the Numeric folder, as seen in Figure A-2.
Examples:

- TANH(0) returns a value of 0.
- TANH(0.3) returns a value of 0.291313.
- TANH(0.5) returns a value of 0.462117.

TO_CHAR (Dates)

Syntax: TO_CHAR(date, format [,nls_parameters])
Description: This function converts a date into a string by applying the specified format. The date provided must be a valid date. The function also takes an optional NLS (National Language Support) string of parameters. For an explanation of NLS, see the function NLS_INITCAP. For a list of all of the date format masks, please refer to the end of this appendix.
Folder: TO_CHAR can be found in the Conversion folder, as seen in Figure A-6.

Examples: In the examples below, suppose the current date is 23-JUL-00 at 3:52 P.M.

- TO_CHAR(SYSDATE, 'fmDay, Month DD, YYYY HH:MI:AM') returns 'Sunday, July 23, 2000 3:51 PM'.
- TO_CHAR(SYSDATE, 'MM/DD/YY') returns '07/23/00'.
- TO_CHAR(TO_DATE('20-JUL-00'), 'Month-YYYY') returns the string 'July-2000'. You cannot supply a string directly to TO_CHAR because the date supplied *must* be a valid date in its own right.

TO_CHAR (Labels)

Syntax: TO_CHAR(label, format [,nls_parameters])
Description: This function converts a label into a string by applying the specified format. The function also takes an optional NLS (National Language Support) string of parameters. For an explanation of NLS, see the function NLS_INITCAP. This function is for use by administrators only.
Folder: TO_CHAR can be found in the Conversion folder, as seen in Figure A-6.

TO_CHAR (Numbers)

Syntax: TO_CHAR(number, [format [,nls_parameters]])
Description: This function converts a number into a string by applying the specified optional format. The function also takes an optional NLS (National Language Support) string of parameters. For an explanation of NLS, see the function NLS_INITCAP. For a list of all of the number format masks, please refer to the end of this appendix.
Folder: TO_CHAR can be found in the Conversion folder, as seen in Figure A-6.
Examples:

- TO_CHAR(678) returns the string '678'.
- TO_CHAR(678.7,'999D99') returns the string '678.70'.
- TO_CHAR(678, 'RN') returns the string 'DCLXXVIII'—that is, 678 in roman numerals.

TO_DATE

Syntax: TO_DATE(string, format)
Description: This function converts a string in the given format into a standard Oracle date. Only if the string is already in the standard Oracle format of

'DD-MON-YY' can the format option be omitted. For a full listing of the valid format options, please see the section dealing with date format masks at the end of this appendix.
Folder: TO_DATE can be found in the Conversion folder, as seen in Figure A-6.
Examples:

- TO_DATE('14/10/58', 'DD/MM/YY') returns the Oracle date 14-OCT-58.
- TO_DATE('09-09-51', 'MM-DD-YY') returns the Oracle date 09-SEP-51.

TO_LABEL

Syntax: TO_LABEL(string, format)
Description: This function converts a string into a label using the label format supplied. This function is for use by administrators only.
Folder: TO_LABEL can be found in the Conversion folder, as seen in Figure A-6.

TO_MULTI_BYTE

Syntax: TO_MULTI_BYTE(string)
Description: This function converts each of the single-byte characters in the string into their multibyte equivalents. If the character has no multibyte equivalent, the function leaves the character unchanged.
Folder: TO_MULTI_BYTE can be found in the Conversion folder, as seen in Figure A-6.

TO_NUMBER

Syntax: TO_NUMBER(string, format [,nls_parameters])
Description: This function converts a string into a number by applying the specified optional format. The function also takes an optional NLS (National Language Support) string of parameters. For an explanation of NLS, see the function NLS_INITCAP. For a list of all of the number format masks, please refer to the end of this appendix. Discoverer is very good at converting strings into numbers, and we recommend you avoid supplying a format mask.
Folder: TO_NUMBER can be found in the Conversion folder, as seen in Figure A-6.
Examples:

- See the functions GREATEST and LEAST.
- TO_NUMBER('765.43') returns the number 765.43.

- TO_NUMBER(order_number) will convert the database field called order_number into a number. Care should be taken when doing this that all of the strings being converted are indeed numbers.
- TO_NUMBER('0.5555','990D9999') returns 0.56, 0.556 or 0.5555, depending upon the format you have applied to the column.

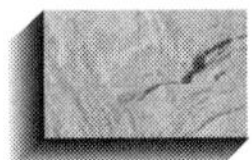

NOTE
Be careful when specifying the optional format mask. If you supply a mask, you must ensure that the mask corresponds exactly to the number within the string. Supplying an incorrect format mask causes Discoverer to error out with an ORA-01722 error. The following function will fail: TO_NUMBER('0.5555','990D99') returns an error because the format mask being applied does not match the actual number of decimal places in the string.

TO_SINGLE_BYTE

Syntax: TO_SINGLE_BYTE(string)
Description: This function converts each of the multibyte characters in the string into their single-byte equivalents. If the character has no single-byte equivalent, the function leaves the character unchanged.
Folder: TO_SINGLE_BYTE can be found in the Conversion folder, as seen in Figure A-6.

TRANSLATE

Syntax: TRANSLATE(string, search, replace)
Description: This function takes the string and looks at each character in the string. It then looks to see if any of the characters in the search string are in the original string. If any of the search characters are there, Discoverer replaces them with the character in the replace string that is in the same position as the character in the search string.
Folder: TRANSLATE can be found in the String folder, as seen in Figure A-4.
Example:

- TRANSLATE('MICHAEL SMITH', 'AEI', '123') returns 'M3CH12L SM3TH'. As you can see, Discoverer has replaced each occurrence of 'A' with a '1', each 'E' with a '2', and each 'I' with a '3'.

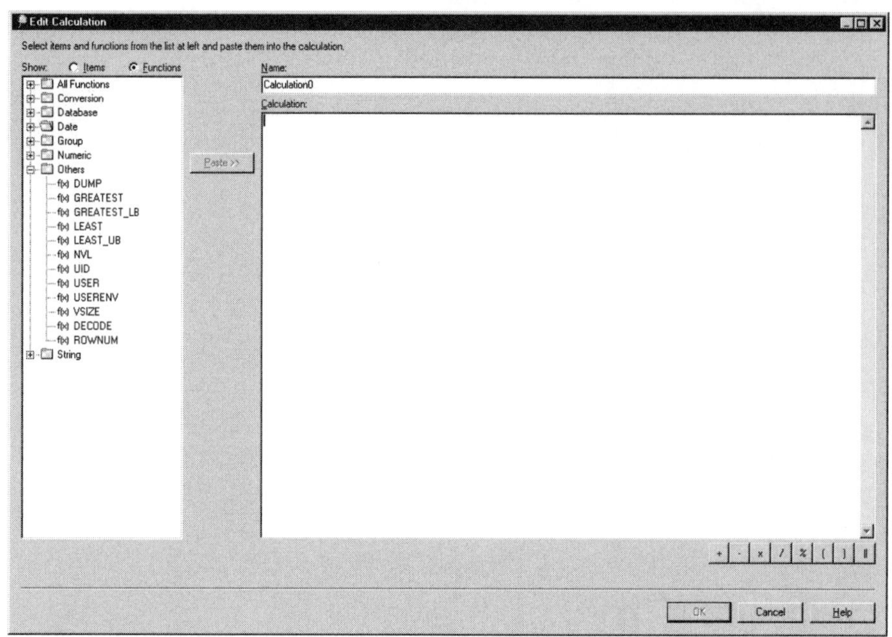

FIGURE A-7. *Discoverer's other functions*

TRUNC (Dates)

Syntax: TRUNC(date, format)
Description: This function takes a date and truncates the time component from it, leaving just the date. Refer to the section entitled "Using Formats when Rounding Dates" later in this appendix.
Folder: TRUNC can be found in the Date folder, as seen in Figure A-3.
Examples:

- TRUNC(SYSDATE) returns the current date minus the time.
- TRUNC(ship date) returns the ship date minus the time. If you have shipped many items in the same day, truncating the date allows you to group all of the items together.

TRUNC (Numbers)

Syntax: TRUNC(number, precision)

Description: This function truncates a number according to the precision specified. If the precision is omitted, or is zero, Discoverer truncates all of the decimal places. If a negative value is supplied for the precision, Discoverer truncates (makes zero) that number of digits to the left of the decimal point. If any decimals are supplied in the precision, these are ignored. This function is not the same as ROUND. We have used the same examples in both functions to show you the difference.
Folder: TRUNC can be found in the Numeric folder, as seen in Figure A-2.
Examples:

- TRUNC(578.666, 2) returns 578.66.
- ROUND(578.666, 0) returns 578.00.
- ROUND(578.667, -1) returns 570.00.
- ROUND(578.667, -2) returns 500.00.

UID

Syntax: UID
Description: This function returns the user ID of the current user as assigned by Oracle. The number is unique on the current database.
Folder: UID can be found in the Others folder, as seen in Figure A-7.

UPPER

Syntax: UPPER(string)
Description: This function uppercases every character in the string.
Folder: UPPER can be found in the String folder, as seen in Figure A-4.
Example: UPPER('Darlene') returns 'DARLENE'.

USER

Syntax: USER
Description: This function returns the user name by which the user is known to the system.
Folder: USER can be found in the Others folder, as seen in Figure A-7.

USERENV

Syntax: USERENV (option)
Description: This function returns information in a string about the current user session. The valid options are 'ENTRYID', 'LANGUAGE', 'SESSIONID', and 'TERMINAL'.

Folder: USERENV can be found in the Others folder, as seen in Figure A-7.
Examples:

- USERENV(TERMINAL) returns the terminal ID you are connected to. If you are using a terminal server, this returns the server name.
- USERENV(LANGUAGE) returns the language and territory currently used by your session along with the database character set in use. In our system, this function returned AMERICAN_AMERICA WE8ISO8859P1. This tells me that the language I am using is American, the territory I am in is America, and the character set I am using is the ISO 8859-1 Western European 8-bit character set.

VARIANCE

Syntax: VARIANCE(number)
Description: This function returns the variance for all values, except null values, of a group of rows. The variance is the authorized deviation.
Folder: VARIANCE can be found in the Group folder, as seen in Figure A-5.

VARIANCE_DISTINCT

Syntax: VARIANCE_DISTINCT(number)
Description: This function returns the variance for all unique values, except null values, of a group of rows. The variance is the authorized deviation.
Folder: VARIANCE_DISTINCT can be found in the Group folder, as seen in Figure A-5.

VSIZE

Syntax: VSIZE(value)
Description: This function tells you how much storage space is being taken up by the item concerned. For strings, the size is the same as the length of the string. For numbers, it is usually smaller because less space is needed to store numbers.
Folder: VSIZE can be found in the Others folder, as seen in Figure A-7.
Examples:

- VSIZE('Michael') returns 7.
- VSIZE(16.8765) returns 4.

Time Zones

The following is a list of the valid time zones that can be used within the Discoverer NEW_TIME date function:

- **'AST', 'ADT'** Atlantic standard or daylight savings time
- **BST', 'BDT'** Bering standard or daylight savings time
- **'CST', 'CDT'** Central standard or daylight savings time
- **'EST', 'EDT'** Eastern standard or daylight savings time
- **'GMT'** Greenwich mean time
- **'HST',' HDT'** Alaska-Hawaii standard or daylight savings time
- **'MST', 'MDT'** Mountain standard or daylight savings time
- **'NST'** Newfoundland standard time
- **'PST', 'PDT'** Pacific standard or daylight savings time
- **'YST', 'YDT'** Yukon standard or daylight savings time

Using Formats when Rounding Dates

When using the ROUND function on a date, the following is a list of formats available, along with an example of each. All of the examples given assume that the current date is 23-JUL-2000, and that the time is 12:35:40 A.M.

- CC, SCC rounds to the first January 1st of the century. It rounds at midnight on the morning of January 1st of 1950, 2050, and so on.
- ROUND(SYSDATE, 'CC') rounds to noon on 01-JAN-2000.
- SYEAR, SYYY, Y, YY, YYY, YYYY, YEAR rounds to January 1st of the year. It rounds at midnight on the morning of July 1st.
- ROUND(SYSDATE, 'YEAR') rounds to noon on 01-JAN-2001.
- Q rounds to the first day of a quarter. Based on quarters beginning January, April, July, and October, it rounds on the 16th day of the second month of the quarter, regardless of how many days there are in the month.
- ROUND(SYSDATE, 'Q') rounds to noon on 01-JUL-2000.

- MONTH, MON, MM rounds to the first date of a month. It rounds on the 16th day of the month, regardless of how many days there are in that month.
- ROUND(SYSDATE, 'MONTH') rounds to noon on 01-AUG-2000.
- WW rounds to the nearest date that has the same day of the week as the beginning of the year.
- ROUND(SYSDATE, 'WW') rounds to noon on 22-JUL-2000.
- W rounds to the nearest date that has the same day of the week as the beginning of the current month.
- ROUND(SYSDATE, 'W') rounds to noon on 22-JUL-2000.
- DDD, DD, J rounds to the next day. This is the same as applying ROUND with no format.
- ROUND(SYSDATE, 'DD') rounds to noon on 23-JUL-2000.
- DAY, DY, D rounds to the following Sunday, the first day of the week. It rounds at noon on Wednesday.
- ROUND(SYSDATE, 'D') rounds to noon on 23-JUL-2000.
- HH, HH12, HH24 rounds to the next whole hour. It rounds at 30 minutes and 30 seconds past the hour.
- ROUND(SYSDATE, 'HH') rounds to 01:00 A.M. on 23-JUL-2000.
- MI Rounds to the next whole minute. It rounds at 30 seconds past the minute.
- ROUND(SYSDATE, 'MI') rounds to 12:36 A.M. on 23-JUL-2000.

Date Format Masks

The following sections contain a full list of the format masks that can be used within the TO_CHAR and TO_DATE functions in Discoverer, along with an example value based on Sunday, July 23, 2000.

Day Format Masks

Mask	Description	Example
D	Number of the day of the week	1
DD	Number of the day of the month	23
DDD	Number of the day in the year, since January 1st	205
DY	Three-letter uppercase abbreviation of the day	SUN
Dy	Three-letter INITCAP abbreviation of the day	Sun
dy	Three-letter lowercase abbreviation of the day	sun
DAY	The uppercase full name of the day	SUNDAY
Day	The INITCAP full name of the day	Sunday
day	The lowercase full name of the day	sunday

Month Format Masks

Mask	Description	Example
MMM	Number of the month	7
RM	Roman numeral for the month	VII
MON	Three-letter uppercase abbreviation of the month	JUL
Mon	Three-letter INITCAP abbreviation of the month	Jul
mon	Three-letter lowercase abbreviation of the month	jul
MONTH	The uppercase full name of the month	JULY
Month	The INITCAP full name of the month	July
month	The lowercase full name of the month	july

Year Format Masks

Mask	Description	Example
Y	Last digit of the year	0
YY	Last two digits of the year	00
YYY	Last three digits of the year	000
YYYY	Full four-digit year	2000
SYYYY	A signed year if the year is BC, for example 255 BC	-255
I	Last digit of the ISO (International Standards Organization) year	0
IY	Last two digits of the ISO year	00
IYY	Last three digits of the ISO year	000
IYYY	Full four-digit ISO year	2000
YEAR	Uppercase year spelled out in full	TWO THOUSAND
Year	The INITCAP year spelled out on full	Two Thousand
year	Lowercase year spelled out in full	two thousand
RR	Last two digits of the year, possibly in another century	00

Other Date Masks

Mask	Description	Example
Q	Number of the current quarter of the year	3
WW	Number of the week in the year	30
W	Number of the week in the month	4
IW	Week of the year, based on the ISO standard	29
J	Number of "Julian" days since December 31, 4713 B.C.	2451749
AD or BC	Displays AD or BC without periods	AD

Mask	Description	Example
ad or bc	Displays AD or BC in lowercase without periods	ad
A.D. or B.C.	Displays AD or BC with periods	A.D.
a.d. or b.c.	Displays AD or BC in lowercase with periods	a.d.
CC	Displays the current century	20
SCC	Displays the current century and prefixes BC dates with '-'	20

Time Format Masks

In this section, suppose the current time is 7:02:22 P.M. This is how Discoverer can format that time:

Mask	Description	Example
HH or hh	The hour of the day with leading zeros	07
HH12 or hh12	The hour of the day with leading zeros	07
HH24	The hour of the day in the 24-hour clock	18
MI or mi	The number of minutes in the hour	02
SS or ss	The number of seconds in the minute	22
SSSSS	The number of seconds since midnight	68542

Special Format Masks

Discoverer allows you to insert special punctuation characters into the TO_CHAR function so that the result is easy to understand. Within the TO_DATE function, you can use the same punctuation to inform Discoverer of the characters that are to be ignored.

Mask	Description	Example
/	Inserts or ignores a forward slash character	23/07/2000
,	Inserts or ignores a comma	23, July, 2000
-	Inserts or ignores a hyphen	23-JUL-00
:	Inserts or ignores a colon	7:02:22
.	Inserts or ignores a period	19.02.22

Prefixes and Suffixes

Within the TO_CHAR function only, Discoverer allows you to add prefixes and suffixes to some of the standard format masks. These prefixes and suffixes further enhance the functionality of the function. The prefixes and suffixes allowed are as follows:

- **fm** This can be prefixed to both Day and Month, such that the format mask looks like fmDay or fmMonth. Using this mask forces Discoverer to suppress padding of the month or day. Without this prefix, the days of the week and months of the year are padded to make them all display as the same length.
- **TH or th** This can be suffixed to dd and DD to force Discoverer to display the date as 23rd or 23RD. The capitalization is applied based on whether you choose dd or DD.
- **SP or sp** This can be suffixed to most date numbers, and forces Discoverer to spell out the number in full. Using this suffix, you can spell out the date—thus, twenty third. Again, the capitalization is applied based on the case of the number to be spelled in full.
- **SPTH or THSP** This suffix is a combination of SP and TH. Using this suffix, you can force Discoverer to apply both of the above two masks.

Number Format Masks

The following is a full list of the format masks that can be used within the TO_CHAR function when working with numbers in Discoverer:

- **9999990** The number of nines or zeroes determines the maximum number of digits that can be displayed.
- **999,999,999.99** Discoverer inserts commas and the decimal point at the places specified in the pattern. If the value is zero, the result will be blank.
- **999990** This causes Discoverer to display zero if the value is zero.
- **099999** This causes Discoverer to display numbers with leading zeros, such that 678 will display as 000678.
- **$99999** This causes Discoverer to insert the dollar symbol in front of every number.

- **B99999** This causes Discoverer to display a blank field when the value is zero.
- **99999MI** For negative numbers, this causes Discoverer to place the minus sign to the right of the number. Normally, Discoverer places the minus sign to the left.
- **99999S** Same as 99999MI above.
- **S99999** For negative numbers, this causes Discoverer to place the minus sign to the left of the number.
- **99D99** This causes Discoverer to insert a decimal point in the position specified.
- **C99999** This causes Discoverer to display the ISO currency character in this position, such that 678 will display as USD678.
- **L99999** This causes Discoverer to display the local currency character in this position, such that if your local currency is the US dollar, 678 will display as $678.
- **RN** This causes Discoverer to display the number in Roman numerals.
- **99999PR** For negative numbers, this causes Discoverer to display the number surrounded by the < and > symbols.
- **9.999EEEE** This causes Discoverer to display the number in scientific notation.
- **999V99** This causes Discoverer to multiply by 10 × *n*, where *n* is the number of digits to the right of the V character. For example, 9753 displays as 975300.

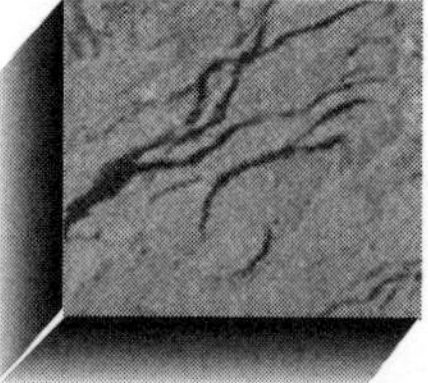

APPENDIX B

Databases and Views

his appendix explains several database concepts. We begin by explaining the difference between traditional schemas, relational schemas, and star schemas. Following this is an in-depth look at database views. We explain why views are used and introduce you to Oracle's Business Views and then Aris Software's Noetix Views.

Database Schemas

There are two basic schemas or types of database structures that you will encounter when working with Discoverer. These are as follows:

- Relational schemas
- Star schemas

Relational Schemas

A relational schema is the traditional type of structure that is used by most databases today. These schemas depend on parent-child relationships, with primary keys and foreign keys. There is also no redundancy in the tables. These schemas are not designed for reporting and can become very complex.

For example, on a typical database of this type, there will be a table of addresses, a table of cities, a table of ZIP codes, and a table of countries, with each one appearing in the database once. Therefore, to print an address, you would have to open up four Discoverer folders.

Using a classroom setting as an example, the following illustration shows a typical relational schema.

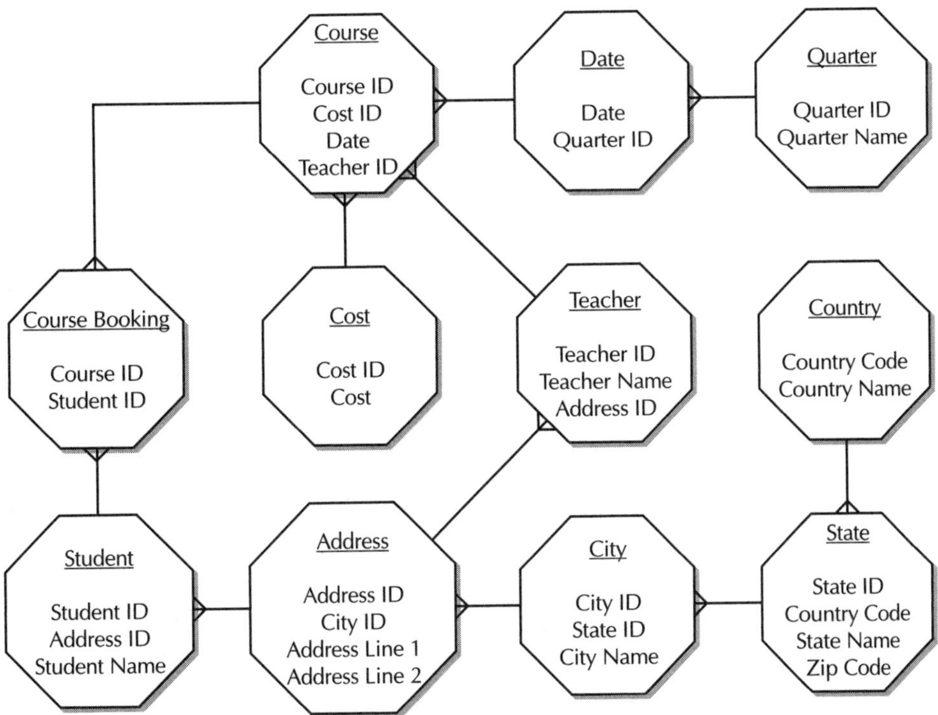

As you can see in the preceding illustration, we have eleven tables. Each table has a unique numeric ID or code. In order to find all of the students who graduated in a particular quarter and then mail them their certificates, you would need to join nine tables together.

Star Schemas

A star schema is traditionally used in a data warehouse. There is no attempt to reduce redundant data, copying data as many times as is needed. In a star schema, you normally have a central fact table, surrounded by many dimension tables. The fact table contains nothing except a foreign key for each of the dimension tables, and facts such as costs, quantities, and so on. Using a star schema with Discoverer, if you select an item from the fact table, all of the other tables are available. If you begin selecting from a dimension table, your next selection must come from the fact table.

Using the same classroom setting from our previous example, the following illustration shows the database as a star schema.

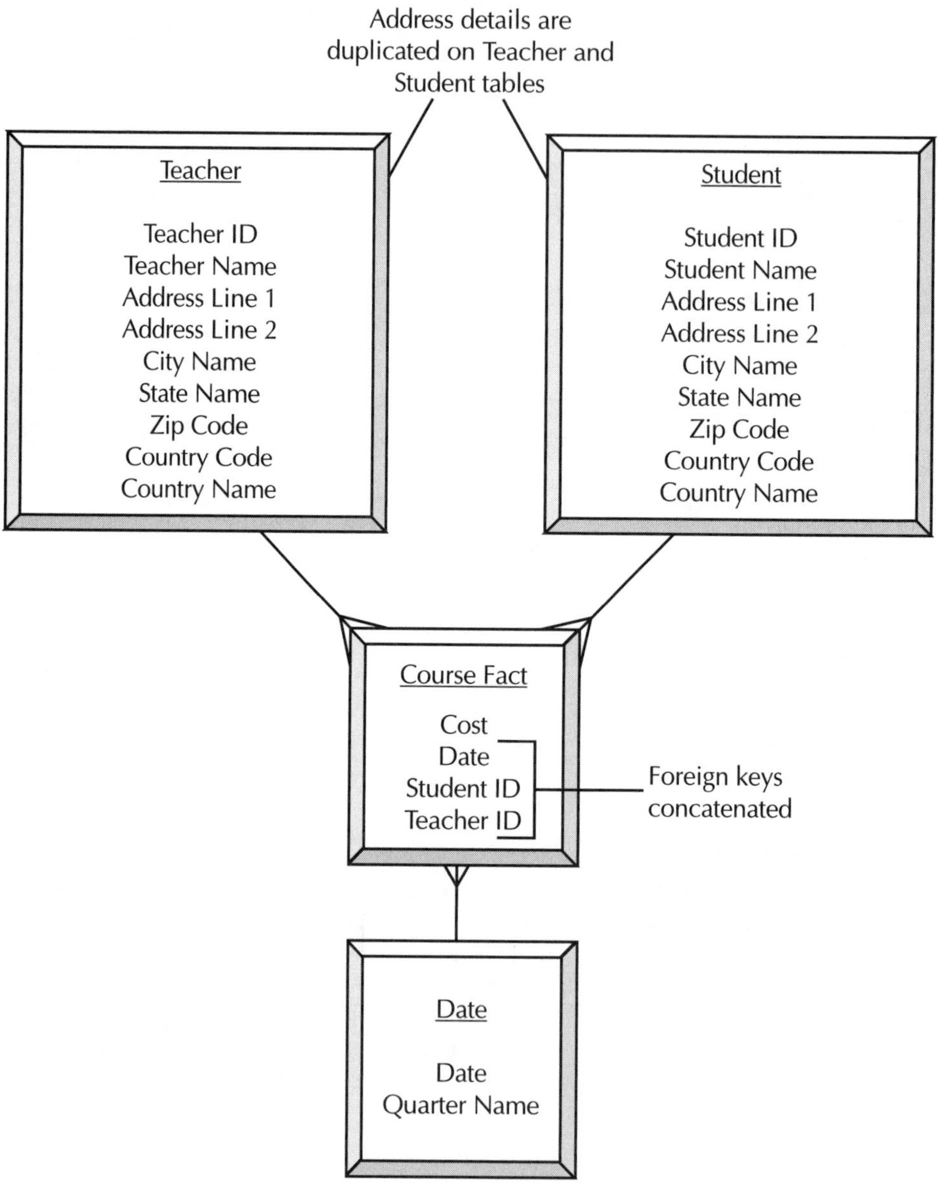

This schema differs from the relational schema as follows:

- The course table has been dropped and has been replaced by a fact table. This fact table contains the foreign-key ID of each of the dimension tables.
- The cost table has been dropped, with the cost of the course added to the fact table.
- The ID of the fact table is made up by concatenating all of the foreign keys together.
- All of the address information is now stored in the Student and Teacher tables.
- All of the time information is in the Date table.

Accessing Oracle Applications Using Discoverer

Oracle Applications provides world-class functionality through transactional power and the ability to support complex business processes. The data stored within its tables is a valuable information asset. Using Discoverer, this data can be leveraged to provide information used across the entire spectrum of decision making. This section deals with and explains various mechanisms for how your company could use Discoverer to access Oracle Applications.

Trying to query from a standard Oracle database can be daunting. In order to enjoy the benefit, you have to know the database structures, the field names, and how the tables are joined together. Added to this is the fact that Oracle has made its applications flexible. By flexible, we mean that they have provided flexfields, fields that you can use to customize your database. The use of these fields causes Oracle Applications to dynamically change the screens that you use for order entry. This is perfect for your data entry staff, but just how do you query these fields? You don't know which flexfield is being used, and you certainly won't know the rules or list of values.

Given that the above makes for difficult querying, Oracle provides the ability to create views of the data. A view is simply a way to pull together data from related tables into one place, in a very efficient manner. A view knows how to join the tables together and can change the Oracle field names to make them more meaningful to you. Views do not contain any data, though; they are only pointers to the data, but you can access them in Discoverer just as if they were tables.

Most companies use views of the database. They simplify querying and they also ensure that the same joins are being made each time, thereby releasing you from having to worry about linking the Oracle tables together. Using a combination of views and an end-user query tool like Discoverer takes away all of the pain and hardship that writing your own queries creates.

Until recently there was only one company, Aris Software, who had taken the approach to building a total set of views against Oracle databases. Their product, Noetix Views, is well known and works very well with Discoverer. More recently, Oracle has released Business Views, a set of views built to query their database. A third option is for your company to build your own views.

We will give you an overview of all three approaches in the next section.

Oracle Applications Business Views

Oracle released Business Views at the same time that this book was being submitted for publication. As such, we have not been able to evaluate their use and are only able to quote you the following information as supplied to us by Oracle.

Oracle is including Business Views as part of Oracle Applications in release 11*i* and beyond. There are nearly 800 views in the Oracle Business Intelligence System (BIS), covering virtually all modules. Using these views you can perform ad hoc and custom reporting using Discoverer. Oracle even plans to provide you with prewritten Discoverer workbooks for use within the business areas. We think this is a wonderful feature.

Oracle Business Views, along with Discoverer, are two of the essential components of Oracle's BIS. Business Views is a layer of database views relating business entity descriptions for use in ad hoc queries against Oracle Applications data. These views deliver the following three important features:

- The ability to present information at a level that is of interest to business users
- The ability to present information in user-friendly terminology
- The ability to present information with consistency across the various Applications products

Oracle Business Views comes in two flavors: base views and full views. The base views are typically created on a single underlying table or view, perhaps joining two at most. Full views, on the other hand, may point to several underlying tables or views. These full views will, therefore, contain several joins and take slightly longer to query from—as opposed to the base views.

Security

Another really wonderful feature of Business Views is that it provides out-of-the-box support for Oracle Applications security—incidentally, enabling Discoverer to be the only ad hoc query solution on the market with this capability. Oracle Applications has a very sophisticated security mechanism, and anyone implementing Discoverer against Oracle Applications using Business Views can leverage the same security structures. This ensures consistent access control across both the main database and business intelligence systems. All of the user accounts and responsibilities that have been set up in your main database are available in Discoverer immediately, without any extra setup by your Discoverer administrator.

In particular, you gain the ability to use existing Oracle Applications usernames, passwords, and responsibilities through Discoverer. Oracle Discoverer is fully cognizant of the Oracle Applications security model, and is capable of returning data that is dependent on the user's userid and Application responsibility combination.

Cross-Organization Support

Discoverer also provides the same level of multiorganization access control that is available through Oracle Applications. Cross-organization reporting is also supported. With cross-organization reporting support, end users have access to a list of organizations within Oracle Applications, as opposed to a single organization. Discoverer's users access the data pertaining to the organizations to which the Applications administrator has granted them access.

Oracle Applications is designed to allow the ability to run reports across multiple organizations captured within your enterprise resource planning (ERP) system. These are distinct operating entities, and are implemented via row-level security within most Applications tables and views. These tables and views are tagged with an org_id column. This column specifies which row in a given table is logically grouped into which organization. Whenever an application user logs in with a given Applications userid and responsibility combination, the system sets up a security mechanism that contains that user's org_id key. Thus, any queries run against a given Application table or view will return only a subset of the data in that table, depending on that user's org_id. This enables Oracle Applications to efficiently store multiple reporting organizations within one set of tables and views.

Oracle Business Intelligence System

Oracle's Business Intelligence System (BIS) is a performance management system for Oracle Applications, built with the proven technology of Oracle Discoverer, Alert, and Workflow. Oracle Discoverer is integrated with BIS to provide powerful analysis solutions for Oracle Applications. BIS is an integrated set of intelligence modules for Financials, Purchasing, Operations, Human Resources, and Process

Manufacturing. Each intelligence module comes with prebuilt Discoverer workbooks that provide ad hoc and detailed analysis of critical day-to-day performance measures, calculated from Oracle Applications. BIS also includes the Oracle Applications end-user layer for Discoverer.

The Oracle Applications EUL is a complete set of easy-to-understand business definitions that represent Oracle Applications data. The EUL simplifies the entire Oracle Applications database and enables users to quickly create and modify analysis reports in any business area. BIS is ideal for customers looking for a prepackaged out-of-the-box solution that has comprehensive coverage of almost all Applications modules. One big advantage of the BIS solution is that it offers a dramatic time reduction over a "do it yourself" approach. Another advantage is that as new releases of Oracle Applications are introduced, the shipped BIS EUL is updated to accommodate these changes, which means less maintenance for you.

Flexfield Management

Companies differ from each other in organizational structure and operational procedures. This is obvious through the differences in information systems. To accommodate these different business processes, Oracle Applications is highly customizable and enables customers to set up and configure their OLTP systems in a flexible manner. Descriptive and key flexfields are one of the features of Oracle Applications that provide this type of flexibility. You can set up these flexfields to suit your particular business practices. The architecture of Discoverer supports flexfields. At each customer site, the flexfield customizations are displayed as EUL items within appropriate folders.

Flexfield configuration information is determined once the Discoverer EUL and Applications Business Views are installed on your site. Each Business View contains placeholders, or tokens, that represent site-specific variable information. These tokens represent the key and descriptive flexfields that you have set up in your system. During the installation and setup process on your site, the Business Views Generator (a new component of the Applications Object Library that is part of Oracle Applications 11*i*) program runs, taking as input the "tokenized" views that have been shipped and your specific flexfield configuration. This program replaces the tokens with columns, derived from the flexfield configuration information, and produces a modified set of views as the output. Discoverer's built-in "refresh" functionality adds the same new columns to the appropriate folders in the EUL. The end result is a complete EUL based on your flexfield customizations, an environment that provides a complete end-user ad hoc query and analysis solution.

Oracle Help and Guides

Oracle has provided comprehensive information and procedures that are of use to both end users and administrators of Oracle Applications. The guides that are of use to Discoverer users are as follows:

- **BIS 11*i* User Guide Online Help** This guide, in HTML format, is provided as an online help from the BIS application and includes information about the various Discoverer workbooks that are available.
- **Oracle Discoverer Administration Guide** This guide provides reference information for your Discoverer administrator. It contains information on how to define security, manage the EUL, create and customize business areas, and for managing summary information.
- **Oracle BIS Implementation Guide** Contains all information necessary to implement the Oracle Business Intelligence System in your company. It contains an overview of the Discoverer workbooks and worksheets that are provided by the system.

Noetix Views

Noetix Views, from Aris Software, converts Oracle Applications data tables into a user-friendly set of business views. Used with Discoverer, Noetix Views delivers a total solution for end-user reporting and ad hoc query. We have seen these in use for several years and can recommend them to anyone considering purchasing a suite of views that you can use against Oracle Applications 10.7 and 11.0.

Currently, Noetix Views look at the data in Oracle Applications Financials, Manufacturing, Supply Chain, Projects, Human Resources, and AOL (Application Object Library). To identify the business areas or roles, Noetix prefixes them with a two- or three-letter code indicating which module is being used. For example, BOM indicates Bills of Materials, INV for Inventory, OE for Order Entry, and so on. During the install, Noetix examines each set of books, business group, operating unit, or organization and creates a separate role for each. It then appends one or two letters to indicate which organization the view belongs to. Let's say you have three organizations: US for America, EU for Europe, and AF for Africa. Using these codes, BOMUS would be the Bills of Materials business area for America, while OEAF would be the Order Entry business area for Africa.

When you open Discoverer, these are the areas that you would look for. Opening one of these business areas displays the folders within. Each folder corresponds to a single Noetix View. When you open up a folder, you can see the items that you need. Noetix uses codes to indicate which items are indexes and which are flexfields. Noetix Views also includes an extensive online help system that is available from both the client and the server. The help system, described later in this section, assists you in finding the right data and understanding its usefulness.

Codes Used Within Noetix Views

When you open a folder based on a view that is part of Noetix Views, you will notice the following codes being used:

- **A$** This code is prefixed to all columns that are indexed. Noetix Views refers to these columns as Search By columns. You should always select indexed columns when you can, and always try to create conditions based on indexed values. Your query will return data much quicker when you do this.

  For example:

  A$CUSTOMER is an index based on the customer name.

  A$SHIP_DATE is an index based on the ship date.

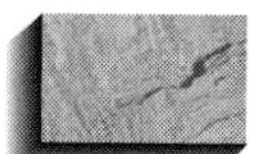

NOTE
Whenever possible, you should always use Search By columns to locate your data. If you do not use these columns, the data will still be located; however, it will take Discoverer much longer. This is because Discoverer has to scan all of the rows in the Oracle table.

- **$** When you see the dollar symbol embedded inside a column name, this indicates that the column is a flexfield. The flexfield can either be an Oracle key flexfield or a descriptive flexfield.

For example, POLIN$Ship_Date is the column associated with the flexfield that you have defined as being the ship date. The word POLIN preceding the dollar symbol is a code for the Oracle table that the field is coming from. The word Ship_Date following the dollar symbol is the name that you have given to one of the flexfields on the purchase order line.

Noetix also provides an excellent help file. The above terminology is repeated in the help file so that you can see at a glance the fields in the system.

Noetix Help File

When you install Noetix Views, it builds a context-sensitive help file for you to use. Opening this help file first of all gives you a list of all of the business areas that Noetix has created. Clicking on a business area allows you to drill down to see a list of the folders that make up that business area. Noetix then gives a brief description of each folder and classifies each as being basic, value added, or cross functional.

These folder types are described as follows:

- **Basic** The folders that are classified as basic draw their information from a single Oracle form or data entry screen. These folders pull their data from a maximum of four tables. Querying from a basic folder is fast.
- **Value added** The folders that are classified as value added draw their information from several forms or data entry screens, but all within the same Oracle module. These folders pull their data from four to eight tables and are slower to query from than basic folders.
- **Cross functional** The folders that are classified as cross functional draw their information from forms or entry screens across two or more Oracle modules. These folders pull their data from eight to fourteen tables and are by far the slowest to query from.

Each view contains hints to give you the quickest and most efficient access to your data. These hints tell you how to choose the best columns upon which to apply conditions. Using these hints to build a query is a very fast way of getting up and running.

The list of column names uses the same dollar codes outlined earlier in this section. In addition, you may also see columns prefixed by Z$. These are joins to other views and give you an indication as to what Discoverer folders will be active should you decide to select a column from this view.

Tips for Using Noetix Views with Discoverer

There are a number of ways that you can help yourself write efficient Discoverer queries when using Noetix Views. The following is a list of tips that we recommend you follow:

- Have the Noetix Views help file open on your desktop.
- Look at the hints given in the help file for clues on how to build queries. When a hint states that you need to apply a certain condition on an item, you should always do so.
- Try to query from basic folders whenever possible.

- Try to use Search By columns whenever possible.
- Always try to apply conditions on the Search By columns.
- Try not to join to more than four other folders in the same query, and even then try to use only basic folders.

Company Built Views

Probably the easiest way to get a quick view of the database is to get someone from your IT department to build a SQL script. Most companies use SQL. If you are lucky enough to have experienced IT staff, fluent in the complexities of writing SQL scripts, you probably already have a number of existing queries that you use today.

In order to use these scripts, you either have your IT department run them for you or you log on to the database and run them yourself. The big disadvantage of this approach is that you cannot quickly modify the script, nor can you use it for ad hoc reporting.

However, it only takes a small step further to turn these scripts into views. Then you have your Discoverer administrator create a new folder based on the view and, voila, there you have converted an SQL script into a Discoverer folder. Now you, and everybody else who has access to the folder, can create ad hoc queries.

APPENDIX C

Comparison Between 3.1 and 3*i*

iscoverer 3*i* is the first release of Discoverer for the Web. Throughout this book we have used Discoverer for the Web or Discoverer 3*i* in reference to Discoverer 3*i* User Edition. Discoverer 3*i* Viewer is also a Discoverer for the Web component but is not discussed in this book. Both 3.1 and 3*i* provide superior ease of use, unsurpassed performance, integration with other desktop products, and powerful data exploration via drill-anywhere capabilities. Discoverer 3.1.42 is, at press time, the latest release of the Windows version, while 3*i* has recently been included amongst Oracle's Business Intelligence suite of software. Oracle will continue parallel development of both the Windows and Web-based systems.

This book was written using Discoverer versions 3.1.36 and 3.3.48 (3*i*). By the time this book is published, Oracle will have published several newer builds of the Discoverer 3*i* User Edition. The following table lists the major differences between Discoverer 3.1 and Discoverer 3*i*:

Features	**3.1**	**3*i***
Platform	Win 95, Win 98, and Win NT.	Internet via Web browser.
Compatibility	A query created in 3*i* can be run and edited in 3.1. 3*i* features not supported are ignored and are not removed.	A query created in 3.1 can be run and edited in 3*i*. 3.1 features not supported are ignored and are not removed.
Login sequence	3.1 remembers the last username and database.	The sticky feature of 3*i* only remembers your login data if you stay within your browser. If you exit your browser, you will have to type in all components of the login sequence again.
Hot keys	Supported.	Not supported in release 3.3.48.
Right mouse context menu	Supported.	Not supported in release 3.3.48.
Renaming columns	Supported.	Not supported in release 3.3.48.
Ordering of columns	Can be done in the Workbook Wizard, Edit Sheet dialog box, and when viewing the results.	Can be done in the Workbook Wizard and the Edit Sheet dialog box only.

Features	3.1	3*i*
Saving workbooks	Can save to My Computer and the database.	Can save to the database only; therefore, no prompt is given.
The Workbook Wizard Discoverer 3*i* has three additional steps in the Workbook Wizard	Six steps: 1. Open existing or new 2. Select items 3. Sheet layout 4. Conditions 5. Sorting 6. Calculations	Nine steps: 1. Open existing or new 2. Select items 3. Sheet layout 4. Conditions 5. Sorting 6. Calculations 7. Percentages 8. Totals 9. Parameters
Workbook Wizard step 5 Sorting	Order referred to as Hi to Lo and Lo to Hi. Can hide a group sorted column. Line width, line spacing, and page breaks can be set for group sorting.	Order referred to as High to Low and Low to High. Can hide all sorted columns. Cannot set line width, line spacing, or page breaks.
Workbook Wizard step 7 Percentages	Not supported in the Workbook Wizard.	Supported in the Workbook Wizard.
Workbook Wizard step 8 Totals	Not supported in the Workbook Wizard.	Supported in the Workbook Wizard.
Workbook Wizard step 9 Parameters	Not supported in the Workbook Wizard.	Supported in the Workbook Wizard.
Subqueries	Fully supported.	Cannot create or edit in 3*i*, but those created in 3.1 will run.

Features	3.1	3*i*
Percentages	When using Page Items, the percentage is based on the current page. A percentage created in 3*i* using all pages will only display based on the current page.	A new look and feel has been given to the dialog box. When using Page Items, percentages can now be based on all pages as well as the current page.
Totals	When using Page Items, the total is based on the current page. A total created in 3*i* using all pages will only display based on the current page.	A new look and feel has been given to the dialog box. When using Page items, totals can be based on all pages as well as the current page. 3*i* also supports several new types of totaling, such as sum distinct.
Calculations	When using Page Items, the calculation is based on the current page. A calculation created in 3*i* using all pages will only display based on the current page.	A new look and feel has been given to the dialog box. When using Page Items, calculations can now be based on all pages as well as the current page.
Creating exceptions	Supported.	Not supported in release 3.3.48, but exceptions created in 3.1 will display.
Ad hoc formatting	Fully supported.	Not supported in release 3.3.48, but will display in the format created in 3.1.
Default formatting	User can set default formats for five major areas: 1. Data 2. Heading 3. Sheet title 4. Total 5. Exceptions	User can set default formats for three major areas: 1. Data 2. Heading 3. Exceptions Sheet title and totals created in 3.1 will display.
Toolbars	Three toolbars available: 1. Standard toolbar 2. Formatting bar 3. Analysis bar	One toolbar available with enhanced analysis tools buttons.

Features	**3.1**	**3*i***
Resizing columns	Supported.	Not supported in release 3.3.48.
Viewing results	No indication of how many pages of data have been returned.	Redesigned results page includes a button for setting the rows per page, and buttons for navigating between the HTML pages of the worksheet.
Edit titles	Supported.	Not supported in release 3.3.48, but titles created in 3.1 will display.
Graphing	Supported.	Not supported in release 3.3.48.
Print preview	Supported.	Not supported in release 3.3.48, but is WYSIWYG.
Page setup	Supported.	Not supported in release 3.3.48.
Headers and footers	Supported.	Not supported in release 3.3.48, but headers and footers created in 3.1 will display.
Drilling	Can drill from the toolbar and when viewing the results, and on any item.	Cannot drill from the toolbar. Can drill when viewing the results, but only on items that have a predefined rollup. Also supports skipping levels in a predefined rollup.
Edit Sheet dialog box	Contains five tabs: 1. Select Items 2. Table Layout 3. Conditions 4. Sort 5. Calculations	Expanded to now contain eight tabs: 1. Select Items 2. Table Layout 3. Conditions 4. Sort 5. Calculations 6. Percentages 7. Totals 8. Parameters

Features	3.1	3*i*
Fan trap detection	Supported, and fan trap resolution introduced in version 3.1.41.	Fan trap detection supported, but resolution not supported in the current release. Oracle will include this in a future release.
Scheduling	Supported.	Not supported in release 3.3.48, but results of scheduled workbooks can be viewed.
Open dialog box	Has four options: 1. My Computer 2. Database 3. Scheduled 4. Recently Used List	Has two options: 1. Database 2. Scheduled
Options dialog box	Contains seven tabs: 1. General 2. Query Governor 3. Table/Crosstab 4. Formats 5. Cache 6. Advanced 7. EUL	Contains six tabs: 1. General 2. Query Governor 3. Sheet Format 4. Formats 5. Advanced 6. EUL The Options dialog box can now be launched by double-clicking the Rows per Page button.
Command-line interface	Supported.	Not supported in release 3.3.48.
Oracle Apps login interface	Not supported.	Supported.

APPENDIX D

Tutorial Database

This appendix contains an entity relationship diagram (ERD) of the tutorial database used in this book. It also contains all table names including primary keys, foreign keys, and data items.

Entity Relationship Diagram for Global Widgets Sales Database

The following is the ERD for the Global Widgets tutorial database.

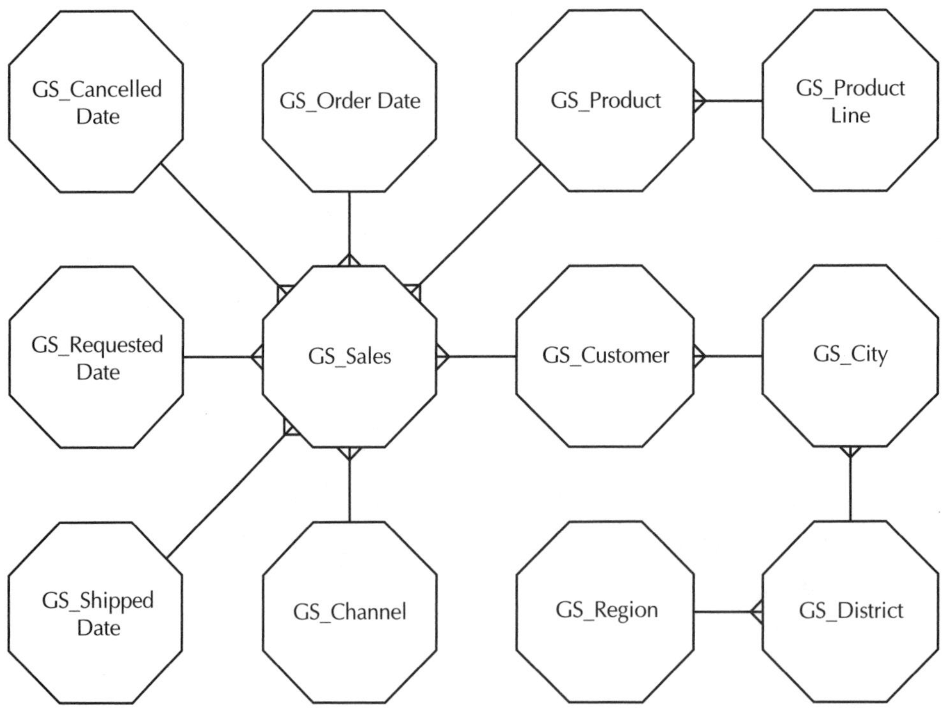

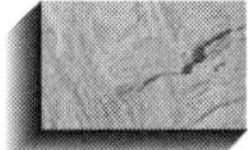

NOTE

For those familiar with data modeling, this is almost a star schema. To change this model into a star schema, you could move the region, district, and city data into the Customer table.

The Global Widgets Tables

The following are the tables contained in the Global Widgets tutorial database:

- Sales Fact Table
- Sales Channel
- Products
- Product Line
- Customer
- City
- District
- Region
- Order Date
- Requested Date
- Cancelled Date
- Ship Date

GS_SALES

This is a fact table and is the main table used in the Global Widgets database. All of the aggregations, costs, and quantities are pulled from this table. The Sales Fact table has the following primary key and foreign keys:

- **ORDID** Primary key
- **CUSTID** Foreign key, links to the Customer table
- **PRODID** Foreign key, links to the Product table
- **CHANNELID** Foreign key, link to the Sales Channel table
- **ORDERDATE** Foreign key, links to the Order Date table
- **REQUESTEDDATE** Foreign key, links to the Requested Date table
- **CANCELDATE** Foreign key, links to the Cancelled Date table (not shown in the following table due to space restrictions)
- **SHIPDATE** Foreign key, links to the Ship Date table

ORDID	CUSTID	PRODID	CHANNELID	ORDERDATE	ORDERQTY	SHIPDATE	SHIPQTY	REQDATE	STATUS	SELLPRICE	COSTPRICE
1059	1	61	1	6/19/98	10000	6/22/98	10000	6/22/98	SHIPPED	212500	98800
1060	2	62	1	6/19/98	1200	6/22/98	1200	6/22/98	SHIPPED	18300	7452
1061	3	63	1	6/19/98	1000	6/26/98	1000	6/22/98	SHIPPED	15250	6210
1062	4	64	1	6/19/98	1920	7/20/98	1920	7/20/98	SHIPPED	51744	22041.6
1063	5	65	1	6/19/98	1920	7/24/98	1920	7/27/98	SHIPPED	51744	22041.6
1064	6	66	1	6/22/98	48	6/25/98	48	6/22/98	SHIPPED	648	346.56
1065	7	67	1	6/22/98	50	6/25/98	50	6/22/98	SHIPPED	637.5	299.5
1066	8	68	1	6/22/98	10000	6/26/98	10000	6/26/98	SHIPPED	212500	98800
1067	9	41	1	6/22/98	1600	6/29/98	1600	6/26/98	SHIPPED	35488	16992
1068	10	42	1	6/22/98	8400	6/29/98	8400	6/26/98	SHIPPED	186312	89208
1069	11	43	1	6/22/98	10000	6/26/98	10000	6/25/98	SHIPPED	221800	106200
1070	12	44	1	6/23/98	15000	6/26/98	15000	6/26/98	SHIPPED	519750	239100

GS_Channel

This is the table for the sales channel. It has the following primary key:

- **CHANNELID** Primary key

ChannelID	Name
1	EXTERNAL
2	INTERNET

GS_PRODUCTS

This is the table for the products. It has the following primary and foreign keys:

- **PRODID** Primary key
- **LINEID** Foreign key, links to the Product Line folder

PRODID	NAME	PRODSIZE	COST	PRICE	LINEID
61	QB-1000	LARGE	12.42	23.45	1
62	QB-2000	LARGE	12.42	23.45	1
63	QB-3000	LARGE	12.42	23.45	1
64	CD-500	LARGE	10.62	22.18	2
65	CD-550	LARGE	10.62	22.18	2
66	CD-625	LARGE	10.62	22.18	2
67	AVR-800	LARGE	15.94	34.65	3
68	AVR-900	LARGE	15.94	34.65	3
41	QB-5000	MEDIUM	8.33	17.66	1
42	QB-5500	MEDIUM	8.33	17.66	1
43	QB-6000	MEDIUM	8.33	17.66	1
44	CD-100	MEDIUM	6.21	15.25	2
45	CD-200	MEDIUM	6.21	15.25	2
46	AVR-500	MEDIUM	11.48	26.95	3
47	AVR-550	MEDIUM	11.48	26.95	3
21	AB-2000	SMALL	7.22	13.5	1
22	AB-2500	SMALL	5.99	12.75	2
23	AB-3000	SMALL	9.88	21.25	3

GS_Prodline

This is the table for the product lines. It has the following primary key:

- **LINEID** Primary key

LineID	Name
1	WONDER WIDGET
2	MEGA WIDGET
3	SUPER WIDGET

GS_CUSTOMER

This is the table for the customers. It has the following primary and foreign keys:

- **CUSTID** Primary key
- **CITYID** Foreign key, links to the City table

CUSTID	NAME	CREDITLIMIT	ADDRESS	CITYID	STATE	POSTCODE
1	CEBU WIDGET CO	100000	217B SMITH AVE	1		99772
2	WONDER WIDGETS	50000	1594 BUSH ST	2	CALIFORNIA	94108
3	WIDGETS ON THE WEB	80000	1234 VIA VINCENZA	8	TERMINI	
4	WIDGETS DE MEXICO	10000	2716 CINCO DE MAYO	13		6500
5	MUM'S WIDGET CO.	0	750 THE CRESCENT	3	MERSEYSIDE	L35 9XX
6	WIDGETS BY THE BAY	50000	21100 MARKET ST	2	CALIFORNIA	94108
7	CASA DE WIDGETS	100000	1782 CORTEZ	9		1200
8	THING'S	50000	112 AVENIDA VERDE	14		1225
9	WIDGETS R US	50000	1711 LOMBARD	2	CALIFORNIA	94108
10	WIDGET O THE MERSEY	50000	1532 DAVIS LN	3	MERSEYSIDE	L29 6BH
11	HONG KONG WIDGETS	80000	98 HIGH STREET	16	VICTORIA	
12	WIDGETS MARKET	100000	1665 MARKET ST	2	CALIFORNIA	94108

CUSTID	NAME	CREDITLIMIT	ADDRESS	CITYID	STATE	POSTCODE
13	MOUNTAIN WIDGETS	50000	9594 COLFAX	10	COLORADO	80203
14	TRICOLOR WIDGETS	50000	RUE DE MADELINE, 52	7	CENTRALE	75006
15	ACE MANUFACTURING	100000	VASCO DE GAMA, 78	4		2750
16	ABC WIDGET CO	100000	123, YOCKSAM-DONG	17	KANGNAM-GU	135-080
17	WIDGETS Y GADGETS	100000	CALLE MARTINEZ, 208	13		6500
18	RIO WIDGETS	100000	AVE DE CENTRAL, 33	5		
19	BIG RIVER WIDGETS	80000	15 IRVING BLVD	20	TEXAS	75207
20	BRIDGE THINGS	80000	1 GOLDEN GATE AVE	2	CALIFORNIA	94108
21	PALMELA WIDGETS	80000	PARQUE DE PALMELA	4		2750
22	WIDGETS SA	0	1550, CHEMIN DU LAC	12	QUEBEC	K156RJ
23	LOTS OF WIDGETS	50000	7870 AMSTERDAM	21	NEW YORK	10023
24	WE'VE GOT WIDGETS	50000	90 S. BROAD ST	11	PENN	19102
25	OXFORD WIDGETS	0	27 OXFORD STREET	6	LONDON	W17
26	LAST RAILWAY WIDGETS	100000	666 MORELAND	19	GEORGIA	30315
27	LAC WIDGETS SA	100000	RUE DE SIMPLON, 5	18	GENEVA	1211
28	PATRIOT'S WIDGET CO.	100000	73 CEDAR	11	PENN	19125
29	WIDGET AIR	50000	SFO INTERNATIONAL	2	CALIFORNIA	94108
30	LONDON WIDGETS LTD.	50000	5 MIDDLE AVENUE	6	LONDON	E18
31	REPUBLIC WIDGETS	100000	PASEO DE LA REPUBLIC	22		PE1
32	WARSAW WIDGETS	75000	PRUSA 15	23		00-600
33	YAMATA WIDGET LTD.	80000	10-3 NAGATA	15		100
34	WIDGET SUPPLY CO.	50000	5002 RIVINGTON	21	NEW YORK	10002
35	THE LITTLE WIDGET	80000	2660 E. 10TH AVE	10	COLORADO	80203

GS_CITY

This is the table for the cities. It has the following primary and foreign keys:

- **CITYID** Primary key
- **DISTRICTID** Foreign key, links to the District table

CITYID	NAME	DISTRICTID	COUNTRYCODE
1	MANILLA	6	PH
2	SAN FRANCISCO	1	US
3	LIVERPOOL	3	GB
4	LISBON	4	PT
5	RIO DE JANEIRO	5	BR
6	LONDON	3	GB
7	PARIS	3	FR
8	ROME	4	IT
9	MADRID	4	ES
10	DENVER	1	US
11	PHILADELPHIA	1	US
12	QUEBEC	1	CA
13	MEXICO CITY	2	MX
14	SAO PAULO	5	BR
15	TOKYO	6	JP
16	HONG KONG	6	HK
17	SEOUL	6	KR
18	GENEVA	3	CH
19	ATLANTA	2	US
20	DALLAS	2	US
21	NEW YORK	2	US
22	LIMA	5	PE
23	WARSAW	7	PL

GS_DISTRICT

This is the table for the districts. It has the following primary and foreign keys:

- **DISTRICTID** Primary key
- **REGIONID** Foreign key, links to the Region table

DISTRICTID	NAME	REGIONID
1	NA NORTH	1
2	NA SOUTH	1
3	EU NORTH	2
4	EU SOUTH	2
5	SA ALL	3
6	FE ALL	4
7	EU EAST	2

GS_REGION

This is the table for the regions. It has the following primary key:

- **REGIONID** Primary key

REGIONID	NAME
1	NORTH AMERICA
2	EUROPE
3	SOUTH AMERICA
4	FAR EAST

DATES

The tutorial database uses four date tables: Order, Requested, Cancelled, and Ship. The definitions for these tables are identical, and so we show the table only once. The four tables and their primary keys are as follows:

- **GS_ORDER_DATE** FS_DATE is the Primary key
- **GS_REQUESTED_DATE** FS_DATE is the Primary key

- **GS_CANCELLED_DATE** FS_DATE is the Primary key
- **GS_SHIP_DATE** FS_DATE is the Primary key

FS_DATE	FS_MONTH	FS_QUARTER	FS_YEAR
9/27/97	Oct-97	1998-Q1	FY1998
9/28/97	Oct-97	1998-Q1	FY1998
9/29/97	Oct-97	1998-Q1	FY1998
9/30/97	Oct-97	1998-Q1	FY1998
10/1/97	Oct-97	1998-Q1	FY1998
10/2/97	Oct-97	1998-Q1	FY1998
10/3/97	Oct-97	1998-Q1	FY1998
10/4/97	Oct-97	1998-Q1	FY1998
10/5/97	Oct-97	1998-Q1	FY1998
10/6/97	Oct-97	1998-Q1	FY1998
10/7/97	Oct-97	1998-Q1	FY1998
10/8/97	Oct-97	1998-Q1	FY1998

Entity Relationship Diagram for Fan Trap

The following is the ERD for the Fan Trap tutorial database.

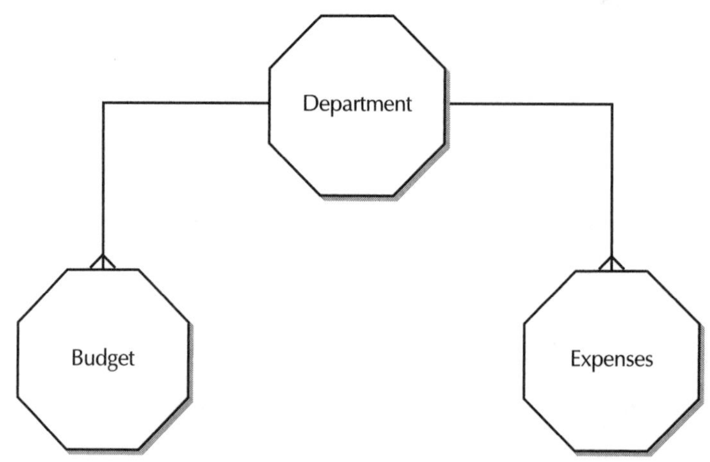

The Fan Trap Tables

The following are the three tables contained in the Fan Trap tutorial database:

- Department
- Expenses
- Budget

FAN_DEPARTMENT

This is the table for the departments. It has the following primary keys:

- **DEPTNO** Primary key

DEPTNO	DEPTNAME
10	SALES
20	HR
30	MIS
40	MARKETING
50	TRAINING

FAN_BUDGET

This is the table for the budgets. It has the following primary and foreign keys:

- **BUDGETID** Primary key
- **DEPTNO** Foreign Key, links to the Department table

BUDGETID	DEPTNO	AMOUNT	REASON	BGT_DATE
1	10	5000	EQUIPMENT	7/24/00
2	20	2000	EQUIPMENT	7/25/00
3	30	25500	EQUIPMENT	8/19/00
4	40	4250	EQUIPMENT	6/30/00
5	50	2090	EQUIPMENT	6/30/00
6	10	40000	TRAVEL	7/24/00

BUDGETID	DEPTNO	AMOUNT	REASON	BGT_DATE
7	20	200	TRAVEL	7/25/00
8	30	10000	TRAVEL	8/19/00
9	40	25000	TRAVEL	6/30/00
10	50	200	TRAVEL	6/30/00

FAN_EXPENSES

This is the table for the expenses. It has the following primary and foreign keys:

- **EXPENSEID** Primary key
- **DEPTNO** Foreign key, links to the Department table

EXPENSEID	DEPTNO	EXPENSES	EXP_DATE
1	10	150	8/1/00
2	10	250	8/20/00
3	10	1000	9/1/00
4	20	1025	8/16/00
5	30	12000	9/1/00
6	40	2750	8/30/00

Index

Symbols

A

D

H

I

Q

T

U

V

W

X

Y

Z

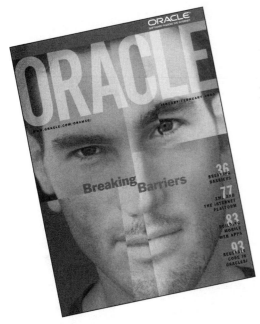

☐ **YES! Please send me a FREE subscription to *Oracle Magazine*.** ☐ **N**

To receive a free bimonthly subscription to *Oracle Magazine*, you must fill out the entire card, sign it, and date it (incomplete cards cannot be processed or acknowledged). You can also fax your application to **+1.847.647.9735. Or subscribe at our Web site at www.oracle.com/oramag/**

SIGNATURE (REQUIRED) X **DATE**

NAME TITLE

COMPANY TELEPHONE

ADDRESS FAX NUMBER

CITY STATE POSTAL CODE/ZIP CODE

COUNTRY E-MAIL ADDRESS

☐ From time to time, Oracle Publishing allows our partners exclusive access to our e-mail addresses for special promotions and announcements. To be included in this program, please check this box.

You must answer all eight questions below.

1 What is the primary business activity of your firm at this location? *(check only one)*
- ☐ 03 Communications
- ☐ 04 Consulting, Training
- ☐ 06 Data Processing
- ☐ 07 Education
- ☐ 08 Engineering
- ☐ 09 Financial Services
- ☐ 10 Government—Federal, Local, State, Other
- ☐ 11 Government—Military
- ☐ 12 Health Care
- ☐ 13 Manufacturing—Aerospace, Defense
- ☐ 14 Manufacturing—Computer Hardware
- ☐ 15 Manufacturing—Noncomputer Products
- ☐ 17 Research & Development
- ☐ 19 Retailing, Wholesaling, Distribution
- ☐ 20 Software Development
- ☐ 21 Systems Integration, VAR, VAD, OEM
- ☐ 22 Transportation
- ☐ 23 Utilities (Electric, Gas, Sanitation)
- ☐ 98 Other Business and Services ____________

2 Which of the following best describes your job function? *(check only one)*

CORPORATE MANAGEMENT/STAFF
- ☐ 01 Executive Management (President, Chair, CEO, CFO, Owner, Partner, Principal)
- ☐ 02 Finance/Administrative Management (VP/Director/ Manager/Controller, Purchasing, Administration)
- ☐ 03 Sales/Marketing Management (VP/Director/Manager)
- ☐ 04 Computer Systems/Operations Management (CIO/VP/Director/ Manager MIS, Operations)

IS/IT STAFF
- ☐ 07 Systems Development/ Programming Management
- ☐ 08 Systems Development/ Programming Staff
- ☐ 09 Consulting
- ☐ 10 DBA/Systems Administrator
- ☐ 11 Education/Training
- ☐ 14 Technical Support Director/ Manager
- ☐ 16 Other Technical Management/Staff
- ☐ 98 Other ____________

3 What is your current primary operating platform? *(check all that apply)*
- ☐ 01 DEC UNIX
- ☐ 02 DEC VAX VMS
- ☐ 03 Java
- ☐ 04 HP UNIX
- ☐ 05 IBM AIX
- ☐ 06 IBM UNIX
- ☐ 07 Macintosh
- ☐ 09 MS-DOS
- ☐ 10 MVS
- ☐ 11 NetWare
- ☐ 12 Network Computing
- ☐ 13 OpenVMS
- ☐ 14 SCO UNIX
- ☐ 24 Sequent DYNIX/ptx
- ☐ 15 Sun Solaris/SunOS
- ☐ 16 SVR4
- ☐ 18 UnixWare
- ☐ 20 Windows
- ☐ 21 Windows NT
- ☐ 23 Other UNIX ____________
- ☐ 98 Other ____________
- 99 ☐ **None of the above**

4 Do you evaluate, specify, recommend, or authorize the purchase of any of the following? *(check all that apply)*
- ☐ 01 Hardware
- ☐ 02 Software
- ☐ 03 Application Development Tools
- ☐ 04 Database Products
- ☐ 05 Internet or Intranet Products
- 99 ☐ **None of the above**

5 In your job, do you use or plan to purchase any of the following products or services? *(check all that apply)*

SOFTWARE
- ☐ 01 Business Graphics
- ☐ 02 CAD/CAE/CAM
- ☐ 03 CASE
- ☐ 05 Communications
- ☐ 06 Database Management
- ☐ 07 File Management
- ☐ 08 Finance
- ☐ 09 Java
- ☐ 10 Materials Resource Planning
- ☐ 11 Multimedia Authoring
- ☐ 12 Networking
- ☐ 13 Office Automation
- ☐ 14 Order Entry/Inventory Control
- ☐ 15 Programming
- ☐ 16 Project Management
- ☐ 17 Scientific and Engineering
- ☐ 18 Spreadsheets
- ☐ 19 Systems Management
- ☐ 20 Workflow

HARDWARE
- ☐ 21 Macintosh
- ☐ 22 Mainframe
- ☐ 23 Massively Parallel Processing
- ☐ 24 Minicomputer
- ☐ 25 PC
- ☐ 26 Network Computer
- ☐ 28 Symmetric Multiprocessing
- ☐ 29 Workstation

PERIPHERALS
- ☐ 30 Bridges/Routers/Hubs/Gateways
- ☐ 31 CD-ROM Drives
- ☐ 32 Disk Drives/Subsystems
- ☐ 33 Modems
- ☐ 34 Tape Drives/Subsystems
- ☐ 35 Video Boards/Multimedia

SERVICES
- ☐ 37 Consulting
- ☐ 38 Education/Training
- ☐ 39 Maintenance
- ☐ 40 Online Database Services
- ☐ 41 Support
- ☐ 36 Technology-Based Training
- ☐ 98 Other ____________
- 99 ☐ **None of the above**

6 What Oracle products are in use at your site? *(check all that apply)*

SERVER/SOFTWARE
- ☐ 01 Oracle8
- ☐ 30 Oracle8*i*
- ☐ 31 Oracle8*i* Lite
- ☐ 02 Oracle7
- ☐ 03 Oracle Application Server
- ☐ 04 Oracle Data Mart Suites
- ☐ 05 Oracle Internet Commerce Server
- ☐ 32 Oracle *inter*Media
- ☐ 33 Oracle JServer
- ☐ 07 Oracle Lite
- ☐ 08 Oracle Payment Server
- ☐ 11 Oracle Video Server

TOOLS
- ☐ 13 Oracle Designer
- ☐ 14 Oracle Developer
- ☐ 54 Oracle Discoverer
- ☐ 53 Oracle Express
- ☐ 51 Oracle JDeveloper
- ☐ 52 Oracle Reports
- ☐ 50 Oracle WebDB
- ☐ 55 Oracle Workflow

ORACLE APPLICATIONS
- ☐ 17 Oracle Automotive
- ☐ 35 Oracle Business Intelligence System
- ☐ 19 Oracle Consumer Packaged Goods
- ☐ 39 Oracle E-Commerce
- ☐ 18 Oracle Energy
- ☐ 20 Oracle Financials
- ☐ 28 Oracle Front Office
- ☐ 21 Oracle Human Resources
- ☐ 37 Oracle Internet Procurement
- ☐ 22 Oracle Manufacturing
- ☐ 40 Oracle Process Manufacturing
- ☐ 23 Oracle Projects
- ☐ 34 Oracle Retail
- ☐ 29 Oracle Self-Service Web Application
- ☐ 38 Oracle Strategic Enterprise Management
- ☐ 25 Oracle Supply Chain Management
- ☐ 36 Oracle Tutor
- ☐ 41 Oracle Travel Management

ORACLE SERVICES
- ☐ 61 Oracle Consulting
- ☐ 62 Oracle Education
- ☐ 60 Oracle Support
- ☐ 98 Other ____________
- 99 ☐ **None of the above**

7 What other database products are in use a your site? *(check all that apply)*
- ☐ 01 Access
- ☐ 02 Baan
- ☐ 03 dbase
- ☐ 04 Gupta
- ☐ 05 IBM DB2
- ☐ 06 Informix
- ☐ 07 Ingres
- ☐ 08 Microsoft Access
- ☐ 09 Microsoft SQL Server
- ☐ 10 PeopleSoft
- ☐ 11 Progress
- ☐ 12 SAP
- ☐ 13 Sybase
- ☐ 14 VSAM
- ☐ 98 Other ____________
- 99 ☐ **None of the above**

8 During the next 12 months, how much do you anticipate your organization will spend on computer hardware, software, peripherals, and services for your location? *(check only one)*
- ☐ 01 Less than $10,000
- ☐ 02 $10,000 to $49,999
- ☐ 03 $50,000 to $99,999
- ☐ 04 $100,000 to $499,999
- ☐ 05 $500,000 to $999,999
- ☐ 06 $1,000,000 and over

If there are other Oracle users at your location who would like to receive a free subscription to *Oracle Magazine*, please photocopy this form and pass it along, or contact Customer Service at +1.847.647.9630

Form 5

OPRESS